THE INTERNATIONAL ALMANAC OF ELECTORAL HISTORY

The INTERNATIONAL ALMANAC of ELECTORAL HISTORY

Fully Revised Third Edition

THOMAS T. MACKIE & RICHARD ROSE

Washington D. C.

First edition 1974
Second edition 1982
Third edition 1991

Published by the Macmillan Press Ltd
Houndmills, Basingstoke, Hampshire RG21 2XS
and London

Published in the United States of America and Canada by
Congressional Quarterly Inc.
1414 22nd Street, N.W.
Washington, D.C. 20037

Library of Congress Cataloging-in-Publication Data

Mackie, Thomas T.
The international almanac of electoral history / Thomas T. Mackie & Richard Rose. – 3rd ed.
p. cm.
ISBN 0–87187–575–6
1. Elections—History. I. Rose, Richard. 1933– . II. Title.
JF1001.M17 1991
324.9—dc20 89–13992
CIP

CONTENTS

	Acknowledgements	vii
	Introduction	ix
1	Australia	1
2	Austria	23
3	Belgium	39
4	Canada	66
5	Denmark	87
6	Finland	109
7	France	130
8	Germany	156
9	Greece	185
10	Iceland	206
11	Ireland	224
12	Israel	243
13	Italy	258
14	Japan	276
15	Luxembourg	298
16	Malta	311
17	The Netherlands	322
18	New Zealand	340
19	Norway	356
20	Portugal	372
21	Spain	385
22	Sweden	400
23	Switzerland	421
24	United Kingdom	438
25	United States of America	456
	Appendix : The Mechanics of Electoral Systems	503

Dedicated to the memory of Fred Craig,
a great craftsman of election statistics

ACKNOWLEDGEMENTS

Even by the standards of a mutually helpful community of scholars, the authors are indebted to a wide variety of individuals for information helpful in revising and expanding the third edition of this book.

National statistical offices, embassies and Commonwealth high commissions gave prompt and courteous replies to requests for information. Working through masses of official materials makes us appreciate consistency and clarity in official government reports of elections.

Three libraries have made particularly valuable contributions to the acquisition of information. The Andersonian Library of the University of Strathclyde promptly responded to many requests for materials from Inter-Library Loan. Time and again the British Library and the Library of the London School of Economics provided materials from the distant past of distant lands.

A large stream of comments about revisions for this edition was received from Arend Lijphart of the University of California, San Diego. Helmut Lang, Virginia Polytechnic Institute and State University, checked the consistency of raw numbers and percentages. Detailed comments on specific chapters were given for Belgium by Nicole Loeb-Mayer, Free University of Brussels; Denmark by Jørgen Elklit, Aarhus University; Finland, Heikki Paloheimo, University of Turku; Greece, Panayote Dimitras, Eurodim, Athens; Iceland, Gudni Baldursson, Statistical Bureau and Viggo Gislason, Parliamentary Librarian; Ireland, Michael Gallagher, Trinity College, Dublin; Israel, Miri Bitton, City University of New York; Japan, David Morris, Pembroke College, Oxford and Matsuo Kazunari, National Diet Library; Portugal, Pedro Tavares de Almeida, Universidade Nova de Lisboa. W. Dean Burnham, University of Texas at Austin, provided the data on American Congressional elections and estimates of the American voting age population.

The impetus to produce the first edition of this book came from comparative research stimulated by conferences and publications of the Committee on Political Sociology of the International Political Science Association and the International Sociological Association. The late Stein Rokkan of the University of Bergen was a founder of the Committee and a great inspiration for comparative electoral analysis.

The preparation of this fully revised third edition was aided by a small grant from the Nuffield Foundation, and also supported by the Centre for the Study of Public Policy at the University of Strathclyde. Susan Rae was responsible for the production of the tables, which required care and persistence beyond the normal call of duty. Anne Shaw prepared the text for publication. Tom Mackie was a Visiting Professor at Virginia Polytechnic Institute and State University while the book was being proofed and corrected, and is grateful to Charles L. Taylor, chair of its political science department, for hospitality and financial support for the project.

Modern technologies make communication across continents a much easier task than for previous editions, but a venture such as this book in the last resort still depends upon the goodwill of friends and colleagues.

THOMAS T. MACKIE RICHARD ROSE

University of Strathclyde

INTRODUCTION

The purpose of this book is to provide a complete and accurate compilation of election results in Western nations since the beginning of competitive national elections. Students of politics can thus be saved much time searching for information, drawing erroneous conclusions from ambiguous information or repeating mistakes enshrined in popular but sometimes inaccurate secondary sources.

Generalizations about parties and elections often err because they are unwittingly restricted to a single country at a particular moment in its history.The publication in a standard format of data about elections in 25 different countries can stimulate awareness of the variety of ways in which elections can be held in democratic political systems, and the choices open to a country introducing free and fair elections (Rose, 1983). Reporting results for each country from the date of its first competitive nationwide election calls attention to changes in parties and party systems, and to elements of persistence too.

Anyone who has ever tried to ascertain seemingly simple political facts will know that the task is neither simple nor is it always obvious. This is as true of an event as public as a general election as it is of the private negotiations of politicians. When information concerns elections distant in time or place, difficulties are much increased. The fundamental problem is that some "facts" are not facts, for the compilation of statistical information under the names of political parties presents choices in the process of aggregation. Problems increase if one wishes to compare results in a series of elections within a country; one must then deal with splits, mergers and successions that sometimes make it difficult to tell whether a party is new or long established.

In developing the terms of reference for this volume, the needs of users have been foremost. A reference volume must be detailed yet clear. Information must be reliable; therefore, wherever possible, we have been careful to use official sources in the original language of the country reported and where more than one interpretation of information is possible to document decisions made in aggregating data.

The countries included here are advanced industrialized nations regularly holding competitive elections since the end of the Second World War. The volume thus covers more than 600 elections in 25 different countries using 17 different languages on four continents. Since the first edition Greece, Portugal and Spain have established or re-established the practice of free elections, and these countries have been added.

The results reported are for the election of representatives to the lower house of a national assembly, whether it be called a parliament, a congress or some other term (Inter-Parliamentary Union, 1986). In countries where presidents are popularly elected, these elections are also reported. In some countries national referendums are held; these deserve and have received separate attention (Butler and Ranney, 1978; Austen, Butler and Ranney, 1987). Results for elections to the multi-national Parliament of the European Community can be found in a series of publications entitled *Europe Votes* (Mackie and Craig, 1980, 1985; Mackie, forthcoming).

Because the electoral histories of Western nations differ greatly from each other, there is no intellectual justification for starting each chapter at the same date. The practice of contesting elections developed at different times in Western nations (Rokkan, 1970). The starting point chosen is the first election in which the great majority of seats for the national parliament were contested, and most candidates fought under party labels common across constituencies. Without competition, no votes need be cast; candidates are elected unopposed. Without parties, no nationwide tabulation of individual votes is possible (for party histories, see Wende, 1981; Day, 1988). The United States has had the longest unbroken history of competitive national elections; in Europe Belgium claims this honour.

Elections are held under a very wide variety of franchise laws. To have confined the elections reported here only to those meeting a rigid criterion of democracy would have involved considerable problems of definition. Is an election democratic from the date at which a majority of a nation's males can vote, or only when the franchise is given to a majority of women as well as men? Or is the franchise democratic only when the whole of the adult population is eligible to vote? What requirements for registering voters are consistent with a democratic franchise? The answers to such questions are not generally agreed. The introductory comments for each chapter describe the evolution of national franchise laws, thus allowing each reader to decide whether or when a country meets a specific definition of democracy. The tables describe the extent to which election outcomes have changed as the franchise was extended.

The mechanics of an electoral system are simple in principle but they are often complex in practice, since laws must allow for many contingent factors that influence the registration of voters, the casting and counting of ballots, and the election of representatives. The introduction to each chapter provides a succinct guide to the workings of a nation's electoral system, and how this has changed through time. The Appendix provides a clear exposition of the operation of the two chief methods of election in use, the plurality or first-past-the-post system favoured in Anglo-American nations, and proportional representation systems used in most countries holding free elections today. Each chapter has a bibliography giving references to more specialized national materials. A variety of comparative compendia give details of electoral systems in many countries (see e.g. Mackenzie, 1958; Sternberger et al., 1969; Lakeman, 1970; Nohlen, 1978; Hand et al., 1979; Cadart, 1983; Bogdanor and Butler, 1983; Lijphart and Grofman, 1984; Grofman and Lijphart, 1986).

The organization of information follows a standard pattern in each chapter. The opening section traces the evolution of the electoral system and franchise laws. A list of political parties includes the name of each party in its national language as well as English, inasmuch as authors writing in English are by no means consistent in translations, nor will a name in English help when referring to source documents published in the country's national language. Detailed notes to this table show that persistence or collapse is not the only alternative in the career of parties; they may also split or merge, or continue through a process of succession (Rose and Mackie, 1988). A table of election dates is included, as this information is surprisingly difficult to locate, especially for earlier contests.

Election results are reported in sets of four standard tables, two giving the total number of votes and percentage share for each party, and two giving the number and percentage of seats that each party wins in the national assembly. Votes are reported for every party that has at least once secured more than one per cent of the vote in a national election. This condition includes many small parties, while avoiding personal parties and esoteric electoral groupings. Parties with fewer votes are reported when this aids comparison cross-nationally (e.g. Communist or Green parties) or when the separatist or regional character of a party confines its appeal to a geographically limited section of the electorate (e.g. the Welsh Nationalist party).

The following conventions have been used in reporting data:

Party did not contest election: -

Data not available: n.a.

Percentages: The vote for each party is a percentage of the valid vote. Percentages are rounded to one decimal place.

Turnout: Valid, invalid and total votes are calculated as a percentage of the electorate. The share of invalid votes as a proportion of the total vote is also calculated.

Bracket: This symbol joins two or more parties for which only aggregated vote or seat figures are available, usually because of an electoral alliance.

The preparation of a third edition of a book initially published in 1974 has involved substantially more than the addition of election results. New parties continue to be created and are added here. Each chapter has been re-examined afresh in the light of recent research and additional original sources consulted. Since nothing changes more than our understanding of the past, many relatively minor alterations have been made in results for elections, especially for the era prior to 1939. Where there are differences between data reported in earlier editions and here, this edition should be considered definitive.

The study is confined to industrial nations because of the many political, social, and economic differences between them and other nations where elections are held. *Competitive Elections in Developing Countries*, edited by Myron Weiner and Ergun Ozbudun (1987) gives a detailed account of free elections in developing nations on four continents (see also Smith, 1960; Nuschler et al., 1978; Landau et al., 1980). *Elections without Choice*, edited by Guy Hermet, Richard Rose and Alain Rouquié (1978), examines the practice of elections which are not free and competitive; this is the practice of the median country in the world today. E.S. Staveley's *Greek and Roman Voting and Elections* (1972) returns to the origins of psephology, when people actually voted by casting pebbles in urns.

Electioneering, in the broad sense of a continuing effort by political parties to attract support, is more than a set of election results. Under the leadership of Howard R. Penniman and Austin Ranney, the American Enterprise Institute has published a series,

At the Polls, describing the electoral system, parties and campaigns in more than thirty countries.

Once the campaign and count are over, a government must be constituted. In countries where no one party wins a majority of seats in the national assembly, control of government is determined by coalition negotiations between two or more parties rather than directly reflecting an election result (Browne and Dreijmanis, 1982; Bogdanor, 1983).

The specialization of knowledge in political science has gone so far that surveys of individual voters have become a field complementary to but separate from examining total votes cast. Virtually every country here has been the subject of one or more sample surveys of voting behaviour, and data archives make surveys available for secondary analysis (Guchteneire et al., 1985). The use of common analytic techniques to examine voting in different countries is characteristically pursued through edited volumes (see e.g. Lipset and Rokkan, 1967; Rose, 1974; Dalton et al., 1984; Franklin et al., forthcoming).

The particular object of this book–the accurate and consistent reporting of national election results–is thus one contribution to a collective enterprise to which scholars with complementary interests have contributed.

Sources:

J. Austen, D. Butler and A. Ranney, 'Referendums, 1978-1986', *Electoral Studies* 6,2 (1987) 139-47

V. Bogdanor (ed.). *Coalition Government in Western Europe* (London: Heineman, 1983)

V. Bogdanor and D. Butler (eds.), *Democracy and Elections* (Cambridge: Cambridge University Press, 1983)

E.C. Browne and J. Dreijmanis (eds.), *Government Coalitions in Western Democracies* (New York: Longman, 1982)

D. Butler and A. Ranney (eds.), *Referendums* (Washington, DC: American Enterprise Institute, 1978)

D. Butler, H.R. Penniman and A. Ranney (eds.), *Democracy at the Polls* (Washington, DC: American Enterprise Institute, 1981)

J. Cadart (ed.), *Les Modes de Scrutin des Dix-huit Pays Libres de l'Europe Occidentale* (Paris: Presses Universitaires de France, 1983)

R.J. Dalton, S.C. Flanagan and P.A. Beck (eds.), *Electoral Change in Advanced Industrial Democracies* (Princeton: Princeton University Press, 1984)

A.J. Day, *Political Parties of the World* (London: Longman, 3rd ed., 1988)

M.N. Franklin, T.T. Mackie and H. Valen, (eds). *Electoral Change* (Cambridge: Cambridge University Press, forthcoming).

B. Grofman and A. Lijphart (eds.), *Electoral Laws and their Political Consequences* (New York: Agathon Press, 1986)

P. de Guchteneire, L. LeDuc and R.G. Niemi, 'A compendium of academic survey studies of elections around the world', *Electoral Studies* 4,2 (1985) 159-74

G. Hand, G. Georgel and C. Sasse (eds.), *European Electoral Systems Handbook* (London: Butterworths, 1979)

G. Hermet, R. Rose and A. Rouquié (eds.), *Elections without Choice* (London: Macmillan, 1978)

Inter-Parliamentary Union, *Parliaments of the World* (Aldershot: Gower, 2nd ed., 1986, 2 volumes)

J. Landau, E. Ozbudun and F. Tachau (eds.), *Electoral Politics in the Middle East* (London: Croom Helm, 1980)

E. Lakeman, *How Democracies Vote* (London: Faber and Faber, 3rd ed., 1970)

A. Lijphart and B. Grofman (eds.), *Choosing an Electoral System* (New York: Praeger, 1984)

S.M. Lipset and S. Rokkan (eds.), *Party Systems and Voter Alignments* (New York: Free Press, 1967)

W.J.M. Mackenzie, *Free Elections* (London: George Allen and Unwin, 1958)

T.T. Mackie and F.W.S. Craig, *Europe Votes* 1,2, (Chichester: Parliamentary Reference Services, 1980, 1985)

T.T. Mackie (ed.) *Europe Votes 3* (Aldershot: Dartmouth, forthcoming).

D. Nohlen, *Wahlsysteme der Welt: Daten und Analysen* (Munich and Zurich: Piper, 1978)

E. Nuschler, K. Ziemer et al., *Politische Organisation und Repräsentation in Afrika* (Berlin: de Gruyter, 1978)

S. Rokkan, *Citizens, Elections, Parties* (Oslo: Universitetsforlaget, 1970)

R. Rose (ed.), *Electoral Behavior: a Comparative Handbook* (New York: Free Press, 1974)

R. Rose, 'Elections and electoral systems: choices and alternatives', in V. Bogdanor and D. Butler (eds.), *Democracy and Elections* (Cambridge: Cambridge University Press, 1983) 20-45

R. Rose and T.T. Mackie, 'Do parties persist or fail? The big trade-off facing organizations', in K. Lawson and P. Merkl (eds.), *When Parties Fail* (Princeton: Princeton University Press, 1988) 533-58

T.E. Smith, *Elections in Developing Countries* (London: Macmillan, 1960)

E.S. Staveley, *Greek and Roman Voting and Elections* (London: Thames and Hudson, 1972)

D. Sternberger, B. Vogel and D. Nohlen, (eds.) *Die Wahl der Parlamente und anderer Staatsorgane: I: Europa* (Berlin: de Gruyter, 1969)

R. Taagepera and M.S. Shugart, *Seats and Votes: the Effects and Determinants of Electoral Systems* (New Haven: Yale University Press, 1989)

F. Wende (ed.), *Lexikon zur Geschichte der Parteien in Europa* (Stuttgart: Alfred Kröner Verlag, 1981)

M. Weiner and E. Ozbudun (eds.), *Competitive Elections in Developing Countries* (Durham, NC: Duke University Press, 1987)

The International Almanac of Electoral History

Chapter 1

AUSTRALIA

The Commonwealth of Australia was established as a federation of six British colonies in 1901. The colonies already enjoyed a large measure of self-government. Their assemblies were elected on a very broad franchise. In South and Western Australia women already had the vote. Elsewhere manhood suffrage was the norm, although there was a small property requirement in Tasmania. In Queensland, Western Australia and Tasmania plural voting on a property basis was in force. Everywhere the ballot was secret (Hughes and Graham, 1968 : 280).

The Commonwealth constitution established a Parliament consisting of a Senate and a House of Representatives. The maximum term for the House is three years; the government can call a dissolution earlier. A government is normally formed by the leader of a party or coalition that commands a majority in the House of Representatives. Seats in the House are apportioned to the states in accord with population, and within states apportioned according to electoral registration. To secure the passage of legislation, the government must also secure endorsement by the Senate, which consists of representatives of the states that constitute the federation. The franchise for Senate elections is the same as for the House elections, but the number of representatives is not. Initially each state had six members in the Senate regardless of its population. This number was increased to 10 in 1949 and 12 in 1984. Since 1975 the Australian Capital Territory and the Northern Territory have each been represented by two Senators. The maximum term for the Senate is six years; normally half the Senate is elected at the time of the election of the whole House, but the whole Senate can be elected simultaneously in prescribed cases of disagreement with the House of Representatives.

In 1922 the Northern Territory was given limited representation in the House of Representatives. Until 1968 the Northern Territory representative had only a limited right to vote in the House. Representation was given the Australian Capital Territory, Canberra, in 1948, and its representative was given full voting rights after the 1966 general election.

In the Commonwealth's first election in 1901 the franchise was granted to all those qualified to vote in the larger of the state assemblies (that is the lower house), with the proviso that plural voting rights were not accepted. In 1902 universal adult suffrage with a minimum age of 21 was introduced; the voting age was reduced to 18 in 1973. House elections have always been for single-member districts. Initially, following British practice, election was by plurality. In 1918 the alternative vote system was introduced. It required voters to rank their choices in order of preference, so that the successful candidate in a constituency must secure an absolute majority of the votes, either on the first ballot or after transfer of additional preferences from candidates with the least support (see Appendix for an explanation). Compulsory voting for both Houses was adopted in 1924. In Senate elections each state forms a single multi-member constituency. Elections were by plurality until 1919 when preferential voting for multi-member constituencies was introduced. Electors were required to express preferences for twice the number of Senators to be elected plus one. Second and lower order preferences were taken into account until three candidates had achieved majorities. In 1934 the expression of preferences for *all* candidates was made compulsory. The single transferable vote was introduced for Senate elections in 1949 and modified in 1984 so that electors might adopt a party ticket of preferences instead of having to rank all candidates in order.

Aboriginal Australians, about one percent of the population as of 1987, were effectively excluded from the federal franchise until the 1960s. The Commonwealth's first electoral laws gave aborigines the federal vote only if they were enfranchised in their state of residence. Effectively this meant that aborigines were disenfranchised everywhere. In 1962 all aborigines were given the right to vote in federal elections, but enrolment and voting both remained voluntary until 1984.

The *Official Returns* first listed party affiliations for the 1975 election. The *Commonwealth Parliamentary Handbook* has reported party affiliations since the publication of its eleventh edition in 1953 beginning with the 1949 elections. For earlier elections the principal source is Hughes and Graham (1968).

Sources:

Australian Electoral Office, *A Summary of Commonwealth Election and Referendum Statistics, 1901-1975* (Canberra: Australian Government Publishing Service, 1976)

Australian Electoral Office, *Senate Election and General Election of Members of the House of Representatives 13 December 1975: Election Statistics* (Canberra: Australian Government Publishing Service, 1976) and subsequent volumes in the same series

C.A. Hughes and B.D. Graham, *A Handbook of Australian Government and Politics* (Canberra: Australian National University Press, 1968)

C.A. Hughes and B.D. Graham, *Voting for the Australian House of Representatives, 1901-1964* (Canberra: Australian National University Press, 1974)

C.A. Hughes, *A Handbook of Australian Government and Politics, 1965-1974* (Canberra: Australian National University Press, 1977)

C.A. Hughes, *A Handbook of Australian Government and Politics, 1975-1984* (Sydney: Australian National University Press/Pergamon Press, 1986)

D. Jaensch, *The Australian Party System* (Sydney: Allen & Unwin, 1983)

J. Jupp, *Australian Party Politics* (Melbourne: Melbourne University Press, 1964)

J. Jupp, *Party Politics in Australia, 1966-1981* (Sydney: Allen & Unwin, 1982)

Australia

P. Loveday, A.W. Martin and R.S. Parker, *The Emergence of the Australian Party System* (Sydney: Hale and Iremonger, 1977)

P. Loveday and D. Jaensch, 'Indigènes and electoral administration, Australia and Canada', *Electoral Studies* 6,1 (1987) 31-40

I. McAllister, M. Mackerras, A. Ascui and S. Moss, *Australian Political Facts* (Melbourne: Longman Cheshire, 1990)

J. Rydon, *A Federal Legislature: the Australian Commonwealth Parliament 1901-1980* (Melbourne: Oxford University Press, 1986)

Table 1.1 POLITICAL PARTIES IN AUSTRALIA SINCE 1901

	Party Names	Elections Contested	
		Years	Number
1	Australian Labor Party - ALP	1901ff	35
2	Free Trade Party [1]	1901-1906	3
3	Protectionists	1901-1906	3
4	Western Australia Party [2]	1906	1
5	Liberal Party [3]	1910-1914	3
6	Nationalist Party [4]	1917-1929	6
7	Country Party; from 1975 to 1982 the National Country Party; since 1982 the National Party [5]	1919ff	28
8	Liberal Union [6]	1922	1
9	Country Progressive Party [7]	1928-1929	2
10	Communist Party [8]	1931-1937; 1943ff	22
11	United Australia Party - UAP [9]	1931-1943	5
12	New South Wales Labor Party [10]	1931-1934	2
13	Social Credit Party	1934-1937	2
14	Non-Communist Labor Party [11]	1940	1
15	State Labor Party [12]	1940-1943	2
16	Liberal Democratic Party [13]	1943	1
17	One Parliament for Australia Party	1943	1
18	Liberal Party of Australia [14]	1946ff	15
19	Lang Labor Party	1946-1949	2
20	Services Party of Australia	1946	1
21	Democratic Labor Party [15]	1955ff	14
22	Queensland Labor Party [16]	1958-1961	2
23	Liberal Reform Group/Australia Party [17]	1966-1975	5
24	Liberal Movement [18]	1974-1975	2
25	National Alliance [19]	1974	1
26	Country-Liberal Party [20]	1975ff	6
27	Australian Democrats [21]	1977ff	5

1 Renamed the Anti-Socialists in 1906.

2 A local anti-Labor alliance.

3 A merger of the Protectionists and the Anti-Socialists in 1909.

4 A merger of the Liberal Party and part of the Labor Party in 1917.

5 The Country Party was formally established in January 1920. Figures for the 1919 election refer to candidates sponsored by the farmers and graziers' organizations (Hughes and Graham, 1968: 320, 325).

6 A dissident faction of Nationalists in Victoria.

7 Country Party dissidents in Victoria. Reunited with the state Country Party in 1930.

8 The Communist Party was outlawed in June 1940. The ban was lifted at the end of 1942.

[9] A merger of the Nationalist Party and former members of the Labor Party in 1931. Includes the Emergency Committee, an electoral alliance formed in the same year by the UAP and the Country Party in South Australia and its successor the Liberal and Country League (LCL) set up in 1932.

[10] Breakaway from the federal Labor Party led by J.T. Lang the Premier of New South Wales, which ran candidates against federal Labor in 1931 and 1934. Reunited with the federal party in 1936.

[11] Labor Party faction in New South Wales led by J.T. Lang.

[12] Splinter groups of the federal Labor Party.

[13] Breakaway from the UAP in New South Wales.

[14] A merger of anti-Labor parties, including the United Australia Party and the Liberal & Country League.

[15] A faction of the Labor Party which contested all states except New South Wales and Queensland as the Australian Labor Party (Anti-Communist) in 1955, being established as the Democratic Labor Party in 1957.

[16] Co-operated with the Democratic Labor Party in the 1958 and 1961 elections and merged with it in 1962.

[17] Founded as the Liberal Reform Group in 1966. Renamed the Australian Reform Movement in 1967 and the Australia Party in 1969.

[18] Breakaway from the Liberal and Country League in South Australia.

[19] A 1973 merger of the Democratic Labor and Country parties in Western Australia, which was dissolved in 1975.

[20] A merger of the Country and Liberal parties in the Northern Territory. Candidates elected to the House of Representatives were free to join either the Country (later National) or Liberal parliamentary group.

[21] Established by Don Chipp, a former Liberal Party minister, in 1977.

Table 1.2 DATES OF ELECTIONS: HOUSE OF REPRESENTATIVES

1.	29 and 30 March 1901	19.	10 December 1949
2.	16 December 1903	20.	28 April 1951
3.	12 December 1906	21.	29 May 1954
4.	13 April 1910	22.	10 December 1955
5.	31 May 1913	23.	22 November 1958
6.	5 September 1914	24.	9 December 1961
7.	5 May 1917	25.	30 November 1963
8.	13 December 1919	26.	26 November 1966
9.	16 December 1922	27.	25 October 1969
10.	14 November 1925	28.	2 December 1972
11.	17 November 1928	29.	18 May 1974
12.	12 October 1929	30.	13 December 1975
13.	19 December 1931	31.	10 December 1977
14.	15 September 1934	32.	18 October 1980
15.	23 October 1937	33.	5 March 1983
16.	21 September 1940	34 .	1 December 1984
17.	21 August 1943	35.	11 July 1987
18.	28 September 1946		

Sources: Australian Electoral Office (1976) and Australian Electoral Office 1977ff.

Table 1.3a AUSTRALIA Total Votes 1901-1922[1]

	1901[2]	1903	1906	1910	1913	1914	1917	1919	1922
Electorate	987,754	1,893,586	2,109,562	2,258,482	2,760,216	2,811,515	2,835,327	2,849,862	2,980,424
Valid Votes	505,972	720,938	951,688	1,322,582	1,900,369	1,686,763	1,883,434	1,909,231	1,572,514
Invalid Votes	8,468	18,463	36,865	27,044	55,354	40,143	51,044	68,612	74,349
Total Votes	514,440	739,401	988,553	1,349,626	1,955,723	1,726,906	1,934,478	1,977,843	1,646,863
PARTY VOTES									
1 Labor Party	82,734	223,163	348,711	660,864	921,099	858,451	827,541	811,244	665,145
2 Free Trade Party	145,611	247,774	363,257	-	-	-	-	-	-
3 Protectionists	189,294	214,091	156,425	-	-	-	-	-	-
4 Western Australia Party	-	-	22,154	-	-	-	-	-	-
5 Liberal Party	-	-	-	596,350	930,076	796,397	-	-	-
6 Nationalist Party	-	-	-	-	-	-	1,021,138	907,249	553,920
7 Country Party	-	-	-	-	-	-	-	130,154	197,513
8 Liberal Union	-	-	-	-	-	-	-	-	73,939
Others	8,284	35,910	61,141[3]	65,368	49,194	31,915	34,755	60,584	81,957

1 Excluding the Northern Territory. From 1919, party votes are first preference votes.
2 Party votes in 1901 exclude constituencies in Southern Australia and Tasmania.
3 Includes 46,074 votes cast for independent Protectionist candidates.

Sources: Hughes and Graham, 1968; Hughes and Graham 1974.

Table 1.3b AUSTRALIA Percentage of Votes 1901-1922

	1901	1903	1906	1910	1913	1914	1917	1919	1922
Total Votes	52.1	39.0	46.9	59.8	70.9	61.4	68.2	69.4	55.3
Valid Votes	51.2	38.1	45.1	58.6	68.8	60.0	66.4	67.0	52.8
Invalid Votes	0.9	1.0	1.7	1.2	2.0	1.4	1.8	2.4	2.5
Share Invalid	1.6	2.5	3.7	2.0	2.8	2.3	2.6	3.5	4.5
PARTY VOTES									
1 Labor Party	19.4	31.0	36.6	50.0	48.5	50.9	43.9	42.5	42.3
2 Free Trade Party	34.2	34.4	38.2	-	-	-	-	-	-
3 Protectionists	44.4	29.7	16.4	-	-	-	-	-	-
4 Western Australia Party	-	-	2.3	-	-	-	-	-	
5 Liberal Party	-	-	-	45.1	48.9	47.2	-	-	-
6 Nationalist Party	-	-	-	-	-	-	54.2	47.5	35.2
7 Country Party	-	-	-	-	-	-	-	6.8	12.6
8 Liberal Union	-	-	-	-	-	-	-	-	4.7
Others	2.0	5.0	6.4	4.9	2.6	1.9	1.8	3.2	5.2

Table 1.3c AUSTRALIA Number of Seats Won in the House of Representatives 1901-1922[1]

	1901	1903	1906	1910	1913	1914	1917	1919	1922
1 Labor Party	15	23 (2)	26 (3)	43 (2)	37 (2)	42 (7)	22 (3)	26 (2)	29
2 Free Trade Party	26	25 (4)	27 (3)	–	–	–	–	–	–
3 Protectionists	32 (6)	26 (11)	16 (1)	–	–	–	–	–	–
4 Western Australia Party	–	–	2	–	–	–	–	–	–
5 Liberal Party	–	–	–	31 (2)	38 (1)	32 (6)	–	–	–
6 Nationalist Party	–	–	–	–	–	–	53 (7)	40	29 (2)
7 Country Party	–	–	–	–	–	–	–	8	14
8 Liberal Union	–	–	–	–	–	–	–	–	2 (1)
Others	2[2]	1	4[3]	1	0	1	0	1[4]	1
Total Seats	75 (6)	75 (17)	75 (7)	75 (4)	75 (3)	75 (13)	75 (10)	75 (2)	75 (3)

1 Figures in parentheses report number of representatives returned unopposed.
2 Including one independent Labor.
3 Independent Protectionists.
4 Independent Nationalist.

Sources: Hughes and Graham, 1968; Hughes and Graham, 1974.

Table 1.3d AUSTRALIA Percentage of Seats Won in the House of Representatives 1901-1922

	1901	1903	1906	1910	1913	1914	1917	1919	1922
1 Labor Party	20.0	30.7	34.7	57.3	49.3	56.0	29.3	34.7	38.7
2 Free Trade Party	34.7	33.3	36.0	–	–	–	–	–	–
3 Protectionists	42.7	34.7	21.3	–	–	–	–	–	–
4 Western Australia Party	–	–	2.7	–	–	–	–	–	–
5 Liberal Party	–	–	–	41.3	50.7	42.7	–	–	–
6 Nationalist Party	–	–	–	–	–	–	70.7	53.3	38.7
7 Country Party	–	–	–	–	–	–	–	10.7	18.7
8 Liberal Union	–	–	–	–	–	–	–	–	2.7
Others	2.7	1.3	5.3	1.3	0.0	1.3	0.0	1.3	1.3

Table 1.4a AUSTRALIA Total Votes 1925-1946[1]

	1925	1928	1929	1931	1934	1937	1940	1943	1946
Electorate	3,302,016	3,444,766	3,539,120	3,649,954	3,902,677	4,080,038	4,239,426	4,466,637	4,739,853
Valid Votes	2,916,638	2,595,085	2,879,250	3,172,034	3,551,385	3,603,341	3,876,986	4,122,491	4,344,744
Invalid Votes	70,562	133,730	78,297	114,440	126,338	95,928	102,023	122,878	109,197
Total Votes	2,987,200	2,728,815	2,957,547	3,286,474	3,677,723	3,699,269	3,979,009	4,245,369	4,453,941
PARTY VOTES									
1 Labor Party	1,313,627	1,158,505	1,406,327	859,513	952,251	1,555,737	1,556,941	2,058,578	2,159,953
6 Nationalist Party	1,238,397	1,014,522	975,979	-	-	-	-	-	-
7 Country Party	-	271,686	295,640	388,544	480,279	560,279	511,482	394,099	493,736
9 Country Progressive Party	-	41,713	27,942	-	-	-	-	-	-
10 Communist Party	-	-	-	8,511	47,499	17,153	-	81,816	64,811
11 United Australia Party[2]	-	-	-	1,330,097	1,274,537	1,240,048	1,171,788	901,452	-
12 New South Wales Labor Party	-	-	-	335,309	510,480	-	-	-	-
13 Social Credit Party	-	-	-	-	166,589	79,432	-	-	-
14 Non-Communist Labor	-	-	-	-	-	-	207,721	-	-
15 State Labor Party	-	-	-	-	-	-	101,191	29,752	-
16 Liberal Democrats	-	-	-	-	-	-	-	42,149	-
17 One Parliament for Australia	-	-	-	-	-	-	-	87,112	-
18 Liberal Party of Australia	-	-	-	-	-	-	-	-	1,402,820
19 Lang Labor Party	-	-	-	-	-	-	-	-	69,138
20 Services Party Of Australia	-	-	-	-	-	-	-	-	54,000
Others	51,251	108,659	173,362[3]	250,060	119,750	150,692	332,863	527,533[4]	100,286

1 Excluding the Northern Territory. All figures for party votes refer to the number of first preference votes polled.
2 Includes the Liberal and Country League merger of the Country and Liberal parties in South Australia.
3 Includes 112,108 votes cast for independent Nationalist Candidates.
4 Includes 26,532 votes cast for a single Lang Labor candidate, J. T. Lang.

Sources: Hughes and Graham, 1968; Hughes and Graham, 1974.

Table 1.4b AUSTRALIA Percentage of Votes 1925-1946

	1925	1928	1929	1931	1934	1937	1940	1943	1946
Total Votes	90.5	79.2	83.6	90.0	94.2	90.7	93.9	95.0	94.0
Valid Votes	88.3	75.3	81.4	86.9	91.0	88.3	91.5	92.3	91.7
Invalid Votes	2.1	3.9	2.2	3.1	3.2	2.4	2.4	2.8	2.3
Share Invalid	2.4	4.9	2.6	3.5	3.4	2.6	2.6	2.9	2.5
PARTY VOTES									
1 Labor Party	45.0	44.6	48.8	27.1	26.8	43.2	40.2	49.9	49.7
6 Nationalist Party	42.5	39.1	33.9	-	-	-	-	-	-
7 Country Party	10.7	10.5	10.3	12.2	13.5	15.5	13.2	9.6	11.4
9 Country Progressive Party	-	1.6	1.0	-	-	-	-	-	-
10 Communist Party	-	-	-	0.3	1.3	0.5	-	2.0	1.5
11 United Australia Party	-	-	-	41.9	35.9	34.4	30.2	21.9	-
12 New South Wales Labor Party	-	-	-	10.6	14.4	-	-	-	-
13 Social Credit Party	-	-	-	-	4.7	2.2	-	-	-
14 Non-Communist Labor	-	-	-	-	-	-	5.4	-	-
15 State Labor Party	-	-	-	-	-	-	2.6	0.7	-
16 Liberal Democrats	-	-	-	-	-	-	-	1.0	-
17 One Parliament for Australia	-	-	-	-	-	-	-	2.1	-
18 Liberal Party of Australia	-	-	-	-	-	-	-	-	32.3
19 Lang Labor Party	-	-	-	-	-	-	-	-	1.6
20 Services Party Of Australia	-	-	-	-	-	-	-	-	1.2
Others	1.8	4.2	6.0	7.9	3.4	4.2	8.6	12.8	2.3

Table 1.4c AUSTRALIA Number of Seats Won in the House of Representatives 1925-1946[1]

	1925	1928	1929	1931	1934	1937	1940	1943	1946
1 Labor Party	23	31 (3)	46 (6)	14	18 (1)	29 (4)	32 (1)	49 (1)	43
6 Nationalist Party	37 (1)	29 (5)	14	–	–	–	–	–	–
7 Country Party	14	13 (4)	10 (3)	16 (3)	15	16	13	9	12
9 Country Progressive Party	–	1	1	–	–	–	–	–	–
10 Communist Party	–	–	–	0	0	0	–	0	0
11 United Australia Party	–	–	–	40 (1)	32	29	23	14	–
12 New South Wales Labor Party	–	–	–	4	9	–	–	–	–
13 Social Credit Party	–	–	–	–	–	0	–	–	–
14 Non-Communist Labor	–	–	–	–	–	–	4	–	–
15 State Labor Party	–	–	–	–	–	–	0	–	–
16 Liberal Democrats	–	–	–	–	–	–	0	0	–
17 One Parliament for Australia	–	–	–	–	–	–	–	0	–
18 Liberal Party of Australia	–	–	–	–	–	–	–	–	17
19 Lang Labor Party	–	–	–	–	–	–	–	–	1
20 Services Party Of Australia	–	–	–	–	–	–	–	–	0
Others	1	1	4[2]	1	0	0	2	2	1
Total Seats	75 (1)	75 (12)	75 (9)	75 (4)	74 (1)	74 (4)	74 (1)	74 (1)	74

1 Figures in parentheses report number of representatives returned unopposed.
2 Including three independent Nationalists.

Sources: Hughes and Graham, 1968; Hughes and Graham, 1974.

Table 1.4d AUSTRALIA Percentage of Seats Won in the House of Representatives 1925-1946

	1925	1928	1929	1931	1934	1937	1940	1943	1946
1 Labor Party	30.7	41.3	61.3	18.7	24.3	39.2	43.2	66.2	58.1
6 Nationalist Party	49.3	38.7	18.7	-	-	-	-	-	-
7 Country Party	18.7	17.3	13.3	21.3	20.3	21.6	17.6	12.2	16.2
9 Country Progressive Party	-	1.3	1.3	-	-	-	-	-	-
10 Communist Party	-	-	-	0.0	0.0	0.0	-	0.0	0.0
11 United Australia Party	-	-	-	53.3	43.2	39.2	31.1	18.9	-
12 New South Wales Labor Party	-	-	-	5.3	12.2	-	-	-	-
13 Social Credit Party	-	-	-	-	0.0	0.0	-	-	-
14 Non-Communist Labor	-	-	-	-	-	-	5.4	-	-
15 State Labor Party	-	-	-	-	-	-	0.0	0.0	-
16 Liberal Democrats	-	-	-	-	-	-	-	0.0	-
17 One Parliament for Australia	-	-	-	-	-	-	-	-	-
18 Liberal Party of Australia	-	-	-	-	-	-	-	-	23.0
19 Lang Labor Party	-	-	-	-	-	-	-	-	1.4
20 Services Party Of Australia	-	-	-	-	-	-	-	-	0.0
Others	1.3	1.3	5.3	1.3	0.0	0.0	2.7	2.7	1.4

Table 1.5a AUSTRALIA Total Votes 1949-1969[1]

	1949	1951	1954	1955	1958	1961	1963	1966	1969
Electorate	4,895,227	4,962,675	5,096,468	5,172,443	5,384,624	5,651,561	5,824,917	6,193,881	6,606,873
Valid Votes	4,604,410	4,565,899	4,557,288	4,395,535	4,993,493	5,246,033	5,474,713	5,709,749	6,114,118
Invalid Votes	93,390	88,507	62,283	130,239	147,616	138,317	101,264	182,578	159,493
Total Votes	4,697,800	4,654,406	4,619,571	4,525,774	5,141,109	5,384,350	5,575,977	5,892,327	6,273,611
PARTY VOTES									
1 Labor Party	2,117,088	2,174,840	2,280,098	1,961,829	2,137,890	2,512,929	2,489,184	2,282,834	2,870,792
7 Country Party	500,349	443,713	388,171	347,445	465,320	446,475	489,498	561,926	523,232
10 Communist Party	40,941	45,759	56,675	51,001	26,337	25,429	32,053	23,056	4,920
18 Australian Liberal Party	1,813,794	1,854,799	1,756,808	1,746,485	1,859,180	1,761,738	2,030,823	2,291,964	2,125,987
19 Lang Labor Party	32,870	-	-	-	-	-	-	-	-
21 Democratic Labor Party	-	-	-	227,083	389,688	399,475	407,416	417,411	367,977
22 Queensland Labor Party	-	-	-	-	80,035	57,487	-	-	-
23 Australia Party	-	-	-	-	-	-	-	49,610	53,646
Others	99,368	46,788	75,536	61,692	35,043	42,500	25,739	82,948	167,564

1 All figures for party votes refer to first preference votes. From 1966 figures include the Northern Territory and the Australian Capital Territory.

Sources: Hughes and Graham, 1968; Hughes and Graham, 1974.

Table 1.5b AUSTRALIA Percentage of Votes 1949-1969

	1949	1951	1954	1955	1958	1961	1963	1966	1969
Total Votes	96.0	93.8	90.6	87.5	95.5	95.3	95.7	95.1	95.0
Valid Votes	94.1	92.0	89.4	85.0	92.7	92.8	94.0	92.2	92.5
Invalid Votes	1.9	1.8	1.2	2.5	2.7	2.4	1.7	2.9	2.4
Share Invalid	2.0	1.9	1.3	2.9	2.9	2.6	1.8	3.1	2.5
PARTY VOTES									
1 Labor Party	46.0	47.6	50.0	44.6	42.8	47.9	45.5	40.0	47.0
7 Country Party	10.9	9.7	8.5	7.9	9.3	8.5	8.9	9.8	8.6
10 Communist Party	0.9	1.0	1.2	1.2	0.5	0.5	0.6	0.4	0.1
18 Liberal Party of Australia	39.4	40.6	38.5	39.7	37.2	33.6	37.1	40.1	34.8
19 Lang Labor Party	0.7	-	-	-	-	-	-	-	-
21 Democratic Labor Party	-	-	-	5.2	7.8	7.6	7.4	7.3	6.0
22 Queensland Labor Party	-	-	-	-	1.6	1.1	-	-	-
23 Australia Party	-	-	-	-	-	-	-	0.9	0.9
Others	2.2	1.0	1.7	1.4	0.7	0.3	0.5	1.5	2.7

Table 1.5c AUSTRALIA Number of Seats Won in the House of Representatives 1949-1969[1]

	1949	1951	1954	1955	1958	1961	1963	1966	1969
1 Labor Party	47	52 (2)	57 (1)	47	45	60	50	41	59
7 Country Party	19	17	17 (3)	18 (5)	19	17	20	21	20
10 Communist Party	0	0	0	0	0	0	0	0	0
18 Liberal Party of Australia	55	52 (1)	47 (3)	57 (5)	58	45	52	61	46
19 Lang Labor Party	0	–	–	–	–	–	–	–	–
21 Democratic Labor Party	0	0	0	0	0	0	0	0	0
22 Queensland Labor Party	–	–	–	–	0	0	–	–	–
23 Australia Party	–	–	–	–	–	–	–	0	0
Others	0	0	0	0	0	0	0	1	0
Total Seats	121	121 (3)	121 (7)	122 (10)	122	122	122	124	125

1 Figures in parentheses report number of representatives returned unopposed.

Sources: Hughes and Graham, 1968; Hughes and Graham, 1974.

Table 1.5d AUSTRALIA Percentage of Seats Won in the House of Representatives 1949-1969

	1949	1951	1954	1955	1958	1961	1963	1966	1969
1 Labor Party	38.8	43.0	47.1	38.5	36.9	49.2	41.0	33.1	47.2
7 Country Party	15.7	14.0	14.0	14.8	15.6	13.9	16.4	16.9	16.0
10 Communist Party	0.0	0.0	0.0	0.0	0.0	0.0	0.0	0.0	0.0
18 Liberal Party of Australia	45.5	43.0	38.8	46.7	47.5	36.9	42.6	49.2	36.8
19 Lang Labor Party	0.0	–	–	–	–	–	–	–	–
21 Democratic Labor Party	–	–	–	–	0.0	0.0	0.0	0.0	0.0
22 Queensland Labor Party	–	–	–	–	0.0	0.0	–	–	–
23 Australia Party	–	–	–	–	–	–	–	0.0	0.0
Others	0.0	0.0	0.0	0.0	0.0	0.0	0.0	0.8	0.0

Table 1.6a AUSTRALIA Total Votes 1972-1987[1]

	1972	1974	1975	1977	1980	1983	1984	1987
Electorate	7,074,070	7,898,922	8,262,413	8,553,780	9,014,920	9,373,580	9,866,266	10,353,213
Valid Votes	6,601,050	7,391,006	7,732,578	7,922,850	8,305,633	8,684,862	8,664,960	9,235,086
Invalid Votes	146,197	144,762	149,295	204,912	208,359	185,312	628,061	480,342
Total Votes	6,747,247	7,535,768	7,881,873	8,127,762	8,513,992	8,870,174	9,293,021	9,715,428
PARTY VOTES								
1 Labor Party	3,273,549	3,644,110	3,313,004	3,141,048	3,749,605	4,297,521	4,120,135	4,232,563
7 National Party[2]	622,826	736,252	869,919	793,445	736,153	799,609	921,153	1,064,230
10 Communist Party	8,105	539	9,393	14,098	11,318	6,398	1,213	535
18 Liberal Party	2,115,085	2,582,968	3,232,159	3,017,894	3,108,517	2,983,856	2,979,891	3,169,391
21 Democratic Labor Party	346,415	104,974	101,750	113,271	25,456	17,318	49,121	3,334
23 Australia Party	159,916	172,176	33,630	-	-	-	-	-
24 Liberal Movement	-	57,817	49,484	-	-	-	-	-
25 National Alliance	-	60,325	-	-	-	-	-	-
26 Country-Liberal Party	-	-	15,976	16,462	18,805	20,479	27,335	21,668
27 Australian Democrats	-	-	-	743,365	546,033	437,265	472,205	557,259
Others	75,154	31,845	107,263	83,267	109,746	122,416	93,907	186,106

1 All figures for party votes refer to first preference votes.
2 In 1972 and 1974 the Country Party. From 1974 to 1980 the National Country Party. Since 1982 the National Party.

Sources: Hughes and Graham, 1974 and Australian Electoral Officer, 1976 ff.

Table 1.6b AUSTRALIA Percentage of Votes 1972-1987

	1972	1974	1975	1977	1980	1983	1984	1987
Total Votes	95.4	95.4	95.4	95.0	94.4	94.6	94.2	93.8
Valid Votes	93.3	93.6	93.6	92.6	92.1	92.7	87.8	89.2
Invalid Votes	2.1	1.8	1.8	2.4	2.3	2.0	6.4	4.6
Share Invalid	2.2	1.9	1.9	2.5	2.4	2.1	6.8	4.9
PARTY VOTES								
1 Labor Party	49.6	49.3	42.8	39.6	45.1	49.5	47.5	45.8
7 National Party	9.4	10.0	11.3	10.0	8.9	9.2	10.6	11.5
10 Communist Party	0.1	0.0	0.1	0.2	0.1	0.1	0.0	0.0
18 Australian Liberal Party	32.0	34.9	41.8	38.1	37.4	34.4	34.4	34.3
21 Democratic Labor Party	5.3	1.4	1.3	1.4	0.3	0.2	0.6	0.0
23 Australia Party	2.4	2.3	0.4	-	-	-	-	-
24 Liberal Movement	-	0.8	0.6	-	-	-	-	-
25 National Alliance	-	0.8	-	-	-	-	-	-
26 Country-Liberal Party	-	-	0.2	0.2	0.2	0.2	0.3	0.2
27 Australian Democrats	-	-	-	9.4	6.6	5.0	5.4	6.0
Others	1.1	0.4	1.4	1.1	1.3	1.4	1.1	2.0

Table 1.6c AUSTRALIA Number of Seats Won in the House of Representatives 1972-1987

	1972	1974	1975	1977	1980	1983	1984	1987
1 Labor Party	67	66	36	38	51	75	82	86
7 National Party	20	21	23[1]	19[1]	20[1]	17[1]	21	19
10 Communist Party	0	0	0	0	0	0	0	0
18 Liberal Party of Australia	38	40	68	67	54	33	44[2]	43
21 Democratic Labor Party	0	0	0	0	0	0	0	0
23 Australia Party	0	0	0	–	–	–	–	–
24 Liberal Movement	–	0	0	–	–	–	–	–
25 National Alliance	–	0	–	–	–	–	–	–
26 Country-Liberal Party	–	–	–	–	–	–	–	0
27 Australian Democrats	–	–	0	0	0	0	1	0
Others	0	0	0	0	0	0	0	0
Total Seats	125	127	127	124	125	125	148	148

1 Includes one M.P. elected as Country-Liberal in Northern Territory.
2 Includes one M.P. elected as Country-Liberal in Northern Territory.

Sources: Hughes and Graham, 1974 and figures provided by the Chief Electoral Officer.

Table 1.6d AUSTRALIA Percentage of Seats Won in the House of Representatives 1972-1987

	1972	1974	1975	1977	1980	1983	1984	1987
1 Labor Party	53.6	52.0	28.3	30.6	40.8	60.0	55.4	58.1
7 National Party	16.0	16.5	18.1	15.3	16.0	13.6	14.2	12.8
10 Communist Party	0.0	0.0	0.0	0.0	0.0	0.0	0.0	0.0
18 Liberal Party of Australia	30.4	31.5	53.5	54.0	43.2	26.4	30.4	29.1
21 Democratic Labor Party	0.0	0.0	0.0	0.0	0.0	0.0	0.0	0.0
23 Australia Party	-	-	-	-	-	-	-	-
24 Liberal Movement	-	0.0	0.0	-	-	-	-	-
25 National Alliance	-	0.0	-	-	-	-	-	-
26 Country-Liberal Party	-	-	-	-	-	-	-	0.0
27 Australian Democrats	-	-	0.0	0.0	0.0	0.0	0.0	0.0
Others	0.0	0.0	0.0	0.0	0.0	0.0	0.0	0.0

Chapter 2

AUSTRIA

Until 1918 the territory that was to become the Republic of Austria consisted of a number of predominantly German-speaking provinces in one part of the multi-national dual monarchy of Austria-Hungary. The House of Assembly of Cisleithanian Austria consisted of four estates or curia, representing large landowners, cities, chambers of commerce and trade, and the rural communes. In 1897 a fifth curia was added in which all men over 24 could vote; this comprised 72 of the 425 seats. Voting figures for the elections of 1897 and 1900/01 are available in *Österreichische Statistik* 49(1) 1897 and 59(3) 1901. The calculation of aggregate voting statistics for these elections is inhibited by the curia system, and by the fact that in most of the fifth curia constituencies elections were indirect.

In 1907 the estates system was abolished and replaced by universal male suffrage. Direct and secret elections in single-member constituencies using the two-ballot majority system were introduced. A detailed description of the complex pattern of Austrian election laws under the Habsburgs may be found in Stiefbold and Metzler-Andelberg, 1969: 15-30. The extension of the franchise was followed by the growth of political parties based on the different linguistic groups which made up Cisleithanian Austria. The Social Democrats and the Christian Social Party, both founded in 1889, dominated the provinces of Upper and Lower Austria, Carinthia, Salzburg, Styria, Tyrol and Vorarlberg, which were later to form the core of the Austrian republic (Table 2.a).

In 1919 various nationality groups of the Habsburg Empire successfully claimed independence; most of these successor states did not institutionalize systems of free nationwide elections. The predominantly German-speaking provinces established an independent Austrian republic. The Constitution of 1920 established a bicameral Parliament. Membership in the upper chamber the Bundesrat was determined by the Land assemblies. Membership in the lower house, the Nationalrat, was by popular election. Proportional representation in 25 constituencies using the d'Hondt highest average system replaced the majority system used in the Empire. Women gained the vote and the voting age was reduced to 20. In 1920 a second-stage seat distribution at national level was introduced, employing the d'Hondt system; 15 of the 165 seats in the Nationalrat were to be distributed at the second stage. In 1923 the Hagenbach-Bischoff system replaced the d'Hondt system at the constituency level. The second stage distribution continued to be calculated according to the d'Hondt method, but in four constituency groupings (Wahlkreisverbände) rather than for the country as a whole. In order to participate in the second stage, a party had to win at least one constituency seat. In 1919 provincial laws prescribed compulsory voting in Nationalrat elections in the Tyrol and Vorarlberg. Styria followed suit in 1949 and Carinthia in 1986.

Table 2.a FIFTH CURIA ASSEMBLY ELECTION RESULTS: AUSTRIAN PROVINCES

	14 May 1907			13 June 1911		
	Votes	%	Seats	Votes	%	Seats
Christian Social Party	658,198	52.3	94	555,986	45.5	70
Social Democrats	264,431	21.0	28	310,663	25.4	33
German Agrarians	16,656	1.3	0	9,214	0.8	1
German Conservative	15,260	1.2	1	12,308	1.0	1
German National Party	8,481	0.7	2	26,779	2.2	5
German People's Party	83,073	6.6	15	55,182	4.5	14
German Progressive Party	20,211	1.6	2	—	—	—
Italian parties	57,704	4.6	10	47,719	3.9	9
Slovene parties	57,020	4.5	8	53,063	4.3	8
German Farmers' League	—	—	—	15,301	1.2	0
German Freedom Party	—	—	—	62,789	5.1	15
Upper Austrian Farmers' League	—	—	—	22,009	1.8	0
Others	77,108	6.1	2	53,214	4.4	6
Total Valid Votes	1,258,142	100	162	1,224,227	100	162
Electorate	1,488,350			1,546,987		

Source: *Österreichische Statistik*, 1912: 8-10.

The constitution of the First Republic provided for a president as the formal head of state, chosen for a four-year term by a joint session of the two houses of parliament. In 1929 a constitutional amendment was passed lengthening the president's term of office to six years and providing for direct popular election, with a second round ballot between the two leading candidates if no one received an absolute majority in the first round. When the first election under the new system was scheduled to take place in 1931, the Christian Social and Social Democratic parties agreed to re-elect the incumbent president Wilhelm Miklas under the old system. Thus, no popular vote for a President occurred in the First Republic.

In 1934 the Social Democratic Party was suppressed and Austria became a one-party corporate state. Four years later the Anschluss led to its absorption as a region of Nazi Germany. After the defeat of Germany in 1945, the Second Austrian Republic was established as a federal system with the same territorial boundaries as the First Republic. Until the signature of the Austrian State Treaty in 1955 the country was under four-power Allied military occupation.

The Second Republic restored the 1920 Constitution, as modified in 1929, with a bicameral Parliament in which the upper house the Bundesrat is chosen by the

Land assemblies and the lower house, the Nationalrat, is elected by the same system in use at the end of the First Republic. The 1945 election law disenfranchised all those who had been members of the Nazi Party or its military affiliates. Voting rights for all but the most heavily incriminated Nazis were restored in 1948, increasing the electorate by about half a million (Ucakar, 1985: 463). In 1968 the voting age was reduced to 19. In 1970 the number of constituencies was reduced to nine and the number of Wahlkreisverbände was reduced to two. The method of computing the constituency quota was altered to the Hare method, starting in 1971.

Voting in presidential elections was compulsory in the whole of Austria until 1982 when a constitutional amendment transferred the authority to impose such a requirement to the provinces. The four provinces where voting for Nationalrat elections is compulsory now also have compulsory voting in presidential elections. The first president of the Second Republic, Karl Renner, a Socialist, was elected by parliament in 1945; the first direct popular election did not take place until 1951 when a Socialist, Theodor Körner, was elected for a four-year term of office (see Table 2.5a). The following have been Presidents of Austria since 1945:

President	*Period in Office*	*Party*
Karl Renner	1945-1951	Socialist
Theodor Körner	1951-1957	Socialist
Adolf Scharf	1957-1965	Socialist
Franz Jonas	1965-1974	Socialist
Rudolf Kirschläger	1974-1986	Socialist [1]
Kurt Waldheim	1986-	People's

[1] Unopposed by the People's Party in 1980.

Sources:

Kaiserlich-Königliche Statistisches Zentral-Commission, 'Ergebnisse der Reichsratswahlen 1911', *Österreichisches Statistik*, vii, 1 (1912)

Österreichischen Statistischen Zentralamt, *Die Nationalratswahl vom 9. Oktober 1949* (Vienna, 1950) and subsequent volumes in the same series

W. Simon, 'Democracy in the shadow of imposed sovereignty: the First Republic of Austria', in J. Linz and A. Stepan (eds.), *The Breakdown of Democratic Regimes* (Baltimore: Johns Hopkins University Press, 1978), 80-121.

R. Stiefbold, A. Leupold-Löwenthal, G. Ress, W. Lichem and D. Marvick (eds.), 'Wahlstatistik', *Wahlen und Parteien in Österreich*, III, C (Vienna: Institute für Höhere Studien, 1966)

R. Stiefbold and R. Metzler-Andelberg, 'Austria', in S. Rokkan and J. Meyriat (eds.), *International Guide to Electoral Statistics* (The Hague and Paris: Mouton, 1969)

M. Sully, *Political Parties and Elections in Austria* (London: Hurst, 1981)

K. Ucakar, *Demokratie und Wahlrecht in Österreich* (Vienna: Verlag für Gesellschaftskritik, 1985)

Table 2.1 POLITICAL PARTIES IN AUSTRIA SINCE 1919

	Party Names	Elections Contested Years	Number
1	Socialists. Initially Sozialdemokratische Arbeiterpartei - SDP ; since 1945 Sozialistische Partei Österreichs - SPÖ	1919ff	18
2	Christian Social Party (Christlichsoziale Partei - CSP); since 1945 the Austrian People's Party (Österreichische Volkspartei - ÖVP)	1919ff	18
3	German Nationalists[1]	1919	1
4	Czechs[2]	1919-1923	3
5	Communist Party (Kommunistische Partei Österreichs - KPÖ)[3]	1920ff	17
6	Greater German People's Party (Grossdeutsche Volkspartei - GdVP)	1920-1930	4
7	Land League (Landbund)[4]	1920-1930	4
8	Carinthian Unity List (Kärntner Einheitsliste)[5]	1923	1
9	National Socialist German Workers' Party: Hitler Movement (Nationalsozialistischer Deutscher Arbeiterpartei: Hitlerbewegung)[6]	1927-1930	2
10	Fatherland Front (Heimatblock)	1930	1
11	League of Independents (Verband der Unabhängigen, VdU); from 1956 the Freedom Party (Freiheitliche Partei Österreichs - FPÖ)[7]	1949ff	12
12	Democratic Progressive Party (Demokratische Fortschrittliche Partei - DFP)[8]	1966-1970	2
13	United Greens of Austria (Vereinte Grünen Österreichs - VGÖ)	1983	1
14	Alternative List (Alternative Liste Österreichs - ALÖ)	1983	1
15	Green Alternative (Die Grüne Alternative) [9]	1986	1

1 Comprises several nationalist parties whose elected deputies formed the Grossdeutsche Partei. These eventually merged to form the Greater German People's Party with the exception of some agrarian parties who united to form the Land League in 1922.

2 Representatives of the Czech-speaking minority in Lower Austria and Vienna.

3 In 1949 the Left Block (Kommunistische Partei Osterreichs und Linkssozialisten - Linksblock); in 1953 the Austrian People's Opposition (Wahlgemeinschaft Osterreichisches Volksopposition); from 1956 to 1966 Communists and Left Socialists (Kommunisten und Linkssozialisten).

4 In 1920 various regional agrarian parties which united to form the Landbund in 1922.

5 An electoral alliance in Carinthia between the Christian Social and Greater German People's parties and the Carinthian Farmers' League.

6 Contested the 1927 election as the Volkisch-sozialer Block.

7 Contested the 1949 election as the Electoral Party of Independents (Wahlpartei der Unabhängigen - WdU). Merged with the Freedom Party (Freiheitspartei) an extreme rightwing party founded in 1955, to form the Freedom Party in 1956.

8 Formed by ex-members of the Socialist Party led by Fritz Olah, a former Minister of the Interior.

9 An alliance of the ALÖ, the VGÖ, Citizens Parliamentary Initiative (Bürgerinitiative Parlament) and various provincial groups including the Slovene Koroska Enstra Lista (the Carinthian Unity List), headed by Frieda Meissner-Blau, the Green candidate in the 1986 presidential election.

Table 2.2a DATES OF ELECTIONS : NATIONALRAT[1]

1	16 February 1919	10	10 May 1959
2	17 October 1920	11	18 November 1962
3	21 October 1923	12	6 March 1966
4	24 April 1927	13	1 March 1970
5	9 November 1930	14	10 October 1971
6	25 October 1945	15	5 October 1975
7	9 October 1949	16	6 May 1979
8	22 February 1953	17	24 April 1983
9	13 May 1956	18	23 November 1986

[1] In 1919 the Nationalversammlung.

Source: Österreichische Statistische Zentralamt.

Table 2.2b DATES OF PRESIDENTIAL ELECTIONS 1951-1986

1	6 and 27 May 1951	5	25 April 1971
2	5 May 1957	6	23 June 1974
3	28 April 1963	7	18 May 1980
4	23 May 1965	8	4 May, 8 June 1986

Source: Österreichische Statistische Zentralamt.

Table 2.3a AUSTRIA Total Votes 1919-1956

	1919	1920[1]	1923	1927	1930	1945	1949	1953	1956
Electorate	3,554,242	3,752,212	3,849,484	4,119,626	4,121,282	3,449,605	4,391,815	4,586,870	4,614,464
Valid Votes	2,973,454	2,980,328	3,312,606	3,641,526	3,688,068	3,217,354	4,193,733	4,318,688	4,351,908
Invalid Votes	24,843	n.a	38,249	35,907	28,098	35,975	56,883	76,831	75,803
Total Votes	2,998,297	n.a	3,350,855	3,677,433	3,716,166	3,253,329	4,250,616	4,395,519	4,427,711
PARTY VOTES									
1 Socialists	1,211,814	1,072,709	1,311,870	1,539,635	1,517,146	1,434,898	1,623,524	1,818,517	1,873,295
2 Christian Social/People's Party	1,068,382	1,245,531	1,459,047	} 1,756,761	1,314,956	1,602,227	1,846,581	1,781,777	1,999,986
6 Greater German People's Party	-	390,013	259,373		471,944[2]	-	-	-	-
3 German Nationalists	545,938	-	-	-	-	-	-	-	-
4 Czechs	67,514	7,580	7,580	-	-	-	-	-	-
5 Communist Party	-	27,386	22,164	16,119	20,951	174,257	213,066	228,159	192,438
7 Land League	-	124,014	99,583	230,157	-	-	-	-	-
8 Carinthian Unity List	-	-	95,465	-	-	-	-	-	-
9 Nazi Party	-	-	-	26,991	111,627	-	-	-	-
10 Fatherland Front	-	-	-	-	227,401	-	-	-	-
11 League of Independents	-	-	-	-	-	-	489,273	472,866	283,749
Others	79,806	112,995	57,522	71,863	24,043	5,972	21,289	17,369	2,440

1 Includes results of elections held in Carinthia on 19 June 1921 and Burgenland on 18 June 1922.

2 Comprises 428,255 votes cast for the Nationaler Wirtschaftsblock und Landbund and 43,689 votes cast for independant Land League lists in Salzburg and Upper Austria.

Source: *Die Nationalratswahl vom 23. November 1986*: 54-61.

Table 2.3b AUSTRIA Percentage of Votes 1919-1956

	1919	1920	1923	1927	1930	1945	1949	1953	1956
Total Votes	84.4	79.4	87.0	89.3	90.2	94.3	96.8	95.8	96.0
Valid Votes	83.7	79.4	86.1	88.3	89.5	93.3	95.5	94.2	94.3
Invalid Votes	0.7	n.a	1.0	0.9	0.7	1.0	1.3	1.7	1.6
Share Invalid	0.8	n.a	1.0	1.0	0.8	1.1	1.3	1.7	1.7
PARTY VOTES									
1 Socialists	40.8	36.0	39.6	42.3	41.1	44.6	38.7	42.1	43.0
2 Christian Social Party/People's Party	35.9	41.8	44.0		35.7	49.8	44.0	41.3	46.0
			}	48.2					
6 Greater German People's Party	-	13.1	7.8		-	-	-	-	-
3 German Nationalists	18.4	-	-	-	-	-	-	-	-
4 Czechs	2.3	0.3	0.2	-	-	-	-	-	-
5 Communist Party	-	0.9	0.7	0.4	0.6	5.4	5.1	5.3	4.4
7 Land League	-	4.2	3.0	6.3	12.8	-	-	-	-
8 Carinthian Unity List	-	-	2.9	-	-	-	-	-	-
9 Nazi Party	-	-	-	0.7	3.0	-	-	-	-
10 Fatherland Front	-	-	-	-	6.2	-	-	-	-
11 League of Independents	-	-	-	-	-	-	11.7	10.9	6.5
Others	2.7	3.7	1.7	2.0	0.7	0.2	0.5	0.4	0.1

Table 2.3c AUSTRIA Number of Seats Won in the Nationalrat 1919-1956

	1919	1920	1923	1927	1930	1945	1949	1953	1956
1 Socialists	72	69	68	71	72	76	67	73	74
2 Christian Social Party/People's Party	69	85	80	73	66	85	77	74	82
6 Greater German People's Party	–	21	6	12	10	–	–	–	–
3 German Nationalists	27	–	–	–	–	–	–	–	–
4 Czechs	1	0	0	–	–	–	–	–	–
5 Communist Party	–	0	0	0	0	4	5	4	3
7 Land League	–	7	5	9	9	–	–	–	–
8 Carinthian Unity List	–	–	6[1]	–	–	–	–	–	–
9 Nazi Party	–	–	–	0	0	–	–	–	–
10 Fatherland Front	–	–	–	–	8	–	–	–	–
11 League of Independents	–	–	–	–	–	–	16	14	6
Others	1	1	0	0	0	0	0	0	0
Total Seats	170	183	165	165	165	165	165	165	165

1 Four deputies joined the Greater German People's Party and two joined the Christian Social Party.

Source: *Die Nationalratswahl vom 23. November 1986*: 54-61

Table 2.3d AUSTRIA Percentage of Seats Won in the Nationalrat 1919-1956

	1919	1920	1923	1927	1930	1945	1949	1953	1956
1 Socialists	42.3	37.7	41.2	43.0	43.6	46.1	40.6	44.2	44.8
2 Christian Social Party/People's Party	40.6	46.4	48.5	44.2	40.0	51.5	46.7	44.8	49.7
6 Greater German People's Party	-	11.5	3.6	7.2	6.1	-	-	-	-
3 German Nationalists	15.9	-	-	-	-	-	-	-	-
4 Czechs	0.6	0.0	0.0	-	-	-	-	-	-
5 Communist Party	-	0.0	0.0	0.0	0.0	2.4	3.0	2.4	1.8
7 Land League	-	3.8	3.0	5.5	5.5	-	-	-	-
8 Carinthian Unity List	-	-	3.6	-	-	-	-	-	-
9 Nazi Party	-	-	-	0.0	0.0	-	-	-	-
10 Fatherland Front	-	-	-	-	4.8	-	-	-	-
11 League of Independents	-	-	-	-	-	-	9.7	8.5	3.6
Others	0.6	0.5	0.0	0.0	0.0	0.0	0.0	0.0	0.0

Table 2.4a AUSTRIA Total Votes 1959-1986

	1959	1962	1966	1970	1971	1975	1979	1983	1986
Electorate	4,696,603	4,805,351	4,886,818	5,045,841	4,984,448	5,019,277	5,186,735	5,316,436	5,461,414
Valid Votes	4,362,856	4,456,131	4,531,885	4,588,961	4,556,990	4,613,432	4,729,251	4,853,417	4,852,188
Invalid Votes	61,802	49,876	52,085	41,890	50,626	49,252	54,922	69,037	88,110
Total Votes	4,424,658	4,506,007	4,583,970	4,630,851	4,607,616	4,662,684	4,784,173	4,922,454	4,940,298
PARTY VOTES									
1 Socialist Party	1,953,935	1,960,685	1,928,985	2,221,981	2,280,168	2,326,201	2,413,226	2,312,529	2,092,024
2 People's Party	1,928,043	2,024,501	2,191,109	2,051,012	1,964,713	1,981,291	1,981,739	2,097,808	2,003,663
5 Communist Party	142,578	135,520	18,636	44,750	61,762	55,032	45,280	31,912	35,104
11 Freedom Party	336,110	313,895	242,570	253,425	248,473	249,444	286,743	241,789	472,205
12 Democratic Progressive Party	-	-	148,528	17,405	-	-	-	-	-
13 United Greens of Austria	-	-	-	-	-	-	-	93,766	-
14 Alternative List	-	-	-	-	-	-	-	65,816	-
15 Green Alternative	-	-	-	-	-	-	-	-	234,028
Others	2,190	21,530	2,057	388	1,874	1,464	2,263	9,777	15,164

Source: *Die Nationalratswahl vom 23. November 1986*: 54-59

Table 2.4b AUSTRIA Percentage of Votes 1959-1986

	1959	1962	1966	1970	1971	1975	1979	1983	1986
Total Votes	94.2	93.8	93.8	91.8	92.4	92.9	92.2	92.6	90.5
Valid Votes	92.9	92.7	92.7	90.9	91.4	91.9	91.2	91.3	88.8
Invalid Votes	1.3	1.0	1.1	0.8	1.0	1.0	1.1	1.3	1.6
Share Invalid	1.4	1.1	1.1	0.9	1.1	1.1	1.1	1.4	1.8
PARTY VOTES									
1 Socialist Party	44.8	44.0	42.6	48.4	50.0	50.4	51.0	47.6	43.1
2 People's Party	44.2	45.4	48.3	44.7	43.1	42.9	41.9	43.2	41.3
5 Communist Party	3.3	3.0	0.4	1.0	1.4	1.2	1.0	0.6	0.7
11 Freedom Party	7.7	7.0	5.4	5.5	5.5	5.4	6.1	5.0	9.7
12 Democratic Progressive Party	-	-	3.3	0.4	-	-	-	-	-
13 United Greens of Austria	-	-	-	-	-	-	-	1.9	-
14 Alternative List	-	-	-	-	-	-	-	1.4	-
15 Green Alternative	-	-	-	-	-	-	-	-	4.8
Others	0.1	0.5	0.0	0.0	0.0	0.0	0.0	0.2	0.3

Table 2.4c AUSTRIA Number of Seats Won in the Nationalrat 1959-1986

	1959	1962	1966	1970	1971	1975	1979	1983	1986
1 Socialist Party	78	76	74	81	93	93	95	90	80
2 People's Party	79	81	85	79	80	80	77	81	77
5 Communist Party	0	0	0	0	0	0	0	0	0
11 Freedom Party	8	8	6	5	10	10	11	12	18
12 Democratic Progressive Party	–	–	0	0	–	–	–	–	–
13 United Greens of Austria	–	–	–	–	–	–	–	0	–
14 Alternative List	–	–	–	–	–	–	–	0	–
15 Green Alternative	–	–	–	–	–	–	–	–	8
Others	0	0	0	0	0	0	0	0	0
Total Seats	165	165	165	165	183	183	183	183	183

Source: *Die Nationalratswahl vom 23. November 1986*: 54-59

Table 2.4d AUSTRIA Percentage of Seats Won in the Nationalrat 1959-1986

	1959	1962	1966	1970	1971	1975	1979	1983	1986
1 Socialist Party	47.3	46.1	44.8	49.1	50.8	50.8	51.9	49.2	43.7
2 People's Party	47.9	49.1	51.5	47.9	43.7	43.7	42.1	44.3	42.1
5 Communist Party	0.0	0.0	0.0	0.0	0.0	0.0	0.0	0.0	0.0
11 Freedom Party	4.8	4.8	3.6	3.0	5.5	5.5	6.0	6.6	9.8
12 Democratic Progressive Party	–	–	0.0	0.0	–	–	–	–	–
13 United Greens of Austria	–	–	–	–	–	–	–	0.0	–
14 Alternative List	–	–	–	–	–	–	–	0.0	–
15 Green Alternative	–	–	–	–	–	–	–	–	4.4
Others	0.0	0.0	0.0	0.0	0.0	0.0	0.0	0.0	0.0

Table 2.5a AUSTRIA Presidential Elections 1951-1986

	1951 (6 May)	1951 (27 May)	1957	1963	1965	1971	1974	1980	1986 (May)	1986 (June)
Electorate	4,513,597	4,513,597	4,630,997	4,869,928	4,874,928	5,024,324	5,031,772	5,215,875	5,436,846	5,436,846
Valid Votes	4,298,347	4,184,953	4,417,859	4,464,120	4,585,324	4,712,048	4,630,837	4,430,889	4,719,980	4,571,810
Invalid Votes	72,227	188,241	81,706	190,537	94,103	75,658	102,179	438,165	144,729	174,039
Total Votes	4,370,574	4,373,194	4,499,565	4,654,657	4,679,427	4,787,706	4,733,016	4,779,054	4,864,709	4,745,849
PARTY VOTES										
1 Socialist Party	1,682,881	2,178,631	2,258,255	2,473,349	2,324,436	2,487,239	2,392,367	} 3,538,748[2]	2,061,104	2,107,023
2 People's Party	1,725,451	2,006,322	2,159,604	1,814,125	2,260,888	2,224,809	2,238,470		2,343,463	2,464,787
5 Communist Party	219,969	–	–	–	–	–	–	–	–	–
13 United Greens	–	–	–	–	–	–	–	–	259,689	–
11 Freedom Party	662,501	–	–	–	–	–	–	751,400	55,724[4]	–
European Federal Party	–	–	–	176,646[1]	–	–	–	–	–	–
National Democrats[3]	–	–	–	–	–	–	–	140,741	–	–
Others	7,545	–	–	–	–	–	–	–	–	–

1 The European Federal Party also contested the 1962 Nationalrat election. It won 21,530 votes.
2 The incumbent President, Dr. Rudolf Kirschläger, elected as the Socialist Party candidate in 1974, was again the Socialist candidate in 1980 and was unopposed by the People's Party.
3 The National Democratic Party is a party of the extreme right wing which also contested the 1970 Nationalrat election winning 2,631 votes.
4 Right-wing member of the Freedom Party, standing as an Independent.

Sources: *Die Wahl des Bundespräsident am 6. und 27. Mai 1951* and subsequent volumes in the same series.

Table 2.5b AUSTRIA Percentage of Votes 1951-1986

	1951 (6 May)	1951 (27 May)	1957	1963	1965	1971	1974	1980	1986 (May)	1986 (June)
Valid Votes	95.2	92.7	95.4	91.7	94.1	93.8	92.0	85.0	86.8	84.1
Invalid Votes	1.6	4.2	1.8	3.9	1.9	1.6	2.0	6.7	2.7	3.2
Total Votes	96.8	96.9	97.2	95.6	96.0	95.3	94.1	91.6	89.5	87.2
Share Invalid	1.7	4.3	1.8	3.9	2.0	1.6	2.2	7.3	3.0	3.7
PARTY VOTES										
1 Socialist Party	39.2	52.1	51.1	55.4	50.7	52.8	51.7		43.7	46.1
							}	79.9		
2 People's Party	40.1	47.9	48.9	40.6	49.3	47.2	48.3		49.6	53.9
5 Communist Party	5.1	-	-	-	-	-	-	-	-	-
11 Freedom Party	15.4	-	-	-	-	-	-	17.0	1.2	-
13 United Greens	-	-	-	-	-	-	-	-	5.5	-
European Federal Party	-	-	-	4.0	-	-	-	-	-	-
National Democrats	-	-	-	-	-	-	-	3.2	-	-
Others	0.2	-	-	-	-	-	-	-	-	-

Chapter 3

BELGIUM

Belgium became an independent state in 1830. The 1831 Constitution set up a two-chamber Parliament consisting of a Chamber of Representatives (In Flemish, Kamer der Volksvertegenwoordigers; in French, Chambre des Représentants) and a Senate (Senaat/Sénat). The government is responsible to both Chambers, which have equal legislative powers. Different political groupings existed from 1830 onwards; unionism was the rule in parliament and government until 1847. Distinct national parties did not exist, although there was a cleavage between clericals and anti-clericals. The Liberals formed a national party organisation in 1846. The process of party formation by the Catholics began in the 1860s and was formally achieved only in 1884. In the following year several workers' organisations united to form the *Parti ouvrier belge* which first gained representation in parliament after the achievement of manhood suffrage in 1893.

From 1830 to 1893, the period of the *régime censitaire*, the right to vote for the Chamber of Representatives was confined to men over 25 who paid a minimum direct tax. Until 1848, when a uniform rate of 20 florins was introduced, the tax qualification varied between rural and urban areas and between provinces. In 1830 only about five percent of the male population aged over 25 could vote. By the early 1880s this had increased to about eight percent. Universal male suffrage, modified by plural voting, was introduced in 1893. Voting was made compulsory. All married men over 35 who occupied a house with a taxable value of at least five francs received an extra vote, as did all owners of property worth more than 2,000 francs, and recipients of rents and dividends of more than 1,000 francs (*Vote censitaire*) Electors with a higher education diploma were entitled to two extra votes (*Vote capacitaire*). No one could have more than three votes. In 1893, of a total of 1,370,000 voters, approximately 850,000 had only one vote, 290,000 had two votes and 220,000 three votes. Plural electors were thus fewer in number than those with only one vote, but in aggregate they cast more ballots (Gilissen, 1958: 125). Plural voting was abolished and the voting age reduced to 21 for the first postwar election in 1919. These changes were incorporated in the Constitution in 1920. Mothers and widows of soldiers who had died in the war were enfranchised, but women were not given the vote on the same basis as men until 1948. The voting age was reduced to 18 for European elections in 1979 and for national elections in 1981.

Until 1899 a majority system was used in predominantly multi-member constituencies; if all the seats in a constituency were not claimed by candidates on a list that won an absolute majority of the vote in the first round, a run-off election was held in which the number of candidates was restricted to twice the number of seats, in order to ensure a majority for all the seats in the constituency (Moyne, 1970: 21). In 1899 the d'Hondt system of proportional representation replaced the majority system. Seats were allocated at the constituency level. The 1919 electoral law provided for a second allocation of seats at the provincial level (*apparentement*) in order to achieve greater proportionality. In each constituency the electoral divisor was the number of votes cast divided by the number of seats. The seats awarded to each party was decided by dividing its total vote by the electoral divisor. If any seats remained unallocated, each party's constituency votes were transferred to a provincial pool, where a second allocation was made using the d'Hondt method.

Until the constitutional reforms of 1920 the usual practice was to have a partial not a general election, that is, voting in about half the provinces at one time. In partial elections, the two groups which alternated in voting firstly consisted of Antwerp, Brabant, West Flanders, Luxembourg and Namur; and secondly of East Flanders, Hainaut, Liège and Limburg. Nationwide elections were held only when the parliament was dissolved; only eight such elections were held from 1847 to 1914. The overall distribution of seats in the chamber after each partial and general election is presented in Tables 3.6a and 3.6b.

The 1831 constitution provided for a directly elected Senate with the same suffrage as the Chamber. Membership of the Senate was, however, limited to the highest tax-payers; only 412 persons were eligible to fill the 106 seats in the Senate in 1842 (Mabille, 1986: 118). In 1893 the membership of the Senate was extended to include Senators elected indirectly by the nine provincial councils, and eligibility provisions were somewhat liberalised. The 1921 constitutional reform provided for a third class of Senators, those coopted by the directly and indirectly elected members. The eligibility rules were further liberalised to include those holding or having held high office in public or private sector organizations, and university graduates. Inflation has so extended the tax-payment qualification that eligibility is now almost universal (Senelle, 1974).

Historically Belgian parties divided along lines of religion and class, divisions that cut across the linguistic differences between francophones and flemish speakers (Lorwin, 1966). In the 1960s the growing significance of the language issue in Belgian politics led first to the growth in support for regionally based parties and then to the breakup along linguistic lines of the major national parties. The Christian Social and Christian People's parties split in 1968, although they still presented a common list in the bilingual area of Brussels in the 1971 election. The Liberals divided in 1971 with a third liberal party emerging in Brussels; all the francophone liberals were reunited as the *Parti réformateur libéral* in 1979. The Socialist Party broke up along linguistic lines in 1978.

Sources:

Annuaire Statistique de la Belgique 1967, 1970 (Brussels: Institut National de Statistique, 1967 and 1970)

R.E. De Smet, R. Evalenko and W. Fraeys, *Atlas des élections belges 1919-1954* (Brussels: Institut de Sociologie Solvay, U.L.B., 1958)

R.E. De Smet, R. Evalenko and W. Fraeys, *Supplement comportant les résultats des élections législatives du ler juin 1958* (1961)

R.E. De Smet, R. Evalenko and W. Fraeys, *Deuxième supplément comportant les résults des élections législatives du 26 mars 1961* (1962)

W. Fraeys, 'Les élections législatives du 17 décembre 1978', *Res Publica* 21,2 (1979) 309-328

W. Fraeys, 'Les élections législatives de 13 octobre 1985' *Res Publica* 28,2 (1986) 213-233

J. Gilissen, *Le régime représentatif en Belgique depuis 1790* (Brussels: Renaissance du Livre, 1958)

T.K. Hill, 'Belgium: political change in a segmented society', in R. Rose (ed.) *Electoral Behavior: a Comparative Handbook* (New York: Free Press, 1974) 29-107

C. Lebas, *L'union des catholiques et des libéraux de 1839 à 1847* (Louvain: Editions Nauwelaerts, 1960)

Les partis politiques en Belgique, Dossier du CRISP, Number 21 (Brussels: Centre de recherche et d'information socio-politiques, 3rd ed., 1986)

V. Lorwin, 'Belgium: religion, class and language in national politics' in R.A. Dahl (ed.), *Political Oppositions in Western Democracies* (New Haven: Yale University Press, 1966) 147-87

Th. Luyckx, *Politieke Geschiednis van België* (Amsterdam/Brussels: Elsevier, fourth edition, 1978)

X. Mabille, *Histoire politique de la Belgique* (Brussels: CRISP, 1986)

Ministère de l'Intérieur, *Élections législatives-Chambre des Représentants: résultats officiels des élections du 23 mai 1965 et du 31 mars 1968* (Brussels: 1969) and subsequent volumes in same series

W. Moyne, *Résultats des élections belges entre 1847 et 1914* (Brussels: Institut Belge de Science Politique, 1970)

R. Senelle, 'The Belgian Constitution - Commentary' *Memo from Belgium No. 166* (Brussels: Ministry of Foreign Affairs, 1974)

G. Van den Berghe, 'Belgium' in G. Hand, J. Georgel and C. Sasse (eds.) *European Electoral Systems Handbook* (London: Butterworths, 1979) 1-28

H. Van Impe, *Le régime parlementaire en Belgique* (Brussels: Bruylant, 1968)

E. Witte and J. Craeybeckx, *La Belgique politique de 1830 a nos jours* (Brussels: Ed. Labor, 1987)

F. Zombek-Fuks and W. Fraeys, 'Belgique' in S. Rokkan and J. Meyriat (eds.), *International Guide to Electoral Statistics* (The Hague and Paris: Mouton, 1969) 47-57

Table 3.1 POLITICAL PARTIES IN BELGIUM SINCE 1847

	Party Names	Elections Contested Years	Number
1	Catholic Party; since 1945 francophone Christian Social Party (Parti social chrétien - PSC) and flemish Christian People's Party (Christelijke Volkspartij - CVP)[1]	1847-1965	51
2	Liberal Party (Liberale Partij/ Parti libéral). In 1961 renamed Party of Liberty and Progress (Partij voor Vrijheid en Vooruitgang - PVV/Parti de la liberté et du progrès - PLP) [2]	1847-1971	53
3	Belgian Workers' Party (Belgische Werkliedenpartij - BWP/Parti ouvrier belge - POB). In 1945 renamed Belgian Socialist Party (Belgische Socialistische Partij - BSP/ Parti socialiste belge - PSB) [3]	1890-1977	31
4	Daensists (Christene Volkspartij) [4]	1894-1914	11
5	Liberal-Workers/Socialist Party cartels [5]	1894-1898; 1906-1912;1946; 1950-1958	11
6	Dissident Catholic Lists [6]	1919-1936; 1945-1954; 1961-1965	12
7	Ex-Servicemen (Anciens combattants)	1919-1922	
8	Flemish Nationalists. Until 1932 the Front Party (Frontpartij); 1936-39 the Flemish National League (Vlaamsch Nationaal Verbond - VNV); 1949 Flemish Concentration (Vlaamsch Concentratie); 1954 Flemish Christian Peoples' Union (Christelijke Vlaamse Volksunie). Since 1954 Volksunie (VU)	1919-1939; 1949; 1954ff	20
9	Middle Class Party (Classes moyennes)	1919-1928	4
10	Communist Party (Kommunistische Partij van België - KPB/Parti communiste de Belgique - PCB)	1921ff	22
11	German Minority. In 1929-32 Christian People's Party (Christlich Volkspartei). In 1939 Heimattreue Front. In 1971 Christlich Unabhängige Wählerverband. From 1972 Partei der Deutschsprächigen Belgier [7]	1929-1932; 1939;1971ff	8
12	Rexists (Rex)	1936-1939	2
13	Democratic Union (Union démocratique belge - UDB)	1946	1
14	Francophone Democratic Front (Front démocratique des Bruxellois francophones - FDF)	1965ff	9

15	Walloon Democratic Front (Front démocratique wallon)	1965	1
16	Walloon Front (Front wallon)	1965	1
17	Walloon Workers' Party (Parti wallon des travailleurs - PWT)	1965-1968	2
18	Walloon Rally (Rassemblement wallon) [8]	1968ff	8
19	Christian People's Party (Christelijke Volkspartij - CVP)	1971ff	7
20	Christian Social Party (Parti social chrétien - PSC)	1971ff	7
21	Party of Liberty and Progress (Partij voor Vrijheid en Vooruitgang - PVV)	1974ff	4
22	Francophone Liberals: Party of Liberty and Progress (Parti de la liberté et du progrès - PLP). From November 1976 Parti des réformes et de la liberté de Wallonie (PRLW). Since 1979 Parti réformateur libéral (PRL) [9]	1974ff	6
23	Brussels Liberal Party (Parti libéral); in 1974 Parti libéral démocrate et pluraliste - PLDP) [10]	1971-1978	4
24	All Power to the Workers (Alle Macht aan de Arbeiders/Tout le pouvoir aux ouvriers-AMADA/ TPO; from 1981 Labour Party (Partij van der Arbeid/Parti du travail de Belgique - PVDA/PTB)	1974ff	6
25	Revolutionary Workers' League (Ligue révolutionnaire des travailleurs/Revolutionaire Arbeidersliga - LRT/RAL); from 1985 Socialist Workers Party (Parti ouvrier socialiste/ Socialistische Arbeiderspartij - POS/SAP)	1977ff	5
26	Écolo - Francophone Greens [11]	1977ff	5
27	Agalev - Flemish-speaking Greens [12]	1977ff	5
28	Democratic Union for the Respect of Labour (Union démocratique pour le respect du travail/ Respect voor Arbeid en Demokratie - UDRT/RAD) [13]	1978ff	4
29	Flemish Block (Vlaamse Blok) [14]	1978ff	4
30	Flemish Socialist Party (Belgische Socialistische Partij - BSP; since March 1980 Socialistische Partij - SP)	1978ff	4
31	Francophone Socialist Party (Parti socialiste - PS)	1978ff	4

[1] Before the First World War Catholic Party organization was very weak. In 1921 a Catholic Union (Union catholique belge) was established as a federation of social groups (*Standen*). In 1937 the party was reformed as the Catholic Block (Bloc catholique belge), a federation of separate flemish and french-speaking parties: the Katholieke Vlaamsche Volkspartij-KVV and the Parti catholique social-PCS. This gave way to the unitary PSC - CVP in 1945. In 1968 the two linguistic wings established themselves as separate parties, numbers 19 and 20 above.

[2] The Walloon and Flemish Liberals established independent parties in 1972, numbers 21 and 22 above.

[3] The walloon and flemish wings of the Socialist Party established independent parties in October 1978 (parties 29 and 30 above).

4 Christian Democrat party founded by the Abbé Daens in 1893.

5 Provincial-level electoral alliances between the Liberal Party and the Workers' Party and later the Socialist Party. For an estimate of the sharing out of the alliance votes see Hill, 1974: 101.

6 Various Catholic lists presented independently of the Catholic and Christian Social parties as identified in de Smet et al. 1958: 10-11, 1961,1962 and Ministère de l'Intérieur 1969ff.

7 Parties representing the German minority in areas annexed by Belgium from Germany after the First World War. The pro-Nazi Heimattreue Front had no connection with the German-language parties which preceded and followed it.

8 Founded as the Parti wallon in 1965 and renamed the Rassamblement wallon before the 1968 election, uniting the Front wallon, a wing of the Parti wallon des travailleurs, and several independents. The Rassemblement wallon did not contest the 1985 election as a separate party. Personalities from the RW and two minor wallon parties combined to run as the Parti wallon.

9 Merged with a faction of the Rassemblement wallon to form the PRLW in November 1976. Reunited with the Brussels Liberals to form the PRL in 1979.

10 Brussels wing of the Parti de la liberté et du progrès. Contested the 1974 election in an electoral alliance with the Francophone Democratic Front. Merged with the walloon Liberals to form the Parti réformateur libéral in 1979.

11 In 1977 and 1978 various independent provincial francophone green lists. From the 1981 election, Écolo: Écologistes-confederés pour l'organisation de luttes originales, founded in 1980.

12 Anders gaan leven - Live Differently, the Flemish green party.

13 The UDRT/RAD list only presented candidates in five provinces in 1987. Some ex-UDRT leaders were candidates on the PSC-ApB (Alliance pour Bruxelles) list in Brussels.

14 Extreme right-wing nationalist party created in 1979 by the merger of two parties, the Flemish People's Party (Vlaamse Volkspartij - VVP) and the Flemish National Party (Vlaamse Nationale Partij - VNP) that had broken away from the Volksunie. They contested the 1978 elections as an electoral alliance under the label Flemish Block.

Table 3.2 DATES OF ELECTIONS : KAMER DER VOLKSVERTEGENWOORDIGERS/CHAMBRE DES REPRÉSENTANTS

1.	8 June 1847 (B)	30.	27 May 1900 (G)
2.	13 June 1848 (G)	31.	25 May 1902 (A)
3.	11 June 1850 (A)	32.	29 May 1904 (B)
4.	8 June 1852 (B)	33.	27 May 1906 (A)
5.	13 June 1854 (A)	34.	24 May 1908 (B)
6.	10 June 1856 (B)	35.	22 May 1910 (A)
7.	10 December 1857 (G)	36.	2 June 1912 (G)
8.	14 June 1859 (A)	37.	24 May 1914 (B)
9.	11 June 1861 (B)	38.	16 November 1919
10.	9 June 1863 (A)	39.	20 November 1921
11.	11 August 1864 (G)	40.	5 May 1925
12.	12 June 1866 (B)	41.	26 May 1929
13.	9 June 1868 (A)	42.	27 November 1932
14.	14 June 1870 (B)	43.	24 May 1936
15.	2 August 1870 (G)	44.	2 April 1939
16.	11 June 1872 (A)	45.	17 February 1946
17.	9 June 1874 (B)	46.	29 June 1949
18.	13 June 1876 (A)	47.	4 June 1950
19.	11 June 1878 (B)	48.	11 April 1954
20.	8 June 1880 (A)	49.	1 June 1958
21.	13 June 1882 (B)	50.	26 March 1961
22.	10 June 1884 (A)	51.	23 May 1965
23.	8 June 1886 (B)	52.	31 March 1968
24.	12 June 1888 (A)	53.	7 November 1971
25.	10 June 1890 (B)	54.	10 March 1974
26.	14 June 1892 (G)	55.	17 April 1977
27.	14 October 1894 (G)	56.	17 December 1978
28.	5 July 1896 (A)	57.	8 November 1981
29.	22 May 1898 (B)	58.	13 October 1985
		59.	13 December 1987

(G) indicates a general election during the period 1847 to 1914. Since 1919 all elections have been general elections.

(A) a partial election in the provinces of Antwerp, Brabant, Luxembourg, Namur and West Flanders.

(B) a partial election in East Flanders, Hainaut, Liège and Limburg.

Election dates from 1847 to 1898 refer to the first ballot.

Sources: Moyne, 1970; Ministère de l'Intérieur, 1969ff.

Table 3.3a BELGIUM Total Votes 1847-1864

	1847	1848*	1850	1852	1854	1856	1857*	1859	1861	1863	1864*
Electorate	22,572	79,076	40,435	42,053	45,884	45,573	90,543	49,672	47,555	52,519	103,717
Valid Votes[1]	17,541	44,311	27,954	29,092	28,008	27,640	71,783	27,778	27,778	39,109	79,566
Total Votes	18,906	52,955[2]	30,150	31,727	32,037	31,261	76,219	37,972[3]	30,538	40,565	83,949
PARTY VOTES											
1 Catholic Party	8,298	13,122	11,618	12,404	11,921	15,168	32,503	12,726	11,799	21,310	39,750
2 Liberal Party	9,142	30,806	15,320	16,688	16,087	12,472	39,280	15,052	15,979	17,799	39,576
Others	101	383	1,016	-	-	-	-	-	-	-	240

Table 3.3b BELGIUM Percentage of Votes 1847-1864

	1847	1848*	1850	1852	1854	1856	1857*	1859	1861	1863	1864*
Total Votes	77.7	56.0	69.1	69.2	61.0	60.6	79.3	55.9	58.4	74.5	76.7
PARTY VOTES											
1 Catholic Party	47.3	29.6	41.6	42.6	42.6	54.9	45.3	45.8	42.5	54.5	50.0
2 Liberal Party	52.1	69.5	54.8	57.4	57.4	45.1	54.7	54.2	57.5	45.5	49.7
Others	0.6	0.9	3.6	-	-	-	-	-	-	-	0.3

1 Until 1900 each elector was entitled to as many votes as there were seats in his constituency. Party votes have been estimated by dividing the number of valid votes cast by the number of seats in the consituency.

2 Excluding the Oudenarde constituency for which party votes are not available.

3 Excluding the Ieper constituency for which party votes are not available.

* Indicates a General Election.

Source: Moyne, 1970: 128-129

Table 3.3c BELGIUM Number of Seats Won in the Chambre des Représentants 1847-1864[1]

	1847	1848*	1850	1852	1854	1856	1857*	1859	1861	1863	1864*
1 Catholic Party	21	26	22	23	26	33	38 (9)	27 (9)	22	34	53
2 Liberal Party	33	82 (1)	32	31	28	21	70 (3)	31 (3)	36	24	63
Others	0	0	0	-	-	-	-	-	-	-	0
Total Seats	54	108 (1)	54	54	54	54	108 (12)	58 (12)	58	58	116

Table 3.3d BELGIUM Percentage of Seats Won in the Chambre des Représentants 1847-1864

	1847	1848*	1850	1852	1854	1856	1857*	1859	1861	1863	1864*
1 Catholic Party	38.9	24.1	40.7	42.6	48.1	61.1	35.2	46.7	37.9	58.6	45.7
2 Liberal Party	61.1	75.9	59.3	57.4	51.9	38.9	64.8	53.4	62.1	41.4	54.3
Others	0.0	0.0	0.0	-	-	-	-	-	-	-	0.0

1 Unopposed candidates reported in parenthesis. General election results are shown in bold type.

* Indicates a general election.

Source: Moyne, 1970: 128-125

Table 3.4a BELGIUM Total Votes 1866-1884

	1866	1868	1870 (June)	1870* (Aug.)	1872	1874	1876	1878	1880	1882	1884
Electorate	51,465	55,297	51,435	107,099	54,933	52,074	63,278	57,640	62,936	55,517	69,276
Valid Votes	36,025	30,721	30,871	72,873	30,470	33,395	42,740	36,051	42,301	41,689	54,790
Total Votes	38,933	34,079	33,373	79,083	36,179[1]	36,082	45,184	38,748	45,787	46,676	58,156
PARTY VOTES											
1 Catholic Party	15,060	16,918	13,698	39,705	20,949	15,864	22,952	17,085	20,700	19,681	33,428
2 Liberal Party	20,965	13,619	17,173	32,448	9,455	17,531	19,788	18,966	21,283	22,001	21,294
Others	-	184	-	720	66	-	-	-	318	7	68

Table 3.4b BELGIUM Percentage of Votes 1866-1884

	1866	1868	1870 (June)	1870* (Aug.)	1872	1874	1876	1878	1880	1882	1884
Total Votes	70.0	55.6	60.0	68.0	55.5	64.1	67.5	62.5	67.2	75.1	79.1
PARTY VOTES											
1 Catholic Party	41.8	55.1	44.4	54.5	68.8	47.5	53.7	47.4	48.9	47.2	61.0
2 Liberal Party	58.2	44.3	55.6	44.5	31.0	52.5	46.3	52.6	50.3	52.8	38.9
Others	-	0.6	-	1.0	0.2	-	-	-	0.8	0.0	0.1

1 Excluding the Nivelles constituency for which party votes are not available.

* Indicates a general election.

Source: Moyne, 1970: 128-125

Table 3.4c BELGIUM Number of Seats Won in the Chambre des Représentants 1866-1884

	1866	1868	1870 (June)	1870* (Aug.)	1872	1874	1876	1878	1880	1882	1884
1 Catholic Party	18	33	30	73	43	26	42	18	40	20	67
2 Liberal Party	43	30	31	51	20	35	21	48	26	49	2
Others	–	–	–	–	–	–	–	–	–	–	–
Total Seats	61	63	61	124	63	61	63	66	66	69	69

Table 3.4d BELGIUM Percentage of Seats Won in the Chambre des Représentants 1866-1884

	1866	1868	1870 (June)	1870* (Aug.)	1872	1874	1876	1878	1880	1882	1884
1 Catholic Party	29.5	52.4	49.2	58.9	68.3	42.6	66.7	27.3	60.6	29.0	97.1
2 Liberal Party	70.5	47.6	50.8	41.1	31.7	57.4	33.3	72.7	39.4	71.0	2.9
Others	–	–	–	–	–	–	–	–	–	–	–

* Indicates a general election.

Table 3.5a BELGIUM Total Votes 1886-1906[1]

	1886	1888	1890	1892*	1894*	1896	1898	1900*	1902	1904	1906
Electorate	57,692	73,276	59,452	136,707	2,111,127	1,076,151	1,093,103	2,269,414	1,164,185	1,216,735	1,259,242
Valid Votes	36,944	53,517	38,210	104,728[2]	1,802,980[3]	884,009	902,944	2,051,014	1,064,926	1,107,940	1,172,828
PARTY VOTES											
1 Catholic Party	17,979	31,273	17,253	56,199	921,607	492,547	373,375	994,245	596,382	486,643	636,446
2 Liberal Party	18,965	19,967	20,829	47,518	503,929	166,794	170,839	498,799	266,891	283,411	197,021
3 Workers' Party	-	-	98	167	237,920	74,762	190,492	461,095	159,370	287,847	72,224
4 Daensists	-	-	-	-	21,849	12,195	22,978	61,131	26,435	-	10,602
5 Liberal-Workers'/ Socialist cartels	-	-	-	-	94,129	129,227	123,256	-	-	20,761	234,677
Others	-	2,277	30	844	23,546	8,484	22,004	35,744	15,848	29,278	21,858

Table 3.5b BELGIUM Percentage of Votes 1886-1906

	1886	1888	1890	1892*	1894*	1896	1898	1900*	1902	1904	1906
Total Votes	64.0	73.0	64.3	76.6	85.4	82.1	82.6	90.4	91.5	91.1	93.1
PARTY VOTES											
1 Catholic Party	48.7	58.4	45.2	53.7	51.1	55.7	41.4	48.5	56.0	43.9	54.3
2 Liberal Party	51.3	37.3	54.5	45.4	27.9	18.9	18.9	24.3	25.1	25.6	16.8
3 Workers' Party	-	-	0.3	0.2	13.2	8.5	21.1	22.5	15.0	26.0	6.2
4 Daensists	-	-	-	-	1.2	1.4	2.5	3.0	2.5	-	0.9
5 Liberal-Workers'/ Socialist cartels	-	-	-	-	5.2	14.6	13.7	-	-	1.9	20.0
Others	-	4.3	0.1	0.8	1.3	1.0	2.4	1.7	1.5	2.6	1.9

1 From 1894 the electorate figures report the total number of votes to which electors were entitled rather than the number of electors..
2 Excludes the Brussels constituency for which no votes are available.
3 Excludes the Tielt constituency for which no votes are available.
* Indicates a general election.

Table 3.5c BELGIUM Number of Seats Won in the Chambre des Représentants 1886-1906

	1886	1888	1890	1892*	1894*	1896	1898	1900*	1902	1904	1906
1 Catholic Party	32	66	29	92	103(1)	72(3)	37(4)	86	54	38	50
2 Liberal Party	37	3	40	60	20	4	9	33	20	22	23
3 Workers' Party[1]	-	-	-	-	28	1	27	32	10	19	12
4 Daensists	-	-	-	-	1	-	-	1	1	1	-
Others	-	0	0	0	0	0	2[3]	0	0	1[4]	0
Total Seats[2]	69	69	69	152	152(1)	77(3)	75(4)	152	85	81	85

Table 3.5d BELGIUM Percentage of Seats Won in the Chambre des Représentants 1886-1906

	1886	1888	1890	1892*	1894*	1896	1898	1900*	1902	1904	1906
1 Catholic Party	46.4	95.7	42.0	60.5	67.8	93.5	49.3	56.6	63.5	46.9	58.8
2 Liberal Party	53.6	4.3	58.0	39.5	13.2	5.2	12.0	21.7	23.5	27.2	27.1
3 Workers' Party	-	-	-	-	18.4	1.3	36.0	21.1	11.8	23.5	14.1
4 Daensists	-	-	-	-	0.7	-	-	0.7	1.2	1.2	-
Others	-	0.0	0.0	0.0	0.0	0.0	2.7	0.0	0.0	1.2	0.0

1 Candidates elected by the Liberal-Workers' Party cartel are assigned to their respective parties.
2 Unopposed candidates reported in parentheses..
3 Independent Catholics.
4 Independent Catholic.

* Indicates a general election.

Source: Moyne, 1970: 128-125

Table 3.6a BELGIUM Overall Distribution of Seats in the Chambre des Représentants 1847-1914[1]

	1847	1848*	1850	1852	1854	1856	1857*	1859	1861	1863	1864*	1866	1868
1 Catholics	53	25	39	51	54	63	38	47	50	57	53	52	50
2 Liberals	55	83	69	57	54	45	70	69	66	59	63	70	72
Total Seats	108	108	108	108	108	108	108	116	116	116	116	122	122

	1870 (June)	1870* (Aug.)	1872	1874	1876	1878	1880	1882	1884	1886	1888	1890	1892*
1 Catholics	61	72	71	68	67	60	58	59	86	98	98	94	92
2 Liberals	61	52	53	56	57	72	74	79	52	40	40	44	60
Total Seats	122	124	124	124	124	132	132	138	138	138	138	138	152

	1894	1896	1898	1900*	1902	1904	1906	1908	1910	1912*	1914
1 Catholics	104	111	112	86	96	93	89	87	86	101	99
2 Liberals	20	13	13	34	34	42	46	43	44	44	45
3 Workers' Party	28	28	27	31	34	29	30	35	35	39	40
4 Daensists	0	0	0	1	2	2	1	1	1	2	2
Total Seats	152	152	152	152	166	166	166	166	166	186	186

1 This table presents the number of seats held by each party in the Chamber after both general and partial elections.

* Indicates a general election.

Source: Gilissen, 1958, 190.

Table 3.6b BELGIUM Overall Percentage Distribution of Seats in the Chambre des Représentants1847-1914

	1847	1848*	1850	1852	1854	1856	1857*	1859	1861	1863	1864*	1866	1868
1 Catholics	49.1	23.1	36.1	47.2	50.0	58.3	35.2	40.5	43.1	49.1	44.8	42.6	41.0
2 Liberals Party	50.9	76.9	63.9	52.8	50.0	41.7	64.8	59.5	56.9	50.9	55.2	57.4	59.0

	1870 (June)	1870* (Aug.)	1872	1874	1876	1878	1880	1882	1884	1886	1888	1886	1864*
1 Catholics	50.0	24.1	57.3	54.8	54.0	45.5	43.9	42.8	62.3	71.0	71.0	68.1	60.5
2 Liberals	50.0	75.9	42.7	45.2	46.0	54.5	56.1	57.2	37.7	29.0	29.0	31.9	39.5

	1894	1896	1898	1900	1902	1904	1906	1908	1910	1912	1914
1 Catholics	68.4	73.0	73.7	56.6	57.8	56.0	53.6	52.4	51.8	54.3	53.2
2 Liberals	13.2	8.6	8.6	22.4	20.5	25.3	27.7	25.9	26.5	23.7	24.2
3 Workers' Party	18.4	18.4	17.8	20.4	20.5	17.5	18.1	21.1	21.1	21.0	21.5
4 Daensists	0.0	0.0	0.0	0.7	1.2	1.2	0.7	0.7	0.6	1.1	1.1

* Indicates a general election.

Table 3.7a BELGIUM Total Votes 1908-1939[1]

	1908[1]	1910[1]	1912	1914[1]	1919	1921	1925	1929	1932	1936	1939
Electorate	1,304,864	1,365,116	2,814,181	1,436,962	2,102,710	2,226,797	2,346,096	2,497,446	2,555,743	2,652,707	2,667,341
Valid Votes	1,200,906	1,274,496	2,621,771	1,334,581	1,760,745	1,931,967	2,079,624	2,230,065	2,335,192	2,362,454	2,338,437
Invalid Votes	38,725	32,258	62,327	n.a	100,145	97,326	98,572	116,664	74,361	148,812	150,442
Total Votes	1,239,631	1,306,754	2,684,098	n.a	1,860,890	2,029,293	2,178,196	2,346,729	2,409,553	2,511,266	2,488,879
PARTY VOTES											
1 Catholic Party	517,679	676,846	1,337,315	570,806	645,462	715,041	751,058	788,914	899,887	653,717	764,843
2 Liberal Party	236,503	232,663	303,895	326,922	310,853	343,929	304,467	369,114	333,567	292,972	401,991
3 Workers'Party	271,870	85,326	243,338	404,701	645,075	672,445	820,116	803,347	866,817	758,485	705,969
4 Daensists	15,396	13,960	48,7162	22,219	-	-	-	-	-	-	-
5 Lib Socialist cartels	135,546	243,063	679,734	-	-	-	-	-	-	-	-
6 Dissident Catholics	-	-	-	-	37,245	82,509	52,400	69,988	4,664	26,460	-
7 Ex-Servicemen	-	-	-	-	19,075	20,633	-	-	-	-	-
8 Flemish Nationalists	-	-	-	-	45,863	58,790	80,407	140,616	138,456	168,355	193,528
9 Middle Class Party	-	-	-	-	18,267	9,754	9,999	3,569	-	-	-
10 Communist Party	-	-	-	-	-	939	34,149	42,237	65,694	143,223	125,428
11 German Minority	-	-	-	-	-	-	-	7,740	7,460	-	7,733
12 Rexists	-	-	-	-	-	-	-	-	-	271,491	103,821
Others	23,912[2]	22,638	8,773	9,933	40,301[3]	27,802	27,324	4,844	18,647	47,751	35,124

1 Partial election
2 Including votes cast for a joint Liberal-Workers' Party - Daensist list in Brugge.
3 Includes 12,246 votes cast for Rénovation nationale.

Sources: Moyne, 1970: 128-129; de Smet et al, 1958: 10-11; *Annuaire Statistique*, 1967: 584.

Table 3.7b BELGIUM Percentage of Votes 1908-1939

	1908	1910	1912	1914	1919	1921	1925	1929	1932	1936	1939
Total Votes	95.0	95.7	95.4	92.9	88.5	91.1	92.8	94.0	94.3	94.7	93.3
Valid Votes	92.0	93.4	93.2	92.9	83.7	86.8	88.6	89.3	91.4	89.1	87.7
Invalid Votes	3.0	2.4	2.2	n.a	4.8	4.4	4.2	4.7	2.9	5.6	5.6
Share Invalid	3.1	2.5	2.3	n.a	5.4	4.8	4.5	5.0	3.1	5.9	6.0
PARTY VOTES											
1 Catholic Party	43.1	53.1	51.0	42.8	36.7	37.0	36.1	35.4	38.5	27.7	32.7
2 Liberal Party	19.7	18.3	11.6	24.5	17.7	17.8	14.6	16.6	14.3	12.4	17.2
3 Workers' Party	22.6	6.7	9.3	30.3	36.6	34.8	39.4	36.0	37.1	32.1	30.2
4 Daensists	1.3	1.1	1.9	1.7	-	-	-	-	-	-	-
5 Lib Socialist cartels	11.3	19.1	25.9	-	-	-	-	-	-	-	-
6 Dissident Catholics	-	-	-	-	2.1	4.3	2.5	3.1	0.2	1.1	-
7 Ex-Servicemen	-	-	-	-	1.1	1.1	-	-	-	-	-
8 Flemish Nationalists	-	-	-	-	2.6	3.0	3.9	6.3	5.9	7.1	8.3
9 Middle Class Party	-	-	-	-	1.0	0.5	0.5	0.2	-	-	-
10 Communist Party	-	-	-	-	-	0.0	1.6	1.9	2.8	6.1	5.4
11 German Minority	-	-	-	-	-	-	-	0.3	0.3	-	0.3
12 Rexists	-	-	-	-	-	-	-	-	-	11.5	4.4
Others	2.0	1.8	0.3	0.7	2.3	1.4	1.3	0.2	0.8	2.0	1.5

Table 3.7c BELGIUM Number of Seats Won in the Chambre des Représentants/Kamer der Volksvertegenwoordigers 1908-1939

	1908[1]	1910[1]	1912	1914	1919	1921	1925	1929	1932	1936	1939
1 Catholic Party	37	49	101	41	73	78	75	71	79	61	73
2 Liberal Party[2]	21	24	44	20	34	33	23	28	24	23	33
3 Workers' Party[2]	22	12	39	26	70	68	78	70	73	70	64
4 Daensists	1	–	2	1	–	–	–	–	–	–	–
6 Dissident Catholics	–	–	–	–	0	2	3	6	0	2	–
7 Ex-Servicemen	–	–	–	–	2	1	–	–	–	–	–
8 Flemish Nationalists	–	–	–	–	5	4	6	11	8	16	17
9 Middle Class Party	–	–	–	–	1	0	0	0	–	–	–
10 Communist Party	–	–	–	–	–	0	2	1	3	9	9
11 German Minority	–	–	–	–	–	–	–	0	0	–	0
12 Rexists	–	–	–	–	–	–	–	–	–	21	4
Others	0	0	0	0	1[3]	0	0	0	0	0	2
Total Seats	81	85	186	88	186	186	187	187	187	202	202

1 Partial election. For the overall distribution of seats in the Chamber after these elections see Table 3.6a.
2 Candidates elected by the Liberal-Workers' Party cartel are assigned to their respective parties.
3 Rénovation nationale.

Source: de Smet et al; 1958: 14-15

Table 3.7d BELGIUM Percentage of Seats Won in the Chambre des Représentants/Kamer der Volksvertegenwoordigers 1908-1939

	1908	1910	1912	1914	1919	1921	1925	1929	1932	1936	1939
1 Catholic Party	45.7	57.6	54.3	46.6	39.2	41.9	40.1	38.0	42.2	30.2	36.1
2 Liberal Party	25.9	28.2	23.7	22.7	18.3	17.7	12.3	15.0	12.8	11.4	16.3
3 Workers' Party	27.2	14.1	21.0	29.5	37.6	36.6	41.7	37.4	39.0	34.7	31.7
4 Daensists	1.2	-	1.1	1.1	-	-	-	-	-	-	-
6 Dissident Catholics	-	-	-	-	0.0	1.1	1.6	3.2	0.0	1.0	-
7 Ex-Servicemen	-	-	-	-	1.1	0.5	-	-	-	-	-
8 Flemish Nationalists	-	-	-	-	2.7	2.2	3.2	5.9	4.3	7.9	8.4
9 Middle Class Party	-	-	-	-	0.5	0.0	0.0	0.0	-	-	-
10 Communist Party	-	-	-	-	-	0.0	1.1	0.5	1.6	4.5	4.5
11 German Minority	-	-	-	-	-	-	-	0.0	0.0	-	0.0
12 Rexists	-	-	-	-	-	-	-	-	-	10.4	2.0
Others	0.0	0.0	0.0	0.0	0.5	0.0	0.0	0.0	0.0	0.0	1.0

Table 3.8a BELGIUM Total Votes 1946-1974

	1946	1949	1950	1954	1958	1961	1965	1968	1971	1974
Electorate	2,724,796	5,635,452	5,635,452	5,863,092	5,954,858	6,036,165	6,091,534	6,170,167	6,271,240	6,322,227
Valid Votes	2,365,638	5,030,886	4,942,807	5,160,486	5,302,353	5,265,025	5,181,935	5,177,952	5,281,633	5,258,531
Invalid Votes	95,158	289,377	276,469	302,644	272,774	308,836	396,941	376,700	459,637	453,465
Total Votes	2,460,796	5,320,263	5,219,276	5,463,130	5,575,127	5,573,861	5,578,876	5,554,652	5,741,270	5,711,996
PARTY VOTES										
1 Catholic Party - CVP/PSC	1,006,293	2,190,898	2,356,608	2,123,408	2,465,549	2,182,652	1,785,211	-	-	-
2 Liberal Party - PVV/PLP	211,143	767,180	556,102	626,983	585,999	649,376	1,120,081	-	-	-
3 SocialistParty	746,738	1,496,539	1,705,781	1,927,015	1,897,646	1,933,424	1,465,503	1,449,172	1,438,626	1,401,725
5 Liberal/Socialist cartels	37,844	-	87,252	109,982	111,284	-	-	-	-	-
6 Dissident Catholics	348	4,327	332	44,796[1]	-	42,081[2]	14,007	-	-	-
8 Volksunie	-	103,896	-	113,632	104,823	182,407	333,409	506,697	586,917	536,287
10 Communist Party	300,099	376,765	234,541	184,108	100,145	162,238	236,702	170,625	161,517	166,008
11 German Minority	-	-	-	-	-	-	-	-	7,801	8,700
13 Democratic Union	51,095	-	-	-	-	-	-	-	-	-
14 Francophone Democratic Front	-	-	-	-	-	-	68,966	130,271	239,829	267,423[5]
15 Walloon Democratic Front	-	-	-	-	-	-	5,709	-	-	-
16 Walloon Front	-	-	-	-	-	-	24,245	-	-	-
17 Walloon Workers' Party	-	-	-	-	-	-	23,582	3,474	-	-
18 Walloon Rally	-	-	-	-	-	-	-	175,181	353,416	308,004
19 Christian People's Party-CVP	-	-	-	-	-	-	-	1,037,309	1,038,998	1,222,646
20 Christian Social Party-PSC	-	-	-	-	-	-	-	606,283[3]	548,197[4]	478,209
21 Party of Liberty and Progress-PVV	-	-	-	-	-	-	-	-	500,614	504,545
22 Francophone Liberals - PLP	-	-	-	-	-	-	-	-	299,089	294,273
23 Brussels Liberal Party	-	-	-	-	-	-	-	-	69,139	-
24 All Power to the Workers - AMADA	-	-	-	-	-	-	-	-	-	19,794
Others	12,078	91,281	2,191	30,562	36,907	112,847	104,520	17,861	40,675	50,857

1 Rassemblement social chrétien de la liberté.
2 Rassemblement national.
3 Includes 236,283 votes for the Van den Boeynants-CVP list in Brussels.
4 Includes 200,359 votes cast for a PSC-CVP list in Brussels.
5 Electoral alliance with the Brussels Liberal Party.

Table 3.8b BELGIUM Percentage of Votes 1946-1974

	1946	1949	1950	1954	1958	1961	1965	1968	1971	1974
Total Votes	90.3	94.4	92.6	93.2	93.6	92.3	91.6	90.0	91.5	90.3
Valid Votes	86.8	89.3	87.7	88.0	89.0	87.2	85.1	83.9	84.2	83.2
Invalid Votes	3.5	5.1	4.9	5.2	4.6	5.1	6.5	6.1	7.3	7.2
Share Invalid	3.9	5.4	5.3	5.5	4.9	5.5	7.1	6.8	8.0	7.9
PARTY VOTES										
1 Catholic Party - CVP/PSC	42.5	43.5	47.7	41.1	46.5	41.5	34.5	-	-	-
2 Liberal Party - PVV/PLP	8.9	15.2	11.3	12.1	11.1	12.3	21.6	-	-	-
3 Socialist Party	31.6	29.7	34.5	37.3	35.8	36.7	28.3	28.0	27.2	26.7
5 Liberal/Socialist cartels	1.6	-	1.8	2.1	2.1	-	-	-	-	-
6 Dissident Catholics	0.0	0.1	0.0	0.9	-	0.8	0.3	-	-	-
8 Volksunie	-	2.1	-	2.2	2.0	3.5	6.4	9.8	11.1	10.2
10 Communist Party	12.7	7.5	4.7	3.6	1.9	3.1	4.6	3.3	3.1	3.2
11 German Minority	-	-	-	-	-	-	-	-	0.1	0.2
13 Democratic Union	2.2	-	-	-	-	-	-	-	-	-
14 Francophone Democratic Front	-	-	-	-	-	-	1.3	2.5	4.5	5.1
15 Walloon Democratic Front	-	-	-	-	-	-	0.1	-	-	-
16 Walloon Front	-	-	-	-	-	-	0.5	-	-	-
17 Walloon Workers' Party	-	-	-	-	-	-	0.5	0.1	-	-
18 Walloon Rally	-	-	-	-	-	-	-	3.4	6.7	5.9
19 Christian People's Party-CVP	-	-	-	-	-	-	-	20.0	19.7	23.3
20 Christian Social Party-PSC	-	-	-	-	-	-	-	11.7	10.4	9.1
21 Party of Liberty and Progress-PVV	-	-	-	-	-	-	-	-	9.5	9.6
22 Francophone Liberals	-	-	-	-	-	-	-	-	5.7	5.6
23 Brussels Liberal Party	-	-	-	-	-	-	-	-	1.3	-
24 All Power to the Workers - AMADA	-	-	-	-	-	-	-	-	-	0.4
Others	0.5	1.8	0.0	0.6	0.7	2.1	2.0	0.3	0.7	0.9

Sources: *Annuaire Statistique*, 1967: 584; de Smet et al., 1958: 10-11; de Smet et al., 1961: 12; de Smet et al., 1962: 3 and Ministère de l'Interieur, 1969 ff.

Table 3.8c BELGIUM Number of Seats Won in the Chambre des Représentants/Kamer der Volksvertegenwoordigers 1946-1974

	1946	1949	1950	1954	1958	1961	1965	1968	1971	1974
1 Catholic Party - CVP/PSC	92	105	108	95	104	96	77	–	–	–
2 Liberal Party - PVV/PLP	17	29	20	25	21	20	48	–	–	–
3 Socialist Party	69	66	77	86	84	84	64	59	61	59
6 Dissident Catholics	0	0	0	1[1]	–	1[2]	0	–	–	–
8 Volksunie	–	0	–	1	1	5	12	20	21	22
10 Communist Party	23	12	7	4	2	5	6	5	5	4
11 German Minority	–	–	–	–	–	–	–	–	0	0
13 Democratic Union	1	–	–	–	–	–	–	–	–	–
14 Francophone Democratic Front	–	–	–	–	–	–	3	7	10	9
15 Walloon Democratic Front	–	–	–	–	–	–	0	–	–	–
16 Walloon Front	–	–	–	–	–	–	1	–	–	–
17 Walloon Worker's Party	–	–	–	–	–	–	1	0	–	–
18 Walloon Rally	–	–	–	–	–	–	–	5	14	13
19 Christian People's Party-CVP	–	–	–	–	–	–	–	50	47	50
20 Christian Social Party-PSC	–	–	–	–	–	–	–	19	20	22
21 Party of Liberty and Progress-PVV	–	–	–	–	–	–	–	–	20	21
22 Francophone Liberals - PLP	–	–	–	–	–	–	–	–	11	9
23 Brussels Liberal Party	–	–	–	–	–	–	–	–	3	3
24 All Power to the Workers' - AMADA	–	–	–	–	–	–	–	–	–	0
Others	0	0	0	0	0	1[3]	0	0	0	0
Total Seats	202	212	212	212	212	212	212	212	212	212

1 Rassemblement social chrétien de la liberté.
2 Rassemblement national
3 Parti social indépendant.

Source: *Annuaire Statistique*, 1967: 592-593 and Ministère de l'Interieur, 1969 ff.

Table 3.8d BELGIUM Percentage of Seats Won in the Chambre des Représentants/Kamer der Volksvertegenwoordigers 1946-1974

	1946	1949	1950	1954	1958	1961	1965	1968	1971	1974
1 Catholic Party - CVP/PSC	45.5	49.5	50.9	44.8	49.1	45.3	36.3	-	-	-
2 Liberal Party - PVV/PLP	8.4	13.7	9.4	11.8	9.9	9.4	22.6	-	-	-
3 Socialist Party	34.2	31.1	36.3	40.6	39.6	39.6	30.2	27.8	28.8	27.8
6 Dissident Catholics	0.0	0.0	0.0	0.5	-	0.5	0.0	-	-	-
8 Volksunie	-	0.0	-	0.5	0.5	2.4	5.7	9.4	9.9	10.4
10 Communist Party	11.4	5.7	3.3	1.9	0.9	2.4	2.8	2.4	2.4	1.9
11 German Minority	-	-	-	-	-	-	-	-	0.0	0.0
13 Democraric Union	0.5	-	-	-	-	-	-	-	-	-
14 Francophone Democratic Front	-	-	-	-	-	-	1.4	3.3	4.7	4.3
15 Walloon Democratic Front	-	-	-	-	-	-	0.0	-	-	-
16 Walloon Front	-	-	-	-	-	-	0.5	-	-	-
17 Walloon Workers' Party	-	-	-	-	-	-	0.5	0.0	-	-
18 Walloon Rally	-	-	-	-	-	-	-	2.4	6.6	6.1
19 Christian People's Party-CVP	-	-	-	-	-	-	-	23.6	22.2	23.6
20 Christian Social Party-PSC	-	-	-	-	-	-	-	9.0	9.4	10.4
21 Party of Liberty and Progress-PVV	-	-	-	-	-	-	-	-	9.4	9.2
22 Francophone Liberals - PLP	-	-	-	-	-	-	-	-	5.2	4.2
23 Brussels Liberal Party	-	-	-	-	-	-	-	-	1.4	1.4
24 All Power to the Workers' - AMADA	-	-	-	-	-	-	-	-	-	0.0
Others	0.0	0.0	0.0	0.0	0.0	0.5	0.0	0.0	0.0	0.0

Table 3.9a BELGIUM Total Votes 1977-1987

	1977	1978	1981	1985	1987
Electorate	6,316,292	6,366,652	6,878,141	7,001,297	7,039,250
Valid Votes	5,575,230	5,533,206	6,024,877	6,064,260	6,141,212
Invalid Votes	430,965	506,710	479,179	487,974	431,833
Total Votes	6,005,195	6,039,916	6,504,056	6,552,234	6,573,045
PARTY VOTES					
3 Socialist Party	1,507,014[1]	-	-	-	-
8 Volksunie	559,634	388,368	588,430	477,755	494,229
10 Communist Party	151,421	181,921	138,992	71,695	51,074
11 German Minority	7,735	9,031	8,392	5,228	5,683
14 Francophone Democratic Front	237,280	235,152	150,616	72,361	71,340
18 Walloon Rally	164,961	158,563	103,087	9,294[2]	12,390
19 Christian People's Party-CVP	1,459,997	1,446,056	1,165,155	1,291,244	1,194,687
20 Christian Social Party-PSC	543,608	560,565	430,712	482,254	491,839
21 Party of Liberty and Progress-PVV	475,912	572,520	776,882	651,806	709,137
22 Francophone Liberals	328,608	287,942	516,291	619,390	577,897
23 Brussels Liberal Party	63,041	42,156	-	-	-
24 All Power to the Workers/ Labour Party	24,876	43,483	45,804	45,685	45,162
25 Revolutionary Workers/ Socialist Workers	14,596	8,980	12,351	14,003	31,442
26 Ecolo	20,132	32,330	153,008	152,483	157,985
27 Agalev	3,081	11,001	138,526	226,758	275,307
28 Respect for Labour	-	48,611	163,725	69,707	6,452
29 Flemish Block	-	75,864	66,422	85,391	116,410
30 Flemish Socialist Party	-	684,465	744,586	882,200	913,975
31 Francophone Socialist Party	-	719,926	765,055	834,488	961,429
Others	12,334	21,262	57,763	72,518	24,774

[1] Includes 33,598 votes cast for a joint Socialist-Walloon Rally List in the province of Luxembourg.
[2] In 1985 the Parti Walloon.

Source: Ministere de l'Intérieur, 1978 ff., and Fraeys, 1979 & 1986.

Table 3.9b BELGIUM Percentage of Votes 1977-1987

	1977	1978	1981	1985	1987
Total Votes	95.1	94.8	94.6	93.6	93.4
Valid Votes	88.3	86.9	87.6	86.6	87.2
Invalid Votes	6.8	8.0	7.0	7.0	6.1
Share Invalid	7.2	8.4	7.4	7.4	6.6
PARTY VOTES					
3 Socialist Party	27.0	-	-	-	-
8 Volksunie	10.0	7.0	9.8	7.9	8.0
10 Communist Party	2.7	3.3	2.3	1.2	0.8
11 German Minority	0.1	0.2	0.1	0.1	0.1
14 Francophone Democratic Front	4.3	4.2	2.5	1.2	1.2
18 Walloon Rally	3.0	2.9	1.7	0.2	0.2
19 Christian People's Party-CVP	26.2	26.1	19.3	21.3	19.5
20 Christian Social Party-PSC	9.8	10.1	7.2	8.0	8.0
21 Party of Liberty and Progress-PVV	8.5	10.3	12.9	10.7	11.5
22 Francophone Liberals	5.9	5.2	8.6	10.2	9.4
23 Brussels Liberal Party	1.1	0.8	-	-	-
24 All Power to the Workers/ Labour Party	0.4	0.8	0.8	0.8	0.7
25 Revolutionary Workers/ Socialist Workers	0.3	0.2	0.2	0.2	0.5
26 Ecolo	0.4	0.6	2.5	2.5	2.6
27 Agalev	0.1	0.2	2.3	3.7	4.5
28 Respect for Labour	-	0.9	2.7	1.1	0.1
29 Flemish Block	-	1.4	1.1	1.4	1.9
30 Flemish Socialist Party	-	12.4	12.4	14.6	14.9
31 Francophone Socialist Party	-	13.0	12.7	13.9	15.7
Others	0.2	0.4	1.0	1.2	0.4

Table 3.9c BELGIUM

Number of Seats Won in the Chambre des Représentants/Kamer der Volksvertegenwoordigers 1977-1987

	1977	1978	1981	1985	1987
3 Socialist Party	62	–	–	–	–
8 Volksunie	20	14	20	16	16
10 Communist Party	2	4	2	0	0
11 German Minority	0	0	0	0	0
14 Francophone Democratic Front	10	11	6	3	3
18 Walloon Rally	5	4	2	–	–
19 Christian People's Party-CVP	56	57	43	49	43
20 Christian Social Party-PSC	24	25	18	20	19
21 Party of Liberty and Progress-PVV	17	22	28	22	25
22 Francophone Liberals	14	14	24	24	23
23 Brussels Liberal Party	2	1	–	–	–
24 All Power to the Workers/ Labour Party	0	0	0	0	0
25 Revolutionary Workers/ Socialist Workers	0	0	0	0	0
26 Ecolo	0	0	2	5	3
27 Agalev	0	0	2	4	6
28 Respect for Labour	–	1	3	1	0
29 Flemish Block	–	1	1	1	2
30 Flemish Socialist Party	–	26	26	32	32
31 Francophone Socialist Party	–	32	35	35	40
Others	0	0	0	0	0
Total Seats	212	212	212	212	212

Table 3.9d BELGIUM

Percentage of Seats Won in the Chambre des Représentants/Kamer der Volksvertegenwoordigers 1977-1987

	1977	1978	1981	1985	1987
3 Socialist Party	29.2	-	-	-	-
8 Volksunie	9.4	6.6	9.4	7.5	7.5
10 Communist Party	0.9	1.9	0.9	0.0	0.0
11 German Minority	0.0	0.0	0.0	0.0	0.0
14 Francophone Democratic Front	4.7	5.2	2.8	1.4	1.4
18 Walloon Rally	2.4	1.9	0.9	-	0.0
19 Christian People's Party-CVP	26.4	26.9	20.3	23.1	20.3
20 Christian Social Party-PSC	11.3	11.8	8.5	9.4	9.0
21 Party of Liberty and Progress-PVV	8.0	10.4	13.2	10.4	11.8
22 Francophone Liberals	6.6	6.6	11.3	11.3	10.8
23 Brussels Liberal Party	0.9	0.5	-	-	-
24 All Power to the Workers/ Labour Party	0.0	0.0	0.0	0.0	0.0
25 Revolutionary Workers/ Socialist Workers	0.0	0.0	0.0	0.0	0.0
26 Ecolo	0.0	0.0	0.9	2.4	1.4
27 Agalev	0.0	0.0	0.9	1.9	2.8
28 Respect for Labour	-	0.5	1.4	0.5	0.0
29 Flemish Block	-	0.5	0.5	0.5	0.9
30 Flemish Socialist Party	-	12.3	12.3	15.1	15.1
31 Francophone Socialist Party	-	15.1	16.5	16.5	18.9
Others	0.0	0.0	0.0	0.0	0.0

Chapter 4

CANADA

The Dominion of Canada was established in 1867 as a federation of British colonies in North America. The Canadian Parliament has always been bicameral. The government is responsible to the popularly elected House of Commons, where seats are distributed roughly in accord with population. Elections for the House of Commons must be held at least once every five years, and may be called earlier by the government. The upper chamber, the Senate, is an appointive body with formal powers virtually equal to the Commons, but traditionally it has not used them. An exception was refusing to pass the proposed free trade agreement with the United States until after a general election was held in 1988.

For House of Commons elections a plurality electoral system in predominantly single-member constituencies has always been used. Until 1921 there were five two-member constituencies, from 1925 to 1930 four, and two from 1935 until 1968. The secret ballot was introduced in 1874. For the first three federal elections the aggregation of votes across constituencies is very uncertain because of the absence of or uncertainty about the partisan affiliation of many candidates (Urquhart, 1965: 620). The distribution of seats in the House of Commons was:

	1867	**1872**	**1874**
Conservatives	101	103	73
Liberals	80	97	133
Total	181	200	206

Suffrage laws were the exclusive concern of the provinces until 1917, except for the period from 1885 to 1897. The franchise therefore varied from province to province; in all cases it was confined to adult males who met income or property requirements. In practice this amounted to a householder franchise with about 15 per cent of the population being entitled to vote (Ward, 1950: 212). In 1888 Manitoba introduced adult male suffrage with very minor restrictions; franchise requirements were gradually lowered elsewhere and by the end of the century manhood suffrage was the norm except in Nova Scotia and Québec, where property qualifications were still retained. Women were given the vote in Manitoba, Saskatchewan and Alberta in 1916 and in British Columbia and Ontario in 1917, and in Nova Scotia in 1918. Federal wartime legislation enfranchised all servicemen and men and women who had close relatives serving in the armed forces. At the same time citizens born in enemy countries and naturalised after 1902 and conscientious objectors were disenfranchised (Boyer, 1987 : 387-8). In 1918 the federal franchise was extended to all women who had the same qualifications as male electors in the respective provinces. This gave the vote to women in Québec. In 1920 the first uniform federal franchise introduced universal adult suffrage with a minimum voting age of 21. The voting age was reduced to 18 in 1970.

There were some important racial exceptions to the universal franchise provisions of the 1920 Act. Native Indians and Inuit (about 1.6 per cent of the population as of 1987) were effectively disenfranchised until 1960, though exceptions were made for those who had served in the armed forces in the two World Wars or Korea. Most Orientals were denied the provincial vote in British Columbia, as were Chinese-Canadians in Saskatchewan. These groups were not enfranchised at the federal level until these qualifications were gradually removed by the provincial governments. Japanese Canadians were disenfranchised during the Second World War. Their franchise was restored in 1948. The 1960 Elections Act repealed all electoral discrimination against Indians and Inuit (Boyer, 1987: 389).

Canadian parties do not necessarily contest seats at both federal and provincial elections. The Social Credit Party, powerful electorally in British Columbia, has no links with the rump Social Credit party which contests federal elections. Québec is the most extreme example of this phenomenon. Parties important in the provincial legislature of Québec, such as the Union Nationale, have never fought federal elections. The Parti Québécois is unique among nationalist parties in the Western world today in not contesting national elections. It contests elections only in Québec, where it succeeded in forming the provincial government from 1976 to 1985.

Sources:

J.M. Beck, *Pendulum of Power: Canada's Federal Elections* (Scarborough, Ontario: Prentice-Hall, 1968)

J.P. Boyer, *Political Rights: the Legal Framework of Elections in Canada* (Toronto and Vancouver: Butterworths, 1981)

J.P. Boyer, *Election Law in Canada: the Law and Procedure of Federal, Provincial and Territorial Elections* (Toronto and Vancouver: Butterworths, 1987)

C. Campbell, *Canadian Political Facts* 1945-1976 (Toronto: Methuen, 1977)

F. Feigert, *Canada Votes, 1935-1985* (Durham: Duke University Press, 1989)

P. Loveday and D. Jaensch, 'Indigènes and electoral administration, Australia and Canada', *Electoral Studies* 6,1 (1987), 31-40

T.H. Qualter, *The Election Process in Canada* (Toronto: McGraw-Hill, 1970)

H.A. Scarrow, *Canada Votes: A Handbook of Federal and Provincial Election Data* (New Orleans: The Hauser Press, 1962)

Twenty-sixth General Election, 1963, Report of the Chief Electoral Officer (Ottawa: the Queen's Printer, 1963) and subsequent volumes in the same series

M.C. Urquhart, ed., *Historical Statistics of Canada* (Toronto: Macmillan & Cambridge: Cambridge University Press, 1965)

N. Ward, *The Canadian House of Commons: Representation* (Toronto: University of Toronto Press, 1950)

Table 4.1 POLITICAL PARTIES IN CANADA SINCE 1878

	Party Names	Elections Contested Years	Number
1	Conservative Party; in 1942 renamed the Progressive Conservative Party	1878ff	31
2	Liberal Party	1878ff	31
3	Patrons of Industry	1891-1896	2
4	McCarthyites	1896	1
5	Labour [1]	1900-1940	11
6	Communist Party/Labour Progressive Party [2]	1921; 1930ff	19
7	National Progressive Party	1921-1930	4
8	Cooperative Commonwealth Federation - CCF; in 1961 renamed the New Democratic Party - NDP	1935ff	17
9	Reconstruction Party	1935	1
10	Social Credit	1935ff	17
11	Bloc populaire canadien	1945	1
12	Ralliement des créditistes du Québec [3]	1965-1968	2
13	Rhinoceros Party	1979ff	4
14	Parti nationaliste du Québec	1984	1
15	Green Party	1984ff	2
16	Confederation of Regions - Western Party	1984ff	2
17	Reform Party [4]	1988	1

1 Comprises numerous provincial labour parties, that at different times contested federal elections, but never formed a single nationwide organisation (Scarrow, 1962: 9-10).

2 Founded in 1921 the party was banned in 1941. It was reorganized as the Labour Progressive Party in 1941 and reverted to its previous name in 1959.

3 Organized as the Québec branch of the Social Credit Party in August 1958, it became a separate party in 1963. Renamed the Ralliement Créditiste/Social Credit Rally in 1968, it was reunited with the rest of the Social Credit Party in 1971.

4 Regional party based in Western Canada.

Table 4.2 DATES OF ELECTIONS : HOUSE OF COMMONS

1.	17 September 1878	16.	26 March 1940
2.	20 June 1882	17.	11 June 1945
3.	22 February 1887	18.	27 June 1949
4.	5 March 1891	19.	10 August 1953
5.	23 June 1896	20.	10 June 1957
6.	7 November 1900	21.	31 March 1958
7.	3 November 1904	22.	18 June 1962
8.	26 October 1908	23.	8 April 1963
9.	21 September 1911	24.	8 November 1965
10.	7 December 1917	25.	25 June 1968
11.	6 December 1921	26.	30 October 1972
12.	29 October 1925	27.	8 July 1974
13.	14 September 1926	28.	22 May 1979
14.	28 July 1930	29.	18 February 1980
15.	14 October 1935	30.	4 September 1984
		31.	21 November 1988

Sources: Beck, 1968 and the Chief Electoral Officer, Ottawa.

Table 4.3a CANADA Total Votes 1878-1908

	1878	1882	1887	1891	1896	1900	1904	1908
Electorate[1]	n.a	n.a	n.a	n.a	1,358,328	1,167,402	1,385,490	1,463,591
Valid Votes	533,941	515,504	722,722	778,522	899,046	950,763	1,030,788	1,174,709
PARTY VOTES								
1 Conservative Party	280,224	261,293	362,632	397,731	414,838	450,790	478,729	550,351
2 Liberal Party	247,043	241,400	352,184	366,817	405,185	487,193	536,370	592,596
3 Patrons of Industry	-	-	-	2,198	36,655	-	-	-
4 McCarthyites	-	-	-	-	17,532	-	-	-
5 Labour	-	-	-	-	-	2,924	2,159	1,320
Others	6,674	12,811	7,906	11,776	24,836	9,856	13,530	30,442

1 Excludes electors in constituencies where the candidate was unopposed.

Sources: Urquhart, 1965: 616; Beck, 1968.

Table 4.3b CANADA Percentage of Votes 1878-1908

	1878	1882	1887	1891	1896	1900	1904	1908
Valid Votes	n.a	n.a	n.a	n.a	66.2	81.4	74.4	80.3
PARTY VOTES								
1 Conservative Party	52.5	50.7	50.2	51.1	46.1	47.4	46.4	46.8
2 Liberal Party	46.3	46.8	48.7	47.1	45.1	51.2	52.0	50.4
3 Patrons of Industry	-	-	-	0.3	4.1	-	-	-
4 McCarthyites	-	-	-	-	2.0	-	-	-
5 Labour	-	-	-	-	-	0.3	0.2	0.1
Others	1.2	2.5	1.1	1.5	2.8	1.0	1.3	2.6

Table 4.3c CANADA Number of Seats Won in the House of Commons 1878-1908[1]

	1878	1882	1887	1891	1896	1900	1904	1908
1 Conservative Party	142 (8)	139 (24)	126 (4)	121 (5)	88 (1)	80 (1)	75	85 (1)
2 Liberal Party	64 (3)	71 (1)	89 (6)	94 (3)	118 (2)	133 (4)	138 (4)	135 (2)
3 Patrons of Industry	–	–	–	–	2	–	–	–
4 McCarthyites	–	–	–	–	4	–	–	–
5 Labour	–	–	–	–	–	0	0	0
Others	0	1	0	0	1	0	1	1
Total Seats	206 (11)	211 (25)	215 (10)	215 (8)	213 (3)	213 (5)	214 (4)	221 (3)

1 Figures in parentheses report the number of MPs returned unopposed.

Source: Beck, 1968 .

Table 4.3d CANADA Percentage of Seats Won in the House of Commons 1878-1908

	1878	1882	1887	1891	1896	1900	1904	1908
1 Conservative Party	68.9	65.9	58.6	56.3	41.3	37.6	35.0	38.5
2 Liberal Party	31.1	33.6	41.4	43.7	55.4	62.4	64.5	61.1
3 Patrons of Industry	-	-	-	-	0.9	-	-	-
4 McCarthyites	-	-	-	-	1.9	-	-	-
5 Labour	-	-	-	-	-	0.0	0.0	0.0
Others	0.0	0.5	0.0	0.0	0.5	0.0	0.5	0.5

Table 4.4a CANADA Total Votes 1911-1940

	1911	1917	1921	1925	1926	1930	1935	1940
Electorate[1]	1,820,742	2,093,799	4,435,310	4,608,636	4,665,381	5,153,971	5,918,207	6,588,888
Valid Votes	1,307,528	1,885,329	3,123,903	3,152,525	3,256,508	3,898,527	4,406,854	4,620,260
Invalid Votes	7,425	7,412	15,403	15,885	16,554	24,100	45,821	52,271
Total Votes	1,314,953	1,892,741	3,139,306	3,168,410	3,273,062	3,922,627	4,452,675	4,672,531
PARTY VOTES								
1 Conservative Party	666,074	1,074,701[2]	945,681	1,465,331	1,474,283	1,903,815	1,305,565	1,416,230
2 Liberal Party	623,554	751,493[3]	1,272,660	1,256,824	1,500,302	1,761,352	1,975,841	2,381,443
5 Labour	1,742	34,558	71,321	55,330	48,352	29,315	15,206	6,270
6 Communist Party	-	-	810	-	-	7,034	31,221	14,616
7 National Progressive Party	-	-	714,620	282,152	171,516	109,745	-	-
8 CCF	-	-	-	-	-	-	387,056	393,230
9 Reconstruction Party	-	-	-	-	-	-	384,095	-
10 Social Credit	-	-	-	-	-	-	180,301	123,033
Others	16,158	24,577	118,811	92,888	62,055	87,266	127,569	285,438

1 Excludes electors in constituencies where the candidate was unopposed, except in 1911 when the electors in four constituencies where the candidate was returned by acclamation are included.
2 Votes cast for candidates supporting the Union Government formed by Conservatives and Unionist Liberals.
3 Votes cast for Liberal candidates opposing the Unionist government and for 13 Labour candidates who ran against government candidates in constituencies where there was no Liberal candidate.

Sources: Urquhart, 1965: 616; Beck, 1968.

Table 4.4b CANADA Percentage of Votes 1911-1940

	1911	1917	1921	1925	1926	1930	1935	1940
Total Votes	72.2	90.4	70.8	68.7	70.2	76.1	75.2	70.9
Valid Votes	71.8	90.0	70.4	68.4	69.8	75.6	74.5	70.1
Invalid Votes	0.4	0.4	0.3	0.3	0.4	0.5	0.8	0.8
Share Invalid	0.6	0.4	0.5	0.5	0.5	0.6	1.0	1.1
PARTY VOTES								
1 Conservative Party	50.9	57.0	30.3	46.5	45.3	48.8	29.6	30.7
2 Liberal Party	47.7	39.9	40.7	39.9	46.1	45.2	44.8	51.5
5 Labour	0.1	1.8	2.3	1.8	1.5	0.8	0.3	0.1
6 Communist Party	-	-	0.0	-	-	0.2	0.7	0.3
7 National Progressive Party	-	-	22.9	9.0	5.3	2.8	-	-
8 CCF	-	-	-	-	-	-	8.8	8.5
9 Reconstruction Party	-	-	-	-	-	-	8.7	-
10 Social Credit	-	-	-	-	-	-	4.1	2.7
Others	1.2	1.3	3.8	2.9	1.9	2.2	2.9	6.2

Table 4.4c CANADA Number of Seats Won in the House of Commons 1911-1940[1]

	1911	1917	1921	1925	1926	1930	1935	1940
1 Conservative Party	134 (1)	153 (14)	50	116	91	137	40	40
2 Liberal Party	87 (3)	82 (18)	116	99	128 (1)	91	173	181
5 Labour	0	0	2	2	3	2	0	0
6 Communist Party	–	–	–	–	–	0	0	0
7 National Progressive Party	–	–	64	24	20	12	–	–
8 CCF	–	–	–	–	–	–	7	8
9 Reconstruction Party	–	–	–	–	–	–	1	–
10 Social Credit	–	–	–	–	–	–	17	10
Others	0	0	3	4	3	3	7	6
Total Seats	221 (4)	235 (32)	235	245 (1)	245 (1)	245 (1)	245	245

[1] Figures in parenthesis report the number of MPs returned unopposed.

Source: Beck, 1968.

Table 4.4d CANADA Percentage of Seats Won in the House of Commons 1911-1940

	1911	1917	1921	1925	1926	1930	1935	1940
1 Conservative Party	60.6	65.1	21.3	47.3	37.1	55.9	16.3	16.3
2 Liberal Party	39.4	34.9	49.4	40.4	52.2	37.1	70.6	73.9
5 Labour	0.0	0.0	0.9	0.8	1.2	0.8	0.0	0.0
6 Communist Party	-	-	-	-	-	0.0	0.0	0.0
7 National Progressive Party	-	-	27.2	9.8	8.2	4.9	-	-
8 CCF	-	-	-	-	-	-	2.9	3.3
9 Reconstruction Party	-	-	-	-	-	-	0.4	-
10 Social Credit	-	-	-	-	-	-	6.9	4.1
Others	0.0	0.0	1.3	1.6	1.2	1.2	2.9	2.4

Table 4.5a CANADA Total Votes 1945-1965

	1945	1949	1953	1957	1958	1962	1963	1965
Electorate[1]	6,952,445	7,893,629	8,401,691	8,902,125	9,131,200	9,700,325	9,910,757	10,274,904
Valid Votes	5,246,130	5,848,971	5,641,272	6,605,980	7,287,297	7,690,134	7,894,076	7,713,316
Invalid Votes	59,063	54,601	60,691	74,710	69,842	82,522	64,560	83,412
Total Votes	5,305,193	5,903,572	5,701,963	6,680,690	7,357,139	7,772,656	7,958,636	7,796,728
PARTY VOTES								
1 Conservative Party	1,435,747	1,736,226	1,749,579	2,572,926	3,908,633	2,865,582	2,591,614	2,499,913
2 Liberal Party	2,146,330	2,897,662	2,751,307	2,702,573	2,447,909	2,861,834	3,293,790	3,099,519
6 Communist Party	109,768	32,833	59,622	7,760	9,869	6,360	4,324	4,285
8 CCF	816,259	782,410	636,310	707,659	692,398	1,036,853	1,037,857	1,381,658
10 Social Credit	214,998	220,415[2]	305,551	436,663	188,356	896,574	940,703	282,454
11 Bloc populaire canadien	186,822	-	-	-	-	-	-	-
12 Ralliement des créditistes	-	-	-	-	-	-	-	359,438
Others	336,206	179,425	138,903	178,399	40,132	22,931	25,788	86,049

1 Excluding electors in constituencies where the candidate was returned unopposed.
2 Including 85,198 votes cast for the Union des électeurs, the Québec affiliate of Social Credit.

Source: Urquhart, 1965: 616 and Beck, 1968.

Table 4.5b CANADA Percentage of Votes 1945-1965

	1945	1949	1953	1957	1958	1962	1963	1965
Total Votes	76.3	74.8	67.9	75.0	80.6	80.1	80.3	75.9
Valid Votes	75.5	74.1	67.1	74.2	79.8	79.3	79.7	75.1
Invalid Votes	0.8	0.7	0.7	0.8	0.8	0.9	0.7	0.8
Share Invalid	1.1	0.9	1.1	1.1	0.9	1.1	0.8	1.1
PARTY VOTES								
1 Conservative Party	27.4	29.7	31.0	38.9	53.6	37.3	32.8	32.4
2 Liberal Party	40.9	49.5	48.8	40.9	33.6	37.2	41.7	40.2
6 Communist Party	2.1	0.6	1.1	0.1	0.1	0.1	0.1	0.1
8 CCF	15.6	13.4	11.3	10.7	9.5	13.5	13.1	17.9
10 Social Credit	4.1	3.8	5.4	6.6	2.6	11.7	11.9	3.7
11 Bloc populaire canadien	3.6	-	-	-	-	-	-	-
12 Ralliement des créditistes	-	-	-	-	-	-	-	4.7
Others	6.4	3.1	2.5	2.7	0.6	0.3	0.3	1.1

Table 4.5c CANADA Number of Seats Won in the House of Commons 1945-1965[1]

	1945	1949	1953	1957	1958	1962	1963	1965
1 Conservative Party	67	41	51	112	208	116	95	97
2 Liberal Party	125	193	171 (2)	105 (1)	49	100	129	131
6 Communist Party	1	0	0	0	0	0	0	0
8 CCF	28	13	23	25	8	19	17	21
10 Social Credit	13	10	15	19	-	30	24	5
11 Bloc populaire canadien	2	-	-	-	-	-	-	-
12 Ralliement des créditistes	-	-	-	-	-	-	-	9
Others	9	5	5 (2)	4 (1)	0	0	0	2
Total Seats	245	262	265 (4)	265 (2)	265	265	265	265

1 Figures in parentheses report the number of representatives returned unopposed.

Sources: Beck, 1968 and the Chief Electoral Officer.

Table 4.5d CANADA Percentage of Seats Won in the House of Commons 1945-1965

	1945	1949	1953	1957	1958	1962	1963	1965
1 Conservative Party	27.3	15.6	19.2	42.3	78.5	43.8	35.8	36.6
2 Liberal Party	51.0	73.7	64.5	39.6	18.5	37.7	48.7	49.4
6 Communist Party	0.4	0.0	0.0	0.0	0.0	0.0	0.0	0.0
8 CCF	11.4	5.0	8.7	9.4	3.0	7.2	6.4	7.9
10 Social Credit	5.3	3.8	5.7	7.2	-	11.3	9.1	1.9
11 Bloc populaire canadien	0.8	-	-	-	-	-	-	-
12 Ralliement des créditistes	-	-	-	-	-	-	-	3.4
Others	3.7	1.9	1.9	1.5	0.0	0.0	0.0	0.8

Table 4.6a CANADA Total Votes 1968-1988

	1968	1972	1974	1979	1980	1984	1988
Electorate	10,860,888	12,909,179	13,620,553	15,234,997	15,890,416	16,700,565	17,639,001
Valid Votes	8,125,996	9,667,760	9,505,908	11,445,702	10,947,914	12,545,973	13,175,599
Invalid Votes	91,920	298,388	165,094	85,298	67,000	89,009	105,592
Total Votes	8,217,916	9,966,148	9,671,002	11,531,000	11,014,914	12,634,982	13,281,191
PARTY VOTES							
1 Conservative Party	2,554,880	3,383,277	3,369,335	4,111,559	3,552,994	6,276,530	5,667,563
2 Liberal Party	3,696,945	3,718,654	4,102,776	4,594,319	4,853,914	3,516,173	4,205,072
6 Communist Party	4,465	6,475	12,100	9,162	6,002	7,616	7,168
8 New Democratic Party	1,378,260	1,714,208	1,467,748	2,048,779	2,164,987	2,358,676	2,685,308
10 Social Credit	62,956	737,421	481,231	527,604	185,486	16,700	3,407
12 Ralliement des créditistes	361,045	-	-	-	-	-	-
13 Rhinoceros Party	-	-	-	62,600	110,597	99,207	52,173
14 Parti nationaliste du Québec	-	-	-	-	-	86,482	-
15 Green Party	-	-	-	-	-	26,921	47,228
16 Western Party	-	-	-	-	-	65,655	41,342
17 Reform Party	-	-	-	-	-	-	275,767
Others	67,445	107,725	72,718	101,679	73,914	92,013	190,571

Table 4.6b CANADA Percentage of Votes 1968-1988

	1968	1972	1974	1979	1980	1984	1988
Total Votes	75.7	77.2	71.0	75.7	69.3	75.7	75.5
Valid Votes	74.8	74.9	69.8	75.1	68.9	75.1	74.9
Invalid Votes	0.8	2.3	1.2	0.6	0.4	0.5	0.6
Share Invalid	1.1	3.0	1.7	0.7	0.6	0.7	0.8
PARTY VOTES							
1 Conservative Party	31.4	35.0	35.4	35.9	32.5	50.0	43.0
2 Liberal Party	45.5	38.5	43.2	40.1	44.3	28.0	31.9
6 Communist Party	0.1	0.1	0.1	0.1	0.1	0.1	0.1
8 New Democratic Party	17.0	17.7	15.4	17.9	19.8	18.8	20.4
10 Social Credit	0.8	7.6	5.1	4.6	1.7	0.1	0.0
12 Ralliement des créditistes	4.4	–	–	–	–	–	–
13 Rhinoceros Party	–	–	–	0.5	1.0	0.8	0.4
14 Parti nationaliste du Québec	–	–	–	–	–	0.7	–
15 Green Party	–	–	–	–	–	0.2	0.4
16 Western Party	–	–	–	–	–	0.5	0.3
17 Reform Party	–	–	–	–	–	–	2.1
Others	0.8	1.1	0.8	0.9	0.7	0.7	1.4

Table 4.6c CANADA Number of Seats Won in the House of Commons 1968-1988

	1968	1972	1974	1979	1980	1984	1988
1 Conservative Party	72	107	95	136	103	211	169
2 Liberal Party	155	109	141	114	147	40	83
6 Communist Party	0	0	0	0	0	0	0
8 New Democratic Party	22	31	16	32	32	30	43
10 Social Credit	0	15	11	0	0	0	0
12 Ralliement des créditistes	14	–	–	–	–	–	–
13 Rhinoceros Party	–	–	–	0	0	0	0
14 Parti nationaliste du Québec	–	–	–	–	–	0	–
15 Green Party	–	–	–	–	–	0	0
16 Western Party	–	–	–	–	–	0	0
17 Reform Party	–	–	–	–	–	–	0
Others	1	2	1	0	0	1	0
Total Seats	264	264	264	282	282	282	295

Table 4.6d CANADA Percentage of Seats Won in the House of Commons 1968-1988

	1968	1972	1974	1979	1980	1984	1988
1 Conservative Party	27.3	40.5	36.0	48.2	36.5	74.8	57.3
2 Liberal Party	58.7	41.3	53.4	40.4	52.1	14.2	28.1
6 Communist Party	0.0	0.0	0.0	0.0	0.0	0.0	0.0
8 New Democratic Party	8.3	11.7	6.1	11.3	11.3	10.6	14.6
10 Social Credit	0.0	5.7	4.2	0.0	0.0	0.0	0.0
12 Ralliement des créditistes	5.3	-	-	-	-	-	-
13 Rhinoceros Party	-	-	-	0.0	0.0	0.0	0.0
14 Parti nationaliste du Québec	-	-	-	-	-	0.0	-
15 Green Party	-	-	-	-	-	0.0	0.0
16 Western Party	-	-	-	-	-	0.0	0.0
17 Reform Party	-	-	-	-	-	-	0.0
Others	0.4	0.8	0.4	0.0	0.0	0.4	0.0

Chapter 5

DENMARK

Four provincial consultative assemblies which met for the first time in 1836 were the first elected bodies in Denmark. A property franchise limited the electorate to two to three per cent of the population. In 1848 a constituent assembly was elected on a broad franchise of all self supporting men aged over 30. The June 1849 Danish Constitution established a two-chamber Parliament, the Rigsdag, in which each house had equal powers. The wide franchise was retained; all men over 30, except those in the service of others and not householders and those in receipt of poor relief, could vote in elections to both the Folketing, the lower house, and the Landsting, the upper house; 73 per cent of men over 30 were enfranchised in 1849, rising to 84 per cent by 1901. Folketing elections were held in single-member constituencies. Voting was first by show of hands. The candidate who won a plurality of the vote in the opinion of the election committee was declared elected. If the election committee's decision was challenged, a roll-call vote took place; in the case of a single candidate, the electors simply voted yes or no. If in such cases the candidate did not win a majority on the yes/no roll-call, a second and final vote took place a week later. In 1901 open voting was replaced by the secret ballot. In constituencies where there was only one candidate, the candidate was declared elected unless at least 50 electors called for a vote. Landsting elections were indirect with the Folketing electorate choosing electors who then voted for Landsting members by plurality in multi-member districts.

In 1854-55 an attempt was made to establish a federal Council of the Realm (Rigsraad) uniting the provinces of Denmark with the duchies Schleswig, Holstein and Lauenburg. In addition to 20 members nominated by the crown, 30 were directly elected and 30 indirectly elected by the provincial councils. The elected members were to be chosen by a version of the single transferable vote invented by the Danish mathematician and minister Carl Andrae (see Appendix for details). The initiative was stillborn. But Andrae's electoral system was retained for elections both to the successor of the first Council of the Realm (1861-66) and to the Landsting following the conservative constitutional reforms of the mid 1860s.

In 1866 the franchise for Landsting elections was made much more restrictive in order to ensure conservative control of the house. Twelve members of the Landsting were to be nominated by the crown, one elected by the Faroese Lagting and 53 indirectly elected. One half of the electoral college in each multi-member constituency were chosen by the Folketing electorate. In Copenhagen the other half of the college was chosen by tax-payers whose tax was based on an income above a fixed threshold. In other constituencies 40 per cent of the electoral college were elected by the Folketing electorate in the countryside, 10 per cent by the Folketing electorate in the towns, 10 per cent by urban taxpayers above a certain income level; the highest tax-payers in the countryside, mainly the large landowners, comprised the remaining 40 per cent of the electoral college.

Political parties in the modern sense began to appear in 1870 with the formation of a Liberal Party group in parliament. The Liberals dominated the Folketing for the rest of the nineteenth century, but the Conservatives who opposed Liberal demands for the establishment of parliamentary government controlled the Landsting. It was not until 1901 that the King appointed a Liberal ministry and thus accepted the principle of government responsible to parliament.

Party votes are not recorded in the official statistics until 1901, but figures for the last five Folketing elections in the nineteenth century, collated from a variety of sources, are presented in Elklit, (1988).

Table 5.a EARLY FOLKETING ELECTIONS

	1887		1890		1892		1895		1898	
	Votes	Seats	Votes	Seats	Votes	Seats	Votes	Seats	Votes	Seats
	%	N	%	N	%	N	%	N	%	N
Conservatives	39	27	40	27	35	31	29	25	26	16
Moderate Liberals	-	-	-	-	24	39	19	27	16	23
Liberals	58	74	53	72	32	30	-	-	-	-
Liberal Reform Party	-	-	-	-	-	-	41	54	47	63
Social Democrats	3	1	7	3	9	2	11	8	14	12
Totals	100	102	100	102	100	102	100	114	100	114
Valid votes in constituencies with a roll-call vote	226,000		233,000		222,000		221,000		225,000	

In 1915 universal adult suffrage was introduced for Folketing elections and the voting age reduced to 29. Proportional representation using the d'Hondt system was introduced in Copenhagen and Frederiksberg. In the rest of the country single member constituencies with election by plurality continued, but a number of supplementary seats were added in order to secure a more proportional representation overall. In 1920 proportional representation was extended to the rest of Denmark, with constituency seats allocated according to the d'Hondt method and supplementary seats by the largest remainder. The allocation of supplementary seats *within* parties and regions was by the Sainte-Laguë method. From the third election in 1920 the voting age was reduced to 25. In 1953 the voting age was lowered to 23 and the Sainte-Laguë system (with an initial divisor of 1.4) replaced the d'Hondt system at the constituency level, with supplementary seats continuing to be allocated by the largest remainder method (Johansen, 1979: 43-47). The voting age was further reduced to 21 in 1961, to 20 in 1971 and to 18 in 1978.

The 1915 reforms saw the introduction of universal suffrage for Landsting elections as well, but with a minimum voting age of 35. Elections continued to be indirect, although the electors were now chosen in multi-member constituencies using the d'Hondt system. A version of Andrae's method was used for the selection of Landsting members. A number of members were also elected by the preceding Landsting and the Faroese Lagting continued to choose one member. The Landsting was abolished as part of the 1953 constitutional reform.

The Faroe Islands have been represented in the Rigsdag since 1850. In 1948 the islands were given internal self government and the number of representatives in the Folketing increased to two. Greenland has sent two representatives to the Folketing since 1953. The Faroes and Greenland are excluded from the following tables unless specifically stated otherwise (Thomas, 1973: 53-57).

Sources:

O. Borre, 'The social bases of Danish electoral behaviour' in R. Rose (ed.), *Electoral Participation* (London: Sage, 1980) 241-282

Danmarks Statistik, *Folketingsvalgene 1901* (Copenhagen: 1901) and subsequent volumes in the same series

J. Elklit, 'Election laws and electoral behaviour in Denmark until 1920', in O. Büsch (ed.), *Wahlerbewegung in der europäischen Geschichte* (Berlin: Colloquium Verlag, 1980) 366-97

J. Elklit, *Fra aaben til hemmelig afstemning: Aspekter af et partisystems udvikling* (Aarhus: Forlaget Politica, 1988)

C. Friisberg, *Paa vej mod et demokrati. Fra junigrundloven 1849 til junigrundloven 1915* (Copenhagen: Fremad, 1975)

A. Holm, *Rigsdagsvalgene i hundrede aar* (Copenhagen: Fremad, 1949)

Institute of Political Science, Aarhus University, 'Denmark', in S. Rokkan and J. Meyriat (eds.) *International Guide to Electoral Statistics* (Paris and the Hague: Mouton, 1969)

L.N. Johansen, 'Denmark', in G. Hand, J. Georgel and C. Sasse (eds.), *European Electoral Systems Handbook* (London: Butterworths, 1979)

P. Møller, *Politisk haandbog: en samling konkrete oplysninger* (Copenhagen: Hagerup, 1950)

A. Thomas, *Parliamentary Parties in Denmark, 1945-1972* (Glasgow: U. of Strathclyde Survey Research Centre, 1973)

Table 5.1 POLITICAL PARTIES IN DENMARK SINCE 1901

	Party Names	Elections Contested Years	Number
1	Conservatives. Until 1915 the Right (Højre). Since 1915 the Conservative People's Party (Konservative Folkeparti)	1901ff	37
2	Moderate Liberals (Moderate Venstre) Literally, Moderate Left	1901-1909	4
3	Liberal Reform Party (Venstrereformparti) [1]	1901-1909	4
4	Social Democrats (Socialdemokratiet)	1901ff	37
5	Radical Party (Radikale Venstre) [2]	1906ff	35
6	Liberals (Venstre) [3]	1910ff	33
7	Industry Party (Erhvervspartiet) [4]	1918-1924	5
8	Schleswig Party (Schleswigsche Partei/Slesvigsk Parti) [5]	Sept. 1920-39; 1947-64; 1968-77	19
9	Communist Party (Danmarks Kommunistiske Parti) [6]	1920-1939; 1945ff	28
10	Justice Party (Retsforbundet) [7]	1924-1987	25
11	Farmers' Party (Bondepartiet) [8]	1935-1943	3
12	National Socialists (Danmarks Nationalsocialistiske Arbejderparti)	1932-1943	4
13	Danish Union (Dansk Samling)	1939-1947; April 1953; 1964	6
14	National Cooperation (Nationalt Samvirke)	1939	1
15	Independents' Party (De Uafhaengige) [9]	Sept. 1953-1968	6
16	Socialist People's Party (Socialistisk Folkeparti) [10]	1960ff	13
17	Liberal Centre (Liberalt Centrum) [11]	1966-1968	2
18	Left Socialist Party (Venstresocialisterne) [12]	1968ff	10
19	Christian People's Party (Kristeligt Folkeparti)	1971ff	9
20	Centre Democrats (Centrum-Demokraterne) [13]	1973ff	8
21	Progress Party (Fremkridtspartiet) [14]	1973ff	8
22	Common Course (Faelles Kurs)	1987ff	2
23	The Greens (De Grønne)	1987ff	2

1 Formed in 1895 following continuous splits in the Liberal Party (the Venstre) throughout the 1880s and early 1890s.

2 Left-wing splinter from the Liberal Reform Party.

3 Reunification of the Liberal Party, combining the Moderate Liberals and Liberal Reform Party.

4 In 1918 the Industry List (Erhvervlisten).

5 The party representing the German-speaking minority. From 1947 to September 1953, non-party candidates were nominated to represent this minority. Votes for these candidates are included with the Schleswig Party. From 1973 to 1977 the party ran with the Centre Democrats.

6 Founded in November 1919 as the Left Socialist Party of Denmark (Danmarks Venstresocialistiske Parti).

7 In 1924 Retspartiet. Often known as the Single-Tax Party. The party did not run in 1988.
8 In 1935 the Free People's Party (Frie Folkeparti).
9 Right-wing splinter from the Liberal Party, founded in 1953.
10 Established in 1959 by Askel Larsen, the former leader of the Communist Party.
11 Splinter from the Liberal Party established in 1965.
12 Founded in 1967 as the result of a split in the Socialist People's Party.
13 Right-wing splinter from the Social Democrats, founded in 1973.
14 Anti-tax party formed by Mogens Glistrup in 1972.

Table 5.2 DATES OF ELECTIONS : FOLKETING

1.	3 April 1901	20.	28 October 1947
2.	16 June 1903	21.	5 September 1950
3.	29 May 1906	22.	21 April 1953
4.	25 May 1909	23.	22 September 1953
5.	20 May 1910	24.	14 May 1957
6.	20 May 1913	25.	15 November 1960
7.	7 May 1915	26.	22 September 1964
8.	22 April 1918	27.	22 November 1966
9.	26 April 1920	28.	23 January 1968
10.	6 July 1920	29.	21 September 1971
11.	21 September 1920	30.	4 December 1973
12.	11 April 1924	31.	9 January 1975
13.	2 December 1926	32.	15 February 1977
14.	24 April 1929	33.	23 October 1979
15.	16 November 1932	34.	8 December 1981
16.	22 October 1935	35.	10 January 1984
17.	3 April 1939	36.	8 September 1987
18.	23 March 1943	37.	10 May 1988
19.	30 October 1945		

Sources: Holm, 1949: 13 and Danmarks Statistik.

Table 5.3a DENMARK Total Votes 1901-1920[1]

	1901	1903	1906	1909	1910	1913	1918	1920 (April)	1920 (July)
Electorate	404,271	416,748	438,341	460,553	470,392	491,422	1,218,901	1,274,377	1,276,302
Valid Votes[2]	225,066	235,699	302,062	324,258	348,856	363,360	916,929	1,024,206	953,561
Invalid Votes	3,510	3,999	3,666	3,126	3,026	2,955	3,468	3,082	2,004
Total Votes	228,576	239,698	305,728	327,384	351,882	366,315	920,397	1,027,288	955,565
PARTY VOTES									
1 Conservatives	54,103	49,109	67,224	66,133	64,904	82,137	167,743	201,499	180,293
2 Moderate Liberals	26,993	19,149	20,487	19,241	-	-	-	-	-
3 Liberal Reform Party	96,481	113,000	95,555	83,569	-	-	-	-	-
4 Social Democrats	38,398	48,117	76,612	93,079	98,718	107,365	262,796	300,345	285,166
5 Radical Party	-	-	41,460	60,261	66,205	67,903	189,521	122,160	109,931
6 Liberals	-	-	-	-	118,902	105,837	269,646	350,563	344,351
7 Industry Party	-	-	-	-	-	-	11,934	29,464	25,627
9 Communist Party	-	-	-	-	-	-	-	3,859	2,493
Others	9,091	6,324	724	1,975	127	118	15,289	16,316	5,700

1 For elections from 1901 to 1913 figures include the Faroe Islands. The results of the 1915 election are not included. The election was held in order to amend the Constitution. Only ten single-member constituencies were contested and in five of these there was only one candidate. (*Folketingsvalget den 15. Maj 1915: 8-9*)

2 From 1901 to 1913 includes 'No" votes in constituencies where there was only one candidate. 'Yes" votes in those constituences are included with the party of the candidate.

Sources: Danmarks Statistik, *Folketingsvalget den 8. September 1987*, *Statistisk Arbog*, 1914: 162, and figures provided by Danmarks Statistik.

Table 5.3b DENMARK Percentage of Votes 1901-1920[1]

	1901	1903	1906	1909	1910	1913	1918	1920 (April)	1920 (July)
Total Votes	56.5	57.5	69.7	71.1	74.8	74.5	75.5	80.6	74.9
Valid Votes	55.7	56.6	68.9	70.4	74.2	73.9	75.2	80.4	74.7
Invalid Votes	0.9	1.0	0.8	0.7	0.6	0.6	0.3	0.2	0.2
Share Invalid	1.5	1.7	1.2	1.0	0.9	0.8	0.4	0.3	0.2
PARTY VOTES									
1 Conservatives	24.0	20.8	22.3	20.4	18.6	22.6	18.3	19.7	18.9
2 Moderate Liberals	12.0	8.1	6.8	5.9	-	-	-	-	-
3 Liberal Reform Party	42.9	47.9	31.6	25.8	-	-	-	-	-
4 Social Democrats	17.1	20.4	25.4	28.7	28.3	29.5	28.7	29.3	29.9
5 Radical Party	-	-	13.7	18.6	19.0	18.7	20.7	11.9	11.5
6 Liberals	-	-	-	-	34.1	29.1	29.4	34.2	36.1
7 Industry Party	-	-	-	-	-	-	1.3	2.9	2.7
9 Communist Party	-	-	-	-	-	-	-	0.4	0.3
Others	4.0	2.7	0.2	0.6	0.0	0.0	1.7	1.6	0.6

1 For elections from 1901 to 1913 figures include the Faroe Islands

Table 5.3c DENMARK Number of Seats Won in the Folketing 1901-1920[1]

	1901	1903	1906	1909	1910	1913	1918	1920 (April)	1920 (July)
1 Conservatives	8	12	14	21	13	7	22	28	26
2 Moderate Liberals	16	12	9	11	–	–	–	–	–
3 Liberal Reform Party	76 (6)	73 (7)	56	40	–	–	–	–	–
4 Social Democrats	14 (2)	16 (2)	24	24	24	32	39	42	42
5 Radical Party	–	–	11	18	20	31	32	17	16
6 Liberals	–	–	–	–	57	44 (1)	44	48	51
7 Industry Party	–	–	–	–	–	–	1	4	4
9 Communist Party	–	–	–	–	–	–	–	0	0
Others	0	1	0	0	0	0	1	0	0
Total Seats	114 (8)	114 (9)	114	114	114	114 (1)	139	139	139

1 For 1901 to 1913 includes the Faroe Islands. Figures in parentheses report unopposed return.

Source: Danmarks Statistik.

Table 5.3d DENMARK Percentage of Seats Won in the Folketing 1901-1920

	1901	1903	1906	1909	1910	1913	1918	1920 (April)	1920 (July)
1 Conservatives	7.0	10.5	12.3	18.4	11.4	6.1	15.8	20.1	18.7
2 Moderate Liberals	14.0	10.5	7.9	9.6	-	-	-	-	-
3 Liberal Reform Party	66.7	64.0	49.1	35.1	-	-	-	-	-
4 Social Democrats	12.3	14.0	21.1	21.1	21.1	28.1	28.1	30.2	30.2
5 Radical Party	-	-	9.6	15.8	17.5	27.2	23.0	12.2	11.5
6 Liberals	-	-	-	-	50.0	38.6	31.7	34.5	36.7
7 Industry Party	-	-	-	-	-	-	0.7	2.9	2.9
9 Communist Party	-	-	-	-	-	-	-	0.0	0.0
Others	0.0	0.9	0.0	0.0	0.0	0.0	0.7	0.0	0.0

Table 5.4a DENMARK Total Votes 1920-1945

	1920 (Sept.)	1924	1926	1929	1932	1935	1939	1943	1945
Electorate	1,576,716	1,637,564	1,742,604	1,786,092	1,902,835	2,044,997	2,159,356	2,280,716	2,381,983
Valid Votes	1,211,583	1,282,937	1,337,647	1,420,246	1,547,082	1,646,438	1,699,889	2,010,783	2,049,184
Invalid Votes	2,673	4,147	3,579	2,904	4,039	4,694	9,667	29,800	6,131
Total Votes	1,214,256	1,287,084	1,341,226	1,423,150	1,551,121	1,651,132	1,709,556	2,040,583	2,055,315
PARTY VOTES									
1 Conservatives	216,733	242,955	275,793	233,935	289,531	293,393	301,625	421,523	373,688
4 Social Democrats	389,653	469,949	497,106	593,191	660,839	759,102	729,619	894,632	671,755
5 Radical Party	147,120	166,476	150,931	151,746	145,221	151,507	161,834	175,179	167,073
6 Liberals	411,661	362,682	378,137	402,121	381,862	292,247	309,355	376,850	479,158
7 Industry Party	27,403	2,102	-	-	-	-	-	-	-
8 Schleswig Party	7,505	7,715	10,422	9,787	9,868	12,617	15,016	-	-
9 Communist Party	5,160	6,219	5,678	3,656	17,179	27,135	40,893	-	255,236
10 Justice Party	-	12,643	17,463	25,810	41,238	41,199	33,783	31,323	38,459
11 Farmers' Party	-	-	-	-	-	52,793	50,829	24,572	-
12 National Socialists	-	-	-	-	757	16,257	31,032	43,309	-
13 Danish Union	-	-	-	-	-	-	8,553	43,367	63,760
14 National Cooperation	-	-	-	-	-	-	17,350	-	-
Others	6,460	12,196	2,117	-	587	188	-	28	55

Source: Danmarks Statistik, *Folketingsvalget den 8. September 1987.*

Table 5.4b DENMARK Percentage of Votes 1920-1945

	1920 (Sept.)	1924	1926	1929	1932	1935	1939	1943	1945
Total Votes	77.0	78.6	77.0	79.7	81.5	80.7	79.2	89.5	86.3
Valid Votes	76.8	78.3	76.8	79.5	81.3	80.5	78.7	88.2	86.0
Invalid Votes	0.2	0.3	0.2	0.2	0.2	0.2	0.4	1.3	0.3
Share Invalid	0.2	0.3	0.3	0.2	0.3	0.3	0.6	1.5	0.3
PARTY VOTES									
1 Conservatives	17.9	18.9	20.6	16.5	18.7	17.8	17.7	21.0	18.2
4 Social Democrats	32.2	36.6	37.2	41.8	42.7	46.1	42.9	44.5	32.8
5 Radical Party	12.1	13.0	11.3	10.7	9.4	9.2	9.5	8.7	8.2
6 Liberals	34.0	28.3	28.3	23.3	24.7	17.8	18.2	18.7	23.4
7 Industry Party	2.3	0.2	-	-	-	-	-	-	-
8 Schleswig Party	0.6	0.6	0.8	0.7	0.6	0.8	0.9	-	-
9 Communist Party	0.4	0.5	0.4	0.3	1.1	1.6	2.4	-	12.5
10 Justice Party	-	1.0	1.3	1.8	2.7	2.5	2.0	1.6	1.9
11 Farmers' Party	-	-	-	-	-	3.2	3.0	1.2	-
12 National Socialists	-	-	-	-	0.0	1.0	1.8	2.2	-
13 Danish Union	-	-	-	-	-	-	0.5	2.2	3.1
14 National Cooperation	-	-	-	-	-	-	1.0	-	-
Others	0.5	1.0	0.2	-	0.0	0.0	-	0.0	0.0

Table 5.4c DENMARK Number of Seats Won in the Folketing 1920-1945

	1920 (Sept.)	1924	1926	1929	1932	1935	1939	1943	1945
1 Conservatives	27	28	30	24	27	26	26	31	26
4 Social Democrats	48	55	53	61	62	68	64	66	48
5 Radical Party	18	20	16	16	14	14	14	13	11
6 Liberals	51	44	46	43	38	28	30	28	38
7 Industry Party	3	0	–	–	–	–	–	–	–
8 Schleswig Party	1	1	1	1	1	1	0	–	–
9 Communist Party	0	0	0	0	2	2	3	–	18
10 Justice Party	–	–	2	3	4	4	3	2	3
11 Farmers' Party	–	–	–	–	–	5	4	2	–
12 National Socialists	–	–	–	–	0	0	3	3	–
13 Danish Union	–	–	–	–	–	–	1	3	4
14 National Cooperation	–	–	–	–	–	–	–	–	–
Others	0	0	0	–	0	0	–	0	0
Total Seats	148	148	148	148	148	148	148	148	148

Source: Danmarks Statistik, *Folketingsvalget den 8. September 1987*.

Table 5.4d DENMARK Percentage of Seats Won in the Folketing 1920-1945

	1920 (Sept.)	1924	1926	1929	1932	1935	1939	1943	1945
1 Conservatives	18.2	18.9	20.3	16.2	18.2	17.6	17.6	20.9	17.6
4 Social Democrats	32.4	37.2	35.8	41.2	41.9	45.9	43.2	44.6	32.4
5 Radical Party	12.2	13.5	10.8	10.8	9.5	9.5	9.5	8.8	7.4
6 Liberals	34.5	29.7	31.1	29.1	25.7	18.9	20.3	18.9	25.7
7 Industry Party	2.0	0.0	-	-	-	-	-	-	-
8 Schleswig Party	0.7	0.7	0.7	0.7	0.7	0.7	-	-	-
9 Communist Party	0.0	0.0	0.0	0.0	1.4	1.4	2.0	-	12.2
10 Justice Party	-	-	1.4	2.0	2.7	2.7	2.0	1.4	2.0
11 Farmers' Party	-	-	-	-	-	3.4	2.7	1.4	-
12 National Socialists	-	-	-	-	0.0	0.0	2.0	2.0	-
13 Danish Union	-	-	-	-	-	-	0.7	2.0	2.7
14 National Cooperation	-	-	-	-	-	-	0.0	-	-
Others	0.0	0.0	0.0	-	0.0	0.0	0.0	0.0	0.0

Table 5.5a DENMARK Total Votes 1947-1968

	1947	1950	1953 (April)	1953 (Sept.)	1957	1960	1964	1966	1968
Electorate	2,435,306	2,516,118	2,571,311	2,695,554	2,772,159	2,842,336	3,088,269	3,162,352	3,208,646
Valid Votes	2,084,141	2,054,330	2,070,903	2,166,391	2,310,175	2,431,947	2,631,384	2,794,007	2,854,647
Invalid Votes	4,874	5,614	6,712	5,645	10,922	7,989	9,472	8,297	10,158
Total Votes	2,089,015	2,059,944	2,077,615	2,172,036	2,321,097	2,439,936	2,640,856	2,802,304	2,864,805
PARTY VOTES									
1 Conservatives	259,324	365,236	358,509	364,960	383,843	435,764	527,798	522,028	581,051
4 Social Democrats	834,089	813,224	836,507	894,913	910,170	1,023,794	1,103,667	1,068,911	974,833
5 Radical Party	144,206	167,969	178,942	169,295	179,822	140,979	139,702	203,858	427,304
6 Liberals	574,895	438,188	456,896	499,656	578,932	512,041	547,770	539,027	530,167
8 Schleswig Party	7,464	6,406	8,438	9,721	9,202	9,058	9,274	-	6,831
9 Communist Party	141,094	94,523	98,940	93,824	72,315	27,298	32,390	21,553	29,706
10 Justice Party	94,570	168,784	116,288	75,449	122,759	52,330	34,258	19,905	21,124
13 Danish Union	24,724	-	16,383	-	-	-	9,747	-	-
15 Independents' Party	-	-	-	58,573	53,061	81,134	65,756	44,994	14,360
16 Socialist People's Party	-	-	-	-	-	149,440	151,697	304,437	174,553
17 Liberal Centre	-	-	-	-	-	-	-	69,180	37,407
18 Left Socialist Party	-	-	-	-	-	-	-	-	57,184
Others	3,775	-	-	-	71	109	9,325	114	127

Source: Danmarks Statistik, *Folketingsvalget den 8. September 1987.*

Table 5.5b DENMARK Percentage of Votes 1947-1968

	1947	1950	1953 (April)	1953 (Sept.)	1957	1960	1964	1966	1968
Total Votes	85.8	81.9	80.8	80.6	83.7	85.8	85.5	88.6	89.3
Valid Votes	85.6	81.6	80.5	80.4	83.3	85.6	85.2	88.4	89.0
Invalid Votes	0.2	0.2	0.3	0.2	0.4	0.3	0.3	0.3	0.3
Share Invalid	0.2	0.3	0.3	0.3	0.5	0.3	0.4	0.3	0.4
PARTY VOTES									
1 Conservatives	12.4	17.8	17.3	16.8	16.6	17.9	20.1	18.7	20.4
4 Social Democrats	40.0	39.6	40.4	41.3	39.4	42.1	41.9	38.3	34.1
5 Radical Party	6.9	8.2	8.6	7.8	7.8	5.8	5.3	7.3	15.0
6 Liberals	27.6	21.3	22.1	23.1	25.1	21.1	20.8	19.3	18.6
8 Schleswig Party	0.4	0.3	0.4	0.4	0.4	0.4	0.4	-	0.2
9 Communist Party	6.8	4.6	4.8	4.3	3.1	1.1	1.2	0.8	1.0
10 Justice Party	4.5	8.2	5.6	3.5	5.3	2.2	1.3	0.7	0.7
13 Danish Union	1.2	-	0.8	-	-	-	0.4	-	-
15 Independents' Party	-	-	-	2.7	2.3	3.3	2.5	1.6	0.5
16 Socialist People's Party	-	-	-	-	-	6.1	5.8	10.9	6.1
17 Liberal Centre	-	-	-	-	-	-	-	2.5	1.3
18 Left Socialist Party	-	-	-	-	-	-	-	-	2.0
Others	0.2	-	-	-	0.0	0.0	0.4	0.0	0.0

Table 5.5c DENMARK Number of Seats Won in the Folketing 1947-1968

	1947	1950	1953 (April)	1953 (Sept.)	1957	1960	1964	1966	1968
1 Conservatives	17	27	26	30	30	32	36	34	37
4 Social Democrats	57	59	61	74	70	76	76	69	62
5 Radical Party	10	12	13	14	14	11	10	13	27
6 Liberals	49	32	33	42	45	38	38	35	34
8 Schleswig Party	0	0	0	1	1	1	0	–	0
9 Communist Party	9	7	7	8	6	0	0	0	0
10 Justice Party	6	12	9	6	9	0	0	–	0
13 Danish Union	0	–	0	–	–	–	–	–	–
15 Independents' Party	–	–	–	0	0	6	5	–	–
16 Socialist People's Party	–	–	–	–	–	11	10	20	11
17 Liberal Centre	–	–	–	–	–	–	–	4	0
18 Left Socialist Party	–	–	–	–	–	–	–	–	4
Others	0	–	–	–	0	0	0	0	0
Total Seats	148	149	149	175	175	175	175	175	175

Table 5.5d DENMARK Percentage of Seats Won in the Folketing 1947-1968

	1947	1950	1953 (April)	1953 (Sept.)	1957	1960	1964	1966	1968
1 Conservatives	11.5	18.1	17.4	17.1	17.1	18.3	20.6	19.4	21.1
4 Social Democrats	38.5	39.6	40.9	42.3	40.0	43.4	43.4	39.4	35.4
5 Radical Party	6.8	8.1	8.7	8.0	8.0	6.3	5.7	7.4	15.4
6 Liberals	33.1	21.5	22.1	24.0	25.7	21.7	21.7	20.0	19.4
8 Schleswig Party	0.0	0.0	0.0	0.6	0.6	0.6	0.0	-	0.0
9 Communist Party	6.1	4.7	4.7	4.6	3.4	0.0	0.0	0.0	0.0
10 Justice Party	4.1	8.1	6.0	3.4	5.1	0.0	0.0	-	0.0
13 Danish Union	0.0	-	0.0	-	-	-	-	-	-
15 Independents' Party	-	-	-	0.0	0.0	3.4	2.5	-	-
16 Socialist People's Party	-	-	-	-	-	6.3	5.7	11.4	6.3
17 Liberal Centre	-	-	-	-	-	-	-	2.3	0.0
18 Left Socialist Party	-	-	-	-	-	-	-	-	2.3
Others	0.0	-	-	-	0.0	0.0	0.0	0.0	0.0

Table 5.6a DENMARK Total Votes 1971-1988

	1971	1973	1975	1977	1979	1981	1984	1987	1988
Electorate	3,332,044	3,460,737	3,477,621	3,552,904	3,730,650	3,776,333	3,829,600	3,907,454	3,329,129
Valid Votes	2,883,900	3,053,203	3,049,452	3,106,297	3,171,002	3,123,563	3,362,010	3,362,557	3,329,129
Invalid Votes	20,196	17,050	18,850	18,670	23,343	19,861	24,723	26,644	23,522
Total Votes	2,904,096	3,070,253	3,068,302	3,124,967	3,194,345	314,424	3,386,733	3,389,201	3,352,651
PARTY VOTES									
1 Conservatives	481,335	279,391	168,164	263,262	395,653	451,478	788,224	700,886	642,048
4 Social Democrats	1,074,777	783,145	913,155	1,150,355	1,213,456	1,026,726	1,062,561	985,906	992,682
5 Radical Party	413,620	343,117	216,553	113,330	172,365	160,053	184,642	209,086	185,707
6 Liberals	450,904	374,283	711,298	371,728	396,484	353,280	405,737	354,291	394,190
8 Schleswig Party[1]	6,743	-	-	-	-	-	-	-	-
9 Communist Party	39,564	110,715	127,837	114,022	58,901	34,625	23,085	28,974	27,439
10 Justice Party	50,231	87,904	54,095	102,149	83,238	45,174	50,381	16,359	-
16 Socialist People's Party	262,756	183,522	150,963	120,357	187,284	353,373	387,122	490,176	433,261
18 Left Socialist Party	45,979	44,843	63,579	83,667	116,047	82,711	89,356	46,141	20,303
19 Christian People's Party	57,072	123,573	162,734	106,082	82,133	72,174	91,623	79,664	68,047
20 Centre Democrats	-	236,784	66,316	200,347	102,132	258,522	154,553	161,070	155,464
21 Progress Party	-	485,289	414,219	453,792	349,243	278,383	120,641	160,461	298,132
22 Common Course	-	-	-	-	-	-	-	72,631	63,263
23 Greens	-	-	-	-	-	-	-	45,076	44,960
Others	919	637	539	27,206	14,066	7,064	4,085	11,836	3,633

[1] From 1973 to 1977 Schleswig Party candidates were included in Centre Democrat lists.

Source: *Folketingsvalget den 8. September 1987*, and figures provided by Danmarks Statistik.

Table 5.6b DENMARK Percentage of Votes 1971-1988

	1971	1973	1975	1977	1979	1981	1984	1987	1988
Total Votes	87.2	88.7	88.2	88.0	85.6	83.2	88.4	86.7	85.7
Valid Votes	86.6	88.2	87.7	87.4	85.0	82.7	87.8	86.1	85.1
Invalid Votes	0.6	0.5	0.5	0.5	0.6	0.5	0.6	0.7	0.6
Share Invalid	0.7	0.6	0.6	0.6	0.7	0.6	0.7	0.8	0.7
PARTY VOTES									
1 Conservatives	16.7	9.2	5.5	8.5	12.5	14.5	23.4	20.8	19.3
4 Social Democrats	37.3	25.6	29.9	37.0	38.3	32.9	31.6	29.3	29.8
5 Radical Party	14.3	11.2	7.1	3.6	5.4	5.1	5.5	6.2	5.6
6 Liberals	15.6	12.3	23.3	12.0	12.5	11.3	12.1	10.5	11.8
8 Schleswig Party	0.2	-	-	-	-	-	-	-	-
9 Communist Party	1.4	3.6	4.2	3.7	1.9	1.1	0.7	0.9	0.8
10 Justice Party	1.7	2.9	1.8	3.3	2.6	1.4	1.5	0.5	-
16 Socialist People's Party	9.1	6.0	5.0	3.9	5.9	11.3	11.5	14.6	13.0
18 Left Socialist Party	1.6	1.5	2.1	2.7	3.7	2.6	2.7	1.4	0.6
19 Christian People's Party	2.0	4.0	5.3	3.4	2.6	2.3	2.7	2.4	2.0
20 Centre Democrats	-	7.8	2.2	6.4	3.2	8.3	4.6	4.8	4.7
21 Progress Party	-	15.9	13.6	14.6	11.0	8.9	3.6	4.8	9.0
22 Common Course	-	-	-	-	-	-	-	2.2	1.9
23 Greens	-	-	-	-	-	-	-	1.3	1.4
Others	0.0	0.0	0.0	0.9	0.4	0.2	0.1	0.4	0.1

Table 5.6c DENMARK Number of Seats Won in the Folketing 1971-1988

	1971	1973	1975	1977	1979	1981	1984	1987	1988
1 Conservatives	31	16	10	15	22	26	42	38	35
4 Social Democrats	70	46	53	65	68	59	56	54	55
5 Radical Party	27	20	13	6	10	9	10	11	10
6 Liberals	30	22	42	21	22	21	22	19	22
8 Schleswig Party[1]	0	1	1	1	–	–	–	–	–
9 Communist Party	0	6	7	7	0	0	0	0	0
10 Justice Party	0	5	0	6	5	0	0	0	–
16 Socialist Peoples Party	17	11	9	7	11	20	21	27	24
18 Left Socialist Party	0	0	4	5	6	5	5	0	0
19 Christian Peoples Party	0	7	9	6	5	4	5	4	4
20 Centre Democrats	–	13	3	10	6	15	8	9	9
21 Progress Party	–	28	24	26	20	16	6	9	16
22 Common Course	–	–	–	–	–	–	–	4	–
23 Greens	–	–	–	–	–	–	–	0	0
Others	0	0	0	0	0	0	0	0	0
Total Seats	175	175	175	175	175	175	175	175	175

1 The Schleswig Party deputies were elected on Centre Democrat lists.

Source: *Folketingsvalget den 8. September 1987*, and figures provided by Danmarks Statistik.

Table 5.6d DENMARK Percentage of Seats Won in the Folketing 1971-1988

	1971	1973	1975	1977	1979	1981	1984	1987	1988
1 Conservatives	17.7	9.1	5.7	8.6	12.6	14.9	24.0	21.7	20.0
4 Social Democrats	40.0	26.3	30.3	37.1	38.9	33.7	32.0	30.9	31.4
5 Radical Party	15.4	11.4	7.4	3.4	5.7	5.1	5.7	6.3	5.7
6 Liberals	17.1	12.6	24.0	12.0	12.6	12.0	12.6	10.9	12.6
8 Schleswig Party	0.0	0.6	0.6	0.6	-	-	-	-	-
9 Communist Party	0.0	3.4	4.0	4.0	0.0	0.0	0.0	0.0	0.0
10 Justice Party	0.0	2.9	0.0	3.4	2.9	0.0	0.0	0.0	-
16 Socialist People's Party	9.7	6.3	5.1	4.0	6.3	11.4	12.0	15.4	13.7
18 Left Socialist Party	0.0	0.0	2.3	2.9	3.4	2.9	2.9	0.0	0.0
19 Christian People's Party	0.0	4.0	5.1	3.4	2.9	2.3	2.9	2.3	2.3
20 Centre Democrats	-	7.4	1.7	5.7	3.4	8.6	4.6	5.1	5.1
21 Progress Party	-	16.0	13.7	14.9	11.4	9.1	3.4	5.1	9.1
22 Common Course	-	-	-	-	-	-	-	2.3	0.0
23 Greens	-	-	-	-	-	-	-	0.0	0.0
Others	0.0	0.0	0.0	0.0	0.0	0.0	0.0	0.0	0.0

Chapter 6

FINLAND

Finland was a Grand Duchy under Russian rule until 1917. The Finnish parliament consisted of a diet of four estates on the Swedish pattern. Political parties appeared before the end of the nineteenth century. There was a Finnish nationalist party which later split into two factions, the Old Finns and the Young Finns; a party representing the Swedish minority, which in 1906 became the Swedish People's Party; and the Finnish Labour Party, founded in 1899 and renamed the Social Democratic Party in 1903. In 1906 the four estates were replaced by a single-chamber legislature, the Eduskunta. Adult suffrage was introduced with a minimum voting age of 24 and deputies chosen by secret ballot in multi-member constituencies by the d'Hondt highest average system of proportional representation.

The electoral system introduced in the Grand Duchy in 1906 was maintained in the 1919 constitution of independent Finland, and has been in effect with only minor revisions since. Constitutional government and free elections continued during the 1930s but the banning of the Communist front party in 1930, which had received 14 per cent of the vote in the 1929 election, was a serious limitation of electoral choice and there was pressure from the rightwing Lapua Movement (Alapuro and Allardt, 1978). The Communist Party was legalised and the semi-fascist Patriotic Peoples' Movement dissolved as a consequence of Finland's defeat by the Soviet Union in 1944. Lapland from 1906 until 1938 and the Aland Islands since 1948 have formed single-member constituencies having their representative chosen by plurality (Törnudd, 1968). The minimum voting age was reduced to 21 in 1944, 20 in 1969 and 18 in April 1972. Beginning in 1975 Finnish citizens resident abroad have had the right to vote.

When Finland became independent the 1919 constitution gave significant powers to an elected President. The Finnish President is popularly elected for a six-year term by a 300-member (since 1982, 301 member) electoral college. Until 1988 the electoral college met on 15 February, and two rounds of voting occurred in which an absolute majority of electoral college votes was required to win. If no candidate secured this, a run-off election was held between the two leading first-round candidates. More than one electoral college ballot was held in 1925, 1931, 1937, 1956 and 1988. Candidates for election to the electoral college have usually stood under party labels, but especially in the earlier elections, parties have not always nominated a candidate for the presidency.

Changes in the presidential election procedure were implemented for the first time in the 1988 election. Voters now have two votes, one for an individual candidate for the presidency and one for a candidate for the electoral college. Only candidates committed to a particular presidential candidate can stand for the electoral college. If a presidential candidate wins an absolute majority of the votes cast he is declared elected. If no candidate wins a majority the electoral college is convened to choose the president.

In practice, the Finnish parliament has sometimes used its legal powers to name the president without the election of an electoral college. In 1940 and 1943 the president was chosen by the electoral college elected in 1937. In 1973 parliament extended President Kekkonen's term of office, due to end the following year, for an additional four years. The following have been Presidents of Finland since 1919:

President	Period in Office	Party
K.J. Ståhlberg	1919-1925	National Progressive
L. Relander	1925-1931	Agrarian Union
P.E. Svinhufvud	1931-1937	National Coalition
K.Kallio	1937-1940	Agrarian Union
R. Ryti	1940-1944	National Progressive
Marshal Mannerheim	1944-1946	Non-party
J.K. Paasikivi	1946-1956	National Coalition
U. Kekkonen	1956-1982	Agrarian Union/Centre Party [1]
M. Koivisto	1982	Social Democrat

[1] For varying multi-party coalitions which supported Kekkonen, giving him an absolute majority of the popular vote in 1968 and 1978, see Table 6.6.

Sources:

R. Alapuro and E. Allardt, 'The Lapua movement: the threat of rightist takeover in Finland, 1930-32', in J. Linz and A. Stepan (eds.), *The Breakdown of Democratic Regimes* (Baltimore: Johns Hopkins Press, 1978) 122-41

D. Arter, *Politics and Policy Making in Finland* (Brighton: Wheatsheaf, 1987)

E. Jutikkala, 'Political parties in the elections of the Finnish Diet of Estates', *Sitzungsberichte der Finnischen Akademie der Wissenschaften 1960* (Helsinki: 1961) 167-184

D.G. Kirby, *Finland in the Twentieth Century* (London: Hurst, 1979)

J. Nousiainen, *The Finnish Political System* (Cambridge, Mass: Harvard University Press, 1971)

Official Statistics of Finland, Series XXIX A, *Vaalitilasto,* 1907 (Helsinki: Central Statistical Office, 1908) and subsequent volumes in the same series

P. Pesonen, 'Finland: party support in a fragmented system', in R. Rose (ed.) *Electoral Behavior: a Comparative Handbook* (New York: Free Press, 1974) 271-314

K. Törnudd, *The Electoral System of Finland* (London: Hugh Evelyn, 1968)

Table 6.1 POLITICAL PARTIES IN FINLAND SINCE 1907

	Party Names	Elections Contested Years	Number
1	Social Democrats (Suomen Sosialidemokraattinen Puolue)	1907ff	30
2	Swedish People's Party (Svenska Folkpartiet/ Ruotsalainen Kansanpuolue) [1]	1907ff	30
3	Christian Labour Union (Suomen Kristillinen Työväen Puolue)	1907-1919	9
4	Agrarian Union (Maalaisliitto). Since 1965 the Centre Party (Keskustapuolue), and since 1988 the Finnish Centre (Suomen Keskusta)	1907ff	30
5	Young Finnish Party (Nuorsuomalainen Puolue)	1907-1917	8
6	Finnish Party (Suomalainen Puolue) [2]	1907-1917	8
7	People's Party (Kansanpuolue)	1917	1
8	National Coalition (Kansallinen Kokoomus)	1919ff	22
9	National Progressive Party (Kansallinen Edistyspuolue). Renamed the Finnish People's Party (Suomen Kansanpuolue) in 1951, and in 1966 the Liberal People's Party (Liberaalinen Kansanpuolue)	1919ff	22
10	Socialist Workers' Party (Suomen Sosialistinen Työväenpuolue) [3]	1922-1930	5
11	Small Farmers' Party (Suomen Pienviljelijain Puolue)	1929-1951	8
12	Patriotic People's Movement (Isanmaallinen Kansanliike) [4]	1933-1939	3
13	Finnish People's Democratic Union (Suomen Kansan Demokraattinen Liitto) [5]	1945ff	13
14	Liberal League (Vapaamielisten Liitto) [6]	1951-1962	4
15	Social Democratic League of Workers and Smallholders (Työväen ja Pienviljelijäin Sosialdemokraattinen Liitto) [7]	1958-1972	5
16	Christian League (Suomen Kristillinen Liitto)	1958ff	9
17	Finnish Smallholders' Party (Suomen Pientalonpoiken Puolue); since 1966 Finnish Rural Party (Suomen Maaseudun Puolue) [8]	1962ff	8
18	Constitutional People's Party (Suomen Perustuslaillinen Kansanpuolue). Renamed Constitutional Party of Finland (Perustuslaillinen Oikeistopuolue) in 1980 [9]	1975ff	4
19	Finnish People's Unity Party (Suomen Kansan Yhtenaisyyden Puolue). In 1983 Union for Democracy (Kansalaisvallan Liitto) [10]	1975-1983	3

20	Greens (Vihreät); since February 1987 the Green Union (Vihreä Liitto)	1983ff	2
21	Pensioners' Party (Suomen Eläkeläisten Puolue)	1987	1
22	Democratic Alternative (Demokraattinen Vaihtoehto) [11]	1987	1

1 From 1919 to 1948 normally includes the Swedish Left Wing group, founded as the Svenska Republikanska Vänstern in 1919, renamed the Svenska Vänstern in 1920 and the Svenska Frisinnade Partiet in 1948. In 1930 and in 1939 the parties ran separate lists. After 1922 Swedish Left representatives formed part of the Swedish People's Party parliamentary group. Includes since 1948 the Aland Coalition (Ålandsk Samling), an electoral grouping representing all non-communist groups in the single-member Åland Islands constituency, where the coalition candidate always receives over 90 per cent of the vote.

2 Also known as the Old Finns (Vahasuomalaiset).

3 Closely connected with the proscribed Finnish Communist Party (Suomen Kommunistinen Puolue). Founded in 1920 as the Socialist Workers' Party. Dissolved by the government, it re-emerged as the Finnish Socialist Workers' Party (Suomen Sosialistinen Työväen Puolue). Renamed the Finnish Labour Party (Suomen Työväen Puolue) in 1923, it was again banned in the same year. Its successor, the Association of Socialist Workers and Smallholders (Sosialistinen Työväen ja Pienviljelijäin Järjesto), was suppressed in 1930.

4 Banned in 1944.

5 The Communist Party (Suomen Kommunistinen Puolue) legalised in 1944, contests national elections as part of this group.

6 Established in 1951 by former members of the Progressive Party. Merged with the Finnish People's Party to form the Liberal People's Party in 1966.

7 After presenting independent Social Democrat lists at the 1958 election, the party was founded in the following year. Returned to the Social Democratic Party in 1978.

8 Splinter from the Agrarian Union.

9 Founded in 1973 by right-wing elements from the National Coalition and Swedish People's parties.

10 Founded in 1973 by 12 deputies previously in the Rural Party.

11 Anti-reformist breakaway group from the Finnish Communist Party.

Table 6.2a DATES OF ELECTIONS : EDUSKUNTA

1.	15-16 March 1907	16.	1-2 July 1936
2.	1-2 July 1908	17.	1-2 July 1939
3.	1-3 May 1909	18.	17-18 March 1945
4.	1-2 February 1910	19.	1-2 July 1948
5.	2-3 January 1911	20.	2-3 July 1951
6.	1-2 August 1913	21.	7-8 March 1954
7.	1-2 July 1916	22.	6-7 July 1958
8.	1-2 October 1917	23.	4-5 February 1962
9.	1-3 March 1919	24.	20-21 March 1966
10.	1-3 July 1922	25.	15-16 March 1970
11.	1-2 April 1924	26.	2-3 January 1972
12.	1-2 July 1927	27.	21-22 September 1975
13.	1-2 July 1929	28.	12-13 March 1979
14.	1-2 October 1930	29.	20-21 March 1983
15.	1-3 July 1933	30.	15-16 March 1987

Source: Central Statistical Office of Finland.

Table 6.2b DATES OF ELECTIONS : PRESIDENTIAL ELECTORAL COLLEGE

1.	15-16 January 1925	6.	15-16 January 1962
2.	15-16 January 1931	7.	15-16 January 1968
3.	15-16 January 1937	8.	15-16 January 1978
4.	16-17 January 1950	9.	17-18 January 1982
5.	16-17 January 1956	10.	31 January-1 February 1

Source: Central Statistical Office of Finland.

Table 6.3a FINLAND Total Votes 1907-1922

	1907	1908	1909	1910	1911	1913	1916	1917	1919	1922
Electorate	1,272,873	1,269,177	1,305,305	1,324,931	1,350,058	1,430,135	1,442,091	1,441,075	1,438,709	1,489,022
Valid Votes	890,990	809,441	846,471	791,559	802,387	724,304	795,209	992,762	961,101	865,421
Invalid Votes	8,357	7,896	6,212	5,010	4,707	6,345	5,725	4,903	4,771	5,404
Total Votes	899,347	825,463	852,683	796,569	807,094	730,649	800,934	997,665	965,872	870,825
PARTY VOTES										
1 Social Democrats	329,946	310,826	337,685	316,951	321,201	312,214	376,030	444,670	365,046	216,861
2 Swedish People's Party	112,267	103,146	104,191	107,121	106,810	94,672	93,555	108,190	116,582	107,414
3 Christian Labour Union	13,790	18,848	23,259	17,344	17,245	12,850	14,626	15,489	14,718	-
4 Agrarian Union	51,242	51,756	56,943	60,157	62,885	56,977	71,608	122,900	189,297	175,401
5 Young Finnish Party	121,604	115,201	122,770	114,291	119,361	102,313	99,419			
6 Finnish Party	243,573	205,892	199,920	174,661	174,177	143,982	139,111	}299,516	-	-
7 People's Party	-	-	-	-	-	-	-			
8 National Coalition	-	-	-	-	-	-	-	-	151,018	157,116
9 National Progressive Party	-	-	-	-	-	-	-	-	123,090	79,676
10 Socialist Workers' Party	-	-	-	-	-	-	-	-	-	128,181
Others	18,568	3,772	1,703	1,034	708	1,296	860	1,997	1,350	772

Sources: Törnudd, 1968: 146-150; Statistical Yearbook, 1970: 374, *Vaalitilasto*, 1907:25.

Table 6.3b FINLAND Percentage of Votes 1907-1922

	1907	1908	1909	1910	1911	1913	1916	1917	1919	1922
Total Votes	70.7	64.4	65.3	60.1	59.8	51.1	55.5	69.2	67.1	58.5
Valid Votes	70.0	63.8	64.8	59.7	59.4	50.6	55.1	68.9	66.8	58.1
Invalid Votes	0.7	0.6	0.5	0.4	0.3	0.4	0.4	0.3	0.3	0.4
Share Invalid	0.9	1.0	0.7	0.6	0.6	0.9	0.7	0.5	0.5	0.6
PARTY VOTES										
1 Social Democrats	37.0	38.4	39.9	40.0	40.0	43.1	47.3	44.8	38.0	25.1
2 Swedish People's Party	12.6	12.7	12.3	13.5	13.3	13.1	11.8	10.9	12.1	12.4
3 Christian Labour Union	1.5	2.3	2.7	2.2	2.1	1.8	1.8	1.6	1.5	-
4 Agrarian Union	5.8	6.4	6.7	7.6	7.8	7.9	9.0	12.4	19.7	20.3
5 Young Finnish Party	13.6	14.2	14.5	14.4	14.9	14.1	12.5		-	-
6 Finnish Party	27.3	25.4	23.6	22.1	21.7	19.9	17.5	}30.2	-	-
7 People's Party	-	-	-	-	-	-	-		-	-
8 National Coalition	-	-	-	-	-	-	-	-	15.7	18.2
9 National Progressive Party	-	-	-	-	-	-	-	-	12.8	9.2
10 Socialist Workers' Party	-	-	-	-	-	-	-	-	-	14.8
Others	2.1	0.5	0.2	0.1	0.1	0.2	0.1	0.2	0.1	0.1

Table 6.3c FINLAND Number of Seats Won in the Eduskunta 1907-1922

	1907	1908	1909	1910	1911	1913	1916	1917	1919	1922
1 Social Democrats	80	83	84	86	86	90	103	92	80	53
2 Swedish People's Party	24	25	25	26	26	26	21	21	22[1]	25[1]
3 Christian Labour Union	2	2	1	1	1	–	1	0	2	–
4 Agrarian Union	9	9	13	17	16	18	19	26	42	45
5 Young Finnish Party	26	27	29	28	28	28	23	32	–	–
6 Finnish Party	59	54	48	42	43	38	33	24	–	–
7 People's Party	–	–	–	–	–	–	–	5	–	–
8 National Coalition	–	–	–	–	–	–	–	–	28	35
9 National Progressive Party	–	–	–	–	–	–	–	–	26	15
10 Socialist Workers' Party	–	–	–	–	–	–	–	–	–	27
Others	0	0	0	0	0	0	0	0	0	0
Total Seats	200	200	200	200	200	200	200	200	200	200

1 Includes one Swedish left wing deputy.

Source: Törnudd, 1968: 146-150.

Table 6.3d FINLAND Percentage of Seats Won in the Eduskunta 1907-1922

	1907	1908	1909	1910	1911	1913	1916	1917	1919	1922
1 Social Democrats	40.0	41.5	42.0	43.0	43.0	45.0	51.5	46.0	40.0	26.5
2 Swedish People's Party	12.0	12.5	12.5	13.0	13.0	13.0	10.5	10.5	11.0	12.5
3 Christian Labour Union	1.0	1.0	0.5	0.5	0.5	-	0.5	0.0	1.0	-
4 Agrarian Union	4.5	4.5	6.5	8.5	8.0	9.0	9.5	13.0	21.0	22.5
5 Young Finnish Party	13.0	13.5	14.5	14.0	14.0	14.0	11.5	16.0	-	-
6 Finnish Party	29.5	27.0	24.0	21.0	21.5	19.0	16.5	12.0	-	-
7 People's Party	-	-	-	-	-	-	-	2.5	-	-
8 National Coalition	-	-	-	-	-	-	-	-	14.0	17.5
9 National Progressive Party	-	-	-	-	-	-	-	-	13.0	7.5
10 Socialist Workers' Party	-	-	-	-	-	-	-	-	-	13.5
Others	0.0	0.0	0.0	0.0	0.0	0.0	0.0	0.0	0.0	0.0

Table 6.4a FINLAND Total Votes 1924-1951

	1924	1927	1929	1930	1933	1936	1939	1945	1948	1951
Electorate	1,539,393	1,638,864	1,719,567	1,722,588	1,789,331	1,872,908	1,956,807	2,284,249	2,420,287	2,448,239
Valid Votes	878,941	910,191	951,270	1,130,028	1,107,823	1,173,382	1,297,319	1,698,376	1,879,968	1,812,817
Invalid Votes	4,884	4,180	5,026	5,517	4,917	5,030	5,029	11,875	13,869	12,962
Total Votes	883,825	914,371	956,296	1,135,545	1,112,740	1,178,412	1,302,348	1,710,251	1,893,837	1,825,779
PARTY VOTES										
1 Social Democrats	255,068	257,572	260,254	386,026	413,551	452,751	515,980	425,948	494,719	480,754
2 Swedish People's Party	105,733	111,005	108,886	122,589[1]	115,433	131,440	130,700[4]	142,298[5]	145,455	137,171
4 Agrarian Union	177,982	205,313	248,762	308,280	249,758	262,917	296,529	362,662	455,635	421,613
8 National Coalition	166,880	161,450	138,008	203,958		121,619	176,215	255,394	320,366	264,044
					} 187,527					
12 Patriotic People's Movement	-	-	-	-		97,891	86,219	-	-	-
9 Progressives	79,937	61,613	53,301	65,830	82,129	73,654	62,387	87,868	73,444	102,933
10 Socialist Workers' Party	91,839	109,939	128,164	11,504	-	-	-	-	-	-
11 Small Farmers' Party	-	-	10,154	20,883	37,544	23,159	27,783	20,061	5,378	4,964
13 Finnish People's Democratic Union	-	-	-	-	-	-	-	398,618	375,820	391,362
14 Liberal League	-	-	-	-		-	-	-	-	4,936
Others	1,502	3,299	3,741	10,958[2]	21,881[3]	9,951	1,506	5,527	9,151	5,040

1 Includes 9,271 votes cast for a separate Swedish Left Party list.
2 Includes 9,390 votes cast for the People's Party (Kansanpuolue).
3 Includes 7,449 votes cast for the People's Party.
4 Includes 5,980 votes cast for a separate Swedish Left Party list.
5 Includes Swedish Left Wing.

Source: Official Statistics of Finland, Series XXIXA.

Table 6.4b FINLAND Percentage of Votes 1924-1951

	1924	1927	1929	1930	1933	1936	1939	1945	1948	1951
Total Votes	57.4	55.8	55.6	65.9	62.2	62.9	66.6	74.9	78.2	74.6
Valid Votes	57.1	55.5	55.3	65.6	61.9	62.7	66.3	74.4	77.7	74.0
Invalid Votes	0.3	0.3	0.3	0.3	0.3	0.3	0.3	0.5	0.6	0.5
Share Invalid	0.6	0.5	0.5	0.5	0.4	0.4	0.4	0.7	0.7	0.7
PARTY VOTES										
1 Social Democrats	29.0	28.3	27.4	34.2	37.3	38.6	39.8	25.1	26.3	26.5
2 Swedish People's Party	12.0	12.2	11.4	10.8	10.4	11.2	10.1	8.4	7.7	7.6
4 Agrarian Union	20.2	22.6	26.2	27.3	22.5	22.4	22.9	21.4	24.2	23.3
8 National Coalition	19.0	17.7	14.5	18.0		10.4	13.6	15.0	17.0	14.6
				}	16.9					
12 Patriotic People's Movement	-	-	-	-		8.3	6.6	-	-	-
9 Progressives	9.1	6.8	5.6	5.8	7.4	6.3	4.8	5.2	3.9	5.7
10 Socialist Workers' Party	10.4	12.1	13.5	1.0	-	-	-	-	-	-
11 Small Farmers' Party	-	-	1.1	1.8	3.4	2.0	2.1	1.2	0.3	0.3
13 Finnish People's Democratic Union	-	-	-	-	-	-	-	23.5	20.0	21.6
14 Liberal League	-	-	-	-	-	-	-	-	-	0.3
Others	0.2	0.4	0.4	1.0	2.0	0.8	0.1	0.3	0.5	0.3

Table 6.4c FINLAND Number of Seats Won in the Eduskunta 1924-1951

	1924	1927	1929	1930	1933	1936	1939	1945	1948	1951
1 Social Democrats	60	60	59	66	78	83	85	50	54	53
2 Swedish People's Party	23[1]	24[1]	23[2]	21[1]	21[1]	21[1]	18	15[1]	14	15
4 Agrarian Union	44	52	60	59	53	53	56	49	56	51
8 National Coalition	38	34	28	42	18	20	25	28	33	28
12 Patriotic People's Movement	–	–	–	–	14	14	8	–	–	–
9 Progressives	17	10	7	11	11	7	6	9	5	10
10 Socialist Workers' Party	18	20	23	–	–	–	–	–	–	–
11 Small Farmers' Party	–	–	–	1	3	1	2	–	0	0
13 Finnish People's Democratic Union	–	–	–	–	–	–	–	49	38	43
14 Liberal League	–	–	–	–	–	–	–	–	–	–
Others	0	0	0	0	2	1	0	0	0	0
Total Seats	200	200	200	200	200	200	200	200	200	200

1 Includes one Swedish Left Wing deputy.
2 Includes two Swedish Left Wing deputies.

Source: Official Statistics of Finland, Series XXIXA.

Table 6.4d FINLAND Percentage of Seats Won in the Eduskunta 1924-1951

	1924	1927	1929	1930	1933	1936	1939	1945	1948	1951
1 Social Democrats	30.0	30.0	29.5	33.0	39.0	41.5	42.5	25.0	27.0	26.5
2 Swedish People's Party	11.5	12.0	11.5	10.5	10.5	10.5	9.0	7.5	7.0	7.5
4 Agrarian Union	22.0	26.0	30.0	29.5	26.5	26.5	28.0	24.5	28.0	25.5
8 National Coalition	19.0	17.0	14.0	21.0	9.0	10.0	12.5	14.0	16.5	14.0
12 Patriotic People's Movement	-	-	-	-	7.0	7.0	4.0	-	-	-
9 Progressives	8.5	5.0	3.5	5.5	5.5	3.5	3.0	4.5	2.5	5.0
10 Socialist Workers' Party	9.0	10.0	11.5	-	-	-	-	-	-	-
11 Small Farmers' Party	-	-	-	0.5	1.5	0.5	1.0	-	0.0	0.0
13 Finnish People's Democratic Union	-	-	-	-	-	-	-	24.5	19.0	21.5
14 Liberal League	-	-	-	-	-	-	-	-	-	-
Others	0.0	0.0	0.0	0.0	1.0	0.5	0.0	0.0	0.0	0.0

Table 6.5a FINLAND Total Votes 1954-1987

	1954	1958	1962	1966	1970	1972	1975	1979	1983	1987
Electorate	2,526,969	2,606,258	2,714,838	2,800,461	3,094,359	3,178,169	3,741,460	3,858,553	3,951,932	4,018,248
Valid Votes	2,008,257	1,944,235	2,301,998	2,370,046	2,535,782	2,577,949	2,749,818	2,894,446	2,979,694	2,880,093
Invalid Votes	10,785	10,162	8,092	8,537	8,728	9,111	11,405	11,620	13,276	15,395
Total Votes	2,019,042	1,954,397	2,310,090	2,378,583	2,544,510	2,587,060	2,761,223	2,906,066	2,992,970	2,895,488
PARTY VOTES										
1 Social Democrats	527,094	450,212	448,930	645,339	594,185	664,724	683,590	691,512	795,953	695,331
2 Swedish People's Party	140,130	130,888	147,655	141,688	144,436	138,079	137,693	131,704	146,881	161,998
4 Centre Party	483,958	448,364	528,409	503,047	434,150	423,039	484,772	500,478	} 525,207	507,460
9 Liberal People's Party[1]	158,323	114,617	136,915	153,259	150,823	132,955	119,534	106,560		27,824
8 National Coalition	257,025	297,094	337,161	326,928	457,582	453,434	505,145	626,764	659,078	666,236
13 Finnish People's Democratic Union	433,528	450,506	507,124	502,635	420,556	438,757	519,483	518,045	416,270[3]	270,433
14 Liberal League	6,810	6,424	12,000	-	-	-	-	-	-	-
15 Social Democratic League	-	33,947	100,396	61,274	35,453	25,527	-	-	-	-
16 Christian League	-	3,358	18,567[2]	10,646	28,547	65,228	90,599	138,244	90,410	74,209
17 Rural Party	-	-	49,773	24,351	265,939	236,206	98,815	132,457	288,711	181,938
18 Constitutional People's Party	-	-	-	-	-	-	43,344	34,958	11,104	3,096
19 Finnish People's Unity Party	-	-	-	-	-	-	45,402	9,316	2,335	-
20 Greens	-	-	-	-	-	-	-	-	42,045	115,988
21 Pensioners' Party	-	-	-	-	-	-	-	-	-	35,100
22 Democratic Alternative	-	-	-	-	-	-	-	-	-	122,181
Others	1,389	8,825	15,068	879	4,111	-	21,441	4,408	1,700	18,299

1 From 1954 to 1962 the Finnish People's Party.
2 Comprises 9,477 votes cast for Christian League candidates on National Coalition lists and 9,090 votes cast for League candidates on Finnish People's Party lists.
3 Includes 15,340 votes cast for a successful independent candidate in the Lapland constituency.

Source: Official Statistics of Finland, Series XXIXA.

Table 6.5b FINLAND Percentage of Votes 1954-1987

	1954	1958	1962	1966	1970	1972	1975	1979	1983	1987
Total Votes[1]	79.9	75.0	85.1	84.9	82.2	81.4	73.8	75.3	75.7	72.1
Valid Votes	79.5	74.6	84.8	84.6	81.9	81.1	73.5	75.0	75.4	71.7
Invalid Votes	0.4	0.4	0.3	0.3	0.3	0.3	0.3	0.3	0.3	0.4
Share Invalid	0.5	0.5	0.4	0.4	0.3	0.4	0.4	0.4	0.4	0.5
PARTY VOTES										
1 Social Democrats	26.2	23.2	19.5	27.2	23.4	25.3	24.9	23.9	26.7	24.1
2 Swedish People's Party	7.0	6.7	6.4	6.0	5.7	5.4	5.0	4.6	4.9	5.6
4 Centre Party	24.1	23.1	23.0	21.2	17.1	16.4	17.6	17.3	17.6	17.6
9 Liberal People's Party	7.9	5.9	5.9	6.5	5.9	5.2	4.3	3.7		1.0
8 National Coalition	12.8	15.3	14.6	13.8	18.0	17.5	18.4	21.7	22.1	23.1
13 Finnish People's Democratic Union	21.6	23.2	22.0	21.2	16.6	17.0	18.9	17.9	14.0	9.4
14 Liberal League	0.3	0.3	0.5	-	-	-	-	-	-	-
15 Social Democratic League	-	1.7	4.4	2.6	1.4	1.0	-	-	-	-
16 Christian League	-	0.2	0.8	0.4	1.1	2.5	3.3	4.8	3.0	2.6
17 Rural Party	-	-	2.2	1.0	10.5	9.2	3.6	4.6	9.7	6.3
18 Constitutional People's Party	-	-	-	-	-	-	1.6	1.2	0.4	0.1
19 Finnish People's Unity Party	-	-	-	-	-	-	1.7	0.3	0.1	-
20 Greens	-	-	-	-	-	-	-	-	1.4	4.0
21 Pensioners' Party	-	-	-	-	-	-	-	-	-	1.2
22 Democratic Alternative	-	-	-	-	-	-	-	-	-	4.2
Others	0.1	0.5	0.7	0.0	0.2	-	0.8	0.2	0.1	0.6

[1] From 1975 citizens resident outside Finland have been eligible to vote their turnout has averaged only seven percent, thus depressing turnout overall. Turnout of electors resident in Finland was 79.7 percent in 1975, 81.2 percent in 1979, 80.9 percent in 1983 and 75.9 percent in 1987.

Table 6.5c FINLAND Number of Seats Won in the Eduskunta 1954-1987

	1954	1958	1962	1966	1970	1972	1975	1979	1983	1987
1 Social Democrats	54	48	38	55	51	55	54	52	57	56
2 Swedish People's Party	13	14	14	12	12	10	10	10	11	13
4 Centre Party	53	48	53	49	37	35	39	36	38	40
9 Liberal People's Party	13	8	13	9	8	7	9	4	0	0
8 National Coalition	24	29	32	26	37	34	35	47	44	53
13 Finnish People's Democratic Union	43	50	47	41	36	37	40	35	27	16
14 Liberal League	–	0	1	–	–	–	–	–	–	–
15 Social Democratic League	–	3	2	7	0	0	–	–	–	–
16 Christian League	–	0	0	0	1	4	9	9	3	5
17 Rural Party	–	–	0	1	18	18	2	7	17	9
18 Constitutional People's Party	–	–	–	–	–	–	1	0	1	0
19 Finnish People's Unity Party	–	–	–	–	–	–	1	0	0	–
20 Greens	–	–	–	–	–	–	–	–	2	4
21 Pensioners' Party	–	–	–	–	–	–	–	–	–	0
22 Democratic Alternative	–	–	–	–	–	–	–	–	–	4
Others	0	0	0	0	0	0	0	0	0	0
Total Seats	200	200	200	200	200	200	200	200	200	200

Source: Official Statistics of Finland, Series XXIXA.

Table 6.5d FINLAND Percentage of Seats Won in the Eduskunta 1954-1987

	1954	1958	1962	1966	1970	1972	1975	1979	1983	1987
1 Social Democrats	27.0	24.0	19.0	27.5	25.5	27.5	27.0	26.0	28.5	28.0
2 Swedish People's Party	6.5	7.0	7.0	6.0	6.0	5.0	5.0	5.0	5.5	6.5
4 Centre Party	26.5	24.0	26.5	24.5	18.5	17.5	19.5	18.0	19.0	20.0
9 Liberal People's Party	6.5	4.0	6.5	4.5	4.0	3.5	4.5	2.0	0.0	0.0
8 National Coalition	12.0	14.5	16.0	13.0	18.5	17.0	17.5	23.5	22.0	26.5
13 Finnish People's Democratic Union	21.5	25.0	23.5	20.5	18.0	18.5	20.0	17.5	13.5	8.0
14 Liberal League	-	0.0	0.5	-	-	-	-	-	-	-
15 Social Democratic League	-	1.5	1.0	3.5	0.0	0.0	-	-	-	-
16 Christian League	-	0.0	0.0	0.0	0.5	2.0	4.5	4.5	1.5	2.5
17 Rural Party	-	-	0.0	0.5	9.0	9.0	1.0	3.5	-	4.5
18 Constitutional People's Party	-	-	-	-	-	-	0.5	0.0	0.5	0.0
19 Finnish People's Unity Party	-	-	-	-	-	-	0.5	0.0	0.0	-
20 Greens	-	-	-	-	-	-	-	-	1.0	2.0
21 Pensioners' Party	-	-	-	-	-	-	-	-	-	0.0
22 Democratic Alternative	-	-	-	-	-	-	-	-	-	2.0
Others	0.0	0.0	0.0	0.0	0.0	0.0	0.0	0.0	0.0	0.0

Table 6.6a FINLAND Elections to the Presidential Electoral College: Total Votes 1925-1988[1]

	1925	1931	1937	1950	1956	1962	1968	1978	1982	1988[14]
Electorate	1,572,485	1,775,982	1,929,868	2,487,230	2,597,738	2,714,883	2,930,635	3,844,279	3,921,005	4,036,169
Valid Votes	621,919	836,758	1,112,646	1,577,043	1,896,655	2,202,204	2,038,592	2,448,384	3,177,525	2,985,709
Invalid Votes	2,258	2,763	3,058	8,792	8,794	9,237	10,192	21,955	10,531	155,651
Total Votes	624,177	839,521	1,115,704	1,585,835	1,905,449	2,211,441	2,048,784	2,470,339	3,188,056	3,141,360
PARTY VOTES										
1 Social Democrats	165,091	252,550	341,408	343,828[2]	442,408	289,366	315,068[7]	569,154[7]	1,370,314	1,175,209[15]
2 Swedish People's Party	78,422[2]	75,382[2]	112,993[3]	139,318[6]	130,145[2]	147,340[8]	115,515[11]	93,385[7]	121,519	-
4 Agrarian Union/Centre Party	123,932[2]	167,574	184,668	309,060	510,783	698,199[7]	421,197[7]	475,372[7]	534,515	647,769
8 National Coalition	141,240[2]	180,378	240,602[4]	360,789[6]	340,311	288,912[2]	432,014	360,310[7]	593,271	603,180
9 Progressive Party/Finnish People's Party/Liberal People's Party	71,119	148,430	123,355[5]	84,956[6]	85,690	176,576[9]	102,831[7]	71,232[7]	56,070	-
10 Socialist Workers' Party	41,213	-	-	-	-	-	-	-	-	-
11 Small Farmers' Party	-	11,772[2]	13,883[5]	-	-	-	-	-	-	-
12 Patriotic People's Movement	-	-	90,378[4]	-	-	-	-	-	-	-
13 Finnish People's Democratic Union	-	-	-	338,035	354,575	451,750	345,609[7]	445,098[7]	348,359	286,833
14 Liberal League	-	-	-	-	32,662	7,898[2]	-	-	-	-
15 Social Democratic League	-	-	-	-	-	66,166	46,833[7]	-	-	-
16 Christian League	-	-	-	-	-	-	-	215,244	59,885	-
17 Rural Party	-	-	-	-	-	-	231,282	114,488	71,947	120,043[15]
18 Constitutional People's Party	-	-	-	-	-	-	-	82,478	9,532	-
19 Finnish People's Unity Party	-	-	-	-	-	-	-	18,548	994	-
22 Democratic Alternative	-	-	-	-	-	-	-	-	-	56,528
Others	822[2]	672[2]	5,359[2]	1,057	81[2]	75,997[10]	28,243[12]	3,080[7]	11,119[13]	96,147[15]

1 In 1919, 1944 and 1946 Parliament elected the President. In 1940 and 1943 the President was chosen by the electoral college elected in 1937.

2 Votes cast for uncommitted candidates.

3 Includes 10,743 votes cast for Swedish Left wing candidates supporting K. J. Ståhlberg.

4 Votes cast for supporters of the re-election of President Svinhufvud.

5 Votes cast for supporters of J. Ståhlberg.

6 Votes cast for supporters of the re-election of President Paasikivi.

7 Votes cast for suppporters of the re-election of President Kekkonen.

8 Includes 35,599 votes cast for supporters of President Kekkonen.

9 Includes 165,489 votes cast for supporters of President Kekkonen.

10 Includes 75,961 votes cast for supporters of President Kekkonen.

11 Includes 70,946 votes cast for supporters of President Kekkonen, 43,892 votes cast for supporters of Matti Virkkunen, the candidate of the National Coalition and 677 votes for a supporter of Veikko Vennamo, the Rural Party candidate.

12 Includes 21,425 votes cast for independent candidates supporting President Kekkonen and 6,787 votes cast for independent candidates supporting Matti Virkkunen.

13 Aland Coalition. The Coalition's elector supported Mannu Koivisto, the Social Democrat Party candidate.

14 Votes cast for members of the electoral college. In the simultaneous vote for the direct election of a President the votes were cast as follows:- President Koivisto (Social Democrat) 1,513,234; P. Väyrinen (Centre and Christian League candidate) 635,735; H. Holkeri (National Coalition) 570,340; K. Kivisto (Communist) 330,672; J. Kajanova (Democratic Alternative) 44,428.

15 Supporters of the re-election of President Koivisto.

Table 6.6b FINLAND Elections to the Presidential Electoral College: Percentage of Votes 1925-1988

	1925	1931	1937	1950	1956	1962	1968	1978	1982	1988
Valid Votes	39.6	47.1	57.7	63.4	73.0	81.1	69.6	63.7	81.0	73.9
Invalid Votes	0.1	0.1	0.1	0.4	0.3	0.3	0.3	0.6	0.3	3.9
Total Votes	39.7	47.2	57.8	63.8	73.3	81.4	69.9	64.3	81.4	77.6
Share Invalid	0.4	0.3	0.3	0.6	0.5	0.4	0.5	0.9	0.4	5.0
PARTY VOTES										
1 Social Democrats	26.2	30.2	30.7	21.8	23.3	13.1	15.5	23.3	43.1	39.4
2 Swedish People's Party	12.6	9.0	10.2	8.8	6.9	6.7	5.7	3.8	3.8	-
4 Centre Party	19.9	20.0	16.6	19.6	26.9	31.7	20.7	19.4	16.8	21.7
8 National Coalition	22.7	21.6	21.6	22.9	17.9	13.1	21.2	14.7	18.7	20.2
9 Progressive Party/Finnish People's Party/Liberal People's Party	11.4	17.7	11.0	5.4	4.5	8.0	5.0	2.9	1.8	-
10 Socialist Workers' Party	6.6	-	-	-	-	-	-	-	-	-
11 Small Farmers' Party	-	1.4	1.2	-	-	-	-	-	-	-
12 Patriotic People's Movement	-	-	8.1	-	-	-	-	-	-	-
13 Finnish People's Democratic Union	-	-	-	21.4	18.7	20.5	17.0	18.2	11.0	9.6
14 Liberal League	-	-	-	-	1.7	0.4	-	-	-	-
15 Social Democratic League	-	-	-	-	-	3.0	2.3	-	-	-
16 Christian League	-	-	-	-	-	-	-	8.7	1.9	-
17 Rural Party	-	-	-	-	-	-	11.3	4.7	2.3	4.0
18 Constitutional People's Party	-	-	-	-	-	-	-	3.4	0.2	-
19 Finnish People's Unity Party	-	-	-	-	-	-	-	0.8	0.0	-
22 Democratic Alternative	-	-	-	-	-	-	-	-	-	1.9
Others	0.1	0.1	0.5	0.1	0.0	3.4	1.3	0.1	0.3	3.2

Table 6.6c FINLAND Presidential Elections: Electoral College Seats by Party 1925-1988

	1925	1931	1937	1950	1956	1962	1968	1978	1982	1988
1 Social Democrats	79	90	95	64	72	36	55	74	144	128
2 Swedish People's Party	35	25	25	24	20	21	15	12	11	–
4 Centre Party	69	69	56	62	88	111	65	64	53	68
8 National Coalition	68	64	63	68	54	37	58	45	58	63
9 Finnish People's/Liberal People's	33	50	36	15	7	22	9	8	1	–
10 Socialist Workers' Party	16	–	–	–	–	–	–	–	–	–
11 Small Farmers' Party	–	2	–	–	–	–	–	–	–	–
12 Patriotic People's Movement	–	–	23	–	–	–	–	–	–	–
13 Finnish People's Democratic Union	–	–	–	67	56	63	56	56	32	26
14 Liberal League	–	–	–	–	3	1	–	–	–	–
15 Social Democratic League	–	–	–	–	–	2	6	–	–	–
16 Christian League	–	–	–	–	–	–	–	24	0	–
17 Rural Party	–	–	–	–	–	–	33	10	1	7
18 Constitutional People's Party	–	–	–	–	–	–	–	6	0	–
19 Finnish People's Unity Party	–	–	–	–	–	–	–	0	0	–
22 Democratic Alternative	–	–	–	–	–	–	–	–	–	0
Others	0	0	2[1]	0	0	7[2]	3[3]	1[4]	1[5]	9[5]
Others	300	300	300	300	300	300	300	300	300	301

1 Swedish Left
2 Non-partisan supporters of Kekkonen (Centre).
3 Two non-partisan supporters of Virkkunen (National Coalition) and one non-partisan supporter of Kekkonen (Centre).
4 Representative of Åland Coalition supporting Kekkonen.
5 Representative of Åland Coalition supporting Koivisto (Social Democrat).
6 Supporters of the re-election of Koivisto.

Chapter 7

FRANCE

The election to the States General in 1789 which preceded the French revolution took place under the rules of the *ancien régime* with separate representation for peers, clergy and the "third estate" and electoral laws varying between provinces and localities. Between the Revolution and 1848 elections were indirect; voters cast ballots for electors who chose the national assembly. The franchise for these indirect elections varied considerably.

The constitution of 1791 extended the vote to all male active citizens above the age of 25 and paying a minimum tax. This excluded only domestic servants, adults living in the parental home and those without a permanent home. Of 7,000,000 adult males about 4,300,000 were qualified to vote. In 1792 adult male suffrage with a voting age of 21 was introduced for elections to the Convention, which, in the following year, introduced a new constitution providing for adult male suffrage and direct elections; however, this constitution was never implemented. In 1795 the franchise was once again limited to tax payers. Under the Consulate and the Napoleonic empire adult male suffrage was in force. Save for the still-born system of 1793, all the elections provided for voters choosing an electoral college, which in turn chose the deputies. After 1795 elections were by a four-stage indirect process effectively controlled by the government.

The fall of Napoleon and the restoration of the monarchy in 1815 led to the institution of a very restrictive *régime censitaire* (a tax-based franchise) with the vote limited to men over 30 who paid at least 300 francs in tax. The electorate was reduced from 6,000,000 to about 110,000. In 1820 the franchise was further limited by the introduction of the plural vote; 258 deputies continued to be elected by electoral colleges, and 172 extra deputies were chosen by the richest quarter of electors in each college. The 1830 revolution led to a modest liberalization of the franchise. The minimum voting age was reduced to 25 and the tax requirement reduced to 200 francs; the plural vote was abolished. Members of the liberal professions and public servants who paid a tax of 100 francs were also given the vote (Cole and Campbell, 1989: 35-44).

Since the establishment of direct popular elections in 1848 there have been 16 major changes in the laws governing elections for the lower house of parliament. (Bon, 1978: 13 and Cole and Campbell, 1989: 35-36).

The 1848 revolution brought about the downfall of the monarchy. A Constituent Assembly was elected later the same year on a franchise giving all males aged 21 or over the right to vote. This increased the electorate from 241,000 to 8,221,000. Members of the Constituent Assembly were chosen by plurality in multi-member constituencies. Each elector had as many votes as there were seats to fill. About 300 monarchists, 100 socialist republicans and about 500 moderate republicans were elected.

The constitution of the Second Republic provided for a popularly elected President and a Legislative Assembly elected by plurality in multi-member constituencies, with each elector having as many votes as there were seats to fill. The presidential election in December 1848 was won by Louis Napoléon Bonaparte (Tudesq, 1985: 206). Three major groups contested the first Legislative Assembly elections in 1849. The Party of Order comprised the conservative supporters of Louis Napoléon; the Constitutional Republicans, the socially conservative but anti-Bonapartist elements who had supported the presidential candidacy of General Cavaignac; and the Democrat-Socialists, the extreme republicans and socialists who supported the presidential candidacy of Ledru-Rolin (Table 7.a).

Table 7.a ELECTION TO THE ASSEMBLÉE LÉGISLATIVE 13 MAY 1849

	Votes	%	Seats
Electorate	9,837,000		
Valid Votes	6,594,000	67.0	750
Party of Order	3,310,000	50.2	500
Constitutional Republicans	834,000	12.6	70
Democrat-Socialists	1,955,000	29.6	180
Others	495,000	7.5	0

Source: Genique, 1921: 34; for a critique, see Bouillon, 1956.

Louis Napoleon's *coup d'état* in December 1851 led to the replacement of the Second Republic by the Second Empire. The constitution of the new regime provided for a single-chamber Parliament, the *Corps Législatif*, elected by universal male suffrage. To secure election a candidate had to win a majority in a single-member constituency. If no candidate won an absolute majority of the votes cast on the first ballot a run-off ballot was held at which anyone could stand, even if not a candidate at the first round. In the second round a plurality sufficed for election. During the Second Empire democratic forms were retained, but elections were 'managed' more or less successfully by the government. Government-sponsored candidates always won a large majority of seats in parliament, but their electoral support dropped sharply, especially in the last election of the Second Empire held in 1869 (Zeldin, 1958).

The collapse of the Second Empire in 1870 was followed the next year by elections to a National Assembly held under the electoral laws of the Second Republic. Monarchist candidates won about 400 of the 650 seats (Bon, 1978: 35). Divisions between Orléanist and legitimist monarchists and growing popular support for a republic made the restoration of the monarchy increasingly impractical and in 1875 the National Assembly finally passed a series of laws which inaugurated the Third Republic.

The constitutional laws established a two-chamber National Assembly consisting of a directly elected Chamber of Deputies and an indirectly elected Senate. The President was elected for a seven-year term by the National Assembly. The Chamber of Deputies was elected by universal male suffrage. The Second Empire's two-ballot system with single-member constituencies was retained and was employed in all the 16 parliamentary elections held under the Third Republic, except for the elections of 1885, 1919 and 1924. The 1885 election was held in multi-member constituencies. Candidates could stand either as individuals or as part of a list. Each elector was allowed as many votes as there were seats in a constituency. Voters could cast their votes for candidates in different lists, but could not cast more than one vote per candidate. In order to be elected on the first ballot a candidate had to win an absolute majority of the valid ballot papers cast. For election on the second ballot a plurality was sufficient. In 1889 the single-member two-ballot system was restored.

In 1919 and 1924 a mixed majority/proportional representation system was used to advantage broad electoral alliances. In each multi-member constituency the elector had as many votes as there were seats to be filled. He could vote for candidates on different lists, but could not cast more than one vote for an individual. Seats were allocated in three stages: first any candidate winning more votes than the total number of electors casting valid votes was declared elected. In the second stage the average vote received by each list was divided by a Hare quota, computed by dividing the number of ballots by the number of deputies to be elected. Thirdly, any seats still unallocated went to the list with the highest average vote.

The introduction of universal suffrage in France came long before the development of national political parties. During the early years of the Third Republic political conflict was based on acceptance or rejection of the régime. The Republicans consistently held an electoral and parliamentary majority in competition with a conservative *tendance*, divided between the Bonapartists and supporters of two rival branches of the French royal family (Table 7.b).

The 1889 election saw an unsuccessful challenge to the regime led by the former War Minister, General Boulanger. The republican government restored the single-member two ballot system they had previously opposed to allow republicans to cooperate at the second ballot against alliances of Boulangist and conservative voters. By the end of the nineteenth century the quarrel over the régime had largely been settled in favour of the Third Republic.

Towards the end of the nineteenth century organised political parties began to develop with divisions between the moderate republicans and the radicals and radical socialists. In 1901 most of the radicals and radical socialists united to form a single party. In 1905 the two main wings of the socialist movement were united as the *Section française de l'Internationale ouvrière* : *SFIO*. After the 1902 election the Catholic *ralliés* who had been reconciled to the Republic formed the *Action libérale populaire*. From 1893 to 1906 uncertainty about the political classification of

Table 7.b VOTES AND SEATS, CHAMBRE DES DÉPUTÉS: 1876-89

	1876	1877	1881	1885	1889
Electorate	9,961,000	9,948,000	10,125,000	10,181,000	10,387,000
Republicans	4,028,000	4,340,000	5,128,000	4,373,000	4,353,000
	(371)	(318)	(455)	(367)	(350)
Conservatives	3,202,000	3,639,000	1,789,000	3,420,000	2,915,000
	(155)	(208)	(96)	(202)	(168)
Boulangists	–	–	–	–	709,000
					(42)
Total votes	7,230,000	7,979,000	6,917,000	7,793,000	7,977,000
Total seats	(526)	(526)	(541)	(569)	(570)

Sources: Lancelot, 1968 : 14; Avenel, 1894 and 1896; Duverger, 1978 : 384-385.

candidates, especially on the centre and right, and inconsistencies between different authors makes only approximate the aggregation of constituency votes under national partisan labels (Table 7.c).

The year 1910 is chosen as the starting point for the reporting of votes and seats under party labels because in that year deputies were forbidden to belong to more than one group in the Assembly. During the twentieth century French party organizations have continued to be ill-defined, especially on the right. The large number of parties, difficulties in assigning party labels to individual candidates and differences between membership in electoral and parliamentary party groups often combine to make reporting of results difficult except in terms of broad political *tendances*.

The membership of parliamentary groups, including overseas deputies may be conveniently found in Bomier Landowski (1951) for the Third Republic, Duverger (1971) for the Fourth Republic and Lancelot (1988) for the Fifth Republic. Only amongst the parties of the left, especially the Socialists and the Communists, is there a complete match between electoral parties and parliamentary groups. With the exception of the Socialists and the Communists, once elected candidates can and do join parliamentary groups other than the one most closely linked with their electoral party. These differences were particularly marked during the Third Republic when important electoral parties such as the *Alliance républicaine démocratique* were *purely* electoral organisations whose successful candidates were free to join any parliamentary group.

The Third French Republic fell with the French surrender to Germany in 1940. It was replaced by a French-led régime at Vichy; political parties were outlawed. After the liberation of France by allied armies in 1944, free elections and political parties were restored. Women were given the vote. A purely proportional representation system using the d'Hondt formula was introduced for the first time for the election of a constituent assembly in 1945. The same system was used in 1946 for the election

Table 7.c ELECTIONS: VOTES AND SEATS CHAMBRE DES DÉPUTÉS, 1893-1906

	1893	1898	1902	1906
Electorate	10,446,178	10,635,206	11,058,702	11,218,644
Conservatives	1,178,007	1,011,398	2,383,080 }	
	(76)	(65)	(147) }	2,257,765
Ralliés/Liberal	458,416	541,576	385,618 }	(109)
Popular Action	(27)	(35)	(18)	
Moderate Repub.	3,187,670	3,347,826	2,501,425	1,238,048
	(279)	(235)	(180)	(69)
Radicals	1,443,915	1,400,416	1,413,931	1,395,946
	(143)	(98)	(120)	(91)
Radical Socialists	171,810	748,412	853,140	2,514,508
	(10)	(82)	(75)	(241)
Socialists	598,206	888,385	875,532	–
	(31)	(57)	(46)	
S.F.I.O.	–	–	–	877,221
				(53)
Independent Soc.	–	–	–	205,081
				(18)
Others	108,596	–	n.a.	9,924
	(0)		(3)	(0)
Total votes	7,146,620	7,833,013	8,412,727	8,812,493
Total seats	(566)	(572)	(589)	(581)

Sources: Lancelot, 1968: 14; Avenel, 1894 and *ibid.*, 1898; Duverger, 1978; 384-385

of a second constituent assembly and for the election of the first National Assembly of the Fourth Republic. In all cases party lists were closed; electors could vote only for a party list and could not express a preference for an individual candidate or candidates. Fourth Republic presidents, like their Third Republic predecessors, were elected for a seven-year term by a joint sitting of both houses of parliament.

In 1951 the electoral system for the National Assembly was altered in an attempt by the pro-régime parties to prevent the anti-system Gaullist and Communist parties from gaining a parliamentary majority. In the Paris region the largest remainder system replaced the d'Hondt system. Elsewhere the d'Hondt system was retained, but with an important modification. In each constituency alliances were allowed between national parties, defined as those presenting lists in at least 30 departments. A list or an alliance of lists which won an absolute majority in a particular constituency was awarded every seat. In the case of an alliance of lists the seats were divided between the member parties by the highest average system.

The Fourth Republic fell in May, 1958, following a military coup in Algiers. A provisional government was established under General Charles de Gaulle, who was charged with drawing up a new constitution. The Constitution was ratified by referendum in September 1958. The electoral laws of the Fifth Republic restored the two-ballot single-member system for elections to the National Assembly. Election to the National Assembly on the first round required an absolute majority of votes cast in a constituency and the support of a quarter of the electorate. No new candidates were admitted at the second ballot, at which a plurality sufficed for election. Candidates winning less than five per cent of the valid vote in the first round were eliminated from the second. This threshold was raised to ten per cent of the electorate in 1967 and to 12.5 per cent in 1976. The voting age was reduced to 18 in 1974.

The electoral law has been substantially modified in the 1980s. The 1981 legislative elections gave President Mitterrand's Socialist Party an overall majority in the National Assembly with only 38 per cent of the vote on the first round ballot. Electoral support for the Socialists soon began to wane with the party winning only 21 percent of the vote in the 1984 European Parliament elections. In order to minimise the party's losses in the legislative elections scheduled for 1986 there was a return to a system of proportional representation quite similar to that applied in the early years of the Fourth Republic. Each department formed a multi-member constituency with one deputy for every 108,000 inhabitants and a minimum of two deputies. Seats were allocated by the d'Hondt formula, but lists gaining less than five percent of the vote were excluded. As in the Fourth Republic the lists were closed. With one-third of the deputies elected in constituencies returning only from two to five deputies, the system was designed to favour larger parties. In the subsequent election the opposition RPR-UDF won an overall majority with the support of conservative independents and formed a government which promptly reintroduced the Fifth Republic's traditional two-ballot system.

Major changes have been made in the election of the President of the Republic. The constitution of the Fifth Republic initially established an electoral college comprised of members of both houses of parliament and of departmental general councils, representatives of communal councils and of Algeria, the overseas territories and the new states of the French Community. On 21 December 1958 General de Gaulle was elected President with 78.5 per cent of the 79,470 votes cast.

In 1962 a referendum approved a constitutional amendment authorizing the direct election of the President by universal suffrage. At the first round an absolute majority is required. If no candidate wins an absolute majority, a second round is held two weeks later. The second round is limited to the two candidates who obtain the largest number of votes in the first ballot. Five elections for the Presidency have been held. The 1969 election was held before the expiration of the President's seven-year term because of the resignation of President de Gaulle, and the 1974 election was held early because of the death of President Pompidou. (Table 7.d)

Table 7.d PRESIDENTIAL ELECTIONS, 1965-1988 [1]

	First Round Votes	%	Second Round Votes	%
		1965		
General de Gaulle	10,828,523	44.6	13,083,699	55.2
François Mitterrand (SFIO, PCF, PSU, Radicals, CIR)	7,694,003	31.7	10,619,735	44.8
Jean Lecanuet (MRP, CNIP and right wing Radicals)	3,777,119	15.6		
Jean-Louis Tixier-Vignancour (Extreme right)	1,260,208	5.2		
Pierre Marcilhacy (Moderate conservative)	415,018	1.7		
Marcel Barbu (Non-party)	279,683	1.2		
Electorate	28,913,422		28,902,704	
Valid Votes	24,254,554	83.9	23,703,434	82.0
Invalid Votes	248,403	0.9	668,213	2.3
Total Votes	24,502,957	84.8	24,371,647	84.3
		1969		
Georges Pompidou (Gaullists, Independent Repub., CDP)	10,051,816	44.6	11,064,371	58.2
Alain Poher (Centre démocrate and Radicals)	5,268,651	23.3	7,943,118	41.8
Jacques Duclos (PS)	4,808,285	21.3		
Gaston Defferre (PS)	1,133,222	5.0		
Michel Rocard (PSU)	816,471	3.6		
Louis Ducatel (Non-party)	286,447	1.3		
Alain Krivine (Trotskyist Ligue communiste révolutionnaire)	239,106	1.1		
Electorate	29,513,361		29,500,334	
Valid Votes	22,603,998	76.6	19,007,489	64.4
Invalid Votes	295,036	1.0	303,798	1.0
Total Votes	22,899,034	77.6	19,311,287	65.5
		1974		
Valéry Giscard d'Estaing (Republicans, Centre démocrate, some Radicals, some Gaullists)	11,044,373	43.2	13,396,203	50.8
François Mitterrand (PS, PCF, PSU and MRG)	8,326,774	32.6	12,971,604	49.2
Jacques Chaban-Delmas (Gaullist UDR, CDP and some Radicals)	3,857,728	15.1		

	First Round		Second Round	
Jean Royer (Rightwing independent)	810,540	3.2		
Arlette Laguiller (Trotskyist Lutte ouvrière)	595,247	2.3		
René Dumont (Ecologists)	337,800	1.3		
Jean-Marie Le Pen (Front national)	190,921	0.7		
Emile Muller (Mouvement démocrate socialiste de France)	176,279	0.7		
Alain Krivine (Trotskyist Ligue communiste révolutionnaire)	93,990	0.4		
Bertrand Renouvin (Royalist Nouvelle Action française)	43,722	0.2		
Jean-Claude Sebag (European Federalist)	42,007	0.2		
Guy Héraud (European Federalist)	19,255	0.1		
Electorate	30,602,953		30,600,775	
Valid Votes	25,538,636	83.5	26,367,807	87.3
Invalid Votes	237,107	0.8	356,788	1.2
Total Votes	25,775,743	84.2	26,724,595	86.2

1981

	First Round		Second Round	
François Mitterrand (Parti socialiste)	7,505,960	25.8	15,708,262	51.8
Valéry Giscard d'Estaing (UDF)	8,222,432	28.3	14,642,306	48.2
Jacques Chirac (Gaullist RPR)	5,225,848	18.0		
Georges Marchais (PCF)	4,456,922	15.3		
Brice Lalonde (Ecologists)	1,126,254	3.9		
Arlette Laguiller (Lutte ouvrière)	668,057	2.3		
Michel Crépeau (MRG)	642,847	2.2		
Michel Debré (Independent Gaullist)	481,821	1.7		
Marie-France Garaud (Independent Gaullist)	386,623	1.3		
Huguette Bouchardeau (PSU)	321,353	1.1		
Electorate	36,398,859		36,398,762	
Valid Votes	29,038,117	79.8	30,350,568	83.4
Invalid Votes	477,965	1.3	898,984	2.5
Total Votes	29,516,082	81.1	31,249,552	85.9

1988

	First Round		Second Round	
François Mitterrand (PS, MRG)	10,367,220	34.1	16,704,279	54.0
Jacques Chirac (RPR)	6,063,514	19.9	14,218,970	46.0

	First Round		Second Round	
Raymond Barre (UDF)	5,031,849	16.5		
Jean-Marie Le Pen (FN)	4,375,894	14.4		
André Lajoinie (PCF)	2,055,995	6.8		
Antoine Waechter (Greens)	1,149,642	3.8		
Pierre Juquin (Independent communist)	639,084	2.1		
Arlette Laguiller (Lutte ouvrière)	606,017	2.0		
Pierre Boussel (Trotskyist)	116,823	0.4		
Electorate	38,128,507		36,168,869	
Valid Votes	30,406,038	79.7	30,923,249	81.0
Invalid Votes	621,664	1.6	1,161,822	3.0
Total Votes	31,027,692	81.4	32,085,071	84.1

1 Principal supporters at the first round indicated in brackets after the candidate's name. Figures include the overseas departments and territories.

The French colonies were first given representation in 1789 and have been continuously represented in the French Parliament since 1871. Until 1945 only residents of French origin and a very limited number of native inhabitants who had been granted French citizenship were entitled to vote. During the Fourth Republic universal adult suffrage was extended to the overseas departments of French Guiana, Guadeloupe, Martinique and Réunion and elsewhere the franchise was broadened. But except in the overseas departments French citizens and the majority of the local population voted in separate constituencies. In general the same electoral system as employed in metropolitan France was used except that in single member constituencies first past the post systems were often employed (Campbell, 1989: 180-181). With the independence of Algeria and the African colonies in the early 1960s, overseas representation in the French Parliament was much reduced. As of 1988 there are 22 overseas deputies. As elections overseas have not been on the same basis as in France, voting figures here usually refer only to metropolitan France.

Most French parliaments have been bicameral. However the constitutions of 1791, 1793 and 1848 provided for single-chamber assemblies. The 1795 constitution provided for a Council of Ancients elected by the same electorate and electoral system as the Council of Five Hundred. From 1815 to 1848 the members Chambers of Peers were nominated for life by the King. The upper houses of the Third, Fourth and Fifth Republics were chosen by different methods and different electorates than those of the lower houses.

The Third Republic's Senate was initially intended to be a conservative counterweight to the Chamber. Seventy-five of its 300 members were elected for life by the National Assembly which drew up the regime's constitution. Replacements for these positions were made by the Senate itself. The remaining Senators were chosen by departmental electoral colleges comprising departmental deputies, departmental and arrondisement councillors and delegates elected by communal councils. A three-ballot system with election by majority on the first two ballots and by a plurality on the third was used. Senators were elected for nine years with one-third being replaced every three years. The provision for nominating a quarter of the Senate and over-representation of rural areas ensured a conservative dominance which was only slightly reduced in 1884 when a republican government modified the electoral law to provide that future vacancies amongst the life senators would not be filled and that their seats should instead be allocated to the more populous departments.

The Fourth Republic's upper chamber, the Council of the Republic, had 300 members. Two hundred were elected by departmental electoral colleges, comprising deputies, members of the departmental general councils and popularly elected delegates. Fifty members were elected by the National Assembly and 65 by overseas electoral colleges. The aim of the electoral system was to mirror representation in the National Assembly. In 1948 the method of election to the Council was changed to exclude the popularly elected delegates from the departmental electoral colleges and also delegates chosen by the National Assembly. The electoral college thus consisted of deputies, departmental councillors and delegates of the communal councils. As in the Third Republic conservative, rural interests were heavily overrepresented.

The Fifth Republic retained an upper house, renamed the Senate. The principle of indirect election by an electoral college of deputies, departmental councillors and representatives of the communal councils was continued. As in the Third Republic Senators serve for nine years with one-third retiring every three (for more detail on upper house elections, see Cole and Campbell, 1989: 182-184).

A note on sources:

Until 1951 French official election returns are fragmentary and do not indicate the party affiliations of candidates. Since the 1951 legislative election the official Ministry of the Interior reports do identify the candidates' parties, but a lack of consistency between elections makes these figures very difficult to interpret. The legislative election results reported here derive from secondary sources. Presidential election results since 1965 are definitively reported in the *Journal officiel.* For Third Republic elections the publications of Georges Lachapelle are the primary source. For the elections of 1945 and 1946 there are very full volumes published by *Le Monde*. From 1956 CEVIPOF, (Centre d'Études de la Vie Politique Française, Paris) and the Institut d'Études Politiques, Grenoble, have compiled a machine-readable date-set of election results, based upon the Ministry of the Interior figures but with a much finer and more consistent breakdown of candidates by partisan affiliation. This data-set is distributed by the Banque de Données Socio-Politiques, Université des Sciences Sociales, Grenoble. This much preferable source is used here for all Fifth Republic elections. The figures for votes are based upon the CEVIPOF figures as presented in Lancelot (1988). The figures for seats are drawn directly from the CEVIPOF data-set, because Lancelot reports only the distribution of seats by parliamentary groups, which can combine more than one electoral party.

Sources:

Association Française de Science Politique, *Les élections législatives du mars 1956* (Paris: Armand Colin, 1956)

H. Avenel, *Comment vote la France. Dix-huit ans de suffrage universel (1876-1893)* (Paris: Quantin, 1894)

H. Avenel, *Le nouveau ministère et la nouvelle chambre* (Paris: Flammarion, 1898)

Banque de Données Sociopolitiques, University of Grenoble, *Résultats des élections législatives, présidentielles et européenes et des référendums de 1956 à 1981 par circonscription législative*

A. Bomier-Landowski, "Les groupes parlementaires de l'Assembleé Nationale et de la Chambre des Députés de 1871 à 1936" in F. Goguel and G. Dupeux (eds.), *Sociologie électorale* (Paris: Armand Colin, 1951)

F. Bon, *Les élections en France* (Paris: Editions du Seuil, 1978)

J. Bouillon, "Les démocrates-socialistes aux elections de 1849", *Revue française de science politique*, 6, (1956), 71-95

J. Chapsal, *La vie politique sous la Ve République* second edition (Paris: Presses Universitaires de France, 1984)

A. Cole and P. Campbell, *French Electoral Systems and Elections since 1789* (Aldershot: Gower, 1989)

M. Duverger, F. Goguel and J. Touchard, *Les élections du 2 janvier 1956* (Paris: Armand Colin, 1957)

M. Duverger, *Constitutions et documents politiques* 6th edition (Paris: Presses Universitaires de France, 1971)

Élections législatives 1988: Résultats, analyses et commentaires (Paris: "Le Figaro", 1988)

G. Genique, *L'election à l'assemblée législative en 1849. Essai d'une répartition géographique des partis en France* (Paris: Rieder, 1921)

F. Goguel, *Chroniques électorales, les scrutins politiques en France de 1945 à nos jours* (Paris: Presses de la Fondation Nationale des Sciences Politiques, 1983)

G. Lachapelle, *Tableau des élections législatives des 24 avril et 10 mai 1910* (Paris: Roustan, 1910)

A. Lancelot, *L'abstentionnisme électorale en France* (Paris: Armand Colin, 1968)

A. Lancelot, *Les élections sous la Ve République*, second edition (Paris: Presses Universitaires de France, 1988)

Ministère de l' Intérieur, *Les élections législatives du 17 juin, 1951* (Paris: La Documentation française, 1953) and subsequent volumes in the same series.

Le Monde, *Élections et référendums des 21 Octobre 1945, 5 mai et 2 juin 1946* (Paris: Le Monde, 1946)

Le Monde, *Élections et référendums des 13 octobre, 10 et 24 novembre et 8 décembre 1946*. (Paris: Le Monde, 1947)

A. Tudesq, *L'élection presidentielle de Louis Napoléon Bonaparte* (Paris: Rieder, 1921)

T. Zeldin, *The Political System of Napoleon III* (London: Macmillan, 1958)

Table 7.1 POLITICAL PARTIES IN FRANCE SINCE 1910

	Party Name	Elections Contested Years	Number
1	Socialist Party (Section française de l'internationale ouvrière - SFIO; since 1969 the Parti socialiste - PS)	1910ff	21
2	Radical Socialist Party (Parti républicain radical et radical socialiste) [1]	1910-73	14
3	Socialist Republicans (Parti républicain socialiste) and Independent Socialists [2]	1910-1936	7
4	Independent Radicals (Radicaux indépendants)	1910-1936	7
5	Left Republicans (Gauche républicaine)	1910-1936	7
6	Republican Union (Union républicaine)	1910-1936	7
7	Liberal Popular Action (Action libérale populaire)	1910	1
8	Conservatives and Independents	1910-1936	7
9	Communist Party (Parti Communiste Français - PCF)	1924ff	18
10	Popular Democratic Party (Parti démocrate populaire - PDP)	1932-1936	2
11	Proletarian Unity (Parti de l'unité prolétaire) [3]	1932-1936	2
12	Conservatives [4]	1945ff	12
13	Popular Republican Movement (Mouvement républicain populaire - MRP)	1945-1962	6
14	Gaullists [5]	1946ff	12
15	Poujadists - Union for the Defence of Traders and Artisans (UDCA Union pour la défence des commerçants et artisans)	1956-1962	3
16	Other Extreme Right [6]	1956ff	10
17	Union of Democratic Forces (Union des forces démocratiques - UFD)	1958	1
18	Other Extreme Left [7]	1962ff	8
19	Unified Socialist Party (Parti socialiste unifié - PSU)	1962-1981	6
20	Independent Republicans (Fédération nationale des Républicains indépendants - FNRI) [8]	1962-73	4
21	Democratic Centre (Centre démocrate); in 1968 Centre du progrès et de la démocratie moderne [9]	1967-73	3
22	Regionalist parties [10]	1967-68; 1978-86	5
23	Centre Democracy and Progress (Centre démocratie et progrès - CDP) [11]	1973	1
24	Workers' Struggle (Lutte ouvrière - LO)	1973-86	4
25	Left Radicals (Mouvement des radicaux de gauche - MRG) [12]	1973ff	5
26	Reformers' Movement (Mouvement réformateur) [13]	1973	1

27	Other Left [14]	1973-86	4
28	Greens (Écologistes)	1978ff	4
29	National Front (Front national - FN)	1978ff	4
30	Union for French Democracy (Union pour la démocratie française - UDF) [15]	1978ff	4

1 Established in 1901 by a merger of the Radicals and Radical Socialists. In October 1945 includes votes cast for various right-wing socialist lists and for the Democratic and Socialist Union of the Resistance (Union demócratique et socialiste de la résistance - UDSR). From 1946 the Radical Party combined with these groups to contest elections as the Rassemblement des Gauches Républicaines (RGR). During the Fifth Republic the Radical Party contested most elections in alliance with other parties. In 1967 and 1968 the party was allied with the Socialist Party (SFIO) in the Fédération de la Gauche démocrate socialiste; a few centrist radicals stood independently in these elections. In 1973 most of the Radical Party formed part of the Mouvement Réformateur. The party was one of the founding partners of the Union for French Democracy in 1978. A left-wing breakaway from the party, the Mouvement des Radicaux de Gauche, has been allied with the Socialist Party since 1973.

2 A *tendance* combining the Parti républicain socialiste and others to the right of the SFIO. Allied with and then largely absorbed by the Radical Party after 1945.

3 Breakaway group from the Communist Party, founded as the Parti ouvrier et paysan in 1929.

4 In the Fourth Republic includes the Parti républicain de la liberté, the Independants républicains, the Parti paysan, the Centre national des indépendants et paysans, Action républicaine et sociale, Centre républicain and other candidates classified as *modérés* or *divers droite*. In the Fifth Republic comprises principally candidates classified by Lancelot (1988) as *modérés* or *Centre national des indépendants, divers centristes, divers droite* and *intérêts locaux.*

5 In the November 1946 election the Union gaulliste; in the 1951 election the Rassemblement du peuple français; in the 1956 election the Républicains sociaux; in 1958 the Union pour la nouvelle république (UNR), the Centre de la Réforme républicaine, Renouveau et fidelité, and independent Gaullist candidates; in 1962 and 1967 an alliance of the UNR and the Union démocratique du travail (UDT), the successor to the Centre de la réforme républicaine. After the 1967 election the party was renamed the Union des démocrates pour la Ve république. It contested the 1968 election as the Union pour la défence de la république and took the name Union des démocrates pour la république (UDR) later in the same year. In December 1976 the party became the Rassemblement pour la république (RPR). During the Fifth Republic also includes candidates classified by Lancelot (1988) as *divers gaullistes* and *RPR dissidents* and (in the 1962 and 1967 elections) as pro-Gaullist centre right.

6 Small extreme right wing parties and candidates, but not the Poujadists or National Front.

7 Various extreme left parties and candidates, excluding the PSU and Lutte ouvrière.

8 Breakaway from the conservative Centre national des indépendants et paysans (CNIP) led by Valéry Giscard d'Estaing who supported the direct election of the President of the Republic, in opposition to the majority of CNIP deputies. Renamed the Republican Party (Parti Republicain-PR in 1977 and merged with the Union for French Democracy (UDF) in 1978.

9 Founded in 1966 by Jean Lecanuet, a former MRP leader and presidential candidate. Included leading figures from the MRP, the Radical Party and conservatives groups. In 1973 part of the Reformers' Movement. Reunited with Centre Democracy and Progress (CDP) to form the Centre Social Democrats (CDS) in 1976. Since 1978 part of the Union for French Democracy (UDF).

10 Various regional parties, mostly in Brittany and Corsica as identified in Lancelot (1988).

11 Breakaway led by Jacques Duhamel, who supported Pompidou in the 1969 presidential election. Reunited with the Democratic Centre to form the Centre Social Democrats (CDS) in 1976.

12 Breakaway Radical group which supported the Common Programme of Socialist and Communist parties in 1972. Since then closely allied to the Socialist Party.

13 Alliance of the Radical Party, the Centre démocrate, the Centre républicain (a splinter from the Radical Party) and the Parti social démocrate (former members of the Socialist Party opposed to an alliance with the PCF).

14 Non-Communist left-wing candidates standing independently of the Socialist Party and the Left Radical Movement.

15 A federation of the Republican Party, the Radical Party, the Centre des démocrates sociaux (CDS, a merger of the Centre démocrate and the Centre démocratie et progrés) and other minor centrist and conservative groups. In Table 7.5a votes cast for a few candidates standing under the labels of these parties without the UDF umbrella are included with the UDF.

Table 7.2a DATES OF ELECTIONS: CHAMBRE DES DÉPUTÉS 1910-1936; ASSEMBLÉE NATIONALE 1945-1988 [1]

1.	24 April 1910	11	17 June 1951
2	26 April 1914	12	2 January 1956
3	16 November 1919	13	23 November 1958
4	11 May 1924	14	18 November 1962
5	22 April 1928	15	5 March 1967
6	1 May 1932	16	23 June 1968
7	26 April 1936	17	4 March 1973
8	21 October 1945 [2]	18	12 March 1978
9	2 June 1946 [2]	19	14 June 1981
10	10 November 1946	20	16 March 1986
		21	5 June 1988

1 Date of first ballot: 1910-14, 1928-30, 1958-81, and 1988.

2 Election of a Constituent Assembly.

Source: Lancelot, 1968: 14-16; and Ministry of the Interior.

Table 7.2b DATES OF PRESIDENTIAL ELECTIONS

1. 5 and 19 December 1965
2. 1 and 15 June 1969
3. 5 and 19 May 1974
4. 26 April and 10 May 1981
5. 24 April and 8 May 1988

Source: *Journal officiel.*

Table 7.3a FRANCE Total Votes 1910-1936[1]

	1910	1914	1919	1924	1928	1932	1936
Electorate	11,204,410	11,183,568	11,445,702	11,070,360	11,395,760	11,561,751	11,768,491
Valid Votes	8,445,773	8,431,056	8,148,070	9,026,837	9,469,844	9,576,422	9,847,266
PARTY VOTES							
1 Socialist Party (SF10)	1,110,561	1,413,044	1,728,663	1,814,000	1,708,972	1,964,384	1,954,906[2]
2 Radical Socialist Party	1,727,064	1,530,188	1,420,381	}1,612,581	1,682,543	1,836,991	1,422,611[2]
3 Socialist Republicans and Independent Socialists	345,202	326,927	430,034		490,324	515,176	749,000[2]
4 Independent Radicals	966,407	1,399,830	504,363	}1,058,293	2,196,243	955,990	
5 Left Republicans	1,018,704	819,184	889,177			1,299,936	
6 Republican Union	1,472,442	1,588,075	1,819,691	3,190,831	2,082,024	1,233,360	4,202,298[3]
7 Liberal Popular Action	153,231	-	-	-	-	-	-
8 Conservatives and Independents	1,602,209	1,297,722	1,139,794	375,806	215,169	582,095	
9 Communist Party	-	-	-	885,993	1,066,099	796,630	1,502,404[2]
10 Popular Democratic Party	-	-	-	-	-	309,336	
11 Proletarian Unity	-	-	-	-	-	78,412	n.a[2]
Others	49,953	56,086	215,967	89,333	28,470	4,112	16,047

1 Includes Algeria.
2 Contested the election as part of the Popular Front.
3 National Front, comprising Independent Radicals, Left Republicans, Republican Union, Popular Democrats and Conservatives and Independents.

Source: Duverger, 1978: 384 - 387.

Table 7.3b FRANCE Percentage of Votes 1910-1936

	1910	1914	1919	1924	1928	1932	1936
Valid Votes	75.4	75.4	71.2	81.5	83.1	82.8	83.7
PARTY VOTES							
1 Socialist Party (SFIO)	13.1	16.8	21.2	20.1	18.0	20.5	19.9
2 Radical Socialist Party	20.4	18.1	17.4	} 17.9	17.8	19.2	14.4
3 Socialist Republicans and Independent Socialists	4.1	3.9	5.3		5.2	5.4	7.6
4 Independent Radicals	11.4	16.6	6.2	} 11.7	23.2	10.0	
5 Left Republicans	12.1	9.7	10.9			13.6	
6 Republican Union	17.4	18.8	22.3	35.3	22.0	12.9	42.7
7 Liberal Popular Action	1.8	-	-	-	-	-	-
8 Conservatives and Independents	19.0	15.4	14.0	4.2	2.3	6.1	
9 Communist Party	-	-	-	9.8	11.3	8.3	15.3
10 Popular Democratic Party	-	-	-	-	-	3.2	
11 Proletarian Unity	-	-	-	-	-	0.8	n.a
Others	0.6	0.7	2.7	1.0	0.3	0.0	0.2

Table 7.3c FRANCE Number of Seats Won in the Chambre des Députés 1910-1936[1]

	1910	1914	1919	1924	1928	1932	1936
1 Socialist Party (SF10)	75	103	67	104	99	129	149[2]
2 Radical Socialist Party	148	140	106	} 162	120	157	109[2]
3 Socialist Republicans and Independent Socialists	25	27	22	–	33	37	56[2]
4 Independent Radicals	60	96	51	} 53	52	62	
5 Left Republicans	70	57	79	–	74	72	
6 Republican Union	116	96	201	204	182	76	} 222[3]
7 Liberal Popular Action	5	–	–	–	–	–	–
8 Conservatives and Independents	86	73	88	25	26	33	
9 Communist Party	–	–	–	26	14	12	72[2]
10 Popular Democratic Party	–	–	–	–	–	16	
11 Proletarian Unity	–	–	–	–	–	11	n.a[4]
Others	2	0	2	0	2	0	0
Total Seats	587	592	616	574	602	605	608

1 Includes deputies from Algeria.
2 Elected as part of the Popular Front electoral alliance with 386 deputies.
3 National Front comprising Independent Radicals, Left Radicals, Republican Union, Popular Democrats and Conservatives and Independents.
4 Some Proletarian Unity deputies included amongst the Popular Front deputies.

Sources: Duverger, 1978: 385 - 387 and Lachapelle, 1910: 258.

Table 7.3d FRANCE Percentage of Seats Won in the Chambre des Députés 1910-1936

	1910	1914	1919	1924	1928	1932	1936
1 Socialist Party (SFIO)	12.8	17.4	10.9	-	16.4	21.3	24.5
2 Radical Socialist Party	25.2	23.6	17.2	} 28.2	19.9	26.0	17.9
3 Socialist Republicans and Independent Socialists	4.3	4.6	3.6	18.1	5.5	6.1	9.2
4 Independent Radicals	10.2	16.2	8.3	} 9.2	8.6	10.2	
5 Left Republicans	11.9	9.6	12.8	-	12.3	11.9	
6 Republican Union	19.8	16.2	32.6	35.5	30.2	12.6	} 36.5
7 Liberal Popular Action	0.9	-	-	-	-	-	-
8 Conservatives and Independents	14.7	12.3	14.3	4.4	4.3	5.5	
9 Communist Party	-	-	-	4.5	2.3	2.0	11.8
10 Popular Democratic Party	-	-	-	-	-	2.6	
11 Proletarian Unity	-	-	-	-	-	1.8	n.a
Others	0.3	0.0	0.0	0.0	0.8	0.0	0.0

Table 7.4a FRANCE Total Votes 1945-1958[1]

	1945	1946 (June)	1946 (Nov)	1951	1956	1958
Electorate	24,622,862	24,696,949	25,052,523	24,530,523	26,772,255	27,244,992
Valid Votes	19,189,799	19,880,741	19,203,071	19,129,004	21,490,886	20,492,368
Invalid Votes	467,804	334,459	362,672	541,591	647,160	534,175
Total Votes	19,657,603	20,215,200	19,565,743	19,670,655	22,138,046	21,026,543
PARTY VOTES						
1 Socialist Party	4,561,411	4,187,818	3,431,954	2,744,842	3,247,431	3,171,459
2 Radical Socialist Party	2,131,763	2,295,119	2,381,385	1,887,583	3,227,484[2]	1,977,710
9 Communist Party	5,005,336	5,199,111	5,489,288	5,056,605	5,514,403	3,870,184
12 Conservatives	2,545,845	2,539,845	2,465,526	2,656,995	3,257,782	4,091,120
13 Popular Republican Movement	4,780,338	5,589,059	5,058,307	2,369,778	2,366,321	2,272,643
14 Gaullists	-	-	312,635	4,125,492	842,351[3]	4,229,145
15 Poujadists	-	-	-	-	2,483,813	301,371
16 Extreme Right	-	-	-	-	260,749	225,273
17 Union of Democratic Forces	-	-	-	-	-	248,262
Others	165,106	69,789	63,976	125,739	98,600	105,201

1 Metropolitan France only.

2 The votes cast for the Radical Socialists comprise two lists. One, led by Pierre Mendès-France won 2,389,163 votes forming part of the Republican Front in alliance with the Socialist Party and some of the Gaullist Social Republicans led by Jacques Chaban-Delmas. The second list led by Edgar Faure was part of a centre-right alliance with the Popular Republican Movement and Conservatives. It won 848,321 votes.

3 Chaban-Delmas' wing of the Social Republicans won 256,587 votes; the centre-right faction won 585,764 votes.

Sources: *Le Monde*, 1946: 260, 266 - 267; *Le Monde*, 1947: 252, 260 - 261; Ministère de l'Intérieur, 1953: 42; Association Française de Science Politique, 1975: 470; Ministère de l'Intérieur, 1957: 72 and Lancelot, 1988: 19.

Table 7.4b FRANCE Percentage of Votes 1945-1958

	1945	1946 (June)	1946 (Nov.)	1951	1956	1958
Total Votes	79.8	81.9	78.1	80.2	82.7	77.2
Valid Votes	77.9	80.5	76.7	78.0	80.3	75.2
Invalid Votes	1.9	1.4	1.4	2.2	2.4	2.0
Share Invalid	2.4	1.7	1.9	2.8	2.9	2.5
PARTY VOTES						
1 Socialist Party	23.8	21.1	17.9	14.5	15.2	15.5
2 Radical Socialist Party	11.1	11.5	12.4	10.0	15.2	9.7
9 Communist Party	26.1	26.2	28.6	26.7	25.9	18.9
12 Conservatives	13.3	12.8	12.8	14.0	15.3	20.0
13 Popular Republican Movement	24.9	28.1	26.3	12.5	11.1	11.1
14 Gaullists	-	-	1.6	21.8	4.0	20.6
15 Poujadists	-	-	-	-	11.7	1.5
16 Extreme Right	-	-	-	-	1.2	1.1
17 Union of Democratic Forces	-	-	-	-	-	1.2
Others	0.9	0.4	0.3	0.6	0.5	0.5

Table 7.4c FRANCE Number of Seats Won in the Assemblée Nationale 1945-1958[1]

	1945	1946 (June)	1946 (Nov)	1951	1956	1958
1 Socialist Party	134	115	90	94	88	44
2 Radical Socialist Party	35	39	55	77	73	23
9 Communist Party	148	146	166	97	147	10
12 Conservatives	62	62	70	87	95	133
13 Popular Republican Movement	141	160	158	82	71	57
14 Gaullists	–	–	5	107	16	198
15 Poujadists	–	–	–	–	51	0
16 Extreme Right	–	–	–	–	0	0
17 Union of Democratic Forces	–	–	–	–	–	0
Others	2	0	0	0	3	0
Total Seats	522	522	544	544	544	465

1 Excludes Algeria and the overseas territories and departments.

Table 7.4d FRANCE Percentage of Seats Won in the Assemblée Nationale 1945-1958

	1945	1946 (June)	1946 (Nov.)	1951	1956	1958
1 Socialist Party	25.7	22.0	16.5	17.3	16.2	9.5
2 Radical Socialist Party	6.7	7.5	10.1	14.2	13.4	4.9
9 Communist Party	28.4	28.0	30.5	17.8	27.0	2.2
12 Conservatives	11.9	11.9	12.9	16.0	17.5	28.6
13 Popular Republican Movement	27.0	30.7	29.0	15.1	13.1	12.3
14 Gaullists	-	-	0.9	19.7	2.9	42.6
15 Poujadists	-	-	-	-	9.4	0.0
16 Extreme Right	-	-	-	-	0.0	0.0
17 Union of Democratic Forces	-	-	-	-	-	0.0
Others	0.4	0.0	0.0	0.0	0.5	0.0

Table 7.5a FRANCE Total Votes 1962-1988

	1962	1967	1968	1973	1978	1981	1986	1988
Electorate	27,540,358	28,242,549	28,178,087	29,883,738	34,424,388	35,536,041	36,614,738	36,977,321
Valid Votes	18,333,788	22,389,474	22,117,138	23,752,321	28,098,115	24,823,537	27,490,874	23,983,568
Invalid Votes	584,361	521,365	383,386	546,889	558,730	359,086	1,245,206	488,761
Total Votes	18,918,154	22,910,839	22,500,524	24,299,210	24,658,645	25,182,623	28,736,080	24,472,329
PARTY VOTES								
1 Socialist Party	2,279,209	4,231,173[1]	3,662,443[1]	4,537,348	6,403,265	9,077,842	8,604,296	8,767,596
2 Radical Socialist Party	1,360,465			-	-	-	-	-
9 Communist Party	4,010,463	5,039,032	4,434,831	5,085,356	5,791,525	4,003,025	2,663,259	2,680,120
12 Conservatives	2,111,167	729,980	428,872	810,076	525,975	674,063	528,508	655,326
13 Popular Republican Movement	1,443,838	-	-	-	-	-	-	-
14 Gaullists	6,177,841	7,378,089	8,422,413	6,167,417	6,416,288	5,272,788	7,379,500	4,575,040
15 Poujadists	50,874	-	-	-	-	-	-	-
16 Other Extreme Right	88,326	124,862	18,933	122,498	128,018	26,931	63,698	31,751
18 Other Extreme Left	6,464	21,220	14,778	100,008	131,633	28,236	246,573	88,197
19 Unified Socialist Party	363,842	473,846	862,515	463,537	311,807	177,005	-	-
20 Independent Republicans/Republican Party	427,821	1,230,870	1,863,371	1,700,806	-	-	-	-
21 Democratic Party	-	3,155,367	2,319,118	-	-	-	-	-
22 Regionalist Parties	-	5,035	6,299	-	44,251	24,445	22,218	-
23 Centre Democracy and Progress - CDP	-	-	-	914,397	-	-	-	-
24 Workers' Struggle	-	-	-	194,685	474,226	99,043	173,759	-
25 Left Radicals	-	-	-	408,734	606,565	364,978	308,719	279,316
26 Reformers' Movement	-	-	-	3,149,118	-	-	-	-
27 Other Left	-	-	-	98,331	385,158	61,860	105,986	-
28 Greens	-	-	-	-	574,136	265,647	341,239	86,256
29 National Front	-	-	-	-	82,743	44,414	2,701,701	2,347,595
30 Union for French Democracy - UDF	-	-	-	-	6,186,269	4,702,625	4,351,418	4,454,600
Others	13,478	-	113,634	-	36,256	43	-	17,771

[1] Fédération de la gauche démocrate socialiste

Sources: compiled from Lancelot (1988) and *Elections Législatives 1988*

Table 7.5b FRANCE Percentage of Votes 1962-1988

	1962	1967	1968	1973	1978	1981	1986	1988
Total Votes	68.7	81.1	80.0	81.3	83.2	70.9	78.5	66.2
Valid Votes	66.6	79.3	78.6	79.5	81.6	69.9	75.1	64.9
Invalid Votes	2.1	1.8	1.4	1.8	1.6	1.0	3.4	1.3
Share Invalid	3.1	2.3	1.7	2.3	1.9	1.4	4.3	2.0
- PARTY VOTES								
1 Socialist Party	12.4			19.1	22.8	36.6	31.3	36.6
		} 18.9	16.5					
2 Radical Socialist Party	7.4			-	-	-	-	-
9 Communist Party	21.9	22.5	20.0	21.4	20.6	16.1	9.7	11.2
12 Conservatives	11.5	3.3	1.9	3.4	1.9	2.7	1.9	2.7
13 Popular Republican Movement	7.8	-	-	-	-	-	-	-
14 Gaullists	33.7	33.0	38.0	26.0	22.8	21.2	26.8	19.1
15 Poujadists	0.3	-	-	-	-	-	-	-
16 Other Extreme Right	0.5	0.6	0.1	0.5	0.5	0.1	0.2	0.1
18 Other Extreme Left	0.0	0.1	0.1	0.4	0.5	0.1	0.9	0.4
19 Unified Socialist Party	2.0	2.1	3.9	2.0	1.1	0.7	-	-
20 Ind. Republicans/Republican Party	2.3	5.5	8.4	7.2	-	-	-	-
21 Democratic Centre	-	14.1	10.5	-	-	-	-	-
22 Regionalist parties	-	0.0	0.0	-	0.2	0.1	0.1	-
23 Centre Democracy & Progress - CDP	-	-	-	3.8	-	-	-	-
24 Workers' Struggle	-	-	-	0.8	1.7	0.4	0.6	-
25 Left Radicals	-	-	-	1.7	2.2	1.5	1.1	1.2
26 Reformers' Movement	-	-	-	13.3	-	-	-	-
27 Other Left	-	-	-	0.4	1.4	0.2	0.4	-
28 Greens	-	-	-	-	2.0	1.1	1.2	0.4
29 National Front	-	-	-	-	0.3	0.2	9.8	9.8
30 Union for French Democracy - UDF	-	-	-	-	22.0	18.9	15.8	18.6
Others	0.1	-	0.5	-	0.1	0.0	-	0.1

Table 7.5c FRANCE Number of Seats Won in the Assemblée Nationale 1962-1988

	1962	1967	1968	1973	1978	1981	1986	1988
1 Socialist Party	64			89	102	268	198	260
		} 118	57					
2 Radical Socialist Party	41			–	–	–	–	–
9 Communist Party	41	72	33	73	86	43	32	24
12 Conservatives	32	7	8	15	10	10	4	8
13 Popular Republican Movement	37	–	–	–	–	–	–	–
14 Gaullists	230	191	282	178	142	80	146	123
15 Poujadists	0	–	–	–	–	–	–	–
16 Other Extreme Right	0	0	0	0	0	0	0	0
18 Other Extreme Left	0	0	0	0	0	0	0	0
19 Unified Socialist Party	2	3	0	2	0	0	–	–
20 Independent Republicans/Republican Party	18	41	64	54	–	–	–	–
21 Democratic Party	–	38	26	–	–	–	–	–
22 Regionalist Parties	–	0	0	–	0	0	0	–
23 Centre Democracy and Progress - CDP	–	–	–	21	–	–	–	–
24 Workers' Struggle	–	–	–	0	0	0	0	–
25 Left Radicals	–	–	–	11	10	14	13	9
26 Reformers' Movement	–	–	–	30	–	–	–	–
27 Other Left	–	–	–	0	0	0	0	–
28 Greens	–	–	–	–	0	0	0	0
29 National Front	–	–	–	–	0	0	35	1
30 Union for French Democracy - UDF	–	–	–	–	124	59	128	130
Others	0	–	0	–	0	0	–	0
Total Seats	465	470	470	473	474	474	556	555

Sources: Banques des Données Socio-Politiques

Table 7.5d FRANCE Percentage of Seats Won in the Assemblée Nationale 1962-1988

	1962	1967	1968	1973	1978	1981	1986	1988
1 Socialist Party	13.7			18.8	21.5	56.5	35.6	46.8
		} 25.1	12.1					
2 Radical Socialist Party	8.8			-	-	-	-	-
9 Communist Party	8.8	15.3	7.0	15.4	18.1	9.2	5.8	4.3
12 Conservatives	6.9	1.5	1.7	3.2	2.1	2.1	0.7	1.4
13 Popular Republican Movement	8.0	-	-	-	-	-	-	-
14 Gaullists	49.5	40.6	60.0	37.6	30.0	16.9	26.3	22.2
15 Poujadists	0.0	-	-	-	-	-	-	-
16 Other Extreme Right	0.0	0.0	0.0	0.0	0.0	0.0	0.0	0.0
18 Other Extreme Left	0.0	0.0	0.0	0.0	0.0	0.0	0.0	0.0
19 Unified Socialist Party	0.4	0.6	0.0	0.4	0.0	0.0	-	-
20 Ind. Republicans/Republican Party	3.8	8.7	13.6	11.4	-	-	-	-
21 Democratic Centre	-	8.1	5.5	-	-	-	-	-
22 Regionalist parties	-	0.0	0.0	-	0.0	0.0	0.0	-
23 Centre Democracy & Progress CDP	-	-	-	4.4	-	-	-	-
24 Workers' Struggle	-	-	-	0.0	0.0	-	-	-
25 Left Radicals	-	-	-	2.3	2.1	3.0	2.3	1.6
26 Reformers' Movement	-	-	-	6.3	-	-	-	-
27 Other Left	-	-	-	0.0	0.0	0.0	0.0	-
28 Greens	-	-	-	0.0	0.0	0.0	0.0	0.0
29 National Front	-	-	-	-	0.0	0.0	6.3	0.2
30 Union for French Democracy - UDF	-	-	-	-	26.2	12.4	23.0	23.4
Others	0.0	-	0.0	-	0.0	0.0	-	0.0

Chapter 8

GERMANY

While free competitive elections have been held in Germany for more than a century, its territory and system of government have been subject to frequent changes. This chapter concerns elections to the Reichstag of the German Empire from 1871 to 1912, the 1919 election to the Constituent Assembly, elections to the Reichstag of the Weimar Republic from 1920 to 1933 and to the Bundestag, the lower chamber of the Parliament of the Federal Republic of Germany since 1949. Major boundary changes occurred at the end of the First and Second World Wars. In addition, Alsace-Lorraine, annexed from France, did not participate in the 1871 election; vote totals for the Federal Republic before 1957 exclude the Saarland; and West Berlin's non-voting representatives in the Bundestag are chosen by its Chamber of Deputies and not by the voters directly.

In the Empire elections to the Reichstag were held under a majority system in single-member constituencies. If no candidate received an absolute majority in the first round, a run-off election was held between the two leading candidates. The franchise was limited to men over 25 years. The ballot was secret. For a description of the complex and varied electoral laws employed in elections to the legislatures of the constituent states of the Empire see Urwin, 1974: 117.

The Weimar period saw the introduction of universal adult suffrage with a minimum voting age of 20. A system of direct proportional representation replaced the majority system. A uniform quota of 60,000 votes was needed to win a seat in one of the 35 constituencies; in 1919 only the quota was 150,000. Parties could combine lists in specified constituencies, such as Baden and Württemberg, to form a multiple constituency (*Wahlkreisverband*) where a total of 60,000 votes would also gain a seat provided that at least 30,000 votes had been received in one of the districts comprising the enlarged constituency. Surplus votes plus votes received in those districts where a party had failed to reach the 60,000 vote quota were grouped in a national pool At this stage a minimum of 30,000 votes was needed to win a seat, but only parties which had already been awarded seats could benefit from this final distribution stage and they could not be awarded more seats than they had previously been allocated. Effectively any party gaining more than 100,000 votes, less than one-third of one per cent of the total cast, could hope to win one or two seats in the Reichstag (Falter et al., 1986: 26-28, Urwin, 1974: 118).

The first President of the Weimar Republic was chosen by the Constituent Assembly. Subsequent Presidents were elected by popular vote in 1925 and 1932 using a two-ballot system, in which a candidate needed more than half the votes cast to be declared elected on the first ballot. If no candidate secured an absolute majority, then any number of candidates could run in the second ballot, and individuals who had not run in the first ballot could enter the contest. The winner of the second ballot was the candidate with the largest number of votes, even if less than an absolute majority.

Table 8.a PRESIDENTIAL ELECTIONS, WEIMAR REPUBLIC

	1925			
	First Round Votes	%	Second Round Votes	%
Hindenburg (DNVP and DVP)	–		14,655,641	48. 5
Jarres (DNVP and DVP)	10,416,658	38.8	–	
Held (BVP)	1,007,450	3.7	–	
Ludendorff (Extreme Nationalist)	285,793	1.1	–	
Braun (SPD)	7,802,497	29.0	–	
Marx (Zentrum)	3,887,734	14.5	13,751,605	45. 2
Hellpach (DDP)	1,568,398	5.8	–	
Thälmann (KPD)	1,871,815	7.0	1,931,151	6. 3
Others	25,761	0.1	13,416	0. 0
Electorate	39,226,136		39,414,316	
Valid Votes	26,866,106	68.5	30,351,813	77. 0
Invalid votes	150,654	0.4	216,061	0. 5
Total Votes	27,016,760	68.9	30,567,874	77.6
	1932			
Hindenburg(DVP, Zentrum, SPD)	8,651,497	49.6	19,359,983	53.0
Duesterberg (Stahlhelm*)	2,557,729	6.8	–	
Hitler (NSDAP)	11,339,446	30.1	13,418,547	36.8
Thälmann (KPD)	4,983,341	13.2	3,706,759	10.2
Others	116,304	0.3	5,472	0.0
Electorate	43,949,681		44,063,095	
Valid Votes	37,648,317	85.7	36,490,761	82.8
Invalid Votes	242,134	0.6	281,026	0.6
Total Votes	37,890,451	86.2	36,771,787	83.5

Sources: Statistisches Reichsamt, Volumes 321 and 427.
*Organization of World War I veterans.

After the November, 1932 election, in which the Nazi Party won a third of the seats in the Reichstag, Adolf Hitler was appointed Chancellor on 30 January 1933. The Reichstag fire of 27 February 1933 was used by Hitler as a pretext to abolish fundamental rights. Hitler promptly called an election on 5 March 1933, in which the Nazi Party won less than half the votes and seats. Hitler coerced the Reichstag to secure the abrogation of the Weimar Constitution and the start of the the Third Reich (Empire); it collapsed in military defeat in 1945 (Bracher, 1973).

The Federal Republic, established for the reduced boundaries of West Germany in 1949, restored free elections. The Parliament consists of a directly elected lower chamber, the Bundestag, and an upper chamber, the Bundesrat, composed of delegates appointed by the *Länder*, the states which form the federal system. The number of seats of a party in the Bundestag is determined by proportional representation, subject to modifications. However, representatives are chosen through a dual system of voting, in which some members are elected directly for single-member constituencies, and while others are elected from party lists by the d'Hondt system of proportional representation.

In the first election in 1949, three-fifths of the deputies were elected by a plurality in single-member constituencies. The remaining deputies were chosen by proportional representation from lists at the level of the *Land*. The allocation of seats starts by totalling the number of individuals elected by each party from single-member districts in a *Land*. Every party that won at least one individual-member seat or five per cent of the vote in the region could then claim a full share of the *Land's* total through allocation by PR. The seats won by each party in single-member seats were deducted from their proportional share, and the remainder allocated from the party's *Land* list. In distributing seats by proportional representation the barrier for qualification can be lowered for parties representing national minorities. So far only one party, the South Schleswig Voters' League, which represents the Danish-speaking minority, has benefited from this provision.

A 1953 law modified the system by reducing the number of constituency-elected deputies to one-half the total, and strengthening the barrier clause by making the five per cent vote minimum a national rather than a *Land* requirement. A 1956 law introduced an initial allocation of seats by the d'Hondt method at the national level. A second allocation is then made within each *Land*. The barrier clause was again raised to provide a minimum requirement of five per cent of the vote or three constituency seats. If a party wins more constituency seats than it would be entitled to under the proportional representation distribution (*Überhangmandate*), it keeps the extra seats. In 1985 the d'Hondt system was replaced by a variant of the largest remainder system devised by Professor Niemeyer.

The Niemeyer quota is calculated by multiplying each party's total second votes by the number of seats to be allocated and dividing the product by the total number of second votes cast. Because of the barrier clause this latter figure will exclude parties gaining less than five percent of the vote. Each party receives one seat for each whole number resulting from the calculation. The few remaining seats are then allocated by largest remainder, effectively the descending order of decimal fractions.

Every adult has the right to vote; the age to qualify for the ballot was reduced from 21 to 18 in 1972. Since 1953 the elector has had two votes, one for a candidate in a single-member constituency and the second for the proportional representation party list. In 1949 the elector had only one vote, which was counted at both constituency and *Land* levels. The two votes are normally cast for the same party. But the number of split ticket votes has increased from 4.3 per cent in 1957 to 13.7 per cent in 1987. Voters for minor parties in particular tend to split their votes. In reporting election results, the convention is that the total of second votes for the proportional representation lists are regarded as determining each party's electoral strength (Jesse 1988).

Sources:

K.D. Bracher *Die Weimarer Republik* (Stuttgart: Klott, 1973)

O. Busch, M. Wolk and W. Wolk (eds.), *Wählerbewegung in der deutschen Geschichte: Analysen und Berichte zu den Reichstagswahlen 1871-1933*. (Berlin: Historische Kommission zu Berlin, 1979).

J. Falter, Th. Lindeberger and S. Schumann, *Wähler und Abstimmungen in der Weimarer Republik* (Munich: Beck, 1986).

D. Fricke, *Die Bürgerlichen Parteien in Deutschland* (Berlin: Europäische Buch, 1968).

E. Jesse, 'Split-voting in the Federal Republic of Germany: an analysis of the federal elections from 1953 to 1987', *Electoral Studies*, 7, 2 (1988) 109-124

E. Jesse, *Wahlrecht zwischen Kontinuität und Reform* (Dusseldorf: Droste, 1985)

P. Schindler (ed.), *Datenhandbuch zur Geschichte des Deutschen Bundestages 1949 bis 1982* (Bonn: Presse-und Informationszentrum des Deutschen Bundestages, 1983)

Statistisches Reichsamt, 'Die Wahlen zum Reichstag am 6. Juni 1920', *Statistik des Deutschen Reichs*, Volume 291 (1920) and subsequent volumes in the same series

Statistisches Bundesamt, *Wahl zum Deutschen Bundestag am 25 Januar 1987* Series 1, *Bevölkerung und Erwerbstätigkeit* (Stuttgart and Mainz: Kohlhammer, 1987)

R. Stöss (ed.), *Parteien Handbuch: Die Parteien der Bundesrepublik Deutschland 1945-1980* (Opladen: Westdeutscher Verlag, 1983)

D. Urwin, 'Continuity and change in German electoral politics', in R. Rose (ed.) *Electoral Behavior: a Comparative Handbook* (New York: Free Press, 1974) 109-170

B. Vogel, D. Nohlen and R.O. Schultze, *Wahlen in Deutschland* (Berlin: de Gruyter, 1971)

W. Woyke and V. Steffens, *Stichwort Wahlen* (Opladen: Leske Verlag and Budrich, 4th ed., 1984).

Table 8.1 POLITICAL PARTIES IN GERMANY SINCE 1871

	Party Names	Elections Contested Years	Number
1	Centre Party (Deutsche Zentrumspartei) [1]	1871-1957;1969	26
2	Social Democrats (Sozialdemokratische Partei Deutschlands - SPD) [2]	1871ff	33
3	German Conservatives (Deutsch-Konservative)	1871-1912	13
4	German People's Party (Deutsche Volkspartei)	1871-1907	12
5	German Reich Party (Deutsche Reichspartei)	1871-1912	13
6	Liberal Reich Party (Liberale Reichspartei)	1871-1874	2
7	National Liberals (Nationalliberale)	1871-1912	13
8	Progressive Party (Fortschrittspartei)	1871-1881	5
9	Danish minority	1871-1912;1920-1930	18
10	Hanoverian Party (Deutsch Hannoversche Partei)	1871-1933	22
11	Polish minority	1871-1912;1920-1932	19
12	Alsatians [3]	1874-1912	12
13	Liberal Union (Liberale Vereinigung - LV) [4]	1877-1881	3
14	Liberal Party (Freisinnige Partei) [5]	1884-1896	3
15	Anti-Semites (Anti-Semiten) [6]	1887-1912	7
16	Liberal People's Party (Freisinnige Volkspartei) [7]	1893-1907	4
17	Liberal Union (Freisinnige Vereinigung - FV) [7]	1893-1907	4
18	Bavarian Farmers' League (Bayerischer Bauernbund); from 1922 the Bayerischer Bauern - und Mittelstands Bund; from 1928 German Farmers' Party (Deutsche Bauernpartei)	1898-1933	13
19	Farmers' League (Bund der Landwirte)	1898-1912	4
20	Economic Union (Wirtschaftsvereinigung)	1907-1912	2
21	Progressive People's Party (Fortschrittliche Volkspartei) [8]	1912	1
22	German Democratic Party (Deutsche Demokratische Partei - DDP). In 1928 renamed the German State Party (Deutsche Staatspartei)	1919-1933	9
23	German National People's Party (Deutschnationale Volkspartei - DNVP)	1919-1933	9
24	German People's Party (Deutsche Volkspartei - DVP)	1919-1933	9
25	Independent Social Democrats (Unabhängige Sozialdemokratische Partei Deutschlands - USPD) [9]	1919-1930	6
26	Bavarian People's Party (Bayerische Volkspartei - BVP) [10]	1920-1933	8
27	German Social Party (Deutschsoziale Partei)	1920-1928	4
28	Communist Party (Kommunistische Partei Deutschlands - KPD); German Communist Party (Deutsche Kommunistische Partei - DKP) [11]	1920-1956; 1972-1983	14

29	Business Party of the German Middle Classes (Wirtschaftspartei des Deutschen Mittelstandes; from 1928 Reichspartei des Deutschen Mittelstandes)	May 1924-1932	6
30	Land League (Landbund) [12]	May 1924-1933	7
31	National Socialists/Nazis (Nationalsozialistische Deutsche Arbeiterpartei - NSDAP)	May 1924-1933	7
32	Christian National Peasants and Farmers' Party (Christlich-Nationale Bauern und Landvolkspartei) [13]	1928-1932	4
33	National Party for People's Rights and Revaluation (Reichspartei für Volksrecht und Aufwertung - VRP)	1928-1932	4
34	Christian People's Service (Christlich-sozialer Volksdienst) [14]	1930-1933	4
35	Conservative People's Party (Konservative Volkspartei) [15]	1930	1
36	Christian Democratic Union (Christlich Demokratische Union - CDU)	1949ff	9
37	Christian Social Union (Christlich Soziale Union - CSU)	1949ff	9
38	Free Democrats (Freie Demokratische Partei - FDP)	1949ff	9
39	Bavarian Party (Bayernpartei - BP)	1949-1957;1969	4
40	Economic Reconstruction League (Wirtschaftliche Aufbauvereinigung - WAV)	1949	1
41	German Party (Deutsche Partei - DP)	1949-1957	3
42	German Reich Party (Deutsche Reichspartei)[16]	1949-1961	4
43	South Schleswig Voters' League (Südschleswigscher Wählerverband - SSW Sydslesvigsk Vaelgerforening)	1949-1961	4
44	All-German People's Party (Gesamtdeutsche Volkspartei - GVP)	1953	1
45	Refugee Party (Gesamtdeutscher Block/Bund der Heimatvertriebenen und Entrechteten - GB/BHE)	1953-1957	2
46	Federal Union (Föderalistische Union - FU) [17]	1957	1
47	All-German Party (Gesamtdeutsche Partei) [18]	1961-1969	3
48	German Peace Union (Deutsche Friedensunion - DFU) [19]	1961-1969	3
49	National Democratic Party (Nationaldemokratische Partei Deutschlands - NPD)	1965ff	7
50	Action for Democratic Progress (Aktion Demokratischer Fortschritt - ADF) [20]	1969	1
51	Greens (Die Grünen)	1980ff	3

1 In 1919 the Christliche Volkspartei - CVP. After 1949 the minority of the former Zentrum that did not join the CDU.

2 In the 1871 and 1874 elections the Allgemeiner Deutscher Arbeiterverein and the Sozialdemokratische Arbeiterpartei, which merged in 1875 to form the Sozialdemokratische Partei Deutschlands (SPD).

3 Particularist candidates standing in Alsace-Lorraine, annexed from France in 1871.

4 Splinter from the Nationalliberale Partei.

5 Merger of the Fortschrittspartei and the Liberale Vereinigung.

6 Includes the Christlichsoziale Partei and the Deutschsoziale Reformpartei, for which separate figures are not available.

7 The Freisinnige Partei split in 1893 to form the Freisinnige Vereinigung and the Freisinnige Volkspartei.

8 A merger of the Freisinnige Vereinigung, the Freisinnige Volkspartei and the Deutsche Volkspartei.

9 Splinter from the SPD established in 1917. The party was reunited with the SPD in 1922, but a splinter group continued to contest elections independently until 1930.

10 Breakaway from the Centre Party.

11 The Communist Party was banned by the Constitutional Court in 1956, but was effectively reconstituted in 1968 as the Deutsche Kommunistische Partei (DKP). It contested the 1969 election as part of the Aktion Demokratischer Fortschritt.

12 The Württembergischer Bauern - und Weingärtnerbund; in alliance with other regional parties in the two 1924 elections.

13 Founded by leaders of regional farmers' organizations who had been members of the DNVP and DVP parliamentary groups in the Reichstag.

14 Splinter from the German National People's Party.

15 Splinter from the German National People's Party founded by Count Westarp.

16 In 1949 the German Rights Party - German Conservative Party (Deutsche Rechtspartei/Deutsche Konservative Partei). Merged with the National Democratic Party to form the German Reich Party in 1950.

17 An electoral alliance of three regionally based parties: the Bayernpartei, the Zentrum and the Deutsch-Hannoversche Partei.

18 A merger of the German Party and the Refugee Party. In 1965 the GDP did not present its own list but GDP candidates were included in the CSU list in Bavaria and in SPD lists in Hesse and Lower Saxony.

19 Contested the 1969 election as part of Action for Democratic Progress.

20 An electoral alliance which included the DFU and the DKP.

Table 8.2 DATES OF ELECTIONS : REICHSTAG, 1871-1933; BUNDESTAG 1949-1987 [1]

1.	3 March 1871	18.	20 May 1928
2.	10 February 1874	19.	14 September 1930
3.	10 January 1877	20.	31 July 1932
4.	30 July 1878	21.	6 November 1932
5.	27 October 1881	22.	5 March 1933
6.	28 October 1884	23.	14 August 1949
7.	21 February 1887	24.	6 September 1953
8.	20 February 1890	25.	15 September 1957
9.	15 June 1893	26.	17 September 1961
10.	16 June 1898	27.	19 September 1965
11.	16 June 1903	28.	28 September 1969
12.	25 January 1907	29.	19 November 1972
13.	12 January 1912	30.	30 October 1976
14.	19 January 1919 [2]	31.	9 October 1980
15.	6 June 1920	32.	6 March 1983
16.	4 May 1924	33.	25 January 1987
17.	7 December 1924		

1 Election dates up to and including 1912 refer to the date of the first ballot.

2 Election of a Constituent Assembly. The election results presented in Tables 8.5a-d include elections held in East Prussia and Schleswig-Holstein on 20 February 1921 and in Oppeln, Silesia, on 19 November 1922, which were postponed pending referenda on whether they wished to be part of Germany.

Table 8.3a GERMANY Total Votes 1871-1890

	1871	1874	1877	1878	1881	1884	1887	1890
Electorate	7,656,200	8,523,400	8,943,000	9,128,300	9,088,300	9,383,100	9,769,800	10,145,900
Valid Votes	3,892,200	5,190,300	5,401,000	5,760,900	5,097,800	5,663,000	7,540,900	7,228,500
Invalid Votes	225,800	29,600	21,600	20,000	20,600	18,700	29,800	33,100
Total Votes	4,148,000	5,219,900	5,422,600	5,780,900	5,118,400	5,681,700	7,570,700	7,261,600
PARTY VOTES								
1 Centre Party	700,400	1,446,000	1,341,300	1,328,100	1,182,900	1,282,000	1,516,200	1,342,100
2 Social Democrats	124,700	352,000	493,300	437,100	312,000	550,000	763,100	1,427,300
3 German Conservatives	549,700	360,000	526,000	749,500	830,800	861,100	1,147,200	895,100
4 German People's Party	18,700	21,700	44,900	66,100	103,400	95,900	88,800	147,600
5 German Reich Party	346,900	375,500	426,600	785,800	379,300	387,700	736,400	482,300
6 Liberal Reich Party	273,900	53,900	-	-	-	-	-	-
7 National Liberals	1,176,600	1,542,500			746,600	997,000	1,678,000	1,177,800
			} 1,604,300	1,486,800				
13 Liberal Union	-	-			429,000	-	-	-
8 Progressive Party	342,400	447,500	417,800	385,100	649,300	-	-	-
9 Danish Minority	18,200	19,900	17,300	16,100	14,400	14,400	12,400	13,700
10 Hanoverian Party	85,300	92,100	97,200	102,600	86,700	96,400	112,800	112,700
11 Polish Minority	176,300	198,400	216,200	210,100	194,900	203,200	220,000	246,800
12 Alsatians	-	234,500	200,000	178,900	153,000	165,600	233,700	101,100
14 Liberal Party	-	-	-	-	-	997,000	973,100	1,159,900
15 Anti-Semites	-	-	-	-	-	-	11,600	47,500
Others	79,100	46,300	16,100	14,700	15,300	12,700	47,600	74,600

Source: Vogel et al., 1971: 290-291

Table 8.3b GERMANY Percentage of Votes 1871-1890

	1871	1874	1877	1878	1881	1884	1887	1890
Total Votes	53.8	61.2	60.6	63.3	56.3	60.6	77.5	71.6
Valid Votes	50.8	60.9	60.4	63.1	56.1	60.4	77.2	71.2
Invalid Votes	2.9	0.3	0.2	0.2	0.2	0.2	0.3	0.3
Share Invalid	5.5	0.6	0.4	0.3	0.4	0.3	0.4	0.5
PARTY VOTES								
1 Centre Party	18.0	27.9	24.8	23.1	23.2	22.6	20.1	18.6
2 Social Democrats	3.2	6.8	9.1	7.6	6.1	9.7	10.1	19.7
3 German Conservatives	14.1	6.9	9.7	13.0	16.3	15.2	15.2	12.4
4 German People's Party	0.5	–	0.8	1.1	2.0	1.7	1.2	2.0
5 German Reich Party	8.9	7.2	7.9	13.6	7.4	6.8	9.8	6.7
6 Liberal Reich Party	7.0	1.0	–	–	–	–	–	–
7 National Liberals	30.2	29.7			14.6	17.6	22.3	16.3
		}	29.7	25.8				
13 Liberal Union	–	–			8.4	–	–	–
8 Progressive Party	8.8	8.6	7.7	6.7	12.7	–	–	–
9 Danish Minority	0.5	0.4	0.3	0.3	0.3	0.3	0.2	0.2
10 Hanoverian Party	2.2	1.8	1.8	1.8	1.7	1.7	1.5	1.6
11 Polish Minority	4.5	3.8	4.0	3.6	3.8	3.6	2.9	3.4
12 Alsatians	–	4.5	3.7	3.1	3.0	2.9	3.1	1.4
14 Liberal Party	–	–	–	–	–	17.6	12.9	16.0
15 Anti-Semites	–	–	–	–	–	–	0.2	0.7
Others	2.0	0.9	0.3	0.3	0.3	0.2	0.6	1.0

Table 8.3c GERMANY Number of Seats Won in the Reichstag 1871-1890

	1871	1874	1877	1878	1881	1884	1887	1890
1 Centre Party	61	91	93	94	100	99	98	106
2 Social Democrats	2	9	12	9	12	15	11	35
3 German Conservatives	57	22	40	59	50	78	80	73
4 German People's Party	1	1	4	3	9	7	0	10
5 German Reich Party	37	33	38	57	28	28	41	20
6 Liberal Reich Party	30	3	-	-	-	-	-	-
7 National Liberals	125	155	128	109	47	51	99	42
13 Liberal Union	-	-	13	10	46	-	-	-
8 Progressive Party	46	49	35	26	60	-	-	-
9 Danish Minority	1	1	1	1	2	1	1	1
10 Hanoverian Party	9	4	10	4	10	11	4	11
11 Polish Minority	13	14	14	14	18	14	13	16
12 Alsatians	-	15	15	15	15	-	15	10
14 Liberal Party	-	-	-	-	-	67	32	66
15 Anti-Semites	-	-	-	-	-	-	1	5
Others	0	0	0	0	0	-	2	2
Total Seats	382	397	397	397	397	397	397	397

Source: Vogel et al., 1971: 290-291

Table 8.3d GERMANY Percentage of Seats Won in the Reichstag 1871-1890

	1871	1874	1877	1878	1881	1884	1887	1890
1 Centre Party	16.0	22.9	23.4	23.7	25.2	24.9	24.7	26.7
2 Social Democrats	0.5	2.3	3.0	2.3	3.0	2.8	2.8	8.8
3 German Conservatives	14.9	5.5	10.1	14.9	12.6	19.6	20.2	18.4
4 German People's Party	0.3	0.3	1.0	0.8	2.3	1.8	0.0	2.5
5 German Reich Party	9.7	8.3	9.6	14.4	7.1	7.1	10.3	5.0
6 Liberal Reich Party	7.9	0.8	-	-	-	-	-	-
7 National Liberals	32.7	39.0	32.2	24.9	11.8	12.8	24.9	10.6
13 Liberal Union	-	-	3.8	2.5	11.6	-	-	-
8 Progressive Party	12.0	12.3	8.8	6.5	15.1	-	-	-
9 Danish Minority	0.3	0.3	0.3	0.3	0.5	0.3	0.3	0.3
10 Hanoverian Party	2.4	1.0	2.5	1.0	2.5	2.8	1.0	2.8
11 Polish Minority	3.4	3.5	3.5	3.5	4.5	3.5	3.3	4.0
12 Alsatians	-	3.8	3.8	3.8	3.8	-	3.8	2.5
14 Liberal Party	-	-	-	-	-	-	8.1	16.6
15 Anti-Semites	-	-	-	-	-	-	0.3	1.3
Others	0.0	0.0	0.0	0.0	0.0	0.0	0.5	0.5

Table 8.4a GERMANY Total Votes 1893-1912

	1893	1898	1903	1907	1912
Electorate	10,628,300	11,441,100	12,531,200	13,352,900	14,441,400
Valid Votes	7,674,000	7,752,700	9,489,000	11,253,400	12,207,500
Invalid Votes	28,300	34,000	44,800	50,100	53,100
Total Votes	7,702,300	7,786,700	9,533,800	11,303,500	12,260,600
PARTY VOTES					
1 Centre Party	1,468,500	1,455,100	1,875,300	2,179,800	1,996,800
2 Social Democrats	1,786,700	2,107,100	3,010,800	3,259,000	4,250,400
3 German Conservatives	1,038,300	859,200	948,500	1,060,200	1,126,300
4 German People's Party	166,800	108,500	91,200	138,600	-
5 German Reich Party	438,400	343,600	333,400	471,900	367,200
7 National Liberals	997,000	971,300	1,317,400	1,630,600	1,662,700
9 Danish Minority	14,400	15,400	14,800	15,400	17,300
10 Hanoverian Party	101,800	105,200	94,300	78,200	84,600
11 Polish Minority	229,500	244,100	347,800	453,900	441,600
12 Alsatians	114,700	107,400	101,900	103,600	162,000
15 Anti-Semites	263,900	284,300	244,500	248,500	51,900
16 Liberal People's Party	666,400	558,300	538,200	736,000	-
17 Liberal Union	258,500	195,700	243,200	359,300	-
18 Bavarian Farmers' League	66,300	140,300	111,400	75,300	48,200
19 Farmers' League	-	110,400	118,800	119,400	29,800
20 Economic Union	-	-	-	104,600	304,600
21 Progressive People's Party	-	-	-	-	1,497,000
Others	62,800	146,800	97,500	219,100	167,100

Source: Vogel et al., 1971: 281-293

Table 8.4b GERMANY Percentage of Votes 1893-1912

	1893	1898	1903	1907	1912
Total Votes	72.5	85.5	76.1	84.7	84.9
Valid Votes	72.2	67.8	75.7	84.3	84.5
Invalid Votes	0.3	0.3	0.4	0.4	0.4
Share Invalid	0.4	0.3	0.5	0.4	0.4
PARTY VOTES					
1 Centre Party	19.1	14.9	19.8	19.4	16.4
2 Social Democrats	23.3	21.6	31.7	29.0	34.8
3 German Conservatives	13.5	8.8	10.0	9.4	9.2
4 German People's Party	2.2	1.1	1.0	1.2	-
5 German Reich Party	5.7	3.5	3.5	4.2	3.0
7 National Liberals	15.3	10.0	13.9	14.5	13.6
9 Danish Minority	0.2	0.2	0.2	0.1	0.1
10 Hanoverian Party	1.3	1.1	1.0	0.7	0.7
11 Polish Minority	3.0	2.5	3.7	4.0	3.6
12 Alsatians	1.5	1.1	1.1	0.9	1.3
15 Anti-Semites	3.4	2.9	2.6	2.2	0.4
16 Liberal People's Party	8.7	5.7	5.7	6.5	-
17 Liberal Union	3.4	2.0	2.6	3.2	-
18 Bavarian Farmers' League	0.9	1.4	1.2	0.7	0.4
19 Farmers' League	-	1.1	1.3	1.1	0.2
20 Economic Union	-	-	-	0.9	2.5
21 Progressive People's Party	-	-	-	-	12.3
Others	0.8	1.5	1.0	1.9	1.4

Table 8.4c GERMANY Number of Seats Won in the Reichstag 1893-1912

	1893	1898	1903	1907	1912
1 Centre Party	96	102	100	105	91
2 Social Democrats	44	56	81	43	110
3 German Conservatives	72	56	54	60	43
4 German People's Party	11	8	6	7	-
5 German Reich Party	28	23	21	24	14
7 National Liberals	53	46	51	54	45
9 Danish Minority	1	1	1	1	1
10 Hanoverian Party	7	9	6	1	5
11 Polish Minority	19	14	16	20	18
12 Alsatians	8	10	9	7	9
15 Anti-Semites	16	13	11	16	3
16 Liberal People's Party	24	29	21	28	-
17 Liberal Union	13	12	9	14	-
18 Bavarian Farmers' League	4	5	4	1	2
19 Farmers' League	-	6	4	8	2
20 Economic Union	-	-	-	5	10
21 Progressive People's Party	-	-	-	-	42
Others	1	7	3	3	2
Total Seats	397	397	397	397	397

Source: Vogel et al., 1971: 291-293

Table 8.4d GERMANY Percentage of Seats Won in the Reichstag 1893-1912

	1893	1898	1903	1907	1912
1 Centre Party	24.2	25.7	25.2	26.4	22.9
2 Social Democrats	11.1	14.1	20.4	10.8	27.7
3 German Conservatives	18.1	14.1	13.6	15.1	10.8
4 German People's Party	2.8	2.0	1.5	1.8	-
5 German Reich Party	7.1	5.8	5.3	6.0	3.5
7 National Liberals	13.4	11.6	12.8	13.6	11.3
9 Danish Minority	0.3	0.3	0.3	0.3	0.3
10 Hanoverian Party	1.8	2.3	1.5	0.3	1.3
11 Polish Minority	4.8	3.5	4.0	5.0	4.5
12 Alsatians	2.0	2.5	2.3	1.8	2.3
15 Anti-Semites	4.0	3.3	2.8	4.0	0.8
16 Liberal People's Party	6.0	7.3	5.2	7.1	-
17 Liberal Union	3.3	3.0	2.3	3.5	-
18 Bavarian Farmers' League	1.0	1.3	1.0	0.5	0.5
19 Farmers' League	-	1.5	1.0	2.0	0.5
20 Economic Union	-	-	-	1.3	2.5
21 Progressive People's Party	-	-	-	-	10.6
Others	0.3	1.8	0.8	0.8	0.5

Table 8.5a GERMANY Total Votes 1919-1933

	1919	1920	1924 (May)	1924 (Dec.)	1928	1930	1932	1932 (July)	1933 (Nov.)
Electorate	37,302,100	35,949,800	38,374,900	38,987,400	41,224,700	42,957,700	44,211,200	44,374,100	44,664,800
Valid Votes	30,400,300	28,196,300	29,281,800	30,311,900	30,753,200	34,960,900	36,882,400	35,470,800	39,343,300
Invalid Votes	124,500	267,300	427,600	391,700	412,600	264,900	279,700	287,500	315,000
Total Votes	30,524,800	28,463,600	29,709,400	30,703,600	31,165,800	35,225,800	37,162,100	35,788,300	39,688,300
PARTY VOTES									
1 Centre Party	5,760,900	3,845,000	3,914,400	4,120,900	3,712,200	4,127,900	4,589,400	4,230,500	4,425,000
2 Social Democrats	11,509,000	6,104,400	6,008,900	7,886,300	9,152,900	8,577,700	7,959,700	7,251,700	7,181,300
9 Danish Minority	-	5,000	7,600	5,100	2,400	1,800	1,700	1,700	-
10 Hanoverian Party	296,100	319,100	314,000	262,800	195,600	144,300	46,900	64,000	47,700
11 Polish Minority	-	140,700	100,300	81,900	64,800	73,400	33,400	33,000	-
18 Bavarian Farmers' League/ Farmers' Party	275,800	218,600	169,000	298,100	481,300	339,600	137,800	149,000	114,100
22 Democratic Party	5,641,800	2,333,700	1,655,100	1,921,300	1,505,700	1,322,400	373,300	338,600	334,300
23 National People's Party	3,121,500	4,249,100	5,696,500	6,209,200	4,381,600	2,458,200	2,177,400	2,959,100	3,136,900
24 People's Party	1,345,600	3,919,400	2,694,400	3,051,300	2,679,700	1,578,200	436,000	660,900	432,200
25 Ind. Social Democrats	2,317,300	5,046,800	235,100	99,200	20,800	11,900	-	-	-
26 Bavarian People's Party	-	1,173,300	946,600	1,135,100	945,600	1,059,100	1,192,700	1,095,400	1,073,600
27 German Social Party	-	23,000	333,400	159,400	46,000	-	-	-	-
28 Communist Party	-	589,500	3,693,300	2,711,800	3,264,800	4,592,100	5,369,702	5,980,600	4,847,900
29 Business Party	-	-	524,600	700,200	1,397,100	1,381,000	146,900	110,300	-
30 Land League	-	-	541,200	499,600	199,500	194,000	96,900	105,200	83,800
31 Nazi Party	-	-	1,918,300	907,900	810,100	6,409,600	13,745,700	11,737,400	17,277,300
32 Peasants and Farmers' Party	-	-	-	-	581,800	1,108,700	90,600	46,400	-
33 People's Justice Party	-	-	-	-	483,200	271,400	40,800	46,200	-
34 Christian People's Service	-	-	-	-	-	870,100	364,500	413,200	384,000
35 Conservative People's Party	-	-	-	-	-	290,000	-	-	-
Others	131,800	228,700	529,000	261,800	828,100	148,900	79,000	247,600	5,200

Sources: Vogel et al., 1971: 296-297, and Falter, 1986: 51

Table 8.5b GERMANY Percentage of Votes 1919-1933

	1919	1920	1924 (May)	1924 (Dec.)	1928	1930	1932 (July)	1932 (Nov.)	1933
Total Votes	81.8	79.2	77.4	78.8	75.6	82.0	84.1	80.6	88.8
Valid Votes	81.5	78.4	76.3	77.7	74.6	81.4	83.4	79.9	88.1
Invalid Votes	0.3	0.7	1.1	1.0	1.0	0.6	0.6	0.6	0.7
Share Invalid	0.4	0.9	1.4	1.3	1.3	0.8	0.8	0.8	0.8
PARTY VOTES									
1 Centre Party	19.0	13.6	13.4	13.6	12.1	11.8	12.4	11.9	11.2
2 Social Democrats	37.9	21.6	20.5	26.0	29.8	24.5	21.6	20.4	18.3
9 Danish Minority	-	0.0	0.0	0.0	0.0	0.0	0.0	0.0	-
10 Hanoverian Party	1.0	1.1	1.1	0.9	0.6	0.4	0.1	0.2	0.1
11 Polish Minority	-	0.5	0.3	0.3	0.2	0.2	0.1	0.1	-
18 Bavarian Farmers' League/ Farmers' Party	0.9	0.8	0.6	1.0	1.6	1.0	0.4	0.4	0.3
22 Democratic Party	18.6	8.3	5.7	6.3	4.9	3.8	1.0	0.9	0.8
23 National People's Party	10.3	15.1	19.5	20.5	14.2	7.0	5.9	8.3	8.0
24 People's Party	4.4	13.9	9.2	10.1	8.7	4.5	1.2	1.9	1.1
25 Ind. Social Democrats	7.6	17.9	0.8	0.3	0.1	0.0	-	-	-
26 Bavarian People's Party	-	4.2	3.2	3.7	3.1	3.0	3.2	3.1	2.7
27 German Social Party	-	0.1	1.1	0.5	0.1	-	-	-	-
28 Communist Party	-	2.1	12.6	8.9	10.6	13.1	14.6	16.9	12.3
29 Business Party	-	-	1.8	2.3	4.5	4.0	0.4	0.3	-
30 Land League	-	-	2.0	1.6	0.6	0.6	0.3	0.3	0.2
31 Nazi Party	-	-	6.6	3.0	2.6	18.3	37.3	33.1	43.9
32 Peasants and Farmers' Party	-	-	-	-	1.9	3.2	0.2	0.1	-
33 People's Justice Party	-	-	-	-	1.6	0.8	0.1	0.1	-
34 Christian People's Service	-	-	-	-	-	2.5	1.0	1.1	1.0
35 Conservative People's Party	-	-	-	-	-	0.8	-	-	-
Others	0.4	0.8	1.8	0.9	2.7	0.4	0.2	0.7	0.0

Table 8.5c GERMANY Number of Seats Won in the Reichstag 1919-1933

	1919	1920	1924 (May)	1924 (Dec.)	1928	1930	1932 (July)	1932 (Nov.)	1933
1 Centre Party	91	64	65	69	62	68	75	70	74
2 Social Democrats	163	102	100	131	153	143	133	121	120
9 Danish Minority	–	0	0	0	0	0	0	0	–
10 Hanoverian Party	1	5	5	4	3	3	0	1	0
11 Polish Minority	–	0	0	0	0	0	0	0	–
18 Bavarian Farmers' League/ Farmers' Party	4	4	3	6	8	6	2	3	2
22 Democratic Party	75	39	28	32	25	20	4	2	5
23 National People's Party	44	71	95	103	73	41	37	52	52
24 People's Party	19	65	45	51	45	30	7	11	2
25 Ind. Social Democrats	22	84	0	0	0	0	–	–	–
26 Bavarian People's Party	–	21	16	19	16	19	22	20	18
27 German Social Party	–	0	4	0	0	–	–	–	–
28 Communist Party	–	4	62	45	54	77	89	100	81
29 Business Party	–	–	7	11	23	23	2	1	–
30 Land League	–	–	10	8	3	3	2	2	1
31 Nazi Party	–	–	32	14	12	107	230	196	288
32 Peasants and Farmers' Party	–	–	–	–	10	19	1	0	–
33 People's Justice Party	–	–	–	–	2	0	1	0	–
34 Christian People's Service	–	–	–	–	–	4	3	5	4
35 Conservative People's Party	–	–	–	–	–	4	–	–	–
Others	2	0	0	0	2	0	0	0	0
Total Seats	421	459	472	493	491	577	608	584	647

Source: Vogel et al., 1971: 296-297

Table 8.5d GERMANY Percentage of Seats Won in the Reichstag 1919-1933

	1919	1920	1924 (May)	1924 (Dec.)	1928	1930	1932 (July)	1932 (Nov.)	1933
1 Centre Party	21.6	13.8	13.8	14.0	12.6	11.8	12.3	12.0	11.4
2 Social Democrats	38.7	21.2	21.2	26.6	31.2	24.8	21.9	20.7	18.5
9 Danish Minority	-	0.0	0.0	0.0	0.0	0.0	0.0	0.0	-
10 Hanoverian Party	0.2	1.1	1.1	0.8	0.6	0.5	0.0	0.2	0.0
11 Polish Minority	-	0.0	0.0	0.0	0.0	0.0	0.0	0.0	-
18 Bavarian Farmers' League /Farmers' Party	1.0	0.9	0.6	1.2	1.6	1.0	0.3	0.5	0.3
22 Democratic Party	17.8	8.5	5.9	6.5	5.1	3.5	0.7	0.3	0.8
23 National People's Party	10.5	15.5	20.1	20.9	14.9	7.1	6.1	8.9	8.0
24 People's Party	4.5	14.2	9.5	10.3	9.2	5.2	1.2	1.9	0.3
25 Ind. Social Democrats	5.2	18.3	0.0	0.0	0.0	0.0	-	-	-
26 Bavarian People's Party	-	4.6	3.4	3.9	3.3	3.3	3.6	3.4	2.8
27 German Social Party	-	0.0	0.8	0.0	0.0	-	-	-	-
28 Communist Party	-	0.9	13.1	9.1	11.0	13.3	14.6	17.1	12.5
29 Business Party	-	-	1.5	2.2	4.7	4.0	0.3	0.2	-
30 Land League	-	-	2.1	1.6	0.6	0.5	0.3	0.3	0.2
31 Nazi Party	-	-	6.8	2.8	2.4	18.5	37.8	33.6	44.5
32 Peasants and Farmers' Party	-	-	-	-	2.0	3.3	0.2	0.0	-
33 People's Justice Party	-	-	-	-	0.4	0.0	0.2	0.0	-
34 Christian People's Service	-	-	-	-	-	2.4	0.5	0.9	0.6
35 Conservative People's Party	-	-	-	-	-	0.7	-	-	-
Others	0.4	0.0	0.0	0.0	0.4	0.0	0.0	0.0	0.0

Table 8.6a GERMANY Total Votes 1949-1969

	1949	1953	1957	1961	1965	1969
Electorate	31,207,620	33,202,287	35,400,923	37,440,715	38,510,395	38,677,325
Valid Votes	23,732,398	27,551,272	29,905,428	31,550,901	32,620,442	32,966,024
Invalid Votes	763,216	928,278	1,167,466	1,298,723	795,765	557,040
Total Votes	24,495,614	28,479,550	31,072,894	32,849,624	33,416,207	33,523,064
PARTY VOTES						
1 Centre Party	727,505	217,078	-	-	-	15,933
2 Social Democrats	6,934,975	7,944,943	9,495,571	11,427,355	12,813,186	14,065,716
27 Communist Party	1,361,706	607,860	-	-	-	-
36 Christian Democratic Union[1]	5,978,636	10,016,594	11,875,339	11,283,901	12,387,562	12,079,535
37 Christian Social Union[1]	1,380,448	2,427,387	3,133,060	3,014,471	3,136,506	3,115,652
38 Free Democrats	2,829,920	2,629,163	2,307,135	4,028,766	3,096,739	1,903,422
39 Bavarian Party	986,478	465,641	-	-	-	49,694
40 Economic Reconstruction League	681,888	-	-	-	-	-
41 German Party	939,934	896,128	1,007,282	-	-	-
42 German Reich Party	429,031	295,739	308,564	262,977	-	-
43 South Schleswig Voters' League	75,388	44,585	32,262	25,449	-	-
44 All-German People's Party	-	318,475	-	-	-[2]	-
45 Refugee Party	-	1,616,953	1,374,066	-	-	-
46 Federal Union	-	-	254,322	-	-	-
47 All-German Party[2]	-	-	-	870,756	-	45,401
48 German Peace Union	-	-	-	609,918	434,182[3]	-
49 National Democratic Party	-	-	-	-	664,193	1,422,010
50 Action for Democratic Progress[3]	-	-	-	-	-	197,331
Others	1,406,489	70,726	117,827	27,308	88,074	72,330

1 The Christian Social Union contested elections only in Bavaria as the counterpart of the Christian Democratic Union.
2 All-German Party candidates were included in both SPD and CSU lists in 1965. There was no separate All-German Party list at this election.
3 Includes German Peace Union and candidates of the revived Communist Party (DKP).

Sources: *Wahl zum Deutschen Bundestag am 25. Januar 1987*: 21-28

Table 8.6b GERMANY Percentage of Votes 1949-1969

	1949	1953	1957	1961	1965	1969
Total Votes	78.5	85.8	87.8	87.7	86.8	86.7
Valid Votes	76.0	83.0	84.5	84.3	84.7	85.2
Invalid Votes	2.4	2.8	3.3	3.5	2.1	1.4
Share Invalid	3.1	3.3	3.8	4.0	2.4	1.7
PARTY VOTES						
1 Centre Party	3.1	0.8	-	-	-	0.0
2 Social Democrats	29.2	28.8	31.8	36.2	39.3	42.7
27 Communist Party	5.8	2.2	-	-	-	-
36 Christian Democratic Union	25.2	36.4	39.7	35.8	38.0	36.6
37 Christian Social Union	5.8	8.8	10.5	9.6	9.6	9.5
38 Free Democrats	11.9	9.5	7.7	12.8	9.5	5.8
39 Bavarian Party	4.2	1.7	-	-	-	0.2
40 Economic Reconstruction League	2.9	-	-	-	-	-
41 German Party	4.0	3.3	3.4	-	-	-
42 German Reich Party	1.8	1.1	1.0	0.8	-	-
43 South Schleswig Voters' League	0.3	0.2	0.1	0.1	-	-
44 All-German People's Party	-	1.2	-	-	-	-
45 Refugee Party	-	5.9	4.6	-	-	-
46 Federal Union	-	-	0.9	-	-	-
47 All-German Party	-	-	-	2.8	-	-
48 German Peace Union	-	-	-	1.9	1.3	-
49 National Democratic Party	-	-	-	-	2.0	4.3
50 Action for Democratic Progress	-	-	-	-	-	0.6
Others	5.9	0.3	0.4	0.1	0.3	0.4

Table 8.6c GERMANY Number of Seats Won in the Bundestag 1949-1969[1]

	1949	1953	1957	1961	1965	1969
1 Centre Party	10	3	–	–	–	0
2 Social Democrats	131	151	169	190	202	224
27 Communist Party	15	0	–	–	–	–
36 Christian Democratic Union[2]	115	191	217	192	196	193
37 Christian Social Union[2]	24	52	53	50	49	49
38 Free Democrats	52	48	41	67	49	30
39 Bavarian Party	17	0	–	–	–	0
40 Economic Reconstruction League	12	–	–	–	–	–
41 German Party	17	15	17	0	–	–
42 German Reich Party	5	0	0	0	–	–
43 South Schleswig Voters' League	1	0	0	0	–	–
44 All-German People's Party	–	0	–	–	–	–
45 Refugee Party	–	27	0	–	–	–
46 Federal Union	–	–	0	–	–	–
47 All-German Party[3]	–	–	–	0	0	0
48 German Peace Union	–	–	–	0	0	–
49 National Democratic Party	–	–	–	–	0	0
50 Action for Democratic Progress	–	–	–	–	–	0
Others	3	0	0	0	0	0
Total Seats	402	487	497	499	496	496

1 Excluding the non-voting deputies of West Berlin.
2 The Christian Democratic Union and the Christian Social Union form a single party (*Fraktion*) in the Bundestag.
3 In 1965 four All-German Party deputies were elected, two on Christian Social Union and two on Social Democrat lists.

Source: *Wahl zum Deutschen Bundestag am 25. Juni 1987*: 34-35

Table 8.6d GERMANY Percentage of Seats Won in the Bundestag 1949-1969

	1949	1953	1957	1961	1965	1969
1 Centre Party	2.5	0.6	-	-	-	0.0
2 Social Democrats	32.6	31.0	34.0	38.1	40.7	45.2
27 Communist Party	3.7	0.0	-	-	-	-
36 Christian Democratic Union	28.6	39.2	43.7	38.5	39.5	38.9
37 Christian Social Union	6.0	10.7	10.7	10.0	9.9	9.9
38 Free Democrats	12.9	9.9	8.2	13.4	9.9	6.0
39 Bavarian Party	4.2	0.0	-	-	-	0.0
40 Economic Reconstruction League	3.0	-	-	-	-	-
41 German Party	4.2	3.1	3.4	-	-	-
42 German Reich Party	1.2	0.0	0.0	0.0	-	-
43 South Schleswig Voters' League	0.2	0.0	0.0	0.0	-	-
44 All-German People's Party	-	0.0	-	-	-	-
45 Refugee Party	-	5.5	0.0	-	-	-
46 Federal Union	-	-	0.0	-	-	-
47 All-German Party	-	-	-	0.0	0.0	0.0
48 German Peace Union	-	-	-	0.0	0.0	-
49 National Democratic Party	-	-	-	-	0.0	0.0
50 Action for Democratic Progress	-	-	-	-	-	0.0
Others	0.7	0.0	0.0	0.0	0.0	0.0

Table 8.7a GERMANY Total Votes 1972-1987

	1972	1976	1980	1983	1987
Electorate	41,446,302	42,058,015	43,231,741	44,088,935	45,327,982
Valid Votes	37,459,750	37,822,500	37,938,981	38,940,687	37,867,319
Invalid Votes	301,839	343,253	353,115	33,884	357,975
Total Votes	37,761,589	38,165,753	38,292,096	38,974,571	38,225,294
PARTY VOTES					
2 Social Democrats	17,175,169	16,099,019	16,260,677	14,865,807	14,025,763
27 Communist Party	113,891	118,581	71,600	64,986	-
36 Christian Democratic Union	16,806,020	18,394,801	16,897,659	14,857,680	16,761,572
37 Christian Social Union	3,615,183	4,027,499	3,908,459	4,140,865	3,715,827
38 Free Democrats	3,129,982	2,995,085	4,030,999	2,706,942	3,449,686
49 National Democratic Party	207,465	122,661	68,096	91,095	227,054
51 Greens	-	-	569,589	2,167,431	3,126,256
Others	27,233	92,353	40,361	45,881	285,763

Source: *Wahl zum Deutschen Bundestag am 25. Januar 1987*: 29-33.

Table 8.7b GERMANY Percentage of Votes 1972-1987

	1972	1976	1980	1983	1987
Total Votes	91.1	90.7	88.6	88.4	84.3
Valid Votes	90.4	89.9	87.8	88.3	83.5
Invalid Votes	0.7	0.8	0.8	0.1	0.8
Share Invalid	0.8	0.9	0.9	0.1	0.9
PARTY VOTES					
2 Social Democrats	45.8	42.6	42.9	38.2	37.0
27 Communist Party	0.3	0.3	0.2	0.2	-
36 Christian Democratic Union	35.2	38.0	34.2	38.2	34.5
37 Christian Social Union	9.7	10.6	10.3	10.6	9.8
38 Free Democrats	8.4	7.9	10.6	7.0	9.1
49 National Democratic Party	0.6	0.3	0.2	0.2	0.6
51 Greens	-	-	1.5	5.6	8.3
Others	0.1	0.2	0.1	0.1	0.8

Table 8.7c GERMANY Number of Seats Won in the Bundestag 1972-1987

	1972	1976	1980	1983	1987
2 Social Democrats	230	214	218	193	186
27 Communist Party	0	0	0	0	-
36 Christian Democratic Union	177	190	174	191	174
37 Christian Social Union	48	53	52	53	49
38 Free Democrats	41	39	53	34	46
49 National Democratic Party	0	0	0	0	0
51 Greens	-	-	0	27	42
Others	0	0	0	0	0
Total Seats	496	496	497	498	497

Source: *Wahl zum Deutschen Bundestag am 25. Januar 1987*: 29-33.

Table 8.7d GERMANY Percentage of Seats Won in the Bundestag 1972-1987

	1972	1976	1980	1983	1987
2 Social Democrats	46.4	43.1	43.9	38.8	37.4
27 Communist Party	0.0	0.0	0.0	0.0	-
36 Christian Democratic Union	35.7	38.3	35.0	38.4	35.0
37 Christian Social Union	9.7	10.7	10.5	10.6	9.9
38 Free Democrats	8.3	7.9	10.7	6.8	9.3
49 National Democratic Party	0.0	0.0	0.0	0.0	0.0
51 Greens	-	-	0.0	5.4	8.5
Others	0.0	0.0	0.0	0.0	0.0

Chapter 9

GREECE

Greece was recognised as an independent state in 1830 with powers of government vested in a monarchy. The first king, Prince Otto of Bavaria assumed office in 1833. In 1844 a constitution provided for a two-chamber parliament consisting of a senate, the Gerousia, appointed for life by the king, and a lower house, the Vouli, elected for three years by near universal manhood suffrage with a minimum voting age of 25. Representatives were chosen by an absolute majority by two ballots in multi-member districts. Incumbent governments managed elections by a combination of bribery and coercion (Contiades, 1969: 561-562).

In 1862 King Otto was deposed and replaced in 1863 by Prince William of Denmark who became King George I of Greece. The 1864 constitution provided for a single chamber parliament elected by plurality by universal manhood suffrage. The voting age was reduced to 21 and a new voting procedure introduced. For each candidate standing in his constituency the elector was obliged to vote either Yes or No by placing a lead ballot (sfairidion) in the appropriate part of a ballot box. The lead ballot was employed throughout Greece until 1923, when the paper ballot was introduced in 17 of the 98 electoral districts. In 1926 the use of the paper ballot was extended throughout the country with the exception of three small island constituencies, which followed in 1928. This voting system makes it impossible to establish a national vote total for the period from 1865 to 1923 (Contiades, 1969: 564).

From 1844 until 1933 special arrangements were made for the three small islands of Hydra, Spetse and Psara, which enjoyed a guaranteed parliamentary representation of three, two and two seats respectively, regardless of population, in recognition of their contribution to the war of independence. In these districts election was always by plurality. In the 1923, 1928, 1932 and 1933 elections there were also separate constituencies to represent the Muslim minority in Thrace recognized by the Treaty of Lausanne in 1923, and the Jewish community in Thessaloniki.

In 1922 a military coup was followed by the abdication of the king. In December 1923 a constituent assembly was elected and in April 1924 a plebiscite approved the establishment of a republic. Following the election of 1926 a new constitution was promulgated in 1927 which provided for a popularly elected two-chamber parliament. The Senate was abolished in 1935; since then, Greece has had a single-chamber parliament. In the same year the monarchy was restored. On 4 August 1936 the constitutionally elected prime minister General Metaxas dissolved parliament and established a military dictatorship which lasted until the German invasion of 1941.

The party system of the republic established in 1924 was polarised by the conflict between a political group dominated by the Liberal Party, founded by Eleftherios Venizelos in 1910, and a group founded in 1915 as the Nationalist Party and renamed the People's Party in 1920.

Free elections were re-established in 1946 and, following a plebiscite in September 1946, King George II returned to Greece. The Communist Party had boycotted the election; following the renewal of civil war in December 1946 it was outlawed. A new constitution was voted by parliament in 1952. Women first voted in national elections in 1956. The voting age was reduced to 20 in 1976 and to 18 in 1982.

The post-1946 period saw the fragmentation of the major pre-war parties, the Liberals and the People's Party. Marshal Papagos's Greek Rally, founded in 1951, absorbed much of the support of the People's Party. In January 1956, following the death of Papagos, the Rally was dissolved and replaced by the National Radical Union, headed by Papagos's successor as prime minister, Konstantinos Karamanlis. Disparate liberal groupings were finally reunited as the Centre Union under Giorgios Papandreou in 1961. The illegal Communist Party operated electorally under the label of the United Democratic Left.

Free elections were suspended following a military coup on 21 April 1967. Civilian rule was restored in 1974 and free elections were held in November 1974 under the 1952 constitution. The following month a plebiscite approved the abolition of the monarchy and a new republican constitution was introduced in 1975.

The main parties contesting elections since 1974 have been New Democracy, essentially the successor to the National Radical Union and led until his election to the presidency in 1980 by Karamanlis; the Communist Party, which was legalised in 1974, and the Pan-Hellenic Socialist Movement a new left-wing party founded by Andreas Papandreou, son of Giorgios Papandreou, the Centre Union prime minister from 1963 to 1965. The Centre Union's support declined rapidly after the 1974 election and its leading figures formed or joined other parties.

The 20 general elections since 1926 have been held under 12 electoral systems. The 1926 election was the first to use proportional representation. In 1928 there was a reversal to a plurality system. Proportional representation was again employed in 1932 and a plurality system in 1933 and 1935. The same proportional representation system was used in 1936, 1946 and 1950. The 1951 election saw the introduction of a system of "reinforced" proportional representation which, with some variants, was employed at most subsequent general elections until 1989, except for 1952 and 1956 where a plurality and mixed plurality/proportional representation systems were used. In all proportional representation elections since 1926 (except 1985) candidates from the party lists have been elected according to the preferential votes of the electors.

Both the choice of proportional or plurality systems and variations within these two options resulted from decisions of Greek governments based upon both immediate partisan advantage and broader political objectives. In the 1920s and

1930s plurality electoral systems were further manipulated by both Venizelist and anti-Venizelist governments principally by varying the sizes of multi-member electoral districts to their advantage (see Mavrogordatos, 1983: 351-353).

In proportional representation elections (except in 1951, 1958, 1961 and 1989) seats have always been allocated in three stages, with an initial seat allocation using the Hagenbach-Bischoff quota; in 1951, 1958 and 1974 a Hare quota was employed. Seats unallocated at the first round were distributed at first regional and then national levels. The system of "reinforced" proportional representation was introduced in order to ensure that the largest party won a parliamentary majority even if it lacked a majority of votes, to discourage the proliferation of parties and to reduce the parliamentary representation of the communist left. This modification of proportional representation limited participation in the second and third rounds of the seat allocation process to parties meeting a varying but high vote threshold. In the calculation for second-round distribution of seats, the total votes won by a party are used rather than remainders. As smaller parties were unlikely to be allocated many seats at the first stage, using total votes benefitted the larger parties (Table 9.a).

Table 9.a PERCENTAGE THRESHOLDS FOR INCLUSION IN SECOND AND THIRD ROUND SEAT ALLOCATIONS 1951-81

	1951	1958	1961-1964	1974-1981
Single parties	17	25	15	17
Two-party alliances	20	35	25	25
Three or more party alliances	20	40	30	30

The 1985 electoral law purported to be an abandonment of the principle of "reinforced" proportional representation, principally because the threshold barriers for inclusion in post-first round seat allocations were abandoned. In fact the system remained highly disproportional, principally because one of the consequences of abandoning the threshold was that fewer seats were allocated at the second round and more at the third. The complex rules for third round distribution greatly advantaged the largest party especially because any seats unallocated in constituencies were given to the party with a plurality vote in that constituency, provided that party also had a plurality nationally.

The electoral system employed in 1989 retained the Hagenbach-Bischoff quota for the first round allocation and did not reintroduce a threshold for inclusion in the second round. The third round allocation was abandoned. The use of remainders rather than total votes in the second round allocation and the guarantee that parties winning one or two percent of the total national vote would receive one or three seats respectively in the second round allocation resulted in a more proportional distribution of seats.

The electoral laws of the post-1975 republic have made major modifications of previous systems. In addition to 288 deputies elected from constituency lists, 12 Deputies of State are chosen by proportional representation from national party lists. Until 1985 only parties that met the threshold rule for inclusion in second-round seat allocation could compete for Deputies of State. The system was introduced to allow for the election of prominent personalities not dependent upon the often clientelistic electoral politics of local constituencies.

Sources:

R. Clogg, "Greece", in V. Bogdanor and D. Butler (eds.) *Democracy and Elections: Electoral Systems and their Political Consequences* (Cambridge: Cambridge University Press, 1983)

R. Clogg, *Parties and Elections in Greece: the Search for Legitimacy* (London: Hurst, 1988)

I. Contiades: 'Griechenland', in D. Sternberger and B. Vogel (eds.) *Die Wahl der Parlamente und anderer Staatsorgane. Ein Handbuch* Volume 1 (Berlin: de Gruyter, 1969): 555-603

P. Dimitras and T. Kalogeropoulou "Greek Election Results 1926-1989" *Greek Opinion,* 6 June 1989 : 2-24.

General Statistical Office: Statistike ton bouletikon eklogon tes 7es' Noembriou 1926/ Statistique des élections des députés du 7 novembre 1926 (Athens: Ministry of the Economy 1928 and subsequent volumes in the same series. In 1951 published by the Ministry of Commerce and subsequently by the Ministry of the Interior)

Greek Opinion, Special Issue on electoral laws Athens, April 1989.

D. Kitsikis, 'Grèce', in S. Rokkan and J. Meyriat (eds.), *International Guide to Electoral Statistics* (The Hague and Paris: Mouton, 1969)

K. Legg, *Politics in Modern Greece* (Stanford: Stanford University Press, 1969)

G.Th. Mavrogordatos: *Stillborn Republic: Social Coalitions and Party Strategies in Greece, 1922-1936* (Berkeley: University of California Press, 1983)

G.Th. Mavrogordatos: 'The 1946 Election and Plebiscite: Prelude to Civil War' in J.O. Iatrides (ed.), *Greece in the 1940's: a Nation in Crisis* (Hanover, New Hampshire: University Press of New England, 1987)

J. Meynaud: *Les forces politiques en Grèce* (Lausanne: Études de Science Politique, 1965)

A. Pantelis and M. Triantafyllou, *Ta Ellenika Eklogika Systemata kai oi Ekloges (1926-1985) Ston Electroniko Ypologiste* (Athens: New Synora, 1988)

P. Vegleris, "Greek electoral law" in H.R. Penniman (ed.), *Greece at the Polls: the National Elections of 1974 and 1977* (Washington, D.C. : American Enterprise Institute, 1981)

Table 9.1 POLITICAL PARTIES IN GREECE SINCE 1926 [1]

	Party Names	Elections Contested Years	Number
1	Liberal Party I (Komma Fileleftheron) [2]	1926-1958	11
2	People's Party (Laikon Komma) [3]	1926-1958	12
3	Agrarian Party I (Agrotikon Komma) [4]	1926-1936	5
4	Communist Party of Greece (Kommounistikon Komma Elladas - KKE) [5]	1926-1936; 1974ff	9
5	Farmer-Labour Party (Agrotikon-Ergatikon Komma) [6]	1926-1936	5
6	Free Opinion Party (Komma Ton Eleftherofronon) [7]	1926-1936	6
7	Conservative Republican Party (Syntiritiko Dimokratikon Komma) [8]	1926-1933	4
8	National Republican Party (Ethnikon Dimokratikon Komma); from 1932 the National Radical Party (Ethnikon Rizospastikon Komma) [9]	1928-1936	4
9	Progressive Party (Proodeftikon Komma) [10]	1928-1936	5
10	Progressive Union (Proodeftiki Enosis) [11]	1928	1
11	Agrarian Republican Party (Agrotikon Dimokratikon Komma) [12]	1933-1936	2
12	Agrarian Party II (Agrotikon Komma) [13]	1933	1
13	National Unity Party (Ethnikon Enotikon Komma); in 1950 National Regeneration Front (Metopon Ethnikis Anadimiourgias) [14]	1936-1950	3
14	National People's Party (Ethnikon Laikon Komma) [15]	1936	1
15	Reformist Party (Metarrythmistikon Komma) [16]	1936-1946	2
16	Democratic Socialist Party (Dimokratikon Socialistikon Komma); in 1950 and 1951 George Papandreou Party (Komma Georgiou Papandreou) [17]	1936-1951	4
17	Venizelist Liberal Party (Komma Venizelikon Fileleftheron) [18]	1946	1
18	National Liberal Party (Ethnikon Fileleftheron Komma) [19]	1946	1
19	National Party of Greece (Ethnikon Komma Ellados) [20]	1946-1950	2
20	Nationalist Party (Komma Ethnikofronon) [21]	1946-1950; 1958	3
21	National Front of the Working People (Ethniki Parataksis Ergazomenou Laou) [22]	1950	1
22	National Progressive Centre Union (Ethniki Proodeftiki Enosis Kentrou - EPEK) [23]	1950-1958	5
23	New Party (Neon Komma) [24]	1950	1

24	Farmers' and Workers' Rally (Synagermos Agroton kai Ergazomenon); from 1956 the Farmers' and Workers' Party (Agrotikon kai Ergatikon Komma) [25]	1950-1958	4
25	United Democratic Left (Eniaia Demokratiki Aristera - EDA); in 1950 Democratic Front (Dimokratiki Parataksis); in 1961 Pan-Agrarian Democratic Front of Greece (Pandimokratikon Agrotikon Metopon Ellados -PAME) [26]	1950ff	13
26	Greek Rally (Ellenikos Synagermos) [27]	1951-1952	2
27	Democratic Party of the Working People (Dimokratikon Komma Ergazomenou Laou) [28]	1956-1958	2
28	Liberal Democratic Union (Fileleftheri Dimokratiki Enosis) [29]	1956	1
29	National Radical Union (Ethniki Rizospastiki Enosis - ERE) [30]	1956-1964	5
30	Popular Social Party (Laikon Koinonikon Komma) [31]	1956-1958	2
31	Party of the Progressives (Komma Proodeftikon)[32]	1956-1964; 1981	6
32	Centre Union (Enosis Kentrou); from 1977 Union of the Democratic Centre (Enosis Dimokratikou Kentrou - EDIK) [33]	1961ff	8
33	Christian Democracy (Christianiki Dimokratia) [34]	1974ff	5
34	National Democratic Union (Ethniki Dimokratiki Enosis) [35]	1974	1
35	Communist Party of Greece - Interior (Kommounistikon Komma Ellados Esoterikou - KKE es.) [36]	1974ff	4
36	New Democracy (Nea Dimokratia) [37]	1974ff	5
37	Pan-Hellenic Socialist Movement (Panhellinio Socialistiko Kinema - PASOK) [38]	1974ff	5
38	National Alignment (Ethniki Parataxis) [39]	1977	1
39	New Liberal Party (Komma Neofileleftheron) [40]	1977	1
40	Liberal Party II (Komma Fileleftheron) [41]	1981ff	3
41	Party for Democratic Socialism (Kommaton Dimokratikou Socialismou - KODISO) [42]	1981ff	3
42	National Political Union (Ethniki Politiki Enosis - EPEN) [43]	1985ff	2
43	Independent Muslim Lists [44]	1985ff	2
44	Democratic Renewal (Dimokratiki Ananeosi - DIANA) [45]	1989	1
45	Greek Left (Elleniki Aristera - EAR) [46]	1989	1
46	Ecological Movement-Political Renaissance (Ikologiko Kinima Politikis Anagennisis - OIKIPA)	1989	1

[1] The party genealogies presented in this table are largely derived from Legg (1969), Mavrogordatos (1983) and Clogg (1988).

2 Founded by Eleftherios Venizelos in 1910. One of the two major parties in pre-World War II Greece. The party suffered numerous divisions both before and after the war. The Liberals were incorporated into the Centre Union in 1961.

3 Major anti-Venizelist party in the pre-World War II period. Former People's Party leaders formed the core of the Greek Rally and then the National Radical Union in the 1950s; the rump of the party continued to contest elections independently until 1958.

4 The Agrarian Party split before the 1933 election. One faction (Party 12, Agrarian Party II) formed part of the anti-Venizelist alliance in that election. A second faction led by Alexandros Mylonas joined a pro-Venizelos coalition; it later became the Agrarian Republican Party. A third faction led by Ioannes Sofianopoulos joined neither alliance.

5 The Communist Party was banned in 1936. After taking part in the resistance to the German occupation as the principal element in the National Liberation Front (Ethnikon Apeleftherotikon Metopon - EAM) and the People's Liberation Army (Ethnikos Laikos Apeleftherofikos Stratos - ELAS) it was defeated in the 1944-1947 civil war. The party was legalised in 1974.

6 Left-wing breakaway from the Liberal Party led by Alexandros Papanastasiou.

7 Right-wing party founded by General Ioannes Metaxas in the 1920s, who became dictator in 1936.

8 Right-wing breakaway from the Liberal Party led by Andreas Michalakopoulos.

9 Breakaway from the Liberal Party led by General Giorgios Kondyles.

10 Breakaway from the Liberal Party led by Giorgios Kafandares.

11 Liberal Party splinter led by Konstantinos Zavitzianos.

12 Part of the Agrarian Party led by Alexandros Mylonas which allied with the Liberal Party in the 1933 election. Renamed the Agrarian Republican Party, it formed part of the Republican Coalition electoral alliance in 1936.

13 Splinter from the Agrarian Party, which formed part of an anti-Liberal alliance with the People's, Free Opinion and National Radical parties in 1933.

14 Republican but anti-Venizelist party founded by Panayiotis Kanellopoulos in 1935. Kanellopoulos later became a leading figure in the Greek Rally and leader of the National Radical Union after Karamanlis's resignation in 1963.

15 Right-wing breakaway from the People's Party led by Ioannes Theotokis.

16 Splinter from the People's Party.

17 Breakaway from the Liberal Party founded by Giorgios Papandreou in 1935. Papandreou was elected to parliament on a Greek Rally list in 1952. He later joined and became leader of the Liberal Party before founding the Centre Union in 1961.

18 Breakaway from the Liberal Party led by Sofoklis Venizelos. Reunited with the Liberal Party in 1947.

19 Breakaway from the Liberal Party led by Stulianos Gonatas. By 1950 most of its members had returned to the Liberal Party.

20 Founded by General Napoleon Zervas and built upon his wartime resistance group the National Democratic Greek Army. Dissolved after the 1950 election with its members joining largely centrist parties.

21 Lead by Theodoros Tourkovasilis. In 1946 part of the Union of the Nationally Minded (Enosis Ethnikifronon) with the Agrarian People's Party (Laikon Agrotikon Komma). In 1950 part of the Independent Political Front (Politiki Anexartitos Parataxis) with the Greek Renaissance Party (Komma Elleniki Anagenniseos). In 1958 allied with the People's Party. Part of Centre Union from 1961.

22 Coalition of right-wing personalist parties, some of whose leaders were former associates of the dictator General Metaxas.

23 In 1950 an alliance of the Progressive Liberal Centre Party (Komma Proodeftikon Fileftheron Kentrou) led by the Venizelist General Nikolaos Plastiras and the Democratic Centre Party (Dimokratikon Proodeftikon Komma) led by Emmanouil Tsouderos. Tsouderos and his followers joined the Greek Rally before the 1951 election. Plastiras's party fought subsequent elections as EPEK the name of the 1950 alliance.

24 Founded by Spyros Markezinis who later joined the Greek Rally (see also party number 32).

25 Agrarian party led by Alexandros Baltatzis. Contested the 1950 election in alliance with the National Agrarian Progressive Party led by Alexandros Mylonas. Incorporated into the Centre Union in 1961.

26 Generally regarded as a front for the illegal Communist Party, the EDA continued as a separate party after the legalisation of the Communist Party in 1974. In 1977 part of the Alliance of Progressive and Left-Wing Forces. In 1981 and 1985 Manolis Glezos, the EDA's leader, was a candidate on the Pasok list. In 1989 part of the Coalition of the Left and Progress List.

27 Founded by Marshal Papagos in 1951. Included many leading personalities from the People's Party, the National Unity Party (Kanellopoulos), the New Party (Markezinis) and the Democratic Centre Party (Tsouderos). Giorgios Papandreou joined the party before the 1952 election. Papagos died in October 1955 and the Rally was dissolved early the following year. Most of its members joined the National Radical Union formed by Papagos's successor as Prime Minister Konstantinos Karamanlis.

28 Left-of-centre party founded in 1953 by a breakaway group from the National Progressive Centre Union led by Giorgios Kartalis and Alexander Svolos whose Socialist Party had previously formed party of the United Democratic Left.

29 Founded by Sofoklis Venizelos after his resignation from the leadership of the Liberal Party. Reunited with the Liberal Party after the 1956 election.

30 Founded by Prime Minister Konstantinos Karamanlis, mainly from former members of the Greek Rally.

31 Founded by a former leading figure in the Greek Rally, Stefanos Stefanopoulos.

32 Founded by Spyros Markezinis whose New Party had been absorbed in the Greek Rally, Markezinis was Prime Minister in 1972-3 during the military dictatorship. He revived his party in 1979.

33 Founded in 1961 by Giorgios Papandreou the Union incorporated the parties of the Venizelist liberal tradition, but also some more conservative parties. Its main components were three factions of the Liberal Party (which had split in 1958), and the National Progressive Centre Union, the Farmers and Workers' Party, the Democratic Union (Dimokratiki Enosis) a breakaway from the United Democratic Left and two conservative parties the Popular Social Party (Stefanopoulos) and the Nationalist Party (Tourkovasilis). After the collapse of the dictatorship the Centre Union was revived as the Centre Union-New Forces to signify its coalition with a number of groups and individuals who had opposed the dictatorship. These groups included New Forces led by Ioannes Pesmazoglou and Christian Democracy led by Nikalaos Psouradakis. The party was renamed Union of the Democratic Centre in 1976. Over the next two years most of the party's deputies left to join other parties or form their own. The rump of the party contested the 1981 and 1989 elections. In 1985 the party's leader was elected on a PASOK ticket.

34 Contested the 1974 election as part of an alliance with New Forces and the 1977 election in alliance with Progressive and Left-Wing Forces. The party ran independently in 1981 and 1989; in 1985 its leader, Nikolaos Psaroudakis, was a successful candidate on a Pasok ticket.

35 Party of the far right led by Petros Garoufalias.

36 Breakaway from the pro-Moscow Communist Party, founded in 1968. In 1987 a majority of the party formed the Greek Left (EAR). A minority group refused to join the EAR and formed the Communist Party of the Interior - Left Renewal (KKE es. AA).

37 Successor party to the National Radical Union founded by that party's former leader Konstantinos Karamanlis and headed by him until his election to the presidency in 1980.

38 Founded by Andreas Papandreou the son of Giorgios Papandreou and a Centre Union minister in the 1960s. The party combined Papandreou's Panhellenic Liberation Movement and other groups opposed to the 1967-1974 military dictatorship.

39 Party of the far right. Its leaders were Stefanos Stefanopoulos a former leader of the conservative wing of the Centre Union and prime minister from 1965 to 1966 who had earlier been a Greek Rally leader, and Spyros Theotokis, a former National Radical Union leader and foreign minister in the 1950s. Theotokis won a seat in the 1981 election on the New Democracy national list.

40 Founded by Konstantinos Mitsotakis a former Centre Union leader. The party contested only constituencies in Crete. After the 1977 election Mitsotakis joined New Democracy and was elected party leader in 1984.

41 Founded in 1981 by Nikitas Venizelos, grandson of Eleftherios Venizelos, founder of the Liberal Party in 1910, who had been elected on on EDIK list in 1977.

42 Founded by John Pesmazoglou, a founding member of New Forces and former leader of EDIK, who was expelled from the party in 1978. Pesmazoglou and the party's secretary general ran on New Democracy lists in the 1985 election and elected as part of the Coalition of the left and Progress in 1989.

43 Party of the extreme right supporting the imprisoned leaders of the 1967-74 military dictatorship.

44 Lists representing the Turkish-speaking Muslim minority in two districts in Thrace.

45 Breakaway from New Democracy formed by Kostis Stefanopoulos, a former contender for the party leadership.

46 Founded in April 1987 and comprising the majority of the Communist Party of Greece-Interior, whose Secretary General Leonidas Kyrkos, became the new party's leader. It contested the 1989 elections as part of the Coalition of the Left and Progress.

Table 9.2 DATES OF ELECTIONS : VOULI

1	7 November 1926	11	19 February 1956
2	19 August 1928	12	11 May 1958
3	25 September 1932	13	29 October 1961
4	5 March 1933	14	3 November 1963
5	9 June 1935	15	16 February 1964
6	26 January 1936	16	17 November 1974
7	31 March 1946	17	20 November 1977
8	5 March 1950	18	18 October 1981
9	9 September 1951	19	2 June 1985
10	16 November 1952	20	18 June 1989

Table 9.3a GREECE Total Votes 1926-1936[1]

	1926	1928	1932	1933	1936
Electorate	1,572,469	n.a	n.a	n.a	n.a
Valid Votes	961,226	1,017,281	1,171,637	1,141,331	1,274,892
Invalid Votes	3,912	4,153	4,346	5,612	4,083
Total Votes	965,138	1,021,434	1,175,983	1,146,943	1,278,085
PARTY VOTES					
1 Liberal Party I	304,727	477,502	391,521	379,968	474,651
2 People's Party	211,972[2]	243,543	395,974	434,550	281,597
3 Agrarian Party I	28,318	17,042	72,311	22,985	13,006
4 Communist Party	41,982	14,325	58,223	51,656	73,411
5 Farmer Labour Party	62,260	68,278	69,057	47,460	
9 Progressive Party	–	25,729	97,836	77,254	} 66,026[6]
11 Agrarian Republican Party	–	–	–	14,302	
16 Democratic Socialist Party	–	–	–	–	
6 Free Opinion Party	151,660	53,958	18,591	25,758	} 50,137
7 Conservative Republican Party	–	15,852	11,494	9,672	–
8 National Republican /Radical Party	–	27,603	47,698	46,692	} 253,384[7]
14 National People's Party	–	–	–	–	
10 Progressive Union	–	13,452	–	–	–
12 Agrarian Party II	–	–	–	20,200	–
13 National Unity Party	–	–	–	–	9,870
15 Reformist Party	–	–	–	–	17,822
Others	160,307[3]	59,997[4]	8,932[5]	10,834	34,098[8]

[1] The election of 9 June 1935 was subject to widespread irregularities and government pressure and was boycotted by the Venizelist parties. It is therefore not reported here. (Mavrogordatos, 1983: 49).
[2] Includes 17,493 votes cast for joint People's Party - Free Opinion Party lists in Lesbos and Euboea.
[3] Including 83,033 votes cast for pro-Venizelist local lists and independents, and 39,600 votes cast for anti-Venizelist local lists and candidates.
[4] Including 18,069 votes cast for pro-Venizelist candidates and 38,556 for anti-Venizelist independents.
[5] Including 1,221 votes for an anti-Venizelist independent list and 305 votes for a pre-Venizelist list.
[6] Republican Coalition electoral alliance of the Progressive Party, the Farmer Labour Party, the Agrarian Republican Party and the Democratic Socialist Party.
[7] General People's Radical Union, an alliance of the National Radical and National People's parties and dissidents from the People's and Free Opinion parties.
[8] Including 22,021 votes cast for a number of local pro-Venizelist lists and 3,357 votes cast for a local anti-Venizelist list.

Sources: adapted from Mavrogordatos, 1983: 31-52 and Dimitras and Kalogeropoulou, 1989: 2-7.

Table 9.3b GREECE Percentage of Votes 1926-1936

	1926	1928	1932	1933	1936
Total Votes	61.4	n.a	n.a	n.a	n.a
Valid Votes	61.1	n.a	n.a	n.a	n.a
Invalid Votes	0.2	n.a	n.a	n.a	n.a
Share Invalid	0.4	0.4	0.4	0.5	0.3
PARTY VOTES					
1 Liberal Party I	31.7	46.9	33.4	33.3	37.3
2 People's Party	22.1	23.9	33.8	38.1	22.1
3 Agrarian Party I	2.9	1.7	6.2	2.0	1.0
4 Communist Party	4.4	1.4	5.0	4.5	5.8
5 Farmer Labour Party	6.5	6.7	5.9	4.2	
9 Progressive Party	–	2.5	8.4	6.8	} 5.2
11 Agrarian Republican Party	–	–	–	1.3	
16 Democratic Socialist Party	–	–	–	–	
6 Free Opinion Party	15.8	5.3	1.6	2.3	3.9
7 Conservative Republican Party	–	1.6	1.0	0.8	–
8 National Republican /Radical Party	–	2.7	4.1	4.1	} 19.9
14 National People's Party	–	–	–	–	
10 Progressive Union	–	1.3	–	1.8	–
12 Agrarian Party II	–	–	–	–	–
13 National Unity Party	–	–	–	–	0.8
15 Reformist Party	–	–	–	–	1.4
Others	16.7	5.9	0.8	0.9	2.6

Table 9.3c GREECE Number of Seats Won in the Vouli 1926-1936[1]

	1926	1928	1932	1933	1936
1 Liberal Party I	108	178	98	80	126
2 People's Party	63	19	95	118	72
3 Agrarian Party I	4	0	11	2	1
4 Communist Party	10	0	10	0	15
5 Farmer Labour Party	17	20	8	13	
9 Progressive Party	–	3	15	10	} 11[4]
11 Agrarian Republican Party	–	–	–	5	
16 Democratic Socialist Party	–	–	–	–	
6 Free Opinion Party	54	1	3	6	7
7 Conservative Republican Party	–	5	2	2	–
8 National Republican /Radical Party	–	9	6	11	} 60[5]
14 National People's Party	–	–	–	–	
10 Progressive Union	–	5	–	–	–
12 Agrarian Party II	–	–	–	1	–
13 National Unity Party	–	–	–	–	0
15 Reformist Party	–	–	–	–	4
Others	30[2]	10[3]	0	0	4[6]
Total Seats	286	250	248	248	300

[1] The anti-Venizelist forces won all 300 seats in the fraudulent June 1935 election. The People's Party won 249 seats and the National Radical Party 32.
[2] Including 18 pro-Venizelos and 10 anti-Venizelos independents.
[3] Comprises six pro and four anti-Venizelos independents.
[4] Republican Coalition.
[5] General People's Radical Union.
[6] Pro-Venizelos independents.

Source: Mavrogordatos, 1983: 31-52.

Table 9.3d GREECE Percentage of Seats Won in the Vouli 1926-1936

	1926	1928	1932	1933	1936
1 Liberal Party I	37.8	71.2	39.5	32.3	42.0
2 People's Party	22.0	7.6	38.5	47.6	24.0
3 Agrarian Party I	1.4	0.0	4.4	0.8	0.3
4 Communist Party	3.5	0.0	4.0	0.0	5.0
5 Farmer Labour Party	5.9	8.0	3.2	5.2	
9 Progressive Party	–	1.2	6.0	4.0	} 3.7
11 Agrarian Republican Party	–	–	–	2.0	
16 Democratic Socialist Party	–	–	–	–	
6 Free Opinion Party	18.9	0.4	1.2	2.4	2.3
7 Conservative Republican Party	–	2.0	0.8	0.8	–
8 National Republican /Radical Party	–	3.6	2.4	4.4	} 20.0
14 National People's Party	–	–	–	–	
10 Progressive Union	–	2.0	–	–	–
12 Agrarian Party II	–	–	–	0.4	–
13 National Unity Party	–	–	–	–	0.0
15 Reformist Party	–	–	–	–	1.3
Others	10.5	4.0	–	0.0	1.3

Table 9.4a GREECE Total Votes 1946-1958

	1946	1950	1951	1952	1956	1958
Electorate	n.a	n.a	2,224,246	2,123,150	4,507,907	5,119,148
Valid Votes	1,108,473	1,688,923	1,708,904	1,591,807	3,364,361	3,847,785
Invalid Votes	13,223	7,223	8,108	8,365	15,084	16,197
Total Votes	1,121,696	1,696,146	1,717,012	1,600,172	3,379,445	3,863,982

PARTY VOTES

	1946	1950	1951	1952	1956	1958
25 United Dem. Left	–	163,824	180,640	152,011		939,902
1 Liberal Party I	159,525	291,083	325,390			795,445
22 National Prog. Centre Union	–	277,739	401,379 }	544,834	} 1,620,007[4]	
24 Farmers and Workers	–	44,308	21,009	10,431	}	408,787[5]
27 Democratic Party	–	–	–	–		
28 Liberal Dem.	–	–	–	–		–
31 Progressives[1]	–	–	–	–	74,545	
2 People's Party		317,512	113,876	16,767		
15 Reformist Party }	610,995[2]	–	–	–	–	–
18 National Liberal		–	–	–	–	–
13 National Unity		88,979				
16 Dem. Socialist /Papandreou }	213,721[3]	180,185	35,810	–	–	–
17 Venizelist Liberals		–	–	–	–	–
19 National Party	66,027	61,575	–	–		–
20 Nationalist	32,538	137,618	–	–	–	
30 Popular Social	–	–	–	–	29,375 }	113,358[6]
21 National Front	–	26,925	–	–	–	–
23 New Party	–	42,157	–	–	–	–
26 Greek Rally	–	–	624,316	783,541	–	–
29 National Radical Union	–	–	–	–	1,594,112	1,583,885
Others	25,667	57,018	6,484	84,223	46,322	6,408

1 In 1958 formed part of the Progressive Agrarian Democratic Union.

2 United Alignment of the Nationally Minded (Inomeni Paataksis Ethnikofronon) combining the People's, National Liberal and Reformist parties with several minor parties and independents.

3 National Political Union (Ethniki Politiki Enosis) combining the Venezelist Liberals and the Democratic Socialist and National Unity parties.

4 Democratic Union (Dimokratiki Enosis) an alliance of all the parties opposed to the National Radical Union except the Progressives.

5 Progressive Agrarian Democratic Union (Proodeftiki Agrotiki Dimokratiki Enosis) combining the Farmer and Workers' Party, the National Progressive Centre Union, the Democratic Party of the Working People the Progressives and the independents.

6 Union of the People's Parties (Enosis Laikon Kommaton) combining the People's, Popular Social and Nationalist parties.

Sources: Official reports of the Ministry of the Interior and Dimitras and Kalogeropoulou (1989): 8-13.

Table 9.4b GREECE Percentage of Votes 1946-1958

	1946	1950	1951	1952	1956	1958
Total Votes	n.a	n.a	77.2	75.4	75.0	75.5
Valid Votes	n.a	n.a	76.8	75.0	74.6	75.2
Invalid Votes	n.a	n.a	0.4	0.4	0.3	0.3
Share Invalid	1.2	0.4	0.5	0.5	0.4	0.4
PARTY VOTES						
25 United Dem. Left	-	9.7	10.6	9.5		24.4
1 Liberal Party I	14.4	17.2	19.0	34.2		20.7
22 National Prog. Centre Union	-	16.4	23.5	- }	48.2	
24 Farmers and Workers	-	2.6	1.2	0.7	}	10.6
27 Democratic Party	-	-	-	-		
28 Liberal Dem.	-	-	-	-		
31 Progressives	-	-	-	-	2.2	
2 People's Party		18.8	6.7	1.1		
15 Reformist Party }	55.1	-	-	-	-	-
18 National Liberal		-	-	-	-	-
13 National Unity		5.3	-	-	-	-
16 Dem. Socialist /Papandreou }	19.3	10.7	2.1	-	-	-
17 Venizelist Liberals		-	-	-	-	-
19 National Party	6.0	3.6	-	-	-	-
20 Nationalist	2.9	8.1	-	-	-	
30 Popular Social	-	-	-	-	0.9}	2.9
21 National Front	-	1.6	-	-	-	-
23 New Party	-	2.5	-	-	-	-
26 Greek Rally	-	-	36.5	49.2	-	-
29 National Radical Union	-	-	-	-	47.4	41.2
Others	2.3	3.4	0.4	5.3	1.4	0.2

Table 9.4c GREECE Number of Seats Won in the Vouli 1946-1958

	1946	1950	1951	1952	1956	1958
25 United Dem. Left	–	18	10	0	18 [5]	79
1 Liberal Party I	48	56	57	24	25 [5]	36
22 National Prog. Centre Union	–	45	74	27	15 [5]	1 [7]
24 Farmers and Workers	–	3	1	0	7 [5]	6 [7]
27 Democratic Party	–	–	–	–	18 [5]	1 [7]
28 Liberal Dem.	–	–	–	–	39 [5]	–
31 Progressives	–	–	–	–	0	2 [7]
2 People's Party	156 [1]	62	2	0	3	2 [8]
15 Reformist Party	5 [1]	–	–	–	–	–
18 National Liberal	34 [1]	–	–	–	–	–
13 National Unity	8 [2]	7	–	–	–	–
16 Rep. Socialist /Papandreou	27 [2]	35	0	–	–	–
17 Venizelist Liberals	30 [2]	–	–	–	–	–
19 National Party	20	7	–	–	–	–
20 Nationalist	9	16 [4]	–	–	–	0
30 Popular Social	–	–	–	–	0	2 [8]
21 National Front	–	0	–	–	–	–
23 New Party	–	1	–	–	–	–
26 Greek Rally	–	–	114	247	–	–
29 National Radical Union	–	–	–	–	165	171
Others	17 [3]	0	0	2	10 [6]	0
Total Seats	354	250	258	300	300	300

1 Elected on the United Alignment of the Nationally Minded alliance lists.
2 Elected on the National Political Union alliance lists.
3 Includes seven deputies elected as part of the United Alignment of the Nationally Minded alliance, three deputies elected as part of the National Political Union alliance and three independents.
4 Nationalist Party four, Greek Renaissance Party five and seven others.
5 Elected on the Democratic Union lists.
6 Includes seven deputies elected as part of the Democratic Union electoral alliance.
7 Elected on the Progressive Agrarian Democratic Union lists.
8 Elected on the Union of the People's Parties lists.

Sources: Official reports of the Ministry of the Interior and Dimitras and Kalogeropoulou, 1989: 8-13.

Table 9.4d GREECE Percentage of Seats Won in the Vouli 1946-1958

	1946	1950	1951	1952	1956	1958
25 United Dem. Left	–	7.2	3.9	0.0	6.0	26.3
1 Liberal Party I	13.6	22.4	22.1	8.0	8.3	12.0
22 National Prog. Centre Union	–	18.0	28.7	9.0	5.0	0.3
24 Farmers and Workers	–	1.2	0.4	0.0	2.3	2.0
27 Democratic Party	–	–	–	–	6.0	0.3
28 Liberal Dem.	–	–	–	–	13.0	–
31 Progressives	–	–	–	–	0.0	0.7
2 People's Party	44.1	24.8	0.8	0.0	1.0	0.7
15 Reformist Party	1.4	–	–	–	–	–
18 National Liberal	9.6	–	–	–	–	–
13 National Unity	2.3	2.8	–	–	–	–
16 Dem. Socialist /Papandreou	7.6	14.0	0.0	–	–	–
17 Venizelist Liberals	8.5	–	–	–	–	–
19 National Party	5.6	2.8	–	–	–	–
20 Nationalist	2.5	6.4	–	–	–	0.0
30 Popular Social	–	–	–	–	0.0	0.7
21 National Front	–	0.0	–	–	–	–
23 New Party	–	0.4	–	–	–	–
26 Greek Rally	–	–	44.2	82.3	–	–
29 National Radical Union	–	–	–	–	55.0	57.0
Others	4.8	0.0	0.0	0.7	3.3	0.0

Table 9.5a GREECE Total Votes 1961-1989

	1961	1963	1964	1974	1977	1981	1985	1989 (June)
Electorate	5,668,298	5,662,965	5,662,965	6,241,066	6,403,738	7,059,778	7,661,588	7,892,904
Valid Votes	4,620,751	4,667,154	4,598,839	4,911,974	5,129,771	5,671,057	6,365,095	6,521,211
Invalid Votes	19,761	35,632	27,451	54,584	64,120	82,421	57,372	143,017
Total Votes	4,640,512	4,702,791	4,626,290	4,966,558	5,193,891	5,753,478	6,421,466	6,669,228
PARTY VOTES								
41 Party for Democratic Socialism[1]	-	-	-	-	-	40,126		
45 Greek Left	-	-	-	-	-	-	-	
4 Communist Party	-	-	-		480,272	620,302	629,525	} 855,944[8]
25 United Democratic Left[2]	675,867	669,267	542,865	} 464,787[6]				
35 Communist Party (Interior)	-	-	-		} 139,356[7]	76,404	117,135	18,114
33 Christian Democracy[3]	-	-	-			8,638		11,450
32 Centre Union[4]	1,555,442	1,962,079	2,424,477	1,002,559	612,786	22,763		7,770
29 National Radical Union	2,347,824	1,837,377	1,621,546	-	-	-	-	-
31 Progressives[5]		173,981		-	-	95,799	-	-
34 National Democratic Union	-	-	-	52,768	-	-	-	-
36 New Democracy	-	-	-	2,669,133	2,146,365	2,034,496	2,599,681	2,887,488
37 Pan-Hellenic Socialist Movement	-	-	-	666,413	1,300,025	2,726,309	2,916,735	2,551,518
38 National Alignment	-	-	-	-	349,988	-	-	-
39 New Liberal Party	-	-	-	-	55,494	-	-	-
40 Liberal Party II	-	-	-	-	-	20,645	10,551	9,001
42 National Political Union	-	-	-	-	-	-	37,965	21,149
43 Independent Muslim lists	-	-	-	-	-	-	20,708	34,145
44 Democratic Renewal	-	-	-	-	-	-	-	65,614
46 Ecological Movement	-	-	-	-	-	-	-	8,182
Others	41,618	24,455	9,951	53,314	45,485	25,575	32,794	50,836

1 Allied with New Democracy in 1985 and in Coalition of the Left and Progress 1989.
2 Part of the United Left in 1977, allied with Communist Party (Interior) in 1977 and Pasok in 1981 and 1985. Part of the Coalition of the Left and Progress in 1989.
3 Allied with the Centre Union in 1977 and with Pasok in 1985.
4 Part of New Democracy in 1985.
5 Contested the 1961 election with the Centre Union and the 1964 election with the National Radical Union.

Table 9.5b GREECE Percentage of Votes 1961-1989

	1961	1963	1964	1974	1977	1981	1985	1989 (June)
Total Votes[9]	81.9	83.0	81.7	79.5	81.1	81.5	83.8	84.5
Valid Votes	81.5	82.4	81.2	78.7	80.1	80.3	83.1	82.6
Invalid Votes	0.3	0.6	0.5	0.9	1.6	1.2	0.7	1.9
Share Invalid	0.4	0.8	0.6	1.1	1.2	1.4	0.9	2.2
41 Party for Democratic Socialism	–	–	–	–	–	0.7		
45 Greek Left	–	–	–	–	–	–	–	} 13.1
4 Communist Party	–	–	–		9.4	10.9	9.9	
25 United Democratic Left	14.6	14.3	11.8	} 9.5				
35 Communist Party (Interior)	–	–	–		} 2.7	1.3	1.8	0.3
33 Christian Democracy	–	–	–	–		0.2		0.2
32 Centre Union	33.7	42.0	52.7	20.4	11.9	0.4		0.1
29 National Radical Union	50.8	39.4	35.3	–	–	–	–	–
31 Progressives	–	3.7	–	–	–	1.7	–	–
34 National Democratic Union	–	–	–	1.1	–	–	–	–
36 New Democracy	–	–	–	54.3	41.8	35.9	40.8	44.3
37 Pan-Hellenic Socialist Movement	–	–	–	13.6	25.3	48.1	45.8	39.1
38 National Alignment	–	–	–	–	6.8	–	–	–
39 New Liberal Party	–	–	–	–	1.1	–	–	–
40 Liberal Party II	–	–	–	–	–	0.4	0.2	0.1
42 National Political Union	–	–	–	–	–	–	0.6	0.3
43 Independent Muslim lists	–	–	–	–	–	–	0.3	0.5
44 Democratic Renewal	–	–	–	–	–	–	–	1.0
46 Ecological Movement	–	–	–	–	–	–	–	0.1
Others	0.9	0.5	0.2	1.1	0.9	0.5	0.5	0.8

6 United Left, comprising the Communist Party, Communist Party Interior and United Democratic Left.
7 Alliance of Communist Party (Interior), EDA, Christian Democracy, Socialist Initiative (splinter from the Centre Union) and Socialist March (splinter from PASOK).
8 Coalition of the Left and Progress comprising the Communist Party, Greek Left, the United Democratic Left, the Party for Democratic Socialism and other minor leftist parties and independents.
9 Percentage turnout and total votes based upon official figures. At least from 1974 these figures overestimate the electorate because deceased persons are not deleted and some electors register in two places. The actual turnout rate was approximately 88 per cent in 1984 and 90 per cent in 1985 and 1989.

Sources: Official Reports of the Ministry of the Interior and Dimitras and Kalogeropoulou, 1989: 8-13.

Table 9.5c GREECE Number of Seats Won in the Vouli 1961-1989

	1961	1963	1964	1974	1977	1981	1985	1989 (June)
41 Party for Democratic Socialism	–	–	–	–	–	0		
45 Greek Left	–	–	–	–	–	–	–	
4 Communist Party	–	–	–	5	11	13	12	} 28[4]
25 United Democratic Left	24	28	22	1	1			
35 Communist Party (Interior)	–	–	–	2	1	0	1	0
33 Christian Democracy	–	–	–	0	0	0	–	0
32 Centre Union	86	138	171	60	16	0	–	0
29 National Radical Union	176	132	100	–	–	–	–	–
31 Progressives	14	2	7	–	–	0	–	–
34 National Democratic Union	–	–	–	0	–	–	–	–
36 New Democracy	–	–	–	220	171	115	126[2]	145
37 Pan-Hellenic Socialist Movement	–	–	–	12	93	172[1]	161[3]	125
38 National Alignment	–	–	–	–	5	–	–	–
39 New Liberal Party	–	–	–	–	2	–	–	–
40 Liberal Party II	–	–	–	–	–	0	0	0
42 National Political Union	–	–	–	–	–	–	0	0
43 Independent Muslim lists	–	–	–	–	–	–	0	1
44 Democratic Renewal	–	–	–	–	–	–	–	1
46 Ecological Movement	–	–	–	–	–	–	–	–
Others	0	0	–	0	0	0	0	0
Total Seats	300	300	300	300	300	300	300	300

1 Includes Manolis Glezos, leader of the United Democratic Left (EDA).
2 Includes Ioannes Zighdis, leader of the Union of the Democratic Centre and Ioannes Pesmazoglou, leader of the Party for Democratic Socialism.
3 Includes Manolis Glezos, leader of the EDA and Nikolaos Psouradakis, leader of Christian Democracy.
4 Communist Party 20, Greek Left four, EDA one and three independents.

Sources: Official reports of the Ministry of the Interior and Dimitras and Kalogeropoulou (1989): 14-23.

Table 9.5d GREECE Percentage of Seats Won in the Vouli 1961-1989

	1961	1963	1964	1974	1977	1981	1985	1989 (June)
41 Party for Democratic Socialism	–	–	–	–	–	0.0	–	
45 Greek Left	–	–	–	–	–	–	–	
4 Communist Party	–	–	–	2.7	3.7	4.3	4.0	} 9.3
25 United Democratic Left	8.0	9.3	7.3	0.1	0.1			
35 Communist Party (Interior)	–	–	–	–	0.7	0.0	0.3	0.0
33 Christian Democracy	–	–	–	0.0	0.0	0.0		0.0
32 Centre Union	28.7	46.0	57.0	20.0	5.3	0.0		0.0
29 National Radical Union	58.7	44.0	33.3	–	–	–	–	–
31 Progressives	4.7	0.7	2.3	–	–	0.0	–	–
34 National Democratic Union	–	–	–	0.0	–	–	–	–
36 New Democracy	–	–	–	73.3	57.0	38.3	42.0	48.3
37 Pan-Hellenic Socialist Movement	–	–	–	4.0	31.0	57.3	53.7	41.7
38 National Alignment	–	–	–	–	1.7	–	–	–
39 New Liberal Party	–	–	–	–	0.7	–	–	–
40 Liberal Party II	–	–	–	–	–	0.0	0.0	0.0
42 National Political Union	–	–	–	–	–	–	0.0	0.0
43 Independent Muslim lists	–	–	–	–	–	–	0.0	0.3
44 Democratic Renewal	–	–	–	–	–	–	–	0.3
46 Ecological Movement	–	–	–	–	–	–	–	0.0
Others	0.0	0.0	0.0	0.0	0.0	0.0	0.0	0.0

Chapter 10

ICELAND

Organized political groups began to compete in Icelandic elections in 1897, reflecting major differences within the country about its constitutional autonomy as regards Denmark, which was then the governing authority. However, the groups lacked stability and cohesion (Grimsson, 1970: 272-273). Iceland gained home rule by the revision of the Danish Constitution of 1915 and gained the equivalent of dominion status by the Danish-Icelandic Act of Union of 1918. The establishment of the Progressive and Social Democratic parties in 1916 marked the beginning of an effective party system in Iceland. No figures for parties are given in official election sources before then.

The 1915 constitutional law provided for direct elections by secret ballot to the Icelandic parliament, the two-chamber Althingi. The Lower House, the Nedri deild, initially consisted of 40 members. A plurality vote was used to elect 34 of these members, 18 in two-member and 16 in single-member constituencies. An additional six members, the landskjör, were elected nationwide for twelve-year terms, with half standing every six years; the landskjör ballot was the d'Hondt highest average system of proportional representation, and the minimum voting age was 35. The landskjör members and eight of the constituency members formed the Upper House, the Efri deild. In 1920 the term of the landskjör members was reduced to eight years, and the number of constituency representatives increased to 36, including four elected by the d'Hondt system of proportional representation in the capital, Reykjavik, and the remainder by plurality, 12 in two-member and 20 in single-member constituencies.

The landskjör members of the Althingi were distributed among the parties as follows: 1916-22: Home Rule Party 3, Hardline Independence Party 2, Independent Farmers 1. 1922-26: Home Rule Party 1, Hardline Independence Party 2, Independent Farmers 1, Progressive Party 1, Women's List 1. 1926-30: Progressive Party 2, Social Democrats 1, Conservative Party 3. 1930-34: Progressive Party 2, Social Democrats 1, Independence Party 3.

The landskjör were abolished in 1934. Since then the upper house of parliament has consisted of one-third of the members of the Althingi elected by parliament as a whole. The 1934 reforms increased the number of constituency seats to 38. In order to achieve greater proportionality 11 supplementary seats were created. They were divided amongst the parties in proportion to their share of the national vote using the d'Hondt formula; to be included in this allocation a party had already to have won at least one constituency seat. In 1942 the number of Althingi seats was increased to 52. Of these 20 were elected by proportional representation, eight in the capital and 12 in two-member constituencies, 21 were elected by plurality in single-member constituencies and the 11 supplementary seats were distributed as before.

Proportional representation was introduced in all constituencies and the total number of members increased to 60 in 1959. Twelve representatives were elected in the capital, which formed a single constituency; 25 in five-member seats and 12 in two six-member constituencies. The 11 supplementary seats were retained.

The 1874 Constitution had limited the franchise to men who were either independent farmers or government officials, or who paid minimum amounts of local government tax or had certain educational qualifications. About ten percent of the population were registered to vote. The tax payment threshold was lowered in 1903, increasing the electorate by one half. The 1915 constitutional reforms extended the vote to 30 percent of the population; the franchise was given to women and to farm labourers aged 40 or above. This age limit was to be reduced by one year each year until a common voting age of 25 was achieved. In 1920 a common voting age of 25 was established. In 1934 persons in receipt of public assistance were enfranchised and the voting age was also reduced to 21 in 1934. The voting age was reduced to 20 in 1968.

Changes in the constitution and the electoral law in 1984 and 1987 increased the number of seats in the Althingi to 63. Of these eight are allocated to constituencies by the Ministry of Justice immediately before each election in order to ensure greater proportionality. Seats are assigned to parties and individual candidates in a complex four-stage procedure. In the first stage seats are allocated within constituencies by a modified version of the largest remainder system. In subsequent stages seats are allocated on a national basis using the d'Hondt formula. The voting age was reduced to 18 in 1984.

In 1944 a national referendum overwhelmingly voted to make Iceland a republic independent of Denmark and the new constitution provided for a president popularly elected by a plurality vote to serve a four-year term. Only four of the ten presidential elections have been contested (Table 10.a). Sveinn Björnsson was returned unopposed in 1946 and 1950. After he died in 1952, Ásgeir Ásgeirsson was elected to succeed him in the first contested election, and served three more terms without opposition. In 1968 Kristján Eldjárn was elected in a contested election, and returned unopposed in 1972 and 1976. In 1980 Vigdís Finnbogadóttir won a contested election; he was returned unopposed in 1984 and reelected by an overwhelming majority in 1988. Although some candidates had previously been active in national politics, presidential elections have not usually been highly partisan contests. Party divisions have only been clear in 1952 when Bishop Bjarni Jónsson was supported by the Progressive and Independence parties against the Social Democrat Ásgeirsson, who stood as an independent without official backing from his own party, and in 1988 when the opponent of the incumbent was backed by the Humanist Party.

Table 10.a CONTESTED PRESIDENTIAL ELECTIONS IN ICELAND

	Votes	%
	29 June	**1952**
Ásgeir Ásgeirsson	32,924	52. 7
Bjarni Jónsson	31,045	41.6
Gísli Sveinssonn	4,255	5.7
Electorate	85,887	
Valid Votes	68,224	79.4
Invalid Votes	2,233	2.6
	30 June	**1968**
Kristján Eldjárn	67,554	65.7
Gunnar Thoroddsen	35,428	34.4
Electorate	112,737	
Valid Votes	102,982	91.3
Invalid Votes	918	0.8
	29 June	**1980**
Vigdís Finnbogadóttir	43,611	33.8
Gudlaugur Thorvaldsson	41,700	32.3
Albert Gudmundsson	25,599	19.8
Pétur J. Thorsteinsson	18,139	14.1
Electorate	143,196	
Valid Votes	129,049	90.1
Invalid Votes	546	0.4
	25 June	**1988**
Vigdís Finnbogadóttir	117,292	94.6
Sigrun Thorsteinsdottir	6,712	5.4
Electorate	173,800	
Valid Votes	124,004	
Invalid Votes	2,531	

Source: Statistical Bureau of Iceland, 1952ff.

Sources:

Ó.R. Grímsson, *Political Power in Iceland Prior to the Period of Class Politics, 1845-1918* (PhD Thesis, University of Manchester, 1970)

Ó.R. Grímsson, 'Iceland' in S. Rokkan and J. Meyriat (eds.) *International Guide to Electoral Statistics* (The Hague and Paris: Mouton, 1969) 183-94

S. Kristjansson, *Conflict and Consensus in Icelandic Politics,1916-1944* (PhD Thesis, University of Illinois at Urbana, 1977)

Statistical Bureau of Iceland, *Althingiskosningar, 1916* (Reykjavik, 1916) and subsequent volumes in the same series

Statistical Bureau of Iceland, *Forsetakjör Arid 1952* (Reykjavik, 1952) and subsequent volumes in the same series

Table 10.1 POLITICAL PARTIES IN ICELAND SINCE 1916

	Party Names	Elections Contested Years	Number
1	Home Rule Party (Heimastjornáflokkur)	1916-1922	4
2	Independence Party I (Sjálfstaedisflokkur)	October 1916-1922	3
3	Hardline Independence Party (Sjálfstaedisflokkur 'thversum')	1916	2
4	Moderate Independence Party (Sjálfstaedisflokkur 'langsum')	1916	2
5	Farmers' Party I (Baendakflokkur)	1916	2
6	Independent Farmers (Óhádir Baendur)	1916	2
7	Social Democrats (Althyduflokkur)	1916ff	28
8	Progressive Party (Framsóknarflokkur) [1]	1919ff	26
9	Women's List (Kvennalisti)	1922, 1926	2
10	Citizens' Party I (Borgaraflokkur) [2]	1923	1
11	Conservative Party (Ìhaldsflokkur)	1926-1927	2
12	Liberal Party (Frjálslyndiflokkur)	1926-1927	2
13	Independence Party II (Sjálfstaedisflokkur) [3]	1930ff	21
14	Communist Party (Kommúnistaflokkur); latterly United Socialist Party and People's Alliance [4]	1931ff	8
15	Farmers' Party II (Baendaflokkur) [5]	1934-1937	2
16	Commonwealth (Thjodveldismenn) [6]	1942	1
17	National Preservation Party (Thjodvarnarflokkur) [7]	1953-1959	4
18	Republic Party (Lydveldisflokkur) [6]	1953	1
19	Independent Democratic Party (Ohádi Lydraedisflokkur)	1967	1
20	Union of Liberals and Leftists (Samtök Frjálslyndra og Vinstri Manna) [8]	1967-1978	4
21	Candidature Party (Frambodsflokkur) [9]	1971	1
22	Social Democratic Federation (Bandalag Jafnatharmanna) [10]	1983ff	1
23	Women's Alliance (Samtök um Kvennalista)	1983ff	2
24	Citizens' Party II (Borgaraflokkur) [11]	1987	1
25	Humanist Party (Flokkur Mannsins)	1987	1
26	National Party (Thjodarflokkur) [12]	1987	1
27	Association for Equality and Justice (Samtök um Jafnrétti og Félagshyggju) [13]	1987	1

1 Merger of the Farmers' and Independent Farmers' parties after the 1916 elections.

2 Electoral alliance of opponents of the Progressive and Social Democratic parties, most of whose deputies combined to found the Conservative Party in 1924.

3 Merger of the Conservative and Liberal parties in 1929.

4 In 1938 the Communist Party merged with a Social Democrat splinter group to form the United Socialist Party (Sósiálistaflokkur). In 1956 the People's Alliance (Althydubandalag) was formed by the United Socialist Party and another Social Democrat splinter group. It was joined by the National Preservation Party in 1963.

5 Splinter from the Progressive Party.
6 Right-wing splinters from the Independence Party.
7 Joined with Communists in the People's Alliance in 1963.
8 In 1967 a dissident People's Alliance list led by Hannibal Valdirmarsson, who formed the Union of Liberals and Leftists in 1971,
9 Protest party founded by students at Reykjavik University. Dissolved immediately after the 1971 election.
10 Breakaway from the Social Democrats, founded in 1982.
11 Formed in 1987 by Albert Gudmundsson, a leading figure in the Independence Party II.
12 Breakaway from the Progressive Party.
13 Regional list in the North-East constituency, formed by a Progressive Party deputy in the outgoing parliament.

Table 10.2 DATES OF ELECTIONS : ALTHINGI

1	5 August 1916 [1]	15	30 June 1946
2	21 October 1916	16	23 October 1949
3	15 November 1919	17	28 June 1953
4	8 July 1922 [1]	18	24 June 1956
5	27 October 1923	19	28 June 1959
6	1 July 1926 [1]	20	25 October 1959
7	9 July 1927	21	9 June 1963
8	15 June 1930 [1]	22	11 June 1967
9	12 June 1931	23	13 June 1971
10	16 July 1933	24	30 June 1974
11	24 June 1934	25	25 June 1978
12	20 June 1937	26	2 December 1979
13	5 July 1942	27	23 April 1983
14	18 October 1942	28	25 April 1987

1 Landskjör elections.

Source: *Althingiskosningar 25. Apríl 1987.*

Table 10.3a ICELAND Total Votes 1916-1931

	1916[1] (Aug.)	1916 (Oct.)	1919	1922[1]	1923	1926[1]	1927	1930[1]	1931
Electorate	24,189	28,529	31,870	29,094	43,932	30,767	46,047	34,467	50,617
Valid Votes	5,829	13,350	14,035	11,794	30,362	13,947	32,009	24,149	38,544
Invalid Votes	44	680	429	168	784	168	919	149	1,064
Total Votes	5,873	14,030	14,464	11,962	31,146	14,115	32,928	24,298	39,608
PARTY VOTES									
1 Home Rule Party	1,950	5,333	6,423[2]	3,258	-	-	-	-	-
2 Independence Party I	1,337	1,014	-	633	-	-	-	-	-
3 Hardline Independence Party	419	2,097	-	-	-	-	-	-	-
4 Moderate Independence Party	-	938	3,548[2]	-	-	-	-	-	-
5 Farmers' Party I	435	1,173	-	-	-	-	-	-	-
6 Independent Farmers	1,290	554	-	-	-	-	-	-	-
7 Social Democrats	398	903	949	2,033	4,912	3,164	6,097	4,893	6,197
8 Progressive Party	-	-	3,115[2]	3,196	8,062	3,481	9,532	7,585	13,844
9 Women's List	-	-	-	2,674	-	489	-	-	-
10 Citizens' Party I	-	-	-	-	16,272	-	-	-	-
11 Conservative Party	-	-	-	-	-	5,501	13,616	-	-
12 Liberal Party	-	-	-	-	-	1,312	1,858	-	-
13 Independence Party II	-	-	-	-	-	-	-	11,671	16,891
14 Communist Party	-	-	-	-	-	-	-	-	1,165
Others	-	1,336	-	-	1,115	-	904	-	446

1 Landskjör elections.
2 Includes votes cast for independents sympathetic to the party.

Source: *Althingiskosningarr*, 1916 ff

Table 10.3b ICELAND Percentage of Votes 1916-1931

	1916 (Aug.)	1916 (Oct.)	1919	1922	1923	1926	1927	1930	1931
Total Votes	24.3	49.2	45.4	41.1	70.9	45.9	71.5	70.5	78.3
Valid Votes	24.1	46.8	44.0	40.5	69.1	45.3	69.5	70.1	76.1
Invalid Votes	0.2	2.4	1.3	0.6	1.8	0.5	2.0	0.4	2.1
Share Invalid	0.7	4.8	3.0	1.4	2.5	1.2	2.8	0.6	2.7
PARTY VOTES									
1 Home Rule Party	33.5	40.0	45.8	27.6	-	-	-	-	-
2 Independence Party I	22.9	7.6	-	5.4	-	-	-	-	-
3 Hardline Independence Party	7.2	15.7	-	-	-	-	-	-	-
4 Moderate Independence Party	-	7.0	25.3	-	-	-	-	-	-
5 Farmers' Party I	7.5	8.8	-	-	-	-	-	-	-
6 Independent Farmers	22.1	4.1	-	-	-	-	-	-	-
7 Social Democrats	6.8	6.8	6.8	17.2	16.2	22.7	19.0	20.3	16.1
8 Progressive Party	-	-	22.2	27.1	26.6	25.0	29.8	31.4	35.9
9 Women's List	-	-	-	22.7	-	3.5	-	-	-
10 Citizens' Party I	-	-	-	-	53.6	-	-	-	-
11 Conservative Party	-	-	-	-	-	39.4	42.5	-	-
12 Liberal Party	-	-	-	-	-	9.4	5.8	-	-
13 Independence Party II	-	-	-	-	-	-	-	48.3	43.8
14 Communist Party	-	-	-	-	-	-	-	-	3.0
Others	-	10.0	-	-	3.7	-	2.8	-	1.2

Table 10.3c ICELAND Number of Seats Won in the Althingi 1916-1931[1]

	1916[2] (Aug)	1916 (Oct)	1919	1922[2]	1923	1926[2]	1927	1930[2]	1931
1 Home Rule Party	3	12 (1)	13 (4)	1	–	–	–	–	–
2 Independence Party I	2	3	11 (4)	0	–	–	–	–	–
3 Hardline Independence Party	0	7	–	–	–	–	–	–	–
4 Moderate Independence Party	–	3 (1)	–	–	–	–	–	–	–
5 Farmers' Party I	0	5	–	–	–	–	–	–	–
6 Independent Farmers	1	1	–	–	–	–	–	–	–
7 Social Democrats	0	1	–	0	1	1	4	0	3
8 Progressive Party	–	–	10 (2)	1	13 (1)	1	17	1	21
9 Women's List	–	–	–	1	–	0	–	–	–
10 Citizens' Party I	–	–	–	–	21 (2)	–	–	–	–
11 Conservative Party	–	–	–	–	–	1	13[1]	–	–
12 Liberal Party	–	–	–	–	–	0	1	–	–
13 Independence Party II	–	–	–	–	–	–	–	2	12
14 Communist Party	–	–	–	–	–	–	–	–	0
Others	–	2	–	–	1	–	1	–	0
Total Seats	6	34 (2)	34 (10)	3	36 (3)	3	36	3	36

1 Figures in parentheses report representatives returned unopposed.
2 Landskjör elections.

Table 10.3d ICELAND Percentage of Seats Won in the Althingi 1916-1931

	1916 (Aug)	1916 (Oct)	1919	1922	1923	1926	1927	1930	1931
1 Home Rule Party	50.0	35.3	38.2	33.3	-	-	-	-	-
2 Independence Party I	33.3	8.8	32.4	0.0	-	-	-	-	-
3 Hardline Independence Party	0.0	20.6	-	-	-	-	-	-	-
4 Moderate Independence Party	-	8.8	-	-	-	-	-	-	-
5 Farmers' Party I	0.0	14.7	-	-	-	-	-	-	-
6 Independent Farmers	16.7	2.9	-	-	-	-	-	-	-
7 Social Democrats	0.0	2.9	0.0	0.0	2.8	33.3	11.1	0.0	8.3
8 Progressive Party	-	-	29.4	33.3	36.1	33.3	47.2	33.3	58.3
9 Women's Party	-	-	-	33.3	-	0.0	-	-	-
10 Citizens' Party I	-	-	-	-	-	-	-	-	-
11 Conservative Party	-	-	-	-	58.3	33.3	36.1	-	-
12 Liberal Party	-	-	-	-	-	0.0	2.8	-	-
13 Independence Party II	-	-	-	-	-	-	-	66.7	33.3
14 Communist Party	-	-	-	-	-	-	-	-	0.0
Others	-	5.9	-	-	2.8	-	2.8	-	0.0

Table 10.4a ICELAND Total Votes 1933-1956

	1933	1934	1937	1942 (July)	1942 (Oct.)	1946	1949	1953	1956
Electorate	52,465	64,338	67,195	73,440	73,560	77,670	82,481	87,601	91,618
Valid Votes	35,680	51,929	58,415	58,131	59,688	66,913	72,219	77,410	82,678
Invalid Votes	1,091	516	681	809	908	982	1,213	1,344	1,677
Total Votes	36,771	52,445	59,096	58,940	60,576	67,895	73,432	78,754	84,355
PARTY VOTES									
7 Social Democrats	6,864	11,269	11,084	8,979	8,455	11,914	11,937	12,093	15,153
8 Progressive Party	8,530	11,377	14,556	16,033	15,809	15,429	17,659	16,959	12,925
13 Independence Party II	17,131	21,974	24,132	22,975	23,001	26,428	28,546	28,738	35,027
14 United Socialist Party[1]	2,673	3,098	4,932	9,423	11,059	13,049	14,077	12,422	15,859
15 Farmers' Party II	-	3,348	3,578	-	-	-	-	-	-
16 Commonwealth	-	-	-	618	1,284	-	-	-	-
17 National Preservation Party	-	-	-	-	-	-	-	4,667	3,706
18 Republic Party	-	-	-	-	-	-	-	2,531	-
Others	480	862	131	103	-	93	-	-	8

1 In 1956 the People's Alliance.

Source: *Althingiskosningar*, 1916 ff.

Table 10.4b ICELAND Percentage of Votes 1933-1956

	1933	1934	1937	1942 (July)	1942 (Oct.)	1946	1949	1953	1956
Total Votes	70.1	81.5	87.9	80.3	82.4	87.4	89.0	89.9	92.1
Valid Votes	68.0	80.7	86.9	79.2	81.1	86.2	87.6	88.4	90.2
Invalid Votes	2.1	0.8	1.0	1.1	1.2	1.3	1.5	1.5	1.8
Share Invalid	3.0	1.0	1.0	1.4	1.5	1.4	1.7	1.7	2.0
PARTY VOTES									
7 Social Democrats	19.2	21.7	19.0	15.4	14.2	17.8	16.5	15.6	18.3
8 Progressive Party	23.9	21.9	24.9	27.6	26.6	23.1	24.5	21.9	15.6
13 Independence Party II	48.0	42.3	41.3	39.5	38.5	39.5	39.5	37.1	42.4
14 United Socialist Party	7.5	6.0	8.4	16.2	18.5	19.5	19.5	16.0	19.2
15 Farmers' Party II	-	6.4	6.1	-	-	-	-	-	-
16 Commonwealth	-	-	-	1.1	2.2	-	-	-	-
17 National Preservation Party	-	-	-	-	-	-	-	6.0	4.5
18 Republic Party	-	-	-	-	-	-	-	3.3	-
Others	1.3	1.7	0.2	0.2	-	0.1	-	-	0.0

Source: *Althingiskosningar*, 1916 ff.

Table 10.4c ICELAND Number of Seats Won in the Althingi 1933-1956

	1933	1934	1937	1942 (July)	1942 (Oct.)	1946	1949	1953	1956
7 Social Democrats	4	10	8	6	7	9	7	6	8
8 Progressive Party	14	15	19	20	15	13	17	16	17
13 Independence Party II	17	20	17	17	20	20	19	21	19
14 United Socialist Party	0	0	3	6	10	10	9	7	8
15 Farmers' Party II	–	3	2	–	–	–	–	–	–
16 Commonwealth	–	–	–	0	0	–	–	–	–
17 National Preservation Party	–	–	–	–	–	–	–	2	–
18 Republic Party	–	–	–	–	–	–	–	0	–
Others	1	1	0	0	–	0	–	–	0
Total Seats	36	49	49	49	52	52	52	52	52

Source: *Althingiskosningar*, 1916 ff.

Table 10.4d ICELAND Percentage of Seats Won in the Althingi 1933-1956

	1933	1934	1937	1942 (July)	1942 (Oct)	1946	1949	1953	1956
7 Social Democrats	11.1	20.4	16.3	12.2	-	17.3	13.5	11.5	15.4
8 Progressive Party	38.9	30.6	38.8	40.8	-	25.0	32.7	30.8	32.7
13 Independence Party II	-	-	-	-	-	-	-	-	-
14 United Socialist Party	47.2	40.8	6.1	12.2	-	19.2	17.3	13.5	15.4
15 Farmers' Party II	-	-	4.1	-	-	-	-	-	-
16 Commonwealth	-	6.1	-	-	-	-	-	-	-
17 National Preservation Party	-	-	-	-	-	-	-	3.8	-
18 Republic Party	-	-	-	-	-	-	-	-	-
Others	2.8	2.0	0.0	0.0	-	-	-	-	-

Table 10.5a ICELAND Total Votes 1959-1987

	1959 (June)	1959 (Oct.)	1963	1967	1971	1974	1978	1979	1983	1987
Electorate	95,050	95,637	99,798	107,101	118,289	126,388	137,782	142,073	150,977	171,402
Valid Votes	84,788	85,095	89,352	96,090	105,395	114,108	122,207	123,751	130,422	152,722
Invalid Votes	1,359	1,331	1,606	1,765	1,580	1,467	2,170	3,178	3,342	1,716
Total Votes	86,147	86,426	90,958	97,855	106,975	115,575	124,377	126,929	133,764	154,438
PARTY VOTES										
7 Social Democrats	10,632	12,909	12,697	15,059	11,020	10,345	26,912	21,580	15,214	23,265
8 Progressive Party	23,061	21,882	25,217	27,029	26,645	28,381	20,656	30,861	24,095	28,902
13 Independence Party II	36,029	33,800	37,021	36,036	38,170	48,764	39,982	43,838	50,251	41,490
14 People's Alliance	12,929	13,621	14,274	13,403	18,055	20,924	27,952	24,401	22,490	20,387
17 National Preservation Party	2,137	2,883	-	-	-	-	-	-	-	-
19 Independent Democratic Party	-	-	-	1,043	-	-	-	-	-	-
20 Union of Liberals and Leftists	-	-	-	3,520	9,395	5,245	4,073	-	-	-
21 Candidature Party	-	-	-	-	2,110	-	-	-	-	-
22 Social Democratic Federation	-	-	-	-	-	-	-	-	9,849	246
23 Women's Alliance	-	-	-	-	-	-	-	-	7,125	15,470
24 Citizens' Party II	-	-	-	-	-	-	-	-	-	16,588
25 Humanist Party	-	-	-	-	-	-	-	-	-	2,434
26 National Party	-	-	-	-	-	-	-	-	-	2,047
27 Equality and Justice	-	-	-	-	-	-	-	-	-	1,893
Others	-	-	143	-	-	449	2,632	3,071	1,398	-

Source: *Althingiskosningar*, 1916 ff.

Table 10.5b ICELAND Percentage of Votes 1959-1987

	1959 (June)	1959 (Oct.)	1963	1967	1971	1974	1978	1979	1983	1987
Total Votes	90.6	90.4	91.1	91.4	90.4	91.4	90.3	89.3	88.6	90.1
Valid Votes	89.2	89.0	89.5	89.7	89.1	90.3	88.7	87.1	86.4	89.1
Invalid Votes	1.4	1.4	1.6	1.6	1.3	1.2	1.6	2.2	2.2	1.0
Share Invalid	1.6	1.5	1.8	1.8	1.5	1.3	1.7	2.5	2.5	1.1
PARTY VOTES										
7 Social Democrats	12.5	15.2	14.2	15.7	10.5	9.1	22.0	17.4	11.7	15.2
8 Progressive Party	27.2	25.7	28.2	28.1	25.3	24.9	16.9	24.9	18.5	18.9
13 Independence Party II	42.5	39.7	41.4	37.5	36.2	42.7	32.7	35.4	38.5	27.2
14 People's Alliance	15.2	16.0	16.0	13.9	17.1	18.3	22.9	19.7	17.2	13.3
17 National Preservation Party	2.5	3.4	-	-	-	-	-	-	-	-
19 Independent Democratic Party	-	-	-	1.1	-	-	-	-	-	-
20 Union of Liberals and Leftists	-	-	-	3.7	8.9	4.6	3.3	-	-	-
21 Candidature Party	-	-	-	-	2.0	-	-	-	-	-
22 Social Democratic Federation	-	-	-	-	-	-	-	-	7.6	0.2
23 Women's Alliance	-	-	-	-	-	-	-	-	5.5	10.2
24 Citizens' Party II	-	-	-	-	-	-	-	-	-	10.9
25 Humanist Party	-	-	-	-	-	-	-	-	-	1.6
26 National Party	-	-	-	-	-	-	-	-	-	1.3
27 Equality and Justice	-	-	-	-	-	-	-	-	-	1.2
Others	-	-	0.2	-	-	0.4	2.2	2.5	1.1	-

Table 10.5c ICELAND Number of Seats Won in the Althingi 1959-1987

	1959 (June)	1959 (Oct.)	1963	1967	1971	1974	1978	1979	1983	1987
7 Social Democrats	6	9	8	9	6	5	14	10	6	10
8 Progressive Party	19	17	19	18	17	17	12	17	14	13
13 Independence Party II	20	24	24	23	22	25	20	21	23	18
14 People's Alliance	7	10	9	9	10	11	14	11	10	8
17 National Preservation Party	0	0	–	–	–	–	–	–	–	–
19 Independent Democratic Party	–	–	–	0	–	–	0	–	–	–
20 Union of Liberals and Leftists	–	–	–	1	5	2	0	–	–	–
21 Candidature Party	–	–	–	–	0	–	–	–	–	–
22 Social Democratic Federation	–	–	–	–	–	–	–	–	4	0
23 Women's Alliance	–	–	–	–	–	–	–	–	3	6
24 Citizens's Party	–	–	–	–	–	–	–	–	–	7
25 Humanist Party	–	–	–	–	–	–	–	–	–	0
26 National Party	–	–	–	–	–	–	–	–	–	0
27 Equality and Justice	–	–	–	–	–	–	–	–	–	1
Others	–	–	–	–	–	0	0	1	0	–
Total Seats	52	60	60	60	60	60	60	60	60	63

Sources: *Althingiskosningar*, 1916 ff.

Table 10.5d ICELAND Percentage of Seats Won in the Althingi 1959-1987

	1959 (June)	1959 (Oct)	1963	1967	1971	1974	1978	1979	1983	1987
7 Social Democrats	11.5	15.0	13.3	15.0	10.0	8.3	23.3	16.7	10.0	15.8
8 Progressive Party	36.5	28.3	31.7	30.0	28.3	28.3	20.0	28.3	23.3	20.6
13 Independence Party II	38.5	40.0	40.0	38.3	36.7	41.7	33.3	35.0	38.3	28.6
14 People's Alliance	13.5	16.7	15.0	15.0	16.7	18.3	23.3	18.3	16.7	12.7
17 National Preservation Party	0.0	0.0	-	-	-	-	-	-	-	-
19 Independent Democratic Party	-	-	-	-	-	-	-	-	-	-
20 Union of Liberals and Leftists	-	-	-	1.7	8.3	3.3	0.0	-	-	-
21 Candidature Party	-	-	-	-	-	-	-	-	-	-
22 Social Democratic Federation	-	-	-	-	-	-	-	-	6.7	0.0
23 Women's Alliance	-	-	-	-	-	-	-	-	5.0	9.5
24 Citizens' Party	-	-	-	-	-	-	-	-	-	11.1
25 Humanist Party	-	-	-	-	-	-	-	-	-	0.0
26 National Party	-	-	-	-	-	-	-	-	-	0.0
27 Equality and Justice	-	-	-	-	-	-	-	-	-	1.6
Others	-	-	0.0	-	-	0.0	0.0	1.7	0.0	-

Chapter 11

IRELAND

From the creation of the United Kingdom of Great Britain and Ireland in 1801 until the establishment of the 26-county Irish Free State in 1922, all 32 counties of the island of Ireland were represented in the British Parliament at Westminster. The first Republican Parliament was constituted by Sinn Féin MPs elected to Westminster in December 1918 under United Kingdom electoral law. Voting was in single-member constituencies and election was by a plurality; in addition, two MPs were returned by Dublin University and one by the National University, the former chosen by Single Transferable Vote. The results for constituencies in the 26 counties that subsequently became independent are:

Table 11.a IRISH MPs, UNITED KINGDOM ELECTION, 1918

	Votes	%	Seats
Sinn Féin	421,522 [1]	65.2	71
Irish Nationalists	189,829	28.9	2
Unionists	38,011	5.9	3
Totals	649,362		76
Electorate	1,381,261		

[1] Twenty Sinn Féin candidates were returned unopposed
Source: calculated from Walker, 1978: 385-398

Elections to the Irish Free State Parliament of 1921 and 1922 had the same franchise requirement as in 1918, but the ballot took the form of the Single Transferable Vote (see Appendix), with allocation of seats in multi-member constituencies. As the May 1921 election was called in the midst of fighting between Irish republicans and British troops, there were no contests; 124 Sinn Féin MPs and four Unionist MPs representing Dublin University were returned unopposed. The June 1922 election was held at a time of great controversy between Irish groups for and against the 1921 Anglo-Irish Treaty that created the Irish Free State. While an attempt was made to ensure that all incumbent Sinn Féin deputies were returned unopposed, Labour, Farmers' Party and independent candidates produced contests in most constituencies. Civil war broke out shortly after the election. This third Dáil Éireann approved the Constitution drafted by the preceding Dáil.

The election of 1923 was the first to take place under an Irish election law and in relatively settled circumstances. Universal adult suffrage, with a minimum voting age of 21, was introduced, and plural voting abolished. The Single Transferable Vote system was retained. In December 1972 a referendum approved the lowering of the voting age to 18. This change took effect with the 1977 election.

The 1922 Constitution of the Irish Free State required proportional representation in Article 26, and statutes confirmed the form as STV. There was a bicameral legislature, the Oireachtas. The lower house, Dáil Éireann, elected the head of government, styled President of the Executive Council. The upper house, the Senate (Seanad Éireann) consisted initially of nominated members and members elected by the Dáil, who were to be gradually replaced by popularly elected members. In fact after the 1925 election the members of the two houses of the Oireachtas formed the Senate electoral college (McCracken, 1958: 139ff). Separate university representation in the Dáil was continued until 1936, when the university seats were transferred to a reformed Seanad.

In 1937 the present Constitution was adopted, retaining a bicameral Parliament with the supremacy of the popularly elected Dáil. The effective head of government was to be the Taoiseach (Prime Minister), leader of the largest party in the Dáil. The rules for Senate elections were also modified and linked to Dáil elections by a provision that a new Senate must be elected within 90 days of a Dáil election. The 60 strong Senate comprises 43 members chosen by an electoral college consisting of county and county borough councillors, outgoing Senators and incoming Dáil deputies from candidates chosen by five panels representing vocational interests, six members elected by graduates of Irish universities and eleven nominated by the Taoiseach. The office of Governor General, the representative of the British monarch, was abolished, and replaced by a President as head of state, and the ambiguous status of the nation's relation with the British crown was resolved by the proclamation of the Republic of Ireland in 1949.

As party affiliations were not shown on the ballot papers until 1965, there are no completely authoritative figures for the total party vote at elections until then, and conflicting figures are to be found in various publications. Up to 1948 details of the counts, constituency by constituency, were not published officially. Figures for elections from 1922 to 1965 were provided by Dr. Michael Gallagher, Trinity College, Dublin and derived from *Annual Reports* of the Department of Local Government, *Election Results and Transfer of Votes* (for elections from 1948 onwards), W.J. Flynn, *Oireachtas Companion and Saorstat Guide*, 1928, 1929 and 1930, *Free State Companion*, 1932 and *Irish Parliamentary Handbook* 1939 and 1945, newspapers and other sources.

The President has a seven-year term; the following have served:

Douglas Hyde	Non-party	1938-1945
Séan T. O'Kelly	Fianna Fáil	1945-1959
Eamon de Valera	Fianna Fáil	1959-1973
Erskine Childers	Fianna Fáil	1973-1974
Cearbhall O Dálaigh	Non-party	1974-1976
Patrick Hillery	Fianna Fáil	1976-1990

While the President is meant to be directly elected by Single Transferable Vote for a seven-year term, only four of the nine presidential elections have been contested. The first President, Douglas Hyde, was elected unopposed as the joint candidate of Fianna Fáil and Fine Gael. His successor, Sean T. O'Kelly, was returned unopposed for his second term. After the death in office of President Childers in 1974, Cearbhall O Dálaigh, Fianna Fáil Attorney General in the 1950s and Chief Justice during the 1960s was the agreed candidate of Fianna Fáil, Fine Gael and the Labour Party. Following the resignation of O Dálaigh in 1976, Patrick Hillery, a European Community Commissioner and former Fianna Fáil Foreign Minister, was nominated by Fianna Fáil and elected unopposed. In 1983 President Hillery was returned unopposed for a second term.

Table 11.b CONTESTED PRESIDENTIAL ELECTIONS

	First Count	%	Second Count	%
		1945		
Sean T. O'Kelly (Fianna Fáil)	537,965	49.5	565,165	52.0
Sean MacEoin (Fine Gael)	335,539	30.9	453,425	48.0
Patrick McCartan (Independent Republican)	212,834	19.6	-	
Electorate	1,803,463			
Valid Votes	1,086,338	60.2		
Invalid Votes	50,287	2.8		
		1959		
Eamon de Valera (Fianna Fáil)	538,003	56.3		
Sean MacEoin (Fine Gael)	417,536	43.7		
Electorate	1,678,450			
Valid Votes	955,539	56.9		
Invalid Votes	24,628	1.5		
		1966		
Eamon de Valera (Fianna Fáil)	558,861	50.5		
Tom O'Higgins (Fine Gael)	548,144	49.5		
Electorate	1,709,161			
Valid Votes	1,107,005	64.8		
Invalid Votes	9,910	0.6		
		1973		
Erskine Childers (Fianna Fáil)	635,867	52.0		
Tom O'Higgins (Fine Gael)	587,771	48.0		
Electorate	1,977,817			
Valid Votes	1,223,638	61.9		
Invalid Votes	6,946	0.4		

Sources:

B. Chubb, *The Government and Politics of Ireland* (London: Longman, 2nd ed., 1982)

J. Coakley, "The Senate elections" in H. Penniman and B. Farrell (eds.), *Ireland at the Polls 1981, 1982 and 1987* (Durham, N.C. : Duke University Press, 1987), 192-205

Communist Party of Ireland, *Communist Party of Ireland: Outline History* (Dublin Books, 1974)

Dáil Éireann, *Election Results and Transfer of Votes in General Election (May 1954) for Fifteenth Dáil* (Dublin, 1955) and subsequent volumes in the same series.

D. Farrell, "Ireland" in F. Müller-Rommel (ed.) *New Politics in Western Europe: the Rise and Success of Green Parties and Alternative Lists* (Boulder, Colorado: Westview, 1989)

M. Gallagher, 'The Pact general election of 1922', *Irish Historical Studies* 21, 84, (1981), 404-421

M. Gallagher, *Political Parties in the Republic of Ireland* (Manchester: Manchester University Press, 1985)

J.L. McCracken, *Representative Government in Ireland: A Study of Dáil Éireann 1919-1948* (London: Oxford University Press, 1958)

M. Milotte, *Communism in Modern Ireland* (Dublin: Gill & Macmillan, 1984)

C. O'Leary, *Irish Elections 1918-1977* (Dublin: Gill & Macmillan, 1979)

Results of Presidential Elections and Referenda, 1937-1984 (Dublin: Department of the Environment, 1984)

J.M. Smyth, *The Theory and Practice of the Irish Senate* (Dublin: Institute of Public Administration, 1972)

B.M. Walker, ed., *Parliamentary Election Results in Ireland, 1801-1922* (Dublin: Royal Irish Academy, 1978)

Table 11.1 POLITICAL PARTIES IN IRELAND SINCE 1918

	Party Names	Elections Contested	
		Years	Number
1	Irish Parliamentary Party	1918	1
2	Sinn Féin I (Ourselves)	1918-1921	2
3	Unionist Party	1918-1921	2
4	Pro-Treaty Sinn Féin [1]	1922	1
5	Anti-Treaty Sinn Féin/Republican Party [1]	1922-1923	2
6	Sinn Féin II [2]	1927; 1957-1961	3
7	Cumann na nGaedheal (League of Gaels) [3]	1923-1933	5
8	Irish Labour Party [4]	1922ff	24
9	Communists [5]	Sept. 1927-1932, 1951-1954; 1961ff	14
10	Fianna Fáil (Warriors of Destiny) [6]	June 1927ff	22
11	Farmers' Party	1922-1932	5
12	National League	1927	2
13	National Centre Party	1933	1
14	Fine Gael/United Ireland Party (Tribe of Gaels) [7]	1937ff	18
15	Clann na Talmhan (Party of the Land)	1943-1961	7
16	National Labour [8]	1944-1948	2
17	Clann na Poblachta (Republican Party)	1948-1965	6
18	National Progressive Democrats [9]	1961	1
19	Workers' Party [10]	1973ff	7
20	National H-Block Committee [11]	1981	1
21	Socialist Labour Party [12]	1981	1
22	Sinn Féin III [13]	Feb. 1982; 1987ff	3
23	Democratic Socialist Party [14]	Nov. 1982ff	3
24	Ecology Party/Green Party/Comhaontas Glas [15]	Nov. 1982ff	3
25	Progressive Democrats [16]	1987	2

1 The Pro-Treaty and Anti-Treaty Sinn Féin parties that contested the 1922 election were the outcome of a split in Sinn Féin over the acceptance of the 1921 Anglo-Irish Treaty, which established the Irish Free State as a Dominion under the British Crown. The anti-Treaty party contested the 1923 election simply as Sinn Féin; they were generally known as the Republicans.

2 The remnant of the Sinn Féin party after de Valera's supporters had left to form Fianna Fáil.

3 Successor to the Pro-treaty wing of Sinn Féin. Founded in 1923.

4 The Irish Labour Party was founded in 1912. Because it did not contest the 1918 and 1921 elections its electoral history dates from 1922.

5 A Communist party was first formed in 1921, but the first Communist party to take part in national elections was the Irish Worker League, founded in 1923. The communist Revolutionary Workers Groups contested the 1932 elections. The Communist Party was reformed in 1931, but never contested Dáil elections and was dissolved in 1941. The party was re-established as the Irish Workers' League in November 1948 and in 1970 it merged with the Communist Party of Northern Ireland to form the Communist Party of Ireland.

6 Founded in May 1926 by Eamon de Valera following a split in Anti-Treaty Sinn Féin. Its bilingual name is Fianna Fáil the Republican Party.

7 Established in 1933 by the merger of the Cumann na nGaedheal and National Centre parties and members of the banned National Guard. Until the 1940s, usually referred to as the United Ireland Party.
8 A splinter party from the Labour Party formed in 1944. The two parties were reunited in 1950.
9 Established in 1958 by two former Clann na Poblachta deputies, Noel Browne and Jack McQuillan. They joined the Labour Party in 1963.
10 Sinn Féin II split into the Official and Provisional wings in 1970. The Official wing was renamed Sinn Féin - the Workers' Party in 1977 and the Workers' Party five years later.
11 Candidates sponsored by the National H-Block Committee, in protest against conditions of I.R.A. and I.N.L.A. prisoners and hunger-strikers in Northern Ireland.
12 Founded in 1977 mainly by Labour Party members, including Noel Browne, elected as an independent labour candidate in June 1977. Browne was reelected as an SLP candidate in 1981 but left the party in November. The SLP was dissolved in 1982.
13 The Provisional wing of Sinn Féin II (see footnote 10), linked with the Irish Republican Army.
14 Founded in 1982 under the leadership of Jim Kemmy, a former Labour Party member who had been an independent TD for East Limerick since 1981. Merged with the Labour Party on 1 May 1990.
15 Founded in 1981 as the Ecology Party of Ireland. Subsequently renamed the Green Alliance/Comhaontas Glas and then the Green Party/Comhaontas Glas.
16 Founded in December 1985 by a former Fianna Fáil minister Desmond O'Malley.

Table 11.2a DATES OF ELECTIONS : DÁIL

1.	14 December 1918	14.	30 May 1951
2.	24 May 1921	15.	18 April 1954
3.	16 June 1922	16.	5 March 1957
4.	27 August 1923	17.	4 October 1961
5.	9 June 1927	18.	7 April 1965
6.	16 September 1927	19	16 June 1969
7.	16 February 1932	20.	28 February 1973
8.	24 January 1933	21.	16 June 1977
9.	1 July 1937	22.	11 June 1981
10.	17 June 1938	23	18 February 1982
11.	22 June 1943	24	24 November 1982
12.	30 May 1944	25.	17 February 1987
13.	4 February 1948	26.	15 June 1989

Table 11.2b DATES OF PRESIDENTIAL ELECTIONS

1.	14 June 1945
2.	17 June 1959
3.	1 June 1966
4.	30 May 1973

Table 11.3a IRELAND Total Votes 1922-1938

	1922	1923	1927 (June)	1927 (Sept.)	1932	1933	1937	1938
Electorate	1,430,104[2]	1,786,436[3]	1,730,177	1,730,177[3]	1,695,175[3]	1,724,420	1,775,055	1,770,422[4]
Valid Votes[1]	621,587	1,053,955	1,146,460	1,170,869	1,274,026	1,386,558	1,324,449	1,286,259
Invalid Votes	19,684	40,047	31,337	21,886	20,804	14,707	27,824	15,811
Total Votes	641,271	1,093,996	1,177,797	1,192,755	1,294,830	1,401,265	1,352,273	1,302,070
PARTY VOTES								
4 Pro-Treaty Sinn Féin	239,195	-	-	-	-	-	-	-
5 Anti-Treaty Sinn Féin	135,310	288,794	-	-	-	-	-	-
6 Sinn Féin II	-	-	41,401	-	-	-	-	-
7 Cumann na nGaedheal	-	410,695	314,703	453,028	449,506	422,495	-	-
8 Irish Labour Party	132,567	111,939	143,849	106,184	98,286	79,221	135,758	128,945
9 Communists	-	-	-	12,473	1,087	-	-	-
10 Fianna Fáil	-	-	299,486	411,777	566,498	689,054	599,040	667,996
11 Farmers' Party	48,718	127,184	101,955	74,626	26,436	-	-	-
12 National League	-	-	83,598	18,990	-	-	-	-
13 National Centre Party	-	-	-	-	-	126,906	-	-
14 Fine Gael	-	-	-	-	-	-	461,171	428,633
Others	65,797	115,343	161,468	93,791	132,213	68,882	128,480[5]	60,685

1 First preference votes.
2 Eight constituencies with 403,815 electors were uncontested.
3 One constituency, Dublin University was uncontested, with 1,400 electors in 1923, 2,084 in 1927 and 3,182 in 1932.
4 Two constituencies with electorate of 73,099 electors were uncontested.
5 Includes 875 votes for Frank Ryan (United Front Against Fascism), who ran with Communist Party support.

Table 11.3b IRELAND Percentage of Votes 1922-1938

	1922	1923	1927 (June)	1927 (Sept.)	1932	1933	1937	1938
Total Votes	44.9	61.2	68.1	69.0	76.5	81.3	76.2	76.7
Valid Votes	43.5	59.0	66.3	67.7	75.3	80.4	74.6	75.8
Invalid Votes	1.4	2.2	1.8	1.3	1.2	0.9	1.6	0.9
Share Invalid	3.2	3.7	2.7	1.8	1.6	1.1	2.1	1.2
PARTY VOTES								
4 Pro-Treaty Sinn Féin	38.5	-	-	-	-	-	-	-
5 Anti-Treaty Sinn Féin	21.8	27.4	-	-	-	-	-	-
6 Sinn Féin II	-	-	3.6	-	-	-	-	-
7 Cumann na nGaedheal	-	39.0	27.5	38.7	35.3	30.5	-	-
8 Irish Labour Party	21.3	10.6	12.6	9.1	7.7	5.7	10.3	10.0
9 Communists	-	-	-	1.1	0.1	-	-	-
10 Fianna Fáil	-	-	26.1	35.2	44.5	49.7	45.2	51.9
11 Farmers' Party	7.8	12.1	8.9	6.4	2.1	-	-	-
12 National League	-	-	7.3	1.6	-	-	-	-
13 National Centre Party	-	-	-	-	-	9.2	-	-
14 Fine Gael	-	-	-	-	-	-	34.8	33.3
Others	10.6	10.9	14.1	8.0	10.3	5.0	9.7	4.7

Table 11.3c IRELAND Number of Seats Won in the Dáil 1922-1938[1]

	1922	1923	1927 (June)	1927 (Sept.)	1932	1933	1937	1938
4 Pro-Treaty Sinn Féin	58 (17)	–	–	–	–	–	–	–
5 Anti-Treaty Sinn Féin	36 (17)	44	–	–	–	–	–	–
6 Sinn Féin II	–	–	5	–	–	–	–	–
7 Cumann na nGaedheal	–	63	47 (1)	62 (1)	57 (1)	48	–	–
8 Irish Labour Party	17	14	22	13	7	8	13	9
9 Communists	–	–	–	1	0	–	–	–
10 Fianna Fáil	–	–	44	57	72	77 (1)	69 (1)	77 (5)
11 Farmers' Party	7	15	11	6	3	–	–	–
12 National League	–	–	8	2	–	–	–	–
13 National Centre Party	–	–	–	–	–	11	–	–
14 Fine Gael	–	–	–	–	–	–	48	45 (2)
Others	10 (4)	17 (3)	16	12 (3)	14 (3)	9 (3)	8	7
Total Seats	128 (38)	153 (3)	153 (1)	153 (4)	153 (4)	153 (4)	138 (1)	138 (7)

1 Figures in brackets report the number of deputies returned unopposed.

Table 11.3d IRELAND Percentage of Seats Won in the Dáil 1922-1938

	1922	1923	1927 (June)	1927 (Sept.)	1932	1933	1937	1938
4 Pro-Treaty Sinn Féin	45.3	-	-	-	-	-	-	-
5 Anti Treaty Sinn Féin	28.2	28.8	-	-	-	-	-	-
6 Sinn Féin II	-	-	3.2	-	-	-	-	-
7 Cumann na nGaedheal	-	41.2	30.7	40.5	37.3	31.4	-	-
8 Irish Labour Party	13.3	9.2	14.4	8.5	4.6	5.2	9.4	6.5
9 Communists	-	-	-	0.7	0.0	-	-	-
10 Fianna Fáil	-	-	28.8	37.3	47.1	50.3	50.0	55.8
11 Farmers' Party	5.5	9.8	7.2	3.9	2.0	-	-	-
12 National League	-	-	5.2	1.3	-	-	-	-
13 National Centre Party	-	-	-	-	-	7.2	-	-
14 Fine Gael	-	-	-	-	-	-	34.8	32.6
Others	7.8	11.1	10.5	7.8	9.2	5.9	5.8	5.1

Table 11.4a IRELAND Total Votes 1943-1965

	1943	1944	1948	1951	1954	1957	1961	1965
Electorate	1,816,142	1,816,142[1]	1,800,210	1,785,144	1,763,209	1,738,278	1,670,860	1,683,019
Valid Votes	1,331,709	1,217,349	1,323,443	1,331,573	1,335,202	1,227,019	1,168,404	1,253,122
Invalid Votes	16,198	12,790	13,185	12,043	12,730	11,540	11,334	11,544
Total Votes	1,347,907	1,230,139	1,336,628	1,343,616	1,347,932	1,238,559	1,179,738	1,264,666
PARTY VOTES								
6 Sinn Féin II	-	-	-	-	-	65,640	36,396	-
8 Irish Labour Party	208,812	106,767	115,073	151,828	161,034	111,747	136,111	192,740
9 Communists	-	-	-	295	375	3,036[2]	277	183
10 Fianna Fáil	557,525	595,259	553,914	616,212	578,960	592,994	512,073	597,414
14 Fine Gael	307,490	249,329	262,393	342,922	427,031	326,699	374,099	427,081
15 Clann na Talmhan	137,700	131,243	73,813	38,872	51,069	28,905	17,693	-
16 National Labour	-	32,732	34,015	-	-	-	-	-
17 Clann na Poblachta	-	-	174,823	54,210	41,249	20,632	13,170	9,427
18 National Progressive Democrats	-	-	-	-	-	-	11,490	-
Others	120,182	102,019	109,412	127,234	75,484	77,366	67,095	26,277

1 One constituency with 39,192 electors was uncontested.
2 Votes cast for Jack Murphy (Unemployed Protest Committee).

Table 11.4b IRELAND Percentage of Votes 1943-1965

	1943	1944	1948	1951	1954	1957	1961	1965
Total Votes	74.2	67.7	74.2	75.3	76.4	71.3	70.6	75.1
Valid Votes	73.3	67.0	73.5	74.6	75.7	70.6	69.9	74.5
Invalid Votes	0.9	0.7	0.7	0.7	0.7	0.7	0.7	0.7
Share Invalid	1.2	1.0	1.0	0.9	0.9	0.9	1.0	0.9
PARTY VOTES								
6 Sinn Féin II	-	-	-	-	-	5.3	3.1	-
8 Irish Labour Party	15.7	8.8	8.7	11.4	12.1	9.1	11.6	15.4
9 Communist	-	-	-	0.0	0.0	0.2	0.0	0.0
10 Fianna Fáil	41.9	48.9	41.9	46.3	43.4	48.3	43.8	47.7
14 Fine Gael	23.1	20.5	19.8	25.8	32.0	26.6	32.0	34.1
15 Clann na Talmhan	10.3	10.8	5.6	2.9	3.8	2.4	1.5	-
16 National Labour	-	2.7	2.6	-	-	-	-	-
17 Clann na Poblachta	-	-	13.2	4.1	3.1	1.7	1.1	0.8
18 National Progressive Democrats	-	-	-	-	-	-	1.0	-
Others	9.0	8.4	8.3	9.6	5.7	6.4	5.7	2.1

Table 11.4c IRELAND Number of Seats Won in the Dáil 1943-1965[1]

	1943	1944	1948	1951	1954	1957	1961	1965
6 Sinn Féin II	–	–	–	–	–	4	0	–
8 Irish Labour Party	17	8	14	16	19 (1)	12 (1)	16 (1)	22 (1)
9 Communists	–	–	–	0	0	1	0	0
10 Fianna Fáil	6 (1)	76 (3)	68 (1)	69 (1)	65	78	70	72
14 Fine Gael	32	30 (1)	31	40	50	40	47	47
15 Clann na Talmhan	13	11	7	6	5	3	2	–
16 National Labour	–	4	5	–	–	–	–	–
17 Clann na Poblachta	–	–	10	2	3	1	1	1
18 National Progressive Democrats	–	–	–	–	–	–	2	–
Others	9	9	12	14	5	8	6	2
Total Seats	138 (1)	138 (4)	147 (1)	147 (1)	147 (1)	147 (1)	144 (1)	144 (1)

1 Figures in brackets represent the number of deputies returned unopposed. Since 1948 this is the Speaker of the Dáil.

Table 11.4d IRELAND Percentage of Seats Won in the Dáil 1943-1965

	1943	1944	1948	1951	1954	1957	1961	1965
6 Sinn Féin II	-	-	-	-	-	2.7	0.0	-
8 Irish Labour Party	12.3	5.8	9.5	10.9	12.9	8.2	11.1	15.3
9 Communists	-	-	-	0.0	0.0	0.7	0.0	0.0
10 Fianna Fáil	48.6	55.1	46.3	46.9	44.2	53.1	48.6	50.0
14 Fine Gael	23.2	21.7	21.1	27.2	34.0	27.2	32.6	32.6
15 Clann na Talmhan	9.4	8.0	4.8	4.1	3.4	2.0	1.4	-
16 National Labour	-	3.0	3.4	-	-	2.7	-	-
17 Clann na Poblachta	-	-	6.8	1.4	2.0	0.7	0.7	0.7
18 National Progressive Democrats	-	-	-	-	-	-	1.4	-
Others	6.5	6.5	8.2	9.5	3.4	5.4	4.2	1.4

Table 11.5a IRELAND Total Votes 1969-1989

	1969	1973	1977	1981	1982 (Feb.)	1982 (Nov.)	1987	1989
Electorate	1,735,388	1,783,604	2,118,606	2,275,450	2,275,450	2,335,153	2,445,515	2,448,810
Valid Votes	1,318,953	1,350,537	1,603,027	1,718,211	1,665,133	1,688,720	1,777,165	1,656,813
Invalid Votes	16,010	15,937	13,743	16,168	14,367	12,665	16,241	20,779
Total Votes	1,334,963	1,366,474	1,616,770	1,734,379	1,679,500	1,701,385	1,793,406	1,677,592
PARTY VOTES								
8 Irish Labour Party	224,498	184,656	186,410	169,990	151,875	158,115	114,551	156,989
9 Communists	242	466	544	358	462	259	725	342
10 Fianna Fáil	602,234	624,528	811,615	777,616	786,951	763,313	784,547	731,472
14 Fine Gael	449,749	473,781	488,767	626,376	621,088	662,284	481,127	485,307
19 Workers' Party	-	15,366	27,209	29,561	36,263	54,888	67,273	82,263
20 National H-Block Committee	-	-	-	42,803	-	-	-	-
21 Socialist Labour Party	-	-	-	7,107	-	-	-	-
22 Sinn Féin III	-	-	-	-	16,894	-	32,933	20,003
23 Democratic Socialist Party	-	-	-	-	-	7,012	7,424	9,836
24 Greens/Comhaontas Glas	-	-	-	-	-	3,716	7,159	24,827
25 Progressive Democrats	-	-	-	-	-	-	210,583	91,013
Others	42,230	51,740	88,668	64,400	51,600	39,133	70,843	54,761

Source: *Election Results and Transfer of Votes* 1969 ff; and for 1989, final figures of the Department of the Environment.

Table 11.5b IRELAND Percentage of Votes 1969-1989

	1969	1973	1977	1981	1982 (Feb.)	1982 (Nov.)	1987	1989
Total Votes	76.9	76.6	76.3	76.2	73.8	72.8	73.3	68.5
Valid Votes	76.0	75.7	75.7	75.5	73.2	72.3	72.7	67.7
Invalid Votes	0.9	0.9	0.6	0.7	0.6	0.5	0.7	0.8
Share Invalid	1.2	1.2	0.9	0.9	0.9	0.7	0.9	1.2
PARTY VOTES								
8 Irish Labour Party	17.0	13.7	11.6	9.9	9.1	9.4	6.4	9.5
9 Communists	0.0	0.0	0.0	0.0	0.0	0.0	0.0	0.0
10 Fianna Fáil	45.7	46.2	50.6	45.3	47.3	45.2	44.1	44.2
14 Fine Gael	34.1	35.1	30.5	36.5	37.3	39.2	27.1	29.3
19 Workers' Party	-	1.1	1.7	1.7	2.2	3.3	3.8	5.0
20 National H-Block Committee	-	-	-	2.5	-	-	-	-
21 Socialist Labour Party	-	-	-	0.4	-	-	-	-
22 Sinn Féin III	-	-	-	-	1.0	-	1.9	1.2
23 Democratic Socialist Party	-	-	-	-	-	0.4	0.4	0.6
24 Greens/Comhaontas Glas	-	-	-	-	-	0.2	0.4	1.5
25 Progressive Democrats	-	-	-	-	-	-	11.8	5.5
Others	3.2	3.9	5.6	3.7	3.1	2.3	4.0	3.3

Table 11.5c IRELAND Number of Seats Won in the Dáil 1969-1989[1]

	1969	1973	1977	1981	1982 (Feb.)	1982 (Nov.)	1987	1989
8 Irish Labour Party	18	19	17 (1)	15	15	16	12	15
9 Communists	0	0	0	0	0	0	0	0
10 Fianna Fáil	75 (1)	69 (1)	84	78 (1)	81	75	81	77
14 Fine Gael	50	54	43	65	63	70	51 (1)	55 (1)
19 Workers' Party	–	–	–	1	3	2	4	7
20 National H-Block Committee	–	–	–	2	–	–	–	–
21 Socialist Labour Party	–	–	–	1	–	–	–	0
22 Sinn Féin III	–	–	–	–	0	–	0	0
23 Democratic Socialist Party	–	–	–	–	–	0	1	1
24 Greens/Comhaontas Glas	–	–	–	–	–	0	0	1
25 Progressive Democrats	–	–	–	–	–	0	14	6
Others	1	2	4	4	4 (1)	3 (1)	3	4
Total Seats	144 (1)	144 (1)	148 (1)	166 (1)	166 (1)	166 (1)	166 (1)	166 (1)

1 The figure in brackets refers to the Speaker of the Dáil who is returned unopposed.

Source: *Election Results and Transfer of Votes*, 1969 ff., and for 1989 figures provided by the Department of the Environment.

Table 11.5d IRELAND Percentage of Seats Won in the Dáil 1969-1989

	1969	1973	1977	1981	1982 (Feb.)	1982 (Nov.)	1987	1989
8 Irish Labour Party	12.5	13.2	11.5	9.0	9.0	9.6	7.2	9.0
9 Communists	0.0	0.0	0.0	0.0	0.0	0.0	0.0	0.0
10 Fianna Fáil	52.1	47.9	56.8	47.0	48.8	45.2	48.8	46.4
14 Fine Gael	34.7	37.5	29.1	39.2	38.0	42.2	30.7	33.1
19 Workers' Party	–	–	–	0.6	1.8	1.2	2.4	4.2
20 National H-Block Committee	–	–	–	1.2	–	–	–	–
21 Socialist Labour Party	–	–	–	0.6	–	–	–	–
22 Sinn Féin III	–	–	–	–	0.0	–	0.0	0.0
23 Democratic Socialist Party	–	–	–	–	–	0.0	0.6	0.6
24 Greens/Comhaontas Glas	–	–	–	–	–	0.0	0.0	0.6
25 Progressive Democrats	–	–	–	–	–	–	8.4	3.6
Others	0.7	1.4	2.7	2.4	2.4	1.8	1.8	2.4

Chapter 12

ISRAEL

The British mandate in Palestine after the First World War continued the old Ottoman custom of governing through representatives of religous groups. The Jewish community in Palestine enjoyed a high degree of communal self-government. In 1920 an Assembly of the Elected (Asefhat Ha'Nivharim) was established. All members of the Jewish community aged 20 or over were entitled to vote. The Israeli party system developed from the system of the mandate period, and a number of post-independence Israeli parties first contested elections under the mandate.

Table 12.a MANDATE ELECTIONS, ASSEMBLY OF THE ELECTED

	1920 [1]	1925		1931		1944	
	Seats	Votes	Seats	Votes	Seats	Votes	Seats
Achdut Ha'avoda	70	8,834	54	–	–	–	–
Mapai	–	–		23,150	31	73,667	63
Hapoel Hatzair	41	5,337	30	–	–	–	–
Communists	–	1,028	6	–	–	3,948	3
Poale Zion Smol	–	–	–	1,793	2}		
					}	24,764	21
Hashomer Hatzair	–	–	–	812	1}		
Tenuat Achdut Ha'avoda	–	–	–	–	–	18,168	16
Centre Groups	63	11,625	69	14,892	23	40,960	35
Ethnic Groups	72	6,307	44	4,707	9	6,012	6
Religious Groups	68	2,856	18	4,107	5	29,707	27
Totals	314	35,987	221	49,461	71	197,226	171
Total lists in Assembly	20		26		10		16
Registered Voters	28,765	64,764		89,656		300,018	

1 No figures available for votes.

Source: Central Zionist Archives, Jerusalem.

Since the establishment of the state of Israel in 1948 the country's unicameral parliament, the Knesset, has been elected by universal adult suffrage under a system of proportional representation, with all of the 120 seats in the Knesset allocated on the basis of nationwide vote totals. In 1949 and since 1973 seats have been allocated according to the d'Hondt system of proportional representation; from 1951 to 1969, the largest remainder system was used. Since 1951 a party must win at least one per cent of the total valid votes in order to be included in the division of seats in the Knesset.

The ballot is secret. Every citizen aged 18 or over on December 31 of the year preceding the election is entitled to vote. The rapid growth of the population by immigration has increased the total number of persons eligible to vote more than fivefold since 1948. The electorate does not include the 1.5 million Palestinians living in the Gaza Strip and land on the West Bank of the Jordan occupied by Israel after the 1967 Six Days War. Apart from Jerusalem and the Golan Heights these territories have not been annexed and are therefore not included in the electorate (Arian, 1989: 27).

The existence of a nationwide proportional representation system and the social heterogeneity of the electorate have resulted in the creation of a large number of parties winning at least one seat in the Knesset. Some parties have joined alliances or presented joint lists, which affects coalition negotiations in the multi-party Knesset (Arian, 1985). The parties forming an electoral alliance retain their independent organization and can withdraw from it at any time. Historically, the main division in the Israeli party system was between the Labour party and its allies, and a group now organized as Likud. The Labour party and its predecessor Mapai contested elections from 1965 to 1984 as part of a broader list, the Alignment, including other parties, principally Mapam. Mapam withdrew from the Alignment after the formation of the Likud-Alignment Unity government in 1984 to fight future elections as a separate party. The Alignment list was challenged by the creation of Gahal in 1965, as a pact between Herut and the Liberal Party, the latter itself a merger of the Progressive and General Zionist parties. The alliance became known as Likud in 1973, sometimes including other smaller parties. In 1988 Likud was constituted as a single party merging organizations that had previously fought on a common list but as separate parties. A second major cleavage is between the religious parties on the one hand, and the basically secular grouping of Labour, its allies and the Herut bloc on the other. The former group are themselves divided between those who are Zionist in sympathy, the National Religious Party and breakaway groups such as Morasha and Tami, and those who are more or less anti-Zionist, the Aguda parties, Shas and Degel Hatorah (Arian 1989: 97). During the early years of the existence of the state of Israel Israeli Arabs tended to support ethnic parties more or less closely linked with Israeli parties, especially Mapai and the Labour Party. More recently the communist Rakah party and the Arab-Jewish Progressive List for Peace have received increasing support amongst Israeli Arabs (Arian and Shamir, 1986: 121-148).

Sources:

Arazi, A., *Le système électoral israélien* (Geneva: Droz, 1963)

Arian, A., (ed.) *The Elections in Israel - 1977* (Jersualem: Jerusalem Academic Press, 1980)

Arian, A. and M. Shamir, (eds.) *The Elections in Israel - 1984* (Tel Aviv: Romot and New Brunswick, U.S.A.: Transaction Books, 1986)

Arian A., *Politics in Israel: the Second Generation* (Chatham, NJ: Chatham House, 2nd ed., 1989)

Eisenstadt, S.N. *Israeli Society* (London: Weidenfeld & Nicolson, 1970)

Inspector General of Elections: *Results of Elections to the Eleventh Knesset* (Jerusalem, 1984)

Schiff, G.S., *Tradition and Politics: the Religious Parties in Israel* (Detroit: Wayne State University Press, 1977)

O. Seliktar, 'Israel: electoral cleavages in a nation in the making', in R. Rose (ed.), *Electoral Participation* (Beverly Hills and London: Sage, 1980) 191-240

Table 12.1 POLITICAL PARTIES AND ELECTORAL LISTS IN ISRAEL SINCE 1949 [1]

	Party Names	Elections Contested Years	Number
1	Mapai (Mifleget Poalei Eretz Israel - Workers' Party of the Land of Israel) [2]	1949-1965	6
2	General Zionists' (Zionim Klalim) [3]	1949-1959	4
3	Progressive Party (Miflaga Progresivit) [4]	1949-1959	4
4	Herut (Freedom Party) [5]	1949-1984	5
5	Maki (Miflaga Kommunistit Isre'elit - Communist Party of Israel) [6]	1949-1969	7
6	Minority Lists [7]	1949-1977	9
7	Mapam (Mifleget Ha'poalim Hameuhedet - United Workers' Party) [8]	1949ff	12
8	Agudat Israel (Association of Israel) [9]	1949ff	12
9	Poalei Agudat Israel (Union of Israel Workers) [10]	1949ff	12
10	Mizrachi (Merkaz Ruchani - Spiritual Centre) [11]	1949-1951	2
11	Hapoel Ha'mizrachi (Workers' Mizrachi Party) [12]	1949-1951	2
12	Sephardim Party	1949-1955	3
13	Yemenite Association	1949-1959	4
14	WIZO (Womens' International Zionist Organisation)	1949	1
15	Lehi (Lohamei Herut Israel - Fighters for Israel's Freedom)	1949	1
16	United Religious Front [13]	1949	1
17	National Religious Party (Mafdal - Miflaga Datit Leumit) [14]	1955ff	10
18	Achdut Ha'avoda Poalei Zion [15]	1955-1961	3
19	Liberal Party (Miflaga Haliberalit) [16]	1961-1984	7
20	Gahal (Gush-Herut Liberalim - Freedom Liberal Block) [17]	1965-1969	2
21	Alignment (Ma'arach) [18]	1965-1984	7
22	Independent Liberal Party (H'Miflaga H'Liberalit H'Atzmaeet) [19]	1965-1984	6
23	Rakah (Reshima Kommunistit Hadasha - New Communist Party) [20]	1965ff	7
24	Haolem Hazeh/Koach Hadash (This World/ New Force) [21]	1965-1973	3
25	Rafi (Reshimat Poalei Israel) [22]	1965-1968	2
26	Israel Labour Party (Mifleget Ha'avoda Ha'Israelit) [23]	1969ff	6
27	Free Centre (Hamerkaz Hahofshi) [24]	1969-1973	2
28	State List (Reshima Mamlachtit) [25]	1969-1973	2
29	Citizens' Rights Movement (Hatnuah Lezhiot Ha'ezrach) [26]	1973ff	5
30	Kach [27]	1973-1984	4

31	Likud (Union) [28]	1973ff	5
32	Moked (Focus) [29]	1973	1
33	Democratic Movement for Change (Dash - Hatnuah Hademokratit Le-shinui) [30]	1977	1
34	Hadash (Hazit Democratit le Shalom ve-Shivayon - Democratic Front for Peace and Equality) [31]	1977ff	4
35	Peace and Development (Pitua ve Shalom) [32]	1977-1984	3
36	Peace for Zion (Shlomzion) [33]	1977	1
37	Shelli (Shalom le'Israel - Shivion le'Israel - Peace in Israel - Equality in Israel) [34]	1977-1981	2
38	Shinui (Change) [35]	1981-1984	2
39	Tami (Tenua le'Masoret Israel - Movement for Israel's Tradition) [36]	1981-1984	2
40	Tehiya (Tenuat Hetehiya - Renaissance Movement) [37]	1981ff	3
41	Telem (Tenua le'Hithadshut Mamlachtit - Movement for State Renewal) [38]	1981	1
42	Morasha (Heritage) [39]	1984	1
43	Ometz (Courage) [40]	1984	1
44	Progressive List for Peace (Hareshima Ha'mitkademet le-Shalom) [41]	1984ff	2
45	Shas (Shomrei Torah Sephardim - Sephardi Torah Guardians) [42]	1984ff	2
46	Tsomet (Crossroads) [43]	1984ff	2
47	Yachad (Together) [44]	1984	1
48	Arab Democratic Party [45]	1988	1
49	Centre Party (Tnuat Hamerkaz - Shinui) [46]	1988	1
50	Degel Hatorah (Torah Flag) [47]	1988	1
51	Moledet (Homeland) [48]	1988	1

[1] In addition to political parties this table includes a number of long established electoral lists.

[2] Mapai was formed in 1930 by a merger of Achdut Ha'avoda (Unity of Labour) and Hapoel Hatzair (The Young Worker). In 1968 it merged with Achdut Ha'avoda Poalei Zion, which had broken away from Mapam in 1954, and Rafi, a splinter from Mapai, to form the Israel Labour Party.

[3] Merged with the Progressive Party to form the Liberal Party in 1961.

[4] Merged with the General Zionists to form the Liberal Party in 1961.

[5] Part of the Gahal Alliance in the 1965 and 1969 elections and thereafter the dominant partner in the Likud Alliance.

[6] Split in 1965, with a predominantly Arab grouping forming Rakah. In 1973 aligned with Haolem Hazeh as Meri - the Israel Radical Party - and in 1977 with various new left groups in Moked.

[7] Parties representing the Arab and Druze minorities affiliated with Mapai and later the Labour Party.

[8] Established in 1948 by Tenuat Achdut Ha'avoda, which had broken away from Mapai in 1944, Hashomer Hatzair (which had remained independent when other socialist groups united to form Mapai in 1930) and Poalei Zion Smol (Left Workers of Zion). From 1969 to 1984 Mapam participated in the Alignment List, but presented its own list in the 1988 election.

[9] Founded in Poland in 1913. In 1949 part of the Torah Religious Front list with Poalei Agudat Israel and the Mizrachi parties. In the 1955 and 1959 elections combined with Poalei Agudat Israel to form the Torah Religious Front.

10 Founded in Poland in 1922 as the labour wing of Agudat Israel. In 1949 part of the United Religious Front. In 1955 and 1959 participated in the Torah Religious Front, and in 1984, part of Morasha.

11 Established in Palestine in 1918. Part of the United Religious Front in the 1949 general election. Merged with Hapoel Ha'mizrachi to form the National Religious Party in 1956.

12 Breakaway from Mizrachi, founded in 1922. Part of the United Religious Front in the 1949 general election. Merged with Mizrachi to form the National Religious Party in 1955.

13 Electoral alliance of Agudat Israel, Poalei Agudat Israel, Mizrachi and Hapoel Ha'mizrachi.

14 Merger of Mizrachi and Hapoel Ha'mizrachi.

15 Broke away from Mapam in 1954. In 1965 participated in the Alignment list with Mapai and in 1968 merged with Mapai and Rafi to form the Israel Labour Party.

16 Merger of the General Zionist and Progressive Parties. Participated in the Gahal and Likud lists from 1965.

17 Electoral list combining the Liberal and Herut parties. Coalesced into the Likud list in the 1973 election.

18 Electoral list initially combining Mapai and Achdut Ha'avoda. After the merger of these two parties to form the Israeli Labour Party the Alignment was expanded to include Mapam. In the 1984 election the Alignment list also included the Independent Liberal Party.

19 Splinter, mostly of former Progressive Party members, from the Liberal Party, opposed to the latter's electoral alliance with Likud. It ran independent lists until 1984, when it was incorporated into the Labour-dominated Alignment. Elements of it were involved in forming the Centre Party in 1988.

20 Formed as a result of a split within Maki. A largely Arab party, since 1977 contesting elections as part of the list of the Democratic Front for Peace and Equality.

21 Party founded by Uri Avneri the owner of a popular magazine called *Ha'olem Hazeh*. In 1973 formed the Meri (Radical Party) list with leaders of Moked.

22 Splinter from Mapai, originally led by David Ben Gurion. Rejoined Mapai to found the Israel Labour Party in 1968.

23 Merger of Mapai, Achdut Ha'avoda Poalei Zion and Rafi in 1968.

24 Established in 1969 by Shmuel Tamir following a split in Herut. Contested the 1973 election as part of the Likud list. In 1977 Tamir and part of his grouping joined the Democratic Movement for Change, whilst the remainder of the group remained part of Likud.

25 Founded in 1969 by former members of Rafi opposed to its reunification with Mapai. From 1973 a component of Likud.

26 Founded in 1973 by Shulamit Aloni, a former Labour Party member of the Knesset.

27 Founded by Rabbi Meir Kahane, the former leader of the Jewish Defence League in the United States. The Central Election Committee refused to accept the Kach list before the 1984 election on the ground that it was racist, but the Israeli Supreme Court overturned this decision and Kach participated. Following changes in the electoral law in 1988 the Supreme Court upheld the Election Committee's ban on Kach.

28 Successor to the Gahal alliance incorporating Herut, the Liberal Party, Free Centre and the National List and later other right-wing parties. The Likud's component parties merged to form a single party in 1988.

29 Merger of Maki, the mainly Jewish communist party and Techelet-Adom, a left Zionist group. Formed part of the Shelli list in the 1977 and 1981 elections.

30 The Democratic Movement for Change was founded in November 1976 by a merger of Amnon Rubinstein's Shinui (Change) party, founded in 1973 and Yigael Yadin's Democratic Movement founded in May 1976.

31 Alliance comprising principally the Rakah communist party and part of the Black Panther Movement, Sephardi Jews protesting about alleged discrimination against themselves.

32 One-man list formed by Samuel Flatto-Sharon, whose election to the Knesset in 1977 gave him immunity from extradition to France,where he was convicted in his absence on fraud and tax evasion charges.

33 Formed by General Ariel Sharon. After the 1977 election the party merged with Herut.

34 Alliance of Moked, Haolem Hazeh and part of the Black Panther Movement.
35 Party led by Amnon Rubinstein, formerly part of the Democratic Movement for Change.
36 Breakaway led by Abu-Hatzeira from the National Religious Party. Merged with Likud in 1988.
37 Right-wing party formed by members of the Gush Emunin and the Land of Israel Movement in 1979. Two of its leaders, Geula Cohen and Moshe Shamir, were Likud deputies opposed to the 1981 Camp David agreement between Israel and Egypt.
38 Group formed by the former foreign Minister Moshe Dayan and former Finance Minister Yigael Hurwitz, consisting mostly of former members of Rafi. After Dayan died in October 1980, the two deputies elected on the Telem list in 1981 joined Likud.
39 A list headed by former deputies of Poalei Agudat Israel (Avraham Verdiger), the National Religious Party (Rabbi Chaim Druckman), and Tehiya (Hanan Porat).
40 Led by Yigael Hurwitz, a former leading figure in Telem, who had joined Likud after the dissolution of his own party in 1982 and had subsequently served as Finance Minister. Merged with Likud in 1988.
41 Alliance of part of Shelli and the Arab Progressive Movement, advocating the establishment of a Palestinian State in the West Bank and the Gaza Strip.
42 Breakaway from Agudat Israel, founded by Rabbi Yitzak Peretz in 1984.
43 Founded by Lieutenant-General Rafael Eitan, former Chief of Staff of the Israeli Defence Forces.
44 Founded in 1984 by General Ezer Weizman, a former Defence Minister. Merged with the Labour Party in 1986.
45 An Arab party led by Abd El-Wahab Daraoushe, elected to the Knesset as a Labour Party deputy in 1984.
46 Founded in February 1988 by the merger of Shinui and the Independent Liberal Party.
47 Breakaway from Agudat Israel.
48 Advocates the expulsion of the Arab population from territories occupied by Israel in 1967.

Table 12.2 DATES OF ELECTIONS : KNESSET

1	25 January 1949	7	28 October 1969
2	30 July 1951	8	31 December 1973
3	26 July 1955	9	17 May 1977
4	3 July 1959	10	30 June 1981
5	15 August 1961	11	23 July 1984
6	2 November 1965	12	1 November 1988

Table 12.3a ISRAEL Total Votes 1949-1965

	1949	1951	1955	1959	1961	1965
Electorate	506,507	924,885	1,057,795	1,218,483	1,274,880	1,449,709
Valid Votes	434,684	687,492	853,219	969,337	1,006,964	1,206,728
Invalid Votes	5,411	7,515	22,969	24,967	30,066	37,978
Total Votes	440,095	695,007	876,188	994,306	1,037,030	1,244,706

PARTY VOTES

	1949	1951	1955	1959	1961	1965
1 Mapai	155,274	256,456	274,735	370,585	349,330	–
21 Alignment	–	–	–	–	–	443,379
18 Achdut Ha'avoda	–	–	62,401	69,468	75,654	–
2 General Zionists	22,661	111,394	87,099	59,700	–	–
3 Progressive Party	17,786	22,171	37,661	44,889	–	–
4 Herut	49,782	45,651	107,190	130,515	138,599	–
20 Gahal	–	–	–	–	–	256,957
19 Liberal Party	–	–	–	–	137,255	–
5 Maki	15,148	27,334	38,492	27,374	42,111	13,617
6 Minority Lists	13,413	32,288	37,777	37,752	35,356	39,894
7 Mapam	64,018	86,095	69,475	58,043	66,170	79,985
8 Agudat Israel		13,799			37,178	39,795
		}	39,836[2]	45,569[2]	–	–
9 Poalei Agudat Israel		11,194			19,428	22,066
16 United Religious Front	52,982[1]	–	–	–	–	–
10 Mizrachi		10,383	–	–	–	–
11 Hapoel Ha'mizrachi		46,347	–	–	–	–
12 Sephardim Party	15,287	12,002	6,826	–	–	–
13 Yemenite Association	4,399	7,965	2,560	1,939	–	–
14 WIZO	5,173	–	–	–	–	–
15 Fighters for Israel's Freedom	5,363	–	–	–	–	–
17 National Religious Party	–	–	77,936	95,581	98,786	107,966
22 Independent Liberals	–	–	–	–	–	45,299
23 Rakah	–	–	–	–	–	27,413
24 New Force	–	–	–	–	–	14,124
25 Rafi	–	–	–	–	–	95,328
Others	13,398	4,413	11,231	27,952	7,077	20,905

1 United Religious Front combining Agudat Israel, Poalei Agudat Israel, Mizrachi and Hapoel Ha'mrizrachi.

2 Torah Religious Front.

Source: Inspector General of Elections, 1984.

Table 12.3b ISRAEL Percentage of Votes 1949-1965

	1949	1951	1955	1959	1961	1965
Total Votes	86.9	75.1	82.8	81.6	81.3	85.9
Valid Votes	85.8	74.3	80.7	79.6	79.0	83.2
Invalid Votes	1.1	0.8	2.2	2.0	2.4	2.6
Share Invalid	1.2	1.1	2.6	2.5	2.9	3.1
PARTY VOTES						
1 Mapai	35.7	37.3	32.2	38.2	34.7	-
21 Alignment	-	-	-	-	-	36.7
18 Achdut Ha'avoda	-	-	7.3	7.2	7.5	-
2 General Zionists	5.2	16.2	10.2	6.2	-	-
3 Progressive Party	4.1	3.2	4.4	4.6	-	-
4 Herut	11.5	6.6	12.6	13.5	13.8	-
20 Gahal	-	-	-	-	-	21.3
19 Liberal Party	-	-	-	-	13.6	-
5 Maki	3.5	4.0	4.5	2.8	4.2	1.1
6 Minority Lists	3.1	4.7	4.4	3.9	3.5	3.3
7 Mapam	14.7	12.5	8.1	6.0	6.6	6.6
8 Agudat Israel		2.0			3.7	3.2
		}	4.7	4.7		
9 Poalei Agudat Israel }		1.6	-	-	1.9	1.8
16 United Relgious Front	12.2	-	-	-	-	-
10 Mizrachi		1.5	-	-	-	-
11 Hapoel Ha'mizrachi	-	6.7	-	-	-	-
12 Sephardim Party	3.5	1.7	0.8	-	-	-
13 Yemenite Association	1.0	1.2	0.3	0.2	-	-
14 WIZO	1.2	-	-	-	-	-
15 Fighters for Israel's Freedom	1.2	-	-	-	-	-
17 National Religious Party	-	-	9.1	9.9	9.8	8.9
22 Independent Liberals	-	-	-	-	-	3.8
23 Rakah	-	-	-	-	-	2.3
24 New Force	-	-	-	-	-	1.2
25 Rafi	-	-	-	-	-	7.9
Others	3.1	0.6	1.3	2.9	0.7	1.7

Table 12.3c ISRAEL Number of Seats Won in the Knesset 1949-1965

	1949	1951	1955	1959	1961	1965
1 Mapai	46	45	40	47	42	–
21 Alignment	–	–	–	–		45[1]
18 Achdut Ha'avoda	–	–	9	8	9	–
2 General Zionists	7	20	13	8	–	–
3 Progressive Party	5	4	5	6	–	–
4 Herut	14	8	15	17	17	–
20 Gahal	–	–	–	–	–	26[2]
19 Liberal Party	–	–	–	–	17	–
5 Maki	4	5	6	3	5	1
6 Minority Lists	2	5	5	4	5	4
7 Mapam	19	15	10	9	7	8
8 Agudat Israel	3	3	4	4	4	4
9 Poalei Agudat Israel	3	2	2	2	2	2
10 Mizrachi	4	2	–	–	–	–
11 Hapoel Ha'mizrachi	6	8	–	–	–	–
12 Sephardim Party	4	2	0	–	–	–
13 Yemenite Association	1	1	0	0	–	–
14 WIZO	1	–	–	–	–	–
15 Fighters for Israel's Freedom	1	–	–	–	–	–
17 National Religious Party	–	–	11	12	12	11
22 Independent Liberals	–	–	–	–	–	5
23 Rakah	–	–	–	–	–	3
24 New Force	–	–	–	–	–	1
25 Rafi	–	–	–	–	–	10
Others	0	0	0	0	0	0
Total Seats	120	120	120	120	120	120

[1] Comprises Labour Party 37 seats and Achdut Ha'avoda eight seats.
[2] Comprises 15 Herut and 11 Liberals.

Source: Inspector General of Elections, 1984.

Table 12.3d ISRAEL Percentage of Seats Won in the Knesset 1949-1965

	1949	1951	1955	1959	1961	1965
1 Mapai	38.3	37.5	33.3	39.2	35.0	–
21 Alignment	–	–	–	–	–	37.5
18 Achdut Ha'avoda	–	–	7.5	6.7	7.5	–
2 General Zionists	5.8	16.7	10.8	6.7	–	–
3 Progressive Party	4.2	3.3	4.2	5.0	–	–
4 Herut	11.7	6.7	12.5	14.2	14.2	–
20 Gahal	–	–	–	–	–	21.7
19 Liberal Party	–	–	–	–	14.2	–
5 Maki	3.3	4.2	5.0	2.5	4.2	0.8
6 Minority Lists	1.7	4.2	4.2	3.3	4.2	3.3
7 Mapam	15.8	12.5	8.3	7.5	5.8	6.7
8 Agudat Israel	2.5	2.5	3.3	3.3	3.3	3.3
9 Poalei Agudat Israel	2.5	1.7	1.7	1.7	1.7	1.7
10 Mizrachi	3.3	1.7	–	–	–	–
11 Hapoel Ha'mizrachi	5.0	6.7	–	–	–	–
12 Sephardim Party	3.3	1.7	0.0	–	–	–
13 Yemenite Association	0.8	0.8	0.0	0.0	–	–
14 WIZO	0.8	–	–	–	–	–
15 Fighters for Israel's Freedom	0.8	–	–	–	–	–
17 National Religious Party	–	–	9.2	10.0	10.0	9.2
22 Independent Liberals	–	–	–	–	–	4.2
23 Rakah	–	–	–	–	–	2.5
24 New Force	–	–	–	–	–	0.8
25 Rafi	–	–	–	–	–	8.3
Others	0.0	0.0	0.0	0.0	0.0	0.0

Table 12.4a ISRAEL Total Votes 1969-1988

	1969	1973	1977	1981	1984	1988
Electorate	1,758,685	2,037,478	2,236,293	2,490,014	2,654,613	2,894,267
Valid Votes	1,367,743	1,566,855	1,747,820	1,937,366	2,073,321	2,283,132
Invalid Votes	60,238	34,243	23,906	17,243	18,081	22,444
Total Votes	1,427,981	1,601,098	1,771,726	1,954,609	2,091,402	2,305,576

PARTY VOTES

	1969	1973	1977	1981	1984	1988
21 Alignment[1]	632,035	621,183	430,023	708,536	724,074	685,363
20 Gahal	296,294	–	–	–	–	–
31 Likud	–	473,309	583,968	718,981	661,302	709,305
5 Maki	15,712	–	–	–	–	–
6 Minority Lists	47,989	48,961	24,185	–	–	–
7 Mapam	–	–	–	–	–	56,345
8 Agudat Israel	44,002		58,652	73,312	36,079	
	}	60,012			}	102,714
9 Poalei Agudat Israel[2]	24,968		23,571	17,090		
17 National Religious Party	133,238	130,349	160,787	95,232	73,530	89,720
22 Independent Liberals	43,933	56,560	20,384	11,764	–	–
23 Rakah	38,827	53,353	–	–	–	–
24 New Force	16,853	10,462	–	–	–	–
27 Free Centre	16,393	–	–	–	–	–
28 National List	42,654	–	–	–	–	–
29 Citizens' Rights	–	35,023	20,621	27,921	49,698	97,513
30 Kach	–	12,811	4,396	5,128	25,907	–
32 Moked	–	22,147	–	–	–	–
33 Democratic Movement	–	–	202,265	–	–	–
34 Hadash	–	–	80,118	64,918	69,815	84,032
35 Peace & Development	–	–	35,049	10,823	2,430	–
36 Peace for Zion	–	–	33,947	–	–	–
37 Shelli	–	–	27,281	8,691	–	–
38 Shinui	–	–	–	29,837	54,747	–
39 Tami	–	–	–	44,466	31,103	–
40 Tehiya	–	–	–	44,700		70,730
				}	83,037	
46 Tsomet	–	–	–	–		45,489
41 Telem	–	–	–	30,600	–	–
42 Morasha	–	–	–	–	33,287	–
43 Ometz	–	–	–	–	23,845	–
44 Progressives for Peace	–	–	–	–	38,012	33,695
45 Shas	–	–	–	–	63,605	107,709
47 Yachad	–	–	–	–	46,302	–
48 Arab Democratic Party	–	–	–	–	–	27,102
49 Centre Party	–	–	–	–	–	39,538
50 Degel Hatorah	–	–	–	–	–	34,279
51 Moledet	–	–	–	–	–	44,174
Others	14,845	42,678	46,969	51,535	94,560	27,012

[1] In 1984 comprises the Labour Party, Mapai and the Independent Liberal Party. In 1988 comprises the Labour Party and Yachad.

[2] In 1984 part of a joint list with Morasha.

Source: Inspector General of Elections, 1984; for 1988 definitive election figures provided by Israeli Embassy, London.

Table 12.4b ISRAEL Percentage of Votes 1969-1988

	1969	1973	1977	1981	1984	1988
Total Votes	81.2	78.6	79.2	78.5	78.8	79.7
Valid Votes	77.8	76.9	78.2	77.8	78.1	78.9
Invalid Votes	3.4	1.7	1.1	0.7	0.7	0.8
Share Invalid	4.2	2.1	1.3	0.9	0.9	1.0
PARTY VOTES						
21 Alignment	46.2	39.6	24.6	36.6	34.9	30.0
20 Gahal	21.7	–	–	–	–	–
31 Likud	–	30.2	33.2	37.1	31.9	31.1
5 Maki	1.1	–	–	–	–	–
6 Minority Lists	3.5	3.1	1.4	–	–	–
7 Mapam	–	–	–	–	–	2.5
8 Agudat Israel	3.2		3.4	3.8	1.7	
	}	3.8			}	4.5
9 Poalei Agudat Israel	1.8		1.3	0.9		
17 National Religious Party	9.7	8.3	9.2	4.9	3.5	3.9
22 Independent Liberals	3.2	3.6	1.2	0.6	–	–
23 Rakah	2.8	3.4	–	–	–	–
24 New Force	1.2	0.7	–	–	–	–
27 Free Centre	1.2	–	–	–	–	–
28 National List	3.1	–	–	–	–	–
29 Citizens' Rights	–	2.2	1.2	1.4	2.4	4.3
30 Kach	–	0.8	0.2	0.3	1.2	–
32 Moked	–	1.4	–	–	–	–
33 Democratic Movement	–	–	11.6	–	–	–
34 Hadash	–	–	4.6	3.4	3.4	3.7
35 Peace & Development	–	–	2.0	0.6	0.1	–
36 Peace for Zion	–	–	1.9	–	–	–
37 Shelli	–	–	1.6	0.4	–	–
38 Shinui	–	–	–	1.5	2.6	–
39 Tami	–	–	–	–	1.5	–
40 Tehiya	–	–	–	2.3		3.1
	–	–	–	– }	4.0	
46 Tsomet	–	–	–	–		2.0
41 Telem	–	–	–	1.6	–	–
42 Morasha	–	–	–	–	1.6	–
43 Ometz	–	–	–	–	1.2	–
44 Progressives for Peace	–	–	–	–	1.8	1.5
45 Shas	–	–	–	–	3.1	4.7
47 Yachad	–	–	–	–	2.2	–
48 Arab Democratic Party	–	–	–	–	–	1.2
49 Centre Party	–	–	–	–	–	1.7
50 Degel Hatorah	–	–	–	–	–	1.5
51 Moledet	–	–	–	–	–	1.9
Others	1.1	2.7	2.7	2.7	4.6	1.2

Table 12.4c ISRAEL Number of Seats Won in the Knesset 1969-1988

	1969	1973	1977	1981	1984	1988
21 Alignment[1]	56	51	32	47	44	39
20 Gahal[2]	26	–	–	–	–	–
31 Likud[3]	–	39	43	48	41	40
5 Maki	1	–	–	–	–	–
6 Minority Lists	4	3	1	–	–	–
7 Mapam	–	–	–	–	–	3
8 Agudat Israel	4	3	4	4	2	4
9 Poalei Agudat Israel	2	2	1	0	–	1
17 National Religious Party	12	10	12	6	4	5
22 Independent Liberals[4]	4	4	1	0	–	–
23 Rakah	3	4	–	–	–	–
24 New Force	2	0	–	–	–	–
27 Free Centre	2	–	–	–	–	–
28 National List	4	–	–	–	–	–
29 Citizens' Rights	–	3	1	1	3	5
30 Kach	–	0	0	0	1	–
32 Moked	–	1	–	–	–	–
33 Democratic Movement	–	–	15	–	–	–
34 Hadash	–	–	5	4	4	4
35 Peace & Development	–	–	1	0	–	–
36 Peace for Zion	–	–	2	–	–	–
37 Shelli	–	–	2	0	–	–
38 Shinui	–	–	–	2	3	–
39 Tami	–	–	–	3	1	–
40 Tehiya	–	–	–	3	4[6]	3
41 Telem	–	–	–	2	–	–
42 Morasha	–	–	–	–	2	–
43 Ometz	–	–	–	–	1	–
44 Progressives for Peace	–	–	–	–	2	1
45 Shas	–	–	–	–	4	6
46 Tsomet	–	–	–	–	1[6]	2
47 Yachad[5]	–	–	–	–	3	–
48 Arab Democratic Party	–	–	–	–	–	1
49 Centre Party	–	–	–	–	–	2
50 Degel Hatorah	–	–	–	–	–	2
51 Moledet	–	–	–	–	–	2
Others	0	0	0	0	0	0
Total Seats	120	120	120	120	120	120

1 Distribution of seats amongst the parties comprising the Alignment: 1969, Labour Party (including Rafi and Achdut Ha'avoda) 56 seats and Mapam seven seats; 1973 Labour Party 44 and Mapam 7; 1977 Labour Party 27 and Mapam five; 1981 Labour Party 40 and Mapam seven; 1984 Labour Party 37, Mapam six and Independent Liberal Party one and in 1988 Labour Party 38 and Yachad one.

2 Distribution of seats among parties forming Gahal; in Herut 15 and Liberal Party eleven.

3 The distribution of seats amongs parties forming Likud was; in 1973 Herut 17, Liberal Party 13, State List (La'am) 5, Free Centre 4; 1977 Herut 19, Liberals 15, State List 8, Achdut (Unity) a list headed by Hillel Zeidel, 1; 1981 Herut 25, Liberal Party 18, State List 5; 1984 Herut 25, Liberal Party 13, State List 3. By 1988 the Likud alliance had become a single party.

4 One deputy elected on the Alignment list in 1984.

5 One deputy elected on the Alignment list in 1988.

6 Elected on Tehiya-Tsomet joint list.

Source: Inspector General of Elections, 1984, and the Israeli Embassy, London.

Table 12.4d ISRAEL Percentage of Seats Won in the Knesset 1969-1988

	1969	1973	1977	1981	1984	1988
21 Alignment	46.7	42.5	26.7	39.2	36.7	32.5
20 Gahal	21.7	-	-	-	-	-
31 Likud	-	32.5	35.8	40.0	34.2	33.3
5 Maki	0.8	-	-	-	-	-
6 Minority Lists	3.3	2.5	0.8	-	-	-
7 Mapam	-	-	-	-	-	2.5
8 Agudat Israel	3.3	2.5	3.3	3.3	1.7	3.3
9 Poalei Agudat Israel	1.7	1.7	0.8	0.0	-	0.8
17 National Religious Party	10.0	8.3	10.0	5.0	3.3	4.2
22 Independent Liberals	3.3	3.3	0.8	0.0	-	-
23 Rakah	2.5	3.3	-	-	-	-
24 New Force	1.7	0.0	-	-	-	-
27 Free Centre	1.7	-	-	-	-	-
28 National List	3.3	-	-	-	-	-
29 Citizens' Rights	-	2.5	0.8	0.8	2.5	4.2
30 Kach	-	0.0	0.0	0.0	0.8	-
32 Moked	-	0.8	-	-	-	-
33 Democratic Movement	-	-	12.5	-	-	-
34 Hadash	-	-	4.2	3.3	3.3	3.3
35 Peace & Development	-	-	0.8	0.0	-	-
36 Peace for Zion	-	-	1.7	-	-	-
37 Shelli	-	-	1.7	0.0	-	-
38 Shinui	-	-	-	1.7	2.5	-
39 Tami	-	-	-	2.5	0.8	-
40 Tehiya	-	-	-	2.5	3.3	2.5
41 Telem	-	-	-	1.7	-	-
42 Morasha	-	-	-	-	1.7	-
43 Ometz	-	-	-	-	0.8	-
44 Progressives for Peace	-	-	-	-	1.7	0.8
45 Shas	-	-	-	-	3.3	5.0
46 Tsomet	-	-	-	-	0.8	1.7
47 Yachad	-	-	-	-	2.5	-
48 Arab Democratic Party	-	-	-	-	-	0.8
49 Centre Party	-	-	-	-	-	1.7
50 Degel Hatorah	-	-	-	-	-	1.7
51 Moledet	-	-	-	-	-	1.7
Others	0.0	0.0	0.0	0.0	0.0	0.0

Chapter 13

ITALY

The unification of Italy, largely completed by the occupation of Rome in 1870, resulted in the extension of the 1848 Piedmontese constitution to the rest of Italy. This provided for a nominated Senate (Senato) and a directly elected Chamber of Deputies (Camera dei Deputati). The franchise was very restricted. Only men aged over 25 who were literate and also met either minimum tax-payment or office-holding qualifications could vote, about eight per cent of that age group. A two-ballot single-member constituency system was used. If no candidate won an absolute majority of the vote, a run-off election was held between the two leading candidates. Apart from a brief experiment with a multi-member constituency plurality system from 1882 to 1891, the two-ballot system remained in use until 1919.

In 1882 the voting age was reduced to 21. Property and tax-payment qualifications were reduced and all men who had completed primary education were enfranchised. About one-quarter of the relevant age group was entitled to vote; by 1909 this proportion had increased to one-third. In 1912 the vote was extended to all men age 30 and over; men from 21 to 30 were qualified if they had either completed military service, finished primary school, paid minimum taxes or held certain official positions. These reforms extended the franchise to about 90 per cent of the adult male population. Universal male suffrage and the d'Hondt system of proportional representation were introduced in 1919.

Political parties were very slow to develop. Until the foundation of the Socialist Party in 1892 there were no organized nationwide parties. During the period of unification the Chamber was divided into two more or less distinct groups, the *Destra* (Right) and the *Sinistra* (Left). Governments were frequently formed by members of both groups and by the 1880s they had in effect coalesced into a 'broad liberal party of the centre, which monopolised political and public life' (Seton-Watson, 1967: 51). Deputies from Southern Italy, where electoral corruption and interference by government officials were endemic, always provided a solid bloc of support for the government. The growth of electoral support for the Socialist Party caused the Vatican to modify its initial opposition to Catholic participation in national politics. Beginning with the 1904 election the Church ceased to oppose voting in certain constituencies. Although Catholic organizations were mobilized in support of moderate and, in a very few constituencies, specifically Catholic candidates the formation of a Catholic political party was not sanctioned by the Vatican until the establishment of the Popular Party in 1919.

In 1922 Benito Mussolini became Prime Minister at the head of a cabinet of Liberals, Nationalists and Fascists. Because of widespread violence and intimidation by the government, the election of 1924 cannot be considered free. The non-fascist parties gained 35 per cent of the vote (Schepis, 1958: 55-57). During the next two years the non-fascist parties were suppressed and a one-party state established. The fall of Mussolini in 1943 was followed by the re-emergence of the political parties. In 1946 a referendum abolished the monarchy. At the same time a Constituent Assembly was elected, and a new Constitution for the Republic of Italy came into force at the beginning of 1948.

The new Constitution provided for a two-chamber parliament consisting of a Senate and Chamber of Deputies directly elected by universal adult suffrage. The minimum voting age for the Chamber was 21. Deputies are chosen by proportional representation using the Imperiali system, a version of the d'Hondt system with an initial divisor of two rather than one. If all the seats in the Chamber have not been allocated at the constituency level, surplus votes are collected into a national pool where a second distribution takes place using the largest remainder method. In the single-member Val d'Aosta constituency the pre-1919 two-ballot majority system was retained in 1946 and 1948. In 1953 it was replaced by the plurality system.

Before the 1953 election an electoral law was passed which provided that any party or alliance of parties which won more than half of the total vote should be awarded 380 of the 590 seats in the Chamber. The Christian Democrats and their allies narrowly failed to win half the votes, and in 1956 the former electoral law was restored. The voting age was reduced to 18 in 1975.

The Senate now comprises 315 elected members, six nominated for life by the President of the Republic and, *ex officio*, former Presidents of the Republic. The suffrage for Senate elections is the same as for the Chamber of Deputies, except that the minimum voting age is twenty five. The constitution originally provided for each region to have one Senator for every 200,000 inhabitants in excess of 100,000, but with a minimum number of six. The 1963 constitutional reform established a fixed number of elected Senators, 315 with a minimum of seven per region (except for the two-member Molise region and the single-member Val d'Aosta). There are 238 single member constituencies. Any candidate who wins more than 65 per cent of the vote in his constituency is automatically elected. In practice this virtually never happens. In each of the three Senate elections held since 1979 only one Senator was so chosen (Di Virgilio, 1987 : 93). The votes cast in those districts where no candidate is elected are grouped at the regional level where the seats are distributed between the parties by the d'Hondt system of proportional representation.

Sources:

M. Amoraso, 'Italy', in G. Hand, J. Georgel and C. Sasse (eds.), *European Electoral Systems Handbook* (London: Butterworth, 1979) 140-70

M. Caciagli and P. Scaramozzino (eds.), *Il voto di chi non vota: l'astensionismo elettorale in Italia e in Europa* (Milan: Edizioni di Comunità, 1983)

A. Di Virgilio, 'Riforma elettorale e collegio unominale', *Quaderni dell 'Osservatorio Elettorale*, 19 (1987), 89-120

P. Farneti, 'Social conflict, parliamentary fragmentation, institutional shift and the rise of fascism: Italy', in J. Linz and A. Stepan (eds.), *The Breakdown of Democratic Regimes* (Baltimore: Johns Hopkins University Press, 1978) 3-31

O. Focardi, 'I partiti politici alle elezioni generali del 1895', *Giornale degli Economisti*, 11 (1895), 133-180

C. Ghini, *Le elezioni in Italia, 1946-1968* (Milan: Edizioni del Calendario, 1968)

U. Giusti, *Le correnti politiche italiane attraverso due riformi elettorali dal 1909 al 1921* (Florence: Alfani e Venturi, 1922)

A. Mastropaolo, 'Electoral processes, political behaviour, and social forces in Italy from the rise of the left to the fall of Giolitti, 1876-1913', in O. Busch (ed.), *Wählerbewegung in der Europäischer Geschichte*. (Berlin: Colloquium Verlag, 1980) 97-124

Ministero dell'Interno, *Elezione della Camera dei Deputati 1948* (Rome: Istituto Poligrafico dello Stato, 1949) and subsequent volumes in the same series

Ministero dell'Interno, *Compendio dei risultati delle elezioni politiche dal 1848 al 1958* (Rome: Istituto Poligrafico dello Stato, 1963)

G. Schepis, *Le consultazioni popolari in Italia dal 1848 al 1957: profilo storico-statistico* (Empoli: Editrice Caparrini, 1958)

A. Schiavi, 'Le ultime elezioni politiche italiane', *La Riforma Sociale*, 14 (1904), 979-988 and 15 (1905), 127-160

A. Schiavi, *Come hanno votati gli elettori italiani* (Milan:Avanti! 1914)

C. Seton-Watson, *Italy from Liberalism to Fascism* (London: Methuen, 1967)

A. Torresin, 'Statistica delle elezioni generali politiche del giugno 1900', *La Riforma Sociale*, 10 (1900) 788-831

Table 13.1 POLITICAL PARTIES IN ITALY 1895-1987

	Party Names	Elections Contested Years	Number
1	Ministerial and Opposition Liberals [1]	1895-1921	8
2	Radical Party (Partito Radicale)	1895-1919	7
3	Socialist Party (Partito Socialista Italiano - PSI) [2]	1895-1963; 1972ff	16
4	Republican Party (Partito Repubblicano Italiano)	1895ff	17
5	Catholics (Cattolici and Conservatori Cattolici) [3]	1904-1913	3
6	Independent Socialists (Socialisti Independenti)	1913-1921	3
7	Reformist Socialist Party (Partito Socialista Riformista Italiano - PSRI) [4]	1913-1919	2
8	Economic Party (Partito Economico)	1919-1921	2
9	Ex-Servicemen (Combattenti)	1919-1921	2
10	Popular Party (Partito Popolare Italiano)	1919-1921	2
11	Communist Party (Partito Comunista Italiano - PCI)	1921ff	12
12	Fascist Party (Partito Nazionale Fascista)	1921	1
13	Slovene minority [5]	1921; 1963-1968; 1976; 1983	5
14	Deutscher Verband [6]	1921	1
15	Sardinian Action Party (Partito Sardo d'Azione - PSd'A)	1921;1946-1958; 1968; 1979ff	8
16	Action Party (Partito d'Azione - Pd'A)	1946	1
17	Christian Democrats (Democrazia Cristiana - DC)	1946ff	9
18	Common Man Front (Fronte dell'Uomo Qualunque)	1946	1
19	Liberal Party (Partito Liberale Italiano - PLI) [7]	1946ff	11
20	Monarchist Party. In 1946 Blocco Nazionale della Libertà. From 1948 to 1958 Partito Nazionale Monarchico - PNM. From 1963 Partito Democratico di Unità Monarchica - PDIUM [8]	1946-1968	7
21	Peasants' Party (Partito Contadini d'Italia - PCd'I) [9]	1946-1948; 1953	3
22	Sicilian Independence Movement (Movimento per l'Independenza della Sicilia); in 1948 Union of Federalist Movements (Unione Movimenti Federalisti) [10]	1946-1948	2
23	Social Democrats. In 1948 Partito Socialista dei Lavoratori Italiani - PSLI. From 1953 Partito Socialista Democratico Italiano - PSDI) [11]	1948-1963;1972ff	10
24	Italian Social Movement (Movimento Sociale Italiano - MSI); since 1972 Movimento Sociale Italiano - Destra Nazionale - MSI - DN) [12]	1948ff	10

25	South Tyrol People's Party (Südtiroler Volkspartei - SVP)	1948ff	10
26	Community (Comunità - Concentrazione della Cultura, degli Operaii et dei Contadini d'Italia) [13]	1958	1
27	Popular Monarchist Party (Partito Monarchico Popolare - PMP) [14]	1958	1
28	Val d'Aosta Union (Union Valdôtaine)	1958ff	8
29	Piedmontese Regional Autonomist Movement (Movimento Autonomista Regionale Piemontese - MARP)	1958	1
30	Socialist Party of Proletarian Unity (Partito Socialista Italiano di Unità Proletaria - PSIUP) [15]	1968-1972	2
31	United Socialist Party (Partito Socialista Unificato - PSU) [16]	1968	1
32	Manifesto/Party of Proletarian Unity for Communism (Manifesto/Partito di Unità Proletaria per il Comunismo - PdUP) [17]	1972-1983	4
33	Workers' Political Movement (Movimento Politica dei Lavoratori - MPL) [18]	1972	1
34	Radical Party (Partito Radicale - PR)	1976ff	4
35	Continuous Struggle (Lotta Continua)	1976	1
36	Workers' Vanguard (Avanguardia Operaia)	1976	1
37	Proletarian Democracy (Democrazia Proletaria - DP) [19]	1979ff	3
38	Friuli Movement (Moviment Friûl/Movimento Friuli)	1979ff	3
39	Trieste List (Lista per Trieste)	1979-1983	2
40	National Pensioners' Party (Partito Nazionale dei Pensionati - PNP)	1983	1
41	Venetian League (Liga Veneta)	1983	1
42	Lombard League (Lega Lombarda)	1987	1
43	Piedmont-Regional Autonomy (Piemont-Autonomia Regionale)	1987	1
44	Piedmont (Piemont)	1987	1
45	Greens (Federazione delle Liste Verdi) [20]	1987	1

[1] Includes all the variously named liberal parliamentary groups. For details see Giusti, 1922, Schepis, 1958 and Farneti, 1978.

[2] The party was renamed the Partito Socialista Italiano di Unità Proletaria in 1943 when it united with the Movimento per l'Unità Proletaria, which had emerged from the underground socialist movement. It reverted to its original name after the party split following the 1947 Rome Congress. The party was reunited with the Social Democrats as the Partito Socialista Unificato from 1966 to 1969.

[3] A *tendance* including different Catholic groups.

[4] Right-wing socialists expelled from the PSI in 1913.

[5] Lists representing the interests of the Slovene-speaking population in Istria annexed by Italy after the First World War. Since 1968 the Slovenska Skupnost (Slovene Union).

[6] Alliance of the Tiroler Volkspartei and the Freiheitliche Partei in the German-speaking South Tyrol annexed by Italy after the First World War.

7 In 1946 the Unione Democratica Nazionale and in 1948 the Blocco Nazionale.

8 After rejoining the breakaway Popular Monarchist Party in 1959, the Partito Democratico di Unità Monarchica - PDIUM. Merged with MSI to form the National Right in 1972.

9 Regional party in Piedmont. Leading figures in the party stood on Monarchist Party lists in 1953. Part of Comunità electoral alliance in 1958.

10 The left wing of the Movement formed part of the PSI-PCI Popular Democratic Front in the 1948 elections. The rest of the party contested the election as the Unione Movimenti Federalisti.

11 A centrist breakaway from the Socialist Party led by Giuseppe Saragat. In 1952 the PSLI merged with the Partito Socialista Unitario led by Giuseppe Romita, formed by another centrist breakaway from the PSI in 1949 and a left-wing PSLI faction. The PSDI was reunited with the PSI in 1966, but a split re-occurred in 1969.

12 Merged with the PDIUM in 1972 to form the MSI-DN.

13 An electoral alliance formed by several regional groups including the Sardinian Action Party and the Peasants' Party

14 A breakaway group from the Partito Nazionale Monarchico. Reunited with the PNM to form the PDIUM in 1959.

15 Left-wing breakaway from the PSI founded in 1964. Merged with the Communist Party in 1972.

16 Partito Socialista Unificato (PSI-PSDI unificati, Sezione Italiana dell'Internazionale Socialista). Merger of the PSI and the PSDI, which lasted from 1966 to 1969.

17 The Manifesto Movement was a breakaway from the Communist Party in 1971, which combined with other far-left groups, including some ex-members of the PSIUP, to form the PdUP in 1972. The PdUP merged with the PCI in 1984.

18 Left wing Catholic party led by a former Christian Democratic deputy whose leaders later joined either the PCI or the PdUP.

19 In the 1979 election New United Left (Nuova Sinistra Unita), an alliance of Democrazia Proletaria (a merger of part of the PdUP and Workers' Vanguard formed in 1977), Continuous Struggle and independent leftist candidates.

20 Literally, Federation of Green Lists.

Table 13.2 DATES OF ELECTIONS : CAMERA DEI DEPUTATI [1]

1.	26 May, 2 June 1895	11.	7 June 1953
2.	21,28 March 1897	12.	25 May 1958
3.	3,10 June 1900	13.	28 April 1963
4.	6,13 November 1904	14.	19 May 1968
5.	7,14 March 1909	15.	7 May 1972
6.	26 October, 2 November 1913	16.	20 June 1976
7.	16 November 1919	17.	3 June 1979
8.	15 May 1921	18.	26 June 1983
9.	2 June 1946 [2]	19.	14 June 1987
10.	18 April 1948		

1 From 1895 to 1913 the pair of dates refer to the first and second ballots.

2 Election of a constituent assembly.

Sources: Ministero dell'Interno, 1963: 2-5, and Ministero dell'Interno 1968ff.

Table 13.3a ITALY Total Votes 1895-1921

	1895	1897	1900	1904	1909	1913	1919	1921
Electorate	2,121,185	2,120,909	2,248,509	2,541,327	2,930,473	8,443,205	10,239,326	11,477,210
Valid Votes	1,221,598	1,208,140	1,269,061	1,527,180	1,827,865	5,014,921	5,684,833	6,608,141
Invalid Votes	34,646	33,346	41,419	66,706	75,822	85,694	108,674	93,355
Total Votes	1,256,244	1,241,486	1,310,480	1,593,886	1,903,687	5,100,615	5,793,507	6,701,496
PARTY VOTES								
1 Ministerial and Opposition Liberals	979,958	994,083	935,116	989,929	1,144,532	2,804,165	2,016,889	2,846,745[2]
2 Radical Party	142,356	51,207	89,872	128,002	181,242	588,193	110,697	-
3 Socialist Party	82,523	108,086	164,946	326,016	347,615	883,409	1,834,792	1,631,435
4 Republican Party	0	54,764	79,127	75,225	81,461	173,666	118,618[1]	124,924
5 Catholics	-	-	-	8,008	73,015	301,949	-	-
6 Independent Socialists	-	-	-	-	-	67,133	33,938	37,892
7 Reformist Socialist Party	-	-	-	-	-	196,406	82,172	-
8 Economic Party	-	-	-	-	-	-	87,450	53,382
9 Ex Servicemen	-	-	-	-	-	-	232,923	78,391
10 Popular Party	-	-	-	-	-	-	1,167,354	1,347,305
11 Communist Party	-	-	-	-	-	-	-	304,719
12 Fascist Party	-	-	-	-	-	-	-	29,545
13 Slovene Minority	-	-	-	-	-	-	-	39,864
14 Deutscher Verband	-	-	-	-	-	-	-	48,784
15 Sardinian Action Party	-	-	-	-	-	-	-	35,448
Others	16,761	-	-	-	-	-	-	29,703

1 Includes 65,412 votes cast for joint lists of Radicals, Republicans, Socialists and Ex-Servicemen.
2 Includes 1,260,007 votes cast for the Blocco Nazionale, an electoral alliance of liberals, nationalists and fascists.

Sources: Ministero dell'Interno, 1963: 4-5, 46-47, 114-119,Torresin, 1900: 819 and 826, Giusti, 1922: 78-79.

Table 13.3b ITALY Percentage of Votes 1895-1921

	1895	1897	1900	1904	1909	1913	1919	1921
Total Votes	59.2	58.5	58.3	62.7	65.0	60.4	56.6	58.4
Valid Votes	57.6	57.0	56.4	60.1	62.4	59.4	55.5	57.6
Invalid Votes	1.6	1.6	1.8	2.6	2.6	1.0	1.1	0.8
Share Invalid	2.8	2.7	3.2	4.2	4.0	1.7	1.9	1.4
PARTY VOTES								
1 Ministerial and Opposition Liberals	80.2	82.3	73.7	64.8	62.6	55.9	35.5	43.1
2 Radical Party	11.7	4.2	7.1	8.4	9.9	11.7	1.9	–
3 Socialist Party	6.8	8.9	13.0	21.3	19.0	17.6	32.3	24.7
4 Republican Party	0.0	4.5	6.2	4.9	4.5	3.5	2.1	1.9
5 Catholics	–	–	–	0.5	4.0	6.0	–	–
6 Independent Socialists	–	–	–	–	–	1.3	0.6	0.6
7 Reformist Socialist Party	–	–	–	–	–	3.9	1.4	–
8 Economic Party	–	–	–	–	–	–	1.5	0.8
9 Ex Servicemen	–	–	–	–	–	–	4.1	1.2
10 Popular Party	–	–	–	–	–	–	20.5	20.4
11 Communist Party	–	–	–	–	–	–	–	4.6
12 Fascist Party	–	–	–	–	–	–	–	0.4
13 Slovene Minority	–	–	–	–	–	–	–	0.6
14 Deutscher Verband	–	–	–	–	–	–	–	0.7
15 Sardinian Action Party	–	–	–	–	–	–	–	0.5
Others	1.4	–	–	–	–	–	–	0.4

Table 13.3c ITALY Number of Seats Won in the Camera dei Deputati 1895-1921

	1895	1897	1900	1904	1909	1913	1919	1921
1 Ministerial and Opposition Liberals	438	437	412	415	382	310	197	221[1]
2 Radical Party	47	29	34	37	45	73	12	-
3 Socialist Party	15	16	33	29	41	52	156	123
4 Republican Party	-	26	29	24	24	17	9	6
5 Catholics	-	-	-	3	16	29	-	-
6 Independent Socialists	-	-	-	-	-	8	1	1
7 Reformist Socialist Party	-	-	-	-	-	19	6	-
8 Economic Party	-	-	-	-	-	-	7	5
9 Ex Servicemen	-	-	-	-	-	-	20	7
10 Popular Party	-	-	-	-	-	-	100	108
11 Communist Party	-	-	-	-	-	-	-	15
12 Fascist Party	-	-	-	-	-	-	-	37[2]
13 Slovene Minority	-	-	-	-	-	-	-	5
14 Deutscher Verband	-	-	-	-	-	-	-	4
15 Sardinian Action Party	-	-	-	-	-	-	-	3
Others	8	-	-	-	-	-	-	0
Total Seats	508	508	508	508	508	508	508	535

1 Includes 70 deputies elected as part of the Blocco Nazionale.
2 Includes 35 deputies elected as part of the Blocco Nazionale.

Sources: Ministero dell'Interno, 1963: 71-77, 136-139; Torresin, 1900: 824.

Table 13.3d ITALY Percentage of Seats Won in the Camera Dei Deputati 1895-1921

	1895	1897	1900	1904	1909	1913	1919	1921
1 Ministerial and Opposition Liberals	86.2	85.0	81.1	81.7	75.2	61.0	38.8	41.3
2 Radical Party	9.3	5.7	6.7	7.3	8.9	14.4	2.4	–
3 Socialist Party	3.0	3.1	6.5	5.7	8.1	10.2	30.7	23.0
4 Republican Party	–	5.1	5.7	4.7	4.7	3.3	1.8	1.1
5 Catholics	–	–	–	0.6	3.1	5.7	–	–
6 Independent Socialists	–	–	–	–	–	1.6	0.2	0.2
7 Reformist Socialist Party	–	–	–	–	–	3.7	1.2	–
8 Economic Party	–	–	–	–	–	–	1.4	0.9
9 Ex Servicemen	–	–	–	–	–	–	3.9	1.3
10 Popular Party	–	–	–	–	–	–	19.7	20.2
11 Communist Party	–	–	–	–	–	–	–	2.8
12 Fascist Party	–	–	–	–	–	–	–	6.9
13 Slovene Minority	–	–	–	–	–	–	–	0.9
14 Deutscher Verband	–	–	–	–	–	–	–	0.7
15 Sardinian Action Party	–	–	–	–	–	–	–	0.6
Others	1.6	–	–	–	–	–	–	0.0

Table 13.4a ITALY Total Votes 1946-1968

	1946	1948	1953	1958	1963	1968
Electorate	28,005,449	29,117,554	30,267,080	32,436,022	34,201,660	35,566,681
Valid Votes	23,016,464	26,268,912	27,092,743	29,560,269	30,758,031	31,803,253
Invalid Votes	1,930,723	585,291	1,218,108	839,439	1,008,027	1,199,996
Total Votes	24,947,187	26,854,203	28,410,851	30,399,708	31,766,058	33,003,249

PARTY VOTES

	1946	1948	1953	1958	1963	1968
11 Communist Party	4,358,243	} 8,137,047	6,121,922	6,704,454	7,768,228	8,557,404
3 Socialist Party	4,765,665		3,441,305	4,206,726	4,257,300	-
31 United Socialist Party	-	-	-	-	-	4,605,832
23 Social Democrats	-	1,858,346	1,223,251	1,345,447	1,876,409	-
4 Republican Party	1,100,776[2]	652,477	437,988	405,782	420,419	626,567
13 Slovene minority	-	-	-	-	5,679	4,521
15 Sardinian Action Party[1]	78,554	61,919	27,228	-	-	40,842
16 Action Party	334,877	-	-	-	-	-
17 Christian Democrats	8,102,828	12,741,299	10,864,282	12,520,207	11,745,262	12,407,172
18 Common Man Front	1,210,021	-	-	-	-	-
19 Liberal Party	1,560,037	1,004,889	816,267	1,047,718	2,143,954	1,851,060
20 Monarchist Party	636,330	729,174	1,855,842	659,997	536,991	414,423
21 Peasants' Party	102,393	96,025	-	-	-	-
22 Sicilian Independence	171,201	52,600	-	-	-	-
24 Social M'ment - MSI	-	526,670	1,580,293	1,407,718	1,569,815	1,414,794
25 South Tyrol People's Party	-	124,385	122,792	135,491	135,458	152,954
26 Community	-	-	-	173,227	-	-
27 Popular Monarchist Party	-	-	-	776,919	-	-
28 Val d'Aosta Union	-	-	-	30,596	31,844	31,557
29 MARP	-	-	-	70,519	-	-
30 Socialist Party of Proletarian Unity	-	-	-	-	-	1,414,544
Others	697,932	-	601,573	75,468	266,672	281,583

1 Participated in the 1958 election as part of the Community list

2 Includes 97,690 votes cast for the Concentrazione Democratica Repubblicana.

Sources: Ministero dell'Interno, 1963:4 and *Elezioni della Camera dei Deputati, 1948-1968.*

Table 13.4b ITALY Percentage of Votes 1946-1968

	1946	1948	1953	1958	1963	1968
Total Votes	89.1	92.2	93.5	93.7	92.9	92.8
Valid Votes	82.2	90.2	89.5	91.1	89.9	89.4
Invalid Votes	6.9	2.0	4.0	2.6	2.9	3.4
Share Invalid	7.7	2.2	4.3	2.8	3.2	3.6
PARTY VOTES						
11 Communist Party	18.9		22.6	22.7	25.3	26.9
	}	31.0				
3 Socialist Party	20.7		12.7	14.2	13.8	-
31 United Socialist Party	-	-	-	-	-	14.5
23 Social Democrats	-	7.1	4.5	4.6	6.1	-
4 Republican Party	4.8	2.5	1.6	1.4	1.4	2.0
13 Slovene minority	-	-	-	-	0.0	0.0
15 Sardinian Action Party	0.3	0.2	0.1	-	-	0.1
16 Action Party	1.5	-	-	-	-	-
17 Christian Democrats	35.2	48.5	40.1	42.4	38.2	39.0
18 Common Man Front	5.3	-	-	-	-	-
19 Liberal Party	6.8	3.8	3.0	3.5	7.0	5.8
20 Monarchist Party	2.8	2.8	6.8	2.2	1.7	1.3
21 Peasants' Party	0.5	0.4	-	-	-	-
22 Sicilian Independence	0.7	0.2	-	-	-	-
24 Social M'ment - MSI	-	2.0	5.8	4.8	5.1	4.4
25 South Tyrol People's Party	-	0.5	0.5	0.5	0.4	0.5
26 Community	-	-	-	0.6		
27 Popular Monarchist Party	-	-	-	2.6	-	-
28 Val d'Aosta Union	-	-	-	0.1	0.1	0.1
29 MARP	-	-	-	0.2	-	-
30 Socialist Party of Proletarian Unity	-	-	-	-	-	4.4
Others	2.6	1.1	2.2	0.3	0.9	0.9

Table 13.4c ITALY Number of Seats Won in the Camera Dei Deputati 1946-1968

	1946	1948	1953	1958	1963	1968
11 Communist Party	104	131	143	140	166	177
3 Socialist Party	115	52	75	84	87	–
31 United Socialist Party	–	–	–	–	–	91
23 Social Democrats	–	33	19	22	32	–
4 Republican Party	25[1]	9	5	6	6	9
13 Slovene minority	–	–	–	–	0	0
15 Sardinian Action Party	2	1	0	–	–	0
16 Action Party	7	–	–	–	–	–
17 Christian Democrats	207	305	263	273	260	266
18 Common Man Front	30	–	–	–	–	–
19 Liberal Party	41	19	13	17	40	31
20 Monarchist Party	16	14	40	11	8	6
21 Peasants' Party	–	–	–	–	–	–
22 Sicilian Independence	4	–	–	–	–	–
24 Social M'ment-MSI	–	6	29	24	27	24
25 South Tyrol People's Party	–	3	3	3	3	3
26 Community Front	–	–	–	1	–	–
27 Popular Monarchist Party	–	–	–	14	–	–
28 Val d'Aosta Union	–	–	–	1	1	0
29 MARP	–	–	–	–	–	–
30 Socialist Party of Proletarian Unity	–	–	–	–	–	23
Others	5	1	0	0	0	0
Total Seats	556	574	590	596	630	630

[1] Including two seats won by the Concentrazione Democratica Repubblicana, whose deputies later joined the Republican Party.

Sources: Ministero dell 'Interno, 1963:483; *Elezioni della Camera dei Deputati; 1948-1968.*

Table 13.4d ITALY Percentage of Seats Won in the Camera dei Deputati 1946-1968

	1946	1948	1953	1958	1963	1968
11 Communist Party	18.7	22.8	24.2	23.5	26.3	28.1
3 Socialist Party	20.7	9.1	12.7	14.1	13.8	-
31 United Socialist Party	-	-	-	-	-	14.4
23 Social Democrats	-	5.7	3.2	3.7	5.1	-
4 Republican Party	4.5	1.6	0.8	1.0	1.0	1.4
13 Slovene minority	-	-	-	-	0.0	0.0
15 Sardinian Action Party	0.4	0.2	0.0	-	-	0.0
16 Action Party	1.3	-	-	-	-	-
17 Christian Democrats	37.2	53.1	44.6	45.8	41.3	42.2
18 Common Man Front	5.4	-	-	-	-	-
19 Liberal Party	7.4	3.3	2.2	2.9	6.3	4.9
20 Monarchist Party	2.9	2.4	6.8	1.8	1.4	1.0
21 Peasants' Party	-	-	-	-	-	-
22 Sicilian Independence Movement	0.7	-	-	-	-	-
24 Social M'ment MSI	-	1.0	4.9	4.0	4.3	3.8
25 South Tyrol Peoples Party	-	0.5	0.5	0.5	0.5	0.5
26 Community	-	-	-	0.2	-	-
27 Popular Monarchist	-	-	-	-	-	-
28 Val d'Aosta Union	-	-	-	0.2	0.2	0.0
29 MARP	-	-	-	-	-	-
30 Socialist Party of Proletarian Unity	-	-	-	-	-	3.7
Others	0.9	0.2	0.0	0.0	0.0	0.0

Table 13.5a ITALY Total Votes 1972-1987

	1972	1976	1979	1983	1987
Electorate	37,049,654	40,423,131	42,181,664	43,936,534	45,583,499
Valid Votes	33,402,246	36,718,525	36,929,707	36,901,170	38,573,054
Invalid Votes	1,121,860	1,022,879	1,502,521	2,213,151	2,675,292
Total Votes	34,524,106	37,741,404	38,112,228	39,114,321	41,248,346
PARTY VOTES					
3 Socialist Party	3,208,317	3,541,353	3,591,579	4,221,785	5,501,980
4 Republican Party	954,270	1,135,089	1,107,826	1,874,638	1,428,358
11 Communist Party	9,069,774	12,620,750	11,129,262	11,029,355[1]	10,249,690
32 Proletarian Unity - PdUP	224,303		502,389	–	–
35 Continuous Struggle	–	} 555,951	–	–	–
36 Workers' Vanguard	–		–	–	–
13 Slovene minority	–	4,763	–	5,523	–
15 Sardinian Action Party	–	–	17,670	91,809	170,394
17 Christian Democrats	12,913,866	14,213,726	14,026,924	12,148,354	13,231,960
19 Liberal Party	1,296,585	4,478,185	713,486	1,068,555	810,961
23 Social Democrats	1,717,539	1,236,988	1,405,008	1,507,294	1,140,086
24 Social M'ment MSI	2,894,686	244,113	1,927,233	2,509,772	2,282,212
25 South Tyrol Peoples Party	153,674	184,324	205,007	184,971	202,005
28 Val d'Aosta Union	31,964	24,080	33,250	28,086	41,701
30 Proletarian Unity - PSIUP	648,800	–	–	–	–
33 Workers' Political M'ment	120,061	–	–	–	–
34 Radical Party	–	394,610	1,264,082	811,466	987,675
37 Proletarian Democracy - DP	–	–	–	542,476	642,021
38 Friuli Movement	–	–	35,235	26,179	13,210
39 Trieste List	–	–	65,637	93,548	–
40 National Pensioners' Party	–	–	–	504,219	–
41 Venetian League	–	–	–	125,242	298,743
42 Lombard League	–	–	–	–	186,220
43 Piedmont-Regional Autonomy	–	–	–	–	72,041
44 Piedmont	–	–	–	–	61,682
45 Greens	–	–	–	–	969,534
Others	168,407	84,553	605,359	127,948	282,581

1 Joint Communist Party-PdUP list.

Sources: *Elezioni della Camera dei Deputati*, 1972-1983 and for 1987 figures provided by the Ministry of the Interior.

Table 13.5b ITALY Percentage of Votes 1972-1987

	1972	1976	1979	1983	1987
Total Votes	93.2	93.4	91.1	89.0	90.5
Valid Votes	90.2	90.8	86.8	84.0	84.6
Invalid Votes	3.0	2.5	3.6	5.0	5.9
Share Invalid	3.2	2.7	3.9	5.7	6.5
PARTY VOTES					
3 Socialist Party	9.6	9.6	9.8	11.5	14.3
4 Republican Party	2.9	3.1	3.0	5.1	3.7
11 Communist Party	27.2	34.4	30.4		26.6
			}	29.9	
32 Proletarian Unity - PdUP	0.7	–	1.4		–
35 Continuous Struggle	–	1.5	–	–	–
36 Workers' Vanguard	–	–	–	–	–
13 Slovene minority	–	0.0	–	0.0	–
15 Sardinian Action Party	–	–	0.0	0.2	0.4
17 Christian Democrats	38.7	38.7	38.3	32.9	34.3
19 Liberal Party	3.9	12.2	1.9	2.9	2.1
23 Social Democrats	5.1	3.4	3.8	4.1	3.0
24 Social Movement MSI	8.7	0.7	5.3	6.8	5.9
25 South Tyrol Peoples Party	0.5	0.5	0.6	0.5	0.5
28 Val d'Aosta Union	0.1	0.1	0.1	0.1	0.1
30 Proletarian Unity - PSIUP	1.9	1.8	–	–	–
33 Workers' Political M'ment	0.4	–	–	–	–
34 Radical Party	–	1.1	3.5	2.2	2.6
37 Proletarian Democracy - DP	–	–	0.8	1.5	1.7
38 Friuli Movement	–	–	0.1	0.1	0.0
39 Trieste List	–	–	0.2	0.2	–
40 National Pensioners' Party	–	–	–	1.4	–
41 Venetian League	–	–	–	0.3	0.8
42 Lombard League	–	–	–	–	0.5
43 Piedmont-Regional Autonomy	–	–	–	–	0.2
44 Piedmont	–	–	–	–	0.2
45 Greens	–	–	–	–	2.5
Others	0.5	0.2	1.6	0.3	0.7

Table 13.5c ITALY Number of Seats Won in the Camera dei Deputati 1972-1987

	1972	1976	1979	1983	1987
3 Socialist Party	61	57	62	73	94
4 Republican Party	14	14	15	29	21
11 Communist Party	179	227	201	192	177
32 Proletarian Unity - PdUP	0	3	6	6	–
35 Continuous Struggle	–	1	–	–	–
36 Workers' Vanguard	–	2	–	–	–
13 Slovene minority	–	0	–	0	–
15 Sardinian Action Party	–	–	0	1	2
17 Christian Democrats	267	263	261	225	234
19 Liberal Party	21	5	9	16	11
23 Social Democrats	29	15	21	23	17
24 Social Movement MSI	56	35	31	42	35
25 South Tyrol Peoples Party	3	3	4	3	3
28 Val d'Aosta Union	0	0	1	1	1
30 Proletarian Unity - PSIUP	0	–	–	–	–
33 Workers Political M'ment	0	–	–	–	–
34 Radical Party	–	4	18	11	13
37 Proletarian Democracy - DP	–	–	0	7	8
38 Friuli Movement	–	–	0	0	0
39 Trieste List	–	–	1	0	–
40 National Pensioners' Party	–	–	–	0	–
41 Venetian League	–	–	–	1	0
42 Lombard League	–	–	–	–	1
43 Piedmont-Regional Autonomy	–	–	–	–	0
44 Piedmont	–	–	–	–	0
45 Greens	–	–	–	–	13
Others	0	1	0	0	0
Total Seats	630	630	630	630	630

Source: *Elezioni della Camera dei Deputati,* 1972-1983 and for 1987 figures provided by the Ministry of the Interior.

Table 13.5d ITALY Percentage of Seats Won in the Camera dei Deputati 1972-1987

	1972	1976	1979	1983	1987
3 Socialist Party	9.7	9.0	9.8	11.6	14.9
4 Republican Party	2.2	2.2	2.4	4.6	3.3
11 Communist Party	28.4	36.0	31.9	30.5	28.1
32 Proletarian Unity - PdUP	0.0	0.5	1.0	1.0	-
35 Continuous Struggle	-	0.2	-	-	-
36 Workers' Vanguard	-	0.3	-	-	-
13 Slovene minority	-	0.0	-	0.0	-
15 Sardinian Action Party	-	-	0.0	0.2	0.3
17 Christian Democrats	42.4	41.7	41.4	35.7	37.1
19 Liberal Party	3.3	0.0	1.5	2.5	1.7
23 Social Democrats	4.6	2.4	3.3	3.7	2.7
24 Social Movement MSI	8.9	5.6	4.9	6.7	5.6
25 South Tyrol Peoples Party	0.5	0.5	0.6	0.5	0.5
28 Val d'Aosta Union	0.0	0.0	0.2	0.2	0.2
30 Proletarian Unity - PSIUP	0.0	0.0	-	-	-
33 Workers' Political M'ment	0.0	-	-	-	-
34 Radical Party	-	-	2.9	1.7	2.1
37 Proletarian Democracy - DP	-	-	0.0	1.1	1.3
38 Friuli Movement	-	-	0.0	0.0	0.0
39 Trieste List	-	-	0.2	0.0	-
40 National Pensioners' Party	-	-	-	0.0	-
41 Venetian League	-	-	-	0.2	0.0
42 Lombard League	-	-	-	-	0.2
43 Piedmont-Regional Autonomy	-	-	-	-	0.0
44 Piedmont	-	-	-	-	0.0
45 Greens	-	-	-	-	2.1
Others	0.0	0.2	0.0	0.0	0.0

Chapter 14

JAPAN

The Meiji Constitution of 1889 established a two-chamber parliament consisting of a House of Peers and a directly elected House of Representatives with equal powers. The Cabinet was responsible to the Emperor and not to Parliament. The franchise for the House of Representatives was initially very restricted. Only men aged over 25 who paid a direct national tax of at least 15 yen for more than one year, or an income tax for more than three years, were entitled to vote. The tax requirements limited the electorate to about one per cent of the population. In 1900 the tax requirement was reduced to 10 yen, increasing the electorate to two per cent of the population, and to three yen in 1919, making nearly six per cent of the population eligible to vote. Adult male suffrage was introduced in 1925, increasing the electorate from three to twelve million.

In the House of Peers, Royal Princes, other Princes and Marquises sat as of right. The lower orders of the peerage elected representatives to sit for seven years. The total number of peers varied; in the 1930's it amounted to about 200. In addition, the Emperor (in practice the Prime Minister) appointed 125 members for distinguished public service or scholarship. They served for life. Sixty-five elected members of the highest tax-payers (those paying over 300 yen per year in direct taxes) and, after 1925, four members elected by the hundred strong Imperial Academy served for seven year terms (Quigley, 1932: 166-67).

The 1889 election law divided the country into 214 single-member constituencies and 43 two member constituencies. Electors had two votes in the two-member constituencies and election was by plurality. In 1900 a multi-member large district system based on the 51 prefectures and cities was introduced. The secret ballot vote was introduced and each elector given one vote only. With the exception of the 1946 election, the single vote system has been used ever since. In 1919, predominantly single-member constituencies were once again adopted with 295 one-member, 68 two-member and 11 three-member constituencies. From 1925 representatives were elected in districts returning three to five members.

Two major parties, the Jiyuto (Liberal Party) and the Kaishinto (Reform Party), emerged and between them won a majority in the first election to the House of Representatives in 1890. These two parties or their descendants dominated the Japanese party system for the next half century. In 1896 the Kaishinto merged with four other parties to form the Shimpoto (Progressive Party). The Shimpoto and the

Jiyuto were briefly united in 1898, but the attempted merger fell apart and the parties resumed their separate identities, though the Jiyuto retained the name of the short lived united party, Kenseito. In 1900 it merged with a number of other groups to form the Rikken Seiyukai which remained one of Japan's major parties until 1940.

Following the break-up of Kenseito, the Progressives reformed to establish the Kenseihonto (Orthodox Constitutional National Party). In 1913 about half the party's 95 strong parliamentary group merged with several other groups to form the Rikken Doshikai (Constitutional Like Minded Thinker's Association). In 1916 this party again merged with several small parliamentary groups to form the Kenseikai (Constitutional Government Association) which merged with a splinter group of the Seiyukai, the Seiyuhonto, to form the Rikken Minseito (Constitutional Democratic Party) in 1927.

The emergence of the first tolerated working class parties in 1928 further fragmented the party system. The Communist Party was formally banned during this period, though some working class parties were regarded as communist front organisations. In 1940 political parties were dissolved and replaced by the Imperial Rule Assistance Association. In April 1942 in an election in which only the Association, a few small extreme nationalist parties and independents were allowed to compete, the Association won 66 per cent of the votes cast.

The number of votes cast for each party in the first six elections to the House of Representatives is unclear, and only very approximate estimates can be made of the distribution of seats by party. Hence the election results reported here begin with the general election of 1902.

Following the American occupation of Japan at the end of the Second World War, political parties were reinstated. The franchise was extended to women and the voting age reduced to 20. The 1946 election to the House of Representatives was conducted in 53 constituencies returning from two to fourteen deputies. In constituencies returning between 4 and 10 members the elector had two votes; in constituencies returning more than ten deputies he or she had three votes. The single vote was retained in constituencies with three or less deputies. In 1947 the traditional district electoral system with constituencies returning from three to five members each and electors using the single non-transferable vote was revived. Since 1953 the Amami-Oshima district has returned a single representative.

The 1947 constitution provided for a two chamber parliament comprising the House of Councillors and the House of Representatives. The Emperor became a constitutional monarch and governments were to be responsible to the House of Representatives. The upper house was now to be elected and its power over legislation was to be reduced by allowing the House of Representatives to overule it by a two-thirds majority vote.

The franchise for the House of Councillors is the same as for the lower house, but in other respects the electoral system differs. One half of the 252 strong House is elected in multi-member constituencies based upon the 47 prefectures. The constituencies range in size from two-member to eight-member; the other half of the House is elected in a single national constituency. The term of office of the House is six years with half of the seats being contested every three years. Initially elections for both the national and the prefectural constituencies were carried out by the single transferable vote. Beginning in the 1983 elections, seats in the national constituency have been allocated by the d'Hondt system of proportional representation. Electors must now vote for a closed party list rather than for individual candidates.

The postwar Japanese party system had some links with the pre-1940 system. Immediately after the Japanese surrender in August 1945 politicians in the Diet formed the Liberal and Progressive parties which were respectively the successors to the Rikken Seiyukai and the Rikken Minseito. The Communist Party was legalised by the allied occupation administration and a Socialist Party combining pre-war labour, farmer and socialist parties was formed. Disputes between and within the Progressive and Liberal parties led to frequent splits and mergers over the next decade until the formation of the Liberal Democratic Party in 1955 united most of Japan's conservative groupings. The Socialist and Communist parties remain the principal opposition groups, but the Socialists have suffered major splits to both the right and left over the years and the party itself was split in two from 1951 to 1955 over the issue of the peace and security treaties with the United States.

A feature of Japanese elections since 1958 is the existence of a number of officially independent candidates who frequently win elections to the House of Representatives. Most of these candidates are not really independents but members of national political parties (overwhelmingly the Liberal Democrats) who were either not endorsed by their own party or who ran as candidates of more than one party. Since 1955 the majority of independent deputies have joined the Liberal Democratic parliamentary group immediately after the election and in 1976, 1979 and 1983 it was these deputies who provided the Liberal Democrats with a parliamentary majority (Baerwald, 1986 : 42-43).

Sources:

H. Baerwald, *Party Politics in Japan* (Boston and London: Allen & Unwin, 1986)

Fair Election League (Komei Senkyo Renmai): *Results of the Elections to the House of Representatives (Shuguin giin senkyo no gesseki)* (Tokyo, 1977)

K. Hayashida, 'Development of election law in Japan', *Jahrbuch des Öffentlichen Rechts der Gegenwart,* 15 (1966)

R. Hrebenar, *The Japanese Party System: from One-Party Rule to Coalition Government* (Boulder, Colorado: Westview Press, 1986)

J. Masumi, *Postwar Politics in Japan, 1945-1955* (Berkeley, California: Institute of East Asian Studies, University of California, 1955)

H.S. Quigley, *Japanese Government and Politics* (New York: Century Company, 1932)

R.A. Scalapino, *Democracy and the Party Movement in Pre-War Japan* (Berkeley, California: University of California Press, 1962)

Table 14.1 POLITICAL PARTIES IN JAPAN SINCE 1902

	Party Names	Elections Contested Years	Number
1	Rikken Seiyukai (Constitution of Friends Association)	1902-1937	14
2	Kenseihonto (Orthodox Constitutional Government Party); from 1912 to 1920 the Rikken Kokuminto (the Constitutional National Party) and in 1924 the Kakushin Club (Reformist Club)	1902-1924	9
3	Teikokuto (Imperial Party)	1902-1904	3
4	Doshi Club	1902-1903	2
5	Jinin Kai	1902-1903	2
6	Chusei Club	1903	1
7	Seiyu Club	1903	1
8	Kushin Club	1904	1
9	Mumei Club	1904	1
10	Jiyu Club	1904	1
11	Daido Club	1908	1
12	Yuko Kai	1908	1
13	Chuo Club	1912	1
14	Rikken Doshikai (Constitutional Like-Minded Thinkers' Association); 1917-1920 the Kenseikai (Constitutional Government Association) [1]	1915-1920	3
15	Chuseikai (Impartiality Association)	1915	1
16	Okuma Haku Koenkai (Count Okuma's Supporters' Association)	1915	1
17	Seiyauhonto [2]	1924	1
18	Reform Party (Kakushinto)	1928-1932	3
19	Rikken Minseito (Constitutional Democratic Party) [3]	1928-1937	5
20	Jitsugo Doshikai (Business Fellow Thinkers' Association); 1930 the Kokumin Doshikai	1928-1930	2
21	Japan Farmers' Party (Nihon Nominto) [4]	1928	1
22	Labour-Farmer Party (Rodo Nominto); in 1930 the New Labour Farmer Party (Shin Ronoto) [5]	1928-1930	2
23	Japan Labour Farmer Party (Nihon Ronoto)[6]	1928	1
24	Socialist People's Party (Shakai Minshuto) [7]	1928-1932	3
25	Japan Masses Party (Nihon Taishuto) [8]	1930	1
26	National Labour Farmer Masses Party (Zenkoku Taishuto) [9]	1932	1
27	Socialist Masses Party (Shakai Taishuto) [10]	1936-1937	2
28	Kokumin Domei (People's League) [11]	1936-1937	2
29	Showakai (Showa Association)	1936-1937	2
30	Eastern Party (Toho Kai)	1937	1
31	Japan Communist Party (Nihon Kyosanto)	1946ff	17

32	Japan Liberal Party (Nihon Jiyuto); in 1949 the Democratic Liberal Party (Minshu Jiyuto); in 1953 the Liberal Party (Jiyuto). [12]	1946-1953	6
33	Japan Progressive Party (Nihon Shimpoto); in 1947 and 1949 the Japan Democratic Party (Nihon Minshuto); in 1952 and 1953 the Progressive Reform Party (Kaishinto) [13]	1946-1953	6
34	Japan Cooperative Party (Nihon Kyodoto); from 1947 the People's Cooperative Party (Kokumin Kyodoto) [14]	1946-1949	3
35	Japan Socialist Party (Nihon Shakaito) [15]	1946-1949; 1958ff	14
36	Labour Farmer Party (Rodosha Nominto) [16]	1949-1955	4
37	Social Reform Party (Shakai Kakushinto) [17]	1949	1
38	Cooperative Party (Kyodoto) [18]	1952	1
39	Left Wing Socialist Party (Saha Shakaito)	1952-1955	3
40	Right Wing Socialist Party (Uha Shakaito)	1952-1955	3
41	Hatoyama Liberal Party (Hatoyama Jiyuto) [19]	1953	1
42	Japan Democratic Party (Nihon Minshuto) [20]	1955	1
43	Liberal Democratic Party (Jiyu Minshuto) [21]	1958ff	11
44	Democratic Socialist Party (Minshu Shakaito) [22]	1960ff	10
45	Komeito (Clean Government Party) [23]	1967ff	8
46	New Liberal Club (Shin Jiyu Club) [24]	1979-1986	5
47	Social Democratic Federation (Shakai Minshu Rengo) [25]	1979ff	4

1 Merger of the Central Club, controlled by the then Prime Minister, General Katsura Taro and about half of the Rikken Kokuminto deputies in 1913. The new party gradually absorbed most of the remaining Rikken Kokuminto deputies in the House of Representatives.

2 Splinter from the Rikken Seiyukai.

3 Merger of the Seiyuhonto and the Kenseikai.

4 United with other parties to form the Japan Masses Party in December 1928.

5 Banned in April 1928. Reformed as the New Labour Farmer Party in 1929. United with other parties to form the National Labour Farmer Masses Party in 1931.

6 United with other parties to form the Japan Masses Party in December 1928.

7 Merged with the National Labour Farmer Masses Party to form the Socialist Masses Party in 1932.

8 December 1928 merger of the Japan Labour Farmer Party, the Japan Farmers' Party and the Proletarian Masses Party (Musan Taishuto) established in September 1928 by some former members of the banned Labour Farmer Party, and some local proletarian parties. United with other proletarian parties to form the National Masses Party (Zenkoku Taishuto) in July 1930.

9 Merger of the New Labour Farmer Party, the National Masses Party in July 1931.

10 Merger of Socialist People's Party and the National Labour Farmer Masses Party in 1932.

11 Splinter from the Minseito.

12 Established principally by former members of the Rikken Seiyukai and led by Hatoyama Ichiro, until he was purged by the allied occupying powers in 1946. In March 1948 merged with a faction of the Democratic Party led by Shiderara Kijuro to form the Democratic Liberal Party. Renamed Liberal Party in March 1950 after adding a faction of the Japan Democratic Party.

13 Established principally by former members of the Rikken Minseito. Merged with the Ashida faction of the Japan Liberal Party to form the Japanese Democratic Party in March 1947. In April 1950 merged with the People's Cooperative Party to form the People's Democratic Party (Kokumin Minshuto). Renamed the Progressive Reform Party (Kaishinto) in February 1952 when it merged with a majority of members of the Farmers' Cooperative Party.

14 Merged with the Japan Democratic Party to form the People's Democratic Party in April 1950.

15 The Socialist Party split in two over the ratification of the peace and security treaties with the United States. They were reunited in October 1955.

16 Left wing breakaway from the Japan Socialist Party formed in December 1948. The party was dissolved in January 1957 and its members joined the Socialist Party.

17 Breakaway from the Socialist Party in March 1948, led by Satake Haruki. Renamed the Social Democratic Party (Shakai Minshuto) in February 1951. Merged with part of the Farmers' Cooperative Party to form the Cooperative Party (Kyodoto) in July 1952.

18 Merger of the Farmers' Cooperative Party (a splinter from the Japan Cooperative Party) and the Social Democratic Party (footnote 10) in July 1952. Merged with the Right Wing Socialist Party after the 1955 election.

19 Breakaway from the Liberal Party led by Hatoyama Ichiro, who had rejoined the party after being allowed to reenter politics in 1951 (Footnote 6).

20 Merger of the Progressive Reform Party and the Hatoyama Liberals.

21 Merger of the Liberal and Democratic parties in November 1955.

22 Right wing splinter from the Socialist Party.

23 Electoral wing of the Buddhist Soka Gakkai (Values Creation Society).

24 Splinter from the Liberal Democratic Party formed in 1976. Reunited with the Liberal Democrats in August 1986.

25 Right wing splinter from the Socialist Party.

Table 14.2 DATES OF ELECTIONS : HOUSE OF REPRESENTATIVES

1.	10 August 1902	16.	25 April 1947
2.	1 March 1903	17.	23 January 1949
3.	1 March 1904	18.	1 October 1952
4.	15 May 1908	19.	19 April 1953
5.	15 May 1912	20.	27 February 1955
6.	25 March 1915	21.	22 May 1958
7.	20 April 1917	22.	20 November 1960
8.	10 May 1920	23.	21 November 1963
9.	10 May 1924	24.	29 January 1967
10.	20 February 1928	25.	27 December 1969
11.	20 February 1930	26.	10 December 1972
12.	20 February 1932	27.	5 December 1976
13.	20 February 1936	28.	7 October 1979
14.	30 April 1937	29.	22 June 1980
15.	10 April 1946	30.	18 December 1983
		31.	6 July 1986

Sources: Fair Election League, 1977 : 1-9 and Ministry of Home Affairs, 1983 : 16.

Table 14.3a JAPAN Total Votes 1902-1917

	1902	1903	1904	1908	1912	1915	1917
Electorate	982,868	958,322	762,445	1,590,045	1,506,143	1,546,411	1,422,126
Valid Votes	860,670	818,299	650,351	1,342,645	1,338,505	1,417,075	1,300,852
PARTY VOTES							
1 Rikken Seiyukai	433,763	373,022	217,691	649,858	689,613	446,934	504,720
2 Kenseihonto/Rikken Kokuminto	220,939	218,689	170,319	288,243	381,465	106,445	125,974
3 Teikokuto	37,749	34,811	27,244	-	-	-	-
4 Doshi Club	24,541	1,517	-	-	-	-	-
5 Jinin Kai	35,950	2,748	-	-	-	-	-
6 Chusei Club	-	37,070	-	-	-	-	-
7 Seiyu Club	-	24,129	-	-	-	-	-
8 Kushin Club	-	-	55,709	-	-	-	-
9 Mumei Club	-	-	31,197	-	-	-	-
10 Jiyu Club	-	-	31,772	-	-	-	-
11 Daido Club	-	-	-	92,477	-	-	-
12 Yuko Kai	-	-	-	99,690	-	-	-
13 Chuo Club	-	-	-	-	113,834	-	-
14 Rikken Doshikai/Kenseikai	-	-	-	-	-	523,228	467,518
15 Chuseikai	-	-	-	-	-	101,970	-
16 Okuma Supporters	-	-	-	-	-	55,684	-
Others	107,678	129,313	116,419	212,377	153,593	182,814	202,640

Source: Fair Election League, 1977: 2-4

Table 14.3b JAPAN Percentage of Votes 1902-1917

	1902	1903	1904	1908	1912	1915	1917
Valid Votes	87.6	85.4	85.3	84.4	88.9	91.6	91.4
PARTY VOTES							
1 Rikken Seiyukai	50.4	45.6	33.5	48.4	51.5	31.5	38.8
2 Kenseihonto/Rikken Kokuminto	25.7	26.7	26.2	21.5	28.5	7.5	9.7
3 Teikokuto	4.4	4.3	4.2	-	-	-	-
4 Doshi Club	2.9	0.2	-	-	-	-	-
5 Jinin Kai	4.2	0.3	-	-	-	-	-
6 Chusei Club	-	4.5	-	-	-	-	-
7 Seiyu Club	-	2.9	-	-	-	-	-
8 Kushin Club	-	-	8.6	-	-	-	-
9 Mumei Club	-	-	4.8	-	-	-	-
10 Jiyu Club	-	-	4.9	-	-	-	-
11 Daido Club	-	-	-	6.9	-	-	-
12 Yuko Kai	-	-	-	7.4	-	-	-
13 Chuo Club	-	-	-	-	8.5	-	-
14 Rikken Doshikai/Kenseikai	-	-	-	-	-	36.9	36.0
15 Chuseikai	-	-	-	-	-	7.2	-
16 Okuma Supporters	-	-	-	-	-	3.9	-
Others	12.5	15.4	17.9	15.8	11.5	12.9	15.6

Table 14.3c JAPAN Number of Seats Won in the House of Representatives 1902-1917

	1902	1903	1904	1908	1912	1915	1917
1 Rikken Seiyukai	191	175	133	187	209	108	165
2 Kenseihonto/Rikken Kokuminto	95	85	90	70	95	27	35
3 Teikokuto	17	17	19	–	–	–	–
4 Doshi Club	13	0	–	–	–	–	–
5 Jinin Kai	28	0	–	–	–	–	–
6 Chusei Club	–	31	–	–	–	–	–
7 Seiyu Club	–	13	–	–	–	–	–
8 Kushin Club	–	–	39	–	–	–	–
9 Mumei Club	–	–	25	–	–	–	–
10 Jiyu Club	–	–	18	–	–	–	–
11 Daido Club	–	–	–	29	–	–	–
12 Yuko Kai	–	–	–	29	–	–	–
13 Chuo Club	–	–	–	–	31	–	–
14 Rikken/Kenseikai	–	–	–	–	–	153	121
15 Chuseikai	–	–	–	–	–	33	–
16 Okuma Supporters	–	–	–	–	–	12	–
Others	32	55	55	64	46	48	60
Total Seats	376	376	379	379	381	381	381

Source: Fair Election League, 1977: 2-4.

Table 14.3d JAPAN Percentage of Seats Won in the House of Representatives 1902-1917

	1902	1903	1904	1908	1912	1915	1917
1 Rikken Seiyukai	50.8	46.5	35.1	49.3	54.9	28.3	43.3
2 Kenseihonto/Rikken Kokuminto	25.3	22.6	23.7	18.5	24.9	7.1	9.2
3 Teikokuto	4.5	4.5	5.0	-	-	-	-
4 Doshi Club	3.5	0.0	-	-	-	-	-
5 Jinin Kai	7.4	0.0	-	-	-	-	-
6 Chusei Club	-	8.2	-	-	-	-	-
7 Seiyu Club	-	3.5	-	-	-	-	-
8 Kushin Club	-	-	10.3	-	-	-	-
9 Mumei Club	-	-	6.6	-	-	-	-
10 Jiyu Club	-	-	4.7	-	-	-	-
11 Daido Club	-	-	-	7.7	-	-	-
12 Yuko Kai	-	-	-	7.7	-	-	-
13 Chuo Club	-	-	-	-	8.1	-	-
14 Rikken/Kenseikai	-	-	-	-	-	40.2	31.8
15 Chuseikai	-	-	-	-	-	8.7	-
16 Okuma Supporters	-	-	-	-	-	3.1	-
Others	8.5	14.6	14.5	16.9	12.1	12.6	15.7

Table 14.4a JAPAN Total Votes 1920-1937

	1920	1924	1928	1930	1932	1936	1937
Electorate	3,069,148	3,288,405	12,408,678	12,812,895	13,103,679	14,304,546	14,402,497
Valid Votes	2,639,069	2,972,958	9,856,196	10,446,196	9,723,116	11,132,678	10,203,686
PARTY VOTES							
1 Rikken Seiyukai	1,471,728	666,317	4,244,385	3,944,511	5,682,647	4,188,029	3,594,863
2 Rikken Kokuminto/Kakushin Club	140,397	182,720	–	–	–	–	–
14 Rikken/Kenseikai	715,500	872,533	–	–	–	–	–
17 Seiyauhonto	–	730,077	–	–	–	–	–
18 Reform Party	–	–	81,324	55,487	36,839	–	–
19 Rikken Minseito	–	–	4,251,771	5,468,096	3,393,935	4,444,413	3,689,355
20 Jitsugo Doshikai/Kokumin Doshikai	–	–	166,250	128,505	–	–	–
21 Japan Farmers' Party	–	–	44,000	–	–	–	–
22 Labour Farmer Party	–	–	184,040	82,707	–	–	–
23 Japan Labour Farmer Party	–	–	94,626	–	–	–	–
24 Socialist People's Party	–	–	120,044	177,333	125,758	–	–
25 Japan Masses Party	–	–	–	160,248	–	–	–
26 National Labour Farmer Masses Party	–	–	–	–	132,747	–	–
27 Socialist Masses Party	–	–	–	–	–	518,844	928,934
28 Kokumin Domei	–	–	–	–	–	421,632	281,834
29 Showakai	–	–	–	–	–	531,772	414,088
30 Eastern Party	–	–	–	–	–	–	221,455
Others	311,444	521,311	669,756	429,309	325,993	1,027,988	1,073,157

Sources: Fair Election League, 1977: 4-6 and 515.

Table 14.4b JAPAN Percentage of Votes 1920-1937

	1920	1924	1928	1930	1932	1936	1937
Total Votes	86.1	91.2	80.3	82.3	74.9	78.6	71.6
Valid Votes	85.4	90.4	79.5	81.5	74.2	77.8	70.8
Invalid Votes	0.7	0.8	0.8	0.8	0.7	0.8	0.8
Share Invalid	0.9	0.8	1.0	0.9	0.9	1.0	1.1
PARTY VOTES							
1 Rikken Seiyukai	56.2	22.2	43.1	37.8	58.7	37.6	35.2
2 Rikken Kokuminto/Kakushin Club	5.4	6.1	-	-	-	-	-
14 Rikken/Kenseikai	27.5	29.3	-	-	-	-	-
17 Seiyauhonto	-	24.8	-	-	-	-	-
18 Reform Party	-	-	0.8	0.5	0.4	-	-
19 Rikken Minseito	-	-	43.1	52.3	34.8	39.9	36.1
20 Jitsugo Doshikai/Kokumin Doshikai	-	-	1.7	1.2	-	-	2.1
21 Japan Farmers' Party	-	-	0.5	-	-	-	-
22 Labour Farmer Party	-	-	1.9	0.8	-	-	-
23 Japan Labour Farmer Party	-	-	0.9	-	-	-	-
24 Socialist People's Party	-	-	1.2	1.7	1.3	-	-
25 Japan Masses Party	-	-	-	1.6	-	-	-
26 National Labour Farmer Masses Party	-	-	-	-	1.4	-	-
27 Socialist Masses Party	-	-	-	-	-	4.7	9.0
28 Kokumin Domei	-	-	-	-	-	3.8	2.8
29 Showakai	-	-	-	-	-	4.8	4.1
30 Eastern Party	-	-	-	-	-	-	-
Others	11.0	17.5	6.8	4.1	3.4	9.2	10.7

Table 14.4c JAPAN Number of Seats Won in the House of Representatives 1920-1937

	1920	1924	1928	1930	1932	1936	1937
1 Rikken Seiyukai	278	103	217	174	301	174	175
2 Kakushin Club/Kakushin Club	29	30	–	–	–	–	–
14 Rikken/Kenseikai	110	151	–	–	–	–	–
17 Seiyauhonto	–	111	–	–	–	–	–
18 Reform Party	–	–	3	3	2	–	–
19 Rikken Minseito	–	–	216	273	146	205	179
20 Jitsugo Doshikai/Kokumin Doshikai	–	–	4	6	–	–	–
21 Japan Farmers' Party	–	–	0	–	–	–	–
22 Labour Farmer Party	–	–	2	1	–	–	–
23 Japan Labour Farmer Party	–	–	1	–	–	–	–
24 Socialist People's Party	–	–	4	2	3	–	–
25 Japan Masses Party	–	–	–	2	–	–	–
26 National Labour Farmer Masses Party	–	–	–	–	2	–	–
27 Socialist Masses Party	–	–	–	–	–	18	37
28 Kokumin Domei	–	–	–	–	–	15	11
29 Showakai	–	–	–	–	–	20	19
30 Eastern Party	–	–	–	–	–	–	11
Others	47	69	19	5	12	34	34
Total Seats	464	464	466	466	466	466	466

Source: Fair Election League, 1977: 4-6 and 515.

Table 14.4d JAPAN Percentage of Seats Won in the House of Representatives 1920-1937

	1920	1924	1928	1930	1932	1936	1937
1 Rikken Seiyukai	59.9	22.2	46.6	37.3	64.6	37.3	37.6
2 Rikken Kokuminto/Kakushin Club	6.3	6.5	–	–	–	–	–
14 Rikken/Kenseikai	23.7	32.5	–	–	–	–	–
17 Seiyauhonto	–	23.9	–	–	–	–	–
18 Reform Party	–	–	0.6	0.6	0.4	–	–
19 Rikken Minseitu	–	–	46.4	58.6	31.3	44.0	38.4
20 Jitsugo Doshikai/Kokumin Doshikai	–	–	0.9	1.3	–	–	–
21 Japan Farmers' Party	–	–	0.0	–	–	–	–
22 Labour Farmer Party	–	–	0.4	0.2	–	–	–
23 Japan Labour Farmer Party	–	–	0.2	–	–	–	–
24 Socialist People's Party	–	–	0.9	0.4	0.6	–	–
25 Japan Masses Party	–	–	–	0.4	–	–	–
26 National Labour Farmer Masses Party	–	–	–	–	0.4	–	–
27 Socialist Masses Party	–	–	–	–	–	3.9	7.9
28 Kokumin Domei	–	–	–	–	–	3.2	2.4
29 Showakai	–	–	–	–	–	4.3	4.1
30 Eastern Party	–	–	–	–	–	–	2.4
Others	10.1	14.9	4.1	1.1	2.6	7.3	7.3

Table 14.5a JAPAN Total Votes 1946-1960

	1946	1947	1949	1952	1953	1955	1958	1960
Electorate	36,878,420	40,907,493	42,105,300	46,772,584	47,090,167	49,235,375	52,013,529	54,312,993
Valid Votes	55,448,879[1]	27,361,607	30,592,519	35,336,705	34,602,445	37,014,837	39,751,661	39,509,123
Invalid Votes	482,000	435,183	582,438	413,004	343,685	319,501	290,828	410,996
Total Votes	26,582,175	27,796,840	31,174,957	35,749,709	34,946,130	37,334,338	40,042,489	39,920,119
PARTY VOTES								
31 Communist Party	2,135,757	1,002,883	2,984,780	896,765	655,990	733,122[1]	1,012,035	1,156,723
32 Liberal Party	13,505,746	7,312,524	13,420,269	16,937,225	13,476,428	9,849,458	-	-
33 Progressive Party	10,350,530	6,960,270	4,798,352	6,421,094	6,186,232	-	-	-
34 Japan Cooperative Party/People's Cooperative Party[2]	1,799,764	1,915,948	1,041,879	-	-	-	-	-
35 Socialist Party	9,924,930	7,176,882	4,129,794	-	-	-	13,093,993	10,887,134
36 Labour Farmer Party	-	-	606,840	261,190	358,773	357,611	-	-
37 Social Reform Party	-	-	387,214	-	-	-	-	-
38 Cooperative Party	-	-	-	390,015	-	-	-	-
39 Left-Wing Socialists	-	-	-	3,493,970	4,516,715	5,683,312	-	-
40 Right-Wing Socialists	-	-	-	4,103,872	4,677,833	5,129,594	-	-
41 Hatoyama Liberals	-	-	-	-	3,054,688	-	-	-
42 Democratic Party	-	-	-	-	-	13,536,044	-	-
43 Liberal Democratic Party	-	-	-	-	-	-	22,976,846	22,740,271
44 Democratic Socialist Party	-	-	-	-	-	-	-	3,464,147
Others	17,732,152	2,993,100	3,223,391	2,922,574	1,675,786	1,725,696	2,668,786	1,260,846

1 Total number of votes cast for party candidates. Each elector had two or three votes.
2 In 1946 the Japan Cooperative Party.

Sources: Fair Election League, 1977: 6 -7.

Table 14.5b JAPAN Percentage of Votes 1946-1960

	1946	1947	1949	1952	1953	1955	1958	1960
Total Votes	151.7	68.0	74.0	76.4	74.2	75.8	77.0	73.5
Valid Votes	73.4	66.9	72.7	75.6	73.5	75.2	76.4	72.7
Invalid Votes	1.3	1.1	1.4	0.9	0.7	0.6	0.6	0.8
Share Invalid	1.8	1.6	1.9	1.2	1.0	0.9	0.7	1.0
PARTY VOTES								
31 Communist Party	3.9	3.7	9.8	2.5	1.9	2.0	2.5	2.9
32 Liberal Party	24.4	26.7	43.9	47.9	38.9	26.6	–	–
33 Progressive Party	18.7	25.4	15.7	18.2	17.9	–	–	–
34 Japan Cooperative Party/People's Cooperative Party	3.2	7.0	3.4	–	–	–	–	–
35 Socialist Party	17.9	26.2	13.5	–	–	–	32.9	27.6
36 Labour Farmer Party	–	–	2.0	0.7	1.0	1.0	–	–
37 Social Reform Party	–	–	1.3	–	–	–	–	–
38 Cooperative Party	–	–	–	1.1	–	–	–	–
39 Left-Wing Socialists	–	–	–	9.9	13.1	15.4	–	–
40 Right-Wing Socialists	–	–	–	11.4	13.5	13.9	–	–
41 Hatoyama Liberals	–	–	–	–	8.8	–	–	–
42 Democratic Party	–	–	–	–	–	36.6	–	–
43 Liberal Democratic Party	–	–	–	–	–	–	57.8	57.6
44 Democratic Socialist Party	–	–	–	–	–	–	–	8.8
Others	32.0	10.9	10.5	8.3	4.8	4.7	6.7	3.2

Table 14.5c JAPAN Number of Seats Won in the House of Representatives 1946-1960[1]

	1946	1947	1949	1952	1953	1955	1958	1960
31 Communist Party	5	4	35	0	1	2	1	3
32 Liberal Party	141	131	264	240	199	112	–	–
33 Progressive Party	94	124	69	85	76	–	–	–
34 Japan Cooperative Party/People's Cooperative Party	14	31	14	–	–	–	–	–
35 Socialist Party	94	143	48	–	–	–	166	145
36 Labour Farmer Party	–	–	7	4	5	4	–	–
37 Social Reform Party	–	–	5	–	–	–	–	–
38 Cooperative Party	–	–	–	2	–	–	–	–
39 Left-Wing Socialists	–	–	–	54	72	89	–	–
40 Right-Wing Socialists	–	–	–	57	66	67	–	–
41 Hatoyama Liberals	–	–	–	–	35	–	–	–
42 Democratic Party	–	–	–	–	–	185	–	–
43 Liberal Democratic Party	–	–	–	–	–	–	287 (11)	296 (4)
44 Democratic Socialist Party	–	–	–	–	–	–	–	17
Others	118	33	24	24	12	8	13	6
Total Seats	466	466	466	466	466	466	467	467

1 Figures in brackets report the number of independent deputies who joined the Liberal Democratic parliamentary group after the House convened..

Sources: Fair Election League, 1977: 6 -9, Baerwald, 1986: 42.

Table 14.5d JAPAN Percentage of Seats Won in the House of Representatives 1946-1960

	1946	1947	1949	1952	1953	1955	1958	1960
31 Communist Party	1.1	0.9	1.5	0.9	1.1	0.9	-	-
32 Liberal Party	30.3	28.1	56.7	51.5	42.7	24.0	-	-
33 Progressive Party	20.2	26.6	14.8	18.2	16.3	-	-	-
34 Japan Cooperative Party/People's Cooperative Party	3.0	6.7	3.0	-	-	-	-	-
35 Socialist Party	20.2	30.7	10.3	-	-	-	35.5	31.0
36 Labour Farmer Party	-	-	1.5	0.9	1.1	0.9	-	-
37 Social Reform Party	-	-	1.1	-	-	-	-	-
38 Cooperative Party	-	-	-	0.4	-	-	-	-
39 Left-Wing Socialists	-	-	-	11.6	15.5	19.1	-	-
40 Right-Wing Socialists	-	-	-	12.2	14.2	14.3	-	-
41 Hatoyama Liberals	-	-	-	-	7.5	7.5	-	-
42 Democratic Party	-	-	-	-	-	39.6	-	-
43 Liberal Democratic Party	-	-	-	-	-	-	61.5	63.4
44 Democratic Socialist Party	-	-	-	-	-	-	-	3.6
Others	25.3	7.1	5.2	5.2	2.6	1.7	2.8	1.3

Table 14.6a JAPAN Total Votes 1963-1986

	1963	1967	1969	1972	1976	1979	1980	1983	1986
Electorate	58,281,678	62,992,796	69,260,424	73,769,636	77,926,588	80,169,924	80,925,034	84,252,608	86,426,845
Valid Votes	41,016,540	45,996,573	46,989,893	52,425,078	56,612,765	54,010,120	59,028,836	56,779,700	60,448,605
Invalid Votes	442,406	602,883	452,508	476,981	619,228	508,395	1,309,603	461,130	1,255,189
Total Votes	41,458,946	46,599,456	47,442,401	52,929,059	57,231,993	54,518,515	60,338,439	57,240,830	61,703,794
PARTY VOTES									
31 Communist Party	1,646,477	2,190,563	3,199,031	5,496,827	5,878,192	5,625,527	5,803,613	5,302,485	5,313,246
35 Socialist Party	11,906,766	12,826,103	10,074,100	11,478,742	11,713,009	10,643,450	11,400,747	11,065,082	10,412,584
43 Liberal Democratic Party	22,423,915	22,447,838	22,381,570	24,563,199	23,653,626	24,084,131	28,262,441	25,982,785	29,875,501
44 Democratic Socialist Party	3,023,302	3,404,463	3,636,590	3,660,953	3,554,076	3,663,691	3,896,728	4,129,947	3,895,858
45 Komeito	-	2,472,371	5,124,666	4,436,755	6,177,300	5,282,682	5,329,942	5,745,751	5,701,277
46 New Liberal Club	-	-	-	-	2,363,985	1,631,811	1,766,396	1,341,584	1,114,800
47 Social Democratic Federation	-	-	-	-	-	368,660	402,832	381,045	499,670
Others	2,016,080	2,655,232	2,573,933	2,788,601	3,272,577	2,710,165	2,166,135	2,831,059	3,635,669

Sources: Japan Fair Election Society, 1977: 7 and figures provided by the Ministry of Home Affairs.

Table 14.6b JAPAN Percentage of Votes 1963-1986

	1963	1967	1969	1972	1976	1979	1980	1983	1986
Total Votes	71.1	74.0	68.5	71.7	73.4	68.0	74.6	67.9	71.4
Valid Votes	70.4	73.0	67.8	71.1	72.6	67.4	72.9	67.4	69.9
Invalid Votes	0.8	1.0	0.7	0.6	0.8	0.6	1.6	0.5	1.5
Share Invalid	1.1	1.3	1.0	0.9	1.1	0.9	2.2	0.8	2.0
PARTY VOTES									
31 Communist Party	4.0	4.8	6.8	10.5	10.4	10.4	9.8	9.3	8.8
35 Socialist Party	29.0	27.9	21.4	21.9	20.7	19.7	19.3	19.5	17.2
43 Liberal Democratic Party	54.7	48.8	47.6	46.9	41.8	44.6	47.9	45.8	49.4
44 Democratic Socialist Party	7.4	7.4	7.7	7.0	6.3	6.8	6.6	7.3	6.4
45 Komeito	-	5.4	10.9	8.5	10.9	9.8	9.0	10.1	9.4
46 New Liberal Club	-	-	-	-	4.2	3.0	3.0	2.4	1.8
47 Social Democratic Federation	-	-	-	-	-	0.7	0.7	0.7	0.8
Others	4.9	5.8	5.5	5.3	5.8	5.0	3.7	5.0	6.0

Table 14.6c JAPAN Number of Seats Won in the House of Representatives 1963-1986[1]

	1963	1967	1969	1972	1976	1979	1980	1983	1986
31 Communist Party	5	5	14	38	17	39	29	26	26
35 Socialist Party	144	140	90	118	123	107	107	112	85
43 Liberal Democratic Party	283 (12)	277 (5)	288 (12)	271 (12)	249 (11)	248 (9)	284 (5)	250 (8)	300
44 Democratic Socialist Party	23	30	31	19	29	35	32	38	26
45 Komeito	-	25	47	29	55	57	33	58	56
46 New Liberal Club	-	-	-	-	17	4	12	8	6
47 Social Democratic Federation	-	-	-	-	-	2	0	3	4
Others	12	9	16	16	21	19	11	16	9
Total Seats	407	486	486	491	511	511	511	511	512

[1] Figures in parenthesis report the number of independent deputies who joined the Liberal Democratic parliamentary group after the House convened. (Baerwald, 1986: 42).

Sources: Ministry of Home Affairs,Baerwald, 1986: 42.

Table 14.6d JAPAN Percentage of Seats Won in the House of Representatives 1963-1986

	1963	1967	1969	1972	1976	1979	1980	1983	1986
31 Communist Party	1.1	1.0	2.9	7.7	3.3	7.6	5.7	5.1	5.1
35 Socialist Party	30.8	28.8	18.5	24.0	24.1	20.9	20.9	21.9	16.6
43 Liberal Democratic Party	60.6	57.0	59.3	55.2	48.7	48.5	55.6	48.9	58.6
44 Democratic Socialist Party	4.9	6.2	6.4	3.9	5.7	6.8	6.3	7.4	5.1
45 Komeito	-	5.1	9.7	5.9	10.8	11.2	6.5	11.4	10.9
46 New Liberal Club	-	-	-	-	3.3	0.8	2.3	1.6	1.2
47 Social Democratic Federation	-	-	-	-	-	0.4	0.0	0.6	0.8
Others	2.6	1.9	3.3	3.3	4.1	3.7	2.2	3.1	1.8

Chapter 15

LUXEMBOURG

Luxembourg was established as an autonomous Grand Duchy under the Dutch crown in 1815, but was administered as an integral part of the Netherlands. From 1830 to 1839 it formed part of newly independent Belgium. In 1839 the territory of the Grand Duchy was divided. Half the population remained part of Belgium. Sovereignty over the remaining territory was restored to the Netherlands, which granted the country its own indirectly elected assembly.

In 1868 a directly elected parliament, the Chambre des Deputés, was introduced. Each parliamentary term lasted for six years, with half the deputies retiring every three years. General elections were held only when the Chamber was dissolved. The electorate was limited to men more than 25 years old who met a minimum tax qualification. Initially, the qualification was 30 francs a year, reduced to 15 francs in 1892 and 10 francs in 1902. The percentage of the population enfranchised increased from 2.9 per cent in 1871 to 6.3 per cent in 1892 and 12.7 per cent in 1902. The secret ballot was introduced in 1879. A two-ballot majority system in multi-member constituencies was used. If sufficient candidates did not win an absolute majority on the first ballot, a second ballot was held, twice as many candidates as there were vacant seats, with those polling the most votes on the first ballot.

Until the end of the nineteenth century political parties were organized only in Parliament. The Chamber was dominated by the Liberals, who formed all the governments from 1867 until 1915 (Fusilier, 1960: 614). The first socialist deputy was elected in 1896, but the Social Democratic Party was not founded until 1902. The Liberals formed their first national organization, the Ligue Libérale, in 1904. The Catholic Parti de la Droite was not established until January, 1914 (Heiderscheid, 1962: 222-224).

A constituent assembly was elected in 1918:

Party	*Seats*
Party of the Right	23
Social Democrats	12
Liberal League	10
Independent People's Party	5
Independent National Party	2
Others	1

Source: *Annuaire statistique rétrospectif*, 1973: 446.

The constituent assembly introduced major electoral reforms. Adult suffrage was granted all men and women and the voting age reduced to 21; it was subsequently lowered to 18 in 1972. Voting was made compulsory. Proportional representation replaced the majority system. The country is divided into four multi-member constituencies. Each elector has as many votes as there are seats in his constituency. An elector may cast up to two votes for a single candidate and may divide votes between candidates of different parties. Seats are allocated at the constituency level by the Hagenbach-Bischoff method. The six-year parliamentary term with renewal of half the Chamber every three years continued until 1956, when a constitutional amendment provided for nation-wide general elections every five years.

Because the number of votes at the disposal of each elector varies with the number of deputies in a constituency, it is not possible to calculate a national party vote simply be summing the four constituency-level vote totals. In order to estimate a national vote, each constituency vote is first divided by the number of seats in the constituency and the four quotients summed. For this reason and because some voters do not use all the votes to which they are entitled, the party votes reported in the following tables are lower than the total number of valid votes, which are the number of valid ballot papers cast.

Sources:

Centre de Recherche et d'Information Socio-Politiques, *Les élections au Grand-Duché de Luxembourg - Données sur les scrutins de 1974, 1979 et 1984* (Brussels, 1985)

R. Fusilier, *Les monarchies parlementaires* (Paris: Éditions ouvrières, 1960)

A. Heiderscheid, *Aspects de la sociologie religieuse du diocèse de Luxembourg* (Luxembourg: Imprimerie St. Paul, 1962)

G. Kintzele, 'Luxembourg', in G. Hand, J. Georgel and C. Sasse (eds.), *European Electoral Systems Handbook* (London: Butterworths, 1979) 170-92

N. Schaeffer, *Les forces politiques au Grand-Duché de Luxembourg* (dissertation, Institut des Études Politiques, Paris, 1961)

Service Central de la Statistique et des Études Économiques, *Annuaire statistique rétrospectif, 1973*

Service Central de la Statistique et des Études Économiques, *Annuaire statistique du Luxembourg 1987/88*

Table 15.1 POLITICAL PARTIES IN LUXEMBOURG SINCE 1918 [1]

	Party Names	Elections Contested Years	Number
1	Party of the Right (Parti de la Droite); since 1945, Christian Social Party (Parti chrétien social/ Chrëstlech Sozial Vollekspartei - PCS/CSV)	1918ff	19
2	Social Democratic Party (Parti social démocrate); since 1924 Socialist Workrs' Party (Parti ouvrier socialiste luxembourgeois/Letzeburger Sozialistisch Arbechterpartei - POSL/LSAP	1918ff	19
3	Liberal League (Ligue libéral)	1918-1922	3
4	Independent National Party (Parti national indépendant) [2]	1918-1925	4
5	People's Independent Party (Parti populaire indépendant)	1918-1919	2
6	Independents of the East (Parti des indepéndants de l'Est)	1919;1925-1928; 1934;1945	5
7	Communist Party (Parti communiste luxembourgeois/ Kommunistesch Partei vu Lëtzebuerg - PCL/KPL)	1922-1925 1931-1934;1945ff	15
8	Liberal Left (Gauche libérale)	1925	1
9	Radical Party (Parti radical)	1925-1931	3
10	Radical Socialist Party (Parti radical socialiste)	1925;1931	2
11	Radical Liberal Party (Parti radical libéral)	1934-1937	2
12	Democratic List (Liste démocratique)	1937	1
13	Free List of Peasants, Middle Classes and Workers (Liste libre des paysans, classes moyennes et ouvriers)	1937	1
14	Liberal Party (Parti libéral)	1937-1945	2
15	Party of Peasants and Middle Classes (Parti des paysans et classes moyennes)	1937	1
16	Democratic Party (Parti démocratique/Demokratesch Partei - PD/DP); from 1945 to 1951 Groupement patriotique et démocratique; in 1954 Groupement démocratique	1945ff	11
17	Middle Class Party (Parti des classes moyennes)	1954	1
18	Popular Independent Movement (Mouvement indépendant populaire); in 1968 Parti de la solidarité nationale [3]	1964-1968	2
19	Social Democratic Party (Parti social-démocrate/ Sozialdemokratische Partei - PSD/SDP) [4]	1974-1979	2
20	Enrôlés de force [5]	1979	1
21	Independent Socialists (Socialistes indépendants-Liste Jean Gremling) [6]	1979-1984	2
22	Alternative List (Alternativ Lescht-Wiert lech) [7]	1979	1
23	Green Alternative (Di Grëng Alternativ - GAP)	1984ff	2

24	Action Committee 5/6 Pensions for All (Aktiouns-komite 5/6Pensioun fir jiddfereen) [8]	1989	1
25	Ecologists for the North (D'Ekologisten fir den Norden) [9]	1989	1
26	Green Left Ecological Initiative (Greng Lëscht Ekologesch Initiativ - GLEI) [10]	1989	1
27	Luxembourg for the Luxembourgers National Movement (Lëtzebuerg fir de Letzebuerger National Bewegong)	1989	1

1 The spoken language of Luxembourg is Letzeburgish; the official languages are French and German. In official publications political parties are usually recorded under their French-language names. Since the Second World War parties have frequently used their Letzeburgish names.

2 Right-wing breakaway from the Parti de la Droite led by Pierre Prüm.

3 One of the two Popular Independent deputies joined the PCS and the rest of the party merged with the Democratic Party immediately before the 1968 election.

4 Right-wing breakaway from the Socialist Workers' Party formed in 1971.

5 Literally 'forcibly enlisted'. A list formed by a pressure group claiming compensation for Luxembourg citizens forcibly enlisted into the German Army during the Second World War.

6 Splinter group from the Socialist Workers' Party led by Jean Gremling. Jean Gremling was the legal adviser to the Enrôlés de Force. The Independant Socialist and Enrôlés de Force lists were allied in the 1979 election with the former's list headed by Gremling, contesting the Centre constituency and the latter the three other constituencies.

7 Literally Alternative List - 'Defend yourselves'.

8 List presented by a pressure group claiming that private sector pensions should be raised to the five sixths of final salary paid to former public sector employees.

9 Electoral alliance of the Green Left Ecological Initiative (GLEI) and the Green Alternative Party (GAP) in the North constituency.

10 Formed as the result of a split in the Green Alternative Party in the Chamber of Deputies during the 1984 to 1989 parliamentary term.

Table 15.2 DATES OF ELECTIONS : CHAMBRE DES DÉPUTÉS

1	28 July 1918 [1]	10	6 June 1948 (P)
2	26 October 1919	11	3 June 1951 (P)
3	28 May 1922 (P)	12	30 May 1954
4	1 March 1925	13	1 February 1959
5	3 June 1928 (P)	14	7 June 1964
6	7 June 1931 (P)	15	15 December 1968
7	3 June 1934 (P)	16	26 May 1974
8	6 June 1937 (P)	17	10 June 1979
9	21 October 1945	18	17 June 1984
		19	18 June 1989

1 Constituent Assembly

(P) indicates a partial election.

Table 15.3a LUXEMBOURG Total Votes 1919-1937

	1919[1]	1922[2]	1925[1]	1928[3]	1931[4]	1934[5]	1937[6]
PARTY VOTES							
1 Party of the Right	55,237	n.a	45,720	41,735	43,408	26,093	33,104
2 Social Democratic Party	16,294	n.a	17,381	34,697	29,697	18,397	17,186
3 Liberal League	14,907	n.a	-	-	-	-	-
4 Independent National Party	7,971	n.a	7,354	-	-	-	-
5 People's Independent Party	4,053	-	-	-	-	-	-
6 Independents of the East	3,151	n.a	5,671	5,253	-	7,244	-
7 Communist Party	-	-	965	-	2,719	3,225	-
8 Liberal Left	-	-	3,038	-	-	-	-
9 Radical Party	-	-	5,126	3,390	4,854	-	-
10 Radical Socialist Party	-	-	10,288	-	11,047	-	-
11 Radical Liberal Party	-	-	-	-	-	6,441	6,602
12 Democratic List	-	-	-	-	-	-	6,801
13 Free List	-	-	-	-	-	-	2,933
14 Liberal Party	-	-	-	-	-	-	2,511
15 Peasants and Middle Classes	-	-	-	-	-	-	1,785
Others	3,023	-	11,779	3,587	10,366	1,204	-

1 General election.
2 Partial election in the Centre and North constituencies. The Ministry of State reports that voting figures are not available for this election.
3 Partial election in the South and East constituencies and a special election in the Centre constituency where an election was held to choose an extra deputy.
4 Partial elections in the Centre and North constituencies and a special election in the South constituency to choose two additional deputies.
5 Partial election in the East and South constituencies.
6 Partial election in the Centre and North constituencies.

Source: Service Central de la Statistique, 1973: 445-447.

Table 15.3b LUXEMBOURG Percentage of Votes 1919-1937

	1919	1922	1925	1928	1931	1934	1937
Valid Votes	83.0	n.a	96.7	95.9	95.6	94.2	96.1
PARTY VOTES							
1 Party of the Right	52.8	n.a	42.6	47.1	42.5	41.7	46.7
2 Social Democratic Party	15.6	n.a	16.2	39.1	29.1	29.4	24.2
3 Liberal League	14.2	n.a	-	-	-	-	-
4 Independent National Party	7.6	n.a	6.9	-	-	-	-
5 People's Independent Party	3.9	-	-	-	-	-	-
6 Independents of the East	3.0	n.a	5.3	5.9	-	11.6	-
7 Communist Party	-	-	0.9	-	2.7	5.2	-
8 Liberal Left	-	-	2.8	-	-	-	-
9 Radical Party	-	-	4.8	3.8	4.8	-	-
10 Radical Socialist Party	-	-	9.6	-	10.8	-	-
11 Radical Liberal Party	-	-	-	-	-	10.3	9.3
12 Democratic List	-	-	-	-	-	-	9.6
13 Free List	-	-	-	-	-	-	4.1
14 Liberal Party	-	-	-	-	-	-	3.5
15 Peasants and Middle Classes	-	-	-	-	-	-	2.5
Others	2.9	-	11.0	4.0	10.2	1.9	-

Table 15.3c LUXEMBOURG Number of Seats Won in the Chambre des Députés 1919-1937

	1919	1922[1]	1925	1928[2]	1931[3]	1934[4]	1937[5]
1 Party of the Right	27	13	22	13	14	12	13
2 Social Democratic Party	8	2	8	10	5	10	7
3 Liberal League	7	6	–	–	–	–	–
4 Independent National Party	3	4	3	–	–	–	–
5 People's Independent Party	2	–	–	–	–	–	–
6 Independents of the East	1	–	2	2	–	3	–
7 Communist Party	–	–	0	–	0	1	–
8 Liberal Left	–	–	1	–	–	–	–
9 Radical Party	–	–	3	2	2	–	–
10 Radical Socialist Party	–	–	5	–	2	–	–
11 Radical Liberal Party	–	–	–	–	–	3	2
12 Democratic List	–	–	–	–	–	–	2
13 Free List	–	–	–	–	–	–	0
14 Liberal Party	–	–	–	–	–	–	1
15 Peasants and Middle Classes	–	–	–	–	–	–	1
Others	0	0	3	1	4	0	–
Total Seats	48	25	47	28	27	29	26

1 Partial election. After the election the overall composition of the Chamber was: Party of the Right 25, Socialist Workers' Party 7, Liberal Party 9, Independent National Party 4, People's Party 2 and Independents of the East one.

2 Partial election. After the election the overall composition of the Chamber was: Party of the Right 23, Socialist Workers' Party 12, Independent National Party 3, Independents of the East 2, Liberal Left 1, Radical Party 3, Radical Socialist Party 5, and others 3.

3 Partial election. After the election the overall composition of the Chamber was: Party of the Right 26, Socialist Workers' Party 15, Radical Party 4, Independents of the East 2, Radical Socialist Party 2, and others 5.

4 Partial election. After the election the overall composition of the Chamber was: Party of the Right 25, Socialist Workers' Party 14, Independents of the East 3, Radical Liberals 3, Radical Socialist Party 2, Radical Party 2, Communist Party 1 and others four.

5 Partial election. After the election the overall composition of the Chamber was: Party of the Right 25, Socialist Workers' Party 17, Independents of the East 3, Radical Liberal Party 5, Democratic List 2, Liberal Party 1, Peasants and Middle Classes one.

Source: Service Central de la Statistique, 1973.

Table 15.3d LUXEMBOURG Percentage of Seats Won in the Chambre des Députés 1919-1937

	1919	1922	1925	1928	1931	1934	1937
1 Party of the Right	56.3	52.0	45.8	46.4	51.9	41.4	50.0
2 Social Democratic Party	16.7	8.0	17.0	35.7	18.5	34.5	26.9
3 Liberal League	14.6	24.0	-	-	-	-	-
4 Independent National Party	6.3	16.0	5.4	-	-	-	-
5 People's Independent Party	4.2	-	-	-	-	-	-
6 Independents of the East	2.1	-	4.3	7.1	-	10.3	-
7 Communist Party	-	-	0.0	-	0.0	3.4	-
8 Liberal Left	-	-	2.2	7.1	-	-	-
9 Radical Party	-	-	5.4	-	7.4	-	-
10 Radical Socialist Party	-	-	10.6	-	7.4	-	-
11 Radical Liberal Party	-	-	-	-	-	10.3	7.7
12 Democratic List	-	-	-	-	-	-	7.7
13 Free List	-	-	-	-	-	-	0.0
14 Liberal Party	-	-	-	-	-	-	3.8
15 Peasants and Middle Classes	-	-	-	-	-	-	3.8
Others	0.0	0.0	5.4	3.6	14.8	0.0	-

Table 15.4a LUXEMBOURG Total Votes 1945-1989

	1945	1948[1]	1951[2]	1954	1959	1964	1968	1974	1979	1984	1989
Electorate	n.a	84,724	92,110	183,590	188,286	191,788	192,601	205,817	212,614	215,792	218,940
Valid Votes	153,596	73,674	79,662	162,063	165,596	163,158	160,184	175,376	175,808	179,994	180,733
Invalid Votes	5,487	4,191	3,951	8,029	8,240	10,544	10,382	10,151	13,101	11,657	10,599
Total Votes	159,083	77,865	83,613	170,092	173,836	173,702	170,566	185,527	188,909	191,651	191,332
PARTY VOTES											
1 Christian Social Party	66,438	25,610	32,254	70,532	61,624	55,144	56,534	49,253	60,595	61,180	54,832
2 Socialist Workers	34,745	26,641	25,907	51,230	52,353	55,539	46,735	44,461	37,492	53,054	44,340
6 Independents of the East	2,330	-	-	-	-	-	-	-	-	-	-
7 Communist Party	16,466	10,105	2,418	11,338	11,423	16,145	19,750	14,438	8,095	7,317	7,436
14 Liberal Party	1,816	-	-	-	-	-	-	-	-	-	-
16 Democratic Party	26,738	8,176	15,959	19,233	32,219	18,903	27,198	38,395	36,437	33,982	29,087
17 Middle Class Party	-	-	-	3,637	-	-	-	-	-	-	
18 Independent Movement	-	-	-	-	-	8,923	641	-	-	-	-
19 Social Dem. Party	-	-	-	-	-	-	-	16,649	10,622	-	-
20 Enrôlés de force	-	-	-	-	-	-	-	-	7,768	-	-
21 Independent Socialists	-	-	-	-	-	-	-	-	3,345	4,051	-
22 Alternative List	-	-	-	-	-	-	-	-	1,571	-	-
23 Green Alternative	-	-	-	-	-	-	-	-	-	7,049	6,197
24 5/6 Pensions Action	-	-	-	-	-	-	-	-	-	-	13,411
25 Ecologists for North	-	-	-	-	-	-	-	-	-	-	1,850
26 Green Left	-	-	-	-	-	-	-	-	-	-	6,315
27 Luxembourg for the Luxembourgers	-	-	-	-	-	-	-	-	-	-	3,952
Others	134	-	-	-	791	-	-	1,645	619	317	1,695

1 Partial elections in the South and East constituencies.
2 Partial elections in the North and Centre constituencies.

Source: Service Central de la Statistique, 1984: 119-121 and figures provided by the Ministry of State.

Table 15.4b LUXEMBOURG Percentage of Votes 1945-1989

	1945	1948	1951	1954	1959	1964	1968	1974	1979	1984	1989
Total Votes	n.a	91.9	90.8	92.6	92.3	90.6	88.6	90.1	88.9	88.8	87.3
Valid Votes	n.a	87.0	86.5	88.2	91.9	85.1	83.2	85.2	82.7	87.4	82.5
Invalid Votes	n.a	4.9	4.3	4.4	4.4	5.5	5.4	4.9	6.2	5.4	4.8
Share Invalid	n.a	5.6	4.9	4.9	4.9	6.4	6.4	5.8	7.3	6.5	5.5
PARTY VOTES											
1 Christian Social Party	44.7	36.3	42.1	45.2	38.9	35.7	37.5	29.9	36.4	36.6	32.4
2 Socialist Workers'	23.4	37.8	33.8	32.9	33.0	35.9	31.0	27.0	22.5	31.8	26.2
6 Independents of the East	1.6	-	-	-	-	-	-	-	-	-	-
7 Communist Party	11.1	14.3	3.2	7.3	7.2	10.4	13.1	8.8	4.9	4.4	4.4
14 Liberal Party	1.2	-	-	-	-	-	-	-	-	-	-
16 Democratic Party	18.0	11.6	20.9	12.3	20.3	12.2	18.0	23.3	21.9	20.4	17.2
17 Middle Class Party	-	-	-	2.3	-	-	-	-	-	-	-
18 Independent Movement	-	-	-	-	-	5.8	0.4	-	-	-	-
19 Social Dem. Party	-	-	-	-	-	-	-	10.1	6.4	-	-
20 Enrôlés de force	-	-	-	-	-	-	-	-	4.6	-	-
21 Independent Socialists	-	-	-	-	-	-	-	-	2.0	2.4	-
22 Alternative List	-	-	-	-	-	-	-	-	0.9	-	-
23 Green Alternative	-	-	-	-	-	-	-	-	-	4.2	3.7
24 5/6 Pensions Action	-	-	-	-	-	-	-	-	-	-	7.9
25 Ecologists for North	-	-	-	-	-	-	-	-	-	-	1.1
26 Green Left	-	-	-	-	-	-	-	-	-	-	3.7
27 Luxembourg for the Luxembourgers	-	-	-	-	-	-	-	-	-	-	2.3
Others	0.1	-	-	-	0.5	-	-	1.0	0.4	0.2	1.1

Table 15.4c LUXEMBOURG Number of Seats Won in the Chambre des Députés 1945-1989

	1945	1948[1]	1951[2]	1954	1959	1964	1968	1974	1979	1984	1989
1 Christian Social Party	25	12	9	26	21	22	21	18	24	25	22
2 Socialist Workers	11	9	10	17	17	21	18	17	14	21	18
6 Independents of the East	1	–	–	–	–	–	–	–	–	–	–
7 Communist Party	5	0	4	3	3	5	6	5	2	2	1
14 Liberal Party	–	–	–	–	–	–	–	–	–	–	11
16 Democratic Party	9	5	3	6	11	6	11	14	15	14	–
17 Middle Class Party	–	–	–	0	–	–	–	–	–	–	–
18 Independent Movement	–	–	–	–	–	2	0	–	–	–	–
19 Social Dem. Party	–	–	–	–	–	–	–	5	2	–	–
20 Enrôlés de force	–	–	–	–	–	–	–	–	1	–	–
21 Independent Socialists	–	–	–	–	–	–	–	–	1	0	–
22 Alternative List	–	–	–	–	–	–	–	–	0	–	
23 Green Alternative	–	–	–	–	–	–	–	–	–	2	2
24 5/6 Pensions Action	–	–	–	–	–	–	–	–	–	–	4
25 Ecologists for North	–	–	–	–	–	–	–	–	–	–	0
26 Green Left	–	–	–	–	–	–	–	–	–	–	2
27 Luxembourg for the Luxembourgers	–	–	–	–	–	–	–	–	–	–	0
Others	0	–	–	0	0	–	–	0	–	0	0
Total Seats	51	26	26	52	52	56	56	59	59	64	60

1 Partial election. After the election the overall composition of the Chamber of Deputies was: Christian Social Party 21, Socialist Workers' Party 15, Democrats 9 and Communist Party five.

2 Partial election. After the election the overall composition of the Chamber of Deputies was: Christian Social Party 21, Socialist Workers' Party 19, Democrats 8 and Communists four.

Source: Service Central de la Statistique and figures provided by the Ministry of State.

Table 15.4d LUXEMBOURG Percentage of Seats Won in the Chambre des Députés 1945-1989

	1945	1948	1951	1954	1959	1964	1968	1974	1979	1984	1989
1 Christian Social Party	49.0	46.2	34.6	50.0	40.4	39.3	37.5	30.5	40.7	39.1	36.7
2 Socialist Workers	21.6	34.6	38.5	32.7	32.7	37.5	32.1	28.8	23.7	32.8	30.0
6 Independents of the East	2.0	-	-	-	-	-	-	-	-	-	-
7 Communist Party	9.8	0.0	15.4	5.8	5.8	8.9	10.7	8.5	3.4	3.1	1.7
14 Liberal Party	-	-	-	-	-	-	-	-	-	-	-
16 Democratic Party	17.6	19.2	11.5	11.5	21.2	10.7	19.6	23.7	25.4	21.9	18.3
17 Middle Class Party	-	-	-	0.0	-	-	-	-	-	-	-
18 Independent Movement	-	-	-	-	-	3.6	0.0	-	-	-	-
19 Social Dem. Party	-	-	-	-	-	-	-	8.5	3.4	-	-
20 Enrôlés de force	-	-	-	-	-	-	-	-	1.7	-	-
21 Independent Socialists	-	-	-	-	-	-	-	-	1.7	0.0	-
22 Alternative Lists	-	-	-	-	-	-	-	-	0.0	-	-
23 Green Alternative	-	-	-	-	-	-	-	-	-	3.1	3.3
24 5/6 Pensions Action	-	-	-	-	-	-	-	-	-	-	6.7
25 Ecologists for North	-	-	-	-	-	-	-	-	-	-	0.0
26 Green Left	-	-	-	-	-	-	-	-	-	-	3.3
27 Luxembourg for the Luxembourgers	-	-	-	-	-	-	-	-	-	-	0.0
Others	0.0	-	-	0.0	0.0	-	-	0.0	-	0.0	0.0

Chapter 16

MALTA

During the nineteenth century Malta was ruled by a British Governor, assisted by a Council of Government. After 1849 the Council included elected members. In 1887 the elected members were given a majority of seats. Nationalist candidates committed to the defence of Italian, the language of the island's traditional social elite, were almost unfailingly elected. Conflict between the elected majority and the governor over the language question led to the suspension of the constitution. In 1903 a Council of Government was introduced in which elected members were in a minority. Nationalist members were regularly returned, often unopposed (Dobie, 1967: 38-79).

In 1921 Malta was granted internal self-government. A bicameral legislature was established. The 32 members of the Legislative Assembly were elected by single transferable vote in multi-member constituencies. The ballot was secret. The vote was confined to literate men aged at least 21, who had an income from property of at least £5 a year or paid rent of at least £5 a year. Those who had received public assistance during the previous three years were disenfranchised. The Senate consisted of ten members elected by Legislative Assembly voters aged over 35 and ten chosen by different organizations: two each by the Archbishop of Malta, the Maltese nobility, university graduates, the Chamber of Commerce and the Trade Union Council.

The 1921 election was the first contested by well organized political parties. Two parties emerged as defenders of the Italian language, the Maltese Political Union and National Democratic Party. They were opposed by the pro-English language Constitutional Party and the Malta Labour Party. The Constitution was suspended in 1930 and restored in 1932. It was revoked in 1936 and replaced by a Council of Government of five ex-officio members plus members nominated by the Governor. In 1939 the composition of the Council was modified to provide for 10 elected members plus eight ex officio and two nominated by the Governor.

In 1947 a single-chamber Legislative Assembly and universal adult suffrage were introduced. Following a political crisis over relations with the United Kingdom the Constitution was again suspended in 1958. In 1962 self-government was restored and in 1964 Malta became independent. The independence Constitution made no changes in the franchise requirements or electoral system, but the Legislative Assembly was renamed the House of Representatives. The voting age was reduced to 18 with effect at the 1976 election.

The use of the single transferable vote has meant that there is not an exact relationship between a party's first preference votes and the seats it wins. A constitutional crisis followed the 1981 general election, when the ruling Labour Party retained its absolute majority in the House of Representatives despite winning fewer votes than the Nationalist Party. After a year-long boycott of the House by the Nationalists, a constitutional reform was introduced to ensure that whichever party won a majority of first preference votes would be awarded a majority of the seats in the House of Representatives. This provision was enforced in the 1987 election when the Labour Party won 34 seats with 49 per cent of the vote, and the Nationalists, with 51 percent won only 31 seats. As the party with an absolute majority of the vote the Nationalists were entitled to a further four seats to ensure that party a parliamentary majority.

Sources:

Annual Abstract of Statistics (Valletta: Central Office of Statistics, 1970)

Colonial Office, Malta, *Report of Constitutional Commissioner* (London: Her Majesty's Stationery Office, 1947)

Department of Information, *The Constitution and the Electoral Commission* (Valletta: 1986)

E. Dobie, *Malta's Road to Independence* (Norman: University of Oklahoma Press, 1967)

H. Frendo, *Party Politics in a Fortress Colony* (Valletta: Midsea Books, 1979)

S. Howe, 'The Maltese general election of 1987', *Electoral Studies*, 6,3, (1987) 235-247

Results of Poll/Rizultat Tal-Vatazzjoni-General Elections/Elezzjonijiet Generali 1976 (Valletta: Government Printer 1976) and subsequent volumes in the same series

M.J. Schiavone, *L'-Elezzjonijiet F'Malta 1849-1981* (Valletta: Pubblikazzjoni Bugelli, 1987)

Table 16.1 POLITICAL PARTIES IN MALTA SINCE 1921

	Party Names	Elections Contested Years	Number
1	Constitutional Party [1]	1921-39; 1950-53	8
2	Democratic Nationalist Party I Partito Nazionalista Democratico	1921	1
3	Labour Party	1921ff	17
4	Maltese Political Union/Unione Politica Maltese	1921	1
5	Nationalist Party/Partit Nazzjonalista [2]	1924-1939; 1947ff	15
6	Jones Party	1945-1947	2
7	Democratic Action Party	1947-1950	2
8	Gozo Party	1947	1
9	Malta Workers' Party [3]	1950-1953	3
10	Progressive Constitutional Party [4]	1953ff	5
11	Christian Workers' Party [5]	1962-1966	2
12	Democratic Nationalist Party II [6]	1962-1966	2
13	Communist Party/Partit Komunista	1987	1

1 The Constitutional Party did not contest the 1945 election because it was opposed to an election before self-government was restored. The party was dissolved in 1946 and revived in June 1950.

2 A merger of the Democratic Nationalist Party and the Maltese Political Union in 1926. The Nationalist Party boycotted the 1945 election because it took place before the restoration of self-government.

3 Formed in October 1949 by Dr. Paul Boffa, the former leader of the Labour Party.

4 Formed in October 1953 by Mabel Strickland, a former leader of the Constitutional Party.

5 Former members of the Nationalist Party led by Dr. Herbert Ganado.

6 Founded in 1961 by Anthony Pellegrini, formerly General Secretary of the Malta Labour Party.

Table 16.2 DATES OF ELECTIONS: LEGISLATIVE ASSEMBLY 1921-1962; HOUSE OF REPRESENTATIVES [1] 1966-

1.	18-19 October 1921	9.	5-7 May 1951
2.	9-10 June 1924	10.	12-14 December 1953
3.	7-9 August 1927	11.	26-28 February 1955
4.	11-13 June 1932	12.	17-19 February 1962
5.	22-24 July 1939	13.	26-28 March 1966
6.	10-12 November 1945	14.	12-14 June 1971
7.	25-27 October 1947	15.	17-18 September 1976
8.	2-4 September 1950	16.	12 December 1981
		17.	5 May 1987

1 In 1939 and 1945 elections to the Council of Government.

Source: the Electoral Registrar, Valletta

Table 16.3a MALTA Total Votes 1921-1951

	1921	1924	1927	1932	1939	1945	1947	1950	1951
Electorate	27,104	27,104	44,089	52,610	46,852	61,206	140,703	140,516	151,977
Valid Votes	20,475	24,069	34,444	47,305	35,139	25,672	105,494	106,129	112,628
Invalid Votes	159	179	277	1,353	378	918	647	691	738
Total Votes	20,634	24,248	34,721	48,658	35,517	26,590	106,141	106,820	113,366
PARTY VOTES									
1 Constitutional Party	5,183	8,128	14,130	13,513	19,156	-	-	10,584	9,151
2 Democratic Nationalist Party I	2,465	-	-	-	-	-	-	-	-
3 Labour Party	4,742	4,891	4,773	4,221	3,100	19,071	63,145	30,332	40,315
4 Maltese Political Union	7,999	-	-	-	-	-	-	-	-
5 Nationalist Party	-	10,777	15,079	28,906	11,618	-	19,041	31,431	39,946
6 Jones Party	-	-	-	-	-	3,786	3,664	-	-
7 Democratic Action Party	-	-	-	-	-	-	14,010	6,361	-
8 Gozo Party	-	-	-	-	-	-	5,491	-	-
9 Malta Workers' Party	-	-	-	-	-	-	-	24,616	21,053
Others	86	273	462	665	1,265	2,815	143	2,805	2,163

Source: *Annual Abstract of Statistics*, 1970 p.74.

Table 16.3b MALTA Percentage of Votes 1921-1951

	1921	1924	1927	1932	1939	1945	1947	1950	1951
Total Votes	76.1	89.5	78.8	92.5	75.8	43.4	75.4	76.0	74.6
Valid Votes	75.5	88.8	78.1	89.9	75.0	41.9	75.0	75.5	74.1
Invalid Votes	0.6	0.7	0.6	2.6	0.8	1.5	0.5	0.5	0.5
Share Invalid	0.8	0.7	0.8	2.8	1.1	3.5	0.6	0.6	0.7
PARTY VOTES									
1 Constitutional Party	25.3	33.8	41.5	28.6	54.5	-	-	10.0	8.1
2 Democratic Nationalist Party I	12.0	-	-	-	-	-	-	-	-
3 Labour Party	23.2	20.3	13.9	8.9	8.8	74.3	59.9	28.6	35.8
4 Maltese Political Union	39.1	-	-	-	-	-	-	-	-
5 Nationalist Party	-	44.8	43.8	61.1	33.1	-	18.0	29.6	35.5
6 Jones Party	-	-	-	-	-	14.7	3.5	-	-
7 Democratic Action Party	-	-	-	-	-	-	13.3	6.0	-
8 Gozo Party	-	-	-	-	-	-	5.2	-	-
9 Malta Workers' Party	-	-	-	-	-	-	-	23.2	18.7
Others	0.4	1.1	1.3	1.4	3.6	11.0	0.1	2.6	1.9

Table 16.3c MALTA Number of Seats Won in the Legislative Assembly 1921-1951[1]

	1921	1924	1927	1932	1939	1945	1947	1950	1951
1 Constitutional Party	7	9	14	10	6	–	–	4	4
2 Democratic Nationalist Party I	4	–	–	–	–	–	–	–	–
3 Labour Party	7	8	3	1	1	9	24	11	14
4 Maltese Political Union	14	–	–	–	–	–	–	–	–
5 Nationalist Party	–	15	15	21	3	–	7	12	15
6 Jones Party	–	–	–	–	–	1	2	–	–
7 Democratic Action Party	–	–	–	–	–	–	4	1	–
8 Gozo Party	–	–	–	–	–	–	3	–	–
9 Malta Workers' Party	–	–	–	–	–	–	–	11	7
Others	0	0	0	0	0	0	0	1	0
Total Seats	32	32	32	32	10	10	40	40	40

[1] In 1939 and 1945 the Council of Government.

Source: *Annual Abstract of Statistics*, 1970 p. 76.

Table 16.3d MALTA Percentage of Seats Won in the Legislative Assembly 1921-1951

	1921	1924	1927	1932	1939	1945	1947	1950	1951
1 Constitutional Party	21.9	28.1	43.8	31.3	60.0	-	-	10.0	10.0
2 Democratic Nationalist Party I	12.5	-	-	-	-	-	-	-	-
3 Labour Party	21.9	25.0	9.4	3.1	10.0	90.0	60.0	27.5	35.0
4 Maltese Political Union	43.8	-	-	-	-	-	-	-	-
5 Nationalist Party	-	46.9	46.9	65.6	30.0	-	17.5	30.0	37.5
6 Jones Party	-	-	-	-	-	10.0	5.0	-	-
7 Democratic Action Party	-	-	-	-	-	-	10.0	2.5	-
8 Gozo Party	-	-	-	-	-	-	7.5	-	-
9 Malta Workers' Party	-	-	-	-	-	-	-	27.5	17.5
Others	0.0	0.0	0.0	0.0	0.0	0.0	0.0	2.5	0.0

Table 16.4a MALTA Total Votes 1953-1987

	1953	1955	1962	1966	1971	1976	1981	1987
Electorate	148,478	149,380	166,936	161,490	181,768	217,724	238,237	246,292
Valid Votes	118,453	120,655	150,606	143,347	168,059	205,440	224,151	235,168
Invalid Votes	880	588	927	1,526	854	1,403	1,315	1,551
Total Votes	119,333	121,243	151,533	144,873	168,913	206,843	225,466	236,719
PARTY VOTES								
1 Constitutional Party	1,385	-	-	-	-	-	-	-
3 Labour Party	52,771	68,447	50,974	61,774	85,448	105,854	109,990	114,936
5 Nationalist Party	45,180	48,514	63,262	68,656	80,753	99,550	114,132	119,721
9 Malta Workers' Party	14,000	-	-	-	-	-	-	-
10 Progressive Constitutional Party	5,117	3,649	7,290	2,086	1,756	-	-	-
11 Christian Workers' Party	-	-	14,285	8,561	-	-	-	-
12 Democratic Nationalist Party II	-	-	13,968	1,878	-	-	-	-
13 Communist Party	-	-	-	-	-	-	-	119
Others	-	45	827	392	102	36	29	392

Source: *Annual Abstract of Statistics*, 1970, pp. 76-77 and *Results of Poll* 1976 ff.

Table 16.4b MALTA Percentage of Votes 1953-1987

	1953	1955	1962	1966	1971	1976	1981	1987
Total Votes	80.4	81.2	90.8	89.7	92.9	95.0	94.6	96.1
Valid Votes	79.8	80.8	90.2	88.8	92.5	94.4	94.1	95.5
Invalid Votes	0.6	0.4	0.6	0.9	0.5	0.6	0.6	0.6
Share Invalid	0.7	0.5	0.6	1.1	0.5	0.7	0.6	0.7
PARTY VOTES								
1 Constitutional Party	1.2	-	-	-	-	-	-	-
3 Labour Party	44.6	56.7	33.8	43.1	50.8	51.5	49.1	48.9
5 Nationalist Party	38.1	40.2	42.0	47.9	48.1	48.5	50.9	50.9
9 Malta Workers' Party	11.8	-	-	-	-	-	-	-
10 Progressive Constitutional Party	4.3	3.0	4.8	1.5	1.0	-	-	-
11 Christian Workers' Party	-	-	9.5	6.0	-	-	-	-
12 Democratic Nationalist Party II	-	-	9.3	1.3	-	-	-	-
13 Communist Party	-	-	-	-	-	-	-	0.1
Others	-	0.0	0.5	0.3	0.1	0.0	0.0	0.2

Table 16.4c MALTA Number of Seats Won in the House of Representatives 1953-1987[1]

	1953	1955	1962	1966	1971	1976	1981	1987
1 Constitutional Party	0	–	–	–	–	–	–	–
3 Labour Party	19	23	16	22	28	34	34	34
5 Nationalist Party	18	17	25	28	27	31	31	35[2]
9 Malta Workers' Party	3	–	–	–	–	–	–	–
10 Progressive Constitutional Party	0	0	1	0	0	–	–	–
11 Christian Workers' Party	–	–	4	0	–	–	–	–
12 Democratic Nationalist Party II	–	–	4	0	–	–	–	–
13 Communist Party	–	–	–	–	–	–	–	0
Others	–	0	0	0	0	0	0	0
Total Seats	40	40	50	50	55	65	65	69

1 From 1953 to 1962 the Legislative Assembly.

2 The Nationalist Party won an absolute majority of votes but only 31 of the 65 constituency seats in the House. As provided in the 1987 constitutional reform the Nationalist Party co-opted four additional members to make a parliamentary majority.

Source: *Annual Abstract of Statistics*, 1970 pp 76-77 and *Results of Poll* 1976 ff.

Table 16.4d MALTA Percentage of Seats Won in the House of Representatives 1953-1987

	1953	1955	1962	1966	1971	1976	1981	1987
1 Constitutional Party	0.0	-	-	-	-	-	-	-
3 Labour Party	47.5	57.5	32.0	44.0	50.9	52.3	52.3	49.3
5 Nationalist Party	45.0	42.5	50.0	56.0	49.1	47.7	47.7	50.7
9 Malta Workers' Party	7.5	-	-	-	-	-	-	-
10 Progressive Constitutional Party	0.0	0.0	2.0	0.0	0.0	-	-	-
11 Christian Workers' Party	-	-	8.0	0.0	-	-	-	-
12 Democratic Nationalist Party II	-	-	8.0	0.0	-	-	-	-
13 Communist Party	-	-	-	-	-	-	-	0.0
Others	-	0.0	0.0	0.0	0.0	0.0	0.0	0.0

Chapter 17

THE NETHERLANDS

Representative government was introduced in the Netherlands in 1848. The Dutch parliament, the States General, consists of two houses, the First Chamber (Eerste Kamer) and the Second Chamber (Tweede Kamer). The government is constitutionally responsible to both Chambers. The Second Chamber is directly elected. The First Chamber is elected by the Provincial States. The powers of the First Chamber are limited; it can only approve or reject bills without amendment.

The 1848 franchise for the Second Chamber was limited to males over 23 who paid a varying minimum of taxes on ownership of land, enterprise or visible signs of wealth. In 1850 eleven per cent of the adult male population was entitled to vote. In 1887 the franchise requirements were lowered, and the size of the electorate doubled. A new electoral system was introduced. Deputies were chosen in single-member constituencies. If no candidate received a majority in the first ballot, a plurality sufficed in the second ballot. In larger cities there were multi-member constituencies, in which each elector had as many votes as seats. In 1896 the qualifications for the suffrage were again reduced, but the minimum voting age was increased to 25. About half of this age group was now able to vote, a figure which increased to two-thirds by 1913. At the same time the multi-member constituencies were replaced by single-member districts.

Until the 1880s the States General was dominated by Liberal, Conservative and Catholic groups, but parties were not organized to contest elections. The establishment of the Anti-Revolutionary Party in 1879 was followed by the development of a popularly based party system. The Conservatives quickly dwindled to a negligible force; the Liberal and later, Catholic and Christian Historical groups began to establish their own party organizations.

In 1917 universal male suffrage was introduced, and with it proportional representation, using the largest remainder system. Voting was made compulsory. In 1919 women were given the vote. Since 1937 the highest average system using the d'Hondt method has been employed to allocate seats. In 1946 the voting age was reduced to 23. In October, 1956 there was a further reduction to 21 and since 1972 the voting age has been 18. Compulsory voting was abolished in 1970.

The country is divided into 18 constituencies (19 from 1986) for the establishment of electoral lists, but the 150 seats are allocated on a nationwide basis. In order to be represented in the Tweede Kamer the law requires a party to secure only a very small percentage share of the vote. The barrier clause has varied from one-half of one per cent in 1918 to three-quarters of one per cent from 1922 to 1933, one per cent from 1937 to 1952 and two-thirds of one per cent since 1956. For generations the Dutch party system was a byword for stability with each of the main parties characterized as a rocksolid 'pillar' (*zuil*). In the 1970s the social cohesion of the traditional established parties began to weaken, especially among religious parties, leading to mergers and the entry of new parties into the Second Chamber (Lijphart, 1975; Andeweg, 1982; Irwin and Dittrich, 1984; Daalder, 1987).

Sources:

R.B. Andeweg, *Dutch Voters Adrift* (Leiden: Political Science Department, 1982)

Central Bureau of Statistics, *Statistiek der Verkiezingen 1959: Tweede Kamer der Staten Generaal* - and subsequent volumes in the same series

H. Daalder, 'Nationale politieke stelsels: Nederland', in L. van der Land (ed.), *Repertorium voor de Sociale Wetenschappen, Volume One, Politiek* (Amsterdam: Elsevier, 1958) 223-9

H. Daalder, 'De kleine politieke partijen: een voorlopige poging tot inventarisatie', *Acta Politica*, 1 (1966) 172-96

H. Daalder, 'The Netherlands: Opposition in a Segmented Society', in R.A. Dahl (ed.), *Political Opposition in Western Democracies* (New Haven: Yale University Press, 1966) 188-236

H. Daalder, 'The Dutch party system: from segmentation to polarization--and then?', in H. Daalder (ed.), *Party Systems in Denmark, Austria, Switzerland, the Netherlands and Belgium* (London: Frances Pinter, 1987) 193-284

G. Irwin and K. Dittrich, 'And the walls came tumbling down : party dealignment in the Netherlands', in R.J. Dalton, S.C. Flanagan and P.A. Beck (eds.), *Electoral Change in Advanced Industrial Democracies* (Princeton: Princeton University Press, 1984) 267-97

A. Lijphart, *The Politics of Accommodation: Pluralism and Democracy in the Netherlands* (Berkeley: University of California, 2nd ed., 1975)

A. Lijphart, 'The Dutch electoral system in comparative perspective', *Netherlands Journal of Sociology*, 14 (1978) 115-133

Table 17.1 POLITICAL PARTIES IN THE NETHERLANDS SINCE 1888

	Party Names	Elections Contested Years	Number
1	Anti-Revolutionary Party (Anti-Revolutionaire Partij - ARP) [1]	1888-1977	25
2	Catholic Party; from 1897 Catholic Electoral League (Rooms-Katholieke Bond van Kiesverenigingen); from 1926 Roman Catholic States Party (Rooms-Katholieke Staatspartij); since 1945 Catholic People's Party (Katholieke Volkspartij - KVP) [2]	1888-1977	25
3	Liberal Union (Liberale Unie) [3]	1888-1918	9
4	Radicals (Radicalen); from 1901 Liberal Democratic League (Vrijzinnig-Democratische Bond) [4]	1888-1937	15
5	Social Democratic League (Sociaal-Democratische Bond); from 1897 Free Socialist (Vrije Socialisten) [5]	1888-1891; 1897-1905	5
6	Christian Historicals; various local lists until the establishment of the Christian Historical Union (Christelijk-Historische Unie - CHU) in 1908 [6]	1894-1977	23
7	Social Democratic Workers' Party (Sociaal-Democratische Arbeiders Partij - SDAP) [7]	1894-1937	13
8	Free Liberal League (Bond van Vrije Liberalen) [8]	1894-1918	8
9	Christian Democrats; various independent parties until the establishment in 1926 of the Christian Democratic Union (Christen-Democratische Unie - CDU) [9]	1918-1937	6
10	Communist Party. In 1918 Social Democratic Party (Sociaal-Democratische Partij); then Communistische Partij Holland - CPH; since 1936 Communistische Partij Nederland - CPN [10]	1918ff	19
11	Economic League (Economische Bond) [11]	1918	1
12	Farmers' League (Plattelandersbond); from 1933 National Party of Farmers, Horticulturalists and Middle Class (Nationaal Boeren, Tuinders en Middenstandspartij)	1918-1937	6
13	Middle Class Party (Middenstandspartij)	1918	1
14	Political Reformed Party (Staatkundig Gereformeerde Partij - SGP) [12]	1918ff	19
15	Socialist Party (Socialistische Partij)	1918-1925	19
16	Liberal States Party: The Freedom League (Liberale Staatspartij: De Vrijheidsbond) [13]	1922-1937	5

17	New Reformed State Party (Hervormd-Gereformeerde Staatspartij) [14]	1922-1937	5
18	Roman Catholic People's Party (Rooms-Katholieke Volkspartij) [15]	1925-1937	4
19	Middle Party for City and Country (Middenpartij voor Stadt en Land)	1929	1
20	Revolutionary Socialist Party (Revolutionair Socialistische Partij)	1929-1933	2
21	League for National Renewal (Verbond voor Nationaal Herstel) [16]	1933-1937	2
22	National Socialist Movement (Nationaal-Socialistische Beweging) [17]	1937	1
23	Labour Party (Partij van der Arbeid-PvdA) [18]	1946ff	13
24	Liberal Party (Volkspartij voor Vrijheid en Democratie - VVD) [19]	1946ff	13
25	Catholic National Party (Katholieke Nationale Partij) [20]	1948-1952	2
26	Reformed Political Union (Gereformeerd Politiek Verbond) [21]	1952ff	11
27	Pacifist Socialist Party (Pacifistisch-Socialistische Partij) [22]	1959ff	9
28	Farmers' Party (Boerenpartij); since 1977 People's Party of the Right (Rechtse-Volkspartij)	1959-1982	8
29	Democrats '66 (Democraten '66-D'66)	1967ff	7
30	Democratic Socialists '70 (Democratische Socialisten '70-DS'70) [23]	1971-1982	5
31	Middle Class Party (Middenstands Partij)	1971-1972	2
32	Radical Political Party (Politieke Partij Radicalen) [24]	1971ff	6
33	Roman Catholic party (Rooms-Katholieke Partij Nederland; in 1971 Nieuwe Roomse Partij) [25]	1971-1981	4
34	Christian Democratic Appeal (Christen Democratisch Appel) [26]	1977ff	4
35	Reformed Political Federation (Reformatorische Politieke Federatie) [27]	1977ff	4
36	Centre Party (Centrumpartij) [28]	1981ff	3
37	Evangelical People's Party (Evangelische Volkspartij - EVP) [29]	1981ff	3

1 Founded in 1879 the ARP was the principal party of Orthodox (Gereformeerd) Calvinism. Merged with the Catholic People's Party and the Christian Historical Union to form the Christian Democratic Appeal in 1977.

2 Merged with the ARP and the CHU to form the Christian Democratic Appeal in 1979.

3 Founded as a federation of liberal election societies in 1885, the Liberal Union was subject to numerous splits before most liberals were reunited as the Freedom League (later the Liberal States Party) in 1921.

4 Breakaway from the Liberal Union. Joined another splinter to form the Liberal Democratic League in 1901. Merged with other parties to form the Labour Party in 1946.

5 Founded in 1891 by F. Doela Nieuwenhuis. The party rejected electoral politics in 1893, but followers of Nieuenhuis continued to contest elections until 1905.

6 Includes the Free Anti-Revolutionaries (Vrij Anti-Revolutionairen), which split from the ARP in 1894; the Christian Electoral Union (Christelijk-Historische Kiezersbond) established in 1896, and joined with the Free-Anti-Revolutionaries to form the Christian Historical Party (Christelijk-Historische Partij) in 1903. The Friesian Christian Historical Party (Bond van Kiesverenigingen op Christelijk Historische Grondslag) was established in 1898. It merged with the Christian Historical Party to form the Christian Historical Union in 1908.

7 Breakaway from the Social Democratic League after the latter decided to abandon electoral politics. Merged with other parties to found the Labour Party in 1946.

8 Conservative breakaway from the Liberal Union.

9 Left-wing Protestant political party which merged with others to form the Labour Party in 1946.

10 Formed by a group expelled from the Social Democratic Workers' Party in 1909.

11 A breakaway group from the Liberal Democratic League. One of the parties forming the Freedom League in 1921.

12 Conservative Calvinist Party which broke away from the Anti-Revolutionary Party in 1918.

13 A merger in 1921 of the Liberal Union, the Free Liberal League, the Economic League and minor liberal groups initially known as the Freedom League (Vrijheidsbond) and renamed the Liberale Staatspartij in 1928.

14 A splinter from the Christian Historical Union.

15 Breakaway from the Catholic Electoral League. Merged with the Rooms-Katholieke Arbeiderspartij and the Katholiek-Democratische Bond to form the Katholieke Democratische Partij. Merged with the Rooms-Katholieke Staatspartij in 1939.

16 Semi-fascist party.

17 Leaders collaborated with the German occupiers from 1940 to 1945. Banned after liberation.

18 A merger of the Social Democratic Workers' Party, the Liberal Democratic League, the Christian Democratic Union, and some left-wing Catholics and Christian Historicals.

19 Successor to the Liberal States Party which was reformed as the Party of Freedom (Partij van de Vrijheid) after the Second World War. The party was renamed the People's Party for Freedom and Democracy in 1948 when it merged with a breakaway group from the Labour Party composed of former members of the Liberal Democratic League.

20 Right-wing breakaway from the Catholic People's Party (KVP). Reunited with the KVP in 1955.

21 Breakaway from the Anti-Revolutionary Party resulting from a schism in the Gereformeerde Church.

22 Left-wing socialist party founded in 1957 by ex-members of the Labour and Communist parties and pacifists.

23 Right-wing breakaway from the Labour Party.

24 Left-wing party founded by four ex-Catholic People's Party deputies.

25 Conservative breakaway from the Catholic People's Party (KVP); it found the KVP too liberal on moral issues.

26 Initially an electoral alliance of the Catholic People's Party, the Anti-Revolutionary Party and the Christian Historical Union; they merged to form a single party in 1979.

27 Right-wing breakaway from the Anti-Revolutionary Party. The new party was opposed to the merger of the ARP in the Christian Democratic Appeal.

28 Extreme right-wing anti-immigrant party.

29 Left-wing breakaway from the ARP.

Table 17.2 DATES OF ELECTIONS : TWEEDE KAMER[1]

1.	6 March 1888	15.	26 May 1937
2.	23 July 1891	16.	17 May 1946
3.	10 April 1894	17.	7 July 1948
4.	9 February 1897	18.	25 June 1952
5.	14 June 1901	19.	13 June 1956
6.	16 June 1905	20.	12 March 1959
7.	11 June 1909	21.	15 May 1963
8.	17 June 1913	22.	15 February 1967
9.	15 June 1917	23.	28 March 1971
10.	3 July 1918	24.	29 November 1972
11.	5 July 1922	25.	25 May 1977
12.	1 July 1925	26.	26 May 1981
13.	3 July 1929	27.	8 September 1982
14.	26 April 1933	28.	21 May 1986

[1] Before 1918 dates refer to the first ballot.

Source: Netherlands Central Bureau of Statistics.

Table 17.3a NETHERLANDS Total Votes 1888-1918[1]

	1888	1891	1894	1897	1901	1905	1909	1913	1918
Electorate	292,613	293,888	299,073	576,598	609,634	752,692	843,487	960,595	1,517,380
Valid Votes	236,168	205,946	164,894	413,714	389,020	583,388	596,060	768,708	1,344,209
PARTY VOTES									
1 Anti Revolutionary Party	74,048	60,738	28,274	108,581	106,670	143,843	166,270	111,081	179,523
2 Catholics	48,922	41,579	33,454	83,826	61,160	76,605	76,087	165,560	402,908
3 Liberal Union	96,157	86,888	49,132	90,178	80,825	116,746	106,086	128,706	83,173
8 Free Liberal League	-	-	32,967	36,021	26,423	47,630	33,464	50,541	51,195
4 Radicals	4,686	4,409	5,151	14,863	28,398	51,595	54,007	56,462	71,582
5 Social Democratic League/Free Socialists	2,020	2,102	-	-	-	-	-	-	-
6 Christian Historicals	-	-	11,118	44,159	26,233	62,770	63,306	80,402	87,983
7 Social Democratic Workers[2]	-	-	365	12,312	36,981	65,501	82,855	142,185	296,145
9 Christian Democrats	-	-	-	-	-	-	-	-	27,221[3]
10 Communist Party	-	-	-	-	-	-	-	-	31,043
11 Economic League	-	-	-	-	-	-	-	-	42,042
12 Farmers' League	-	-	-	-	-	-	-	-	9,068
13 Middle Class Party	-	-	-	-	-	-	-	-	12,663
14 Political Reformed Party	-	-	-	-	-	-	-	-	5,129
15 Socialist Party	-	-	-	-	-	-	-	-	8,950
Others	10,335	10,230	4,433	23,774	22,330	18,638	13,985	33,771	35,584[4]

1 The 1917 election figures are not reported. By prior agreement among the political parties the distribution of seats after the election was to remain unchanged; 51 candidates were returned unopposed and only 21.4 percent of the electorate voted.

2 From 1897 to 1905 the Social Democrat Workers vote includes some votes cast for Free Socialist candidates.

3 Comprises Christen-Democratische Partij, 10,653 votes; Christelijk Sociale Partij, 8,152 votes and Bond van Christen-Socialisten, 8,416 votes.

4 Includes Neutrale Partij, 7,186 votes and the Verbond Democratiseering Weermacht, 6,830 votes.

Sources: 1888 to 1913 Jan Verhoef and 1918 Robbert van den Helm, both of the University of Leiden.

Table 17.3b NETHERLANDS Percentage of Votes 1888-1918

	1888	1891	1894	1897	1901	1905	1909	1913	1918
Total Votes	80.7	70.1	55.1	71.8	63.8	77.5	70.7	80.0	88.6
Valid Votes	80.7	70.1	55.1	71.8	63.8	77.5	70.7	80.0	88.6
PARTY VOTES									
1 Anti Revolutionary Party	31.4	29.5	17.1	26.2	27.4	24.7	27.9	14.5	13.4
2 Catholics	20.7	20.2	20.3	20.3	15.7	13.1	12.8	21.5	30.0
3 Liberal Union	40.7	42.2	29.8	21.8	20.8	20.0	17.8	16.7	6.2
8 Free Liberal League	–	–	20.0	8.7	6.8	8.2	5.6	6.6	3.8
4 Radicals	2.0	2.1	3.1	3.6	7.3	8.8	9.1	7.3	5.3
5 Social Democratic League/Free Socialists	0.9	1.0	–	–	–	–	–	–	–
6 Christian Historicals	–	–	6.7	10.7	6.7	10.8	10.6	10.5	6.5
7 Social Democratic Workers	–	–	0.2	3.0	9.5	11.2	13.9	18.5	22.0
9 Christian Democrats	–	–	–	–	–	–	–	–	2.0
10 Communist Party	–	–	–	–	–	–	–	–	2.3
11 Economic League	–	–	–	–	–	–	–	–	3.1
12 Farmers' League	–	–	–	–	–	–	–	–	0.7
13 Middle Class Party	–	–	–	–	–	–	–	–	0.9
14 Political Reformed Party	–	–	–	–	–	–	–	–	0.4
15 Socialist Party	–	–	–	–	–	–	–	–	0.7
Others	4.4	5.0	2.7	5.7	5.7	3.2	2.3	4.4	2.6

Table 17.3c NETHERLANDS Number of Seats Won in the Tweede Kamer 1888-1918[1]

	1888	1891	1894	1897	1901	1905	1909	1913	1918
1 Anti Revolutionary Party	27	21	15	17	22 (1)	15	25 (1)	11	13
2 Catholics	25	25	25	22 (7)	25 (9)	25 (6)	25 (10)	25 (5)	30
3 Liberal Union	46	53		35	18	25	20	22	6
		}	57						
8 Free Liberal League	–	–		13	8	9	4	10	4
4 Radicals	0	1	3	4	9	11	9	7	5
5 Social Democratic League/Free Socialists	1	0	–	1	1	1	–	–	–
6 Christian Historicals	–	–	0	6	10	8	10	10	7
7 Social Democratic Workers	–	–	0	2	6	6	7	15	22
9 Christian Democrats	–	–	–	–	–	–	–	–	3[2]
10 Communist Party	–	–	–	–	–	–	–	–	2
11 Economic League	–	–	–	–	–	–	–	–	3
12 Farmers' League	–	–	–	–	–	–	–	–	1
13 Middle Class Party	–	–	–	–	–	–	–	–	1
14 Political Reformed Party	–	–	–	–	–	–	–	–	0
15 Socialist Party	–	–	–	–	–	–	–	–	1
Others	1	0	0	0	1	0	0	0	2[3]
Total Seats	100	100	100	100 (7)	100 (10)	100 (6)	100 (11)	100 (5)	100

1 Figures in parentheses identify the number of deputies returned unopposed.
2 Christen-Democratische Partij, one; Christelijk Sociale Partij, one, and Bond van Christen-Socialisten, one.
3 Neutrale Partij one, and Verbond Democratiseering Weermacht, one.

Sources: 1888 to 1913 Jan Verhoef and 1918 Robbert van den Helm, both of the University of Leiden.

Table 17.3d NETHERLANDS Percentage of Seats Won in the Tweede Kamer 1888-1918

	1888	1891	1894	1897	1901	1905	1909	1913	1918
1 Anti Revolutionary Party	27.0	21.0	15.0	17.0	22.0	15.0	25.0	11.0	13.0
2 Catholics	25.0	25.0	25.0	22.0	25.0	25.0	25.0	25.0	30.0
3 Liberal Union	46.0	53.0		35.0	18.0	25.0	20.0	22.0	6.0
		}	57.0						
8 Free Liberal League	–	–		13.0	8.0	9.0	4.0	10.0	4.0
4 Radicals	0.0	1.0	3.0	4.0	9.0	11.0	9.0	7.0	5.0
5 Social Democratic League/Free Socialists	1.0	0.0	–	1.0	1.0	1.0	–	–	–
6 Christian Historicals	–	–	0.0	6.0	10.0	8.0	10.0	10.0	7.0
7 Social Democratic Workers	–	–	0.0	2.0	6.0	6.0	7.0	15.0	22.0
9 Christian Democrats	–	–	–	–	–	–	–	–	3.0
10 Communist Party	–	–	–	–	–	–	–	–	2.0
11 Economic League	–	–	–	–	–	–	–	–	3.0
12 Farmers' League	–	–	–	–	–	–	–	–	1.0
13 Middle Class Party	–	–	–	–	–	–	–	–	1.0
14 Political Reformed Party	–	–	–	–	–	–	–	–	0.0
15 Socialist Party	–	–	–	–	–	–	–	–	1.0
Others	1.0	0.0	0.0	0.0	1.0	0.0	0.0	0.0	2.0

Table 17.4a NETHERLANDS Total Votes 1922-1956

	1922	1925	1929	1933	1937	1946	1948	1952	1956
Electorate	3,299,672	3,543,058	3,821,612	4,126,490	4,462,859	5,275,888	5,433,633	5,792,679	6,125,210
Valid Votes	2,929,569	3,085,862	3,379,503	3,721,828	4,058,077	4,760,711	4,932,959	5,335,747	5,727,742
Invalid Votes	n.a	150,729	162,482	177,827	154,826	152,304	156,623	165,981	121,910
Total Votes	n.a	3,236,591	3,541,985	3,899,655	4,212,903	4,913,015	5,089,582	5,501,728	5,849,652
PARTY VOTES									
1 Anti Revolutionary Party	402,277	377,426	391,832	499,890	665,501	614,201	651,612	603,329	567,535
2 Catholics/Catholic People's Party	874,745	883,333	1,001,589	1,037,343	1,170,431	1,466,582	1,531,154	1,529,508	1,815,310
4 Radicals	134,595	187,183	208,979	188,950	239,502	-	-	-	-
6 Christian Historical Union	318,669	305,587	354,548	339,808	302,829	373,217	453,226	476,195	482,918
7 Social Democratic Workers	567,769	706,689	804,714	798,632	890,661	-	-	-	-
9 Christian Democrats	40,300[1]	13,944	12,780	38,459	85,004	-	-	-	-
10 Communist Party	53,664	36,770	67,541[2]	118,236	136,026	502,963	382,001	328,621	272,054
12 Farmers' League	45,816	62,639	34,805	47,653	6,891	-	-	-	-
14 Political Reformed Party	26,744	62,513	76,709	93,273	78,619	101,759	116,937	129,081	129,517
15 Socialist Party	12,412	11,790	-	-	-	-	-	-	-
16 Liberal States Party	271,358	269,564	249,105	258,732	160,260	-	-	-	-
17 New Reformed State Party	20,431	30,258	35,931	33,988	24,543	-	-	-	-
18 Roman Catholic People's Party	-	36,571	23,804	40,894	27,665	-	-	-	-
19 Middle Party for City and Country	-	-	39,955	-	-	-	-	-	-
20 Revolutionary Socialist Party	-	-	21,812	48,905	-	-	-	-	-
21 League for National Renewal	-	-	-	30,329	6,270	-	-	-	-
22 National Socialist Movement	-	-	-	-	171,137	-	-	-	-
23 Labour Party	-	-	-	-	-	1,347,940	1,263,058	1,545,867	1,872,209
24 Liberal Party	-	-	-	-	-	305,287	391,923	471,040	502,530
25 Catholic National Party	-	-	-	-	-	-	62,376	144,520	-
26 Reformed Political Union	-	-	-	-	-	-	-	35,497	37,206
Others	160,789	101,595	55,399	146,736	92,728	48,762	80,672	72,087	48,463

1 Comprises Christen-Democratische Partij, 20,760 votes and Christelijk Sociale Partij, 19,540 votes.
2 Comprises 29,863 votes cast for the Wijnkoop Communist Party and 36,578 votes cast for the de Wisser Communist Party.

Source: figures provided by Robbert van den Helm, University of Leiden.

Table 17.4b NETHERLANDS Percentage of Votes 1922-1956

	1922	1925	1929	1933	1937	1946	1948	1952	1956
Total Votes	n.a	91.4	92.7	94.5	94.4	93.1	93.7	95.0	95.5
Valid Votes	88.8	87.1	88.4	90.2	90.9	90.2	90.8	92.1	93.5
Invalid Votes	n.a	4.3	4.3	4.3	3.5	2.9	2.9	2.9	2.0
Share Invalid	n.a	4.7	4.6	4.6	3.7	3.1	3.1	3.0	2.1
PARTY VOTES									
1 Anti Revolutionary Party	13.7	12.2	11.6	13.4	16.4	12.9	13.2	11.3	9.9
2 Catholics/Catholic People's Party	29.9	28.6	29.6	27.9	28.8	30.8	31.0	28.7	31.7
4 Radicals	4.6	6.1	6.2	5.1	5.9	-	-	-	-
6 Christian Historical Union	10.9	9.9	10.5	9.1	7.5	7.8	9.2	8.9	8.4
7 Social Democratic Workers	19.4	22.9	23.8	21.5	21.9	-	-	-	-
9 Christian Democrats	1.4	0.5	0.4	1.0	2.1	-	-	-	-
10 Communist Party	1.8	1.2	2.0	3.2	3.4	10.6	7.7	6.2	4.7
12 Farmers' League	1.6	2.0	1.0	1.3	0.2	-	-	-	-
14 Political Reformed Party	0.9	2.0	2.3	2.5	1.9	2.1	2.4	2.4	2.3
15 Socialist Party	0.4	0.4	-	-	-	-	-	-	-
16 Liberal States Party	9.3	8.7	7.4	7.0	3.9	-	-	-	-
17 New Reformed State Party	0.7	1.0	1.1	0.9	0.6	-	-	-	-
18 Roman Catholic People's Party	-	1.2	0.7	1.1	0.7	-	-	-	-
19 Middle Party for City and Country	-	-	1.2	-	-	-	-	-	-
20 Revolutionary Socialist Party	-	-	0.6	1.3	-	-	-	-	-
21 League for National Renewal	-	-	-	0.8	0.2	-	-	-	-
22 National Socialist Movement	-	-	-	-	4.2	-	-	-	-
23 Labour Party	-	-	-	-	-	28.3	25.6	29.0	32.7
24 Liberal Party	-	-	-	-	-	6.4	7.9	8.8	8.8
25 Catholic National Party	-	-	-	-	-	-	1.3	2.7	-
26 Reformed Political Union	-	-	-	-	-	-	-	0.7	0.6
Others	5.5	3.3	1.6	3.9	2.3	1.0	1.6	1.4	0.8

Table 17.4c NETHERLANDS Number of Seats Won in the Tweede Kamer 1922-1956

	1922	1925	1929	1933	1937	1946	1948	1952	1956
1 Anti Revolutionary Party	16	13	12	14	17	13	13	12	15
2 Catholics/Catholic People's Party	32	30	30	28	31	32	32	30	49
4 Radicals	5	7	7	6	6	–	–	–	–
6 Christian Historical Union	11	11	11	10	8	8	9	9	13
7 Social Democratic Workers	20	24	24	22	23	–	–	–	–
9 Christian Democrats	0	0	0	1	2	–	–	–	–
10 Communist Party	2	1	2[1]	4	3	10	8	6	7
12 Farmers' League	2	1	1	1	–	–	–	–	–
14 Political Reformed Party	1	2	3	3	2	2	2	2	3
15 Socialist Party	0	0	–	–	–	–	–	–	–
16 Liberal States Party	10	9	8	7	4	–	–	–	–
17 New Reformed State Party	0	1	1	1	0	–	–	–	–
18 Roman Catholic People's Party	–	1	0	1	0	–	–	–	–
19 Middle Party for City and Country	–	–	1	–	–	–	–	–	–
20 Revolutionary Socialist Party	–	–	0	1	–	–	–	–	–
21 League for National Renewal	–	–	–	1	0	–	–	–	–
22 National Socialist Movement	–	–	–	–	4	–	–	–	–
23 Labour Party	–	–	–	–	–	29	27	30	50
24 Liberal Party	–	–	–	–	–	6	8	9	13
25 Catholic National Party	–	–	–	–	–	–	1	2	–
26 Reformed Political Union	–	–	–	–	–	–	–	0	0
Others	1	0	0	0	0	0	0	0	0
Total Seats	100	100	100	100	100	100	100	100	150

[1] One each for the Wijnkoop and de Wisser Communist Party.

Source: figures provided by Robbert van den Helm, University of Leiden.

Table 17.4d NETHERLANDS Percentage of Seats Won in the Tweede Kamer 1922-1956

	1922	1925	1929	1933	1937	1946	1948	1952	1956
1 Anti Revolutionary Party	16.0	13.0	12.0	14.0	17.0	13.0	13.0	12.0	10.0
2 Catholics/Catholic People's Party	32.0	30.0	30.0	28.0	31.0	32.0	32.0	30.0	32.7
4 Radicals	5.0	7.0	7.0	6.0	6.0	–	–	–	–
6 Christian Historical Union	11.0	11.0	11.0	10.0	8.0	8.0	9.0	9.0	8.7
7 Social Democratic Workers	20.0	24.0	24.0	22.0	23.0	–	–	–	–
9 Christian Democrats	0.0	0.0	0.0	1.0	2.0	–	–	–	–
10 Communist Party	2.0	1.0	2.0	4.0	3.0	10.0	8.0	6.0	4.7
12 Farmers' League	2.0	1.0	1.0	1.0	–	–	–	–	–
14 Political Reformed Party	1.0	2.0	3.0	3.0	2.0	2.0	2.0	2.0	2.0
15 Socialist Party	0.0	0.0	–	–	–	–	–	–	–
16 Liberal States Party	10.0	9.0	8.0	7.0	4.0	–	–	–	–
17 New Reformed State Party	0.0	1.0	1.0	1.0	0.0	–	–	–	–
18 Roman Catholic People's Party	–	1.0	0.0	1.0	0.0	–	–	–	–
19 Middle Party for City and Country	–	–	1.0	–	–	–	–	–	–
20 Revolutionary Socialist Party	–	–	0.0	1.0	–	–	–	–	–
21 League for National Renewal	–	–	–	1.0	0.0	–	–	–	–
22 National Socialist Movement	–	–	–	–	4.0	–	–	–	–
23 Labour Party	–	–	–	–	–	29.0	27.0	30.0	33.3
24 Liberal Party	–	–	–	–	–	6.0	8.0	9.0	8.7
25 Catholic National Party	–	–	–	–	–	–	1.0	2.0	–
26 Reformed Political Union	–	–	–	–	–	–	–	0.0	0.0
Others	1.0	0.0	0.0	0.0	0.0	0.0	0.0	0.0	0.0

Table 17.5a NETHERLANDS Total Votes 1959-1986

	1959	1963	1967	1971	1972	1977	1981	1982	1986
Electorate	6,427,864	6,748,611	7,452,776	8,048,726	8,916,947	9,506,318	10,040,121	10,216,634	10,727,701
Valid Votes	5,999,531	6,258,521	6,878,030	6,318,152	7,394,045	8,317,612	8,690,837	8,236,516	9,172,159
Invalid Votes	143,878	161,443	198,298	46,567	51,242	48,217	47,401	37,115	27,462
Total Votes	6,143,409	6,419,964	7,076,328	6,364,719	7,445,287	8,365,829	8,738,238	8,273,631	9,199,621
PARTY VOTES									
1 Anti Revolutionary Party	563,091	545,836	681,060	542,742	653,609	-	-	-	-
2 Catholic People's Party	1,895,914	1,995,352	1,822,904	1,379,672	1,305,401	-	-	-	-
6 Christian Historical Union	486,429	536,801	560,033	399,106	354,463	-	-	-	-
34 Christian Democratic Appeal	-	-	-	-	-	2,652,278	2,677,259	2,420,441	3,172,918
10 Communist Party	144,542	173,325	248,318	246,569	330,398	143,481	178,292	147,753	57,847
14 Political Reformed Party	129,678	143,818	138,069	148,192	163,114	177,010	171,324	156,636	159,740
23 Labour Party	1,821,285	1,753,084	1,620,112	1,554,280	2,021,454	2,813,793	2,458,452	2,503,517	3,051,678
24 Liberal Party	732,658	643,839	738,202	653,370	1,068,375	1,492,689	1,505,311	1,900,763	1,596,991
26 Reformed Political Union	39,972	46,324	59,156	101,790	131,236	79,421	70,878	67,163	88,381
27 Pacifist Socialist Party	110,499	189,373	197,206	90,738	111,262	77,972	184,422	187,567	110,182
28 Farmers' Party	39,423	133,231	327,953	69,656	143,239	69,914	17,371	21,987	-
29 Democrats '66	-	-	307,810	428,067	307,048	452,423	961,121	351,278	562,466
30 Democratic Socialists '70	-	-	-	336,714	304,714	59,487	48,568	-	-
31 Middle Class Party	-	-	-	95,706	32,970	-	-	-	-
32 Radical Political Party	-	-	-	116,049	354,829	140,910	171,042	136,446	115,203
33 Roman Catholic Party	-	-	-	23,047	67,658	33,227	20,812	-	-
35 Reformed Political Federation	-	-	-	-	-	53,220	108,364	124,235	83,582
36 Centre Party	-	-	-	-	-	-	12,242	68,423	36,741
37 Evangelical People's Party	-	-	-	-	-	-	45,189	56,466	21,998
Others	36,040	97,538	177,207	132,449	44,275	71,787	60,190	93,841	114,432

Source: Central Bureau of Statistics, *Statistiek der Verkiezingen*.

Table 17.5b NETHERLANDS Percentage of Votes 1959-1986

	1959	1963	1967	1971	1972	1977	1981	1982	1986
Total Votes	95.6	95.1	94.9	79.1	83.5	88.0	87.0	81.0	85.8
Valid Votes	93.3	92.7	92.3	78.5	82.9	87.5	86.6	80.6	85.5
Invalid Votes	2.2	2.4	2.7	0.6	0.6	0.5	0.5	0.4	0.3
Share Invalid	2.3	2.5	2.8	0.7	0.7	0.6	0.5	0.4	0.3
PARTY VOTES									
1 Anti Revolutionary Party	9.4	8.7	9.9	8.6	8.8	-	-	-	-
2 Catholic People's Party	31.6	31.9	26.5	21.8	17.7	-	-	-	-
6 Christian Historical Union	8.1	8.6	8.1	6.3	4.8	-	-	-	-
34 Christian Democratic Appeal	-	-	-	-	-	31.9	30.8	29.4	34.6
10 Communist Party	2.4	2.8	3.6	3.9	4.5	1.7	2.1	1.8	0.6
14 Political Reformed Party	2.2	2.3	2.0	2.3	2.2	2.1	2.0	1.9	1.7
23 Labour Party	30.4	28.0	23.6	24.6	27.3	33.8	28.3	30.4	33.3
24 Liberal Party	12.2	10.3	10.7	10.3	14.4	17.9	17.3	23.1	17.4
26 Reformed Political Union	0.7	0.7	0.9	1.6	1.8	1.0	0.8	0.8	1.0
27 Pacifist Socialist Party	1.8	3.0	2.9	1.4	1.5	0.9	2.1	2.3	1.2
28 Farmers' Party	0.7	2.1	4.8	1.1	1.9	0.8	0.2	0.3	-
29 Democrats '66	-	-	4.5	6.8	4.2	5.4	11.1	4.3	6.1
30 Democratic Socialists '70	-	-	-	5.3	4.1	0.7	0.6	-	-
31 Middle Class Party	-	-	-	1.5	0.4	-	-	-	-
32 Radical Political Party	-	-	-	1.8	4.8	1.7	2.0	1.7	1.3
33 Roman Catholic Party	-	-	-	0.4	0.9	0.4	0.2	-	-
35 Reformed Political Federation	-	-	-	-	-	0.6	1.2	1.5	0.9
36 Centre Party	-	-	-	-	-	-	0.1	0.8	0.4
37 Evangelical People's Party	-	-	-	-	-	-	0.5	0.7	0.2
Others	0.6	1.5	2.6	2.1	0.6	0.9	0.7	1.4	1.1

Table 17.5c NETHERLANDS Number of Seats Won in the Tweede Kamer 1959-1986

	1959	1963	1967	1971	1972	1977	1981	1982	1986
1 Anti Revolutionary Party	14	13	15	13	14	–	–	–	–
2 Catholic People's Party	49	50	42	35	27	–	–	–	–
6 Christian Historical Union	12	13	12	10	7	–	–	–	–
34 Christian Democratic Appeal	–	–	–	–	–	49	48	45	54
10 Communist Party	3	4	5	6	7	2	3	3	0
14 Political Reformed Party	3	3	3	3	3	3	3	3	3
23 Labour Party	48	43	37	39	43	53	44	47	52
24 Liberal Party	19	16	17	16	22	28	26	36	27
26 Reformed Political Union	0	1	1	2	2	1	1	1	1
27 Pacifist Socialist Party	2	4	4	2	2	1	3	3	1
28 Farmers' Party	0	3	7	1	3	1	0	0	–
29 Democrats '66	–	–	7	11	6	8	17	6	9
30 Democratic Socialists '70	–	–	–	8	6	1	0	–	–
31 Middle Class Party	–	–	–	2	0	–	–	–	–
32 Radical Political Party	–	–	–	2	7	3	3	2	2
33 Roman Catholic Party	–	–	–	0	1	0	0	–	–
35 Reformed Political Federation	–	–	–	–	–	0	2	2	1
36 Centre Party	–	–	–	–	–	–	0	1	0
37 Evangelical People's Party	–	–	–	–	–	–	0	1	0
Others	0	0	0	0	0	0	0	0	0
Total Votes	150	150	150	150	150	150	150	150	150

Source: Central Bureau of Statistics *Statistiek der Verkiezingen*.

Table 17.5d NETHERLANDS Percentage of Seats Won in the Tweede Kamer 1959-1986

	1959	1963	1967	1971	1972	1977	1981	1982	1986
1 Anti Revolutionary Party	9.3	8.7	10.0	8.7	9.3	-	-	-	-
2 Catholic People's Party	32.7	33.3	28.0	23.3	18.0	-	-	-	-
6 Christian Historical Union	8.0	8.7	8.0	6.7	4.7	-	-	-	-
34 Christian Democratic Appeal	-	-	-	-	-	32.7	32.0	30.0	36.0
10 Communist Party	2.0	2.7	3.3	4.0	4.7	1.3	2.0	2.0	0.0
14 Political Reformed Party	2.0	2.0	2.0	2.0	2.0	2.0	2.0	2.0	2.0
23 Labour Party	32.0	28.7	24.7	26.0	28.7	35.3	29.3	31.3	34.7
24 Liberal Party	12.7	10.7	11.3	10.7	14.7	18.7	17.3	24.0	18.0
26 Reformed Political Union	0.0	0.7	0.7	1.3	1.3	0.7	0.7	0.7	0.7
27 Pacifist Socialist Party	1.3	2.7	2.7	1.3	1.3	0.7	2.0	2.0	0.7
28 Farmers' Party	0.0	2.0	4.7	0.7	2.0	0.7	0.0	0.0	-
29 Democrats '66	-	-	4.7	7.3	4.0	5.3	11.3	4.0	6.0
30 Democratic Socialists '70	-	-	-	5.3	4.0	0.7	0.0	-	-
31 Middle Class Party	-	-	-	1.3	0.0	-	-	-	-
32 Radical Political Party	-	-	-	1.3	4.7	2.0	2.0	1.3	1.3
33 Roman Catholic Party	-	-	-	0.0	0.7	0.0	0.0	-	-
35 Reformed Political Federation	-	-	-	-	-	0.0	1.3	1.3	0.7
36 Centre Party	-	-	-	-	-	-	0.0	0.7	0.0
37 Evangelical People's Party	-	-	-	-	-	-	0.0	0.7	0.0
Others	0.0	0.0	0.0	0.0	0.0	0.0	0.0	0.0	0.0

Chapter 18

NEW ZEALAND

Representative institutions were first established in 1852 when New Zealand was a British colony; limited internal self-government was achieved in 1856. A bi-cameral parliament was created, consisting of a nominated Legislative Council and an elected House of Representatives. The Legislative Council was abolished in 1950.

The franchise established in the 1852 Constitution was originally limited to men aged 21 or over with a minimum property qualification or who paid a minimum annual rent. By 1866 17 per cent of the total European population was entitled to vote (Lipson, 1948:20). In 1879 manhood suffrage for Europeans was established, increasing the proportion of the population who could vote to 24 per cent. Women were given the vote in 1893. The secret ballot was introduced in European constituencies in 1870. The voting age was reduced to 20 in 1965 and 18 in 1974.

Plurality voting in single-member constituencies has been the norm in New Zealand elections with two exceptions. Between 1890 and 1904 inclusive there were four three-member constituencies in the major urban centres. In the 1908 and 1911 elections a two-ballot system was used. In the event of no candidate winning an absolute majority a run-off election was held a week later between the two leading candidates. Since 1914 the simple plurality single ballot single-member constituency system has been continuously in use.

Since 1867 special franchise provisions have been employed for the indigenous Maori, who numbered 8.8 per cent of the population in the 1981 census. Some Maoris were able to meet the property qualifications laid down in 1852, but because most Maori land was held in common their number was very limited. In 1867 in what was intended to be a temporary solution to this political problem, four Maori constituencies were established in which all adult Maori men could vote. The franchise was extended to Maori women in 1893. Public voting continued in the Maori constituencies until 1939.

Organized political parties did not develop until the 1890s. The initial electoral success of the Liberal Party was followed by the gradual disintegration of the Conservatives. The parliamentary Opposition consisted of individuals rather than a coherent party. By 1911 the Opposition had coalesced as the Reform Party. Labour candidates began standing independently of the Liberal Party at the end of the nineteenth century, but did not organise as the Labour Party until 1916 (Gustafson, 1980). Its growing strength led to the formation of an electoral alliance between the Liberal and Reform parties, and to their eventual merger as the National Party in 1936 (Milne, 1966: 28ff).

A major change in voting rights was made in 1975, allowing Maoris to choose whether to register in Maori or general electorates. About half are now registered in the four Maori electorates and about half on the general roll.

In 1986 a Royal Commission on electoral reform produced a report,'Towards a Better Democracy', which endorsed proportional representation for House of Representatives elections, with 60 members were to be elected by plurality in single member constituencies and 60 from a national constituency in which voters could only choose between closed party lists. At the 1987 election the Labour Prime Minister promised that there would be a referendum on proportional representation; in April 1989 it was announced that no referendum would be held.

Sources:

J. Boston,'Electoral reform in New Zealand: the report of the Royal Commission', *Electoral Studies*, 6 (1987) 105-114

General Election, 1957, Parliamentary Paper H33; from 1972, Parliamentary Paper E9 (Wellington, 1957ff) and subsequent volumes in the same series

B. D. Graham,'The Country Party idea in New Zealand politics, 1901-1935', *Studies in a Small Democracy*, ed. R. Chapman and K. Sinclair (Auckland: Paul's Book Arcade for the University of Auckland, 1963) 175-99

B.S. Gustafson, *Constitutional Changes Since 1870* (Auckland and London: Heineman, 1969)

B.S. Gustafson, *Labour's Path to Independence: the Origins and Establishment of the New Zealand Labour Party* (Auckland: Auckland University Press, 1980)

B.S. Gustafson, *The First Fifty Years: A History of the New Zealand National Party* (Auckland: Reed Methuen, 1986)

L. Lipson, *The Politics of Equality* (Chicago: University of Chicago Press, 1948)

E.M. McLeay,'Political argument about representation: the case of the Maori seats', *Political Studies*, 28 (1980) 43-62

A.H. McLintock (ed.), *An Encyclopaedia of New Zealand* (Wellington: Government Printer, 1976)

A. McRobie,'The electoral system and the 1978 election', *New Zealand at the Polls*, ed. H. Penniman (Washington, DC: American Enterprise Institute, 1980)

R.S. Milne, *Political Parties in New Zealand* (Oxford: Clarendon Press, 1966)

New Zealand Parliament, *House of Representatives: Appendices to the Journals*

C. Norton, *New Zealand Parliamentary Election Results 1946-1987*, Occasional Publication No. 1. Victoria University of Wellington, New Zealand, 1988

Royal Commission on the Electoral System, *Towards a Better Democracy* (Wellington: Government Printer, 1986)

H. Roth, 'The Communist vote in New Zealand', *Political Science*, 17 (1965) 26-35

J.D. Wilson, *New Zealand Parliamentary Record 1840-1984* (Wellington: Government Printer, 1985)

Table 18.1 POLITICAL PARTIES IN NEW ZEALAND SINCE 1890

	Party Names	Elections Years	Contested Number
1	Conservative Party	1890-1908	7
2	Liberal Party [1]	1890-1935	15
3	Labour Party [2]	1902ff	28
4	Reform Party	1911-1935	8
5	Country Party	1925-1935	4
6	Ratana Independent Movement [3]	1928-1935	3
7	Communist Party	1931-1935; 1946-1969	11
8	Democratic Party [4]	1935	1
9	National Party [5]	1938ff	17
10	Democratic Soldier Labour Party [6]	1943	1
11	Social Credit /Democratic Party [7]	1954ff	12
12	Socialist Unity Party [8]	1972-1984	5
13	Values Party	1972ff	6
14	Mana Motuhake [9]	1981ff	3
15	New Zealand Party [10]	1984ff	2

[1] Includes Liberal-Labour candidates in 1919 and National in 1925. In 1928 the United Party.

[2] Before 1916 various labour and socialist parties that amalgamated in 1916 to form the New Zealand Labour Party.

[3] The Maori Ratana Movement was founded in the early 1920s by T.W. Ratana. After the 1935 election it merged with the Labour Party.

[4] Established by former members of the United Party in 1934. Amalgamated with the National Party in 1936.

[5] A merger of the Reform and Liberal parties in 1936. The two parties had formed electoral alliances in the elections of 1931 and 1935.

[6] Founded as the Democratic Labour Party by John A. Lee, a leading figure in the Labour Party after his expulsion from it in 1940. Later renamed the Democratic Soldier Labour Party.

[7] Founded as the Social Credit Political League in 1953, the party was renamed the Social Credit Party in 1982 and the New Zealand Democratic Party in 1984.

[8] Breakaway from the Communist Party, founded in 1966.

[9] Mana Motuhake o Aotearoa - Dignity and Self Respect for Aotearoa (the Maori name for New Zealand). Breakaway from the Labour Party founded by Matiu Rata, a former Minister of Maori Affairs, in 1979.

[10] Founded in 1983 by Robert Jones, a businessman, to protest against the economic policies of the National Party government. It effectively disbanded by 1987, but a fringe group with the same name put up candidates in 31 of New Zealand's 97 electorates.

Table 18.2 DATES OF ELECTIONS : HOUSE OF REPRESENTATIVES

1	5 December 1890	17	25 September 1943
2	28 November 1893	18	27 November 1946
3	4 December 1896	19	30 November 1949
4	6 December 1899	20	1 September 1951
5	25 November 1902	21	13 November 1954
6	6 December 1905	22	30 November 1957
7	17 and 24 November 1908[1]	23	26 November 1960
8	7 and 14 December 1911[1]	24	30 November 1963
9	10 December 1914	25	26 November 1966
10	17 December 1919	26	29 November 1969
11	7 December 1922	27	25 November 1972
12	4 November 1925	28	29 November 1975
13	14 November 1928	29	25 November 1978
14	2 December 1931	30	28 November 1981
15	27 November 1935	31	14 July 1984
16	15 October 1938	32	15 August 1987

[1] In 1908 and 1911 the two dates given are for the first and second ballots.

Sources: *New Zealand Parliamentary Record,* 1969: 25 and the Chief Electoral Officer. Until 1951 European and Maori constituencies voted on different days. The dates refer to the European polling day.

Table 18.3a NEW ZEALAND Total Votes 1890-1922[1]

	1890	1893	1896	1899	1902	1905	1908	1911	1914	1919	1922
Electorate[1]	183,171	302,997	339,230	373,744	415,798	476,473	537,003	599,092	616,043	683,420	707,717
Valid Votes[2]	136,337	304,176	359,404	387,629	416,962	407,234	426,871	477,336	534,457	552,971	634,728
Invalid Votes[3]	n.a	n.a	n.a	n.a	4,974	5,468	4,596	4,143	5,618	7,587	6,580
Total Votes	73,332	220,082	258,254	279,330	318,859	396,657	428,648	492,912	521,525	550,327	620,650
PARTY VOTES											
1 Conservative Party	39,338	74,482	134,397	141,758	85,769	120,810	-	-	-	-	-
2 Liberal Party	76,548	175,814	165,259	204,331	215,845	216,312	250,445	194,089	230,336	155,877	166,708
3 Labour Party	-	-	-	-	10,501	3,623	17,492	40,759	49,482	131,402	150,448
4 Reform Party	-	-	-	-	-	-	118,773	165,127	250,424	199,010	249,735
Others	20,451	53,880	59,748	41,540	104,847	66,489	40,161	77,361	4,215	66,682	67,837

1 Number of registered voters in the European constituencies. There was no electoral register in the four Maori constituencies until 1949. Figures include electors registered in constituencies where there was no contest. Electors in these constituencies (numbers of seats in brackets): 1890, 13,688 (6); 1893; 10,539 (3); 1899, 13,626 (3); 1911, 9,050 (1); and 1922, 7,601 (1).

2 From 1890 to 1902 excludes votes cast in the Maori constituencies. From 1883 to 1902 includes additional votes cast in the four three-member constituencies.

3 Invalid and total votes figures refer to the European constituencies only. No record of invalid votes was kept in the Maori constituencies until 1938

Source: Wilson, 1985: 286, 289 and 294.

Table 18.3b NEW ZEALAND Percentage of Votes 1890-1922

	1890	1893	1896	1899	1902	1905	1908	1911	1914	1919	1922
Valid Votes	74.4	72.6	76.1	74.7	76.7	82.1	79.0	82.8	83.7	79.4	87.7
PARTY VOTES											
1 Conservative Party	28.9	24.5	37.4	36.6	20.6	29.7	27.8	-	-	-	-
2 Liberal Party	56.1	57.8	46.0	52.7	51.8	53.1	58.7	40.7	43.1	28.9	26.3
3 Labour Party	-	-	-	-	2.5	0.9	4.1	8.5	9.3	23.8	23.7
4 Reform Party	-	-	-	-	-	-	-	34.6	46.9	36.0	39.4
Others	15.0	17.7	16.6	10.7	25.1	16.3	9.4	16.2	0.8	12.1	10.7

Table 18.3c NEW ZEALAND Number of Seats Won in the House of Representatives 1890-1922[1]

	1890	1893	1896	1899	1902	1905	1908	1911	1914	1919	1922
1 Conservative Party	25	13	25	19	19	16	26	-	-	-	-
2 Liberal Party	38	51	39	49	47	58	50	33	33	21	22
3 Labour Party	-	-	-	-	0	0	1	4	6	8	17
4 Reform Party	-	-	-	-	-	-	-	37	41	47	37
Others	7	6	6	2	10	6	3	6	-	4	4
Total Seats	70	70	70	70	70	80	80	80	80	80	80

1 Until 1905 excludes the four Maori seats.

Source: Wilson, 1985: 287.

Table 18.3d NEW ZEALAND Percentage of Seats Won in the House of Representatives 1890-1922

	1890	1893	1896	1899	1902	1905	1908	1911	1914	1919	1922
1 Conservative Party	35.7	18.6	35.7	27.1	25.0	20.0	32.5	-	-	-	-
2 Liberal Party	54.3	72.9	55.7	70.0	61.8	72.5	62.5	41.3	41.3	26.3	27.5
3 Labour Party	-	-	-	-	0.0	0.0	1.3	5.0	7.5	10.0	21.3
4 Reform Party	-	-	-	-	-	-	-	46.3	51.3	58.8	46.3
Others	10.0	8.6	8.6	2.9	13.2	7.5	3.8	7.5	0.0	5.0	5.0

Table 18.4a NEW ZEALAND Total Votes 1925-1957[1]

	1925	1928	1931	1935	1938	1943	1946	1949	1951	1954	1957
Electorate[2]	754,113	844,633	838,344	919,798	995,173	1,021,034	1,081,898	1,113,852	1,205,762	1,209,670	1,252,329
Valid Votes	687,285	756,331	714,511	852,637	946,393	941,828	1,047,205	1,073,181	1,069,791	1,096,893	1,157,365
Invalid Votes	6,906	8,300	4,955	6,887	6,373	9,957	7,999	6,724	3,632	8,716	5,696
Total Votes	n.a	n.a	n.q	n.a	n.a	n.a	1,055,204	1,079,905	1,073,423	1,105,609	1,163,061
PARTY VOTES											
2 Liberal Party	139,887	225,042	-	-	-	-	-	-	-	-	-
3 Labour Party	187,378	198,092	244,881	392,965	528,290	447,919	536,994	506,100	490,143	484,082	559,096
4 Reform Party	319,810	263,382	-	-	-	-	-	-	-	-	-
5 Country Party	2,398	11,990	16,710	21,048	-	-	-	-	-	-	-
6 Ratana Movement	-	5,108	7,157	8,569	-	-	-	-	-	-	-
7 Communist Party	-	-	639	600	-	-	1,181	3,499	528	1,134	706
8 Democrat Party	-	-	-	66,965	-	-	-	-	-	-	-
9 National Party	-	-	396,004[3]	280,222[3]	381,081	402,887	507,139	556,805	577,630	485,630	511,699
10 Democratic Soldier Labour Party	-	-	-	-	-	40,443	-	-	-	-	-
11 Social Credit Party	-	-	-	-	-	-	-	-	-	122,068	83,498
Others	37,812	52,717	49,120	82,268	37,022	50,599	1,891	6,777	1,490	3,979	2,366

1 From 1925 to 1943 figures for the electorate and invalid and total votes refer to the European constituencies only.
2 Figures include voters registered in constituencies where there was no contest. Electors in these constituencies numbered (seats in brackets): 1925, 7,428 (1), 1931, 36,443 (4) and 1943, 20,837 (2).
3 In 1931 and 1935 an electoral alliance of the Liberal and Reform parties.

Source: Wilson, 1985: 286, 287 and 294, and Roth, 1985.

Table 18.4b NEW ZEALAND Percentage of Votes 1925-1957

	1925	1928	1931	1935	1938	1943	1946	1949	1951	1954	1957
Total Votes	90.0	88.0	83.3	90.7	92.9	92.1	97.5	94.0	89.0	91.4	93.4
Valid Votes	89.1	87.1	82.7	90.0	92.2	91.1	96.8	93.4	88.7	90.7	93.0
Invalid Votes	0.9	1.0	0.6	0.7	0.6	1.0	0.7	0.6	0.3	0.7	0.5
Share Invalid	1.0	1.1	0.7	0.8	0.7	1.1	0.8	0.6	0.3	0.8	0.5
PARTY VOTES											
2 Liberal Party	20.4	29.8	-	-	-	-	-	-	-	-	-
3 Labour Party	27.3	26.2	34.3	46.1	55.8	47.6	51.3	47.2	45.8	44.1	48.3
4 Reform Party	46.5	34.8	-	-	-	-	-	-	-	-	-
5 Country Party	0.3	1.6	2.3	2.5	-	-	-	-	-	-	-
6 Ratana Movement	-	0.7	1.0	1.0	-	-	-	-	-	-	-
7 Communist Party	-	-	0.1	0.1	-	-	0.1	0.3	0.0	0.1	0.1
8 Democrat Party	-	-	-	7.8	-	-	-	-	-	-	-
9 National Party	-	-	55.4	32.8	40.3	42.8	48.4	51.9	54.0	44.3	44.2
10 Democratic Soldier Labour Party	-	-	-	-	-	4.3	-	-	-	-	-
11 Social Credit Party	-	-	-	-	-	-	-	-	-	11.1	7.2
Others	5.5	7.0	6.9	9.6	3.9	5.4	0.2	0.6	0.1	0.4	0.2

Table 18.4c NEW ZEALAND Number of Seats Won in the House of Representatives 1925-1957

	1925	1928	1931	1935	1938	1943	1946	1949	1951	1954	1957
2 Liberal Party	11	27	–	–	–	–	–	–	–	–	–
3 Labour Party	12	19	24	53	53	45	42	34	30	35	41
4 Reform Party	55	27	–	–	–	–	–	–	–	–	–
5 Country Party	–	1	1	2	–	–	–	–	–	–	–
6 Ratana Movement	–	0	0	2	–	–	–	–	–	–	–
7 Communist Party	–	–	0	0	–	–	0	0	0	0	0
8 Democrat Party	–	–	–	0	–	–	–	–	–	–	–
9 National Party	–	–	51[1]	19[1]	25	34	38	46	50	45	39
10 Democratic Soldier Labour Party	–	–	–	–	–	0	–	–	–	–	–
11 Social Credit Party	–	–	–	–	–	–	–	–	–	0	0
Others	2	6	4	4	2	1	0	0	0	0	0
Total Seats	80	80	80	80	80	80	80	80	80	80	80

[1] An electoral alliance of the Liberal and Reform parties.

Source: Wilson, 1985: 286, 287 and 294.

Table 18.4d NEW ZEALAND Percentage of Seats Won in the House of Representatives 1925-1957

	1925	1928	1931	1935	1938	1943	1946	1949	1951	1954	1957
2 Liberal Party	13.8	33.8	-	-	-	-	-	-	-	-	-
3 Labour Party	15.0	23.8	30.0	66.3	66.3	56.3	52.5	42.5	37.5	43.8	51.3
4 Reform Party	68.8	33.8	-	-	-	-	-	-	-	-	-
5 Country Party	-	1.3	1.3	2.5	-	-	-	-	-	-	-
6 Ratana Movement	0.0	0.0	0.0	2.5	-	-	-	-	-	-	-
7 Communist Party	-	-	0.0	0.0	-	-	0.0	0.0	0.0	0.0	0.0
8 Democrat Party	-	-	-	-	-	-	-	-	-	-	-
9 National Party	-	-	63.8	23.8	31.3	42.5	47.5	57.5	62.5	56.3	48.8
10 Democratic Soldier Labour Party	-	-	-	-	-	0.0	-	-	-	-	-
11 Social Credit Party	-	-	-	-	-	-	-	-	-	-	-
Others	2.5	7.5	5.0	5.0	2.5	1.3	0.0	0.0	0.0	0.0	0.0

Table 18.5a NEW ZEALAND Total Votes 1960-1987

	1960	1963	1966	1969	1972	1975	1978	1981	1984	1987
Electorate	1,311,536	1,335,836	1,409,600	1,519,889	1,583,256	1,953,050	2,057,840[1]	2,034,747	2,111,651	2,114,658
Valid Votes	1,170,503	1,198,045	1,205,095	1,340,168	1,401,152	1,603,733	1,710,173	1,801,311	1,929,201	1,831,777
Invalid Votes	6,460	7,277	7,032	11,645	9,088	8,287	11,270	8,985	7,565	11,184
Total Votes	1,176,963	1,205,322	1,212,127	1,351,813	1,410,240	1,612,020	1,721,443	1,810,296	1,936,766	1,842,961
PARTY VOTES										
3 Labour Party	508,179	524,066	499,392	592,055	677,669	634,453	691,076	702,601	829,154	878,448
7 Communist Party	2,423	3,167	1,060	368	-	-	-	-	-	-
9 National Party	557,046	563,875	525,945	605,960	581,422	763,136	680,991	698,504	692,494	806,306
11 Social Credit Party	100,905	95,176	174,515	121,576	93,231	119,147	274,756	372,097	147,162	105,081
12 Socialist Unity Party	-	-	-	-	408	306	156	-	-	-
13 Values Party	-	-	-	-	27,467	83,241	41,220	3,460	3,826	1,759
14 Mana Motuhake	-	-	-	-	-	-	-	-	5,989	9,789
15 New Zealand Party	-	-	-	-	-	-	-	-	236,385	5,306
Others	1,950	11,761	4,183	20,209	20,955	3,450	21,974	24,649	14,191	25,088

1 Population age 18 and over on 31 December 1977. The number of names on the electoral register was recorded as 2,487,594, an excess of 429,754 over the population of voting age, because of large scale errors in the compilation of the register following the introduction of a new system of compiling the rolls.

Source: Wilson, 1985: 286 and 290 and *General Election 1987*.

Table 18.5b NEW ZEALAND Percentage of Votes 1960-1987

	1960	1963	1966	1969	1972	1975	1978	1981	1984	1987
Total Votes	89.7	90.2	86.0	88.9	89.1	82.5	83.7	89.0	91.7	87.2
Valid Votes	89.2	89.7	85.5	88.2	88.5	82.1	83.1	88.5	91.4	86.6
Invalid Votes	0.5	0.5	0.5	0.8	0.6	0.4	0.5	0.4	0.4	0.5
Share Invalid	0.5	0.6	0.6	0.9	0.6	0.5	0.7	0.5	0.4	0.6
PARTY VOTES										
3 Labour Party	43.4	43.7	41.4	44.2	48.4	39.6	40.4	39.0	43.0	48.0
6 Communist Party	0.2	0.3	0.1	0.0	-	-	-	-	-	-
9 National Party	47.6	47.1	43.6	45.2	41.5	47.6	39.8	38.8	35.9	44.0
11 Social Credit Party	8.6	7.9	14.5	9.1	6.7	7.4	16.1	20.7	7.6	-
12 Socialist Unity Party	-	-	-	-	0.0	0.0	0.0	-	-	5.7
13 Values Party	-	-	-	-	2.0	5.2	2.4	0.2	0.2	0.1
14 Mana Motuhake	-	-	-	-	-	-	-	-	0.3	0.5
15 New Zealand Party	-	-	-	-	-	-	-	-	12.3	0.3
Others	0.2	1.0	0.3	1.5	1.5	0.2	1.3	1.4	0.7	1.4

Table 18.5c NEW ZEALAND Number of Seats Won in the House of Representatives 1960-1987

	1960	1963	1966	1969	1972	1975	1978	1981	1984	1987
3 Labour Party	34	35	35	39	55	32	40	43	57	57
6 Communist Party	0	0	0	0	–	–	–	–	–	–
9 National Party	46	45	44	45	32	55	51	47	36	40
11 Social Credit Party	0	0	1	0	0	0	1	2	2	0
12 Socialist Unity Party	0	0	–	0	0	0	0	–	–	
13 Values Party	–	–	–	–	0	0	0	0	0	–
14 Mana Motuhake	–	–	–	–	0	0	–	–	0	0
15 New Zealand Party	–	–	–	–	–	–	–	–	0	0
Others	0	0	0	–	0	0	0	0	0	0
Total Seats	80	80	80	84	87	87	92	92	95	97

Source: Wilson, 1985: 286 and *General Election 1987*.

Table 18.5d NEW ZEALAND Percentage of Seats Won in the House of Representatives 1960-1987

	1960	1963	1966	1969	1972	1975	1978	1981	1984	1987
3 Labour Party	42.5	43.8	43.8	46.4	63.2	36.8	43.5	46.7	60.0	58.8
6 Communist Party	0.0	0.0	0.0	0.0	–	–	–	–	–	–
9 National Party	57.5	56.3	55.0	53.6	36.8	63.2	55.4	51.1	37.9	41.2
11 Social Credit Party	0.0	0.0	1.3	0.0	0.0	0.0	1.1	2.2	2.1	0.0
12 Socialist Unity Party	–	–	–	–	0.0	0.0	0.0	–	–	–
13 Values Party	–	–	–	–	0.0	0.0	0.0	0.0	0.0	0.0
14 Mana Motuhake	–	–	–	–	–	–	–	–	0.0	0.0
15 New Zealand Party	–	–	–	–	–	–	–	–	0.0	0.0
Others	0.0	0.0	0.0	0.0	0.0	0.0	0.0	0.0	0.0	0.0

Chapter 19

NORWAY

Electoral competition began in the nineteenth century, when Norway was governed as a kingdom under the Swedish Crown. It had its own parliament, the Storting. Under the 1814 Constitution the voters consisted of royal officials, freehold and leasehold farmers, owners of urban property, and citizens licensed as merchants and artisans (Rokkan, 1969: 262). About 28 percent of the adult male population was enfranchised. In 1884 citizens paying more than a minimum amount of income tax were also enfranchised and the secret ballot was introduced. In 1898 all men age 25 or over except bankrupts and men receiving public assistance were given the vote. Until 1905 elections were indirect. In each constituency the voters elected members of an electoral college, who then chose the representatives on a plurality basis.

The 1882 election to the Storting was the first expressly partisan contest in Norwegian history (Rokkan, 1967: 376). The initial political division between the Left, an alliance of urban radicals and the peasantry, and the right, which supported the royal prerogative, remained the basic political cleavage until the emergence of the Labour Party as a major competitor for working-class votes.

In 1905 Norway declared the union with Sweden dissolved, and thus gained complete independence as a constitutional monarchy with a parliamentary system of government. The Storting, while elected as a single unit, divides itself into two groups, the *Lagting*, composed of one-quarter of the whole, and the *Odelsting*, composed of three-quarters.

In 1905 direct elections in single-member constituencies replaced the indirect system. An absolute majority was required on the first ballot and a plurality on the second. In 1919 proportional representation in multi-member constituencies using the d'Hondt system was introduced. In 1953 the Sainte-Laguë system of proportional representation, with an initial divisor of 1.4, replaced the d'Hondt system.

Voting rights were granted to bankrupts in 1914 and those in receipt of public assistance in 1919. Women were enfranchised in 1907, but only if their own or their husband's income was above a minimum figure. In 1913 women were granted equal voting rights. The voting age was reduced to 23 in 1919, 21 in 1946, 20 in 1969 and 18 in 1978.

Sources:

B.O. Aardal and H. Valen, *Velgere, partier og politisk avstand* (Oslo: Central Bureau of Statistics, 1989)

Central Bureau of Statistics: *Historical Statistics*, 1968 (Oslo, 1969)

C.O. Heidar, *Norske Politiske Fakta, 1884-1982* (Oslo: Norwegian University Press, 1983)

Norges officielle statistik, sub-series *Stortingsvalget* (Oslo, 1906) and subsequent volumes in the same series

S. Rokkan, 'Geography, religion and social class: crosscutting cleavages in Norwegian politics', in S.M. Lipset and S. Rokkan (eds.), *Party Systems and Voter Alignments* (New York: Free Press, 1967) 307-444

S. Rokkan, 'Norway', in S. Rokkan and J. Meyriat (eds.), *International Guide to Electoral Statistics* (The Hague and Paris: Mouton, 1969) 261-80

H. Valen, *Valg og politikk : et samfunn i endring* (Oslo: NKS Forlaget, 1981)

Table 19.1 POLITICAL PARTIES IN NORWAY SINCE 1882

	Party Names	Elections Contested Years	Number
1	Liberals (Venstre - literally Left)	1882ff	30
2	Conservatives (Høyre - literally Right); from 1903 to 1913 known as the Unionist Party (Samlingspartiet) [1]	1882ff	30
3	Moderates (Moderate Venstre - literally, Moderate Left)	1888-1903	6
4	Labour Party (Det Norske Arbeiderparti - DNA)	1894ff	26
5	Worker Democrats (Arbeiderdemokratene); from 1921 Radical People's Party (Radikale Folkeparti)	1906-1936	11
6	Liberal Left (Frisinnede Folkeparti) [2]	1909-1936	10
7	Agrarian League (Landmandsforbundet); from 1921 the Farmers' Party (Bondepartiet); re-named Centre Party (Senterpartiet) in 1959	1915ff	19
8	Social Democratic Workers' Party (Norges Socialdemokratiske Arbeiderparti)[3]	1921-1924	2
9	Communist Party (Norges Kommunistiske Parti - NKP) [4]	1924ff	15
10	Christian People's Party (Kristelig Folkeparti)	1933ff	13
11	Commonwealth Party (Samfunnspartiet) [5]	1933-1949	4
12	National Socialists (Nasjonal Samling - literally National Unity)	1933-1936	2
13	Joint Non-Socialist Lists [6]	1949-1981	9
14	Socialist People's Party (Sosialistisk Folkeparti); since 1975 Socialist Left Party (Sosialistisk Venstreparti) [7]	1961ff	7
15	Anders Lange's Party (Anders Langes Parti); since 1977 Progress Party (Fremskrittspartiet) [8]	1973ff	4
16	New People's Party (Det Nye Folkepartiet); since 1980 Liberal People's Party (Det Liberale Folkeparti)[9]	1973ff	4

1 In 1903 and 1906 the Conservatives made an electoral alliance with a section of the Liberals, the Liberale Venstre.

2 The Liberal Left, a breakaway group from the Venstre, included many of the Liberale Venstre allied with the Conservatives in 1903 and 1906.

3 The Social Democrats left the Labour Party in 1919 when the latter decided to join the Third International. The two parties were reunited in 1927.

4 In 1973 contested the election as part of the Socialist Electoral Alliance. In 1975 the party split, with the NKP reemerging as a separate party, but a large section of the party (including its former leader) remaining in the Alliance to form the Socialist Left Party.

5 The party contested the 1945 election under the name Nytt Norge (New Norway).

6 Local electoral alliances formed by the Conservative, Liberal, Agrarian (Centre), Christian People's and Liberal People's parties.

7 In 1973 contested the election as part of the Socialist Electoral Alliance with the Communist Party, a breakaway group from the Labour Party, and independent socialists. In 1975 the majority of the Communist Party resumed its separate identity, and the remaining components of the alliance became the Socialist Left Party.

8 Literally Anders Lange's Party for Substantial Reduction of Taxes, Duties and Governmental Intervention (Anders Langes parti til sterk nedsettelse av skatter, avgifter og offentlige inngrep).

9 Breakaway of Venstre members who favoured Norwegian membership in the European Community. Reunited with Venstre in 1988.

Table 19.2 DATES OF ELECTIONS : STORTING

1	1882 [1]	16	17 October 1927
2	1885 [1]	17	20 October 1930
3	8 July-15 November 1888	18	16 October 1933
4	8 June-18 November 1891	19	19 October 1936
5	11 August-13 November 1894	20	8 October 1945
6	14 August-15 November 1897	21	10 October 1949
7	13 August-10 September 1900	22	12 October 1953
8	5 August-7 September 1903	23	7 October 1957
9	5 August-28 August 1906	24	11 September 1961
10	2 October-25 October 1909	25	12 September 1965
11	21 October 1912	26	7 September 1969
12	11 October 1915	27	9 September 1973
13	21 October 1918	28	11 September 1977
14	24 October 1921	29	14 September 1981
15	21 October 1924	30	8 September 1985

1 The dates of elections were fixed by individual communes.

Source: Central Bureau of Statistics, Oslo.

Table 19.3a NORWAY Total Votes 1882-1909

	1882	1885	1888	1891	1894	1897	1900	1903	1906[2]	1909[2]
Electorate	99,501	122,952	128,368	139,690	184,124	195,956	426,593	433,448	446,705	760,277
Valid Votes	71,304	90,967	89,629	101,839	165,147	166,177	235,410	236,641	269,281	422,684
PARTY VOTES										
1 Liberals	44,803	57,683	37,320	51,780	83,165	87,548	127,142	101,142	121,562	128,367
6 Liberal Left[1]	–	–	–	–	–	–	–	–	–	
2 Conservatives[1]	26,501	33,284	34,564	} 50,059	81,462	77,682	96,092	106,042	88,323	} 175,388
3 Moderates[1]	–	–	17,745						– –	– –
4 Labour Party	–	–	–	–	520	947	7,013	22,948	43,134	91,268
5 Worker Democrats	–	–	–	–	–	–	–	–	12,819	15,550
Others	–	–	–	–	–	–	5,163	6,509	3,443	12,111

1 Separate figures are not available for the Conservatives and the Moderates from 1891 to 1906 or for the Conservatives and the Liberal Left in 1909.
2 Two-ballot elections. The figures are for the first ballot.

Sources: Rokkan, 1969, pp. 275-276; Central Bureau of Statistics; 1969, p. 631.

Table 19.3b NORWAY Percentage of Votes 1882-1909

	1882	1885	1888	1891	1894	1897	1900	1903	1906	1909
Total Votes	71.7	74.0	69.8	72.9	89.7	84.8	55.2	54.6	60.3	55.6
Valid Votes	71.7	74.0	69.8	72.9	89.7	84.8	55.2	54.6	60.3	55.6
PARTY VOTES										
1 Liberals	62.8	63.4	41.6	50.8	50.4	52.7	54.0	42.7	45.1	30.4
6 Liberal Left	-	-	-	-	-	-	-	-		} 41.5
2 Conservatives	37.2	36.6	38.6	} 49.2	49.3	46.7	40.8	44.8	32.8	
3 Moderates	-	-	19.8						-	-
4 Labour Party	-	-	-	-	0.3	0.6	3.0	9.7	16.0	21.6
5 Worker Democrats	-	-	-	-	-	-	-	-	4.8	3.7
Others	-	-	-	-	-	-	2.2	2.8	1.3	2.9

Table 19.3c NORWAY Number of Seats Won in the Storting 1882-1909

	1882	1885	1888	1891	1894	1897	1900	1903	1906	1909
1 Liberals	83	84	39	63	59	79	77	50	73	46
6 Liberal Left	–	–	–	–	–	–	–	–	–	23
2 Conservatives	31	30	51	35	40	25	31	52	36	41
3 Moderates	–	–	24	16	15	10	6	11	–	–
4 Labour Party	–	–	–	–	–	–	–	4	10	11
5 Worker Democrats	–	–	–	–	–	–	–	–	4	2
Others	–	–	–	–	–	–	0	0	0	0
Total Seats	114	114	114	114	114	114	114	117	123	123

Sources: Rokkan, 1969, pp. 278-279; *Stortingsvalget*, 1906 ff.

Table 19.3d NORWAY Percentage of Seats Won in the Storting 1882-1909

	1882	1885	1888	1891	1894	1897	1900	1903	1906	1909
1 Liberals	72.8	73.7	34.2	55.3	51.8	69.3	67.5	42.7	59.3	37.4
6 Liberal Left	-	-	-	-	-	-	-	-	-	18.7
2 Conservatives	27.2	26.3	44.7	30.7	35.1	21.9	27.2	44.4	29.3	33.3
3 Moderates	-	-	21.1	14.0	13.5	8.9	5.3	9.4	-	-
4 Labour Party	-	-	-	-	-	-	-	3.4	8.1	8.9
5 Worker Democrats	-	-	-	-	-	-	-	-	3.3	1.6
Others	-	-	-	-	-	-	0.0	0.0	-	-

Table 19.4a NORWAY Total Votes 1912-1945

	1912[2]	1915[2]	1918[2]	1921	1924	1927	1930	1933	1936	1945
Electorate	809,582	1,086,557	1,186,602	1,351,183	1,412,441	1,484,409	1,550,077	1,643,498	1,741,905	1,961,977
Valid Votes	488,903	617,670	662,521	904,699	973,941	999,297	1,194,755	1,248,686	1,455,238	1,485,225
Invalid Votes	n.a	n.a	n.a	13,037	13,244	11,328	7,346	6,352	8,230	12,969
Total Votes	n.a	n.a	n.a	917,736	987,185	1,010,625	1,202,101	1,255,038	1,463,468	1,498,194
PARTY VOTES										
1 Liberals		204,243	187,657	181,989	180,979	172,568	241,355	213,153	232,784	204,852
	}195,526									
5 Worker Democrats[1]		25,658	21,980	22,970	17,144	13,459	9,228	6,858	6,407	-
2 Conservatives[1]						240,091	327,731	252,506	310,324	252,608
	}162,074	179,028	201,325	301,372	316,846					
6 Liberal Left[1]						14,439	31,003	20,184	19,236	-
4 Labour Party	128,455	198,111	209,560	192,616	179,567	368,106	374,854	500,526	618,616	609,348
7 Farmers' Party[3]	-	6,351	30,925	118,657	131,706	149,026	190,220	173,634	168,038	119,362
8 Social Democratic Worker's Party	-	-	-	83,629	85,743	-	-	-	-	-
9 Communist Party	-	-	-	-	59,401	40,075	20,351	22,773	4,376	176,535
10 Christian People's Party	-	-	-	-	-	-	-	10,272	19,612	117,813
11 Commonwealth Party	-	-	-	-	-	-	-	18,786	45,109	1,845
12 National Socialists	-	-	-	-	-	-	-	27,850	26,577	-
Others	2,848	4,279	11,074	3,466	2,555	1,533	13	2,144	4,159	2,862

1 Separate figures are not available for the Liberals and Worker Democrats in 1912 and the Conservatives and the Liberal Left from 1912 to 1924.
2 Two-ballot elections. The figures are for the first ballot.
3 Before 1921 the Agrarian League.

Sources: *Stortingsvalget*, 1912-1945.

Table 19.4b NORWAY Percentage of Votes 1912-1945

	1912	1915	1918	1921	1924	1927	1930	1933	1936	1945
Total Votes	60.4	56.8	55.8	67.9	69.9	68.1	77.6	76.4	84.0	76.4
Valid Votes	60.4	56.8	55.8	67.0	69.0	67.3	77.1	76.0	83.5	75.7
Invalid Votes	0.0	0.0	0.0	1.0	0.9	0.8	0.5	0.4	0.5	0.7
Share Invalid	0.0	0.0	0.0	1.4	1.3	1.1	0.6	0.5	0.6	0.9
PARTY VOTES										
1 Liberals		33.1	28.3	20.1	18.6	17.3	20.2	17.1	16.0	13.8
}	40.0									
5 Worker Democrats		4.2	3.3	2.5	1.8	1.3	0.8	0.5	0.4	-
2 Conservatives						24.0	27.4	20.2	21.3	17.0
}	33.2	29.0	30.4	33.3	32.5					
6 Liberal Left					-	1.4	2.6	1.6	1.3	-
4 Labour Party	26.3	32.1	31.6	21.3	18.4	36.8	31.4	40.1	42.5	41.0
7 Farmers' Party	-	1.0	4.7	13.1	13.5	14.9	15.9	13.9	11.5	8.0
8 Social Democratic Workers' Party	-	-	-	9.2	8.8	-	-	-	-	-
9 Communist Party	-	-	-	-	6.1	4.0	1.7	1.8	0.3	11.9
10 Christian People's Party	-	-	-	-	-	-	-	0.8	1.3	7.9
11 Commonwealth Party	-	-	-	-	-	-	-	1.5	3.1	0.1
12 National Socialists	-	-	-	-	-	-	-	2.2	1.8	-
Others	0.6	0.7	1.7	0.4	0.3	0.2	0.0	0.2	0.3	0.2

Table 19.4c NORWAY Number of Seats Won in the Storting 1912-1945

	1912	1915	1918	1921	1924	1927	1930	1933	1936	1945
1 Liberals	70	74	51	37	34	30	33	24	23	20
5 Worker Democrats[1]	6	6	3	2	2	1	1	1	0	-
2 Conservatives	20	20	40	42	43	30	41	30	36	25
4 Labour Party	23	19	18	29	24	59	47	69	70	76
6 Liberal Left	4	1	10	15	11	1	3	1	0	-
7 Farmers' Party[2]	-	1	3	17	22	26	25	23	18	10
8 Social Democratic Workers Party	-	-	-	8	8	-	-	-	-	-
9 Communist Party	-	-	-	-	6	3	0	0	0	11
10 Christian People's Party	-	-	-	-	-	-	-	1	2	8
11 Commonwealth Party	-	-	-	-	-	-	-	1	1	0
12 National Socialists	-	-	-	-	-	-	-	-	0	-
Others	0	2	1	0	0	0	0	-	0	0
Total Seats	123	123	126	150	150	150	150	150	150	150

1 From 1921 the Radical People's Party.
2 Before 1921 the Agrarian League.

Source: *Stortingsvalget*, 1912 to 1945.

Table 19.4d NORWAY Percentage of Seats Won in the Storting 1912-1945

	1912	1915	1918	1921	1924	1927	1930	1933	1936	1945
1 Liberals	56.9	60.2	40.5	24.7	22.7	20.0	22.0	16.0	15.3	10.5
5 Worker Democrats	4.9	4.9	2.4	1.3	1.3	0.7	0.7	0.7	0.0	-
2 Conservatives	16.3	16.3	31.7	28.0	28.7	20.0	27.3	20.0	24.0	13.2
4 Labour Party	18.7	15.4	14.3	19.3	16.0	39.3	31.3	46.0	46.7	40.0
6 Liberal Left	3.3	0.8	7.9	10.0	7.3	0.7	2.0	0.7	0.0	-
7 Farmers' Party	-	0.8	2.4	11.3	14.7	17.3	16.7	15.3	12.0	5.3
8 Social Democratic Workers' Party	-	-	-	5.3	5.3	-	-	-	-	-
9 Communist Party	-	-	-	-	4.0	2.0	0.0	0.0	0.0	5.8
10 Christian People's Party	-	-	-	-	-	-	-	0.7	1.3	4.2
11 Commonwealth Party	-	-	-	-	-	-	-	0.7	0.7	0.0
12 National Socialists	-	-	-	-	-	-	-	-	0.0	-
Others	0.0	1.6	0.8	0.0	0.0	0.0	0.0	0.0	0.0	0.0

Table 19.5a NORWAY Total Votes 1949-1985

	1949	1953	1957	1961	1965	1969	1973	1977	1981	1985
Electorate	2,159,005	2,256,799	2,298,376	2,340,495	2,406,866	2,579,566	2,686,676	2,780,190	3,003,093	3,100,479
Valid Votes	1,758,366	1,779,831	1,791,128	1,840,225	2,047,394	2,158,712	2,152,204	2,301,110	2,458,755	2,601,817
Invalid Votes	12,531	10,500	9,027	10,323	8,697	3,884	3,530	3,386	3,387	3,619
Total Votes	1,770,897	1,790,331	1,800,155	1,850,548	2,056,091	2,162,596	2,155,734	2,304,496	2,462,142	2,605,436
PARTY VOTES										
1 Liberals	218,866	177,662	171,407	132,429	207,834	202,553	49,668	54,243	79,064	81,202
2 Conservatives	279,790	327,971	301,395	354,369	415,292	406,209	370,370	563,783	780,372	791,537
4 Labour Party	803,471	830,448	865,675	860,526	883,319	1,004,348	759,499	972,434	914,749	1,061,712
7 Farmers'/Centre	85,418	157,018	154,761	125,643	192,022	194,128	146,312	184,087	103,753	171,770
9 Communist Party	102,722	90,422	60,060	53,678	27,996	21,517	-	8,448	6,673	4,245
14 Socialist People's/Left	-	-	-	43,996	122,721	73,284	241,851	96,248	121,561	141,950
10 Christian People's Party	147,068	186,627	183,243	171,451	160,332	169,303	255,456	224,355	219,179	214,969
11 Commonwealth Party	13,088	-	-	-	-	-	-	-	-	-
13 Joint Non-Socialist Lists	107,913	9,661	51,360	95,231	37,513	83,073	128,091	111,412	88,969	-
15 Anders Lange/Progress	-	-	-	-	-	-	107,784	43,351	109,564	96,797
16 New People's/ Liberal People's Party	-	-	-	-	-	-	73,854	22,524	13,334	12,958
Others	30	22	3,227	2,902	365	4,297	19,319	20,225	21,537	24,677

Source: *Stortingsvalget*, 1949 to 1985.

Table 19.5b NORWAY Percentage of Votes 1949-1985[1]

	1949	1953	1957	1961	1965	1969	1973	1977	1981	1985
Total Votes	82.0	79.3	78.3	79.1	85.4	83.8	80.2	82.9	82.0	84.0
Valid Votes	81.4	78.9	77.9	78.6	85.1	83.7	80.1	82.8	81.9	83.9
Invalid Votes	0.6	0.5	0.4	0.4	0.4	0.2	0.1	0.1	0.1	0.1
Share Invalid	0.7	0.6	0.5	0.6	0.4	0.2	0.2	0.1	0.1	0.1
PARTY VOTES										
1 Liberals	12.4 (13.1)	10.0	9.6	7.2 (8.8)	10.2 (10.4)	9.4	2.3 (3.5)	2.4 (3.2)	3.2 (3.9)	3.1
2 Conservatives	15.9 (18.3)	18.4 (18.6)	16.8 (18.9)	19.3 (20.0)	20.3 (21.1)	18.8 (19.5)	17.2 (17.4)	24.5 (24.8)	31.7	30.4
4 Labour Party	45.7	46.7	48.3	46.8	43.1	46.5	35.3	42.3	37.2	40.8
7 Farmers'/Centre	4.9 (7.9)	8.8 (9.9)	8.6 (9.3)	6.8 (9.4)	9.4 (9.9)	9.0 (10.5)	6.8 (11.0)	8.0 (8.6)	4.2 (6.7)	6.6
9 Communist Party	5.8	5.1	3.4	2.9	1.4	1.0	-	0.4	0.3	0.2
14 Socialist People's/Left	-	-	-	2.4	6.0	3.4	11.2	4.2	4.9	5.5
10 Christian People's Party	8.4	10.5	10.2	9.3 (9.6)	7.8 (8.1)	7.8 (9.4)	11.9 (12.3)	9.7 (12.4)	8.9	8.3
11 Commonwealth Party	0.7	-	-	-	-	-	-	-	-	-
13 Joint Non-Socialist Lists	6.1	0.5	2.9	5.2	1.8	3.8	6.0	4.8	3.6	-
15 Anders Lange/Progress	-	-	-	-	-	-	5.0	1.9	4.5	3.7
116 New People's/ Liberal People's Party	-	-	-	-	-	-	3.4	1.0 (1.4)	0.5	0.5
Others	0.0	0.0	0.2	0.2	0.0	0.2	0.9	0.9	0.9	0.9

1 Figures in parentheses are estimates made by the Central Bureau of Statistics of the vote share of each party including a proportion of the votes cast for joint non-socialist lists in some constituencies. The estimates were based upon the distribution of votes in the constituency concerned in the most recent Storting election in which separate party lists were presented.

Source: *Stortingsvalget*, 1949-1985.

Table 19.5c NORWAY Number of Seats Won in the Storting 1949-1985

	1949	1953	1957	1961	1965	1969	1973	1977	1981	1985
1 Liberals	21	15	15	14	18	13	2	2	2	0
2 Conservatives	23	27	29	29	31	29	29	41	54	50
4 Labour Party	85	77	78	74	68	74	62	76	65	71
7 Farmers'/Centre Party	12	14	15	16	18	20	21	12	11	12
9 Communist Party	0	3	1	0	0	0	0	0	0	0
14 Socialist People's/Left	–	–	–	2	2	0	16	2	4	6
10 Christian People's Party	9	14	12	15	13	14	20	22	15	16
11 Commonwealth Party	0	–	–	–	–	–	–	–	–	–
15 Anders Lange/Progress	–	–	–	–	–	–	4	0	4	2
16 New People's/ Liberal People's Party	–	–	–	–	–	–	1	0	0	0
Others	0	–	0	0	0	0	0	0	0	–
Total Seats	150	150	150	150	150	150	155	155	155	157

Source: *Stortingsvalget*, 1949 to 1985.

Table 19.5d NORWAY Percentage of Seats Won in the Storting 1949-1985

	1949	1953	1957	1961	1965	1969	1973	1977	1981	1985
1 Liberals	14.0	10.0	10.0	9.3	12.0	8.7	1.3	1.3	1.3	0.0
2 Conservatives	15.3	18.0	19.3	19.3	20.7	19.3	18.7	26.5	34.8	31.8
4 Labour Party	56.7	51.3	52.0	49.3	45.3	49.3	40.0	49.0	41.9	45.2
7 Farmers'/Centre	8.0	9.3	10.0	10.7	12.0	13.3	13.5	7.7	7.1	7.6
9 Communist Party	0.0	2.0	0.7	0.0	0.0	0.0	0.0	0.0	0.0	0.0
14 Socialist People's/Left	-	-	-	1.3	1.3	0.0	10.3	1.3	2.6	3.8
10 Christian People's Party	6.0	9.3	8.0	10.0	8.7	9.3	12.9	14.2	9.7	10.2
11 Commonwealth Party	0.0	-	-	-	-	-	-	-	-	-
15 Anders Lange/Progress	-	-	-	-	-	-	2.6	0.0	2.6	1.3
116 New People's/ Liberal People's Party	-	-	-	-	-	-	0.6	0.0	0.0	0.0
Others	0.0	-	0.0	0.0	0.0	0.0	0.0	0.0	0.0	0.0

Chapter 20

PORTUGAL

Portugal's first parliamentary regime was established by the Constitution of 1822, which provided for a single chamber parliament elected by all men aged over 25, except sons living in their parents' households, domestic servants and friars. The regime was overthrown the following year and after a period of absolute monarchy a new constitution, the Carta Constitucional, was promulgated in 1826. The Charter of 1826 established a two-chamber parliament, the Cortes, consisting of a House of Peers (Câmara dos Pares) and a Chamber of Deputies (Câmara dos Deputados). Except for intervals from 1828-34 and 1836-42, the Charter remained in force until the overthrow of the monarchy in 1910.

In the nineteenth century changes in the franchise requirements were frequent. The Charter gave the vote to all men over 25 with an income of at least 100 milreis a year (reduced to 80 from 1838-42) except sons living in their parents' households, domestic servants and members of religious orders. The qualifying age was reduced to 21 for clergy, married men, service officers and persons with a higher education. No reliable figures are available for the number of persons entitled to vote. The franchise was slightly extended in 1852. Persons entitled to vote on the basis of an educational qualification, such as teachers, university graduates and clergy no longer had to meet an income requirement. In 1878 a major reform extended the franchise to all men over 21 who were literate or heads of families. This increased the size of the electorate from about 40 to 70 percent of the adult male population. (Tavares de Almeida, 1988) In 1895 the income threshold for illiterates was halved, but the abolition of the head of household qualification reduced the electorate to only 47 percent of all adult men.

Changes in the electoral system were also frequent during the period of the Charter. Election to the Chamber of Deputies was initially indirect; the electors chose the members of provincial electoral colleges, who in turn elected the deputies by plurality. Until 1852, candidates for the electoral college required a minimum income of 200 milreis a year. Direct elections were held in 1822, 1836, 1838 and 1840 . In 1852 direct election to the Chamber in multi-member constituencies was definitively introduced. In order to be elected, candidates had to poll at least a quarter of the votes cast in a constituency; in the event of a run-off election the number of candidates was limited to three times the number of seats to be filled. Single-member constituencies with a two-ballot system were introduced in 1859. If no candidate won an absolute majority on the first round a run-off election was held. Participation in the second round was not limited to candidates who had participated in the first round, but second round contests were very uncommon (Tavares de Almeida, 1988).

In 1884 a system combining single-member and multi-member constituencies was introduced; 79 deputies were elected in single-member districts by plurality and 72 in multi-member districts returning between three and six deputies. To assist the representation of minorities, a limited vote system operated in the multi-member constituencies. Each elector had one less vote than there were deputies to elect in three and four member constituencies, and four votes in Lisbon, the only six member constituency. In 1895 the single-member constituencies and the limited vote were both abolished. The following year single member constituencies were reintroduced everywhere except in Lisbon and Oporto. In 1901 multi-member constituencies with the limited vote were re-established throughout the country.

Elections during the period of the monarchy were manipulated by the incumbent government. Electoral competition was very limited. In ten of the 13 elections held between 1868 and 1890 deputies were returned unopposed in about 70 per cent of the constituencies. Although the 1822 constitution and subsequent electoral laws provided for a secret ballot these provisions were largely ineffective. Between 1871 and 1910 there were 22 elections, of which the government only lost one (Wheeler, 1978: 25). Parties were slow to develop and until the last quarter of the nineteenth century were personalist in character. Beginning in the 1870s a relatively stable two-party system was established with the Partido Regenerador and the Partido Progressista regularly alternating in office; these groups were essentially loose coalitions of local notables.

In 1910 the monarchy was overthrown and a republic proclaimed. A constituent assembly elected in May 1911 established a two-chamber parliament in which a Senate replaced the House of Peers. The President was to be elected by a joint session of both houses. The franchise for the Chamber was modelled on the 1878 electoral law. The vote was limited to literate males and male heads of households, but the tax qualification was abolished. The limited vote system in multi-member constituencies was also retained, except in Lisbon and Oporto, where proportional representation using the d'Hondt formula was introduced. In 1913 the head of household qualification was abolished, thus reducing the size of the electorate. In 1915 the proportional representation system introduced in Lisbon and Oporto four years earlier was abolished and replaced by the limited vote system.

Although not entirely free from governmental coercion and restrictions on non-republican parties, the elections of the republic were freer than under the monarchy. In the constituent assembly elections, only the Republicans (the Partido Republicano Português) and a few republican independents were allowed to compete. But later the same year the Republican Party split and two more conservative Republican groups emerged, the Partido Evolucionista and the União Republicana. Reliable voting figures are only available for the June 1915 election.

The Evolutionist Party and the Republican Union united to form the Partido Republicano Liberal in 1919 and won the 1921 election. The party was disbanded in 1923 and replaced by the Partido Republicano Nacionalista as the principal opponent of the Republican Party. Other minor breakaways from the three principal republican

Table 20.a ELECTION TO THE CÂMARAS LEGISLATIVAS, 1915

	Votes	%	Seats
Electorate	471,557		
Republican Party	176,939	55.5	105
Evolutionist Republican Party	62,845	19.7	25
Republican Union Party	41,865	13.1	14
Catholics	11,463	3.6	1
Socialist Party	5,141	1.6	2
Independents	20,596	6.5	5
Totals	318,849	100.0	152

Source: *Censo Eleitoral da Metrópole (Câmaras Legislativas)*, Lisbon, 1916.

parties and socialist and catholic groups also contested elections. Although the Republicans won six of the eight elections from 1911 to 1926 opposition parties were always strongly represented in the Chamber (Oliveira Marques, 1980: 126-128).

In December 1917 a military coup brought Sidónio Pais to power. Pais became President in April 1918 in an election in which all Portuguese men over 21 were given the vote. His supporters gained an overwhelming parliamentary majority in a simultaneous election which was boycotted by the established parties. Pais was assassinated in December 1918. The 1911 constitution was restored and the franchise again restricted to literates.

In 1926 the republic was overthrown by a military coup. Two years later Dr. Antonio Salazar was appointed Minister of Finance. In 1932 he became Prime Minister and the dominant figure in the regime until his retirement in 1968. The constitution of the Salazar dictatorship, promulgated in 1933, provided for a two-chamber parliament with an elected lower house, the Assembleia Nacional. The franchise for Assembly elections and for the popularly elected President was very restricted. Men who were literate or paid at least 100 escudos a year in taxes were entitled to vote. Women were given the vote for the first time, but only if they had completed secondary or university education. In 1946 the vote was extended to women who were heads of households and married women who paid 200 escudos a year in taxes, but it was not until 1968 that women were given the vote on the same restricted basis as men (Braga da Cruz : 195-197). The upper house, the Corporative Chamber (Câmara Corporativa) comprised representatives of agricultural, commercial, industrial, church and university organisations and of the local authorities. Its role was purely consultative.

Until 1945 candidates for both presidential and legislative elections were limited to supporters of the regime, but a significant number of them were not formally members of the government party the Uniao Nacional. After 1945 opposition candidates were allowed and political censorship was lifted for the month before an election. But no active opposition was allowed at other times and those opposition groups who were allowed to compete sometimes withdrew from the contest on the eve of election day. In 1958 an opposition candidate for the Presidency, General Humberto Delgado, according to the official statistics, won one-quarter of the popular vote. The following year popular election of the President was abolished. Following the retirement of Salazar a new electoral law liberalised the franchise for the 1969 National Assembly elections. All adults who were literate could now vote. Elections were still managed by the regime. In 1969 the National Union was officially recorded as having won 88 percent of the vote (Gallagher, 1983: 167).

The first free competitive elections occurred in 1975 for a constituent assembly, after a military coup had overthrown the one-party regime the previous year. All citizens 18 and over were entitled to vote. Representatives were elected in multi-member constituencies using the d'Hondt formula. The constitution promulgated in 1976 established a single-chamber legislature, the Assembleia da República, elected for a four-year term by the same franchise and by the same electoral system as the constituent assembly and a President (Table 20.b). Special arrangements were made for Portuguese citizens resident overseas to elect four deputies in two constituencies. The President was to be popularly elected and could serve no more than two five-year terms. For election on the first ballot an absolute majority of votes cast is required. If no candidate wins an absolute majority, a run-off election is held between the two leading candidates.

Table 20.b PRESIDENTIAL ELECTIONS UNDER THE 1976 CONSTITUTION

	First Round Votes	%	Second Round Votes	%
		1976		
António Ramalho Eanes [1]	2,967,414	61.6		
Otelo Saraiva de Carvalho [2]	796,392	16.5		
José Pinheiro de Azevedo [3]	692,382	14.4		
Octávio Rodrigues Pato [4]	365,371	7.6		
Electorate	6,477,484			
Valid Votes	4,821,559	74.4		
Invalid Votes	64,065	1.0		
		1980		
António Ramalho Eanes [5]	3,258,731	56.4		
António Soares Carneiro [6]	2,322,548	40.2		
Otelo Saraiva de Carvalho [7]	85,555	1.5		
Carlos Galvão de Melo [8]	48,434	0.8		
António Pires Veloso [8]	45,054	0.8		
António Aires Rodrigues [9]	12,657	0.2		
Electorate	6,931,641			
Valid Votes	5,772,979	83.3		
Invalid Votes	61,810	0.9		
		1986		
Diogo Freitas do Amaral [10]	2,631,029	46.3	2,867,911	48.7
Mário Soares [11]	1,443,654	25.4	3,016,062	51.3
Francisco Salgado Zenha [12]	1,185,552	20.9	-	
Maria de Lourdes Pintasilgo [13]	418,334	7.4	-	
Electorate	7,602,205		7,600,001	
Valid Votes	5,678,569	74.7	5,883,973	77.4
Invalid Votes	65,307	0.9	55,398	0.7

1 Army Chief of Staff supported by Socialists, Popular Democrats and Centre Social Democrats.
2 Supported by the Movement of the Socialist Left and the Popular Democratic Union.
3 Incumbent Prime Minister, unsupported by any political party.
4 Communist Party candidate.
5 Supported by the Socialist Party, the Communist Party and the Democratic Movement.
6 Candidate of the Democratic Alliance of the Centre Social Democrats, Social Democrats and Popular Monarchists.
7 Candidate of the extreme left United Popular Front.
8 Independents.
9 Candidate of the Trotskyist Partido Operário de Unidade Socialista.
10 Supported by the Social Democrat and the Centre Social Democrat parties.
11 Former Prime Minister and candidate of the Socialist Party.
12 Supported by Democratic Renewal Party, the Communists and Democratic Movement.
13 Former Prime Minister, supported by small left-wing parties and groups.

Sources:

M. Braga da Cruz, *O Partido e o Estado no Salazarismo* (Lisbon: Editorial Presença, 1988)

M. Caetano, *História Breve des Constituições Portuguesas* third edition (Lisbon: Editorial Verbo, 1971)

J. Gaspar, 'Les élections portugaises 1975/1976', in J. Cadart (ed.), *Les Modes de Scrutin des Dix Huit Pays Libres de l'Europe Occidentale* (Paris: Presses Universitaires de France, 1983) 145-182

T. Gallagher, *Portugal: a Twentieth Century Interpretation* (Manchester: Manchester University Press, 1983)

Ministério da Administraçao Interna/Instituto Nacional de Estatistíca, *Eleição para a Assembleia da República - 1976* (Lisbon: 1976) and subsequent volumes in the same series

Ministério da Administracao Interna/Instituto Nacional de Estatistíca, *Eleição para a Presidência da República - 1976* (Lisbon: 1976) and subsequent volumes in the same series

A.H. Oliveira Marques, *A Primeira República Portuguesa* (Lisbon: Livros Horizonte, 1980)

W. Opello, *Portugal's Political Development: a Comparative Approach* (Boulder, Colorado: Westview Press, 1985)

P. Schmitter, 'Elections in authoritarian Portugal, 1933-1974', in G. Hermet, R. Rose and A. Rouquié (eds.), *Elections without Choice* (London: Macmillan, 1978) 145-68

P. Tavares de Almeida 'Comportamentos eleitorais em Lisboa, 1878-1910', *Análise Social,* XXI,1, (1985) 111-53

P. Tavares de Almeida, *Eleições e Caciquismo no Portugal Oitocentista 1868-1890* (Mimeo, Lisbon: Faculdade de Ciências Sociais e Humanas, Universidade Nova de Lisboa, 1988)

D.L. Wheeler, *Republican Portugal: a Political History 1910-1926* (Madison: University of Wisconsin Press, 1978)

H. Wiarda, 'Portugal', in M. Weiner and E. Ozbudun (eds.), *Competitive Elections in Developing Countries* (Durham, NC: Duke University Press, 1987) 283-327

Table 20.1 POLITICAL PARTIES IN PORTUGAL SINCE 1975

	Party Name	Elections Contested Years	Number
1	Centre Social Democrats (Partido do Centro Democrático Social - CDS)	1975ff	7
2	Communist Party (Partido Comunista Português - PCP)	1975ff	7
3	Popular Democratic Party (Partido Popular Democrático - PPD); since October 1976 the Social Democratic Party (Partido Social Democráta - PSD)	1975ff	7
4	Socialist Party (Partido Socialista Portuguêsa - PSP)	1975ff	7
5	Democratic Movement (Movimento Democrático Português - MDP) [1]	1975; 1979ff	6
6	Movement of the Socialist Left (Movimento de Esquerda Socialista - MES) [2]	1975-1976	2
7	Popular Democratic Union (Uniao Democratica Popular - UDP)	1975ff	7
8	Popular Monarchist Party (Partido - Popular Monárquico - PPM) [3]	1975-1983; 1987	6
9	Popular Socialist Front (Frente Socialista Popular - FSP) [4]	1975-1976	2
10	Christian Democratic Party (Partido da Democracia Crista - PDC)	1976ff	6
11	Reformists (Reformadores) [5]	1979	1
12	Revolutionary Socialist Party (Partido Socialista Revolucionário - PSR)	1979ff	5
13	Union of the Socialist and Democratic Left (Uniao de Esquerda para a Democracia Socialista - UEDS) [6]	1979-1980	2
14	Independent Social Democrats (Associacao Social Democrata Independente - ASDI) [7]	1980	1
15	Socialist Unity Party (Partido Operário de Unidade Socialista - POUS) [8]	1980ff	4
16	Greens (Partido Ecologista 'Os Verdes' - PEV)	1983ff	3
17	Democratic Renewal Party (Partido Renovador Democrático - PRD) [9]	1985ff	2
18	Democratic Intervention (Intervençao Democrática) [10]	1987	1

1 The MDP contested the 1975 election independently and did not contest the 1976 election. From 1979 until 1985 it formed part of the Alianca Povo Unido list with the Communist Party. In 1987 a split occurred in the party with the majority running as a separate list and a minority continuing the electoral alliance with the Communist Party as Democratic Intervention.

2 This party was dissolved in 1981.

3 Contested the 1979 and 1980 elections as part of the Alianca Démocratica with the Centre Social Democrats and the Social Democrats. The party did not contest the 1985 election, but the party's leader was elected on a Socialist Party list in Porto.

4 Breakaway group from the Socialist Party founded by Manuel Serra, whose Movimento Socialista Popular had merged with the Socialist Party in January 1974. The party was dissolved in 1979.

5 A group formed by two former leading members of the Socialist Party, political notables who failed to establish themselves as an organised political party.

6 Founded in January 1978 by A. Lopez Cardoso, a former leading figure in the Socialist Party. The UEDS contested the 1980 election as part of the Republican and Socialist Front. Some UEDS candidates were included in Socialist Party lists in the 1985 election. The party was dissolved in the following year and many party members, including Lopez Cardoso, rejoined the PSP

7 ASDI was formed in April 1979 following a split in the Socialist Party. It was dissolved in January 1985.

8 Formed by two Socialist Party deputies who had been expelled from the party in 1977.

9 Officially founded in July 1985 by leading members of the committee who had supported General Eanes' presidential candidacy in 1980. General Eanes became leader of the party in October 1986 and resigned after the July 1987 election.

10 Breakaway from the Democratic Movement.

Table 20.2a DATES OF ELECTIONS : ASSEMBLEIA DA REPÚBLICA

1. 25 April 1975 [1]
2. 25 April 1976
3. 5 October 1979
4. 5 October 1980
5. 25 April 1983
6. 6 October 1985
7. 19 July 1987

1 Election of a Constituent Assembly.

Table 20.2b DATES OF PRESIDENTIAL ELECTIONS

1. 27 June 1976
2. 7 December 1980
3. 26 January and 16 February 1986

Table 20.3a PORTUGAL Total Votes 1975-1987[1]

	1975	1976	1979	1980	1983	1985	1987
Electorate	6,177,698	6,477,619	6,757,152	6,925,243	7,159,349	7,621,504	7,741,149
Valid Votes	5,273,477	5,135,758	5,746,276	5,617,890	5,481,574	5,594,025	5,498,461
Invalid Votes	393,219	258,095	168,892	139,465	148,422	150,296	124,667
Total Votes	5,666,696	5,393,853	5,915,168	5,917,355	5,629,996	5,744,321	5,623,128
PARTY VOTES							
1 Centre Social Democrats - CDS	433,343	857,179			697,127	559,527	244,076
3 Popular/Social Democrats - PPD/PSD	1,495,017	1,296,246 }	2,662,859[2]	2,788,320[4]	1,522,152	1,711,001	2,819,984
8 Popular Monarchist Party - PPM	31,809	28,160			27,499	-	23,152
11 Reformists	-	-		-	-	-	-
5 Democratic Movement - MDP	233,380	-				-	32,020
2 Communist Party - PCP	709,659	785,594 }	1,121,374[3]	1,000,975[3]	1,024,475[3]	893,216[3]	
16 Greens	-	-	-	-	-	- }	685,109[3]
18 Democratic Intervention	-	-	-	-	-	-	
13 Union of the Socialist and Democratic Left - UEDS	-	-	42,205		-	-	-
4 Socialist Party	2,145,618	1,886,932	1,622,515 }	1,658,266[5]	2,046,733	1,195,722	1,254,205
14 Independent Social Democrats - ASDI	-	-	-		-	-	-
6 Movement of the Socialist Left	57,695	31,063	-	-	-	-	-
7 Popular Democratic Union - UDP	44,546	91,364	127,846	81,920	27,268[6]	72,944	50,812
9 Popular Socialist Front	66,163	41,945	-	-	-	-	-
10 Christian Democratic Party	-	28,178	65,417	20,489	36,365	39,675	30,724
12 Revolutionary Socialist Party - PSR	-	-	36,443	60,160	13,011[6]	34,832	33,493
15 Socialist Unity Party	-	-	12,573	82,464	19,383	18,666	9,115
17 Democratic Renewal Party	-	-	-	-	-	1,036,323	277,449
Others	56,247	89,096	55,044	85,296	67,561	32,119	38,322

1 Metropolitan Portugal including Madeira and the Azores. Excludes votes cast by Portuguese citizens resident in foreign countries who are separately represented in parliament.

2 Democratic Alliance (Alianca Democrática). Comprises the CDS, PSD, PPM and Reformists. Includes 164,532 votes cast for CSD and PSD lists in Madeira and the Azores where the Democratic Alliance did not present lists.

3 From 1979 to 1985 the United People's Alliance (Alianca do Povo Unido). Combines the PCP, the MDP and from 1983 the Greens. In 1987 the United Democratic Coalition (Coligação Democrática Unitária) of the PCP, Greens and Democratic Intervention.

4 Includes 161,407 votes cast for separate CDS and PSD lists in Madeira and the Azores where the Democratic Alliance did not present lists.

5 Republican and Socialist Front (Frente Republicana e Socialista). Comprises the PSP, the UEDS and ASDI.

6 In Lisbon, Oporto and Coimbra the UDP and the PSR presented joint lists. Their 24,910 votes are included with Others.

Table 20.3b PORTUGAL Percentage of Votes 1975-1987

	1975	1976	1979	1980	1983	1985	1987
Total Votes	91.7	83.3	87.5	85.4	78.6	75.4	72.6
Valid Votes	85.4	79.3	85.0	83.4	76.6	73.4	71.0
Invalid Votes	6.4	4.0	2.5	2.0	2.1	2.0	1.6
Share Invalid	6.9	4.8	2.9	2.4	2.7	2.7	2.2
PARTY VOTES							
1 Centre Social Democrats - CDS	8.2	16.7			12.7	10.0	4.4
3 Popular/Social Democrats - PPD/PSD	28.3	25.2 }	46.3	48.3	27.8	30.6	51.3
8 Popular Monarchist Party - PPM	0.6	0.5			0.5	–	0.4
11 Reformists	–	–		–	–	–	–
5 Democratic Movement - MDP	4.4	–		–			0.6
2 Communist Party - PCP	13.5 }	15.3	19.5	17.4	18.7	16.0	
16 Greens	–	–	–	–	–	–	} 12.5
18 Democratic Intervention	–	–	–	–	–	–	
13 Union of the Socialist and Democratic Left - UEDS	–	–	0.7		–	–	–
4 Socialist Party	40.7	36.7	28.2	} 28.7	37.3	21.4	22.8
14 Independent Social Democrats - ASDI	–	–	–		–	–	–
6 Movement of the Socialist Left	1.1	0.6	–	–	–	–	–
7 Popular Democratic Union - UDP	0.8	1.8	2.2	1.4	0.5	1.3	0.9
9 Popular Socialist Front	1.3	0.8	–	–	–	–	–
10 Christian Democratic Party	–	0.5	1.1	0.4	0.7	0.7	0.6
12 Revolutionary Socialist Party - PSR	–	–	0.6	1.0	0.2	0.6	0.6
15 Socialist Unity Party	–	–	0.2	1.4	0.4	0.3	0.2
17 Democratic Renewal Party	–	–	–	–	–	18.5	5.0
Others	1.1	1.7	1.0	1.5	1.2	0.6	0.7

Source: *Eleição para a Assembleia da República* series.

Table 20.3c PORTUGAL Number of Seats Won in the Assembleia da República 1975-1987[1]

	1975	1976	1979	1980	1983	1985	1987
1 Centre Social Democrats - CDS	16	42	42	82	30	22	4
3 Popular/Social Democrats - PPD/PSD	81	73	76	46	75	88	148
8 Popular Monarchist Party - PPM	0	0	5	6	0	–	0
11 Reformists	–	–	5	–	–	–	–
5 Democratic Movement - MDP	5	–	3	2	3	3	0
2 Communist Party - PCP	30	40	44	39	40	34	28
16 Greens	–	–	–	–	1	1	1
18 Democratic Intervention	–	–	–	–	–	–	2
13 Union of the Socialist and Democratic Left - UEDS	–	–	0	4	–	–	–
4 Socialist Party	116	107	74	66	101	57	60
14 Independent Social Democrats - ASDI	–	–	–	4	–	–	–
6 Movement of the Socialist Left	0	0	–	–	–	–	–
7 Popular Democratic Union - UDP	1	1	1	1	0	0	0
9 Popular Socialist Front	0	0	–	–	–	–	–
10 Christian Democratic Party	–	0	0	0	0	0	0
12 Revolutionary Socialist Party - PSR	–	–	0	0	0	0	0
15 Socialist Unity Party	–	–	0	0	0	–	0
17 Democratic Renewal Party	–	–	–	–	–	45	7
Others	1	0	0	0	0	0	0
Total Seats	250[2]	263[3]	250[4]	250[4]	250[5]	250[5]	250[6]

1 In 1975 the Constituent Assembly. Includes deputies representing Portuguese resident overseas.
2 Includes one Socialist, one Popular Democrat and one independent deputy representing Portuguese resident overseas.
3 Includes two Popular Democrat, one Centre Social Democrat and one Socialist deputy representing Portuguese resident overseas.
4 Includes three Democratic Alliance and one Socialist deputy representing Portuguese resident overseas.
5 Includes two Social Democrat, one Centre Social Democrat and one Socialist deputy representing Portuguese resident overseas.
6 Includes three Social Democrat and one Socialist deputy representing Portuguese resident overseas.

Source: *Eleição para a Assembleia da República* series.

Table 20.3d PORTUGAL Percentage of Seats Won in the Assembleia da República 1975-1987

	1975	1976	1979	1980	1983	1985	1987
1 Centre Social Democrats - CDS	6.4	16.0	16.8	32.8	12.0	8.8	1.6
3 Popular/Social Democrats - PPD/PSD	32.4	27.8	30.4	18.4	30.0	35.2	59.2
8 Popular Monarchist Party - PPM	0.0	0.0	2.0	2.4	0.0	-	0.0
11 Reformists	-	-	2.0	-	-	-	-
5 Democratic Movement - MDP	2.0	-	1.2	0.8	1.2	1.2	0.0
2 Communist Party - PCP	12.0	15.2	17.6	15.6	16.0	13.6	11.2
16 Greens	-	-	-	-	0.4	0.4	0.4
18 Democratic Intervention	-	-	-	-	-	-	0.8
13 Union of the Socialist and Democratic Left - UEDS	-	-	0.0	1.6	-	-	-
4 Socialist Party	46.4	40.7	29.6	26.4	40.4	22.8	24.0
14 Independent Social Democrats - ASDI	-	-	-	1.6	-	-	-
6 Movement of the Socialist Left	0.0	0.0	-	-	-	-	-
7 Popular Democratic Union - UDP	0.4	0.4	0.4	0.4	0.0	0.0	0.0
9 Popular Socialist Front	0.0	0.0	-	-	-	-	-
10 Christian Democratic Party	-	0.0	0.0	0.0	0.0	0.0	0.0
12 Revolutionary Socialist Party - PSR	-	0.0	0.0	0.0	0.0	0.0	0.0
15 Socialist Unity Party	-	-	0.0	0.0	0.0	0.0	0.0
17 Democratic Renewal Party	-	-	-	-	-	18.0	2.8
Others	0.4	0.0	0.0	0.0	0.0	0.0	0.0

Chapter 21

SPAIN

Nineteenth- and twentieth-century Spain has been marked by great institutional and political instability. The invasion of the country by Napoleon in 1808 was followed by the collapse of the *ancien régime* absolutism of the Bourbon monarchy. In 1810 a parliament (Cortes) indirectly elected by all heads of household aged over 25 met in Cadiz. This broad franchise, with the voting age reduced to 21, was confirmed in the constitution of 1812, which provided for a constitutional monarchy. In 1814 the exiled King Ferdinand VII returned and restored the absolute monarchy. In 1820 the king was forced to reinstate the 1812 constitution by the army, but he was able to restore royal absolutism three years later with the help of a French army.

In 1834 the Royal Statute (Estatuto Real) established a two-chamber parliament with a nominated upper house and a lower house elected by an extremely restricted property franchise: the electorate of 18,000 comprised less than 0.2 per cent of the population. In 1836 a military coup led to the temporary restoration of the 1812 constitution and the election of a constituent Cortes, which in 1837 voted a new constitution providing for a broader franchise. Tax payment and educational qualifications were liberalised and the vote given to all peasant farmers who owned a yoke of cattle, increasing the electorate from some 65,000 to about 265,000, two per cent of the population. In 1845 the 1837 constitution was revised. New franchise laws reduced the electorate from half a million to 100,000. In 1854 another coup led to the election of a constituent assembly on a slightly expanded suffrage. The liberalisation of the franchise was confirmed in the 1856 constitution. (See Nohlen, 1969: 229-40.)

In 1868 the regime was again overthrown by the army. A constitutional monarchy with a two-chamber parliament, both elected by universal manhood suffrage, was approved in 1869 and Prince Amadeo of Savoy elected king. In 1873 Amadeo abdicated and the first Spanish republic was declared. Amidst growing disorder a military coup restored the Bourbon monarchy in 1874.

Elections to the constituent assembly in 1876 were conducted under the manhood suffrage provisions of the 1869 constitution, but only groups supporting a constitutional monarchy under the Bourbon dynasty were allowed to participate. The new constitution, which remained in force until 1923, provided for a limited monarchy with a two-chamber parliament. The lower house, the Congreso de Diputados, was to be elected on a franchise limited to men aged 25 and over meeting minimum tax-paying requirements. About five per cent of the population were entitled to vote. In 1890 adult manhood suffrage was restored. The deputies were elected by plurality, 307 in single-member constituencies and 88 in multi-member constituencies returning between three and eight deputies. A limited vote system in the multi-member constituencies restricted the number of votes an elector could cast to less than the number of seats.

The party system of the restoration was dominated by the Liberal and Conservative parties. By agreement between the parties they alternated in office. This arrangement, the so-called *turno pacifico*, was implemented by the management of elections by the Ministry of the Interior with the collaboration of local political bosses, the *caciques* (Tusell, 1976). From 1881 to 1923 no government lost a general election. Opposition to the dynastic parties' monopoly of power came from several sources. The Carlist supporters of the claims of a rival branch of the royal family to the throne sought the establishment of an absolutist Catholic monarchy. The republicans were increasingly divided between a middle class reformist group led by Melquiades Alvarez and the Radical Republicans led by Alejandro Lerroux. Parties supporting regional claims against the central government began to emerge towards the end of the nineteenth century. The most important were the Basque Nationalist Party (founded in 1894) and the Lliga Regionalista (founded in 1901), a conservative Catalan party. The Spanish Socialist Party, PSOE, was founded in 1879. Although the dynastic parties remained the dominant element in the Cortes, the opposition parties were able to win parliamentary representation in rural areas where local support was sometimes overwhelming, and increasingly in cities, where the government was unable to manage elections effectively.

Division within the Liberal and Conservative parties and defeat of the Spanish army in Morocco in 1921 led to the military pronunciamento of 1923 and the dictatorship of General Primo de Rivera. From 1923 until 1931 Spain was a dictatorship in which political parties were banned. In August 1930 in San Sebastian, the republican opponents of the regime allied with some ex-leaders of the old dynastic parties in a pact to overthrow the monarchy. In April 1931 municipal elections showed that the Republican-Socialist alliance had won an overwhelming majority in the larger towns. King Alfonso XIII left the country.

The signatories of the San Sebastian pact formed a provisional government and called elections for a constituent Cortes. The members of the single-chamber Cortes were elected by universal manhood suffrage with a minimum voting age of 23 in 61 multi-member constituencies. The North African territories of Ceuta and Melilla each returned one member. In the multi-member constituencies a limited vote system was used. Electors had from 16 votes in 20-member constituencies to one vote in two-member constituencies. Parties or alliances of parties which won a plurality, provided that it was at least 20 per cent of the vote, won as many seats in the constituency as the electors had votes. The second largest party or alliance was awarded the balance of the seats (Linz and Miguel, 1977). If no party or alliance reached this threshold a second round was held a week later at which plurality sufficed for the election of individual candidates.

The constituent Cortes elected an overwhelming republican majority and the constitution of the Second Spanish Republic was promulgated in 1931. It provided for a unicameral parliament elected by universal suffrage. The first round threshold was raised from 20 to 40 per cent with participation in the second round being limited to parties winning eight per cent of the first round vote. In a very fragmented party system, parties able to form broad electoral alliances were particularly favoured. In the 1933 election divisions amongst the left republican and socialist parties allowed the Radicals and the right-wing parties to gain a majority in the Cortes. In 1936 the Popular Front alliance of Communists, Socialists, Left Republicans and the Catalan Left was able to win 280 of the 474 seats in the Cortes with 48 per cent of the vote.

In July 1936 a military uprising against the Popular Front government was followed by a three-year civil war in which the nationalists led by General Franco were victorious. A one-party regime with General Franco as head of state was established. In 1947 a referendum approved the re-establishment of the monarchy and in 1969 Franco nominated Prince Juan Carlos, the grandson of Spain's last king, as his heir. An advisory parliament was set up in 1942. Initially its members comprised ex-officio figures including members of the government and the judiciary, the mayors of the provincial capitals and the leading figures of the Falange Española Tradicionalista, the only legal political party and indirectly elected representatives of the Movement, employers and workers syndicates, local authorities and public institutions, and 50 members appointed by the Head of State. In 1967 a number of members directly elected by heads of households were added. In the election held under this provision in 1971 42 per cent of the 17,250,000 electors voted for 104 representatives of a Cortes of 561 members. General Franco died in November 1975 and Prince Juan Carlos became king.

In November 1976 the old Francoist Cortes passed a Law of Political Reform allowing a two-chamber Cortes to draw up a new constitution. It was elected by universal adult suffrage with a minimum voting age of 21 Political parties were legalised and a constituent parliament was elected in June 1977. A constitution was approved by referendum in 1978. It provided for a constitutional monarchy with a two-chamber parliament consisting an elected Congress of Deputies and a partly elected and partly nominated Senate. In addition to directly elected Senators there were to be representatives of the Autonomous Communities. For the 1977 election the Law of Political Reform allowed the King to nominate a number of Senators. The constitution also lowered the voting age to 18.

In the Congress of Deputies each of the 50 provinces form a single constituency returning at least three and a maximum of 33 deputies; the two North African territories of Ceuta and Melilla each returns one deputy. Electors vote for a party list and cannot express a preference for individual candidates. In the multi-member constituencies deputies are chosen by the d'Hondt highest average system; in Ceuta and Melilla election is by plurality. A constituency level threshold limits representation to parties gaining at least three per cent of the vote. The Senate comprises both directly elected and nominated Senators. The elected Senators number 207, four from each of the 47 peninsular provinces, three from each of the larger islands (Mallorca, Gran Canaria and Tenerife), one each from six smaller islands and two each from Ceuta and Melilla. Senators are elected by a plurality, limited-vote system. Electors vote for individual candidates and are entitled to cast up to three votes in the peninsular constituencies, two in Mallorca, Gran Canaria, Tenerife, Ceuta and Melilla and one in the six single-member constituencies. The representatives of the Autonomous Communities are nominated by their respective legislative assemblies. Each Community is entitled to a minimum of one Senator plus one more for every million inhabitants.

The post-Franco party system has not been stable, especially on the centre and the right. Two parties emerged as the victors in the 1977 constituent elections, the Socialist Party (PSOE) and the Union of the Democratic Centre (UCD) led by the Prime Minister, Adolfo Suarez. Together they won nearly two-thirds of the vote. To the left and right were the Communist Party (PCE) and the Popular Alliance, the latter led by Manuel Fraga, a cabinet minister under Franco. All these parties contested the 1979 election, but the Popular Alliance stood as Coalición Democrática in alliance with a number of small centre-right groups. After the election the UCD group in the Congress began to disintegrate. Suarez resigned as Prime Minister and party leader in 1981. The following year he founded a new party, the Democratic and Social Centre (CDS). Another faction formed its own group and then joined the Socialist Party. A group of Christian Democrats led by Oscar Alzaga formed the Popular Democratic Party. The rump of the UCD won only 11 seats in the 1982 elections and the following year the party was disbanded. In 1982 and 1986 the Popular Alliance was the dominant party on the right in an alliance called Coalición Popular with Alzaga's Popular Democrats and in 1986, the Liberal Party. In 1982 the coalition also included a number of conservative regional parties, but these parties ran independently in 1986. In 1989 the Popular Alliance was reformed as the Popular Party and later the same year both the Liberal Party and the Popular Democrats (the latter having meantime adopted the name Christian Democracy) merged with that party. The Communist Party suffered breakaways by both Eurocommunist and hard-line factions. Before the 1986 elections the PCE and most of these parties combined with a number of non-communist left-wing parties to form the United Left.

Sources:

M. Cuadadro, *Elecciones y Partidos Politicos de España, 1868-1931* (Madrid: Taurus 1969)

R. Gunther, G. Sani and G. Shabad, *Spain after Franco: The Making of a Competitive Party System* (Berkeley: University of California Press, 1986)

J. de Esteban and L. Lopez Guerrá, *Las Elecciones Legislativas de 1 de Marzo de 1979* (Madrid: Centro de Investigaciones Sociologicas, 1979)

J. Linz and J.M. de Miguel, 'Hacia un análysis regional de las elecciones de 1936 en España', *Revista Española de la Opinión Publica* 48, (1977)

J. Linz, 'From great hopes to civil war: the breakdown of democracy in Spain' in J. Linz and A. Stepan (eds.) *The Breakdown of Democratic Regimes: Europe* (Baltimore: Johns Hopkins University Press, 1978)

J. Linz, 'The new Spanish party system' in R. Rose (ed.) *Political Participation* (London and Beverly Hills: Sage 1980)

L. López Nieto and M.A. Ruiz de Azua, 'La publicación oficial de los resultados electorales del 28 de octubre de 1982' *Revista Española de Investigaciones Sociologicas,* 28 (1984) 245-264

Ministerio del Interior (n.d.) *Elecciones Generales 1977 - 1979 - 1982 - 1986 Segun Actas Juntas Electorales Central y Provinciales - Resultados Congreso por Provincias*

D. Nohlen, 'Spanien' in D. Sternberger and B. Vogel (eds.), *Die Wahl der Parlamente* Part 1: *Europa* (Berlin: de Gruyter, 1969)

H.R. Penniman and E. Mujal-Léon (eds.) *Spain at the Polls, 1977 and 1979* (Washington, D.C.: American Enterprise Institute, 1985)

J. Santamaria, *Los partidos politicos en España*, second edition (Madrid: Centro de Investigaciones Sociologicas, 1989)

J. Tusell, *Las Elecciones del Frente Popular* (Madrid: Edicusa, 1971)

J. Tusell, *Oligarquía y Caciquismo in Andalucia* (1890-1923) (Barcelona: Editorial Planeta, 1976)

Table 21.1 POLITICAL PARTIES IN SPAIN SINCE 1931

	Party Names	Elections Contested Years	Number
1	Socialist Party (Partido Socialista Obrero Espanõl - PSOE)	1931ff	7
2	Communist Party (Partido Comunista de España-PCE/PSUC) [1]	1931ff	7
3	Catalan Republican Left (Esquerra Republicana de Catalunya) [2]	1931ff	7
4	Republican Action (Acción Republicana)	1931-1933	2
5	Radical Socialist Party (Partido Republicana Radical Socialista) [3]	1931-1933	2
6	Independent Radical Socialist Party (Partido Radical-Socialista Independiente)	1931-1933	2
7	Galician Republicans (Organización Republicana Gallega Autonomista - ORGA)	1931-1936	3
8	Federal Party (Partido Federal)	1931-1933	2
9	Progressives (Progresistas)	1931-1936	3
10	Group at the Service of the Republic (Agrupación al Servicio de la República) [4]	1931	1
11	Republican Liberal Democratic Party (Partido Republicano Liberal Demócrata) [5]	1931-1936	3
12	Republican Right (Derecha Republicana)	1931	1
13	Radical Party (Partido Republicano Radical)	1931-1936	3
14	Lliga Regionalista (Regional League); from 1933 the Lliga Catalana [6]	1931-1936	3
15	Basque Nationalist Party (Partido Nacionalista Vasco/Euskadi Alberdi Jetzale - PNV/EAJ)	1931ff	7
16	Agrarians (Agrarios)	1931-1936	3
17	National Action (Acción Nacional); in 1933 and 1936 part of the Spanish Confederation of Autonomous Right Wing Groups (Confederación Española de Derechas Autónomas-CEDA) [7]	1931-1936	3
18	Spanish Renewal (Renovación Española); in 1936 the National Block (Bloque Nacional)	1931-1936	3
19	Carlist Party (Partido Carlista) [8]	1931ff	7
20	Conservative Republicans (Republicanos Conservadores)	1933-1936	2
21	Falange (Falange Española) [9]	1933-1936	2
22	Centre [10]	1936	1
23	Republican Left (Izquierda Republicana) [11]	1936	1
24	Republican Union (Unión Republicana) [12]	1936	1
25	Syndicalist Party (Partido Sindicalista)	1936	1
26	Workers' Party of Marxist Unification (Partido Obrero de Unificación Marxista - POUM) [13]	1936	1

27	Carlist Party II (Partido Carlista)	1977-82	3
28	Union of the Democratic Centre (Unión del Centro Democrático - UCD) [14]	1977-1982	3
29	Popular Alliance (Alianza Popular -AP)	1977ff	4
30	Christian Democrats (Equipo de la Democracia Cristiana)	1977	1
31	New Force (Fuerza Nueva) [15]	1977-1982	3
32	Popular Socialist Party (Partido Socialista Popular-PSP) [16]	1977	1
33	Spanish Labour Party (Partido del Trabajo de España - PTE)	1977-1979	2
34	National Alliance (Alianza Nacional 18 del Julio) [17]	1977-1979	2
35	Andalusian Socialist Party (Partido Socialista Andaluz/Partido Andaluz - PSA/PA)	1977ff	4
36	Aragonese Regionalist Party (Partido Aragonés Regionalista-PAR) [18]	1977ff	4
37	Catalan Centre Party (Partit de Centre Catalá - PCC)	1977	1
38	Democratic Union of Catalonia (Unió Democrática de Catalunya-UDC)	1977	1
39	Democratic Convergence of Catalonia (Convergència Democrática de Catalunya - CDC) [19]	1977	1
40	Democratic Left of Catalonia (Esquerra Democrática de Catalunya-EDC) [20]	1977	1
41	Basque Left (Euzkadiko Ezkerra) [21]	1977ff	4
42	Galician National Popular Block (Bloque Nacional Popular Galego-BNPG) [22]	1977-79; 1986	3
43	Galician Socialist Party (Partido Socialista Galego-PSG) [23]	1977ff	4
44	Convergence and Unity (Convergència y Unió - CiU) [24]	1979ff	3
45	National Union (Unión Nacional) [25]	1979-1982	2
46	Herri Batasuna (literally United People) [26]	1979ff	3
47	Canary People's Union (Coalición Unión del Pueblo Canario-UPC)	1979-1982	2
48	Valencian Union (Unió Valenciana)	1979ff	3
49	Navarre People's Union (Unión del Pueblo Navarro)	1979ff	3
50	Democratic and Social Centre (Centro Democrático y Social - CDS) [27]	1982ff	2
51	Popular Democratic Party (Partido Demócrata Popular - PDP) [28]	1982ff	2
52	Liberal Party (Partido Liberal)	1986	1
53	Communist Unity (Mesa per la Unididad de los Comunistas) [29]	1986	1
54	Galician Coalition (Coalición Galega)	1986	1
55	Independent Canary Islands Group (Agrupación Independientes de Canarias - AIC)	1986	1

56	Democratic Reform Party (Partido Reformista Democrático - PRD)	1986	1
57	Greens [30]	1986	1

1 From 1977 includes the United Socialist Party of Catalonia, (the Partit Socialist Unificat de Catalunya-PSUC). In 1986 the United Left (Izquierda Unida) electoral alliance comprising the PCE/PSUC, the Partido Comunista de los Pueblos de España (PCPE) formed in 1984 by a breakaway group from the PCE led by Ignacio Gallego, the Federación Progresista led by a former PCE deputy Ramon Tamames, the Partido de Acción Socialista (PASOC) led by Alonso Puerta, the Partido Humanista, the Partido Carlista and Izquierda Republicana.

2 Alliance of left Republican parties in Catalonia.

3 Breakaway from the Radical Party in 1929.

4 Group of republican intellectuals led by Ortega y Gasset.

5 Successor to the Reformist Liberals of the period before the Primo de Rivera dictatorship; led by Melquiades Alvarez.

6 Conservative party in Catalonia.

7 National Action, renamed Popular Action in 1932, formed a nationwide coalition of conservative groups, the CEDA, in 1933.

8 Often known as the Traditionalists (Communión Tradicionalista).

9 Founded in 1933 the Falange merged with JONS (Juntas de Ofensiva Nacional Sindicalista) to form the Falange Española y de las Juntas de Ofensiva Nacional Sindicalista in February 1934.

10 Grouping of centrist candidates sponsored by the incumbent prime minister Portela Valladares.

11 Merger of Acción Republicana, the Galician Republicans and the Independent Radical Socialists in 1934.

12 Merger of the Radical Socialists and Martinez Barrio's Partido Radical Democrata, which had broken away from the Radical Party in 1934.

13 Founded in 1936 by a merger of the Catalan Bloc Obrer i Camperol led by Joaquín Maurin and the Trotskyite Izquierda Comunista led by Andrés Nin.

14 Founded in 1977 as an electoral alliance of 14 centre and right-wing parties and many independents under the leadership of the incumbent Prime Minister Aldolfo Suarez. Merged to form a single party in 1978.

15 Neo-fascist party led by Blas Piñar. Part of Unión Nacional in the 1979 election, it ran independently in 1982. Piñar dissolved the party later in the same year, but it was revived under his leadership before the 1987 European Parliament elections.

16 Merged with PSOE in 1978.

17 In 1979 part of Unión Nacional.

18 In 1977 the list Candidatura Aragonesa Independiente del Centro, which won a seat in the Congress of Deputies. Reformed as the Aragonese Regionalist Party in 1978.

19 Contested the 1977 election in alliance with the Democratic Left of Catalonia (EDC) and other minor parties as the Democratic Pact for Catalonia (Pacte Democratic per Catalunya).

20 Merged with Democratic Convergence (CDC) in 1978.

21 Electoral alliance of left-wing Basque parties.

22 An electoral alliance whose dominant party is the Marxist Unión do Pobo Galego.

23 Leading party in a series of electoral alliances which contested the 1977 and 1979 elections as Unidade Galega, the 1982 election as Bloque Partido Socialista Galega and the 1986 election as Partido Socialista Galega - Esquerda Galega.

24 Electoral alliance of the Democratic Union of Catalonia (UDC) and the Democratic Convergence of Catalonia (CDC) headed by the latter party's leader, Jorgi Pujol.

25 Formed in January 1979 by Blas Piñar the leader of Fuerza Nueva. The National Union also included Falange Española, the Alianza Nacional and other neo-fascist groups.

26 Formed in 1979 as an electoral alliance of extreme left wing groups supporting independence for the Basque country and allied with the ETA terrorist movement.

[27] Founded in 1982 by the former Prime Minister and UCD leader Adolfo Suarez.
[28] Founded in 1982 by former members of the UCD led by Oscar Alzaga.
[29] Led by the former leader of the PCE Santiago Carrillo.
[30] Comprises four separate Green lists: Los Verdes, Vertice Español Revindicación del Desarollo Ecológico (VERDE), Alternativa Verde - MEC, and Partido Ecologista de Catalunya Verde.

Table 21.2 DATES OF ELECTIONS TO THE CORTES, 1931-1936; CONGRESO DE LOS DEPUTADOS SINCE 1977

1	28 June 1931
2	19 November 1933
3	16 February 1936
4	15 June 1977
5	1 March 1979
6	28 October 1982
7	22 June 1986

Table 21.3a SPAIN Number and Percentage of Votes cast in Elections to the Cortes 1933-1936[1]

	1933	(%)	1936	(%)
Electorate	12,954,652		13,553,710	
Valid Votes	8,509,655	(65.7)	9,684,236	(71.5)
PARTY VOTES				
1 Socialist Party	1,673,648	(19.7)		
2 Communist Party	171,040	(2.0)		
26 P.O.U.M.	-			
25 Syndicalist Party	-			
3 Catalan Republican Left	372,932	(4.4) }	4,654,116[4]	(48.1)
4 Republican Action				
5 Radical Socialist Party				
6 Independent Radical Socialists	}635,705[2]			
7 Galician Republicans				
23 Republican Left	-			
24 Republican Union	-			
15 Basque Nationalists	183,190	(2.2)	125,714	(1.3)
22 Centre	-	-	400,901	(4.1)
13 Radical Party	1,351,100	(15.9)		
8 Federal Party	n.a			
9 Progressives	58,477	(0.7)		
11 Republican Liberal Democrats	77,609	(0.9)		
20 Conservative Republicans	321,754	(3.8) }	4,503,505[5]	(46.5)
14 Lliga Regionalista	307,730	(3.6)		
17 National Action/CEDA				
16 Agrarians				
18 Spanish Renewal/National Block	}3,085,676[3]	(36.3)		
19 Carlists				
21 Falange				
Others	270,804	(3.2)		

1 No figures are available for the election of the Constituent Cortes in 1931.
2 Electoral alliance of Republican Action, Radical Socialists, Independent Radical Socialists and Galician Republicans.
3 Groups National Action, Agrarians, Spanish Renewal, the Carlists and Falange.
4 Popular Front alliance comprising principally the Socialist Party, the Communist Party, the Republican Left, the Republican Union, the Syndicalist Party, the Catalan Republican Left and P.O.U.M.
5 Comprises competing right and centre-right lists principally the CEDA, the Radical Party, the National Block, the Republican Liberal Democrats, the Agrarians, the Conservative Republicans, the Falange, the Carlists and the Catalan League.

Source: Tusell, 1971: 13 and 341

Table 21.3b SPAIN Number and Percentage of Seats Won in the Cortes 1933-1936[1]

	1931	(%)	1933	(%)	1936	(%)
1 Socialist Party	114	(24.3)	59	(12.4)	100	(21.1)
2 Communist Party	0	(0.0)	1	(0.2)	17	(3.6)
26 P.O.U.M.	–	–	–	–	1	(0.2)
25 Syndicalist Party	–	–	–	–	1	(0.2)
3 Catalan Republican Left	37	(7.9)	22	(4.6)	36	(7.6)
4 Republican Action	31	(6.6)	5	(1.1)	–	–
5 Radical Socialist Party	55	(11.7)	1	(0.2)	–	–
6 Independent Radical Socialists	2	(0.4)	2	(0.4)	–	–
7 Galician Republicans	18	(3.8)	3	(0.6)	–	–
23 Republican Left	–	–	–	–	87	(18.4)
24 Republican Union	–	–	–	–	38	(8.0)
15 Basque Nationalists	11[2]	(2.3)	12	(2.4)	10	(2.1)
22 Centre	–	–	–	–	16	(3.4)
13 Radical Party	89	(19.0)	102	(21.5)	4	(0.8)
8 Federal Party	13	(3.0)	1	(0.2)	–	–
9 Progressive Party	8	(1.7)	3	(0.6)	6	(1.3)
10 Group at the Service of the Republic	13	(2.8)	–	–	–	–
11 Republican Liberal Democrats	2	(0.4)	10	(2.1)	1	(0.2)
12 Republican Right	14	(3.0)	–	–	–	–
20 Conservative Republicans	–	–	16	(3.4)	3	(0.6)
14 Lliga Regionalista	4	(0.9)	26	(5.5)	12	(2.5)
17 National Action/CEDA	5	(1.1)	115	(24.3)	88	(18.6)
16 Agrarians	24	(5.1)	32	(6.8)	12	(2.5)
18 Spanish Renewal/National Block	2	(0.3)	15	(3.2)	13	(2.7)
19 Carlists	6	(1.2)	21	(4.4)	9	(2.1)
21 Falange	–	–	1	(0.2)	0	(0.0)
Others	21[3]	(4.5)	27[4]	(5.7)	23[5]	(4.2)
Total Seats	469		474		474	

1 The distribution of seats amongst the political parties in the Cortes is uncertain. There is no complete official record and secondary sources differ. The figures presented here are based upon those published in Linz, 1978: 146-147 and Tusell, 1971: 265-301.

2 Includes four Carlist deputies elected as part of an electoral pact with the Basque Nationalist Party.

3 Comprises Right-wing and Centre-Right independents and a few deputies whose party cannot be identified.

4 Includes eight vacant seats.

5 Includes three vacant seats.

Table 21.4a SPAIN Total Votes 1977-1986

	1977	1979	1982	1986
Electorate	23,616,421	26,836,500	26,855,301	29,117,613
Valid Votes	17,861,309	17,958,404	20,932,951	20,074,434
Invalid Votes	314,018	326,544	506,201	415,217
Total Votes	18,175,327	18,284,948	21,439,152	20,489,651

PARTY VOTES

	1977	1979	1982	1986
1 Socialist Party	5,420,464	5,475,389	10,127,392	8,901,718
2 Communist Party/United Left	1,655,744	1,938,904	865,440	768,258
3 Catalan Republican Left	134,953	123,266	138,116	123,912
15 Basque Nationalists	304,244	296,597	395,656	309,610
27 Carlist Party II	11,139	50,665	224	-
28 Union of the Democratic Centre	6,220,889	6,293,878	1,425,293	-
51 Popular Democratic Party	-	-		
			} 5,548,377[1]	5,247,677[2]
29 Popular Alliance	1,503,376	1,160,009		
52 Liberal Party	-	-	-	
30 Christian Democrats	250,904	-	-	-
31 New Force	5,516		108,578	-
32 Popular Socialist Party	804,382	-	-	-
33 Spanish Labour Party	124,887	192,440	-	-
34 National Alliance	65,001		-	-
35 Andalusian Socialists	-	325,842	84,474	94,008
36 Aragonese Regionalists	37,183	59,343		73,004
37 Catalan Centre Party		-	-	-
	} 167,654			
38 Democratic Union of Catalonia		-	-	-
44 Convergence and Unity	-	482,479	772,726	1,014,258
39 Democratic Convergence of Catalonia		-	-	-
	} 498,889			
40 Democratic Left of Catalonia		-	-	-
41 Basque Left	60,996	85,667	100,326	107,053
42 Galician National Popular Block	23,036	63,446	-	27,049
43 Galician Socialist Party	27,323	57,795	38,508	45,574
45 National Union	-	379,560	-	-
46 Herri Batasuna	-	172,110	210,601	231,732
47 Canary People's Union	-	38,042	35,013	-
48 Valencian Union	-	13,594		64,403
49 Navarre People's Union	-	28,248		
50 Democratic and Social Centre	-	-	604,293	1,838,799
53 Communist Unity	-	-	-	219,440
54 Galician Coalition	-	-	-	79,972
55 Canary Islands Group	-	-	-	66,153
56 Democratic Reform Party	-	-	-	194,538
57 Greens	-	-	-	89,794
Others	544,729	721,130	477,934	577,482

[1] Coalición Popular: the Popular Alliance and the Popular Democrats, including 135,152 votes cast for an alliance with the UCD in the Basque provinces, and regional conservatives.

[2] Coalición Popular: the Popular Alliance, the Popular Democrats, the Liberal Party and regional conservatives.

Sources: Ministerio del Interior (n.d.) and Lopez Nieto, 1984.

Table 21.4b SPAIN Percentage of Votes 1977-1986

	1977	1979	1982	1986
Total Votes	77.0	68.1	79.8	70.6
Valid Votes	75.6	66.9	77.9	69.1
Invalid Votes	1.3	1.2	1.9	1.4
Share Invalid	1.7	1.8	2.4	2.1
PARTY VOTES				
1 Socialist Party	30.3	30.5	48.4	44.3
2 Communist Party/United Left	9.3	10.8	4.1	3.8
3 Catalan Republican Left	0.8	0.7	0.7	0.6
15 Basque Nationalists	1.7	1.7	1.9	1.5
27 Carlist Party II	0.1	0.3	0.0	–
28 Union of the Democratic Centre	34.8	35.0	6.8	–
51 Popular Democratic Party	–	–		
			} 26.5	} 26.1
29 Popular Alliance	8.4	6.5		
52 Liberal Party	–	–	–	
30 Christian Democrats	1.4	–	–	–
31 New Force	0.0		0.5	–
32 Popular Socialist Party	4.5	–	–	–
33 Spanish Labour Party	0.7	1.1	–	–
34 National Alliance	0.4		–	–
35 Andalusian Socialists	–	1.8	0.4	0.5
36 Aragonese Regionalists	0.2	0.3		0.4
37 Catalan Centre Party		–	–	–
}	0.9			
38 Democratic Union of Catalonia		–	–	–
44 Convergence and Unity	–	2.7	3.7	5.1
39 Democratic Convergence of Catalonia		–	–	–
}	2.8			
40 Democratic Left of Catalonia		–	–	–
41 Basque Left	0.3	0.5	0.5	0.5
42 Galician National Popular Block	0.1	0.4	–	0.1
43 Galician Socialist Party	0.2	0.3	0.2	0.2
45 National Union	–	2.1	–	–
46 Herri Batasuna	–	1.0	1.0	1.2
47 Canary People's Union	–	0.2	0.2	–
48 Valencian Union	–	0.1		0.3
49 Navarre People's Union	–	0.2		
50 Democratic and Social Centre	–	–	2.9	9.2
53 Communist Unity	–	–	–	1.1
54 Galician Coalition	–	–	–	0.4
55 Canary Islands Group	–	–	–	0.3
56 Democratic Reform Party	–	–	–	1.0
57 Greens	–	–	–	0.4
Others	3.1	4.0	2.3	3.0

Table 21.4c SPAIN Number of Seats Won in the Congress of Deputies 1977-1986

	1977	1979	1982	1986
1 Socialist Party	118	121	202	184
2 Communist Party/United Left	20	23	4	7[1]
3 Catalan Republican Left	1	1	1	0
15 Basque Nationalists	8	7	8	6
27 Carlist Party II	0	0	0	–
28 Union of the Democratic Centre	165	168	12	–
51 Popular Democratic Party	–	–	} 106	21
29 Popular Alliance	16	9		73
52 Liberal Party	–	–	–	11
30 Christian Democrats	0	–	–	–
31 New Force	0		0	–
32 Popular Socialist Party	5	–	–	–
33 Spanish Labour Party	0	0	–	–
34 National Alliance	0	–	–	–
35 Andalusian Socialists	1	5	0	0
36 Aragonese Regionalists	1	1		1
37 Catalan Centre Party	1	–	–	–
38 Democratic Union of Catalonia	1	–	–	–
44 Convergence and Unity	–	8	12	18
39 Democratic Convergence of Catalonia	} 11	–	–	–
40 Democratic Left of Catalonia		–	–	–
41 Basque Left	1	1	1	2
42 Galician National Popular Block	0	0	–	0
43 Galician Socialist Party	0	0	0	0
45 National Union	–	1	–	–
46 Herri Batasuna	–	3	2	5
47 Canary People's Union	–	1	0	–
48 Valencian Union	–	0		1
49 Navarre People's Union	–	1		
50 Democratic and Social Centre	–	–	2	19
53 Communist Unity	–	–	–	0
54 Galician Coalition	–	–	–	1
55 Canary Islands Group	–	–	–	1
56 Democratic Reform Party	–	–	–	0
57 Greens	–	–	–	0
Others	1	0	0	0
Total Seats	350	350	350	350

[1] Comprising four seats for PCE and one each for the PSUC, PCPE and the Progressive Federation.

Sources: Ministerio del Interior (n.d.) and Lopez Nieto, 1984:

Table 21.4d SPAIN Percentage of Seats Won in the Congress of Deputies 1977-1986

	1977	1979	1982	1986
1 Socialist Party	33.7	34.6	57.7	52.6
2 Communist Party/United Left	5.7	6.6	1.1	2.0
3 Catalan Republican Left	0.3	0.3	0.3	0.0
15 Basque Nationalists	2.3	2.0	2.3	1.7
27 Carlist Party II	0.0	0.0	0.0	
28 Union of the Democratic Centre	47.1	48.0	3.4	–
51 Popular Democratic Party	–	–		6.0
			} 30.6	
29 Popular Alliance	4.6	2.6		20.9
52 Liberal Party	–	–	–	3.3
30 Christian Democrats	0.0	–	–	–
31 New Force	0.0		0.0	–
32 Popular Socialist Party	1.4	–	–	–
33 Spanish Labour Party	0.0	–	–	–
34 National Alliance	0.0	–	–	–
35 Andalusian Socialists	0.3	1.4	0.0	0.0
36 Aragonese Regionalists	0.3	0.3		0.5
37 Catalan Centre Party	0.3	–	–	–
38 Democratic Union of Catalonia	0.3	–	–	–
44 Convergence and Unity	–	2.3	3.4	5.1
39 Democratic Convergence of Catalonia		–	–	–
}	3.1			
40 Democratic Left of Catalonia		–	–	–
41 Basque Left	0.3	0.3	0.3	0.6
42 Galician National Popular Block	0.0	0.0	0.0	0.0
43 Galician Socialist Party	0.0	0.0	–	0.0
45 National Union	–	0.3	–	–
46 Herri Batasuna	–	0.9	0.6	1.4
47 Canary People's Union	–	0.3	0.0	–
48 Valencian Union	–	0.0		0.3
49 Navarre People's Union	–	0.3	–	
50 Democratic and Social Centre	–	–	0.6	5.4
53 Communist Unity	–	–	0.0	0.0
54 Galician Coalition	–	–	–	0.3
55 Canary Islands Group	–	–	–	0.3
56 Democratic Reform Party	–	–	–	0.0
57 Greens	–	–	–	0.0
Others	0.3	0.0	0.0	0.0

Chapter 22

SWEDEN

The modern Swedish party system dates from the controversy over tariff reform in the 1880s. The first election contested by nationally organized political parties was held in 1887 (Stjernquist, 1966: 120). Elections were held under the electoral law of 1866, which replaced the traditional form of representation by estates with a two-chamber parliament, the Riksdag, consisting of an upper house, the First Chamber (*Första Kammaren*) and a lower house, the Second Chamber (*Andra Kammaren*) with equal powers. The franchise for elections to the Second Chamber was limited to men over 21 years of age who met minimum property or income requirements, about one quarter of that age group in the 1880s, increasing to about 30 per cent by 1905. The First Chamber was indirectly elected by the provincial and city councils. Although the local government franchise was in principle broader than that for Second Chamber elections, multiple votes for higher tax payers in fact resulted in an even more restricted electorate.

Deputies were chosen by a plurality system. Single-member constituencies were used, except for the five largest towns, which each formed a multi-member constituency. In the larger towns elections were direct. In other constituencies elections could be either direct or indirect, according to the wishes of the locality. The number of constituencies where indirect elections were held declined steadily from 139 in 1866 to 39 in 1890 and one in 1908 (Lewin et al., 1972: 31). The ballot was secret.

The 1907 election reform abolished the property requirement for the franchise, for Second Chamber elections and liberalised it for local elections and thus indirectly for the Second Chamber. Proportional representation in multi-member constituencies was introduced, using the d'Hondt system for both local and Chamber elections. In 1921 universal adult suffrage was introduced for both local and Second Chamber elections and the voting age reduced to 23. In 1941 the voting age was again reduced to 21. In 1952 the Sainte-Laguë system, with an initial divisor of 1.4, replaced the d'Hondt system.

In 1970 a major reform of the constitution abolished the First Chamber and turned the Riksdag into a single-chamber parliament with 350 members. (In 1974 the number of seats was reduced to 349 to prevent a tie between two groups of parties in a Riksdag vote). Of the seats, 310 are elected in multi-member constituencies as previously. The remaining 40 seats are allocated to parties whose total number of constituency seats is less than their share of the national vote. A barrier clause denies parliamentary representation to any party which does not win at least four per cent of the total vote, with the proviso that any party which won at least 12 per cent of the vote in a particular constituency would still be allowed to compete for seats in that constituency.

The minimum voting age was reduced in 1970, so that all Swedish citizens became entitled to vote in the year following their nineteenth birthday. In 1974 the voting age was lowered to 18.

Sources:

S. Berglund and U. Lindstrom, *The Scandinavian Party System(s)* (Lund: Studentlitteratur, 1978)

S. Carlsson and J. Rosen, *Svensk historia, II* (Stockholm, 1961)

Central Bureau of Statistics, *Sveriges officiella statistik*, sub series *Almänna val* (Stockholm, 1914ff) and subsequent volumes in the same series

Central Bureau of Statistics: *Historisk statistik för Sverige: statistiska oversiktstabeller* (Stockholm: Scandinavian University Books, 1961)

L. Lewin, B. Jansson and D. Sorböm: *The Swedish Electorate, 1887-1968* (Stockholm: Almqvist & Wicksell, 1972)

N. Stjernquist, 'Sweden: stability or deadlock?', in R.A. Dahl (ed.), *Political Oppositions in Western Democracies* (New Haven: Yale University Press, 1966), pp. 116-46

D.V. Verney: *Parliamentary Reform in Sweden, 1866-1921* (Oxford: Clarendon Press, 1957)

Table 22.1 POLITICAL PARTIES IN SWEDEN SINCE 1887

	Party Names	Elections Contested Years	Number
1	Protectionists (Protektionistiska Högerman; literally Protectionist Right)	1887-1896	5
2	Free Traders (Frihandelssinade)	1887-1890	3
3	Liberals (Liberaler) [1]	1893-1921	2
4	Moderate Free Traders (Frihandelssinade Högerman; literally Free Trade Right)	1893-1896	2
5	Social Democrats (Sveriges Socialdemokratistiska Arbetareparti)	1890ff	33
6	Conservatives (Hogerpartiet; literally the Right Party). In 1969 renamed the Moderate Unity Party (Moderate Samlingspartiet)	1899ff	30
7	Agrarian Party (Bondeforbundet). In 1957 renamed the Centre Party (Centerpartiet)	1917ff	23
8	Farmers' Union (Jordbrukarnas Riksförbund) [2]	1917-1921	2
9	Left Socialists (Vänstersocialister) [3]	1917-1921	3
10	Communist Party (Sveriges Kommunistiska Parti). In 1967 renamed the Left Party Communists (Vänsterpartiet Kommunisterna)	1921ff	21
11	Prohibitionist Liberals (Frisinnade Folkpartiet)	1924-1932	3
12	Swedish Liberal Party (Sveriges Liberale Parti)	1924-1932	3
13	Socialist Left Party (Socialistiska Vänsterparti) [4]	1924	1
14	Kilbom Communists (Kilbomskommunister) [5]	1932	1
15	Nationalist Socialist Party (Sveriges National-socialistiska Parti)	1932-1936	2
16	National League (Sveriges Nationella Förbund) [6]	1936; 1944	2
17	National Socialist Workers' Party (Sveriges National-socialistiska Arbetareparti) [7]	1936; 1944	2
18	People's Party (Folkpartiet)	1936ff	17
19	Socialist Party (Socialistiska Parti) [8]	1936-1944	3
20	Christian Democratic Union (Kristen Demokratisk Samling)	1964ff	9
21	Citizens' Coalition (Medborgelig Samling) [9]	1964-1968	2
22	Middle Parties (Mittenpartierna) [10]	1964-1968	2
23	Ecology Party (Miljöpartiet); since 1985 the Miljöpartiet de gröna	1982ff	3

[1] In 1923 the Liberals split on the prohibition issue, forming two parties, the Frisinnade Folkpartiet and the Sveriges Liberale Parti. They were reunited as the People's Party in 1934.

[2] Merged with the Bondeförbundet in 1921.

[3] A splinter from the Social Democrats established in 1917. In 1921 a majority of the Left Socialists joined the Third International and formed the Communist Party. A minority decided to remain independent and contested the 1921 election under the old party label, rejoining the Social Democratic Party in 1924.

[4] Splinter from the Communist Party led by Zeth Höglund and hence often known as the Höglundkommunister. The party was dissolved in 1926 and Höglund rejoined the Social Democratic Party.

[5] Anti-Comintern communist party formed in 1929 and led by Karl Kilbom. The pro-Comintern party, led by Hugo Sillén, was often known as the Sillénkommunister.

[6] Extreme nationalist party formed in 1934 by the youth wing of the Conservative Party.

[7] Splinter from the Nationalist Socialist Party in 1933. Renamed the Sveriges Socialistisk Samling in 1938.

[8] Successor to the Kilbom Communists, many of whom, including Kilbom himself, returned to the Social Democratic Party.

[9] An electoral alliance in the Four Cities constituency (Malmö, Helsinborg, Lund and Landskrona) of the Conservative, Centre and People's parties. In 1968 an alliance of the Conservatives and People's parties only, known as Coalition 68 (Samling-68)

[10] An electoral alliance of the Centre and People's parties in the Gotland constituency. Known as the Intermediate Parties (Mellanpartierna) in 1964.

Table 22.2 DATES OF ELECTIONS: ANDRA KAMMAREN 1887-1968; RIKSDAG, 1970ff

1	29 March-30 April 1887	19	20 September 1936
2	9 August-29 September 1887	20	15 September 1940
3	14 July-29 September 1890	21	17 September 1944
4	2 July-30 September 1893	22	19 September 1948
5	28 June-29 September 1896	23	21 September 1952
6	16 July-30 September 1899	24	26 September 1956
7	7-13 September 1902	25	1 June 1958
8	10-16 September 1905	26	18 September 1960
9	6-12 September 1908	27	20 September 1964
10	9-24 September 1911	28	15 September 1968
11	29 March-7 April 1914	29	20 September 1970
12	5-13 September 1914	30	16 September 1973
13	1-16 September 1917	31	19 September 1976
14	4-17 September 1920	32	16 September 1979
15	10-26 September 1921	33	19 September 1982
16	19-21 September 1924	34	15 September 1985
17	15-21 September 1928	35	18 September 1988
18	17-18 September 1932		

Source: Swedish Central Bureau of Statistics.

Table 22.3a SWEDEN Total Votes 1887-1911

	1887	1887	1890	1893	1896	1899	1902	1905	1908	1911
Electorate	274,733	278,039	288,096	298,810	309,889	339,876	382,075	432,099	503,128	1,066,200
Valid Votes	129,717	95,874	105,807	126,617	140,588	136,945	180,527	217,323	308,389	603,974
Invalid Votes	n.a	n.a	n.a	n.a	n.a	n.a	n.a	n.a	n.a	3,513
Total Votes	n.a	n.a	n.a	n.a	n.a	n.a	n.a	n.a	n.a	607,487
PARTY VOTES										
1 Protectionists	53,692	44,915	45,149	48,963	54,282	-	-	-	-	-
2 Free Traders	76,025	50,959	60,658[1]	-	-	-	-	-	-	-
3 Liberals	-	-	-	44,618[1]	53,388[1]	64,145[1]	92,503	98,287	144,426	242,795
4 Moderate Free Traders	-	-	-	33,036	32,918	-	-	-	-	-
5 Social Democrats	-	-	-	-	-	-	6,321	20,677	45,155	172,196
6 Conservatives	-	-	-	-	-	72,800	81,703	98,359	118,808	188,691
Others	-	-	-	-	-	-	-	-	-	292

1 Includes a few votes cast for joint lists with Social Democrats.

Sources: *Historisk Statistik*, 1960: 270 and Lewin, 1972: 120.

Table 22.3b SWEDEN Percentage of Votes 1887-1911

	1887	1887	1890	1893	1896	1899	1902	1905	1908	1911
Total Votes	47.2	34.5	36.7	42.4	45.4	40.3	47.2	50.3	61.3	57.0
Valid Votes	47.2	34.5	36.7	42.4	45.4	40.3	47.2	50.3	61.3	56.6
Invalid Votes	n.a	n.a	n.a	n.a	n.a	n.a	n.a	n.a	n.a	0.3
Share Invalid	n.a	n.a	n.a	n.a	n.a	n.a	n.a	n.a	n.a	0.6
PARTY VOTES										
1 Protectionists	41.4	46.8	42.7	38.7	38.6	-	-	-	-	-
2 Free Traders	58.6	53.2	57.3	-	-	-	-	-	-	-
3 Liberals	-	-	-	35.2	38.0	46.8	51.2	45.2	46.8	40.2
4 Moderate Free Traders	-	-	-	26.1	23.4	-	-	-	-	-
5 Social Democrats	-	-	-	-	-	-	3.5	9.5	14.6	28.5
6 Conservatives	-	-	-	-	-	53.2	45.3	45.3	38.5	31.2
Others	-	-	-	-	-	-	-	-	-	0.0

Table 22.3c SWEDEN Number of Seats Won in the Andra Kammaren 1887-1911

	1887	1887	1890	1893	1896	1899	1902	1905	1908	1911
1 Protectionists	112	85	88	86	98	–	–	–	–	–
2 Free Traders	102	136	140	–	–	–	–	–	–	–
3 Liberals	–	–	–	76	73	92	107	109	105	101
4 Moderate Free Traders	–	–	–	66	58	–	–	–	–	–
5 Social Democrats[1]	–	–	0	0	1	1	4	13	34	64
6 Conservatives	–	–	–	–	–	137	119	108	91	65
Others	–	–	–	–	–	–	–	–	–	0
Total Seats	214	221	228	228	230	230	230	230	230	230

1 In 1896 and 1899 the successful Social Democratic candidate had been included in joint lists with the Liberals.

Source: Carlsson, 1961: 595

Table 22.3d SWEDEN Percentage of Seats Won in the Andra Kammaren 1887-1911

	1887	1887	1890	1893	1896	1899	1902	1905	1908	1911
1 Protectionists	52.3	38.5	38.6	37.7	42.6	-	-	-	-	-
2 Free Traders	47.7	61.5	61.4	-	-	-	-	-	-	-
3 Liberals	-	-	-	33.3	31.7	40.0	46.5	47.4	45.7	43.9
4 Moderate Free Traders	-	-	-	28.9	25.2	-	-	-	-	-
5 Social Democrats	-	-	0.0	0.0	0.4	0.4	1.7	5.7	14.8	27.8
6 Conservatives	-	-	-	-	-	59.6	51.7	47.0	39.6	28.3
Others	-	-	-	-	-	-	-	-	-	0.0

Table 22.4a SWEDEN Total Votes 1914-1928

	1914 (March)	1914 (Sept.)	1917	1920	1921	1924	1928
Electorate	1,092,454	1,111,767	1,123,969	1,192,922	3,222,917	3,338,892	3,505,672
Valid Votes	760,194	731,361	735,984	657,583	1,741,952	1,765,586	2,358,811
Invalid Votes	3,229	4,124	3,069	2,610	5,601	5,021	4,357
Total Votes	763,423	735,485	739,053	660,193	1,747,553	1,770,607	2,363,168
PARTY VOTES							
3 Liberals	245,107	196,493	202,936	143,355	325,608	-	-
5 Social Democrats	228,712	266,133	228,777	195,121	630,855	725,407	873,931
6 Conservatives	286,250	267,124	182,070	183,019	449,302	461,257	692,434
7 Agrarian Party	-	1,507	39,262	52,318	192,269	190,396	263,501
8 Farmers' Union	-	-	22,659	40,623	-	-	-
9 Left Socialists	-	-	59,243	42,056	56,241	-	-
10 Communist Party	-	-	-	-	80,355	63,601	151,567
11 Prohibitionist Liberals	-	-	-	-	-	228,913	303,995
12 Swedish Liberal Party	-	-	-	-	-	69,627	70,820
13 Socialist Left Party	-	-	-	-	-	26,301	-
Others	125	104	1,037	1,091	7,322	84	2,563

Source: *Almänna Val* series

Table 22.4b SWEDEN Percentage of Votes 1914-1928

	1914 (March)	1914 (Sept.)	1917	1920	1921	1924	1928
Total Votes	69.9	66.2	65.8	55.3	54.2	53.0	67.4
Valid Votes	69.6	65.8	65.5	55.1	54.0	52.9	67.3
Invalid Votes	0.3	0.4	0.3	0.2	0.2	0.2	0.1
Share Invalid	0.4	0.6	0.4	0.4	0.3	0.3	0.2
PARTY VOTES							
3 Liberals	32.2	26.9	27.6	21.8	18.7	-	-
5 Social Democrats	30.1	36.4	31.1	29.7	36.2	41.1	37.0
6 Conservatives	37.7	36.5	24.7	27.8	25.8	26.1	29.4
7 Agrarian Party	-	0.2	5.3	8.0	11.0	10.8	11.2
8 Farmers' Union	-	-	3.1	6.2	-	-	-
9 Left Socialists	-	-	8.0	6.4	3.2	-	-
10 Communist Party	-	-	-	-	4.6	3.6	6.4
11 Prohibitionist Liberals	-	-	-	-	-	13.0	12.9
12 Swedish Liberal Party	-	-	-	-	-	3.9	3.0
13 Socialist Left Party	-	-	-	-	-	1.5	-
Others	0.0	0.0	0.1	0.2	0.4	0.0	0.1

Table 22.4c SWEDEN Number of Seats Won in the Andra Kammaren 1914-1928

	1914 (March)	1914 (Sept.)	1917	1920	1921	1924	1928
3 Liberals	71	57	62	47	41	–	–
5 Social Democrats	73	87	86	75	93	104	90
6 Conservatives	86	86	59	70	62	65	73
7 Agrarian Party	–	–	9	19	21	23	27
8 Farmers' Union	–	–	3	10	–	–	–
9 Left Socialists	–	–	11	7	6	–	–
10 Communist Party	–	–	–	–	7	4	8
11 Prohibitionist Liberals	–	–	–	–	–	28	28
12 Swedish Liberal Party	–	–	–	–	–	5	4
13 Socialist Left Party	–	–	–	–	–	1	–
Others	0	0	0	2	0	0	0
Total Seats	230	230	230	230	230	230	230

Sources: 1911, *Historisk Statistik,* 1960: 269; 1914-1928: *Almänna Val* series

Table 22.4d SWEDEN Percentage of Seats Won in the Andra Kammaren 1914-1928

	1914 (March)	1914 (Sept.)	1917	1920	1921	1924	1928
3 Liberals	30.9	24.8	27.0	20.4	17.8	-	-
5 Social Democrats	31.7	37.8	37.4	32.6	40.4	45.2	39.1
6 Conservatives	37.4	37.4	25.7	30.4	27.0	28.3	31.7
7 Agrarian Party	-	0.0	3.9	8.3	9.1	10.0	11.7
8 Farmers' Union	-	-	1.3	4.3	-	-	-
9 Left Socialists	-	-	4.8	3.0	2.6	-	-
10 Communist Party	-	-	-	-	3.0	1.7	3.5
11 Prohibitionist Liberals	-	-	-	-	-	12.2	12.2
12 Swedish Liberal Party	-	-	-	-	-	2.2	1.7
13 Socialist Left Party	-	-	-	-	-	0.4	-
Others	0.0	0.0	0.0	0.9	0.0	0.0	0.0

Table 22.5a SWEDEN Total Votes 1932-1960

	1932	1936	1940	1944	1948	1952	1956	1958	1960
Electorate	3,698,935	3,924,598	4,110,720	4,310,241	4,707,783	4,805,216	4,902,114	4,992,421	4,972,177
Valid Votes	2,495,106	2,917,753	2,874,417	3,086,304	3,878,991	3,783,707	3,879,330	3,844,252	4,254,114
Invalid Votes	5,663	7,502	14,720	12,799	16,170	17,577	22,784	20,711	17,496
Total Votes	2,500,769	2,925,255	2,889,137	3,099,103	3,895,161	3,801,284	3,902,114	3,864,963	4,271,610
PARTY VOTES									
5 Social Democrats	1,040,689	1,338,120	1,546,804	1,436,571	1,789,459	1,742,284	1,729,463	1,776,667	2,033,016
6 Conservatives	585,248	512,781	518,346	488,921	478,786	543,825	663,693	750,332	704,365
7 Agrarian Party	351,215	418,840	344,345	421,094	480,421	406,183	366,612	486,760	579,007
10 Communist Party	74,245	96,519	101,424	318,466	244,826	164,194	194,016	129,319	190,560
11 Prohibitionist Liberals	244,577	-	-	-	-	-	-	-	-
12 Swedish Liberal Party	48,722	-	-	-	-	-	-	-	-
14 Kilbom Communists	132,564	-	-	-	-	-	-	-	-
15 National Socialists	15,170	3,025	-	-	-	-	-	-	-
16 National League	-	26,750	-	3,819	-	-	-	-	-
17 Nat. Socialist Workers' Party	-	17,483	-	4,204	-	-	-	-	-
18 People's Party	-	376,161	344,113	398,293	882,437	924,819	923,564	700,019	744,142
19 Socialist Party	-	127,832	18,430	5,279	-	-	-	-	-
Others	2,676	242	955	9,657	3,062	2,402	1,982	1,155	3,024

Table 22.5b SWEDEN Percentage of Votes 1932-1960

	1932	1936	1940	1944	1948	1952	1956	1958	1960
Total Votes	67.6	74.5	70.3	71.9	82.7	79.1	79.6	77.4	85.9
Valid Votes	67.5	74.3	69.9	71.6	82.4	78.7	79.1	77.0	85.6
Invalid Votes	0.2	0.2	0.4	0.3	0.3	0.4	0.5	0.4	0.4
Share Invalid	0.2	0.3	0.5	0.4	0.4	0.5	0.6	0.5	0.4
PARTY VOTES									
5 Social Democrats	41.7	45.9	53.8	46.5	46.1	46.0	44.6	46.2	47.8
6 Conservatives	23.5	17.6	18.0	15.8	12.3	14.4	17.1	19.5	16.6
7 Agrarian Party	14.1	14.4	12.0	13.6	12.4	10.7	9.5	12.7	13.6
10 Communist Party	3.0	3.3	3.5	10.3	6.3	4.3	5.0	3.4	4.5
11 Prohibitionist Liberals	9.8	-	-	-	-	-	-	-	-
12 Swedish Liberal Party	2.0	-	-	-	-	-	-	-	-
14 Kilbom Communists	5.3	-	-	-	-	-	-	-	-
15 National Socialists	0.6	0.1	-	-	-	-	-	-	-
16 National League	-	0.9	-	0.1	-	-	-	-	-
17 Nat. Socialist Workers' Party	-	0.6	-	0.1	-	-	-	-	-
18 People's Party	-	12.9	12.0	12.9	22.7	24.4	23.8	18.2	17.5
19 Socialist Party	-	4.4	0.6	0.2	-	-	-	-	-
Others	0.1	0.0	0.0	0.3	0.1	0.1	0.1	0.0	0.1

Table 22.5c SWEDEN Number of Seats Won in the Andra Kammaren 1932-1960

	1932	1936	1940	1944	1948	1952	1956	1958	1960
5 Social Democrats	104	112	134	115	112	110	106	111	114
6 Conservatives	58	44	42	39	23	31	42	45	39
7 Agrarian Party	36	36	28	35	30	26	19	32	34
10 Communist Party	2	5	3	15	8	5	6	5	5
11 Prohibitionist Liberals	20	–	–	–	–	–	–	–	–
12 Swedish Liberal Party	4	–	–	–	–	–	–	–	–
14 Kilbom Communists	6	–	–	–	–	–	–	–	–
15 National Socialists	0	0	–	–	–	–	–	–	–
16 National League	–	0	–	–	–	–	–	–	–
17 Nat. Socialist Workers' Party	–	0	–	–	–	–	–	–	–
18 People's Party	–	27	23	26	57	58	58	38	40
19 Socialist Party	–	6	0	0	–	–	–	–	–
Others	0	0	0	0	0	0	0	0	0
Total Seats	230	230	230	230	230	230	231	231	232

Source: *Almänna Val* series

Table 22.5d SWEDEN Percentage of Seats Won in the Andra Kammaren 1932-1960

	1932	1936	1940	1944	1948	1952	1956	1958	1960
5 Social Democrats	45.2	48.7	58.3	50.0	48.7	47.8	45.9	48.1	49.1
6 Conservatives	25.2	19.1	18.3	17.0	10.0	13.5	18.2	19.5	16.8
7 Agrarian Party	15.7	15.7	12.2	15.2	13.0	11.3	8.2	13.9	14.7
10 Communist Party	0.9	2.2	1.3	6.5	3.5	2.2	2.6	2.2	2.2
11 Prohibitionist Liberals	8.7	-	-	-	-	-	-	-	-
12 Swedish Liberal Party	1.7	-	-	-	-	-	-	-	-
14 Kilbom Communists	2.6	-	-	-	-	-	-	-	-
15 National Socialists	0.0	0.0	-	-	-	-	-	-	-
16 National League	-	0.0	-	-	-	-	-	-	-
17 Nat. Socialist Workers' Party	-	0.0	-	-	-	-	-	-	-
18 People's Party	-	11.7	10.0	11.3	24.8	25.2	25.1	16.5	17.2
19 Socialist Party	-	2.6	-	-	-	-	-	-	-
Others	0.0	0.0	0.0	0.0	0.0	0.0	0.0	0.0	0.0

Table 22.6a SWEDEN Total Votes 1964-1988

	1964	1968	1970	1973	1976	1979	1982	1985	1988
Electorate	5,095,850	5,445,333	5,645,804	5,690,333	5,947,077	6,040,461	6,130,993	6,249,445	6,330,023
Valid Votes	4,245,780	4,829,379	4,976,196	5,160,146	5,437,748	5,448,638	5,554,602	5,567,022	5,373,719
Invalid Votes	27,815	32,522	8,011	8,850	19,295	31,488	52,001	48,200	67,331
Total Votes	4,273,595	4,861,901	4,984,207	5,168,996	5,457,043	5,480,126	5,606,603	5,615,242	5,441,050
PARTY VOTES									
5 Social Democrats	2,006,923	2,420,277	2,256,369	2,247,727	2,324,603	2,356,234	2,533,250	2,487,551	2,321,826
6 Moderate Unity Party	582,609	621,031	573,812	737,584	847,672	1,108,406	1,313,337	1,187,335	983,226
7 Centre Party	559,632	757,215	991,208	1,295,246	1,309,669	984,589	859,618	691,258[1]	607,240
10 Communist Party	221,746	145,172	236,659	274,929	258,432	305,420	308,899	298,419	314,031
18 People's Party	720,733	688,456	806,667	486,028	601,556	577,063	327,770	792,268	655,720
20 Christian Democratic Union	75,389	72,377	88,770	90,388	73,844	75,993	103,820	-	158,182
21 Citizens' Coalition	64,807	82,082	-	-	-	-	-	-	-
22 Middle Parties	13,557	41,307	-	-	-	-	-	-	-
23 Ecology Party	-	-	-	-	-	-	91,787	83,645	296,935
Others	384	1,462	22,711	28,244	21,972	40,933	16,121	26,546	36,559

1 Electoral alliance of the Centre Party and the Christian Democrats.

Source: *Almänna Val* series

Table 22.6b SWEDEN Percentage of Votes 1964-1988

	1964	1968	1970	1973	1976	1979	1982	1985	1988
Total Votes	83.9	89.3	88.3	90.8	91.8	90.7	91.4	89.9	86.0
Valid Votes	83.3	88.7	88.1	90.7	91.4	90.2	90.6	89.1	84.9
Invalid Votes	0.5	0.6	0.1	0.2	0.3	0.5	0.8	0.8	1.1
Share Invalid	0.7	0.7	0.2	0.2	0.4	0.6	0.9	0.9	1.2
PARTY VOTES									
5 Social Democrats	47.3	50.1	45.3	43.6	42.7	43.2	45.6	44.7	43.2
6 Moderate Unity Party	13.7	12.9	11.5	14.3	15.6	20.3	23.6	21.3	18.3
7 Centre Party	13.2	15.7	19.9	25.1	24.1	18.1	15.5	12.4	11.3
10 Communist Party	5.2	3.0	4.8	9.4	4.8	5.6	5.6	5.4	5.8
18 People's Party	17.0	14.3	16.2	-	11.1	10.6	5.9	14.2	12.6
20 Christian Democratic Union	1.8	1.5	1.8	-	1.4	1.4	1.9	12.4	2.9
21 Citizens' Coalition	1.5	1.7	-	-	-	-	-	-	-
22 Middle Parties	0.3	0.9	-	-	-	-	-	-	-
23 Ecology Party	-	-	-	-	-	-	1.7	1.5	5.5
Others	0.0	0.0	0.5	-	0.4	0.8	0.3	0.5	0.7

Table 22.6c SWEDEN Number of Seats Won in the Riksdag[1] 1964-1988

	1964[3]	1968[4]	1970	1973	1976	1979	1982	1985	1988
5 Social Democrats	113	125	163	156	152	154	166	159	156
6 Moderate Unity Party[2]	32	29	41	51	55	73	86	76	66
7 Centre Party	33	37	71	90	86	64	56	43	42
10 Communist Party	8	3	17	19	17	20	20	19	21
18 People's Party	42	32	58	34	39	38	21	51	44
20 Christian Democratic Union	0	–	0	0	0	0	0	1	0
21 Citizens' Coalition	3[3]	4[4]	–	–	–	–	–	–	–
22 Middle Parties	2[3]	3[4]	–	–	–	–	–	–	–
23 Ecology Party	–	–	–	–	–	–	0	0	20
Others	–	–	–	–	–	–	0	–	0
Total Seats	233	233	350	350	349	349	349	349	349

1 In 1964 and 1968 the Andra Kammaren.
2 In 1964 and 1968 the Conservatives.
3 The two Middle Parties deputies joined the Liberal parliamentary group. One Citizens' Coalition deputy joined the Conservatives, and one joined the People's Party.
4 Three Citizens' Coalition deputies joined the Centre Party and one joined the People's Party. Two Middle Party deputies joined the Centre Party and one joined the People's Party.

Source: *Almänna Val* series

Table 22.6d SWEDEN Percentage of Seats Won in the Riksdag 1964-1988

	1964	1968	1970	1973	1976	1979	1982	1985	1988
5 Social Democrats	48.5	53.6	46.6	44.6	43.6	44.1	47.6	45.6	44.7
6 Moderate Unity Party	13.7	12.4	11.7	14.6	15.8	20.9	24.6	21.8	18.9
7 Centre Party	14.2	15.9	20.3	25.7	24.6	18.3	16.0	12.3	12.0
10 Communist Party	3.4	1.3	4.9	5.4	4.9	5.7	5.7	5.4	6.0
18 People's Party	18.0	13.7	16.6	9.7	11.2	10.9	6.0	14.6	12.6
20 Christian Democratic Union	0.0	0.0	0.0	0.0	0.0	0.0	0.0	0.3	0.0
21 Citizens' Coalition	1.3	1.7	-	-	-	-	-	-	-
22 Middle Parties	0.9	1.3	-	-	-	-	-	-	-
23 Ecology Party	-	-	-	-	-	-	0.0	0.0	5.7
Others	0.0	0.0	0.0	0.0	0.0	0.0	0.0	0.0	0.0

Chapter 23

SWITZERLAND

The Swiss Federal Assembly (in German, Bundesversammlung; in French, Assemblée fédérale) is bicameral. It consists of the Council of States (Standerat/Conseil des États), composed of two representatives from each of the cantons and one from each of the half cantons that make up the federation and a National Council (Nationalrat/Conseil national). The federal government (the Bundesrat/Conseil fédéral) is elected by the Federal Assembly. Since 1848 all Swiss males aged 20 and over and resident in the country have been entitled to vote in elections to the National Council. The right to vote was only granted women after a referendum in 1971. The secret ballot was introduced in 1872. Cantonal law determines the mode of election and duration of service of members of the Council of States. As of 1990 all members are popularly elected, usually by a two ballot majority system.

Initially, a multi-ballot system was employed for National Council elections, usually in multi-member constituencies; each elector had as many votes as there were seats to be filled. At the first ballot an absolute majority was required for election. In the event of insufficient candidates obtaining a majority, a second ballot was held. At this stage an absolute majority was still required. If any seats were still unfilled, a third ballot was held at which a plurality sufficed for election. After 1900 the third ballot was abandoned and a plurality at the second ballot secured election.

Until the end of the nineteenth century Swiss party organization was almost entirely cantonal. Three broad political tendances have been identified (Gruner and Frei, 1966: 82-83). The Protestant Left, which favoured a strong federal government, dominated the Assembly until 1919. The Right defended the autonomy of the Catholic cantons. The Centre was a conservative offshoot of the Left. The present-day party system began to emerge in the 1890s. In 1894 the historic Left formed the Radical Democratic Party. The Social Democratic Party, formed in 1888, won its first seat in the National Council in 1893. In the same year the Right came together as the Popular Catholic Party. The Centre had formed the Liberal Democratic group in the National Council in 1893 but without creating a national party organization. The Liberal Democratic Party was only established in 1913. For a detailed record of election results in Switzerland prior to the development of national party organisations, see Gruner (1978).

In 1919 proportional representation using the Hagenbach-Bischoff system was introduced. Each elector has as many votes as there are seats in the constituency, and may simply vote for a party list or distribute the votes between different lists and give two votes on any one candidate (Codding, 1983: 26-27). Representation in the National Council is proportional to population with the proviso that every canton or half-canton is entitled to at least one representative. Five very small cantons - Uri, Obwald, Nidwald, Appenzell Innerrhoden and since 1971 Glarus - benefit from this exception. In these single-member constituencies election is by plurality.

The federal structure of the Swiss state limits the significance of nationwide political organization. The smaller parties do not contest elections throughout the country and their support is confined to a few cantons only. In some of the smallest cantons unopposed returns have been frequent (Girod, 1964: 154-61). The importance of cantonal politics is such that parties give it priority in choosing party labels and alliances. Hence there are inconsistencies between the labels applied to political groups at the cantonal level, in federal elections and in the National Council.

Sources:

G.A. Codding, 'The Swiss political system and the management of diversity' in H.R. Penniman (ed.) *Switzerland at the Polls: the National Elections of 1979* (Washington, DC: American Enterprise Institute, 1983) 1-29

Federal Bureau of Statistics, *Statistik der Nationalratswahlen / Statistique des élections au Conseil national, 1918, 1919, 1922, 1925, 1928* (Bern, 1929). Volumes in the same series have been published for each subsequent election except 1939, which is included in the volume for the 1943 election

R. Girod, 'Geography of the Swiss party system', in E. Allardt and Y. Littunen (eds), *Cleavages, Ideologies and Party Systems* (Helsinki: Westermark Society, 1964) 132-61

E. Gruner, *Die Wahlen in den Schweizerischen Nationalrat 1848-1919 Les élections au Conseil national suisse 1848-1919* four volumes (Bern: Francke, 1978)

E. Gruner and K. Frei, *Die Schweizerische Bundesversammlung 1848-1920* (Bern: A. Francke, 1966).

H. Kerr, 'The Swiss party system: steadfast and changing', in H. Daalder (ed.), *Party Systems in Denmark, Austria, Switzerland, the Netherlands and Belgium* (London: Frances Pinter, 1987) 107-192

Swiss Federal Council, *Bericht des Bundesrates an den Nationalrat über die Nationalratswahlen für die XL. Legislatur periode (Vom 19 November 1975)* (Bern, 1975) and subsequent volumes in the same series.

Table 23.1 POLITICAL PARTIES IN SWITZERLAND SINCE 1896

	Party Names	Elections Contested Years	Number
1	Catholic Conservatives. From 1912 Conservative People's Party (Schweizerische Konservative Volkspartei/Parti populaire conservateur suisse). In 1957 renamed Conservative Christian Social Party (Konservativ-Christlich Soziale Partei/Parti conservateur chretien social); since 1971 Christian Democratic People's Party (Christlich Demokratische Volkspartei/Parti démocrate-chrétien suisse) [1]	1896ff	27
2	Democrats (Demokraten/Groupe des démocrates) [2]	1896-1967	22
3	Liberal Conservatives. From 1913 Liberal Democratic Party (Liberal-Demokratische Partei/ Parti libéral démocratique. From 1961 Liberal Democratic Union of Switzerland (Liberal - Demokratische Union der Schweiz/Union libérale - démocratique suisse. Renamed Liberal Party of Switzerland (Liberale Partei der Schweiz/Parti libéral suisse) in 1977	1896ff	27
4	Radical Democrats (Freisinnig-demokratische Partei/Parti radical-démocratique)	1896ff	27
5	Social Democrats (Sozialdemokratische Partei der Schweiz/Parti socialiste suisse)	1896ff	27
6	Farmers, Traders, and Citizens' Party (Schweizerische Bauern, Gewerbe und Burger Partei - BGB/Parti suisse des paysans, artisans et bourgeois); from 1971 Swiss People's Party (Schweizerische Volkspartei/Union démocratique du centre) [3]	1919ff	19
7	Grütli Union (Grütliverein/Association des Grutléens)	1919-1925	3
8	Protestant People's Party (Evangelische Volkspartei/Parti populaire evangelique)	1919ff	19
9	Communist Party (Kommunistische Partei der Schweiz/Parti communiste suisse). Banned in 1940 and reformed in 1944 as Labour Party (Partei der Arbeit der Schweiz/Parti suisse du travail)	1922-1939; 1947ff	17
10	Free Market Party (Freiwirtschafter/Parti de l'économie franche)	1922-1925; 1935-1955	8
11	Front Party (Fronten/Parti des fronts)	1935	1
12	Independents' Party (Landesring der Unabhängigen/Alliance des indépendants)	1935ff	14
13	Young Peasants (Jungbauern/Jeunes paysans) [4]	1935-1947	4

14	National Action against Foreign Domination (Nationale Aktion gegen die Überfremdung von Volk und Heimat/Action nationale contre l'emprise et la surpopulation etrangère); from 1979 Nationale Action for People and Fatherland (Nationale Aktion für Volk und Heimat/Action national pour le peuple et la patrie)	1967ff	6
15	Vigilance [5]	1967ff	6
16	Republican Movement (Schweizerische Republikanische Bewegung/ Mouvement nationale d'action républicaine et sociale) [6]	1971-1979	3
17	Autonomous Socialist Party (Partito Socialista Autonomo) [7]	1971ff	5
18	Progressive Organisations of Switzerland (Progressive Organisationen/Organisations progressistes suisses) [8]	1971ff	5
19	Greens. In 1983 Federation of Green Parties (Föderation der Grünen Parteien der Schweiz/ Fédération suisse des partis écologistes); in 1987 Green Party of Switzerland (Grüne Partei der Schweiz/Parti écologiste suisse) [9]	1979ff	3
20	Alternative Greens (Alternative verte de Suisse/ Grüne Alternative Schweiz)	1983ff	2
21	Free Liste (Freie Liste) [10]	1983	1
22	Swiss Motorists' Party (Schweizer Auto Partei/Parti automobiliste suisse)	1987	1

1 In the nineteenth and early twentieth century often known as the Catholic Conservatives, the name of the party's parliamentary group.

2 The Democrats were not a national party, but a group of cantonal parties forming the core of the Social-Political Group in the National Council from 1896 to 1931, and subsequently forming the Democratic Group. In 1971 the Democratic parties of Glarus and Grisons merged with the Swiss People's Party, and the Democratic Party of Zürich merged with the Radicals. For details, see Federal Bureau of Statistics, 1929: 29-30 and Ibid. 1968: 142.

3 Founded as the Farmers' and Citizens' Party in 1918. Merged with minor groups to form the Farmers, Traders and Citizens' Party in 1921.

4 Breakaway from the Farmers Traders and Citizens' Party.

5 Anti-immigrant party in Geneva. Allied in federal elections with the Republican Movement from 1975 to 1983.

6 Created in 1971 by James Schwarzenbach, the founder and former leader of National Action.

7 Left-wing breakaway from the Social Democrats in Ticino.

8 Founded early in the 1970s by groups who had broken away from the communist Labour Party.

9 In 1979 Grüne Partei des Kantons Zürich and the Groupement pour la protection de l'environnement in Vaud. Daniel Brelaz of the Vaud party was elected to the Nationalrat in 1979. These parties merged with other cantonal green parties to form the Federation of Green Parties in May 1983. Joined by other cantonal groups, re-formed as the Green Party of Switzerland in 1987.

10 Bern ecology party founded by Leni Rokert, who had broken away from the Radical Party. She was elected to the Nationalrat in 1983. The party later merged with the Federation of Green Parties.

Table 23.2 DATES OF ELECTIONS: NATIONALRAT [1]

1.	25 October 1896	15.	29 October 1939
2.	29 October 1899	16.	31 October 1943
3.	26 October 1902	17.	26 October 1947
4.	29 October 1905	18.	28 October 1951
5.	25 October 1908	19.	30 October 1955
6.	29 October 1911	20.	25 October 1959
7.	25 October 1914	21.	27 October 1963
8.	28 October 1917	22.	29 October 1967
9.	26 October 1919	23.	31 October 1971
10.	29 October 1922	24.	26 October 1975
11.	25 October 1925	25.	21 October 1979
12.	28 October 1928	26.	23 October 1983
13.	25 October 1931	27.	18 October 1987
14.	27 October 1935		

[1] Elections to the Nationalrat take place on the last Sunday in October. For elections before 1919 the dates refer to the first ballot.

Source: Secretariat of the Federal Assembly, Bern.

Table 23.3a SWITZERLAND Total Votes 1896-1919

	1896	1899	1902	1905	1908	1911	1914	1917	1919
Electorate	713,367	737,696	760,252	779,835	809,508	830,102	851,377	915,222	959,971
Valid Votes	371,924	368,735	407,322	411,419	398,224	400,870	340,250	515,022	749,954
Invalid Votes	n.a	n.a	n.a	n.a	n.a	n.a	n.a	n.a	10,646
Total Votes	n.a	n.a	n.a	n.a	n.a	n.a	n.a	n.a	760,600
PARTY VOTES									
1 Catholic Conservatives	85,484	76,845	94,031	92,600	81,733	76,726	71,668	84,784	156,702
2 Democrats	19,946	18,003	15,053	18,028	14,414	12,610	9,069	16,818	14,677
3 Liberal Conservatives	54,012	51,764	34,928	27,643	23,597	27,062	25,142	25,188	28,497
4 Radical Democrats	181,028	183,216	205,235	202,605	202,732	198,300	191,054	210,323	215,566
5 Social Democrats	25,304	35,488	51,338	60,308	70,003	80,050	34,204	158,450	175,292
6 Farmers, Traders and Citizens' Party	-	-	-	-	-	-	-	-	114,537
7 Grütli Union	-	-	-	-	-	-	-	-	20,559
8 Protestant People's Party	-	-	-	-	-	-	-	-	6,031
Others	5,750	3,409	6,737	10,235	5,745	6,122	9,133	19,459	18,093

Sources: Gruner, 1978: 369, 398 and Federal Bureau of Statistics, 1929: 24-25

Table 23.3b SWITZERLAND Percentage of Votes 1896-1919

	1896	1899	1902	1905	1908	1911	1914	1917	1919
Total Votes	52.1	50.0	53.6	52.8	49.2	48.3	40.0	56.3	79.2
Valid Votes	52.1	50.0	53.6	52.8	49.2	48.3	40.0	56.3	78.1
Invalid Votes	0.0	0.0	0.0	0.0	0.0	0.0	0.0	0.0	1.1
Share Invalid	0.0	0.0	0.0	0.0	0.0	0.0	0.0	0.0	1.4
PARTY VOTES									
1 Catholic Conservatives	23.0	20.8	23.1	22.5	20.5	19.1	21.1	16.5	20.9
2 Democrats	5.4	4.9	3.7	4.4	3.6	3.1	2.7	3.3	2.0
3 Liberal Conservatives	14.5	14.0	8.6	6.7	5.9	6.8	7.4	4.9	3.8
4 Radical Democrats	48.7	49.7	50.4	49.2	50.9	49.5	56.2	40.8	28.7
5 Social Democrats	6.8	9.6	12.6	14.7	17.6	20.0	10.1	30.8	23.4
6 Farmers,Traders and Citizens' Party	-	-	-	-	-	-	-	-	15.3
7 Grütli Union	-	-	-	-	-	-	-	-	2.7
8 Protestant People's Party	-	-	-	-	-	-	-	-	0.8
Others	1.5	0.9	1.7	2.5	1.4	1.5	2.7	3.8	2.4

Table 23.3c SWITZERLAND Number of Seats Won in the Nationalrat 1896-1919

	1896	1899	1902	1905	1908	1911	1914	1917	1919
1 Catholic Conservatives	31	32	36	36	35	38	37	42	41
2 Democrats	8	6	4	6	5	6	4	7	4
3 Liberal Conservatives	20	20	20	19	15	14	15	12	9
4 Radical Democrats	87	85	100	104	105	114	112	103	60
5 Social Democrats	1	4	7	2	7	15	19	20	41
6 Farmers,Traders and Citizens' Party	–	–	–	–	–	–	–	–	30
7 Grütli Union	–	–	–	–	–	–	–	–	2
8 Protestant People's Party	–	–	–	–	–	–	–	–	1
Others	0	0	0	0	0	2	2	5	1
Total Seats	147	147	167	167	167	189	189	189	189

Source: Gruner, 1978: 417-424.

Table 23.3d SWITZERLAND Percentage of Seats Won in the Nationalrat 1896-1919

	1896	1899	1902	1905	1908	1911	1914	1917	1919
1 Catholic Conservatives	21.1	21.8	21.6	21.6	21.0	20.1	19.6	22.2	21.7
2 Democrats	5.4	4.1	2.4	3.6	3.0	3.2	2.1	3.7	2.1
3 Liberal Conservatives	13.6	13.6	12.0	11.4	9.0	7.4	7.9	6.3	4.8
4 Radical Democrats	59.2	57.8	59.9	62.3	62.9	60.3	59.3	54.5	31.7
5 Social Democrats	0.7	2.7	4.2	1.2	4.2	7.9	10.1	10.6	21.7
6 Farmers,Traders and Citizens' Party	-	-	-	-	-	-	-	-	15.9
7 Grütli Union	-	-	-	-	-	-	-	-	1.1
8 Protestant People's Party	-	-	-	-	-	-	-	-	0.5
Others	0.0	0.0	0.0	0.0	0.0	1.1	1.1	2.6	0.5

Table 23.4a SWITZERLAND Total Votes 1922-1951

	1922	1925	1928	1931	1935	1939[1]	1943	1947	1951
Electorate	983,238	1,018,191	1,066,500	1,118,841	1,194,910	1,232,643	1,310,445	1,374,740	1,414,308
Valid Votes	737,423	747,138	807,472	866,575	917,575	623,740	887,676	966,680	967,989
Invalid Votes	13,436	17,456	14,917	15,361	18,181	16,125	20,570	18,819	18,948
Total Votes	750,859	764,594	822,389	881,936	935,756	639,865	908,246	985,499	986,937
PARTY VOTES									
1 Catholic Conservatives	153,836	155,467	172,516	184,602	185,052	105,018	182,916	203,202	216,616
2 Democrats	19,287	16,362	15,116	10,726	10,665	16,891	29,627	28,096	21,606
3 Liberal Conservatives	29,041	30,523	23,752	24,573	30,476	10,241	28,434	30,492	24,813
4 Radical Democrats	208,144	206,485	220,135	232,562	216,664	128,163	197,746	220,486	230,687
5 Social Democrats	170,974	192,208	220,141	247,946	255,843	160,377	251,576	251,625	249,857
6 Farmers,Traders and Citizens' Party	118,382	113,512	126,961	131,809	100,300	91,182	101,998	115,976	120,819
7 Grütli Union	9,313	427	-	-	-	-	-	-	-
8 Protestant People's Party	6,306	6,888	5,618	8,454	6,780	5,726	3,627	9,072	9,559
9 Communist Party	13,441	14,837	14,818	12,778	12,569	15,962	-	49,353	25,659
10 Free Market Party	1,106	1,602	-	-	11,078	10,865	9,031	4,626	8,194
11 Front Party	-	-	-	-	13,740	-	-	-	-
12 Independents' Party	-	-	-	-	37,861	43,735	48,557	42,428	49,100
13 Young Peasants' Party	-	-	-	-	28,161	27,708	18,310	-	-
Others	4,574	5,368	5,550	9,841	4,334	7,872	14,930	4,931	4,588

1 In nine cantons returning 55 deputies the election was uncontested.

Sources: *Statistik der Nationalratswahlen 1919, 1922, 1925 und 1928*: 26-31 and *Nationalratswahlen 1971*: 160-194

Table 23.4b SWITZERLAND Percentage of Votes 1922-1951

	1922	1925	1928	1931	1935	1939	1943	1947	1951
Total Votes	76.4	75.1	77.1	78.8	78.3	51.9[1]	69.3	71.7	69.8
Valid Votes	75.0	73.4	75.7	77.5	76.8	50.6	67.7	70.3	68.4
Invalid Votes	1.4	1.7	1.4	1.4	1.5	1.3	1.6	1.4	1.3
Share Invalid	1.8	2.3	1.8	1.7	1.9	2.5	2.3	1.9	1.9
PARTY VOTES									
1 Catholic Conservatives	20.9	20.9	21.4	21.4	20.3	16.8	20.8	21.2	22.5
2 Democrats	2.6	2.2	1.9	1.2	1.2	2.7	3.4	2.9	2.2
3 Liberal Conservatives	4.0	4.0	3.0	2.8	3.3	1.6	3.2	3.2	2.6
4 Radical Democrats	28.3	27.8	27.4	26.9	23.7	20.5	22.5	23.0	24.0
5 Social Democrats	23.3	25.8	27.4	28.7	28.0	25.7	28.6	26.2	26.0
6 Farmers,Traders and Citizens' Party	16.1	15.3	15.8	15.3	11.0	14.6	11.6	12.0	12.6
7 Grütli Union	1.3	0.1	-	-	-	-	-	-	-
8 Protestant People's Party	0.9	0.9	0.7	1.0	0.7	0.9	0.4	0.9	1.0
9 Communist Party	1.8	2.0	1.8	1.5	1.4	2.6	-	5.1	2.7
10 Free Market Party	0.1	0.2	-	-	1.2	1.7	1.0	0.5	0.8
11 Front Party	-	-	-	-	1.5	-	-	-	-
12 Independents' Party	-	-	-	-	4.1	7.0	5.5	4.4	5.1
13 Young Peasants' Party	-	-	-	-	3.1	4.4	2.1	-	-
Others	0.6	0.7	0.7	1.1	0.5	1.3	0.9	0.5	0.5

1 The turnout in the 16 cantons where voting took place was 74.3 percent.

Table 23.4c SWITZERLAND Number of Seats Won in the Nationalrat 1922-1951[1]

	1922	1925	1928	1931	1935	1939	1943	1947	1951
1 Catholic Conservatives	44	42	46	44	42	43 (17)	43 (1)	44	48
2 Democrats	4 (1)	5 (1)	3	2	3	7 (1)	5	5	4
3 Liberal Conservatives	10	7	6	6	6	6 (3)	8	7	5
4 Radical Democrats	60 (3)	60 (3)	58	52	48	47 (20)	47	52 (1)	51 (2)
5 Social Democrats	43 (1)	49 (1)	50	49	50	45 (10)	56 (1)	48 (1)	49
6 Farmers,Traders and Citizens' Party	34	30	31	30	21	22 (2)	22	21	23
7 Grütli Union	0	0	–	–	–	–	–	–	–
8 Protestant People's Party	1	1	1	1	1	–	1	1	1
9 Communist Party	2	3	2	2	2	4 (2)	–	7	5
10 Free Market Party	–	–	–	–	–	1	–	1	–
11 Front Party	–	–	–	–	1	–	–	–	–
12 Independents' Party	–	–	–	–	7	9	7	8	10
13 Young Peasants' Party	–	–	–	–	4	3	3	–	–
Others	–	1	1	1	2	0	2	0	0
Total Seats	198 (5)	198 (5)	198	187	187	194 (55)	194 (2)	194 (2)	196 (2)

1 Figures in parentheses report the number of deputies returned unopposed.

Source: *Nationalratswahlen, 1971*: 160-194

Table 23.4d SWITZERLAND Percentage of Seats Won in the Nationalrat 1922-1951

	1922	1925	1928	1931	1935	1939	1943	1947	1951
1 Catholic Conservatives	22.2	21.2	23.2	23.5	22.5	23.0	22.2	22.7	24.5
2 Democrats	2.0	2.5	1.5	1.1	1.6	3.7	2.6	2.6	2.0
3 Liberal Conservatives	5.1	3.5	3.0	3.2	3.2	3.2	4.1	3.6	2.6
4 Radical Democrats	30.3	30.3	29.3	27.8	25.7	25.1	24.2	26.8	26.0
5 Social Democrats	21.7	24.7	25.3	26.2	26.7	24.1	28.9	24.7	25.0
6 Farmers,Traders and Citizens' Party	17.2	15.2	15.7	16.0	11.2	11.8	11.3	10.3	11.7
7 Grütli Union	0.0	0.0	-	-	-	-	-	-	-
8 Protestant People's Party	0.5	0.5	0.5	0.5	0.5	-	0.5	0.5	0.5
9 Communist Party	1.0	1.5	1.0	1.1	1.1	2.1	-	3.6	2.6
10 Free Market Party	-	-	-	-	-	0.5	-	0.5	-
11 Front Party	-	-	-	-	0.5	-	-	-	-
12 Independents' Party	-	-	-	-	3.7	4.8	3.6	4.1	5.1
13 Young Peasants' Party	-	-	-	-	2.1	1.6	1.5	-	-
Others	0.0	0.5	0.5	0.5	1.1	0.0	1.0	0.0	0.0

Table 23.5a SWITZERLAND Total Votes 1955-1987

	1955	1959	1963	1967	1971	1975	1979	1983	1987
Electorate	1,453,807	1,473,155	1,531,164	1,599,479	3,548,860	3,733,113	3,863,169	4,068,532	4,191,731
Valid Votes	982,020	989,005	969,037	1,001,863	1,974,320	1,931,397	1,833,205	1,959,915	1,934,457
Invalid Votes	16,861	19,558	17,960	18,044	25,815	24,355	23,484	30,097	0.0
Total Votes	998,881	1,008,563	986,997	1,019,907	2,000,135	1,955,752	1,856,689	1,990,012	0.0
PARTY VOTES									
1 Christian Democrats	226,122	229,088	225,160	219,184	407,878	407,285	394,272	399,929	387,372
2 Democrats	21,003	21,170	16,978	14,270	-	-	-	-	-
3 Liberal Conservatives	21,688	22,934	21,501	23,208	43,343	47,256	51,258	55,340	52,537
4 Radical Democrats	227,370	232,557	230,200	230,095	428,089	428,922	441,241	457,864	443,634
5 Social Democrats	263,664	259,139	256,063	233,873	451,768	480,398	447,995	447,925	356,274
6 Swiss People's Party[1]	117,847	113,611	109,202	109,621	217,884	192,052	212,703	217,219	213,252
8 Protestant People's Party	10,581	14,038	15,690	15,728	42,305	37,960	40,745	40,851	-
9 Communist Party	25,060	26,346	21,088	28,723	50,833	45,801	38,185	17,497	15,527
12 Independents' Party	53,450	54,049	48,224	89,950	150,680	117,218	74,624	78,523	80,691
14 National Action	-	-	-	6,275	63,201	47,798	24,258	57,570	57,602
15 Vigilance	-	-	-	1,696	4,319	5,111	4,492	10,128	5,060
16 Republican Movement	-	-	-	-	79,604	57,193	11,590	-	-
17 Autonomous Socialist Party	-	-	-	-	5,263	6,707	8,149	9,962	10,880
18 Progressive Organisations	-	-	-	-	-	19,170	31,125	43,668	24,343
19 Greens	-	-	-	-	-	-	10,997	34,437	95,959
20 Alternative Greens	-	-	-	-	-	-	-	7,093	53,109
21 Free List	-	-	-	-	-	-	-	14,635	-
22 Swiss Motorists' Party	-	-	-	-	-	-	-	-	50,366
Others	5,639	9,438	17,643	21,225	29,153	38,523	41,571	67,274	50,588

[1] Until 1971 the Farmers, Traders and Citizens' Party.

Sources: Calculated from *Nationalratswahlen,1967*: 120-144, *Nationalratswahlen,1975*: 27-30, Swiss Federal Council (1975) and subsequent volumes in the same series and other figures provided by the Federal Bureau of Statistics.

Table 23.5b SWITZERLAND Percentage of Votes 1955-1987

	1955	1959	1963	1967	1971	1975	1979	1983	1987
Total Votes	68.7	68.5	64.5	63.8	56.4	52.4	48.1	48.9	46.1
Valid Votes	67.5	67.1	63.3	62.6	55.6	51.7	47.5	48.2	46.1
Invalid Votes	1.2	1.3	1.2	1.1	0.7	0.7	0.6	0.7	0.0
Share Invalid	1.7	1.9	1.8	1.8	1.3	1.2	1.3	1.5	0.0
PARTY VOTES									
1 Christian Democrats	23.2	23.3	23.4	22.1	20.7	21.1	21.5	20.4	20.0
2 Democrats	2.2	2.2	1.8	1.4	–	–	–	–	–
3 Liberal Conservatives	2.2	2.3	2.2	2.3	2.2	2.4	2.8	2.8	2.7
4 Radical Democrats	23.4	23.7	23.9	23.2	21.7	22.2	24.1	23.4	22.9
5 Social Democrats	27.1	26.4	26.6	23.5	22.9	24.9	24.4	22.9	18.4
6 Swiss People's Party	12.1	11.6	11.4	11.0	11.0	9.9	11.6	11.1	11.0
8 Protestant People's Party	1.1	1.4	1.6	1.6	2.1	2.0	2.2	2.1	1.9
9 Communist Party	2.6	2.7	2.2	2.9	2.6	2.4	2.1	0.9	0.8
12 Independents' Party	5.5	5.5	5.0	9.1	6.1	6.1	4.1	4.0	4.2
14 National Action	–	–	–	0.6	2.5	2.5	1.3	2.9	3.0
15 Vigilance	–	–	–	0.2	0.2	0.3	0.2	0.5	0.2
16 Republican Movement	–	–	–	–	4.0	3.0	0.6	–	–
17 Autonomous Socialist Party	–	–	–	–	0.3	0.3	0.4	0.5	0.6
18 Progressive Organisations	–	–	–	–	–	1.0	1.7	2.2	1.3
19 Greens	–	–	–	–	–	–	0.6	1.8	5.0
20 Alternative Greens	–	–	–	–	–	–	–	0.4	2.7
21 Free List	–	–	–	–	–	–	–	0.7	–
22 Swiss Motorists' Party	–	–	–	–	–	–	–	–	2.6
Others	0.6	–	1.8	2.1	1.5	2.0	2.3	3.4	2.6

Table 23.5c SWITZERLAND Number of Seats Won in the Nationalrat 1955-1987[1]

	1955	1959	1963	1967	1971	1975	1979	1983	1987
1 Christian Democrats	47	47	48	45	44	46	44	41	42
2 Democrats	4	4	4	3	–	–	–	–	–
3 Liberal Conservatives	5	5	6	6	6	6	8	8	9
4 Radical Democrats	50 (2)	51 (1)	51 (3)	49 (3)	49	47	51 (1)	54	51 (1)
5 Social Democrats	53	51 (1)	53 (1)	51 (1)	46	55	51 (1)	47	41
6 Swiss People's Party	22	23	22	21	23	21	23	23	25
8 Protestant People's Party	1	2	2	3	3	3	3	3	3
9 Communist Party	4	3	4	5	5	4	3	1	1
12 Independents' Party	10	10	10	16	13	11	8	8	8
14 National Action	–	–	–	1	4	2	1	5	3
15 Vigilance	–	–	–	0	0	1	1	1	0
16 Republican Movement	–	–	–	–	7	3	1	–	–
17 Autonomous Socialist Party	–	–	–	–	0	1	1	1	1
18 Progressive Organisations	–	–	–	–	0	0	3	3	3
19 Greens	–	–	–	–	–	–	1	4	9
20 Alternative Greens	–	–	–	–	–	–	–	–	1
21 Free List	–	–	–	–	–	–	–	1	–
22 Swiss Motorists' Party	–	–	–	–	–	–	–	–	2
Others	0	0	0	0	0	0	1	0	1 (1)
Total Seats	196 (2)	196 (2)	200 (4)	200 (4)	200	200	200 (2)	200	200 (2)

[1] Figures in parentheses report the number of deputies returned unopposed.

Source: Federal Bureau of Statistics.

Table 23.5d SWITZERLAND Percentage of Seats Won in the Nationalrat 1955-1987

	1955	1959	1963	1967	1971	1975	1979	1983	1987
1 Christian Democrats	24.0	24.0	24.0	22.5	22.0	23.0	22.0	21.0	21.0
2 Democrats	2.0	2.0	2.0	1.5	-	-	-	-	-
3 Liberal Conservatives	2.6	2.6	3.0	3.0	3.0	3.0	4.0	4.0	4.5
4 Radical Democrats	25.5	26.0	25.5	24.5	24.5	23.5	25.5	27.0	25.5
5 Social Democrats	27.0	26.0	26.5	25.5	23.0	27.5	25.5	23.5	20.5
6 Swiss People's Party	11.2	11.7	11.0	10.5	11.5	10.5	11.5	11.5	12.5
8 Protestant People's Party	0.5	1.0	1.0	1.5	1.5	1.5	1.5	1.5	1.5
9 Communist Party	2.0	1.5	2.0	2.5	2.5	2.0	1.5	0.5	0.5
12 Independents' Party	5.1	5.1	5.0	8.0	6.5	5.5	4.0	4.0	4.5
14 National Action	-	-	-	0.5	2.0	1.0	1.0	1.5	1.5
15 Vigilance	-	-	-	0.0	0.0	1.5	1.5	1.5	0.0
16 Republican Movement	-	-	-	-	3.5	1.5	1.5	-	-
17 Autonomous Socialist Party	-	-	-	-	0.0	0.5	0.5	0.5	0.5
18 Progressive Organisations	-	-	-	-	0.0	0.0	1.5	1.5	1.5
19 Greens	-	-	-	-	-	-	0.5	2.0	4.5
20 Alternative Greens	-	-	-	-	-	-	-	-	0.5
21 Free List	-	-	-	-	-	-	-	0.5	-
22 Swiss Motorists' Party	-	-	-	-	-	-	-	-	1.0
Others	0.0	0.0	0.0	0.0	0.0	0.0	0.5	0.0	0.5

Chapter 24

UNITED KINGDOM

The origins of the United Kingdom Parliament can be traced directly to the English Parliament of the Middle Ages. Since the thirteenth century Parliament has consisted of a House of Lords of hereditary peers and ex-officio leaders of law and church, and a directly elected House of Commons. The tradition of election by plurality dates back to the Middle Ages. Since the Act of Union of 1707 Scotland has been represented in the House of Commons and MPs from Ireland were included in 1801 after the abolition of the Irish Parliament. Franchise laws varied enormously from constituency to constituency and nation to nation. (For statutes concerning elections since 1696, see Gwyn, 1962: 255f and Craig 1989: 189-195).

The Reform Act of 1832 led to a small increase in the electorate, from 2.1 per cent of the total population to 3.3 per cent. It also began a century-long process of rationalization of the claim to the vote, abolishing the grossest anomalies in population between constituencies and establishing uniform franchise requirements (Seymour, 1915). In 1867 household suffrage was introduced in the English and Scottish boroughs, subject to the payment of rates on property, and minor extensions of the franchise occurred elsewhere. The secret ballot was introduced in 1872.

A national party system evolved slowly from 1832 to 1885. In the period 1832 to 1880 at least 100 seats were always uncontested and as many as 58 per cent were uncontested in 1859 (Craig, 1989: 160). Party labels lacked a standard meaning, and there was no nationwide party organization until the latter part of the nineteenth century (Hanham, 1959; Craig, 1977).

The 1884 Reform Act introduced a uniform franchise for the United Kingdom. The majority of adult males (15.6 per cent of the population) was now entitled to vote. By 1911 88 per cent of the adult male population was eligible to claim a vote but stringent registration procedures reduced the proportion actually registered to 68 per cent (Blewett, 1965: 31-34). The number of unopposed returns between 1885 and 1910 varied from 43 in 1885 to 243 in 1900. The average was 139, 21 per cent of the seats in the House of Commons.

In 1918 adult male suffrage based on a simple residence requirement was introduced (Pugh, 1978). Women over 30 were given the vote if they or their husbands were householders; in 1928 women were enfranchised on the same basis as men. The traditional practice of allowing a person more than one vote on the basis of an additional claim for a vote as a university graduate or a businessman continued.

University graduates elected 12 MPs by single transferable vote. In 1922 there were 72,000 university voters in the United Kingdom, 0.3 per cent of the electorate (Butler, 1953: 148-153). Occupiers of business premises worth over £10 a year were allowed to vote in the constituency where their business was located as well as from their residence. In 1922 there were 209,000 business voters in England and Wales, or 1.1 per cent of the electorate (Butler, 1953: 146-148). In 1948 the university and the business franchises were abolished. The voting age was reduced from 21 to 18 in 1969.

Until 1832 MPs were usually elected in two-member constituencies in which each elector had two votes. The 1832 Reform Act removed one MP from some two-member constituencies and new single-member constituencies were created. The Reform Act of 1867 created a number of three-member constituencies in larger cities; electors had only two votes. This limited vote system was designed to ensure some representation for the Conservative minority. The 1884 Reform Act abolished all the three-member and most of the two-member constituencies, making the single-member constituency with the MP elected by plurality the norm. The remaining two-member constituencies were abolished in 1948.

Table 24.a NUMBER OF SEATS PER CONSTITUENCY IN THE HOUSE OF COMMONS 1830-1950

	One	Two	Three	Four	Total Constituencies	MPs
1830	106	270	0	3	379	658
1832	153	240	7	1	401	658
1868	196	211	12	1	420	658
1885	616	27	0	0	643	670
1918	670	17	1	0	688	707
1922	576	18	1	0	595	615
1945	601	18	1	0	620	640
1950	625	0	0	0	625	625

Sources: Brock, 1973: 19-20 and Craig, 1989: 161f.

The boundary of the United Kingdom was altered in 1921 when 26 counties of Southern Ireland became self-governing as the Irish Free State, thus removing 89 Irish constituencies from the House of Commons. Northern Ireland remained part of the United Kingdom with its own Parliament at Stormont as well as 12 seats in the United Kingdom Parliament. A separate Northern Ireland House of Commons was first elected in 1921; it was suspended in 1972 (Elliott, 1973). The total of Ulster MPs at Westminster was raised to 17 after the 1979 general election.

Political divisions in Northern Ireland have normally been along lines of religion and national identity. However, there have been frequent changes in the party labels of Protestant and Unionist politicians campaigning in favour of the United Kingdom and of Catholic and nationalist politicians in favour of a United Ireland. In this volume, votes for Ulster Unionist candidates who took the whip of the Conservatives Party in Parliament are included with the British Conservative Party until the February 1974 election, and votes for the Northern Ireland Labour Party (which never elected a Westminster MP) with the British Labour Party totals until 1974. The votes reported for Irish Unity candidates include individuals standing under a variety of labels but having a common allegiance to a united Ireland. The basis of groupings is set out in Rose and McAllister, 1982, Tables 4.1, 4.2, and 4.3.

The Scottish National Party and Plaid Cymru, the Welsh Nationalists, can sometimes win a significant share of the vote within a Scottish or Welsh context. But because Scotland returns only 72 MPs, and Wales 36, their impact on United Kingdom totals is limited (see Rose and McAllister, 1982, chapter 4).

In 1981 a group of Labour MPs, including four former Cabinet ministers led by Roy Jenkins, broke away to form a new Social Democratic Party. It promptly concluded an agreement with the Liberal Party, and the two parties agreed to contest elections under an Alliance banner. Bargaining between leaders of the Liberals and the SDP led to the nomination of a single Alliance candidate for by-elections and for each constituency at the 1983 and 1987 general elections. Each party retained a separate organization and leader (Butler and Kavanagh, 1984: chapter 5). The votes and seats reported in Tables 24.5a - 24.5d are for each Alliance party. Immediately following the 1987 election the leader of the Liberal Party, David Steel, proposed a merger of the two parties, and this was formally approved by each, resulting in 1988 in the creation of a merged party, named the Social and Liberal Democrats: the name was shortened to Liberal Democrats in 1989. However, the vote by SDP members in favour of merger was not accepted by the SDP leader, David Owen, who continued to lead his own Social Democratic Party.

Sources:

N. Blewett, 'The franchise in the United Kingdom, 1885-1918', *Past and Present*, 45 (1965) 27-56

V.Bogdanor, *The People and the Party System: the Referendum and Electoral Reform in British Politics* (Cambridge: Cambridge University Press, 1981)

M. Brock, *The Great Reform Act* (London: Hutchinson, 1973)

D.E. Butler, *The Electoral System of Britain since 1918* (Oxford: Clarendon Press, 1953)

D.E. Butler and D. Kavanagh, *The British General Election of 1983* (London: Macmillan, 1985)

F.W.S. Craig, *Minor Parties at British Parliamentary Elections, 1885-1974* (London: Macmillan, 1975)

F.W.S. Craig, *British Parliamentary Election Results, 1832-1885* (London: Macmillan, 1977)

F.W.S. Craig, *Chronology of British Parliamentary By-Elections, 1833-1987* (Chichester: Parliamentary Research Services, 1987).

F.W.S. Craig, *British Electoral Facts, 1832-1987* (Aldershot: Gower, 1989)

S. Elliott, *Northern Ireland Parliamentary Election Results 1921-1972* (Chichester: Political Reference Publications, 1973)

W.B. Gwyn, *Democracy and the Cost of Politics in Britain* (London: Athlone Press, 1962)

H.J. Hanham, *Elections and Party Management: Politics in the Age of Disraeli and Gladstone* (London: Longmans, 1959. Reprinted with a new introduction by Harvester Press, 1978).

I. McAllister and R. Rose, *The Nationwide Competition for Votes* (London: Frances Pinter, 1984)

M. Pugh, *Electoral Reform in War and Peace 1906-1918* (London: Routledge & Kegan Paul, 1978)

M. Pugh, *The Evolution of the British Electoral System 1832-1987* (London: The Historical Association, 1988)

R. Rose and I. McAllister, *United Kingdom Facts* (London: Macmillan, 1982)

C. Seymour, *Electoral Reform in England and Wales* (New Haven: Yale University Press, 1915. Reprinted by David and Charles, Newton Abbot, 1971)

Table 24.1 POLITICAL PARTIES IN THE UNITED KINGDOM SINCE 1885

	Party Names	Elections Contested Years	Number
1	Conservative Party [1]	1885ff	28
2	Liberal Party [2]	1885-1987	28
3	Irish Nationalist Party [3]	1885-1918	9
4	Liberal Unionists [2]	1886-1910	7
5	Independent Labour Party - ILP [5]	1895-1945	13
6	Labour Party [6]	1900ff	24
7	United Ireland [7]	1918ff	20
8	Lloyd George Liberals [8]	1918-1922;1931	3
9	National Democratic and Labour Party	1918-1922	2
10	Communist Party	1922ff	19
11	Scottish National Party - SNP	1929ff	16
12	Plaid Cymru (Party of Wales)	1929ff	16
13	National Labour	1931-1935	2
14	National Liberal Party [9]	1931-1945	3
15	National Front	1970-1983	5
16	Ulster Unionists and Loyalists [10]	1974ff	5
17	Alliance Party of Northern Ireland	1974ff	5
18	Social Democratic and Labour Party	1974ff	5
19	Ecology/Green Party [11]	1974ff	5
20	Social Democratic Party [12]	1983ff	2
21	The Alliance [13]	1983-1987	2

1 In Scotland formerly known as the Unionist Party, and until the February 1974 election in alliance with the Ulster Unionist Party.

2 For a century subject to splits and mergers; see notes 2, 8, and 9. Formally merged with the Social Democratic Party in 1988 to create the Social and Liberal Democrats, subsequently Liberal Democrats.

3 Known in Ireland as the Irish Parliamentary Party.

4 The Liberal Unionists, led by Joseph Chamberlain, broke away from the Liberal Party in June 1886, being opposed to the granting of Home Rule to Ireland. They then contested elections in alliance with the Conservatives; the two parties were amalgamated on 9 May 1912.

5 The ILP participated in the establishment of the Labour Representation Committee in 1900. Until 1932 it was affiliated to the Labour Party. A few ILP candidates have stood at elections since 1945, but have never won more than 4,000 votes nationwide.

6 Since 1918 the Labour Party vote includes that for Co-operative Party candidates. From 1950 to 1970 also includes votes for the Northern Ireland Labour Party.

7 In 1918 Sinn Féin; from 1918 to 1935 those classified as Irish Nationalist/Anti-Partitionist by Craig, 1981; since 1945 all classified as United Ireland in Rose and McAllister, 1982, Table 4.3, except for the Social Democratic and Labour Party, listed separately as party 18.

8 In 1918 the followers of Lloyd George who contested the election as supporters of the Coalition government with Conservatives. Reunited with the Liberal Party in November 1923, they again stood independently in 1931 in opposition to the Liberal Party's support of the National Government.

9 The Liberal National Organization broke away from the Liberal Party in 1931, and contested elections in alliance with the Conservatives.

10 Unionist and Loyalist parties banded together in the short-lived United Ulster Unionist Council (UUUC) their offshoots include Democratic Unionist Party led by Dr. Ian Paisley (see Rose and McAllister, 1982: 75-79, 89-92).

11 Founded under the name "People" in 1973. Renamed the Ecology Party in 1975 and the Green Party in 1985.

12 Formed by 13 Labour Party MPs who broke away from the Labour Party in 1981. Contested the 1983 and 1987 elections in alliance with the Liberal Party, and merged with the Liberals in 1988 to form the Social and Liberal Democrats. A minority of the SDP continued to follow Dr. David Owen as SDP leader until it ceased in June, 1990.

13 An electoral alliance of the Liberal and Social Democrat parties.

Table 24.2 DATES OF ELECTIONS : HOUSE OF COMMONS [1]

1	24 November-9 December 1885	15	14 November 1935
2	1 July-17 July 1886	16	5 July 1945 [2]
3	4-19 July 1892	17	23 February 1950
4	13-29 July 1895	18	25 October 1951
5	1-15 October 1900	19	26 May 1955
6	12-29 January 1906	20	8 October 1959
7	15-31 January 1910	21	15 October 1964
8	3-19 December 1910	22	31 March 1966
9	14 December 1918	23	18 June 1970
10	15 November 1922	24	28 February 1974
11	6 December 1923	25	10 October 1974
12	29 October 1924	26	3 May 1979
13	30 May 1929	27	9 June 1983
14	27 October 1931	28	11 June 1987

1 Until 1918 the day of polling for individual constituencies was spaced over several weeks. The dates of the first and last polls noted above exclude the University constituencies, where the poll remained open for five days; voting was either in person or by post. Until 1918 Orkney and Shetland voted a week after the rest of the United Kingdom.

2 The poll was delayed for one week in 22 constituencies and a fortnight in one constituency, because the date of the election fell during some local holiday weeks. To allow time for postal votes of servicemen to be collected, the count did not begin until 25 July 1945 and the results were announced the next day.

Source: Craig, 1989: 151-152.

Table 24.3a UNITED KINGDOM Total Votes 1885-1922

	1885	1886	1892	1895	1900	1906	1910 (Jan.)	1910 (Dec.)	1918[3]	1922
Electorate	5,708,030	5,708,030	6,160,541	6,330,519	6,730,935	7,264,608	7,694,741	7,709,981	21,392,220	20,874,456
Total Votes[1]	4,407,507	2,771,287	4,343,252	3,606,666	3,282,711	5,278,637	6,253,495	4,902,797	10,478,983	13,809,720
PARTY VOTES										
1 Conservative Party	2,020,927								4,144,192	5,502,298
}		1,520,886	2,159,150	1,894,772	1,767,958	2,422,071	3,104,407	2,420,169		
4 Liberal Unionists	-								-	-
2 Liberal Party	2,199,998	1,353,581	2,088,019	1,765,266	1,572,323	2,751,057	2,866,157	2,293,869	1,388,784	2,668,143
3 Irish Nationalists	310,608	97,905	311,509	152,959	91,055	35,031	126,647	131,720	228,902	-
5 Ind. Labour Party/ILP[2]	-	-	-	44,325	-	-	-	-	-	-
6 Labour Party	-	-	-	-	62,698	321,663	505,657	371,802	2,357,524	4,237,349
7 United Ireland	-	-	-	-	-	-	-	-	497,107	102,667
8 Lloyd George Liberals	-	-	-	-	-	-	-	-	1,396,590	1,471,317
9 National Democratic and Labour	-	-	-	-	-	-	-	-	181,331	-
10 Communist Party	-	-	-	-	-	-	-	-	-	33,637
Others	106,702	1,791	39,641	3,730	29,448	96,269	64,532	17,678	284,553	376,919

1 The total number of electors casting valid ballots. Because some electors were entitled to more than one vote in a constituency the total number of votes cast exceeds this figure.

2 From 1900 included with the Labour Party.

3 At this election the Conservatives and Lloyd George Liberals formed an electoral alliance together with most of the National Democratic and Labour candidates. At least half of the independent candidates also supported the coalition without being formally affiliated to it.

Source: Craig, 1989: 13-25

Table 24.3b UNITED KINGDOM Percentage of Votes 1885-1922

	1885	1886	1892	1895	1900	1906	1910 (Jan.)	1910 (Dec.)	1918	1922
Valid Votes	77.2	48.6	70.5	57.0	48.8	72.7	81.3	63.6	49.0	66.2
PARTY VOTES[1]										
1 Conservative Party	43.5								39.5	38.5
}		51.4	47.0	49.1	50.3	43.4	46.8	46.6		
4 Liberal Unionists	–								–	–
2 Liberal Party	47.4	45.0	45.1	45.7	45.0	44.4	43.5	44.2	13.3	18.9
3 Irish Nationalists	6.9	3.5	7.0	4.0	2.6	0.7	1.9	2.5	2.2	–
5 Ind. Labour Party/ILP	–	–	–	1.0	–	–	–	–	–	–
6 Labour Party	–	–	–	–	1.3	4.8	7.0	6.4	22.5	29.7
7 United Ireland	–	–	–	–	–	–	–	–	4.7	0.4
8 Lloyd George Liberals	–	–	–	–	–	–	–	–	13.3	9.9
9 National Democratic and Labour	–	–	–	–	–	–	–	–	1.7	–
10 Communist Party	–	–	–	–	–	–	–	–	–	0.2
Others	2.2	0.1	0.9	0.1	0.8	1.7	0.8	0.3	2.7	2.4

1 Percentages have been adjusted to allow for two-member seats; each vote in a two-member seat in which an elector had two votes has been counted as half a vote. (cf. Table 24.a)

Table 24.3c UNITED KINGDOM Number of Seats Won in the House of Commons 1885-1922[1]

	1885	1886	1892	1895	1900	1906	1910 (Jan.)	1910 (Dec.)	1918	1922
1 Conservative Party[2]	249 (10)	316	268	340	334	131	240	235	382 (41)	344 (42)
4 Liberal Unionists	–	77	45	71	68	25	32	36	–	–
2 Liberal Party	319 (14)	192 (40)	272 (13)	177 (11)	184 (22)	399 (27)	274 (1)	272	36	62
3 Irish Nationalists	86 (19)	85 (66)	81 (9)	82 (46)	82 (58)	83 (74)	82 (55)	84 (53)	7	–
5 Ind. Labour Party	–	–	–	–	–	–	–	–	–	–
6 Labour Party	–	–	–	–	2	29	40	42	61	142
7 United Ireland	–	–	–	–	–	–	–	–	73 (25)	3
8 Lloyd George Liberals	–	–	–	–	–	–	–	–	127	53 (4)
9 National Democratic and Labour	–	–	–	–	–	–	–	–	9	–
10 Communist Party	–	–	–	–	–	–	–	–	–	1
Others	16[3]	0	4	0	0	3	2	1	12[4]	10
Total Seats	670 (43)	670 (224)	670 (62)	670 (189)	670 (243)	670 (114)	670 (75)	670 (163)	707 (107)	615 (57)

1 Figures in parentheses report the number of MPs returned unopposed.
2 The number of Conservative and Liberal Unionist MPs returned unopposed were: 1886, 118; 1892, 40; 1895, 132; 1900, 163; June 1910, 19; and December 1910, 72.
3 Comprises eleven independent Liberals, three independent Liberal-Crofter and one independent Liberal-Labour.
4 Includes one independent and four Labour candidates elected as part of the Conservative-dominated Coalition.

Source: Craig, 1989: 13-25

Table 24.3d UNITED KINGDOM Percentage of Seats Won in the House of Commons 1885-1922

	1885	1886	1892	1895	1900	1906	1910 (Jan.)	1910 (Dec.)	1918	1922
1 Conservative Party	37.2	47.2	40.0	50.7	49.9	19.6	35.8	35.1	54.0	55.9
4 Liberal Unionists	–	11.5	6.7	10.6	10.1	3.7	4.8	5.4	–	–
2 Liberal Party	47.6	28.7	40.5	26.4	27.5	59.6	40.9	40.6	5.1	10.1
3 Irish Nationalists	12.8	12.7	12.1	12.2	12.2	12.2	12.2	12.5	1.0	–
5 Ind. Labour Party/ILP	–	–	–	–	–	–	–	–	–	–
6 Labour Party	–	–	–	–	0.3	4.3	6.2	6.3	8.6	23.1
7 United Ireland	–	–	–	–	–	–	–	–	10.3	0.5
8 Lloyd George Liberals	–	–	–	–	–	–	–	–	17.9	8.6
9 National Democratic and Labour	–	–	–	–	–	–	–	–	1.3	–
10 Communist Party	–	–	–	–	–	–	–	–	–	0.2
Others	2.4	0.0	0.5	0.0	0.0	0.4	0.1	0.1	1.7	1.6

Table 24.4a UNITED KINGDOM Total Votes 1923-1955

	1923	1924	1929	1931	1935	1945	1950	1951	1955
Electorate	21,283,085	21,730,988	28,854,748	29,952,361	31,374,449	33,240,391	34,412,255	34,919,331	34,852,179
Valid Votes[1]	13,960,590	15,906,127	21,755,397	21,716,039	21,016,676	24,117,191	28,771,124	28,596,594	26,759,729
PARTY VOTES									
1 Conservative Party	5,514,541	7,933,078	8,656,225	12,006,118	10,549,489	9,234,278	12,492,404	13,718,199	13,310,891
2 Liberal Party	4,301,481	3,035,257	5,308,738	1,372,595	1,443,093	2,252,430	2,621,487	730,546	722,402
5 Ind. Labour Party/ILP	-	-	-	317,354	139,577	46,769	-	-	-
6 Labour Party	4,439,780	5,489,087	8,370,417	6,324,737	8,325,491	11,967,746	13,266,176	13,948,883	12,405,254
7 United Ireland	97,993	46,457	24,177	123,053	158,327	148,078	141,288	125,961	168,360
8 Lloyd George Liberals	-	-	-	103,528	-	-	-	-	-
10 Communist Party	39,448	55,346	50,634	74,824	27,117	102,780	91,765	21,640	33,144
11 Scottish National Party	-	-	3,313	20,954	29,517	30,595	9,708	7,299	12,112
12 Plaid Cymru	-	-	609	2,050	2,534	16,017	17,580	10,920	45,119
13 National Labour	-	-	-	341,370	339,811	-	-	-	-
14 National Liberal Party	-	-	-	809,302	866,354	737,732	-	-	-
Others	154,452	81,054	234,262	159,804	115,744	558,770	130,716	33,146	62,447

[1] From 1923 to 1945 the number of electors casting valid ballots. Because some electors were entitled to more than one vote the total number of votes cast exceeds this figure.

Source: Craig, 1989: 26-38.

Table 24.4b UNITED KINGDOM Percentage of Votes 1923-1955

	1923	1924	1929	1931	1935	1945	1950	1951	1955
Total Votes	65.6	73.2	75.4	72.5	67.0	72.6	83.6	81.9	76.8
Valid Votes	65.6	73.2	75.4	72.5	67.0	72.6	83.6	81.9	76.8
PARTY VOTES									
1 Conservative Party	38.0	47.6	38.1	55.5	48.1	36.8	43.4	48.0	49.7
2 Liberal Party	29.7	18.2	23.5	6.5	6.7	9.0	9.1	2.6	2.7
5 Ind. Labour Party/ILP	-	-	-	1.5	0.7	0.2	-	-	-
6 Labour Party	30.7	33.3	37.1	29.2	38.0	48.0	46.1	48.8	46.4
7 United Ireland	0.4	0.2	0.1	0.3	0.8	0.4	0.4	0.4	0.6
8 Lloyd George Liberals	-	-	-	0.5	-	-	-	-	-
10 Communist Party	0.2	0.3	0.2	0.3	0.1	0.4	0.3	0.1	0.1
11 Scottish National Party	-	-	0.0	0.1	0.1	0.1	0.0	0.0	0.0
12 Plaid Cymru	-	-	0.0	0.0	0.0	0.1	0.1	0.0	0.2
13 National Labour	-	-	-	1.6	1.5	-	-	-	-
14 National Liberal Party	-	-	-	3.7	3.7	2.9	2.9	-	-
Others	1.0	0.4	1.0	0.7	0.6	2.2	2.2	0.1	0.2

Table 24.4c UNITED KINGDOM Number of Seats Won in the House of Commons 1923-1955[1]

	1923	1924	1929	1931	1935	1945	1950	1951	1955
1 Conservative Party	258 (35)	415 (16)	260 (4)	474 (49)	388 (23)	199 (1)	298	321	345
2 Liberal Party	158 (11)	44 (6)	59	32 (7)	21 (3)	12	9	6	6
5 Ind. Labour Party/ILP	–	–	–	5	4	3	–	–	–
6 Labour Party	191 (3)	151 (9)	287	47 (6)	154 (13)	393 (2)	315	295	277
7 United Ireland	3 (1)	1 (1)	3 (3)	2	2	2	2	3	2
8 Lloyd George Liberals	–	–	–	4	–	–	–	–	–
10 Communist Party	0	1	0	0	1	2	0	0	0
11 Scottish National Party	–	–	0	0	0	0	0	0	0
12 Plaid Cymru	–	–	0	0	0	0	0	0	0
13 National Labour	–	–	–	13	8	–	–	–	–
14 National Liberal Party	–	–	–	35	33	11	–	–	–
Others	5	3	6	3	4	18 (3)	1	0	0
Total Seats	615 (50)	615 (32)	615 (7)	615 (62)	615 (46)	640 (3)	625 (2)	625 (4)	630

1 Figures in parenthesis report the number of MPs returned unopposed.

Source: Craig, 1989: 26-38.

Table 24.4d UNITED KINGDOM Percentage of Seats Won in the House of Commons 1923-1955

	1923	1924	1929	1931	1935	1945	1950	1951	1955
1 Conservative Party	42.0	67.5	42.3	77.1	63.1	31.1	47.7	51.4	54.8
2 Liberal Party	25.7	7.2	9.6	5.2	3.4	1.9	1.4	1.0	1.0
5 Ind. Labour Party/ILP	-	-	-	0.8	0.7	0.5	-	-	-
6 Labour Party	31.1	24.6	46.7	7.6	25.0	61.4	50.4	47.2	44.0
7 United Ireland	0.5	0.2	0.5	0.3	0.3	0.3	0.3	0.5	0.3
8 Lloyd George Liberals	-	-	-	0.6	-	-	-	-	-
10 Communist Party	0.0	0.2	0.0	0.0	0.2	0.3	0.0	0.0	0.0
11 Scottish National Party	-	-	0.0	0.0	0.0	0.0	0.0	0.0	0.0
12 Plaid Cymru	-	-	0.0	0.0	0.0	0.0	0.0	0.0	0.0
13 National Labour	-	-	-	2.1	1.3	-	-	-	-
14 National Liberal Party	-	-	-	5.7	5.4	1.7	-	-	-
Others	0.8	0.5	1.0	0.6	0.7	2.8	0.2	0.0	0.0

Table 24.5a UNITED KINGDOM Total Votes 1959-1987

	1959	1964	1966	1970	1974 (Feb,)	1974 (Oct,)	1979	1983	1987
Electorate	35,397,304	35,894,054	35,957,245	39,342,013	39,753,863	40,072,970	41,095,490	42,192,999	43,180,573
Valid Votes	27,862,652	27,657,148	27,264,747	28,344,798	31,340,162	29,189,104	31,221,362	30,671,137	32,529,578
Invalid Votes	n.a	41,073	49,899	41,341	42,252	37,706	117,846	51,104	36,945
Total Votes	n.a	27,698,221	27,314,646	28,386,145	31,382,414	29,226,810	31,233,208	30,722,241	32,566,523
PARTY VOTES									
1 Conservative Party	13,750,875	12,002,642	11,418,455	13,145,123	11,872,180	10,462,565	13,697,923	13,012,316	13,760,583
3 Liberal Party[1]	1,640,760	3,099,283	2,327,457	2,117,035	6,059,519	5,346,704	4,313,804	(4,210,115)	(4,173,450)
21 Alliance	-	-	-	-	-	-	-	7,780,949	7,341,633
20 Social Democratic Party[1]	-	-	-	-	-	-	-	(3,570,834)	(3,168,183)
6 Labour Party	12,216,172	12,205,808	13,096,629	12,208,758	11,645,616	11,457,079	11,532,218	8,456,934	10,029,807
7 United Ireland	63,415	116,306	125,886	181,928	55,079	54,428	57,582	117,351	102,683
10 Communist Party	30,896	46,442	62,092	37,978	32,743	17,426	16,858	11,606	6,078
11 Scottish National Party	21,738	64,044	128,474	306,802	633,180	839,617	504,259	331,975	416,473
12 Plaid Cymru	77,571	69,507	6,107,199	175,016	171,374	166,321	132,544	125,309	123,599
15 National Front	-	-	-	11,449	76,865	113,843	191,719	27,065	-
16 Social Democratic and Labour Party	-	-	-	-	160,437	154,193	137,110	137,012	154,087
17 Ulster Unionists and Loyalists	-	-	-	-	366,703	415,450	402,398	436,696	400,430
18 Alliance Party of Northern Ireland	-	-	-	-	22,660	44,644	82,892	61,275	72,671
19 Ecology/Green Party	-	-	-	-	4,576	1,996	39,918	53,848	89,753
Others	61,225	53,116	44,683	160,717	239,230	143,838	112,137	118,801	31,781

1 Figures in parentheses indicate votes cast for the party's candidates standing for the Alliance.

Sources: Craig, 1989: 39-50; McAllister and Rose, 1984: 89-90.

Table 24.5b UNITED KINGDOM Percentage of Votes 1959-1987

	1959	1964	1966	1970	1974 (Feb.)	1974 (Oct.)	1979	1983	1987
Total Votes	n.a	77.2	76.0	72.2	78.9	72.9	76.3	72.8	75.4
Valid Votes	78.7	77.1	75.8	72.0	78.8	72.8	76.0	72.7	75.3
Invalid Votes	n.a	0.1	0.1	0.1	0.1	0.1	0.3	0.1	0.1
Share Invalid	n.a	0.1	0.2	0.1	0.1	0.1	0.4	0.2	0.1
PARTY VOTES									
1 Conservative Party	49.4	43.4	41.9	46.4	37.9	35.8	43.9	42.4	42.3
3 Liberal Party[1]	5.9	11.2	8.5	7.5	19.3	18.3	13.8	(13.7)	(12.8)
21 Alliance Parties	-	-	-	-	-	-	-	25.4	22.6
20 Social Democratic Party[1]	-	-	-	-	-	-	-	(11.6)	(9.7)
6 Labour Party	43.8	44.1	48.0	43.1	37.2	39.3	36.9	27.6	30.8
7 United Ireland	0.2	0.4	0.5	0.6	0.2	0.2	0.2	0.4	0.3
10 Communist Party	0.1	0.2	0.2	0.1	0.1	0.1	0.1	0.0	0.0
11 Scottish National Party	0.1	0.2	0.5	1.1	2.0	2.9	1.6	1.1	1.3
12 Plaid Cymru	0.3	0.3	22.4	0.6	0.5	0.6	0.4	0.4	0.4
15 National Front	-	-	-	0.0	0.2	0.4	0.6	0.1	-
16 Social Democratic and Labour Party	-	-	-	-	0.5	0.5	0.4	0.4	0.5
17 Ulster Unionists and Loyalists	-	-	-	-	1.5	1.5	1.3	1.4	1.2
18 Alliance Party of Northern Ireland	-	-	-	-	0.1	0.2	0.3	0.2	0.2
19 Ecology/Green Party	-	-	-	-	0.0	0.0	0.1	0.2	0.3
Others	0.2	0.2	0.2	0.6	0.5	0.3	0.4	0.4	0.1

1 Figures in parentheses indicate share of vote cast for the party's candidates standing for the Alliance.

Sources: Craig, 1989: 39-46; McAllister and Rose, 1984: 89-90; Craig, 1984: 96f and Craig 1989: 190f.

Table 24.5c UNITED KINGDOM Number of Seats Won in the House of Commons 1959-1987

	1959	1964	1966	1970	1974 (Feb.)	1974 (Oct.)	1979	1983	1987
1 Conservative Party	365	304	253	330	297	277	339	397	376
3 Liberal Party[1]	6	9	12	6	14	13	11	(17)	(17)
21 Alliance	–	–	–	–	–	–	–	23	22
20 Social Democratic Party[1]	–	–	–	–	–	–	–	(6)	(5)
6 Labour Party	258	317	364	288	301	319	269	209	229
7 United Ireland	0	0	1	3	0	1	1	1	1
10 Communist Party	0	0	0	0	0	0	0	0	0
11 Scottish National Party	0	0	0	1	7	11	2	2	3
12 Plaid Cymru	0	0	0	0	2	3	2	2	3
15 National Front	–	–	–	0	0	0	0	0	–
16 Social Democratic and Labour Party	–	–	–	–	1	1	1	1	3
17 Ulster Unionists and Loyalists	–	–	–	–	11	10	10	15	13
18 Alliance Party of Northern Ireland	–	–	–	–	0	0	0	0	0
19 Ecology/Green Party	–	–	–	–	0	0	0	0	0
Others	1	0	0	2	2	0	0	0	0
Total Seats	630	630	630	630	635	635	635	650	650

1 Figures in parentheses indicate the seats won by the party's candidates standing for the Alliance.

Sources: Craig, 1989: 39-46; McAllister and Rose, 1984: 89-90; Craig, 1984: 96f and Craig 1989: 190f.

Table 24.5d UNITED KINGDOM Percentage of Seats Won in the House of Commons 1959-1987

	1959	1964	1966	1970	1974 (Feb.)	1974 (Oct.)	1979	1983	1987
1 Conservative Party	57.9	48.3	40.2	52.4	46.8	43.6	53.4	61.1	57.8
3 Liberal Party[1]	1.0	1.4	1.9	1.0	2.2	2.0	1.7	(2.6)	(2.6)
21 Alliance	-	-	-	-	-	-	-	3.5	3.4
20 Social Democratic Party[1]	-	-	-	-	-	-	-	(0.9)	(0.8)
6 Labour Party	41.0	50.3	57.8	45.7	47.4	50.2	42.4	32.2	35.2
7 United Ireland	-	-	0.2	0.5	-	0.2	0.2	0.2	0.2
10 Communist Party	0.0	0.0	0.0	0.0	0.0	0.0	0.0	0.0	0.0
11 Scottish National Party	0.0	0.0	0.0	0.2	1.1	1.7	0.3	0.3	0.5
12 Plaid Cymru	0.0	0.0	0.0	0.0	0.3	0.5	0.3	0.3	0.5
15 National Front	-	-	-	0.0	0.0	0.0	0.0	0.0	-
16 Social Democratic and Labour Party	-	-	-	-	0.2	0.2	0.2	0.2	0.5
17 Ulster Unionists and Loyalists	-	-	-	-	1.7	1.6	1.6	2.3	2.0
18 Alliance Party of Northern Ireland	-	-	-	-	0.0	0.0	0.0	0.0	0.0
19 Ecology/Green Party	-	-	-	-	0.0	0.0	0.0	0.0	0.0
Others	0.2	0.0	0.0	0.3	0.3	0.0	0.0	0.0	0.0

1 Figures in parentheses indicate share of vote cast for the party's candidates standing for the Alliance.

Sources: Craig, 1989: 39-46; McAllister and Rose, 1984: 89-90; Craig, 1984: 96f and Craig 1989: 190f.

Chapter 25

UNITED STATES OF AMERICA

The American Constitution of 1787 created the office of President, who was to be elected by an electoral college in which each state is entitled to as many electors as it has members of Congress. If no candidate receives a majority the election falls to the House of Representatives, where each state delegation has a single vote; this procedure was used in 1801 and 1825. The Constitution allows each state to decide how its electors are chosen. Initially, in a majority of the states electors were chosen by the state legislature. In a few states there was a popular election, with electors chosen by plurality, either in districts or by the state as a whole. In the latter case, the list of electors that won a plurality obtained all the state's electoral college votes, a procedure known as the unit rule. Although the Constitution did not anticipate the formation of political parties, voting in the electoral college soon occurred along partisan lines.

By 1828 all but two states had decided to choose their electors by popular vote; from that date, it is possible to speak of the election of the President as a nationwide vote. Delaware began direct elections of its electors in 1832; the South Carolina legislature continued to choose the state's electors until 1860. Since 1828 a state's electoral college votes have, with very rare exceptions, been cast as a block for the candidate with a plurality of votes in the state (Moore, 1985: 256).

Prior to the formation of the United States each colony had had its own charter and form of government, incorporating a variety of eighteenth century English practices of representation (Pole, 1966). The federal nature of the Constitution allowed each state to set more or less generous qualifications for voting, and laws have varied enormously from state to state (Harris, 1934). From the 1840s until 1910 many states allowed aliens to vote. The 1928 presidential election was the first in which citizenship was a voting requirement in all states.

The Constitution also provided for the election of a bicameral Congress. All the 435 members of the House of Representatives are elected every two years from all 50 states, and popular election of Representatives occurred before the popular election of members of the presidential electoral college. In many Congressional districts seats have not been contested, because only one candidate has stood. Until 1960 all state laws provided that even in such cases a poll is held. In the South from the 1890s to the 1960s the dominance of the Democratic Party meant that party primary elections were effectively general elections.

Members of the United States Senate were chosen by the legislature of each state until 1913, when the Seventeenth Amendment to the Constitution required direct popular election. The 100 members of the Senate are elected on a staggered basis for six-year terms; one-third is up for election every two years. Thus, the total votes received by each party in a Senate election depends upon the particular contests being held (Austin, 1986: 181-239).

By 1860 income and property qualifications had mostly been abolished and white manhood suffrage became the rule (Williamson, 1960: 278; Harris, 1934). Women were first given the vote in Wyoming in 1869; by 1917 women had the vote in 12 states. In 1920 a constitutional amendment forbade the denial of the vote on the grounds of sex. The minimum voting age was 21 until 1945, when Kentucky enfranchised 18-year-olds. Georgia followed suit in 1955 and Alaska and Hawaii had already done so before being admitted to the union in 1958 and 1959 respectively. In 1971 the Twenty-sixth Amendment to the Constitution reduced the national voting age to 18. The District of Columbia was given the right to vote in Presidential elections in 1961; but its representative in Congress has no vote.

For most of American history blacks were excluded from the franchise in many states by law or practice. On the eve of the Civil War blacks were legally eligible to vote only in six New England states (Porter, 1918, 89-90). After the end of the Civil War, the 1867 Reconstruction Act and the Fifteenth Amendment to the Constitution in 1870 formally enfranchised blacks on the same basis as whites. However, states had the right to set requirements for voting registration, and especially in the eleven states of the old Confederacy a wide variety of legal devices, such as literacy tests and poll taxes, were used to exclude blacks from the electorate. These devices often effectively disfranchised many whites as well (Key, 1949; Kousser, 1979).

Civil rights groups challenged exclusion from the franchise in the federal courts before and after the Second World War, and the courts normally found in their favour. Civil rights demonstrations demanding the right to vote in the early 1960s publicized the non-enforcement of the Fifteenth Amendment. The effective veto that Southern Democratic congressmen had used to prevent federal legislation on franchise laws was quickly eroded. Federal Civil Rights Acts were passed in 1957, 1960, 1964 and 1965 thus removing restrictions preventing blacks (and many poorer or less educated whites) from voting in the South (US Commission on Civil Rights, 1975; Ball *et al*, 1982; Thernstrom, 1988). The laws also authorized enforcement procedures to ensure compliance. Poll tax requirements for voting were prohibited by the Twenty-fourth Amendment to the Constitution, ratified in 1964.

Unlike almost every other western country, there is no nationwide system of permanent voter registration. In most states persons legally qualified to vote must register individually prior to election day to be entitled to vote (Wolfinger and Rosenstone, 1980; Piven and Cloward, 1988). The electorate figures reported in Tables 25.3a - 25.7a and used as the basis for calculating turnout are estimates of the potential electorate and allow for state-level differences in age, sex, racial and citizenship requirements for the franchise

The exclusion of blacks from the franchise in the South for more than a century creates problems in defining the electorate for purposes of measuring turnout. Before 1868 blacks are only included in the electorate of those states where the franchise allowed freedmen (that is, non-slave blacks) to vote. From 1870 blacks are counted in the electorate of all the states, including those where registration and other state laws effectively prevented blacks from voting until the 1960s.

Voting practices have varied considerably from state to state. In 1845 Congress voted to establish a common day for voting for presidential electors, the Tuesday after the first Monday in November. The traditional English system of oral voting was abandoned by most states by 1800, but because of the use of easily identified ballot papers provided by the contestants and public voting the vote was not effectively secret. In 1888 Massachusetts introduced secret voting and an official ballot paper, and by 1896, 90 per cent of the states had followed suit.

The decentralized character of the American electoral process makes the task of calculating national vote and seat totals peculiarly difficult, especially for House of Representatives elections. Election returns at district and county levels have been compiled for all House elections from 1824 onwards and are available in machine readable form from the Inter-University Consortium for Political and Social Research (ICPSR) at the University of Michigan. The widespread practice in the late nineteenth century of fusion tickets, whereby a candidate was sponsored by more than one party and the use of different party labels by candidates representing the same party in different districts inhibits the compilation of national totals from this otherwise comprehensive source. *Congressional Quarterly's Guide to U.S. Elections* (second edition, 1985) reports district level results for all these elections based upon the ICPSR data. But the exclusion from this source of all candidates winning less than five percent of the votes in any particular district means that it cannot be used to calculate national totals. The *American Votes* series edited by Richard Scammon, provides a complete record of House votes, but this series only goes back to the 1946 House election. The Congressional votes and seats reported here were compiled by Professor W. Dean Burnham, based in part upon the ICPSR data but supplemented and modified by information from other sources.

Until Congress set a standard date effective with the 1880 election the dates of House elections varied from state to state. Most states voted in even years, not always in November, but in some states the election was in the following odd year. Odd-year elections were mostly abandoned after the Civil War but a handful of states, including California continued the practice until 1879. This was possible because, until the adoption of the Twentieth ("lame-duck") Amendment in 1933, the first regular session of Congress began in December in the odd-numbered year. Even after 1870 elections were not all held at the same time as presidential elections, because of the admission of new states to the Union after the November presidential poll and the convening of the Congress 13 months later. Votes cast and seats won in all these elections have been merged in order to provide a single nationwide vote. Unless otherwise noted the distribution of seats reported here details the immediate results of the poll. In some cases the political composition of the House by the time it convened differed because of deaths of elected Congressmen in the interim and subsequent by-election changes and because partisan majorities in the House (especially Republicans in the second half of the nineteenth century) sometimes (especially Republicans in the second half of the nineteenth century) sometimes unseated elected representatives of the opposing party.

Figures from 1960 have been modified to include estimates of votes cast in the four states which no longer held polls in districts where there was only a single candidate in the November election. In three cases (Arkansas, Florida and Oklahoma) a notional vote for the single candidate has been included. Since 1976 Louisiana has held an all-party primary in September, followed by a November poll only if one of the candidates failed to win an absolute majority in the primary. Generally the primary has been the decisive round. For instance in the 1988 election there was a November poll in only one of the eight Louisiana districts. Where it was the decisive ballot, the primary vote has been included in the general election total.

Sources:

Erik W. Austin, *Political Facts of the United States since 1789* (New York: Columbia University Press, 1986)

H. Ball, D. Krane and T.P. Lauth, *Compromised Compliance: Implementation of the 1965 Voting Rights Act* (Westport: Greenwood Press, 1982)

W.D. Burnham, *Presidential Ballots, 1836-1892* (Baltimore: Johns Hopkins University Press, 1955)

C. Catt and N. Shuler, *Woman Suffrage and Politics* (Seattle: University of Washington Press, 1923)

J.A. Harris, *Election Administration in the United States* (Washington DC: Brookings Institution, 1934)

V.O. Key, Jr., *Southern Politics in State and Nation* (New York: Knopf, 1949)

J.M. Kousser, *The Shaping of Southern Politics: Suffrage Restriction and the Establishment of the One-Party South, 1880-1910* (New Haven: Yale University Press, 1979)

S. Lawson, *Black Ballots: Voting Rights in the South, 1944-1969* (New York: Columbia University Press, 1976)

K.C. Martis, *The Historical Atlas of Political Parties in the United States Congress, 1789-1989* (New York: Macmillan, 1989).

J.L. Moore (ed.), *Congressional Quarterly's Guide to U.S. Elections* (Congressional Quarterly Press, 2nd edition, 1985)

N.R. Pierce and L.D. Longley, *The People's President, The Electoral College in American History and the Direct Vote Alternative* (New Haven: Yale University Press, 1981)

F.F. Piven and R.A. Cloward, *Why Americans Don't Vote* (New York: Pantheon, 1988)

J.R. Pole, *Political Representation in England and the Origins of the American Republic* (London: Macmillan, 1966)

K.H. Porter, *A History of Suffrage in the United States* (Chicago: University of Chicago Press, 1918)

R.M. Scammon and A.V. McGillivray, *America Votes 18: A Handbook of Contemporary American Election Statistics* (Washington, D.C. : Elections Research Center/Congressional Quarterly 1989)

A. Thernstrom, *Whose Votes Count? Affirmative Action and Minority Voting Rights* (Cambridge: Harvard University Press, 1988)

U.S. Bureau of the Census, *Historical Statistics of the United States, Colonial Times to 1970, Bicentennial Edition,* Part 2 (Washington D.C.: Government Printing Office, 1975)

U.S. Commission on Civil Rights. *The Voting Rights Act: Ten Years After* (Washington D.C.: Government Printing Office, 1975)

C. Williamson, *American Suffrage from Property to Democracy, 1760-1860* (Princeton: Princeton University Press, 1960)

R. Wolfinger and S. Rosenstone, *Who Votes?* (New Haven: Yale University Press, 1980)

Table 25.1 POLITICAL PARTIES IN THE UNITED STATES SINCE 1828

	Party Names	Elections Contested [1] Years	Number
1	Democratic Party	1828ff	41
2	National Republican Party [2]	1828-1832	2
3	Anti-Masonic Party [3]	1832	1
4	Whig Party [4]	1836-1856	6
5	Liberty Party [5]	1840-1844	2
6	Free Soil Party [6]	1848-1852	2
7	American Party (Know Nothings) [7]	1856	1
8	Republican Party [8]	1856ff	34
9	Constitutional Union Party [9]	1860	1
10	Southern Democrat (Breckinridge) [10]	1860	1
11	Greenback-Labor Party [11]	1876-1884	7
12	Prohibition Party [12]	1872-1976	30
13	Union Labor Party	1888	1
14	People's Party (Populists) [13]	1892-1908	8
15	Socialist Labor Party [14]	1892-1972	22
16	National Democratic Party [15]	1896	1
17	Socialist Party [16]	1900-1920; 1928-1956;	23
18	Progressive Party (T. Roosevelt) [17]	1912-1914	1
19	Farmer-Labor Party [18]	1920	1
20	Progressive Party (La Follette) [19]	1924	1
21	Communist Party [20]	1924-1940; 1968-1984	11
22	Wisconsin Progressive Party [21]	1934-1942	0
23	Union Party	1936	1
24	Progressive Party (H. Wallace) [22]	1948-1952	2
25	State's Rights Party [23]	1948	1
26	American Independent Party/American Party [24]	1968ff	6
27	Libertarian Party	1972ff	5
28	Independent (J. Anderson) [25]	1980	1

1 The number of elections contested refers to Presidential elections. The notes attached to this table largely derive from the party profiles included in Moore (1985) and Martis (1989).

2 The National Republican Party disintegrated after the 1832 election. Its members and supporters formed the core of the Whig Party.

3 A radical anti-slavery, anti-urban and pro-temperance party in New England and the Mid-Atlantic states. Backed William Henry Harrison, the Whig Party candidate in the 1836 presidential election and thereafter united with the Whig Party.

4 Successor to the National Republican Party as the main opponent of the Democratic Party. In the 1856 presidential election the party did not put up its own candidate, but supported the Know-Nothing candidate, Millard Fillmore, a former Whig President.

[5] Founded in 1839 as the first anti-slavery party. Merged with the Free Soil Party in 1848.

[6] Founded by anti-slavery elements from both the Whig and Democratic parties to campaign against the extension of slavery in the western territories. The party disintegrated after the 1852 election and its constituency was taken over by the Republican Party.

[7] Nativist, anti-immigrant and anti-Catholic party. The party broke up over the slavery question, with the pro-slavery wing supporting Millard Fillmoore in the 1856 presidential election and the northern anti-slavery wing of the party backing the candidate of the newly formed Republican Party with which it merged after the election.

[8] Founded in 1854 as an anti-slavery party supported by former Whig, Know Nothing and Free Soil activists and voters and by some Democrats in the northern United States.

[9] An attempt to bridge differences between northern and southern states over slavery.

[10] Breakaway from the Democratic Party based largely in what became the Confederate States, but also with some support in the western states.

[11] Radical party which campaigned against the return to the gold standard, favouring the paper greenbacks first issued during the Civil War.

[12] Founded in 1869. Contested the 1980 election as the National Statesman Party.

[13] Organised in 1891 by former activists in the Greenback Labor Party and southern and western farmers' cooperative associations. The 1880 Greenback Presidential candidate Jim Weaver, was its first presidential candidate in 1892. The Populists endorsed the Democratic Party candidate, William Jennings Bryan, for the Presidency in 1896, but ran their own vice-presidential candidate.

[14] Formed in 1874 as the Social Democratic Workingmens' Party. Renamed the Socialist Labor Party in 1877. Cooperated with Greenback and other labor-oriented candidates in the 1880s and only ran its own presidential candidate from 1892.

[15] Conservative, pro-gold standard faction of the Democratic Party, opposed to the party's 1896 presidential candidate, William Jennings Bryan.

[16] In the 1900 presidential election votes cast for Eugene Debs, the Social Democratic Party candidate who was also backed by a faction of the Socialist Labor Party. The two groups merged to form the Socialist Party in 1901. It ran presidential candidates in every presidential election until 1956, except 1924 when it backed Robert F. La Follette's Progressive candidacy.

[17] Backed the former President Theodore Roosevelt in opposition to the official Republican party candidate, the incumbent President William Howard Taft. Often known as the Bull Moose Party.

[18] Mostly Middle West groups that backed the presidential candidacy of Parley P. Christensen in 1920, and formed a key element in Robert La Follette's 1924 candidacy. From 1928 onwards the Farmer-Labor Party in Minnesota, which campaigned only in congressional and state-level races and merged with the state Democratic Party in 1944 to form the Democratic Farmer Labor Party, the Minnesota branch of the Democratic party.

[19] Alliance backing the presidential candidacy of the progressive Republican governor of Wisconsin Robert La Follette. Included former Bull Moose activists, farmers' cooperative organizations and the Socialist Party.

[20] Founded in 1921 as the Workers' Party.

[21] A party limited to Wisconsin and founded by the sons of Governor Robert La Follette in 1934. The party was disbanded in 1946 with most of its members returning to the Republican Party. The party contested five Congressional elections, but never put up a Presidential candidate.

[22] A left-wing breakaway from the Democratic Party headed by Henry Wallace, a former Vice President and cabinet secretary.

[23] A southern splinter opposed to the inclusion of a civil rights commitment in the Democratic Party 1948 election platform. Strom Thurmond was its Presidential candidate. In subsequent elections a number of independent or state's rights tickets ran in several southern states; they are identified in the footnotes to Table 25.7a and 25.7c.

[24] Founded to support the Presidential candidacy of George Wallace, the Democratic governor of Alabama. After the 1968 election Wallace returned to the Democrats; the party continued to contest presidential elections. In many states it ran under the American Party label in the 1972 election and it officially changed its name to the American Party after the poll. A breakaway group retained the original party label.

[25] Candidacy of John Anderson, a liberal Republican opposed to Ronald Reagan.

Table 25.2 DATES OF PRESIDENTIAL ELECTIONS [1]

1.	7 November 1848	19.	2 November 1920
2.	2 November 1852	20.	4 November 1924
3.	4 November 1856	21.	6 November 1928
4.	6 November 1860	22.	8 November 1932
5.	8 November 1864	23.	3 November 1936
6.	3 November 1868	24.	5 November 1940
7.	5 November 1872	25.	7 November 1944
8.	7 November 1876	26.	2 November 1948
9.	2 November 1880	27.	4 November 1952
10.	4 November 1884	28.	6 November 1956
11.	6 November 1888	29.	8 November 1960
12.	8 November 1892	30.	3 November 1964
13.	3 November 1896	31.	5 November 1968
14.	6 November 1900	32.	7 November 1972
15.	8 November 1904	33.	2 November 1976
16.	3 November 1908	34.	4 November 1980
17.	5 November 1912	35.	6 November 1984
18.	7 November 1916	36.	8 November 1988

1 The dates refer to the election of presidential electors. Before 1848 presidential elections were held over a period, generally from early October to mid-November. Since 1848 the election has been held on the Tuesday following the first Monday in November. Until 1870 elections to the House were staggered over a thirteen month period. Since then they have been held on the same day as presidential elections.

Table 25.3a UNITED STATES OF AMERICA Presidency: Total Votes 1828-1860

	1828	1832	1836	1840	1844	1848	1852	1856	1860
Electorate	2,003,000	2,286,000	2,607,000	3,004,000	3,423,000	3,957,000	4,548,000	5,109,000	5,725,000
Valid Votes	1,148,018	1,293,973	1,503,534	2,411,808	2,703,659	2,879,184	3,161,830	4,054,647	4,685,561
PARTY VOTES									
1 Democratic Party	642,553	701,780	764,176	1,128,854	1,339,494	1,223,460	1,607,510	1,836,072	1,380,202
2 National Republican Party	500,897	484,205	-	-	-	-	-	-	-
3 Anti-Masonic Party	-	100,715	-	-	-	-	-	-	-
4 Whig Party	-	-	738,124[1]	1,275,390	1,300,004	1,361,393	1,386,942	-	-
5 Liberty Party	-	-	-	6,797	62,103	-	-	-	-
6 Free Soil Party	-	-	-	-	-	291,501	155,210	-	-
7 American Party (Know Nothings)	-	-	-	-	-	-	-	873,053[2]	-
8 Republican Party	-	-	-	-	-	-	-	1,342,345	1,865,908
9 Constitutional Union Party	-	-	-	-	-	-	-	-	590,901
10 Southern Democrats (Breckinridge)	-	-	-	-	-	-	-	-	848,019
Others	4,568	7,273	1,234	767	2,058	2,830	12,168	3,177	531

1 There were three Whig candidates, General William H. Harrison, 550,816 votes, Hugh L. White, 146,107 votes and Daniel Webster, 41,201 votes.
2 The American Party candidate, Millard Filmore, was also endorsed by the Whig Party.

Source: *Congressional Quarterly's Guide to U.S. Elections*, 1985: 329-335-367.

Table 25.3b UNITED STATES OF AMERICA Presidency: Percentage of Votes 1828-1860

	1828	1832	1836	1840	1844	1848	1852	1856	1860
Valid Votes	57.3	56.6	57.7	80.3	79.0	71.8	69.5	79.4	81.8
PARTY VOTES									
1 Democratic Party	56.0	54.2	50.8	46.8	49.5	42.5	50.8	45.3	29.5
2 National Republican Party	43.6	37.4	–	–	–	–	–	–	–
3 Anti-Masonic Party	–	7.8	–	–	–	–	–	–	–
4 Whig Party	–	–	49.1	52.9	48.1	47.3	43.9	–	–
5 Liberty Party	–	–	–	0.3	2.3	–	–	–	–
6 Free Soil Party	–	–	–	–	–	10.1	4.9	–	–
7 American Party (Know Nothings)	–	–	–	–	–	–	–	21.5	–
8 Republican Party	–	–	–	–	–	–	–	33.1	39.8
9 Constitutional Union Party	–	–	–	–	–	–	–	–	12.6
10 Southern Democrats (Breckinridge)	–	–	–	–	–	–	–	–	18.1
Others	0.4	0.6	0.1	0.0	0.1	0.1	0.4	0.1	0.0

Table 25.3c UNITED STATES OF AMERICA Number of Seats Won in the Electoral College 1828-1860

	1828	1832	1836	1840	1844	1848	1852	1856	1860
1 Democratic Party	178	219	170	60	170	127	254	174	12
2 National Republican Party	83	49	–	–	–	–	–	–	–
3 Anti-Masonic Party	–	7	–	–	–	–	–	–	–
4 Whig Party	–	–	113[3]	234	105	163	42	–	–
5 Liberty Party	–	–	–	0	0	–	–	–	–
6 Free Soil Party	–	–	–	–	–	0	0	–	–
7 American Party (Know Nothings)	–	–	–	–	–	–	–	8	–
8 Republican Party	–	–	–	–	–	–	–	114	180
9 Constitutional Union Party	0	–	–	–	–	–	–	–	39
10 Southern Democrats (Breckinridge)	–	–	–	–	–	–	–	–	72
Others	0	11[1]	11[4]	0	0	0	0	0	0
Total Seats	261	286	294	294	275	290	296	296	303

1 Votes cast by the South Carolina electors for William Wirt.
2 Excludes two of the Maryland electors who did not vote.
3 Comprises 73 votes for General Harrison, 26 votes for Hugh White and 14 votes for Daniel Webster.
4 Votes cast by South Carolina delegates for Senator Willie Mangum.

Source: *Congressional Quarterly's Guide to U.S. Elections*, 1985: 329-335, 367.

Table 25.3d UNITED STATES OF AMERICA Percentage of Seats Won in the Electoral College 1828-1860

	1828	1832	1836	1840	1844	1848	1852	1856	1860
1 Democratic Party	68.2	76.6	57.8	20.4	61.8	43.8	85.8	58.8	4.0
2 National Republican Party	31.8	17.1	–	–	–	–	–	–	–
3 Anti-Masonic Party	–	2.4	–	–	–	–	–	–	–
4 Whig Party	–	–	38.4	79.6	38.2	56.2	14.2	–	–
5 Liberty Party	–	–	–	0.0	0.0	–	–	–	–
6 Free Soil Party	–	–	–	–	–	0.0	0.0	–	–
7 American Party (Know Nothings)	–	–	–	–	–	–	–	2.7	–
8 Republican Party	–	–	–	–	–	–	–	38.5	59.4
9 Constitutional Union Party	0.0	–	–	–	–	–	–	–	12.9
10 Southern Democrats (Breckinridge)	–	–	–	–	–	–	–	–	23.8
Others	0.0	3.8	3.7	0.0	0.0	0.0	0.0	0.0	0.0

Table 25.4a UNITED STATES OF AMERICA Presidency: Total Votes 1864-1896

	1864[1]	1868[2]	1872	1876[4]	1880	1884	1888	1892	1896
Electorate	5,284,000	7,062,000	8,929,999	10,096,000	11,371,000	12,715,000	14,078,000	15,844,000	17,486,000
Valid Votes	4,031,887	5,722,440	6,467,679	8,413,101	9,210,420	10,049,754	11,383,320	12,056,097	13,935,738
PARTY VOTES									
1 Democratic Party	1,812,807	2,708,744	2,834,761[3]	4,288,546	4,444,260	4,874,621	5,534,488	5,551,883	6,511,495[5]
8 Republican Party	2,218,388	3,013,650	3,598,235	4,034,311	4,446,158	4,448,936	5,443,892	5,179,244	7,108,480
11 Greenback-Labor Party	-	-	3,371	75,973	305,997	175,096	249,813	270,770	125,072
12 Prohibition Party	-	-	-	6,743	9,674	147,482	-	-	-
13 Union Labor	-	-	-	-	-	-	146,602	-	-
14 Populists	-	-	-	-	-	-	-	1,024,280	-
15 Socialist Labor Party	-	-	-	-	-	-	-	21,163	36,356
16 National Democratic Party	-	-	-	-	-	-	-	-	133,435
Others	692	46	31,312	7,528	4,331	3,709	8,525	8,757	20,900

1 Eleven Confederate states did not participate because of the Civil War.
2 Mississippi, Texas and Virginia did not participate. In Florida the state legislature chose the electors.
3 Votes cast for Horace Greeley, the candidate of the Liberal Republican Party, a Republican faction opposed to President Grant, whose candidacy was also endorsed by the Democratic Party.
4 In Colorado the state legislature chose the electors.
5 Votes case for William Jennings Bryan, the Populist presidential candidate in 1892 as a joint Populist/Democratic Party candidate.

Source: *Congressional Quarterly's Guide to U.S. Elections*, 1985: 336-344, 367-368.

Table 25.4b UNITED STATES OF AMERICA Presidency: Percentage of Votes 1864-1896

	1864	1868	1872	1876	1880	1884	1888	1892	1896
Valid Votes	76.8	81.0	72.4	83.3	81.0	79.0	80.9	76.1	79.7
PARTY VOTES									
1 Democratic Party	45.0	47.3	43.8	51.0	48.3	48.5	48.6	46.1	46.7
8 Republican Party	55.0	52.7	55.6	48.0	48.3	48.3	47.8	43.0	51.0
11 Greenback-Labor Party	-	-	0.1	0.9	3.3	1.7	2.2	2.2	0.9
12 Prohibition Party	-	-	-	0.1	0.1	1.5	-	-	-
13 Union Labor	-	-	-	-	-	-	1.3	-	-
14 Populists	-	-	-	-	-	-	-	8.5	-
15 Socialist Labor Party	-	-	-	-	-	-	-	0.2	0.3
16 National Democratic Party	-	-	-	-	-	-	-	-	1.0
Others	0.0	0.0	0.5	0.1	0.0	0.0	0.1	0.1	0.1

Table 25.4c UNITED STATES OF AMERICA Number of Seats Won in the Electoral College 1864-1896

	1864[1]	1868[2]	1872[3]	1876	1880	1884	1888	1892	1896
1 Democratic Party	21	80	66	184	155	219	168	277	176
8 Republican Party	212	214	286	185	214	182	233	145	271
11 Greenback-Labor Party	–	–	–	0	0	0	–	–	–
12 Prohibition Party	–	0	0	0	0	0	0	0	0
13 Union Labor	–	–	–	–	–	–	0	0	–
14 Populists	–	–	–	–	–	–	–	22	–
15 Socialist Labor Party	–	–	–	–	–	–	–	0	0
16 National Democratic Party	–	–	–	–	–	–	–	–	0
Others	0	0	0	0	0	0	0	0	0
Total Seats	233[1]	294[2]	352[3]	369	369	401	401	444	447

1 Excluding the 11 Confederate states and one Nevada elector who did not vote.

2 Excludes Mississippi, Texas and Virginia who had not been readmitted to the Union.

3 Horace Greeley, the Democratic candidate, died before the Presidential electors met. The Democratic electors split their votes between four other politicians; three Georgia electors voted for Greeley. Congress refused to accept the 17 votes cast by Arkansas and Louisiana electors and these votes are not included in the figures reported here.

Source: *Congressional Quarterly's Guide to U.S. Elections*, 1985: 336-344, 367-368.

Table 25.4d UNITED STATES OF AMERICA Percentage of Seats Won in the Electoral College 1864-1896

	1864	1868	1872	1876	1880	1884	1888	1892	1896
1 Democratic Party	9.0	27.2	18.8	49.9	42.0	54.6	41.9	62.4	39.4
8 Republican Party	91.0	72.8	81.3	50.1	58.0	45.4	58.1	32.7	60.6
11 Greenback-Labor Party	-	-	-	0.0	0.0	0.0	-	-	-
12 Prohibition Party	-	0.0	0.0	0.0	0.0	0.0	0.0	0.0	0.0
13 Union Labor	-	-	-	-	-	-	0.0	0.0	-
14 Populists	-	-	-	-	-	-	-	5.0	-
15 Socialist Labor Party	-	-	-	-	-	-	-	0.0	0.0
16 National Democratic Party	-	-	-	-	-	-	-	-	0.0
Others	0.0	0.0	0.0	0.0	0.0	0.0	0.0	0.0	0.0

Table 25.5a UNITED STATES OF AMERICA Presidency: Total Votes 1900-1924

	1900	1904	1908	1912	1916	1920	1924
Electorate	18,937,000	20,593,000	22,624,000	25,503,000	30,008,000	54,313,000	59,503,000
Valid Votes	13,970,470	13,518,964	14,882,734	15,040,963	18,535,022	26,753,786	29,075,959
PARTY VOTES							
1 Democratic Party	6,358,345	5,082,898	6,406,801	6,293,152	9,126,300	9,140,884	8,386,169
8 Republican Party	7,218,039	7,626,593	7,676,258	3,486,333	8,546,789	16,133,314	15,717,553
12 Prohibition Party	209,004	258,596	252,821	207,972	221,030	188,391	54,833
14 Populists	50,340	114,051	28,376	-	-	-	-
15 Socialist Labor Party	40,900	33,156	14,018	29,374	15,284	30,418	28,368
17 Socialist Party	86,935	402,489	420,380	900,369	589,924	913,664	-
18 Progressive (T. Roosevelt)	-	-	-	4,119,207	-	-	-
19 Farmer-Labor Party	-	-	-	-	-	264,540	-
20 Progressive (R. La Follette)	-	-	-	-	-	-	4,814,050
21 Communist Party	-	-	-	-	-	-	38,080
Others	6,907	1,181	84,080	4,556	35,695	82,575	36,906

Source: *Congressional Quarterly's Guide to U.S. Elections*, 1985: 345-351, 369-370

Table 25.5b UNITED STATES OF AMERICA Presidency: Percentage of Votes 1900-1924

	1900	1904	1908	1912	1916	1920	1924
Valid Votes	73.8	65.6	65.8	59.0	61.8	49.3	48.9
PARTY VOTES							
1 Democratic Party	45.5	37.6	43.0	41.8	49.2	34.2	28.8
8 Republican Party	51.7	56.4	51.6	23.2	46.1	60.3	54.1
12 Prohibition Party	1.5	1.9	1.7	1.4	1.2	0.7	0.2
14 Populists	0.4	0.8	0.2	-	-	-	-
15 Socialist Labor Party	0.3	0.2	0.1	0.2	0.1	0.1	0.1
17 Socialist Party	0.6	3.0	2.8	6.0	3.2	3.4	-
18 Progressive (T. Roosevelt)	-	-	-	27.4	-	-	-
19 Farmer-Labor Party	-	-	-	-	-	1.0	-
20 Progressive (R. La Follette)	-	-	-	-	-	-	16.6
21 Communist Party	-	-	-	-	-	-	0.1
Others	0.0	0.0	0.6	0.0	0.2	0.3	0.1

Table 25.5c UNITED STATES OF AMERICA Number of Seats Won in the Electoral College 1900-1924

	1900	1904	1908	1912	1916	1920	1924
1 Democratic Party	155	140	162	435	277	127	136
8 Republican Party	292	336	321	8	254	404	382
12 Prohibition Party	0	–	0	0	0	0	0
14 Populists	0	0	0	–	–	–	–
15 Socialist Labor Party	0	0	0	0	0	0	0
17 Socialist Party	0	–	0	0	0	0	–
18 Progressive (T. Roosevelt)	–	–	–	88	–	–	–
19 Farmer-Labor Party	–	–	–	–	–	0	–
20 Progressive (R. La Follette)	–	–	–	–	–	–	13
21 Communist Party	–	–	–	–	–	–	0
Others	0	0	0	0	0	0	0
Total Seats	447	476	483	531	531	531	531

Source: *Congressional Quarterly's Guide to U.S. Elections*, 1985: 345-351, 369-370

Table 25.5d UNITED STATES OF AMERICA Percentage of Seats Won in the Electoral College 1900-1924

	1900	1904	1908	1912	1916	1920	1924
1 Democratic Party	34.7	29.4	33.5	81.9	52.2	23.9	25.6
8 Republican Party	65.3	70.6	66.5	1.5	47.8	76.1	71.9
12 Prohibition Party	0.0	-	0.0	0.0	0.0	0.0	0.0
14 Populists	0.0	0.0	0.0	-	-	-	-
15 Socialist Labor Party	0.0	0.0	0.0	0.0	0.0	0.0	0.0
17 Socialist Party	0.0	-	0.0	0.0	0.0	0.0	-
18 Progressive (T. Roosevelt)	-	-	-	16.6	-	-	-
19 Farmer-Labor Party	-	-	-	-	-	0.0	-
20 Progressive (R. La Follette)	-	-	-	-	-	-	2.4
21 Communist Party	-	-	-	-	-	-	0.0
Others	0.0	0.0	0.0	0.0	0.0	0.0	0.0

Table 25.6a UNITED STATES OF AMERICA Presidency: Total Votes 1928-1952

	1928	1932	1936	1940	1944	1948	1952
Electorate	64,694,000	69,804,000	74,834,000	79,863,000	85,839,000	91,408,000	96,466,000
Valid Votes	36,790,364	39,749,382	45,642,303	49,840,443	47,974,819	48,692,442	61,551,118
PARTY VOTES							
1 Democratic Party	15,000,185	22,825,016	27,747,636[1]	27,263,448[1]	25,611,936[2]	24,105,587[3]	27,314,649[3]
8 Republican Party	21,411,991	15,758,397	16,679,543	22,336,260	22,013,372	21,970,017	33,936,137
12 Prohibition Party	34,489	81,916	37,668	58,685	74,733	103,489	74,413
15 Socialist Labor Party	21,608	34,028	12,790	14,883	45,179	29,038	30,250
17 Socialist Party	266,453	883,990	187,785	116,827	79,000	138,973	20,065
21 Communist Party	48,170	102,221	79,211	48,548	-	-	-
23 Union Party	-	-	892,492	-	-	-	-
24 Progressive	-	-	-	-	-	1,157,057	140,416
25 State's Rights Party	-	-	-	-	-	1,169,134	-
Others	7,468	63,814	5,178	1,792	150,599	19,147	35,188

1 Includes votes cast for American Labor Party candidates in New York state.
2 Includes votes cast for American Labor and Liberal Party candidates in New York state.
3 Includes votes cast for Liberal Party candidates in New York state.

Source: *Congressional Quarterly's Guide to U.S. Elections*, 1985: 352-358, 371-372

Table 25.6b UNITED STATES OF AMERICA Presidency: Percentage of Votes 1928-1952

	1928	1932	1936	1940	1944	1948	1952
Valid Votes	56.9	53.4	61.0	62.4	55.9	53.3	63.8
PARTY VOTES							
1 Democratic Party	40.8	57.4	60.8	54.7	53.4	49.5	44.4
8 Republican Party	58.2	39.6	36.5	44.8	45.9	45.1	55.1
12 Prohibition Party	0.1	0.2	0.1	0.1	0.2	0.2	0.1
15 Socialist Labor Party	0.1	0.2	0.0	0.0	0.1	0.1	0.0
17 Socialist Party	0.7	2.2	0.4	0.2	0.2	0.3	0.0
21 Communist Party	0.1	0.3	0.2	0.1	-	-	-
23 Union Party	-	-	2.0	-	-	-	-
24 Progressive	-	-	-	-	-	2.4	0.2
25 State's Rights Party	-	-	-	-	-	2.4	-
Others	0.0	0.2	0.0	0.0	0.3	0.0	0.1

Table 25.6c UNITED STATES OF AMERICA Number of Seats Won in the Electoral College 1928-1952

	1928	1932	1936	1940	1944	1948	1952
1 Democratic Party	87	472	523	449	432	303	89
8 Republican Party	444	59	8	82	99	189	442
12 Prohibition Party	0	0	0	0	0	0	0
15 Socialist Labor Party	0	0	0	0	0	0	0
17 Socialist Party	0	0	0	0	0	0	0
21 Communist Party	0	0	0	0	–	–	–
23 Union Party	–	–	0	–	–	–	–
24 Progressive	–	–	–	–	–	0	0
25 State's Rights Party	–	–	–	–	–	39	–
Others	0	0	0	0	0	0	0
Total Seats	531	531	531	531	531	531	531

Source: *Congressional Quarterly's Guide to U.S. Elections*, 1985: 352-358, 371-372

Table 25.6d UNITED STATES OF AMERICA Percentage of Seats Won in the Electoral College 1928-1952

	1928	1932	1936	1940	1944	1948	1952
1 Democratic Party	16.4	88.9	98.5	84.6	81.4	57.1	16.8
8 Republican Party	83.6	11.1	1.5	15.4	18.6	35.6	83.2
12 Prohibition Party	0.0	0.0	0.0	0.0	0.0	0.0	0.0
15 Socialist Labor Party	0.0	0.0	0.0	0.0	0.0	0.0	0.0
17 Socialist Party	0.0	0.0	0.0	0.0	0.0	0.0	0.0
21 Communist Party	0.0	0.0	0.0	0.0	-	-	-
23 Union Party	-	-	0.0	-	-	-	-
24 Progressive	-	-	-	-	-	0.0	0.0
25 State's Rights Party	-	-	-	-	-	7.3	-
Others	0.0	0.0	0.0	0.0	0.0	0.0	0.0

Table 25.7a UNITED STATES OF AMERICA Presidency: Total Votes 1956-1988

	1956	1960	1964	1968	1972	1976	1980	1984	1988
Electorate	100,724,000	105,292,000	111,612,000	117,438,000	136,162,000	146,219,000	156,973,000	165,774,000	173,628,000
Valid Votes	62,026,908	68,838,219	70,644,592	73,211,875	77,718,554	81,555,889	86,515,221	92,652,842	91,594,809
PARTY VOTES									
1 Democratic Party[1]	26,022,752	34,226,731	43,129,566	31,275,166	29,170,383	40,830,763	35,483,883	37,577,185	41,809,074
8 Republican Party[2]	35,590,472	34,108,157	27,178,188	31,785,480	47,169,911	39,147,793	43,904,153	54,455,075	48,886,097
12 Prohibition Party	41,937	46,203	23,267	15,123	13,505	15,934	7,212	4,242	8,002
15 Socialist Labor Party	44,450	47,522	45,219	52,588	53,814	9,616	-	-	-
17 Socialist Party	2,126	-	-	-	-	-	-	-	-
21 Communist Party	-	-	-	1,075	25,595	58,992	45,023	36,386	-
26 American Independent Party/American Party	-	-	-	9,906,473	1,099,482	160,773	6,647	13,161	3,475
27 Libertarian Party	-	-	-	-	3,673	173,011	921,299	228,314	432,116
28 Independent (J. Anderson)	-	-	-	-	-	-	5,720,060	-	-
Others	325,171 [3]	409,606 [4]	268,352 [5]	175,970	182,191	1,159,007[6]	426,944[7]	338,479[8]	456,045[9]

1 Includes votes cast for Liberal Party electors in New York State.
2 From 1972 includes votes cast for Conservative Party electors in New York State.
3 Includes 110,178 votes cast for a State's Rights ticket and 196,318 votes independent or unpledged state's rights tickets in several southern states.
4 Includes 169,572 votes cast for independent electors in Louisiana and 116,248 votes for an unpledged Democratic ticket in Mississippi.
5 Includes 210,732 votes cast for an unpledged Democratic ticket in Alabama.
6 Includes 756,691 votes cast for Eugene McCarthy running as an independent, and 170,531 for an American Independant ticket.
7 Includes 234,294 votes cast for the Citizens' Party ticket headed by Barry Commoner and 41,268 votes for an American Independent Party ticket.
8 Includes 72,200 votes cast for the Citizens' Party.
9 Includes 217,219 votes cast for Lenora B. Fulani (New Alliance Party), 30,905 votes cast for former Senator Eugene McCarthy (Consumer Party) and 27,818 votes for the American Independent Party.

Sources: Scammon, 1987: 24-40; 1988 figures provided by the Elections Research Center, Washington D.C.

Table 25.7b UNITED STATES OF AMERICA Presidency: Percentage of Votes 1956-1988

	1956	1960	1964	1968	1972	1976	1980	1984	1988
Valid Votes	61.6	65.4	63.3	62.3	57.1	55.8	55.1	55.0	52.8
PARTY VOTES									
1 Democratic Party	42.0	49.7	61.1	42.7	37.5	50.1	41.0	40.6	45.6
8 Republican Party	57.4	49.5	38.5	43.4	60.7	48.0	50.7	58.8	53.3
12 Prohibition Party	0.1	0.1	0.0	0.0	0.0	0.0	0.0	0.0	0.0
15 Socialist Labor Party	0.1	0.1	0.1	0.1	0.1	0.0	-	-	-
17 Socialist Party	0.0	-	-	-	-	-	-	-	-
21 Communist Party	-	-	-	0.0	0.0	0.1	0.1	0.0	-
26 American Independent Party /American Party	-	-	-	13.5	1.4	0.2	0.0	0.0	0.0
27 Libertarian Party	-	-	-	-	0.0	0.2	1.1	0.2	0.5
28 Independent (J. Anderson)	-	-	-	-	-	-	6.6	-	-
Others	0.5	0.6	0.4	0.2	0.2	1.4	0.5	0.4	0.5

Table 25.7c UNITED STATES OF AMERICA Number of Seats Won in the Electoral College 1956-1988

	1956	1960	1964	1968	1972	1976	1980	1984	1988
1 Democratic Party	73	303	486	191	17	297	49	13	112[5]
8 Republican Party	457	219	52	301	520	241[4]	489	525	426
12 Prohibition Party	0	0	0	0	0	0	0	–	0
15 Socialist Labor Party	0	0	0	0	0	0	–	–	–
17 Socialist Party	0	–	–	–	–	–	–	–	–
21 Communist Party	–	–	–	0	0	0	0	0	–
26 American Independent Party/American Party	–	–	–	46	0	0	0	–	0
27 Libertarian Party	–	–	–	–	1[3]	0	0	0	0
28 Independent (J. Anderson)	–	–	–	–	–	–	0	–	–
Others	1[1]	15[2]	0	0	0	0	0	0	0
Total Seats	531	537	538	538	538	538	538	538	538

1 One of the Democratic Party electors from Alabama voted for Walter B. Jones and Herman Talmadge rather than the national Democratic Party candidates, Adlai Stevenson and Estes Kefauver.

2 Six of the Democratic electors from Alabama, all eight unpledged Democratic electors from Mississippi and one Republican elector from Oklahoma voted for Senator Harry F. Byrd rather than their national party candidate.

3 One Republican elector from Virginia voted for John Hospers, the Libertarian Party candidate.

4 One Republican elector from Washington voted for Ronald Reagan rather than the Republican Party's national candidate Gerald Ford.

5 One Democratic elector from West Virginia voted for Lloyd Bentsen for President and Michael Dukakis for Vice President.

Source: Scammon and McGillivray, 1989: 24-40.

Table 25.7d UNITED STATES OF AMERICA Percentage of Seats Won in the Electoral College 1956-1988

	1956	1960	1964	1968	1972	1976	1980	1984	1988
1 Democratic Party	13.7	56.4	90.3	35.5	3.2	55.2	9.1	2.4	20.8
8 Republican Party	86.1	40.8	9.7	55.9	96.7	44.8	90.9	97.6	79.2
12 Prohibition Party	0.0	0.0	0.0	0.0	0.0	0.0	0.0	0.0	0.0
15 Socialist Labor Party	0.0	0.0	0.0	0.0	0.0	0.0	–	–	–
17 Socialist Party	0.0	–	–	–	–	–	–	–	–
21 Communist Party	–	–	–	0.0	0.0	0.0	0.0	0.0	–
26 American Independent Party /American Party	–	–	–	8.6	0.0	0.0	0.0	–	0.0
27 Libertarian Party	–	–	–	–	0.2	0.0	0.0	0.0	–
28 Independent (J. Anderson)	–	–	–	–	–	–	0.0	–	–
Others	0.2	2.8	0.0	0.0	0.0	0.0	0.0	0.0	0.0

Table 25.8a UNITED STATES OF AMERICA House of Representatives Total Votes 1828-1846[1]

	1828	1830	1832	1834	1836	1838	1840	1842	1844	1846
Electorate[2]	1,297,000	1,235,000	1,577,000	2,350,000	2,389,000	2,761,000	2,806,000	3,074,000	2,725,000	3,685,000
Valid Votes	757,897	705,256	1,036,446	1,458,386	1,463,942	1,887,972	2,048,242	1,946,566	2,084,937	2,220,653
PARTY VOTES										
1 Democrats	394,014	339,794	510,257	699,123	705,447	947,702	982,266	993,028	1,043,777	1,076,544
2 National Republicans	346,081	326,919	476,831	-	-	-	-	-	-	-
3 Anti-Masonic Party	8,400	27,889	15,691	23,473	-	-	-	-	-	-
4 Whig Party	-	-	-	649,014	747,835	936,356	1,059,149	901,013	943,200	1,042,621
5 Liberal Party	-	-	-	-	-	-	2,729	25,758	45,764	67,165
Others	9,402	10,654	33,667	86,776	10,660	3,654	4,098	26,767	52,193	37,323

Table 25.8b UNITED STATES OF AMERICA Percentage of Votes 1828-1846

	1828	1830	1832	1834	1836	1838	1840	1842	1844	1846
Valid Votes	58.4	57.1	65.7	62.1	61.3	68.4	73.0	63.3	76.5	60.3
PARTY VOTES										
1 Democrats	52.0	48.2	49.2	47.9	48.2	50.2	48.0	51.0	50.1	48.5
2 National Republicans	45.7	46.4	46.0	-	-	-	-	-	-	-
3 Anti-Masonic Party	1.1	4.0	1.5	1.6	-	-	-	-	-	-
4 Whigs	-	-	-	44.5	51.1	49.6	51.7	46.3	45.2	47.0
6 Free Soil	-	-	-	-	-	-	0.1	1.3	2.2	2.9
Others	1.2	1.5	3.2	6.0	0.7	0.2	0.2	1.4	2.5	1.7

1 Until 1880 the dates of Congressional elections varied between states. Many states held elections in the following odd-numbered year.
2 Estimate of number of persons entitled to vote. Data are missing for some congressional districts. Where no data exists for an entire state the electorate figure excludes that state. Where some, but not all district data are available statewide totals have been estimated on the basis of these figures.

Table 25.8 c UNITED STATES OF AMERICA Number of Seats Won in the House of Representatives 1828-1846

	1828	1830	1832	1834	1836	1838	1840	1842	1844	1846
1 Democratic Party	142	132	142	142	122	126	99	142	142	112
2 National Republican Party	71	77	87	-	-	-	-	-	-	-
3 Anti-Masonic Party	0	4	7	5	-	-	-	-	-	-
4 Whig Party	-	-	-	81	120	116	143	81	76	116
5 Liberty Party	-	-	-	-	-	-	-	-	-	-
Others	0	0	3	3	0	0	0	0	6	1
Total Seats	213	213	239	239	242	242	242	223	224	230

Table 25.8 d UNITED STATES OF AMERICA Percentage of Seats Won in the House of Representatives 1828-1846

	1828	1830	1832	1834	1836	1838	1840	1842	1844	1846
1 Democratic Party	66.7	62.0	59.4	58.9	50.4	52.1	40.9	63.7	63.4	48.7
2 National Republican Party	33.3	36.2	36.4	-	-	-	-	-	-	-
3 Anti-Masonic Party	0.0	1.9	2.9	2.1	-	-	-	-	-	-
4 Whig Party	-	-	-	34.9	49.6	47.9	59.1	36.3	33.9	50.4
5 Liberty Party	-	-	-	-	-	-	-	-	-	-
Others	0.0	0.0	1.3	3.3	0.0	0.0	0.0	0.0	2.7	0.4

Table 25.9 a UNITED STATES OF AMERICA House of Representatives Total Votes 1848-1864

	1848	1850	1852	1854	1856	1858	1860	1862	1864
Electorate	3,990,000	4,320,000	4,464,000	4,873,000	5,125,000	5,505,000	4,700,000	4,995,000	5,475,000
Valid Votes	2,677,006	2,581,253	3,007,796	3,190,295	3,817,771	3,782,384	3,818,297	3,231,125	3,809,672
PARTY VOTES									
1 Democratic Party	1,172,039	1,211,063	1,521,245	1,431,977	1,820,543	1,862,603	1,696,998	1,517,156	1,657,712
4 Whig Party	1,229,230	1,098,936	1,316,922	387,285	-	-	-	-	-
6 Free Soil Party	236,504	79,574	106,950	-	-	-	-	-	-
7 American Party	-	-	-	801,717	582,558	410,580	212,623	67,074	-
8 Republican Party	-	-	-	531,975	1,405,983	1,467,734	1,851,545	1,635,193	2,144,579
Others	39,233	191,680	59,679	37,341	8,687	41,467	57,131	11,702	7,781

Table 25.9 b UNITED STATES OF AMERICA House of Representatives Percentage of Votes 1848-1864

	1848	1850	1852	1854	1856	1858	1860	1862	1864
Valid Votes	67.1	59.8	67.4	65.5	74.5	68.7	81.3	64.7	69.6
PARTY VOTES									
1 Democratic Party	43.8	46.9	50.6	44.9	47.7	49.2	44.4	47.0	43.5
4 Whig Party	45.9	42.6	43.8	12.1	-	-	-	-	-
6 Free Soil Party	8.8	3.1	3.6	-	-	-	-	-	-
7 American Party	-	-	-	25.1	15.3	10.9	5.6	2.1	-
8 Republican Party	-	-	-	16.7	36.8	38.8	48.5	50.6	56.3
Others	1.5	7.4	2.0	1.2	0.2	1.1	1.5	0.4	0.2

Table 25.9 c UNITED STATES OF AMERICA Number of Seats Won in the House of Representatives 1848-1864

	1848	1850	1852	1854	1856	1858	1860	1862	1864
1 Democratic Party	116	139	159	81	128	100	53	75	43
4 Whig Party	106	88	71		–	–	–	–	–
			}	117[1]					
6 Free Soil Party	10	6	4		–	–	–	–	–
8 Republican Party	–	–	–	–	92	114	106	103	149
7 American Party	–	–	–	36	14	23	28	6	0
Others	1	0	0	0	0	0	0	0	0
Total Seats	233	233	234	234	234	237	187	184	192

Table 25.9 d UNITED STATES OF AMERICA Percentage of Seats Won in the House of Representatives 1848-1864

	1848	1850	1852	1854	1856	1858	1860	1862	1864
1 Democratic Party	49.8	59.7	67.9	34.6	54.7	42.2	28.3	40.8	22.4
4 Whig Party	45.5	37.8	30.3		–	–	–	–	–
			}	50.0					
6 Free Soil Party	4.3	2.6	1.7	–	–	–	–	–	–
8 Republican Party	–	–	–	–	39.3	48.1	56.7	56.0	77.6
7 American Party	–	–	–	15.4	6.0	9.7	15.0	3.3	0.0
Others	0.4	0.0	0.0	0.0	0.0	0.0	0.0	0.0	0.0

1 Combines Congressmen opposed to the Kansas-Nebraska Act of 1854.

Table 25.10a UNITED STATES OF AMERICA House of Representatives Total Votes 1866-1882

	1866	1868	1870	1872	1874	1876	1878	1880	1882
Electorate	5,796,000	7,694,000	8,369,000	8,932,000	9,531,000	10,155,000	10,762,000	11,371,000	12,033,000
Valid Votes	4,114,968	6,038,662	5,594,877	6,639,610	6,179,307	8,310,809	7,010,929	9,064,956	7,904,273
PARTY VOTES									
1 Democratic Party	1,862,923	2,890,313	2,679,296	3,093,695	3,256,715	4,250,947	3,189,492	4,376,304	3,974,819
8 Republican Party	2,242,209	3,139,825	2,814,959	3,497,044	2,812,962	3,941,749	2,854,607	4,228,616	3,559,627
11 Greenback-Labor Party	-	-	-	-	-	91,082	906,722	424,324	250,137
Others	9,836	8,524	102,622	48,871	109,630	27,031	60,108	35,712	119,690

Table 25.10b UNITED STATES OF AMERICA House of Representatives Percentage of Votes 1866-1882

	1866	1868	1870	1872	1874	1876	1878	1880	1882
Valid Votes	71.0	78.5	66.9	74.3	64.8	81.8	65.1	79.7	65.7
PARTY VOTES									
1 Democratic Party	45.3	47.9	47.9	46.6	52.7	51.1	45.5	48.3	50.3
8 Republican Party	54.5	52.0	50.3	52.7	45.5	47.4	40.7	46.6	45.0
11 Greenback-Labor Party	-	-	-	-	-	1.1	12.9	4.7	3.2
Others	0.2	0.1	1.8	0.7	1.8	0.3	0.9	0.4	1.5

Table 25.10c UNITED STATES OF AMERICA Number of Seats Won in the House of Representatives 1866-1882

	1866	1868	1870	1872	1874	1876	1878	1880	1882
1 Democratic Party	49	66	104	93	179	152	150	135	196
8 Republican Party	144	152	139	199	111	141	130	147	126
11 Greenback-Labor Party	-	-	-	-	-	0	13	9	1
Others	0	0	0	0	3	0	0	2	2
Total Seats	193	218	243	292	293	293	293	293	325

Table 25.10d UNITED STATES OF AMERICA Percentage of Seats Won in the House of Representatives 1866-1882

	1866	1868	1870	1872	1874	1876	1878	1880	1882
1 Democratic Party	25.4	30.3	42.8	31.8	61.3	51.9	51.2	46.1	60.3
8 Republican Party	74.6	69.7	57.2	68.2	38.0	48.1	44.4	50.2	38.8
11 Greenback-Labor Party	-	-	-	-	-	0.0	4.4	3.1	0.3
Others	0.0	0.0	0.0	0.0	1.0	0.0	0.0	0.7	0.6

Table 25.11a UNITED STATES OF AMERICA House of Representatives Total Votes 1884-1900

	1884	1886	1888	1890	1892	1894	1896	1898	1900
Electorate	12,715,000	13,396,000	14,414,000	15,124,000	15,844,000	16,660,000	17,486,000	18,207,000	18,937,000
Valid Votes	9,892,009	8,554,219	11,446,280	9,773,461	11,830,064	11,234,070	13,621,379	10,934,850	13,717,471
PARTY VOTES									
1 Democratic Party	4,953,623	4,185,098	5,592,339	4,951,753	5,586,042	4,292,855	6,198,791	5,227,761	6,433,649
8 Republican Party	4,714,275	3,943,800	5,488,884	4,160,116	4,900,431	5,398,146	6,816,272	5,304,206	6,963,527
11 Greenback-Labor Party	97,037	143,710	106,676	-	-	-	-	-	-
12 Prohibition Party	-	-	-	-	-	-	93,802	135,582	146,332
14 Populists	-	-	-	407,224	1,100,023	1,292,677	372,716	179,316	51,889
Others	127,074	281,631	258,381	244,368	243,568	250,392	140,098	87,985	122,074

Table 25.11b UNITED STATES OF AMERICA House of Representatives Percentage of Votes 1884-1900

	1884	1886	1888	1890	1892	1894	1896	1898	1900
Valid Votes	77.8	63.9	79.4	64.6	74.7	67.4	77.9	60.1	72.4
PARTY VOTES									
1 Democratic Party	50.1	48.9	48.9	50.7	47.2	38.2	45.5	47.8	46.7
8 Republican Party	47.7	46.1	48.0	42.6	41.4	48.1	50.0	48.5	50.8
11 Greenback-Labor Party	1.0	1.7	0.9	-	-	-	-	-	-
12 Prohibition Party	-	-	-	-	-	-	0.7	1.2	1.1
14 Populists	-	-	-	4.2	9.3	11.5	2.7	1.6	0.4
Others	1.3	3.3	2.3	2.5	2.1	2.2	1.0	0.8	0.9

Table 25.11c UNITED STATES OF AMERICA Number of Seats Won in the House of Representatives 1884-1900

	1884	1886	1888	1890	1892	1894	1896	1898	1900
1 Democratic Party	183	169	161	235	216	104	128	166	152
8 Republican Party	141	154	171	88	128	245	204	182	198
11 Greenback-Labor Party	1	-	-	-	-	-	-	-	-
12 Prohibition Party	-	-	0	0	0	0	0	0	0
14 Populists	-	-	-	9	12	7	25	9	7
Others	0	2	0	0	0	0	0	0	0
Total Seats	325	325	332	332	356	356	357	357	357

Table 25.11d UNITED STATES OF AMERICA Percentage of Seats Won in the House of Representatives 1884-1900

	1884	1886	1888	1890	1892	1894	1896	1898	1900
1 Democratic Party	56.3	52.0	48.5	70.8	60.7	29.2	35.9	46.5	42.6
8 Republican Party	43.4	47.4	51.5	26.5	36.0	68.8	57.1	51.0	55.5
11 Greenback-Labor Party	0.3	-	-	-	-	-	-	-	-
12 Prohibition Party	-	-	0.0	0.0	0.0	0.0	0.0	0.0	0.0
14 Populists	-	-	-	2.7	3.4	2.0	7.0	2.5	2.0
Others	0.0	0.6	0.0	0.0	0.0	0.0	0.0	0.0	0.0

Table 25.12a UNITED STATES OF AMERICA House of Representatives Total Votes 1902-1918

	1902	1904	1906	1908	1910	1912	1914	1916	1918
Electorate	19,753,000	20,593,000	21,749,000	22,624,000	23,615,000	25,503,000	27,227,000	28,416,000	31,958,000
Valid Votes	10,983,723	13,149,577	11,143,798	14,400,237	12,207,596	14,216,896	13,641,262	16,720,865	12,760,404
PARTY VOTES									
1 Democratic Party	5,078,058	5,385,825	4,840,018	6,544,563	5,746,616	6,213,813	5,752,099	7,606,008	5,460,195
8 Republican Party	5,479,705	7,157,199	5,700,173	7,186,270	5,664,909	4,628,780	5,839,627	8,088,363	6,670,333
12 Prohibition Party	163,594	217,525	154,444	185,310	155,363	197,825	222,547	263,576	120,850
17 Socialist Party	178,914	320,525	289,628	339,351	531,624	907,322	635,264	607,048	404,224
18 Progressive Party	-	-	-	-	-	2,227,249	1,142,900	-	-
Others	83,452	68,503	159,535	144,743	109,084	41,907	48,828	154,940	104,802

Table 25.12b UNITED STATES OF AMERICA House of Representatives Percentage of Votes 1902-1918

	1902	1904	1906	1908	1910	1912	1914	1916	1918
Valid Votes	55.6	63.9	51.2	63.6	51.7	55.7	50.1	58.8	39.9
PARTY VOTES									
1 Democratic Party	46.2	41.0	43.4	45.4	47.1	43.7	42.2	45.5	42.8
8 Republican Party	49.9	54.4	51.2	49.9	46.4	32.5	42.8	48.4	52.3
12 Prohibition Party	1.5	1.7	1.4	1.3	1.3	1.4	1.6	1.6	0.9
17 Socialist Party	1.6	2.4	2.6	2.4	4.4	6.4	4.7	3.6	3.2
18 Progressive Party	-	-	-	-	-	15.7	8.4	-	-
Others	0.8	0.5	1.4	1.0	0.9	0.3	0.4	0.9	0.8

Table 25.12c UNITED STATES OF AMERICA Number of Seats Won in the House of Representatives 1902-1918

	1902	1904	1906	1908	1910	1912	1914	1916	1918
1 Democratic Party	178	135	168	172	227	291	231	214	192
8 Republican Party	208	251	223	219	163	135	194	215	240
12 Prohibition Party	0	0	0	0	0	0	0	1	1
17 Socialist Party	0	0	0	0	1	0	1	1	1
18 Progressive Party	–	–	–	–	–	9	8	–	–
Others	0	0	0	0	0	0	1	4	1
Total Seats	386	386	391	391	391	435	435	435	435

Table 25.12d UNITED STATES OF AMERICA Percentage of Seats Won in the House of Representatives 1902-1918

	1902	1904	1905	1908	1910	1912	1914	1916	1918
1 Democratic Party	46.1	35.0	43.0	44.0	58.1	66.9	53.1	49.2	44.1
8 Republican Party	53.9	65.0	57.0	56.0	41.7	31.0	44.6	49.4	55.2
12 Prohibition Party	0.0	0.0	0.0	0.0	0.0	0.0	0.0	0.2	0.2
17 Socialist Party	0.0	0.0	0.0	0.0	0.3	0.0	0.2	0.2	0.2
18 Progressive Party	–	–	–	–	–	2.1	1.8	–	–
Others	0.0	0.0	0.0	0.0	0.0	0.0	0.2	0.9	0.2

Table 25.13a UNITED STATES OF AMERICA House of Representatives Total Votes 1920-1936

	1920	1922	1924	1926	1928	1930	1932	1934	1936
Electorate	54,313,000	56,908,000	59,503,000	62,099,000	64,694,000	67,289,000	69,804,000	72,319,000	74,834,000
Valid Votes	25,379,149	20,321,731	26,694,022	20,414,478	34,203,771	24,728,483	37,190,922	32,165,695	42,982,422
PARTY VOTES									
1 Democratic Party	9,060,567	8,961,360	10,654,902	8,217,650	14,210,466	11,034,126	20,114,288	17,495,729	24,209,352
8 Republican Party	14,762,503	10,614,065	14,919,521	11,658,738	19,365,483	13,019,211	15,676,830	13,221,800	17,025,022
17 Socialist Party	711,096	360,121			-	211,915	605,455	358,306	-
		}	962,340	444,379					
19 Farmer-Labor Party	504,418	314,245	-	-	251,126	271,599	326,804	376,927	462,714
24 Wisconsin Progressive Party	-	-	-	-	-	-	-	334,345	479,263
Others	340,565	71,940	128,259	93,711	376,696	191,632	467,545	378,588	806,071

Table 25.13b UNITED STATES OF AMERICA House of Representatives Percentage of Votes 1920-1936

	1920	1922	1924	1926	1928	1930	1932	1934	1936
Valid Votes	46.7	35.7	44.9	32.9	52.9	36.7	53.3	44.5	57.4
PARTY VOTES									
1 Democratic Party	35.7	44.1	39.9	40.3	41.5	44.6	54.1	54.4	56.3
8 Republican Party	58.2	52.2	55.9	57.1	56.6	52.6	42.2	41.1	39.6
17 Socialist Party	2.8	1.8			-	0.9	1.6	1.1	-
		}	3.6	2.2					
19 Farmer-Labor Party	2.0	1.5	-	-	0.7	1.1	0.9	1.2	1.1
24 Wisconsin Progressive Party	-	-	-	-	-	-	-	1.0	1.1
Others	1.3	0.4	0.5	0.5	1.1	0.8	1.3	1.2	1.9

Table 25.13c UNITED STATES OF AMERICA Number of Seats Won in the House of Representatives 1920-1936

	1920	1922	1924	1926	1928	1930[1]	1932	1934	1936
1 Democratic Party	131	208	184	194	166	216	313	320	334
8 Republican Party	303	224	247	238	268	218	117	105	89
17 Socialist Party	1	1	1	1	–	0	0	0	–
19 Farmer-Labor Party	–	1	3	2	1	1	5	3	5
24 Wisconsin Progressive Party	–	–	–	–	–	–	–	7	7
Others	0	1	0	0	0	0	0	0	0
Total Seats	435	435	435	435	435	435	435	435	435

Table 25.13d UNITED STATES OF AMERICA Percentage of Seats Won in the House of Representatives 1920-1936

	1920	1922	1924	1926	1928	1930	1932	1934	1936
1 Democratic Party	30.1	47.8	42.3	44.6	38.2	49.7	72.0	73.6	76.8
8 Republican Party	69.7	51.5	56.8	54.7	61.6	50.1	26.9	24.1	20.5
17 Socialist Party	0.2	0.2	0.2	0.2	–	0.0	0.0	0.0	–
19 Farmer-Labor Party	–	0.2	0.7	0.5	0.2	0.2	1.1	0.7	1.1
24 Wisconsin Progressive Party	–	–	–	–	–	–	–	1.6	1.6
Others	0.0	0.2	0.0	0.0	0.0	0.0	0.0	0.0	0.0

1 By the time the House convened in December 1931, deaths concentrated on the Republican side of the House and Democratic victories in subsequent by-elections gave control of the House to the Democrats, with 220 seats to the Republicans 214.

Table 25.14a UNITED STATES OF AMERICA House of Representatives Total Votes 1938-1954

	1938	1940	1942	1944	1946	1948	1950	1952	1954
Electorate	77,349,000	79,863,000	82,851,000	85,278,000	88,388,000	91,408,000	94,403,000	96,466,000	98,527,000
Valid Votes	36,067,245	46,503,435	28,051,822	45,013,459	34,279,158	45,839,622	40,253,267	57,582,333	42,509,905
PARTY VOTES									
1 Democratic Party	17,921,079	24,102,011	13,235,745	23,448,545	15,433,876	24,137,381	19,938,673	28,636,552	22,346,852
8 Republican Party	16,910,323	21,330,192	14,180,557	21,135,547	18,345,812	20,810,931	19,758,927	28,412,420	19,955,662
19 Farmer-Labor Party	338,684	298,250	151,684	-	-	-	-	-	-
24 Wisconsin Progressive Party	330,828	469,063	185,114	-	-	-	-	-	-
Others	566,331	303,919	298,722	429,367	499,470	891,310	555,697	533,361	207,391

Table 25.14b UNITED STATES OF AMERICA Percentage of Votes 1938-1954

	1938	1940	1942	1944	1946	1948	1950	1952	1954
Valid Votes	46.6	58.2	33.9	52.8	38.8	50.1	43.0	59.7	43.1
PARTY VOTES									
1 Democratic Party	49.7	51.8	47.2	52.1	45.0	52.7	49.5	49.7	52.6
8 Republican Party	46.9	45.9	50.6	47.0	53.5	45.4	49.1	49.3	46.9
19 Farmer-Labor Party	0.9	0.6	0.5	-	-	-	-	-	-
24 Wisconsin Progressive Party	0.9	1.0	0.7	-	-	-	-	-	-
Others	1.6	0.7	1.1	0.9	1.5	1.9	1.4	0.9	0.5

Table 25.14c UNITED STATES OF AMERICA Number of Seats Won in the House of Representatives 1938-1954

	1938	1940	1942	1944	1946	1948	1950	1952	1954
1 Democratic Party	261	263	222	243	189	263	235	213	232
8 Republican Party	171	162	209	190	245	171	199	221	203
19 Farmer-Labor Party	1	1	1	–	–	–	–	–	–
24 Wisconsin Progressive Party	2	3	2	1	–	–	–	–	–
Others[1]	0	1	1	1	1	1	1	1	0
Total Seats	435	435	435	435	435	435	435	435	435

Table 25.14d UNITED STATES OF AMERICA Percentage of Seats Won in the House of Representatives 1938-1954

	1938	1940	1942	1944	1946	1948	1950	1952	1954
1 Democratic Party	60.0	61.5	51.0	55.9	43.4	60.5	54.0	49.0	53.3
8 Republican Party	39.3	37.2	48.0	43.7	56.3	39.3	45.7	50.8	46.7
19 Farmer-Labor Party	0.2	0.2	0.2	–	–	–	–	–	–
24 Wisconsin Progressive Party	–	0.7	0.5	0.2	–	–	–	–	–
Others	0.0	0.2	0.2	0.2	0.2	0.2	0.2	0.2	0.0

1 From 1940 to 1948 Vito Marcontonio, American Labor Party, who was initially elected as a Republican. In 1950 and 1952, F. Reams, (Ninth District, Ohio).

Table 25.15a UNITED STATES OF AMERICA House of Representatives Total Votes 1956-1972

	1956	1958/9	1960	1962	1964[1]	1966	1968	1970	1972
Electorate	100,724,000	103,221,000	105,292,000	108,210,000	111,612,000	114,046,000	116,904,000	119,882,000	135,654,000
Valid Votes	58,434,811	45,966,070	64,214,301	51,391,977	66,288,513	53,153,072	66,558,086	55,251,136	72,220,430
PARTY VOTES									
1 Democratic Party	29,844,664	25,952,307	35,136,959	26,679,519	38,254,998	27,174,857	33,635,378	30,042,115	37,972,557
8 Republican Party	28,467,748	19,827,729	28,660,314	24,500,625	27,781,406	25,512,466	32,172,890	24,443,577	33,344,891
Others	122,319	186,034	417,028	211,833	252,109	465,749	749,818	765,444	902,982

Table 25.15b UNITED STATES OF AMERICA House of Representatives Percentage of Votes 1956-1972

	1956	1958/9	1960	1962	1964[1]	1966	1968	1970	1972
Valid Votes	58.0	44.5	61.0	47.5	59.7	46.6	56.9	46.1	53.2
PARTY VOTES									
1 Democratic Party	51.1	56.5	54.7	51.9	57.7	51.1	50.5	54.4	52.6
8 Republican Party	48.7	43.1	44.6	47.7	41.9	48.0	48.3	44.2	46.2
Others	0.2	0.4	0.6	0.4	0.4	0.9	1.1	1.4	1.2

[1] Since 1964 the District of Columbia votes for Presidential electors and a non-voting member of the House. The House electorate excludes the District, and is thus approximately half a million smaller than the Presidential electorate.

Table 25.15c UNITED STATES OF AMERICA Number of Seats Won in the House of Representatives 1956-1972

	1956	1958	1960	1962	1964	1966	1968	1970	1972
1 Democratic Party	234	284	262	259	295	249	243	255	243
8 Republican Party	201	153	175	176	140	186	192	180	192
Others	0	0	0	0	0	0	0	0	0
Total Seats	435	437	437	435	435	435	435	435	435

Table 25.15d UNITED STATES OF AMERICA Percentage of Seats Won in the House of Representatives 1956-1972

	1956	1958	1960	1962	1964	1966	1968	1970	1972
1 Democratic Party	53.8	65.3	60.2	59.5	67.8	57.2	55.9	58.6	55.9
8 Republican Party	46.2	35.2	40.2	40.5	32.2	42.8	44.1	41.4	44.1
Others	0.0	0.0	0.0	0.0	0.0	0.0	0.0	0.0	0.0

Table 25.16a UNITED STATES OF AMERICA House of Representatives Total Votes 1974-1988

	1974	1976	1978	1980	1982	1984	1986	1988
Electorate	140,690,000	145,725,000	151,110,000	156,494,000	160,966,000	165,300,000	169,077,000	173,154,000
Valid Votes	53,149,732	75,257,137	55,961,674	78,201,975	64,851,109	84,557,538	61,279,777	83,490,507
PARTY VOTES								
1 Democratic Party	30,907,396	42,646,571	30,141,809	39,580,511	35,982,778	44,276,883	33,654,209	44,827,304
8 Republican Party	21,286,562	31,372,788	25,047,095	37,496,096	27,986,623	39,555,836	27,146,534	37,739,811
Others	955,774	1,237,778	772,770	1,125,368	881,708	724,819	479,034	923,392

Table 25.16b UNITED STATES OF AMERICA House of Representatives Percentage of Votes 1974- 1988

	1974	1976	1978	1980	1982	1984	1986	1988
Valid Votes	37.8	51.6	37.0	50.0	40.3	51.2	36.2	48.2
PARTY VOTES								
1 Democratic Party	58.2	56.7	53.9	50.6	55.5	52.4	54.9	53.7
8 Republican Party	40.1	41.7	44.8	47.9	43.2	46.8	44.3	45.2
Others	1.8	1.6	1.4	1.4	1.4	0.9	0.8	1.1

Table 25.16c UNITED STATES OF AMERICA Number of Seats Won in the House of Representatives 1974-1988

	1974	1976	1978	1980	1982	1984	1986	1988
1 Democratic Party	291	292	277	243	269	253	258	260
8 Republican Party	144	143	158	192	166	182	177	175
Others	0	0	0	0	0	0	0	0
Total Seats	435	435	435	435	435	435	435	435

Table 25.16d UNITED STATES OF AMERICA Percentage of Seats Won in the House of Representatives 1974-1988

	1974	1976	1978	1980	1982	1984	1986	1988
1 Democratic Party	66.9	67.1	63.7	55.9	61.8	58.2	59.3	59.8
8 Republican Party	33.1	32.9	36.3	44.1	38.2	41.8	40.7	40.2
Others	0.0	0.0	0.0	0.0	0.0	0.0	0.0	0.0

Appendix

THE MECHANICS OF ELECTORAL SYSTEMS

The conversion of votes cast in a parliamentary election into seats in a legislature involves a number of related but distinct stages; at each stage choices can be made between different ways of accomplishing this end (Rose, 1983). Electoral systems can conveniently be divided into two major categories. *Majority* systems award a seat to the candidate who gets the most votes in a given constituency, whether a plurality of votes or an absolute majority, that is, one vote more than half of the total. *Proportional representation* (PR) systems attempt to allocate seats in proportion to votes. There is more than one form of proportional representation; it is the most frequently used method in Western nations today.

In plurality systems (often known as 'first past the post') the candidate with the largest number of votes wins, even if this is less than an absolute majority. In a single-member constituency, electors have one vote. In multi-member constituencies, electors usually have as many votes as there are seats and candidates are ranked in order of the number of votes until all the seats in the constituency have been filled.

Variants of the plurality system have been employed in order to assist in the representation of minorities in multi-member constituencies. The limited vote, used in Spain and Portugal in the 19th and early 20th centuries and in 13 United Kingdom constituencies between 1868 and 1880, restricts the number of votes an elector may cast to less than the total number of seats in a multi-member constituency. The single non-transferable vote, used in Japan today, is a version of the limited vote; the elector may cast only one vote regardless of the number of seats in the constituency (Lijphart et al., 1986).

The alternative vote, used in elections to the Australian House of Representatives since 1918, ensures that the winning candidate has an absolute majority. An absolute majority may be obtained on the first count, but with three or more candidates this is by no means certain. Hence each elector is required to rank alternative candidates in order of preference 1, 2, 3 etc. If no majority is secured on the first count the candidate with the lowest number of votes is eliminated and his or her second preferences distributed among the remaining candidates. If this does not produce an absolute majority, then the next lowest candidate is eliminated and his or her second preferences distributed and so on until an absolute majority is secured (Wright, 1986).

The two-ballot system, widely used in continental European countries in the 19th century and in the French Third and Fifth Republics, is a variant on the alternative vote (Fisichella, 1984). Instead of voters marking their preference in order at a single point in time two ballots may be held. If no candidate wins an absolute majority on the first ballot a second vote takes place. A majority at the second ballot may be guaranteed by eliminating all but the two leading first round contenders (as in Imperial Germany or the presidential elections of the French Fifth Republic). If more than two candidates are allowed to survive in the second round, a plurality can suffice for victory, as in the legislative elections of the Third or Fifth Republic. In France today, a candidate's first round vote must amount to at least 12.5 per cent of the total electorate in order to proceed to the second round. In Third Republic France there were no restrictions on proceeding to the second round, and candidates could enter the second round even if they did not contest the first.

Proportional representation systems are designed to ensure a high degree of correspondence between a party's share of the popular vote and its share of seats in the legislature. Whereas plurality systems may operate with either single or multi-member constituencies, PR must employ multi-member constituencies so that seats can be shared amongst the parties. In a single-member constituency, the candidate with the most votes wins and there is no representation for those favouring other candidates. That is the consequence of the election of a single individual to a unique office, such as a President.

In PR systems the initial step in allocating seats is the identification of the quota of votes required to win a seat. In the simplest method of calculating a quota (often known as the *Hare* quota), the total number of valid votes is divided by the number of seats to be allocated. Three alternatives are the *Hagenbach-Bischoff* quota, in which the number of votes is divided by the number of seats plus one; the *Droop* quota, in which the number of votes is divided by the number of seats plus one and adding one to the quotient, and the *Imperiali* quota, used in Italy, where the number of votes is divided by the number of seats plus two. Thus, in a constituency with 60,000 votes and five seats, the respective quotas would be: Hare 12,000; Hagenbach-Bischoff 10,000; Droop 10,001; Imperiali 8,572.

After the electoral quota for a constituency has been determined, the next step is to allocate the seats between the parties. Three major systems are in use.

(i) *Largest remainder.* The vote for each party is divided by the electoral quota. A seat is awarded to each party for each bloc of votes equal to a quota. Smaller parties that have not been awarded any seat will have all their votes counted as a remainder, and a party that has won seats will have a remainder that is short of a full quota. There may also be seats remaining unallocated on the basis of requiring the winner to have a full quota. These seats are then allocated in strict sequence to the parties with the largest remainders. This system enables a small party to win a seat in a constituency, even if its share of the vote is less than a quota, provided that its initial vote is more than the remainder of parties that have already won a seat.

In the example in Table 1 (adapted from Mackenzie, 1956: 77-79), 24,000 valid votes have been cast in a five-member constituency. The Hare quota is therefore 24,000/5 = 4,800. In the first stage parties A, B and C each secure a seat, but party D does not because its total vote is less than the quota. Two seats remain to be allocated at the second stage. One quota is subtracted from the votes cast for parties A, B and C, because they have each won a seat; party D's vote remains unchanged. Since Party A has the largest remainder and party D the second largest remainder they are awarded the two remaining seats.

Table 1: DISTRIBUTION OF SEATS BY THE LARGEST REMAINDER SYSTEM

Party	First Round Votes	Hare Quota	Seats	Second Round Remainder	Seats	Total Seats
A	8,700	4,800	1	3,900	1	2
B	6,800	4,800	1	2,000	0	1
C	5,200	4,800	1	400	0	1
D	3,300	–	0	3,300	1	1
Total	24,000					5

(ii) *Highest average system (d'Hondt version).* In a series of rounds, each party's vote is divided by the number of seats it has been allocated in the first round quota plus one, then two, and so on. The remaining seats are allocated in turn to the party which has the highest average vote in each of these divisions. Table 2 considers a five-seat constituency contested by four parties, with the distribution of votes as in Table 1. In the first round parties A, B and C have been allocated one seat by passing the Hare quota of 4,800. Their divisor in the next round is therefore two. Party D has not yet won a seat so its divisor is still one. In the second round Party A, with an average of 4,350, has the highest average and therefore wins a seat. In the third and final round A's divisor is now three, because it has now won two seats, whereas the other parties' divisors remain the same. Party B, with 3,400 votes, now has the highest average, so it is awarded the last seat.

Table 2: DISTRIBUTION OF SEATS BY THE D'HONDT HIGHEST AVERAGE SYSTEM

	First Round			Second Round			Third Round			
Party	Votes	Hare Quota	Seats Won	Divisor	Average	Seats Won	Divisor	Average	Seats Won	Total Seats Won
A	8,700	4,800	1	2	4,350	1	3	2,900	0	2
B	6,800	4,800	1	2	3,400	0	2	3,400	1	2
C	5,200	4,800	1	2	2,600	0	2	2,600	0	1
D	3,300	4,800	0	1	3,300	0	1	3,300	0	0
Total	24,000									5

Another method of computation for allocating seats under the highest average system (which produces an identical outcome) uses the Hagenbach-Bischoff quota. Because this quota is smaller than the Hare quota, a larger number of seats may be allocated initially. For the case quoted in Table 2, the Hagenbach-Bischoff quota would be 4,000, and thus four seats would be allocated in the first round, including two to party A, with a vote more than twice the size of the quota.

A third alternative under the d'Hondt system is to allocate seats simply by the highest average without any use of a quota. Each seat is allocated in turn to a party which, after the allocation of an extra seat, will have the highest average number of votes per seat. In the first round, when no party has yet won a seat, the party with a plurality of votes has the highest average, so the first seat goes to Party A. (The order in which the seats are assigned to a party is indicated in brackets in Table 3). After the allocation of a second seat Party B would have the highest average and therefore gains the seat. In the next round Party C has the highest average, then A and the last seat goes to party B.

Table 3: DISTRIBUTION OF SEATS BY THE D'HONDT HIGHEST AVERAGE SYSTEM WITHOUT AN INITIAL ALLOCATION BY QUOTA

Party	Votes	1st seat Divisor	2nd seat Divisor	3rd seat Divisor	4th seat Divisor	5th seat Divisor	Total
A	8,700	8,700(1)	4,350	4,350	4,350(4)	2,900	2
B	6,800	6,800	6,800(2)	3,400	3,400	3,400(5)	2
C	5,200	5,200	5,200	5,200(3)	2,600	2,600	1
D	3,300	3,300	3,300	3,300	3,300	3,300	0
	24,000						5

(iii) *Highest average system (Sainte-Laguë version).* This system is identical to d'Hondt except that the divisors used are odd numbers; instead of being 1,2,3,4 etc. they are 1, 3, 5, 7 etc. Because the increase in the size of the divisor is greater under the Sainte-Laguë system it is more difficult for a party, once it has been successful, to win each further seat. It is therefore more favourable to smaller parties than the d'Hondt system. In Table 4 parties A, B and C have each passed the quota of 4,800 in the first round and have each been awarded one seat. Their divisor in the next round is therefore three. Party D, which has not yet won a seat still has a divisor of one. In the second round D wins a seat with a highest average of 3,350. In the final round the divisor is three for all the parties, so the last seat goes to the party with a plurality of votes, Party A.

Table 4: DISTRIBUTION OF SEATS BY THE SAINTE-LAGUË HIGHEST AVERAGE SYSTEM

		First Round			Second Round			Third Round		
Party	Votes	Hare Quota	Seats Won	Divisor	Average	Seats Won	Divisor	Average	Seats Won	Total Seats Won
A	8,700	4,800	1	3	2,900	0	3	2,900	1	2
B	6,800	4,800	1	3	2,267	0	3	2,267	0	1
C	5,200	4,800	1	3	1,733	0	3	1,733	0	1
D	3,350	4,800	0	1	3,350	1	3	1,117	0	1
Total	24,000									5

When a full quota is required to win a seat, it can result in not all the seats in a constituency being allocated. In Table 4 only three parties, A, B, and C have as many votes as a Hare quota of 4,800. Since no party has as many votes as two full quotas, only three seats can be allocated on the basis of full quotas, and two seats remain. With a Hagenbach-Bischoff quota of 4,000 or an Imperiali quota of 3,429, Party A would be awarded two seats because its total vote is more than twice the quota, but one seat would still not be allocated. If the quota is combined with either the largest remainder or one of the versions of the highest average system, then all the seats in a constituency can be shared out. In some cases however this second stage calculation is carried out in a regional or even a national grouping. This tends to advantage smaller parties whose support is geographically widespread and whose votes may not be sufficient to reach a constituency quota. Unallocated seats are shared out in this way in Austria, Belgium, Greece and Italy.

In three countries, Denmark, Germany and Sweden, some seats in the parliament are allocated in a nationwide constituency. The seats that the parties have won at constituency level are deducted from the national total, thus compensating for constituency-level disproportionality. Threshold clauses may limit the parties which can participate in the higher-level allocation. For instance, in Germany a party must win either five per cent of the national vote or three single-member constituency seats and in Sweden a party must win four per cent of the national vote or 12 per cent of the vote in one constituency to be included in the nationwide distribution.

The final stage in a proportional representation system is the allocation of seats to particular candidates. In some countries the elector can vote only for the party list, and the ranking of the candidates on the list is determined by the political party. The voter chooses a closed party list and the party list determines the order in which individual candidates can be elected. In many systems electors are able to cast one or more preference votes for individual candidates (Katz, 1986). In Finland, for example, a voter must actually vote for an individual candidate. Votes are then summed according to the candidates' parties and seats allocated proportionately to parties, and within a party, in accord with individual vote totals. More commonly, the elector must choose a party list and then has the option of expressing a preference for individual candidates within that list. In a few cases voters may vote for candidates on different party lists (*panachage*).

In the Single Transferable Vote system, used in Ireland, Malta and elections to the Australian Senate, the voter ranks the individual candidates rather than voting for a party list. In elections to the Irish Dáil, a candidate must receive a Droop quota in order to be elected in a multi-member constituency (Gallagher, 1978). Any candidate whose first preference votes equal or exceed the Droop quota is declared elected. As there usually remain several seats to be filled, a second count is held. Votes surplus to the quota cast for the successful candidates are transferred amongst the remaining candidates according to the second preferences recorded by the voter. This is calculated by counting all the second preference votes recorded on the ballots of the successful candidate and dividing them in proportion to the number of surplus votes. Any candidate who has now achieved a Droop quota is declared elected. If at any count no candidate is elected the candidate with the smallest number of votes is excluded and all his or her next preference votes are allocated to other candidates. This procedure continues until all the seats have been filled or the number of candidates remaining without a quota is one more than the seats remaining to be filled. Then, the candidate with the least votes is eliminated and the top candidate or candidates are elected without a quota.

A country's electoral law may combine features of several systems. For instance Germany overall achieves a proportional representation distribution, but half the members of the Bundestag are elected by a plurality in single-member constituencies.

Table 5 records the main features of the electoral systems operating today in the countries included in this Almanac. The country chapters provide a historical summary of changes in the electoral systems and further details of national variations.

The index of proportionality (Table 5) shows that the proportionality of electoral systems is a matter of degree (Rose, 1983: 49ff; Lijphart, 1990). The degree of proportionality, according to this index, ranges from 79 per cent in the United Kingdom to 100 per cent in Malta. The index of proportionality ranges from 83 per cent in Spain to 100 per cent among PR systems and among plurality systems from 79 per cent to 94 per cent in the United States Congress. Thus, it is empirically possible for a plurality system to produce a more proportional result than a PR system. On average, a PR system scores 94 per cent on the index, and a plurality system, 86 per cent.

Table 5 **BASIC FEATURES OF ELECTORAL SYSTEMS** [1]

	Compulsory Voting	Voting Age	Work or Rest Day	Turnout [5] %	Seats N	Constituencies N
1 Australia	Yes	18	Rest	89.2	148	148
2 Austria	No [2]	19	Rest	88.8	183	9 [13]
3 Belgium	Yes	18	Rest	87.2	212	30 [14]
4 Canada	No	18	Work	74.9	295	295
5 Denmark	No	18	Work	85.1	175 [8]	18
a) Constituency					135	17
b) National					40	1
6 Finland	No	18	Sunday & Monday	71.7	200	15
7 France	No	18	Rest	64.9	555 [9]	555
8 Germany	No	18	Rest	83.5	496 [10]	249
a) Constituency					248	248
b) National					248	1
9 Greece	Yes	18	Rest	82.6	300	56 [15]
10 Iceland	No	18	Rest	89.1	63	9
a) Constituency					50	8
b) National					13	1
11 Ireland	No	18	Work	67.7	166	41
12 Israel	No	18	Rest	78.9	120	1
13 Italy	Yes [3]	18	Sunday & Monday	84.6	630	32 [16]
14 Japan	No	20	Rest	69.9	512	131
15 Luxembourg	Yes	18	Rest	82.5	60	4
16 Malta	No	18	Work	95.5	65	13
17 Netherlands	No [4]	18	Work	85.5 [6]	150	1
18 New Zealand	No	18	Rest	86.6	97	97
19 Norway	No	18	Sunday & Monday	83.9	157	19
20 Portugal	No	18	Rest	71.0	246 [11]	20
21 Spain	No	18	Work	69.1	350	52
22 Sweden	No	18	Rest	84.9	349	29
a) Constituency					310	28
b) National					39	1
23 Switzerland	No	20	Rest	46.1	200	26
24 United Kingdom	No	18	Work	75.3	650	650
25 United States Congress	No	18	Work	48.2 [7]	435 [12]	435

[1] At most recent election for lower house of national parliament.

[2] Compulsory voting in Carinthia, Styria, Tyrol and Vorarlberg.

[3] Voting is not legally compulsory, but is regarded as a civic duty and failure to vote is recorded for five years on an elector's identity card.

[4] Voting was compulsory from 1917 to 1967.

[5] At latest election reported in this book.

[6] Voting was compulsory until 1971. From 1946 to 1967 turnout averaged 94.7 per cent.

Seats per Constituency Average	Range [17]	Electors per Representative	Constituency Seat Allocation	Higher Level Seat Allocation	Candidate Choice	Index of Proportionality [20]	
1	0	69,954	Alternative Vote	–	Yes: individual	87	1
20	6-39	29,844	PR: Hare quota	d'Hondt highest avg.	Yes: from party list	99	2
7	2-34	33,346	PR: Hare quota	d'Hondt highest avg.	Yes from party list	92	3
1	0	59,793	Plurality	–	Yes: individual	86	4
					Yes: from party list	95	5
8	2-21	19,024	PR: Ste Laguë highest	Largest remainder			
40	0		avg. [18]				
14	8-29	20,181	PR: d'Hondt highest avg.	–	Yes: from party list	89	6
1	0	65,973	Two-ballot plurality	–	Yes: individual	81	7
						99	8
1	0	182,774	Plurality	Largest remainder	Yes: individual		
248	0	182,774	–		No: strict party list		
5	2-32	24,607	PR: Hagenbach-Bischoff quota	Largest remainder	Yes: from party list	93	9
					Yes: from party list	96	10
6	5-12	2,721	PR: largest remainder	d'Hondt highest avg.			
13	0	13,184					
4	3-5	14,752	PR: single transferable vote	–	Yes: individual	95	11
120	0	24,119	PR: d'Hondt highest avg.	–	No: strict party list	94	12
20	2-53		PR: imperiali quota	Largest remainder	Yes: from party list	95	13
4	3-5	168,802	Single non-transferable vote	–	Yes: individual	89	14
15	7-23	3,649	PR: Hagenbach-Bischoff highest avg.	–	Yes: from party lists (*panachage*) [19]	91	15
5	0	3,789	PR: single transferable vote	-	Yes: individual	100	16
150	0	71,518	PR: d'Hondt highest avg.	–	Yes: from party list	96	17
1	0	21,801	Plurality	–	Yes: individual candidate	88	18
8	4-15	19,748	PR: Ste Laguë highest average [18]	–	Yes: from party lists	91	19
12	3-56	30,965	PR: d'Hondt highest avg.	–	No: strict party list	91	20
7	2-33	84,582	PR: d'Hondt highest avg.	–	No: strict party list	87	21
					Yes: from party list	97	22
11	3-36	18,138	PR: Ste Laguë highest	PR:Ste Laguë highest			
39	0		average [18]	average [18]			
10	2-35	20,959	PR: Hagenbach-Bischoff highest avg.	–	Yes: from party lists (*panachage*)	91	23
1	0	66,432	Plurality	–	Yes: individual	79	24
1	0	403,630	Plurality	–	Yes: individual	94	25

7 Percentage turnout of citizen population of voting age.

8 Excludes four seats for representatives from the Faroe Islands and Greenland.

9 Excludes 22 seats for the overseas departments and territories.

10 Excludes the representatives of West Berlin. Total number of seats in the Bundestag may be more than 496, because parties who win more single-member constituency seats than they would have been allocated by nationwide PR (Überhangmandate) are allowed to keep the additional seats.

11 Excludes four seats for representatives of Portugese citizens resident abroad.

12 Excludes the non-voting representatives of the District of Columbia, Puerto Rico, the U.S. Virgin Islands, Guam, and American Samoa.

13 Each of Austria's nine provinces forms a constituency. Seats not allocated at the constituency stage are allocated in two regions, one comprising Vienna, Lower Austria and Burgenland, and the other the remaining six provinces.

14 Seats not allocated at the constituency level are allocated within groups of constituencies matching Belgium's nine provinces.

15 Seats not allocated at the constituency level are allocated in 13 regional groupings of constituencies.

16 Any seats not allocated at the constituency level are allocated at the national level.

17 Range excludes a number of single-member districts in predominantly proportional representation systems, namely: Finland (Åland Islands), Greece (Evrytania, Kefallinia, Lefkas, Samos and Zakynthos), Italy (Val d'Aosta), Japan (Amami-Oshima Islands), Spain (Ceuta and Melilla) and Switzerland (Appenzell Inner-Rhoden, Glarus, Nidwalden, Obwalden and Uri).

18 A modified version of the Ste Laguë system with an initial divisor of 1.4 instead of one.

19 Electors may vote for more than one candidate including those on the lists of different parties.

20 The Index of Proportionality is calculated by summing the difference between each party's percentage share of seats and its share of votes, dividing by two and subtracting the result from 100. The formula is applied to the latest election reported in this book.

Sources:

D. Fisichella, 'The double-ballot system as a weapon against anti-system parties', in A. Lijphart and B. Grofman (eds.) *Choosing an Electoral System* (New York: Praeger, 1984) 181-90

M. Gallagher, 'Party solidarity, exclusivity and inter-party relationships in Ireland : 1922-1977' *Economic and Social Review* 10, 1 (1978) 1-22

R. Katz, 'Intraparty preference voting' in B. Grofman and A. Lijphart (eds.), *Electoral Laws and their Political Consequences* (New York: Agathon, 1986)

A. Lijphart, 'The Political Consequences of Electoral Laws, 1945-85', *American Political Science Review* 85,2 (1990) 481-96

A. Lijphart, R. Lopez Pintor and Y. Sone, 'The limited vote and the single nontransferable vote', in B. Grofman and A. Lijphart (eds.), *Electoral Laws and their Political Consequences* (New York: Agathon, 1986) 154-169

W.J.M. Mackenzie, *Free Elections* (London: George Allen & Unwin, 1956)

R. Rose, 'Elections and electoral systems: choices and alternatives', in V. Bogdanor and D. Butler (eds.), *Democracy and Elections* (Cambridge: Cambridge University Press, 1983) 20-45

J.F.H. Wright, 'Australian experience with majority-preferential and quota-preferential systems', in B. Grofman and A. Lijphart, (eds.), *Electoral Laws and their Political Consequences* (New York: Agathon, 1986) 124-138